A Bridge of Ships

JAMES PRITCHARD

A Bridge of | SHIPS

Canadian Shipbuilding during the Second World War

McGill-Queen's University Press
Montreal & Kingston | London | Ithaca

Legal deposit second quarter 2011
Bibliothèque nationale du Québec

Printed in Canada on acid-free paper that is 100% ancient forest free
(100% post-consumer recycled), processed chlorine free

This book has been published with the help of a grant from the
Canadian Federation for the Humanities and Social Sciences,
through the Aid to Scholarly Publications Program, using funds
provided by the Social Sciences and Humanities Research Council
of Canada and a grant from the Archives and Collections (ACS)
Society

McGill-Queen's University Press acknowledges the support of the
Canada Council for the Arts for our publishing program. We also
acknowledge the financial support of the Government of Canada
through the Canada Book Fund for our publishing activities.

Frontispiece: Louis Muhlstock, *Shipyard*, 1944, pastel on paper.
Collection of the Agnes Etherington Art Centre, Queen's University,
Kingston. Gift from the Douglas M. Duncan Collection 1970 (13-
083). Reproduced by the kind permission of David Muhlstock.

Library and Archives Canada Cataloguing in Publication

Pritchard, James S., 1939-
A bridge of ships : Canadian shipbuilding during the Second World
War / James Pritchard.

Includes bibliographical references and index.
ISBN 978-0-7735-3824-5

1. Shipbuilding industry – Canada – History – 20th century.
2. Shipbuilding – Canada – History – 20th century.   I. Title.

VM299.7.C3P75 2011   338.4'7623820097109044   C2010-908017-3

Set in 10.2/12.2 Adobe Minion Pro with Trade Gothic
Book design & typesetting by Garet Markvoort, zijn digital

Dedicated to the memory of the thousands of men and women

who laboured for victory in Canada's shipyards

between 1939 and 1945

Contents

List of Figures and Tables

Figures

Tables

List of Illustrations

List of Abbreviations

ABWC	Amalgamated Building Workers of Canada
ACCL	All Canadian Congress of Labour
AFL	American Federation of Labor
Algoma	Algoma Steel Corporation
AO	Archives of Ontario
BANQ-CAQ	Bibliothèque et Archives Nationales de Quebec – Central Archives Quebec
BATM	British Admiralty Technical Mission
BCARS	British Columbia Archives and Records Service
bhp	brake horsepower
BISUC	Boilermakers and Iron Shipbuilders Union of Canada (ACCL; later CCL)
CB	Companion of the Order of the Bath
CCCL	Canadian and Catholic Confederation of Labour
CCF	Cooperative Commonwealth Federation
CCL	Canadian Congress of Labour
CFL	Canadian Federation of Labour
CIO	Congress of Industrial Organizations
CMG	Companion of the Order of St Michael and St George
CNEC	chief of naval engineering and construction
CNS	chief of the naval staff
CNR	Canadian National Railway

CPRB	Combined Production and Resources Board
CS&MEN	*Canadian Shipping and Marine Engineering News*
CSL	Canada Steamship Lines
CSSRA	Canadian Shipbuilders and Ship Repairing Association
CTA	City of Toronto Archives
CTCC	Confédération des travailleurs catholique du Canada
CVA	City of Vancouver Archives
CVE	carrier-vessel escort
CWMA	Canadian War Museum Archives
DBS	Dominion Bureau of Statistics
DHH	Directorate of History and Heritage, DND
DIR	director of industrial relations
DMS	Department of Munitions and Supply
DND	Department of National Defence
Dofasco	Dominion Foundries and Steel Corporation
Dosco	Dominion Steel and Coal Company
DUA	Dalhousie University Archives
dwt	deadweight tons
Elco	Electric Boat Company
EMA	Esquimalt Municipal Archives
GCA	Grey County Archives
grt	gross registered tons
HA/LA	high angle/low angle
HMC	His Majesty's Canadian
HMCS	His Majesty's Canadian Ship
HMS	His Majesty's Ship
hp	horsepower
HSL	high-speed launch
HSRL	high-speed rescue launch

IDIA	Industrial Disputes Investigation Act
ihp	indicated horsepower
IUMSWA	Industrial Union of Marine and Shipyard Workers of America
IUMSWC	Industrial Union of Marine and Shipbuilding Workers of Canada (CCL)
IWA	International Woodworkers of America
KBE	Knight Commander of the British Empire
KC	King's Counsel
LAC	Library and Archives Canada
LCT	tank-landing craft
LST	tank-landing ship
LST3	transport ferry, or tank-landing ship
MG	Manuscript Group
MINCA	Made in Canada
MMA	Maritime Museum of the Atlantic
MMBC	Maritime Museum of British Columbia
MMGLK	Marine Museum of the Great Lakes at Kingston
MSHS	Muskoka Steamship and Historical Society
MTB	motor torpedo boat
MV	motor vessel (i.e., diesel-powered)
NARA	National Archives and Records Administration (US)
NEO	naval engineering overseer
NFB	National Film Board
NSARM	Nova Scotia Archives and Records Management
NSHQ	naval service headquarters
NSS	National Selective Service
NVMA	North Vancouver Museum and Archives
NWLB	National War Labour Board
OBE	Officer of the Order of the Britsh Empire

OFA	Ontario Fairmile Association
QUA	Queen's University Archives
RCAF	Royal Canadian Air Force
RCMP	Royal Canadian Mounted Police
RCN	Royal Canadian Navy
RCNVR	Royal Canadian Navy Volunteer Reserve
RG	Record Group
RN	Royal Navy
RNO	resident naval overseer
RNN	Royal Netherlands Navy
rpm	rotations per minute
SS	steamship
SHPS	Société Historique de Pierre-de-Saurel Inc.
SR&SB	*Shipping Register and Shipbuilder*
Stelco	Steel Company of Canada
TLC	Trades and Labour Congress of Canada
UBCSC	University of British Columbia, Rare Books and Special Collections
UMCP	University of Maryland at College Park
USN	United States Navy
USS	United States Ship
UVA	University of Victoria Archives
VMD	Victoria Machinery Depot
VMM	Vancouver Maritime Museum
WMSL	Wartime Merchant Shipping Limited
WPB	War Production Board (US)

Acknowledgments

In researching *A Bridge of Ships*, I have incurred many debts of gratitude. Although no mother lode of shipbuilding records exists, without Library and Archives Canada this book would not have been possible. Its holdings, including what is left of the records of the Department of Munitions and Supply, were essential. It is unfortunate that during research for this book, the National Archives of Canada ceased to be an independent agency of the Crown and was merged with the National Library of Canada to form Library and Archives Canada (LAC). Archivists and librarians do not carry out similar jobs; so two cheers for all archivists. The records collections in provincial, municipal, and private archives were just as important to this project as those in the national repository. The records of Burrard Dry Dock Company Limited at the North Vancouver Museum and Archives (NVMA) and of Marine Industries Limited at the Société Historique de Pierre-de-Saurel Incorporated (SHPS) at Sorel-Tracy, Quebec, are exceptional and deserve to be better known by maritime historians. Papers and collections in more than twenty-five archives in Canada, the United Kingdom, and the United States listed in the bibliography provided important evidence for this history.

Many individuals gave their time and advice to assist me with this project. For generously sharing their knowledge, materials, and memories, I am indebted to Roland Aubert, Stephen Briggs, George Cuthbertson, Paul Doddington, Joe Fossey, Edison Horton, Fiona Hyslop, Eben James II, Ken Mackenzie, Chris Madsen, Eileen Marcil, Peter Moogk, David Page, Bill Rawling, Jim Taylor, David Walker, and Ron Wallis. I also thank research assistants Richard Goette, David Rudkin, and Eric Wagner, as well as many others who worked on my behalf. Special thanks are due to Frank Lewis and Marvin McInnis, who read early draft chapters; to W.A.B. "Alec" Douglas and Gerry Tulchinsky, who read the entire manuscript and saved me from several egregious errors; and to my wife, Suzanne, who patiently bore my obsession with shipbuilding for half a decade and carefully proofread the manuscript. I am responsible for any sins of omission and commission.

Earlier versions of parts of several chapters were presented at conferences at Manitowac, Wisconsin, Quebec City, and Victoria, British Columbia, all sponsored by the Canadian Nautical Research Society, and at the 2007 Naval History Symposium, Annapolis, Maryland, sponsored by the US Naval Academy. Material that originally appeared in the *Northern Mariner* in 2006 and 2010 and in *Labour/Le Travail* in 2010 appears here in different form with the gracious permission of the editors of these journals. Finally, I gratefully acknowledge a research grant in 2005 from the Social Sciences and Humanities Research Council of Canada and thank the Office of Research Services of Queen's University for administering the award. I also thank the Archives and Collections (ACS) Society for supporting the publication of this book. The book's title was inspired by a wartime poster stating, "The Road to Victory Is over a Bridge of Ships," published by Wartime Merchant Shipping Limited and posted in the nation's shipyards.[1]

Preface

October 21, 1944, marked the 139th anniversary of the Battle of Trafalgar. Canada observed the date by officially commencing the seventh victory-loan campaign and launching nine ships, each representing a province in the Dominion. The national ceremony was held on Parliament Hill in Ottawa and presided over by Prime Minister Mackenzie King and Miss Shirley Temple of Hollywood, California, and local ceremonies occurred in each province. They took the form of a welcome home to repatriated servicemen. Each man in Ottawa gave a signal to his wife, mother, or sister in a shipyard to christen the vessel representing his own province. The events concluded at Toronto with the wife of the minister of munitions and supply, Mrs Clarence Decatur Howe, launching the 1,000th ship built in Canada since the beginning of the war.[1]

The Canadian shipbuilding program, to which these ceremonies gave visible witness, had become a large focus of Canada's industrial war effort. It included expanding shipyards; building small warships, large and small cargo ships, and countless auxiliary vessels; a vigorous program to build small boats; and a large ship-repair program. Yet in 1939 Canada's shipbuilding industry had been dormant – indeed, it was moribund – for nearly twenty years. No steel-hulled, ocean-going vessel had been built since 1921.

The history of Canada's shipbuilding industry during the Second World War is as astonishing as the history of the nation's wartime navy. The personnel of both expanded by an order of fifty times. Yet, whereas the story of the Royal Canadian Navy (RCN) is sufficiently well known as to arouse vigorous debates among historians, the history of Canada's wartime shipbuilding industry remains virtually unknown. Where the topic has been treated at all, it has been subject to errors of both omission and commission. *A Bridge of Ships* aims primarily to tell the story of the wartime shipbuilding industry, which grew into the largest single wartime industrial activity in the country.

The Canadian shipbuilding industry has disappeared from both the land and memory. Now is the time to recall and assess its contribution to Allied victory during the Second World War, as well as to explain why such an enormous accomplishment left such a meager, short-lived legacy. This book attempts to answer several questions. How did the demand for ships emerge and develop in Canada, and how did the government respond? Who owned the shipyards, where were the ships built, and how did the industry expand to meet the demand? How important was ship repairing within the larger context of the shipbuilding industry? Whence came the thousands of workers? How were they recruited and trained? Why did men and women keep working in the shipyards? How was the labour force organized? Did trade unions help the workers in their struggle with companies and government for recognition, better wages, and improved working conditions? How did the shipbuilding industry acquire the steel for all the ships built in Canada? What role did the United States play? How did numerous foundries, structural-steel firms, engineering and machine shops, and parts manufacturers across the country meet the demands of the rapidly growing industry? What significance ought to be attached to the various boatbuilding programs that were introduced during the war? Finally, can a reliable and even definitive summary of Canadian ship production be assembled and presented?

Of Tonnage Gross and Otherwise

Tonnage is a complex and bewildering term extending back to the fourteenth century to describe a ship's cargo capacity. One easy way to remember differences is to note that marine tonnage refers to volume and that, when ashore, tonnage refers to weight. A long ton, a unit of weight often applied to quantities of pig iron, is equal to 2,240 pounds avoirdupois (1,016.05 kg). A short ton, a unit of weight applied to steel, is equal to 2,000 pounds avoirdupois (907.19 kg). A tonne, or metric ton, equal to 1,000 kilograms (2,205 lb), is increasingly being used as equivalent to a long ton and as a unit of displacement tonnage in ships, but it is not so used in this monograph.

At sea, ship owners, shipbuilders, and naval personnel are interested in the gross, net, deadweight, and displacement tonnage of ships. Gross tonnage is also called registered tonnage, hence the abbreviation grt, for "gross registered tons." It is a measure of actual capacity of a ship's hull below the upper deck measured in cubic feet and dividing the result by 100. This is only important because it appears on a ship's certificate of registration. It bears no relation to cargo-carrying capacity, which is determined by deducting the volume taken up by engine and machinery spaces, fuel, stores, and crew's quarters to arrive at net tonnage, which also appears on a ship's registration certificate. This study makes little use of gross and net tonnage. The latter chiefly interests harbour authorities and customs officers interested in levying fees and duties on a ship's earning capacity.

This study is concerned with deadweight and displacement tonnage. Deadweight tonnage is the weight of cargo a ship can carry without overloading (i.e., when trimmed down to her allotted Plimsoll marks); it is normally reserved for merchant ships. Displacement tonnage, the actual weight of a ship after it has been loaded, is the weight of water displaced by a fully loaded ship. Displacement tonnage is normally measured in warships, which have no earning capacity. Moreover, displacement tonnage includes the weight of crew, armament, stores, and munitions, in addition to the ship; in short, it describes a warship being in all respects ready for sea.[2]

The ratio of gross registered tons to deadweight tons varies from ship to ship, but it is important to determine, as British authors tended to refer to gross tons, whereas during the war Americans and Canadians employed deadweight tons. At the beginning of the war, the ratio of gross registered tonnage to deadweight tonnage in British tramp (i.e., general purpose) ships was 5:8 or 1:1.6.[3] Another author gives the same ratio as about 1:1.4.[4] The use of the larger number, deadweight tons, was a deliberate attempt to emphasize the intense wartime need for increased carrying capacity.[5]

A Bridge of Ships

Noah found grace in the eyes of the Lord

Genesis 6:8

1 | Introduction

Shipbuilding in Prewar Canada

During the nineteenth century, enterprising Canadians created one of the world's largest fleets of merchant ships as shipwrights transformed the timber resources of almost limitless forests into cheap vessels to get their product to market. Converting some timber to ships reduced the risks and costs of shipping raw wood to Britain. But the competitive advantages enjoyed by Quebec and Maritimes entrepreneurs declined after Confederation along with the timber trade and its adjunct trades. They already faced fierce competition from steam power and iron hulls. Canadians enjoyed no advantages in the new era of shipbuilding. Indeed, as the nation adopted protective tariffs on basic iron and steel products, shipbuilders faced real constraints.[1] By the end of the nineteenth century, there was no place for Canadian-built, iron- and steel-hulled, deep-water ships, and by 1914 Canadian shipping and shipbuilding had all but disappeared.[2]

Canada enjoyed no factor endowments, resources, cheap labour, or sufficient capital investment that would allow iron- and steel-hulled, steam-driven ships to be built at competitive prices. Iron ore was poor in quality and sparsely deposited. Coal was in the wrong place, and capitalists saw better investment opportunities in railways and manufacturing. Until well after the Second World War, primary steel used in shipbuilding continued to enter duty free from Britain to allow manufacturers of agricultural implements and other steel products access to cheap steel. British shipbuilders also supplied Canada's shipping needs, even on the Great Lakes, for their ships freely entered the country. The majority of the 100 new canallers purchased between 1900 and 1914 were constructed in the United Kingdom.[3] A steel industry was a long time coming to Canada.[4]

Despite the constraints on developing a steel shipbuilding industry, new factors, chief among them the wheat trade, encouraged a few entrepreneurs to try their fortunes. In 1901 Collingwood Shipyard and Dry Dock Company launched a 3,300-ton, steel-hulled, passenger and package freight ship to work the upper Great Lakes. This was followed by a number of steam-powered vessels over 500 feet long until the eve of the First World War. But the Canadian deep-sea shipbuilding industry languished.

The Dominion government played a minor role in Canadian shipbuilding, enacting a number of acts subsidizing dry docks beginning in 1882 but to little effect.[5] The original aim was to encourage development of a limited ship-repair industry, but the subsidies found few takers. The government also built graving docks at Quebec, Halifax, and Esquimalt. Smaller dry docks intended to overcome the limits imposed by small canals that prevented steel-hulled ships from reaching the Great Lakes and to allow locally owned ships to be repaired during the winter months in Canada were built at Collingwood and Kingston. The government also subsidized shipbuilding directly by ordering vessels for its own account. Three small ships were laid down at Kingston and completed before 1914.[6]

New concepts of imperial defence and economic solidarity, coupled with Canada's own growth and progress, encouraged new interest in the industry shortly before the First World War. The Naval Services Act of 1910, which reflected the Liberal government's desire to build a small fleet of warships for the nascent Canadian navy, provided additional stimulus. Despite the absence of a suitable shipbuilding yard, the government introduced a new act subsidizing dry docks to encourage development of local, modern facilities for shipbuilding and ship repair.[7] The Naval Services Act was never implemented, but its passage, along with a revised act subsidizing dry docks and generous concessions by property developers, encouraged Vickers Sons and Maxim Limited of Great Britain[8] to establish a branch of the company at Montreal.

Canadian Vickers Limited was incorporated in 1911 with a capital of $5 million and a construction budget of $2.5 million. The completed shipyard contained a large floating dry dock and five berths, including one that was enclosed to permit year-round construction. Although anticipated Canadian naval construction was not forthcoming, in 1914 the government obligingly placed an order for a large icebreaker to be built for the Department of Marine and Fisheries. It was the first vessel launched at Montreal's new shipyard.

The same force – rising imperial rivalry – also affected Canada's West Coast, where British shipping met British Columbia's ocean-going transportation needs. The prospect of naval construction attracted Sir Alfred Yarrow, founder of Yarrows and Company of Glasgow. He purchased the British Columbia Marine Railway at Esquimalt in December 1913 and established Yarrows Limited the following June.[9] Nevertheless, except for on the upper Great Lakes, no steel shipbuilding industry existed in Canada before the First World War.

Following the outbreak of war, and in spite of Prime Minister Sir Robert Borden's desire, the British Admiralty resisted every Canadian attempt to secure a modern naval shipbuilding industry by obtaining British shipbuilding orders.[10] It was in submarines that Canadian Vickers made its main contribution to the First World War, albeit from prefabricated parts shipped from the United States. All told, the yard at Montreal built twenty-four submarines, fourteen of which were for the Russian and Italian governments. The company also armed 214 motorboats and seven cargo vessels, in addition to trawlers and drifters, while manufacturing 1.5 million shells and projectiles.[11]

Modern Canadian shipbuilding owes its origins to the Imperial Munitions Board, a British agency set up in Canada to process British war orders. Most of the board's work involved manufacturers with technical and labour problems and the supervision of the production of shells.[12] But responding to Great Britain's growing loss of merchant ships in 1916, the board placed orders in Canada for eighty-seven ships, including thirty-nine steel steamships, ranging in size from 1,800 to 8,800 deadweight tons (dwt).[13] The Canadian shipbuilding industry was so unformed and immature, however, that the largest single order for steel ships was contracted to J. Coughlan and Sons at Vancouver, a West Coast metal fabrication company with no previous shipbuilding experience.[14] Most ships ordered in 1917 were not completed until after the war ended.

In eastern Canada the Imperial Munitions Board let contracts for thirty-five cargo ships totalling 128,900 dwt before the end of 1916.[15] The following year, it contracted for sixty armed, steel-hulled, steam-driven trawlers, twelve of which were to be assigned to the Canadian navy.[16] Of British design, the construction of these small vessels to exacting Admiralty specifications in a year and a half was a significant achievement for the budding industry.

In 1915 the total value of production of Canada's shipbuilding industry had stood at just over $5 million. In 1917 it increased more than sixfold to $35,281,350, and in 1918 it more than doubled to $74,700,000.[17] Nevertheless, shipbuilding had been the most disagreeable of the Imperial Munitions Board's operations.[18]

The desire to develop Canada's export trade and growing constraints on Canadian shipping, now under complete British control, led the Canadian government to prolong shipbuilding beyond the period of hostilities. In 1918 the government incorporated the Canadian Government Merchant Marine and ordered twenty-five ships. The first of these was launched late in November. In 1919 plans for a new rolling mill to produce Canada's first ship plate at Sydney, Nova Scotia, were in hand, and a new yard for steel shipbuilding was being constructed at Halifax.[19] When the last ship came down the ways on 29 January 1920, the Canadian government was the owner of a fleet of sixty-three new steamships totalling 379,300 dwt, ranging in size from 2,800-ton, canal-size freighters to substantial ocean-going merchant ships of 10,500 tons. They had been built in seventeen yards across the country. The total cost came to nearly $73 million. At its peak, shipbuilding had employed 25,000 men in Montreal alone.[20]

The giant postwar boom that the project anticipated quickly turned to bust. Although British ship owners had lost 4.5 million gross registered tons (grt) of shipping during the war, more than 18 million grt of new ships had been launched in British yards by 1922, which produced a glut of ships that world trade was unable to absorb.[21] Canada's tiny shipbuilding industry, which had been created without regard to production costs, came to a grinding halt. Canadian-built ships were less fuel-efficient and less efficient at cargo handling than were newly built postwar ships constructed elsewhere.[22] Canadian shipbuilding was 30 per cent more costly than in Great Britain, and the Dominion government declined to advance any more investment. Moreover, government policy continued to allow British ships to enter the country duty free and to engage in Canadian coastal trade without paying any customs duties on either ships or cargos.[23]

Except on the upper Great Lakes, no additional steel, ocean-going ships were built for nearly twenty years. The ambitious plan to merge all the principal shipyards in eastern Canada with modernized steel and coal companies in Nova Scotia under British Empire Steel and Coal Corporation (Besco) and to manufacture steel for shipbuilding on Cape Breton Island had collapsed by 1925, and the industrial decline that affected Nova Scotia spread across Canada during the remainder of the decade.[24]

The Dominion government had financed construction of two large dry docks during the war, one at St John, New Brunswick, which opened in 1923, and the other at Esquimalt, British Columbia, which officially opened on Dominion Day, 1927, as part of Canada's diamond jubilee celebrations. Despite such encouragement, ship repairs could not keep the shipbuilding industry alive. Canadian ship owners increasingly purchased their vessels overseas. In 1922 alone, forty-seven ships were ordered from foreign yards. Canadian shipbuilders had no hope of being able to compete outside or inside Canada. Between 1922 and 1936, British shipbuilders constructed 137 ships for Canadian Great Lakes ship owners and companies.[25]

Canadian shipyards were being consolidated. In 1925 Davie Shipbuilding and Repairing Company, which traced its origins to the early nineteenth century, became a wholly owned subsidiary of Canada Steamship Lines (CSL).[26] At Montreal, Vickers's parent company, which was facing major financial difficulties in England, got rid of its Canadian subsidiary, selling it in 1926 to two Montreal financiers.

Consolidation also occurred on the Great Lakes in 1926 when Collingwood Shipbuilding Company, which already owned Kingston Shipbuilding Company, was reorganized as Collingwood Shipyards Limited.[27] The new company acquired Port Arthur Shipbuilding Company, established in 1910 as Western Ship Building and Dry Dock Company, a subsidiary of American Ship Building Company at Cleveland. Port Arthur Shipbuilding Company, so named in 1916, continued to operate under its existing name. The shipbuilding and repair facility at Kingston continued to be operated by Collingwood Shipbuilding and was not transferred to the new company.[28] The same year, 1926, Canada Steamship Lines acquired Midland Shipbuilding Company.[29] That year, the yard launched the largest bulk freighter to be built on the Great Lakes, but between 1927 and 1938 the company operated at a loss in all but two years. In 1939, because most of the equipment was obsolete, appraisers recommended that CSL sell the plant for scrap.[30]

Well before the Second World War, most Canadian shipyards lay idle or had found other work. Three ships were built at Collingwood during the 1930s, but at Port Arthur the shipbuilding company survived between 1924 and 1940 by carrying out repair work on lake vessels and direct manufacturing to meet the demands of north-western Ontario's pulp and paper industry.[31] West Coast shipbuilders, who barely survived during the interwar years, received a foretaste of the future in 1938 when they launched two modified Basset-class trawler minesweepers at Vancouver and Victoria for the Royal Canadian Navy (RCN).[32] Shipyard owners and business-men with visions of the contracts to come began readying for the war that was not far off, but no similar activity prevailed on the East Coast, where St John Dry Dock and Shipbuilding Company remained idle except for the odd repair job and where Halifax Shipyards Limited, having built its last ship in 1930, continued to struggle with just ship repairing.[33]

At the outbreak of war, sixteen yards existed capable of building small to moderate-size vessels, together with twenty-five shipyards capable of building small auxiliary vessels. Some were on the Atlantic and Pacific Coasts, but most were on the Great Lakes and St Lawrence River.[34] In 1939 the value of work carried out in Canadian shipyards amounted to $11.2 million, compared with $10.4 million and $6.2 million in 1938 and 1937, respectively. Ship repairing, manufacturing of industrial machinery, and fabrication of structural steel, which together brought in $8.9 million, accounted for nearly 80 per cent of the total. The wages and salaries paid to 3,796 employees in 1939 amounted to $4.8 million. The twenty-nine vessels launched across the country had a finished value of less than $1 million, including the value of work done on them the previous year. Seven were steel-hulled, and only three, worth $457,000, were steam-driven. Four years later, the value of production from Canada's shipyards reached $376,560,974, and eighty-seven shipyards employing an average of 75,847 workers paid out $153,595,336 in wages and salaries.[35] Canada's move from one situation to the other is the subject of much of this book.

The Royal Canadian Navy provided little stimulus to Canada's shipbuilding industry before the war. Its officers had designed the navy as an adjunct to Great Britain's Royal Navy and relied on it for technical and operational support. The navy had neither Canadian identity nor any desire to acquire Canadian-built ships, which was in keeping with the wishes of the Canadian government. It was a colonial navy whose regular officers were inordinately proud of the junior-imperial relationship, and although recent historiography identifies the Second World War as a period of increasing Canadianization of the navy, older attitudes and values persisted well afterward.[36] Lacking both the infrastructure and the technical expertise to build even the smallest of large warships, destroyers, Canadian shipbuilders began constructing small emergency-type warships and minesweepers. Then, as the navy's small demand began to be met sooner than expected, the government turned enthusiastically to building simple dry-cargo ships urgently needed to transport supplies across the Atlantic to a desperate Britain.

Major Ship Types

Of more than 500 warships built in Canadian shipyards during the war, three types predominated. First and foremost was the Flower-class corvette, the Royal Canadian Navy's primary antisubmarine vessel and ocean escort. Designed by William Reed of Smith's Dock Company near Middlesborough, Yorkshire, and patterned after his firm's whale-catcher, *Southern Pride*, of 1936, 30 feet were added to the length, which

A Flower-class corvette in original configuration with short fo'c'sle, open bridge, main mast stepped before the bridge, mizzen mast, and minesweeping gear, including white-painted dan buoys, but lacking secondary armament. Photo probably taken during builder's trials. This corvette remains in its anonymity simply one of the first. George Metcalf Archival Collection, acc. no. 19920085-1001, © Canadian War Museum.

resulted in a standard displacement of 950 tons.[37] This vessel became the mainstay of Canada's escort navy. Originally known as "patrol vessel, whaler type," Winston Churchill named it "corvette," which was in common use by 1940.[38] Sixty-four original Flower-class corvettes, including ten built for the Royal Navy in return for two Tribal-class destroyers laid down in Britain for the RCN, were the chief warships ordered in the first program. They were simple ships propelled by a single triple-expansion, steam-powered reciprocating engine that was capable of developing 16 knots. Six more of the short-forecastle ships, but lacking Oropesa minesweeping gear, were built under the second program, of 1940–41, along with ten "Revised" corvettes.[39] The Revised vessel was built with a longer forecastle and increased sheer and flare to the bow and had greater rake to the stem; they were also 3 feet longer and displaced 1,015 tons. Lessons of wartime experience were incorporated into the final twenty-seven Revised corvettes, known as "Increased Endurance." They improved the shear and flare of the Revised version, raised the bridge a full deck higher, and were built to Admiralty standards. The gun platform was raised to improve the 4-inch gun's field of fire and increased in area to mount the new antisubmarine weapon, hedgehog. Scrapping the minesweeping machinery allowed augmented fuel tanks to be fitted, thereby doubling these ships' range to 7,400 miles.[40] In all, Canadians built 122 corvettes.[41]

The same William Reed who had designed the original corvette designed the second type of warship, first called a twin-screw corvette, for the Royal Navy. His intention was to remedy the latter's shortcomings in range, speed, gun power, and seaworthiness. The Admiralty adopted the name "frigate" at the suggestion of the Canadian chief of the naval staff, Vice Admiral Percy W. Nelles, who also had a keen awareness of history. Considerably larger than a corvette, the River-class frigate was a more effective ocean escort and antisubmarine vessel. Propulsion was provided by the same engine as powered the corvette, but two engines were installed rather than one. The Cabinet War Committee approved construction of the first ten of these new ships on 10 July 1941, but nearly two years passed before the first vessel was commissioned into the RCN.[42] Canadian shipbuilders constructed seventy frigates.

Minesweepers were the third type of warship. More than 200 of them were built during the war. Table 1.1 identifies six types of minesweepers. The Bangor-class was a great improvement over the coal-fired Basset-class vessels built in 1938. The Western Isles trawlers were an educational order placed by the Royal Navy, which quickly began ordering the much larger fleet minesweepers known as Algerine-class. The wooden, diesel-powered minesweepers were chiefly built for the Royal Navy in response to magnetic mines laid around the coast of Great Britain. Those built for the

HMS *Qualicum*, Bangor-class minesweeper, built by Toronto Shipbuilding Company, undergoing sea trials in Lake Ontario, spring 1942. AO, C5, Gordon W. Powley Fonds, 10011152.

Table 1.1 | Characteristics of the principal types of warships built in Canada, 1940–45

Type	Length (overall)	Beam (extreme)	Draught (mean)	Tonnage displacement	Speed (knots)	No. built
Corvette, Flower class	205' 1"	33' 1"	13' 6"	950	16	70
Corvette, Revised Flower class	208' 0"	33' 0"	15' 7"	1,015	16	25
Corvette, Revised Increased Endurance	208' 4"	33' 1"	16' 0"	970	16	27
Frigate, River class	301' 6"	36' 7"	13' 0"	1,445	19	70
Minesweeper:						
Bangor, steam	180' 0"	28' 6"	10' 0"	672	16	50
Bangor, diesel	162' 0"	28' 0"	8' 8"	590	15.5	10
Western Isles trawler	164' 0"	28' 8"	8' 7"	545	12	16
Algerine class	225' 0"	35' 6"	10' 5"	990	16	62
105-foot, wooden	119' 4"	22' 0"	8' 8"	228	9	42
126-foot, wooden	140' 0'"	27' 11"	10' 6"	360	10	30
Fairmile B-type motor launch	112' 0"	17' 10"	4' 10"	79	20	88
Motor torpedo boat	70' 0"			44		27
Transport ferry (LST3)	345' 10"	54' 0"	27' 0"	4,290 (grt)		15
Total						*532*

Sources: Tucker, *Naval Service of Canada*, vol. 2, 502–14; Elliott, *Allied Escort Ships of World War II*; SHPS, P006, series 2, subseries 2, subsubseries 1, D25.

RCN were in response to German mines laid off Canada's East Coast later in the war. The eighty-eight Fairmile motor launches built as small antisubmarine vessels in selected boatyards across the country were a reflection of the desperation of the times, and the motor torpedo boats were an early experiment. In addition to twelve built for the RCN, sixteen were built for the Royal Netherlands Navy.

In addition to the warships shown in table 1.1, the Royal Navy had aircraft carriers modified in Canada. Between July 1943 and July 1944, Canadian shipbuilders in Vancouver modified nineteen Smiter-class carrier-vessel escorts (CVEs) from Seattle-Tacoma Shipbuilding Corporation at Tacoma, Washington. They were powered by Allis-Chalmers turbines, which gave a speed of 16 knots, displaced 15,160 tons, and could carry up to twenty aircraft. The British also ordered seventy-one "transport ferries" to be built in Canada, but only fifteen of these 4,290-ton vessels were completed before the end of 1945. Commonly known as "transport ferries," they were actually tank-landing ships (LST3s), designed to carry armoured vehicles, trucks, and personnel. The snub-nosed, nearly flat-bottomed ships were fitted with bow-opening doors. The bridge, accommodations, and twin engines were all located aft, and the longitudinal system of framing posed challenges to the builders.[43]

The British Ministry of Transport decided the main types of cargo ships to be built in Canada.[44] The largest and most important was the 9,300-ton North Sands type, and

SS *Fort Chilcotin*, the first 10,000-ton North Sands–type freighter built by West Coast Shipbuilders Limited, Vancouver, launched 7 March 1942. Photo by W.J. Moore. CVA, City of Vancouver Photo Collection, 195-1.

the other was the 4,700-ton Gray or Scandinavian type. Neither was a modern efficient ship constructed with a view to the future. Like corvettes, they were emergency-built vessels to be constructed as quickly as possible to meet a desperate need. The North Sands type was a coal-burning steamer of typical British design. It was named after the North Sands shipyard of J.L. Thompson and Company Limited at Sunderland, located at the mouth of the River Wear in the heart of England's northeast shipbuilding region. The British Merchant Shipbuilding Mission, headed by Robert Cyril Thompson of the North Sands shipyard, brought plans for the ship from the United Kingdom in 1940. Plans for the 2,500-horsepower (hp) engine designed by staff of North-Eastern Marine Engineering Company Limited at Wallsend-on-Tyne arrived at the same time. Unlike the Canadian automotive and aircraft industries, which did not build engines during the war, Canadian shipbuilders had long built marine steam engines. This is why these ships could be constructed so rapidly.

The ship plans were amended slightly at New York in January and March 1941, and from them the entire Canadian program originated.[45] The standard North Sands vessel was 440 feet overall, with a beam of 57 feet, 2 inches, and a load draught of 26 feet, 11.5 inches. Gross tonnage was 7,167, and total loaded displacement tonnage was 13,770. Modifications in design and a change from an open to a closed shelter deck increased the ship's deadweight tonnage from 9,300 to 10,300 tons.[46]

The ship carried 9,000 tons of cargo with a full load of fuel. It was common, however, for it to haul more. Most sailed with holds filled and with loads holding them to their Plimsoll marks or deeper with a 10,000-ton payload. The ship had five holds, three forward of the engine room and two aft. Cargo capacity equalled about 300

Table 1.2 | Characteristics of the principal types of cargo ships built in Canada, 1941–45

Type	Length (BP)*	Breadth (moulded)	Depth (moulded)	Tonnage (dwt)	Speed (knots)	No. built
10,000 tons						
North Sands	424' 6"	57' 2"	34' 9"	10,300	10.5	200
Victory						81
Victory tankers						12
Canadian						28
Stores-issuing						12
Maintenance						15
Subtotal						*348*
4,700 tons						
Gray	315' 6"	46' 5"	25' 2"	4,700	10	27
Revised						10
Dominion						6
Subtotal						*43*
Great Lakes tanker	251' 6"	44' 0"	20' 0"	3,600	10.5	6
Total						*397*

* Between perpendiculars.

Source: Canada, Department of External Affairs, *Canadian War Data*, table 55.

railway freight cars. One of these dry-cargo freighters could carry in a single voyage enough flour, cheese, bacon, ham, and canned and dried fruit to feed 225,000 persons in Britain for a week; 2,150 tons of steel bars and slabs; enough gun carriers, trucks, and motorcycles to motorize an infantry battalion; bombs sufficient to load 950 medium bombers or 225 heavy bombers; enough lumber, plywood, wall board, and nails to build ninety four-room cottages; two complete bombers stowed on the aft deck; and aluminum sufficient to build 310 medium bombers or 640 fighter planes.[47] Like their sisters, the American Liberty ships, they were the ships that won the war. They formed a bridge of ships linking the New World to the Old.

The Victory and Canadian types were slightly improved versions of the North Sands ship. The Victory type must not be confused with the larger, faster, turbine-powered ship of the same name being built by the US Maritime Commission. The Canadian vessel was the same as the North Sands type except for its conversion to an oil-burner.[48] Two oil-fired, water-tube boilers replaced the three original Scotch boilers, which saved fuel consumption and the cost of firemen. Assumptions that Americans would continue to buy Canadian-built 10,000-tonners after 1942 and easy availability of oil in the West Indies and California inspired this change.[49] The elimination of coal-loading hatches allowed the boat deck amidships to be extended forward, enabling the small lifeboats to be moved from the captain's-bridge deck to the amidships boat deck, and so altered the vessel's profile.

The Canadian type appeared late in the war and reflected renewed concern about the availability of fuel-oil supplies. Both coal bunkers and alternative fuel-oil capacity were installed, the water-tube boilers were scrapped, and the type reverted to the original three Scotch boilers, as did the profile.[50] Victory tankers were a response to the enormous tanker losses of 1942. Surprisingly, only a dozen were constructed. Oil tanks were installed in the holds, and all the usual piping and pumps common to tankers were added. They did not look like tankers, which may have given some reassurance to their crews when their ships were crossing the Atlantic.

Maintenance and stores-issuing ships were 10,000-tonners built to accompany the Royal Navy fleet train in the Pacific war. Although commissioned into the Royal Navy, they were basically Victory-type ships built to commercial marine standards with extensive additions and alterations to the number of decks, internal configuration, auxiliary machinery, and accommodations. As with all warships, their tonnage was given as 8,580 displacement tons; however, deadweight tons are employed in chapter 11 to aggregate construction data.

The Gray type was a medium-size cargo ship intended to meet Canada's own needs where trade volumes were small and waters shallow, as in Newfoundland, Labrador, and West Indies trades. Although designed as a coaster, she was looked upon as a general-purpose vessel, being large enough for deep-sea voyages.[51] "Gray" referred to the original builders, William Gray and Company Limited at West Hartlepool, not far from Thompson's North Sands yard. In Britain these ships were called Scandinavian type because they were built for the Baltic and northern Russian timber trade, which made good use of their long unencumbered decks for additional loads of lumber.[52] They were 328 feet overall, with a beam of 46.5 feet. Gross tonnage was 2,875, displacement tonnage 6,550, and deadweight tonnage 4,700. As with their larger counterparts, a single triple-expansion, steam-driven reciprocating engine, capable of developing 1,176 hp, gave them a speed of 10 knots.[53] The slow speed of this ship and its larger counterpart reflected their wartime emergency origins. Both vessels were intended to sail in convoys that proceeded slowly across the ocean's vastness. Two variations of the Gray type appeared late in the war in order to make them more suitable for postwar employment. Ships of the Revised type had altered derrick arrangements and some improvements in crew accommodations, whereas the Dominion type had a 'tween deck fitted to suit them for Canadian National Steamships' postwar West Indies service, in addition to improved cargo handling arrangements.

Three distinctive features single out the Great Lakes tankers (shown in table 1.2) for attention: they were the largest all-welded vessels to be built in Canada during the war, they were wholly Canadian in design, and they were fitted with diesel engines. Designed to transit the Great Lakes–St Lawrence canals system, the naval architectural firm of German and Milne at Montreal added the capability to serve the Atlantic seaboard as well.[54]

Considered together, these merchant ships and warships built during the war were truly remarkable. No ocean-going, steel-hulled vessel had been constructed in Canada for nearly twenty years, and many of those with the skills to build them came out of retirement to do so and to teach the men and women of the next generation how.

Stages of Shipbuilding

The Dominion Bureau of Statistics, which prepared the annual surveys of the shipbuilding industry, included ship repairing and new construction in its definition of the industry. Shipyards comprising the industry ranged from small enterprises employing a few workers to very large, integrated establishments employing several thousand. Two distinct stages of work occur during ship construction. The first is the erection of the hull up to the time that the ship is launched, and the second encompasses fitting-out operations that commonly begin before the hull leaves the ways. Hull construction is a relatively simple and straightforward process that can be covered in five stages: first, making templates and marking off the steel plates and structural members of the ship; second, processing this material through the specialized shops in the yards up to the point where it is ready for assembly; third, erection of the material in the ship; fourth, riveting, caulking, and welding operations; and fifth, boring out for the propeller shaft, fitting of shipside valves, and installing shaft, propellers, and rudder.[55] Only steel plate and shapes, a small number of steel castings and shipside valves, and the tail shafts for the propellers are required. Also, the materials and actual construction are almost entirely under the control of the shipbuilding company. Shipyard departments vary considerably in name and function from yard to yard but commonly include a mould loft, fabrication shop, machine shop, woodworking or carpentry shop, punch shop, paint shop, pipe shop, foundry, blacksmith shop, tin or sheet-metal shop, and electrical shop.

Fitting-out activities, which are normally completed in a fitting-out basin or alongside a fitting-out wharf, involve many more kinds of work that can be broadly classed under several more headings: installation of main propelling machinery and boilers; installation of auxiliary machinery, such as pumps and generators; installation of piping and valves; electrical installation; installation of navigational equipment, guns, and signal systems; carpentry and joinery, including manufacturing and installing furniture; installation of deck equipment, boats, masts, rigging, and winches; and lastly, installation of special equipment and devices required by the nature of the service for which the ship is designed.

It is clear from this very brief description that fitting-out operations involved many more people than a shipbuilding company's employees. The work involved the installation of products often manufactured in distant machine shops at virtually every stage of construction. Hundreds of subcontractors and manufactures were involved. Materials varied tremendously, and regular deliveries were vital to production. Sources of supply were very diversified, and orderly progress of fitting-out operations

A triple-expansion, steam-driven reciprocating engine being lowered into the engine room of the corvette HMCS *Belleville* during the summer of 1944. Ernie Verrier, foreman of the riggers' gang, sits in the foreground supervising the lift, and Mike Sullivan, a member of the gang, stands aft. Photo by Francis MacLachlan. MMGLK, Francis MacLachlan Collection, 1984.0006.0066.

depended on deliveries of each item of equipment at the required time. During the early war years, delays caused by nondeliveries abounded.

Warships, the first ships built during the war, were constructed to exacting specifications that had never been experienced in Canada before. Shipbuilding companies were driven by cost-reduction methods of construction. As naval inspectors, originally from the British Admiralty Technical Mission and later also from the RCN, forced attention to their exacting standards, shipbuilding companies gradually developed a culture of excellence that took the industry beyond anything seen before in the country. Resistance was strong at first, but change came rapidly, all things considered. Employees of new yards where no traditions existed were easily trained to new standards, but in Great Lakes and St Lawrence River yards, change came more slowly. Expansion of the labour force probably assisted the changes.

How Canadians responded to the challenges that faced them is truly astonishing. In 1939 Canada's population numbered slightly more than 11 million men, women, and children – the 1941 census of Canada counted 11.2 million. Not only was the population small, but Canada was still in the early stages of industrialization. Fewer than half a million workers, or 9.9 per cent of the labour force, were engaged in all types of manufacturing.[56] During the Second World War, Canadian shipbuilders and workers constructed more than 500 warships, nearly 400 cargo ships, over 400 auxiliary vessels, more than 3,300 landing craft, and more than 5,000 small craft both with and without power. They also carried out more than 36,000 ship repairs, refits, and conversions. At peak production, the Canadian shipbuilding, marine-engineering, and ship-repair industries employed about 126,000 men and women, or nearly 15 per cent of Canada's total labour force engaged in war production. The $1.2 billion spent on shipbuilding and ship repairs between 1939 and 1945 represented over 12 per cent of Canada's total expenditure on wartime production. This great national effort was achieved by an industry that had nearly ceased to be.[57]

Conclusion

The following chapters aim to tell a story of the evolution of a wartime industry and to account for its failure to leave a lasting legacy despite its size. Chapter 2 outlines the development of government policy with regard to wartime shipbuilding. History has made much of the government's response to the Second World War, but stress on the roles played by politicians and bureaucrats has inevitably distorted the picture of Canada at war by ignoring the activities of businessmen and industrial workers, implicitly casting them as the tools of Ottawa's puppet masters.[58] Chapters 3 through 7 attempt to redress that picture by focusing on the men and women without whom the ships would not have been built. Chapters 3 and 4 focus on the shipyards and their owners. Ship repairing consumed one in every six dollars spent on shipbuilding; added to marine conversions and naval modernization, it is the subject of chapter 5. Chapters 6 and 7 shed some light on the workers. How the workforce was recruited and trained and what kept them working at their jobs are the subjects of one chapter, and how shipyard workers organized in the face of government coercion and constraint is the subject of the other. Chapters 8 and 9 examine the materials employed in shipbuilding, and chapter 10 deals with thousands of marine craft that were built, in addition to the more than 1,000 ships; although often ignored and forgotten, they represented an important part of the story. Chapter 11 brings together the main story of ship production, providing data about the whole wartime experience. Finally, a concluding chapter attempts to explain why, despite the astonishing record and unlike the wartime aircraft industry, wartime shipbuilding left no legacy. Canada's wartime ships were, it seems, little more than expensive shells fired at the enemy and then forgotten.

Organizing Shipbuilding

Introduction

The number and variety of organizations employed by the government to foster shipbuilding in Canada were unnecessarily complicated and confirm that no plan of production existed at the outbreak of war. Canadians had to learn to plan the use of their shipbuilding resources, which, like war production generally, did not occur seamlessly as C.D. Howe and his admirers wanted Canadians to believe.[1] Planning consisted initially of extracting reluctant half-promises from private firms and calling the result a program. Before the war progressed very far, Canada had three shipbuilding programs, each with a different organizational form. A branch within the Department of Munitions and Supply (DMS) that managed naval shipbuilding and that might be said to have operated two programs for the department initiated a small-boat program very early in the war. A Crown corporation ran all merchant shipbuilding, and a single controller within the DMS was responsible for ship repairs and salvage. These different forms of government organization, products of contingent events, led to blurring of responsibilities and to competition for scarce material and human resources among shipyards, especially where there was naval and cargo shipbuilding and manufacturing of machinery and parts.[2]

Even more than in Great Britain, not only were Canadian naval officers and senior civil servants ignorant about planning, but they also knew next to nothing about the country's industry and its capabilities.[3] They had little or no experience to fall back upon. The Imperial Munitions Board had learned a great deal about planning during the First World War, but it had been set up in Canada under the British Ministry of Munitions in order to circumvent any Canadian responsibility and to avoid further charges of incompetence and corruption being aimed at Sir Robert Borden's government. It left no planning legacy for the government to call upon.[4] During the Second World War, planning came into its own as war production was organized and programs established. But the process was lengthy, taking almost as long as the war itself in the matter of shipbuilding. The initial steps were uncertain and unsteady.

The Department of National Defence was unorganized for war purchasing owing to its own inadequate arrangements and the patronage system of the minister, Ian

Mackenzie. Successive efforts at organization came through the appointment of the Defence Purchasing Board and the War Supply Board and through establishment of the Department of Munitions and Supply. Even under a new, aggressive, no-nonsense minister, problems continued, compounded by C.D. Howe's casual approach to planning despite his obsession with control, which left coordination of deliveries in a shambles.

The Royal Canadian Navy (RCN) was least able to plan for ship acquisition. Designed as an adjunct to Great Britain's Royal Navy (RN), the Canadian naval service relied on it for operational guidance and support. The chief of the naval staff (CNS), Rear Admiral Percy W. Nelles, was a bureaucrat of less than dynamic personality who was quite unprepared to manage the fiftyfold expansion of the wartime navy and continued to send untrained crews to sea in poorly equipped ships in keeping with his strategic vision of the RCN as an adjunct to the RN. Moreover, Nelles was obsessed with acquiring Tribal-class destroyers chiefly as a ploy to preserve the navy after the war was over. Any claim that he attempted to develop shipbuilding in Canada during the 1930s is unconvincing.[5]

Technical liaison between the RCN and the RN was weak to nonexistent. During the summer of 1939, it was in the hands of the director of naval engineering, Engineer Commander A.D.M. Curry, and two assistants.[6] The true weakness of the liaison became apparent in September when the navy learned of the existence of two new warships, the first to be built in wartime Canada, from a member of a delegation of the Canadian Manufacturers Association on its return from Great Britain rather than from the British Admiralty. Chance alone directed information about the Flower-class corvette and Bangor-class minesweeper to the chief of the naval staff.[7] This was hardly surprising and did not improve for many years. Until mid-1943 the navy maintained only a single technical liaison officer in London to keep in touch with the details of the many projects being carried out by the RN in the United Kingdom.[8]

Naval Service Headquarters (NSHQ) also remained inadequate during the first two years of the war. In response to the minister's complaint, a new organizational framework was adopted in July 1941. A naval board and naval staff replaced the unofficial naval council that had been set up in August 1940 after Angus L. Macdonald had been appointed minister for the naval service.[9] But this never worked satisfactorily. The chief of the naval staff allowed himself and the naval secretary to become overwhelmed with piddling detail while failing to anticipate the need for expanded technical expertise at NSHQ. The British Admiralty remained responsible for the strength, stability, and seaworthiness of RCN ships for more than two years. During that period, Captain Curry recognized that he had lost the confidence of the CNS and asked to be relieved. On 1 February 1941 he exchanged positions with Engineer Captain George L. Stephens as engineer-in-chief at Naval Service Headquarters. Stephens immediately set about dealing with the navy's repair problems. After visiting Halifax, he recommended introducing civilian supervisory officers owing to the paucity of naval engineers.[10] But this was only the first of several reorganizations that continued throughout the war. Indeed, the navy's first official historian concluded that the RCN established machinery for thoroughgoing technical work at NSHQ only early in 1944. Throughout the Second World War, the Royal Canadian Navy relied upon British officers in Canada for technical expertise.[11]

Just as the Canadian government refused to become involved with British efforts to stimulate the shipbuilding industry during the late 1930s, no government shipbuilding program existed at the outbreak of war, nor had any attempt been made to organize the country's shipbuilding industry. Writing to Governor General Lord Tweedsmuir in August 1938, Prime Minister Mackenzie King declared that although his government would not interfere with Canadian Vickers Limited if it contracted with the British Admiralty to build destroyers in Canada, neither would it participate in negotiations, nor would it place a concurrent order for the Royal Canadian Navy.[12] The Admiralty did not proceed with the Vickers order, and it was only a year later, after war had been declared, during the conversion of privately owned vessels to auxiliary warships, that RCN officers discovered that Canadian shipyards were incapable of building warships to naval standards, even the Halcyon-class of minesweepers the navy had in mind.[13] The Flower-class corvette to come was built to first-class mercantile standards that applied to hull, propulsion, and machinery, and it made possible the entire Canadian naval shipbuilding program and the use of surveyors from Lloyd's Register of Shipping and from British Corporation Register of Shipping and Aircraft to oversee construction.[14] But not a single ship was under construction for the navy when Canada's Parliament voted on 10 September to declare war on Germany. There followed the first efforts to organize shipbuilding, but during the next six years, contingent events and rapidly changing wartime conditions rather than foresight or rational planning drove the large shipbuilding programs that emerged. This was perhaps inevitable given the emergency nature of shipbuilding, the lack of Canadian long-term interest and technical expertise, and subservience to British interests. Consequently, confusion, contradiction, and chaos often accompanied the industry's growth.

The War Measures Act and the use of orders-in-council, the Defence of Canada Regulations, and after June 1941 the National Resources Mobilization Act undermined and suborned Canadian democracy during the war. In effect, Canada became an executive dictatorship where habeas corpus had been suspended and members of Parliament reduced to ciphers. Their bombast was theatre while government ministers and senior civil servants promulgated regulations and orders that had the force of law. The Conservative Party of Canada failed to provide even a minimally competent Opposition. During the war, the party had five leaders and was characterized by internal feuding, lacklustre leadership, and general ineptitude. In both 1935 and 1940 the party won just 40 of 245 seats in the House of Commons.[15] The curtailment of individual freedom in the name of its defence and the expansion of federal powers by statute and nearly 6,500 orders-in-council created a corporatist state ruled by experts and specialists who relied on professional propagandists to deliver the correct message of victory through unity.[16] The Cabinet War Committee, comprising nine members, represented an inner sanctum of executive power.[17]

The First Shipbuilding Program

Organization of Canadian war supply and production emerged very slowly. On 6 September 1939, the day before Parliament met in emergency session, C.G. Power, at Prime Minister King's request, drafted a bill establishing a supply department. The hastily drafted measure received royal assent the following week but was proclaimed into law only seven months later.[18] During the interim, the government relied on the Defence Purchasing Board and the War Supply Board to meet its needs. Just why it chose to use these inadequate, temporary organizations remains moot, but this choice illustrates the government's reluctance to plan for the future.

Established in mid-July 1939, the Defence Purchasing Board was a political instrument created in response to charges of political patronage in the awarding of Department of National Defence contracts. Designed to extract the government from unsavory allegations of impropriety, the board had been established with such constraints on its activities as to render it unable to carry out its task of placing government orders with private business and industry.[19] The act required as a principle that competitive bids be solicited for all defence purchases and that when these were not forthcoming, a maximum profit of 5 per cent per annum be allowed on the capital employed. After war was declared, the government was unable to place a single contract on the 5 per cent basis.[20] Profit control was removed in October, and about $35 million worth of defence purchases was contracted for, but clearly the government was not planning for war production. It had no interest in undertaking war production in government-owned factories, nor did it have the required expertise – hence the need to deal with private industry. During this period, "shipbuilding" came between "sheets, galvanized" and "shirts" in the index of the board's minute book, and the category included a contract worth $180 for boat hooks for the Royal Canadian Air Force.[21] The chief significance of the creation of the Defence Purchasing Board was that on the eve of war, scandal had forced the Department of National Defence to surrender control of military procurement to civilian authority, where it would remain for the duration.[22]

Civilian control continued with the War Supply Board, set up on 1 November 1939 under the chairmanship of Wallace R. Campbell, president of Ford Motor Company of Canada, in response to the arrival in Ottawa the previous month of a British supply and technical mission. The Admiralty representative was Admiral Sir Percy Addison, KBE, CB, CMG, RN, who was soon replaced by Engineer Rear Admiral H.A. Sheridan, RN, the first of many technical officers from the Royal Navy who made naval shipbuilding in Canada possible.[23] First called the British Purchasing Mission in Canada and the United States, it was soon named the British Supply Board of Canada and the United States with responsibility to arrange for North American war supplies. Its initial task was "to sponsor, encourage, and finance development and expansion of Canadian industrial capacity" for war production.[24]

With the creation of the War Supply Board, the British board ceased to be a direct-purchasing agency because the Canadian agency took over the task on behalf of the

United Kingdom in Canada. From 7 November 1939, the task of purchasing in the United States was transferred to the British Purchasing Commission in New York. On 23 November responsibility for the War Supply Board was shifted from the minister of finance, J.L. Ralston, to the minister of transport, C.D. Howe, which marked the beginning of the latter's rise to power as virtual czar of Canadian war production.[25]

The government appointed David B. Carswell as director of shipbuilding when it set up the War Supply Board, but during the early months, it awarded just one shipbuilding contract to Burrard Dry Dock Company and one to Halifax Shipyards Limited. Each was for a small ammunition lighter of about 100 deadweight tons.[26] Contracts worth a little more than half a million dollars were also let to the British Admiralty for turbine blading, tail shafts, torpedoes, and parts for RCN destroyers; ten small contracts went to Halifax Shipyards Limited largely for repairs, alterations, and conversions to ships and naval vessels. On the West Coast, three contracts placed at Victoria had nothing to do with shipbuilding or ship repair.[27] During the first ten months of the war, until after the fall of France in June 1940, the British placed no meaningful war orders in Canada.

David Ballantyne Carswell, marine superintendent of the Department of Transport, was the government's senior technical marine engineer. Appointed director of shipbuilding at the War Supply Board in October 1939, he became director general of the shipbuilding branch of the new Department of Munitions and Supply in April 1940. The following November, he was also named controller of ship repairs, but five months later he was reduced to supervising the latter, and a year later, on 1 May 1942, salvage operations were added to his responsibility for ship repairing.[28] He had probably run afoul of C.D. Howe's aversion to civil servants.

Born in Paisley, Scotland, in 1884 and trained in mechanical and marine engineering, Carswell served at sea in China and Australia before joining the design staff of Henry Simon Limited at Manchester, England, in 1908. He became works manager the following year and continued until coming to Canada in 1913. The next year, he joined Detroit Shipbuilding Company, where he served as superintendent until 1918. He was appointed superintendent engineer of Canadian National Steamship Company at Montreal in 1922 and became marine advisor to Sir Henry Thornton on all matters affecting the company. In 1927 he became general manager of Montreal Dry Dock Limited and, two years later, took over as managing director of the new Canadian Vickers Limited before joining the Department of Transport as marine superintendent.[29] Although Carswell had occupied senior management positions in Canadian shipbuilding for thirty years, he failed to convince C.D. Howe that he should have chief direction of Canada's wartime shipbuilding programs.

On 19 September 1939 the Cabinet War Committee approved a modest shipbuilding program of $10 million.[30] But what ships were to be built was changing very rapidly. On 6 September, Rear Admiral Nelles submitted almost the same building program as he had nine months before: two destroyers, four antisubmarine minesweepers of the improved Halcyon-class, and eighteen Fundy-class minesweepers (increased from twelve in January), to be built immediately. Eleven days later, the naval staff submitted to the Cabinet estimates to build thirty small antisubmarine ships, ten minesweepers, and thirty-two motor torpedo boats.

The four Bramble-class antisubmarine escorts, thirty-six smaller antisubmarine vessels, and twenty Fundy-class minesweepers included in an earlier request had all been scrapped in favour of ships the naval staff had learned about only during the previous week! It speaks well of staff members, however, that they so quickly recognized the superior qualities of the new ships. At the end of November, it was officially announced that Canadian shipyards would build thirty of the new whale-catcher-type patrol vessels, including ten for the Royal Navy, and twelve Bangor class mine sweepers, in addition to eight 38-foot motorboats for aircraft-salvage purposes.[31]

This was far from a significant shipbuilding program. Indeed, on 8 December 1939 the prime minister recorded his satisfaction that his Cabinet colleagues had convinced him not to begin a shipbuilding program.[32] But reality was slowly forcing the government to begin planning. At a press conference held at Ottawa on 24 January 1940, C.D. Howe stated the government's intention to build forty-six whale-catcher-type antisubmarine vessels, twenty-eight minesweepers, and forty-one boats of various kinds: ammunition and provision lighters, refuelling scows, aircraft-salvage boats, tenders, and bomb tenders.[33] Finally, on 7 February, five months after Canada's declaration of war and several shipbuilding plans later, the Cabinet approved a revised program to build ninety corvettes and minesweepers for an anticipated cost of $54.2 million. January's forty-six corvettes had grown to sixty-four.[34] Approval was apparently without discussion, which should cause no surprise. The decision was taken in the midst of a federal election campaign, and fierce debates had already taken place between the naval staff and officials of the finance department.

Canada's shipbuilding industry, like the automotive industry, had a large amount of capital equipment lying idle at the beginning of the war. Although much machinery was old and worn out, shipbuilders were able to begin production of these small ships within a relatively short time after receiving the government's orders, which were placed through the War Supply Board and the director of shipbuilding.

Table 2.1, containing the identity and location of fourteen shipyards across Canada that were contracted by 1 March 1940 to build sixty-four corvettes and fourteen minesweepers, together with the prices of the first ships ordered, shows unequivocally what firms were available for shipbuilding at the beginning of the industry's expansion. Prices varied. The cheapest corvettes would be built along the St Lawrence River and in the Great Lakes, and a premium of more than 11 per cent would be paid for ships built at West Coast yards. Higher labour and transportation costs accounted for the difference. No ships in this first order were to be built at Halifax. The contracts anticipated delivery of twenty-eight corvettes before the close of navigation in 1940 and the remaining thirty-six during the following season. The delivery schedule was extremely unrealistic, reflecting both the absence of knowledge in Ottawa of the poor state of the shipbuilding industry and contractors' optimism. Nevertheless, Davie Shipbuilding and Repairing's delivery of HMS (later HMCS) *Windflower* to British authorities on 19 October 1940, nine months from the date of order (eight months

Table 2.1 | Distribution of the first naval shipbuilding contracts among shipbuilding companies, 1 March 1940

No. ships	Builder	Price per vessel	Location
ANTISUBMARINE VESSELS			
3	St John Dry Dock and Shipbuilding Co.	540,000	St John, NB
10	Davie Shipbuilding and Repairing Co.	530,000	Lauzon, QC
3	George T. Davie and Sons	532,000	Lauzon, QC
4	Morton Engineering and Dry Dock Co.	530,000	Quebec, QC
7	Marine Industries Ltd	530,000	Sorel, QC
8	Canadian Vickers Ltd	530,000	Montreal, QC
3	Kingston Shipbuilding Co.	532,000	Kingston, ON
8	Collingwood Shipyards Ltd	528,000	Collingwood, ON
8	Port Arthur Shipbuilding Co.	540,000	Port Arthur, ON
4	Burrard Dry Dock Ltd	605,000	North Vancouver, BC
3	Victoria Machinery Depot	606,000	Victoria, BC
64	*Total antisubmarine vessels*	*33,123,600*	
MINESWEEPERS			
6	North Van Ship Repairs	620,000	North Vancouver, BC
6	Burrard Dry Dock Ltd	620,000	North Vancouver, BC
2	Prince Rupert Dry Dock and Shipbuilding Co.	625,000	Prince Rupert, BC
14	*Total minesweepers*	*8,690,000*	
78	*Combined total warships*	*41,813,600*	
	Miscellaneous contracts	1,625,730	
	Total expenditure	*43,439,330*	

Source: Tucker, *Naval Service of Canada*, vol. 2, 38, 43.

from keel laying) was a great achievement, as was delivery of the second corvette, HMS *Trillium*, from Canadian Vickers eleven days later.[35] The great shipbuilding firm of Harland and Wolff at Belfast had taken eight and a half months to deliver the first British corvette.[36]

The estimated expenditure totalled $43.5 million. Fifty-seven ships worth $34.2 million (72 per cent) were to be built in Quebec and British Columbia, and three ships worth $1.6 million (3.6 per cent) were allocated to the Maritimes. Nineteen ships worth nearly $11 million (23 per cent) went to the three Great Lakes yards. The distribution illustrates clearly that from the beginning Canada's wartime shipbuilding was a political as well as an industrial process. It also shows that the government was not interested in using the contracts to alter the location of the industry in the country.

A contract for four additional minesweepers was let on 1 April 1940 to a new shipyard being built at Toronto, but builders could not be found for the last ten of the twenty-eight minesweepers until naval authorities acknowledged that no more marine steam-driven reciprocating engines could be manufactured in the next two years and decided to install diesel engines in the ten remaining vessels. Late in August contracts for these hulls were let to Davie Shipbuilding and Repairing Company at Lauzon and to Marine Industries Limited at Sorel, both in Quebec.[37] The placement of so few contracts in East Coast shipyards reflected other realities. Shipyards in the Maritimes were small and were needed to effect emergency repairs to vessels suffering from war damage and perils of the sea. Within a year, growing demands on their resources would overwhelm them.

Late in March 1940 Sir Edward Beatty, former president of the Canadian Pacific Railway, acting as British representative of shipping in Canada, was informed by Britain that no merchant shipbuilding was contemplated in Canada, and in June the minister of transport made a similar statement in the House of Commons.[38] Naval shipbuilding appeared sufficient to get the near-dead industry on its legs again, but no plan had been developed to sustain the program beyond 1941. Nothing yet encouraged significant, large-scale capital investment in the industry.

In March 1940 Roy Wolvin, the major owner of the three Great Lakes shipyards, purchased the former Midland Shipbuilding Company property from Canada Steamship Lines and set about reopening the plant in order to bid on additional vessels, and James Franceschini, a Toronto paving contractor, incorporated Dufferin Shipbuilding Company to bid on outstanding minesweeper contracts (see chapter 3). In February the director of the shipbuilding branch had sought to let contracts for prototypes of high-speed, air-sea rescue launches for the British Royal Air Force and suggested that the Canadian navy and air force get involved, but the naval staff demurred. After the Royal Canadian Air Force expressed interest and Carswell went ahead, naval planners took advantage of the situation to return to their original want list. They argued that a need existed for fast patrol boats fitted with asdic, an early version of sonar, for the St Lawrence River and possibly on the Pacific Coast. They chose the B-type Fairmile motor launch, and although the Cabinet authorized their acquisition in May, lengthy delays obtaining detailed drawings and specifications from Britain led to postponement in issuing the first contracts until April 1941.[39]

The navy also revived its desire for torpedo-carrying motorboats for surface warfare, which had been in its original September proposal. The arrival of the controversial designer and boat builder Hubert Scott-Paine in Montreal in May 1940 to establish Canadian Power Boat Company provided the opportunity to acquire some of the new untried craft. They were to be a strike force for the defence of Canada's harbours.[40] By mid-summer 1940 twelve untried motor torpedo boats and all contracts for the navy's program to build ninety ships had been let, sufficient to revive

Riveters at work on a minesweeper under construction by Toronto Shipbuilding Company, c. 1942. AO, C5, Gordon W. Powley Fonds, 1002723.

the Canadian shipbuilding industry but insufficient to encourage significant expansion or development and growth.

The long dearth of shipbuilding during the interwar years had depleted Canadian shipyards' technical and drawing-office staffs to such an extent that few had competent help to engineer properly and to produce the necessary working drawings for the construction of ships. W. Harold Milne, a naval architect, doubted whether the industry could muster sixty men in the entire country.[41] Foreseeing a need for skilled draughtsmen, his firm, German and Milne, had created a central drawing office at Montreal as early as 1937 in order to attract shipyard business. Its members gradually increased and until 1940 were engaged in private construction. Thereafter, until 1945, the drawing office produced much for the Canadian navy and the Department of Munitions and Supply.[42] On 1 April 1940 Donald Page, a recent graduate of Queen's University in mechanical engineering, joined Kingston Shipbuilding Company and was put in charge of its new drawing room. There, he learned the shipbuilding business and three years later, at age twenty-eight, became general superintendent of the yard.[43] Across the country, in similar manner, old men and new men began to fill the reviving industry's needs.

During the spring of 1940, between the invasion of Denmark in early April and the fall of France in mid-June, the Canadian government grew increasingly frustrated as an industrial war producer. On 8 April, fresh from his electoral triumph, Prime Minister King activated the Department of Munitions and Supply. Although partly a reaction to the worsening situation overseas, the new department's appearance was chiefly a response to failings at home. The new department resulted from the aboli-tion of the War Supply Board and de facto dismissal of Wallace R. Campbell, who had allegedly resisted the prime minister's demand that a labour representative sit on the board. A more honest reason was that the board was ineffective; it had no initiating authority and purchased only what the Cabinet ordered. It was a reflection of the government's indisposition to plan a war-production program without greater assurance of British orders.[44] The issue of Campbell's dismissal had arisen in Janu-ary, but in order to avoid controversy during the election campaign, C.D. Howe had persuaded Mackenzie King to wait until after the election before getting rid of the hard-nosed business executive.[45]

The Department of Munitions and Supply possessed almost unlimited powers to buy, organize for manufacture, sell, regulate, and otherwise secure war production. The shipbuilding branch of the War Supply Board and its director were transferred to the new department, and David Carswell was appointed director general.[46] The chief problem, the paucity of British war orders, which led the prime minister to com-plain directly to Winston Churchill on 18 May 1940, remained. The value of British war orders for munitions and supplies was still "very low," only some $90 million in all, and King also protested the slow and cumbersome methods of UK purchasing.[47] Reluctant to spend scarce funds in Canada, the British were trying to panic the Can-adians into agreeing to grant unlimited credit for their orders.[48]

British planners had not foreseen a shipping shortage in wartime and had recom-mended total UK naval and merchant shipbuilding capacity be kept to 1.5 million gross registered tons (grt), which proved wholly inadequate, and shortages of labour, steel, and propelling machinery limited apparent capacity to 1.1 million grt.[49] By 1940 the Royal Navy's likely demands exceeded 1 million grt. A certain confusion about shipbuilding also reigned in the Canadian government. Replying in the House of Commons on 14 June to a demand that the government initiate a steel shipbuilding program in order to construct cargo ships up to 10,000 tons, C.D. Howe denied there was any need. "The shipping situation," he told the House, "instead of growing more acute, has eased off." Moreover, he added, ships of neutral nations as well as British ones were being diverted to Canada. Howe also doubted the capacity of Canadian shipyards to find additional skilled labour or steel given that established yards were fully engaged in naval construction and repairs.[50] Howe was only voicing accepted British wisdom of the day.

Four changes that same month marked the beginning of a new war situation in Canada. First, on 16 June the British divided their North American purchasing oper-ations into separate Canadian and American organizations. Second, British author-ities agreed their officials should deal directly with the Department of Munitions and Supply and established a new body to be known as the British Admiralty Technical Mission (BATM) in order to carry this out. Third, the Canadian government agreed to absorb excess costs above fair prices of war production. And fourth, the Department of Finance agreed to accumulate sterling or absorb Britain's trade deficit with Canada above previously agreed upon limits.[51] The Department of Munitions and Supply was also getting a handle on Canada's industrial production using detailed surveys of more than 2,200 plants carried out by the War Supply Board during its brief five-month existence.[52] An unforeseen event forced the department's new shipbuilding branch into the shipbuilding business itself when the Royal Canadian Mounted Police (RCMP) suddenly swooped down and interned the owner of the new Dufferin Shipbuilding Company, James Franceschini.[53] The branch took over directly running the company for more than a year, during which time four minesweepers were completed and commissioned and construction began on two more.

Also in June 1940 Prime Minister King asked Angus L. Macdonald, the Liberal premier of Nova Scotia, to come to Ottawa to serve in the Cabinet, and on 12 July he was sworn in as minister of national defence for naval services.[54] Macdonald arrived in Ottawa with a sterling reputation for integrity, intelligence, and commitment. As premier of Nova Scotia, he had delivered three consecutive surpluses after fourteen years of deficits.[55] But he proved to be ineffective in Ottawa. He moved to the capital on the prime minister's terms, and as the member for Kingston, Ontario, he had no political power base. He did not represent Nova Scotia in Cabinet or wield any influence in Ontario.[56] Although he was a member of the Cabinet War Committee, he definitely played second fiddle to Howe. He also failed to develop a good relationship with the Ottawa press corps. Within eighteen months of his arrival in Ottawa, he had come to despise the prime minister for his equivocating, and Mackenzie King came to regret his decision to invite the Nova Scotian into his Cabinet.[57] After 1941 Macdonald increasingly favoured conscription, and by the middle of 1944 he knew he would not stand in the coming general election. He resigned from the government in April 1945, thereby terminating a disappointing wartime Ottawa appointment. Although he had come to Ottawa to do a job, Macdonald was not a strong naval minister.

A keen promoter of Nova Scotian industry and anxious to see ships built in the province, Macdonald was not particularly interested in the navy or the multitude of problems associated with its rapid expansion.[58] Although he attended meetings of the naval council set up at his instruction and listened to all the problems, he never took a hand. He did not attend meetings of the naval board established later. Macdonald's abiding concern was his political flanks.[59] According to naval historian Marc Milner, "There is little evidence that the minister ever took much interest in the navy outside the routine administration of accounts and liaison with other government departments."[60]

During the second half of July, members of the British Admiralty Technical Mission arrived in Ottawa, and under Vice Admiral A.E. Evans, CB, OBE, RN, began to seek out firms to develop war production. The mission's purpose was to locate production facilities for the Royal Navy rather than to assist the RCN to meet its own needs. Engineer Rear Admiral Sheridan, RN, in Ottawa since 1939, became deputy head of mission and, in view of his earlier work, was able to advise various technical officers when they arrived as to local sources of supply.[61] Engineer Captain W.R. Horton, RN, assumed Sheridan's old job of representing the Admiralty's engineer-in-chief's department. Before the war ended, the BATM would grow from an initial staff of eighteen, including technical officers from all branches of the controller's department of the Admiralty and civil officers, to nearly 2,000.[62] Virtually unknown today, the BATM was vital to the success of Canada's naval shipbuilding and naval armament and equipment programs during the Second World War.[63]

Warships were beginning to come down the ways. Canadian Vickers launched the first Canadian-built corvette on 26 June 1940, Rear-Admiral Sheridan officiating.[64] Two more were launched on Dominion Day at a yard near Quebec City, and on 22 July another launching took place at Montreal when Lady Campbell, wife of the British high commissioner, christened the ship. She also christened two more that had been launched previously and were lying in the fitting-out basin. Ship launchings had not attracted a great deal of publicity. Large crowds had not attended. But with Lady Campbell's activities, ship launchings became increasingly important occasions for displays of national unity and patriotism.

As of 25 July keels of seven minesweepers and twenty-seven corvettes, in addition to the ten started for British account, had been laid down.[65] Speaking in the House of Commons, the minister of munitions and supply claimed contracts worth $151.4 million had been let for all the ships initially proposed in February and that sixteen yards were now involved in the construction program. Eighteen smaller shipyards were working on the small-boat program. Ever the optimist, Howe anticipated twenty-eight corvettes and five minesweepers would be delivered to the navy before the year's end. The 14,000 men employed in Canada's shipyards and allied industries represented a trebling of the workforce during the previous three months.[66] Throughout the war, Howe tended to exaggerate when reporting his department's achievements, heaping praise on both himself and his minions, with a little reserved for the men and women who actually built the ships. Employment may have passed 10,000 at the end of the third quarter of 1940, and only ten vessels, including eight built for the Royal Navy, were delivered by the year's end. Nevertheless, the navy's program was advancing well.

As hulls were launched, however, the previous want of planning led to growing fears of workers being left idle, and on 3 August 1940 Howe asked Angus L. Macdonald for new shipbuilding orders. The naval staff responded quickly, and less than two weeks later the government authorized construction of sixteen additional corvettes and minesweepers. These new orders did not meet the larger problem of keeping the shipyards busy, and the director of shipbuilding proposed that cargo ship construction commence in the spring of 1941.

Carswell thought the country's yards could build three sizes of merchant ships from 3,500 to 9,000 tons. Nine berths were available to build the largest vessels, and keels laid in May and June 1940 could result in ships delivered eleven months later. If the navy planned no additional ships, he proposed that Canada undertake to construct sixty-eight cargo vessels of all three sizes to be completed by October 1942.[67] But the naval staff ordered twenty more fighting ships in September 1940, and the launching of six vessels during the first two weeks of the month encouraged its optimism. In all, seventy corvettes and forty-eight Bangor-class minesweepers had been ordered to date, and the first proposal to build cargo ships for Canada's own account was forgotten.[68] In addition, the BATM inquired about constructing wooden minesweepers in Canada and on 26 October requested that the DMS negotiate with selected builders. Following extended tendering, acceptances, and withdrawals, on 31 January 1941 "go-ahead" instructions to build two vessels each were issued to five companies. But this initial British exploration of shipbuilding possibilities in Canada was not encouraging. Difficulties during the summer of 1941, equipment not delivered, changes demanded by the BATM, and delays by outside contractors were all causing delays. No deliveries had been made by September 1942.[69]

In September 1941 Howe appointed Frank M. Ross as director general of naval armament and equipment in direct response to the needs of the BATM, whose staff possessed only rudimentary knowledge of Canadian firms and their capabilities.[70] A prominent Montreal businessman closely connected to Canada's shipbuilding and ship-repair industries and to the Liberal Party, Ross was an ideal choice.[71] During the fall, certain irregularities occurred in the DMS's relationship with the BATM as Canadian officials began dealing directly with members of the British mission, leaving Ross out of the loop, but by December such looseness had been corrected; all correspondence and other dealings were routed through Ross's office, and the problem disappeared. Ross proved to be an excellent conduit through which the Admiralty's business was conducted in so far as naval armament and equipment were concerned.[72] This activity, which was all in relation to naval shipbuilding, was to change; Canada was about to face a sudden new demand for a merchant shipbuilding program.

The Second Shipbuilding Program

Shipping losses rose sharply during the second quarter of 1940 to 1 million deadweight tons (dwt).[73] In August the British government decided to send a mission of British shipbuilders to North America to try to arrange for the building of sixty merchant ships. British shipbuilding, severely reduced during the 1930s, was failing to respond to the war's challenges for increased production. Management, government, the navy, and labour refused to tackle owner, institutional, and trade-union barriers to increased production. Some second-hand cargo vessels had been purchased from the US Maritime Commission and private American owners, but as the former would not transfer contracts for ships under construction, the British were forced to initiate their own with US yards. Shrinking currency reserves dictated that only sixty cargo ships displacing about 500,000 dwt could be contracted for. Even this small order augmented British shipbuilding capacity by one-third, although it could replace only one-seventh of current British loses and would do so only fifteen months hence.[74]

In September 1940 the Technical Merchant Shipbuilding Mission arrived in New York under the leadership of Robert Cyril Thomson, head of Joseph L. Thompson Limited at Sunderland, England, and Harry Hunter of North-Eastern Marine Engineering Company Limited at Wallsend-on-Tyne. The mission carried detailed blueprints for the type of simple dry-cargo ship that was wanted.[75] Its focus was to find shipbuilding capacity in the United States, but its members also visited Canada, where they talked with C.D. Howe and David Carswell, inspected Canadian shipyards across the country, and began negotiating contracts. On 20 November Howe announced that negotiations to build eighteen large merchant ships for British account had recently been completed and that contracts were in the process of being awarded.[76] On 20 December the mission, acting through the DMS, issued contracts for twenty dry-cargo ships.[77] On-site inspection had shown that only four shipyards in the country were capable of handling vessels of 10,000 dwt. On the St Lawrence River, Canadian Vickers Limited at Montreal and Davie Shipbuilding and Repairing Company Limited at Lauzon had three and two berths, respectively, and on the West Coast, Burrard Dry Dock Limited at North Vancouver and Prince Rupert Dry Dock and Shipbuilding Company had two berths each.[78] The first three yards were assigned the original order. In January 1941 each received orders for six ships, later increased to eight in the case of Burrard. The order was increased to twenty-six ships in April.[79] By building cargo ships in Canada as well as the United States, the British had increased their shipbuilding capacity by more than 40 per cent. Indeed, to everyone's surprise, nearly one-third of the initial British order in North American was to be built in Canada. But with Canadian industrial production apparently reaching full capacity, absence of planning and other priorities were beginning to have consequences.

C.D. Howe's great strength was his ability to delegate to others, but his casual management of his six-month-old department with its vast purchase orders and expenditures on munitions was presenting the Cabinet with a serious problem.[80] Following a meeting wherein the Department of National Defence's plans and estimates for 1941–42, which included the naval service, had been prepared and submitted without reference to their practicability from the perspectives of labour, material, foreign exchange, or finance and without any consideration of current Canadian production for the United Kingdom, the deputy minister of finance, Dr W. Clifford Clark, proposed that a war requirements committee or board be formed with Harvey R. MacMillan as its chairman.[81] The prime minister agreed, and on 16 November 1941 order-in-council PC 6601 set up the War Requirements Board and appointed MacMillan as chairman. The new board was to secure, coordinate, and analyze information respecting war requirements for all industries. It seems that Howe's Cabinet colleagues forced MacMillan on him.

Harvey R. MacMillan was born in 1885 in Ontario and received his professional education at Yale University, where he earned a master of science degree in forestry. He became chief forester of British Columbia in 1912. During the First World War, he became assistant director of the Imperial Munitions Board. In 1919 he left government service and established H.R. MacMillan Export Company Limited. During the next score years, he developed his business, emerging as the largest lumber exporter and ship charterer in Canada. By 1939 he was a self-made millionaire lumber baron.[82]

In October 1940 MacMillan was already working for Howe and doing an excellent job. The minister had invited the industrialist to come to Ottawa in May, and on 5 June the two met and Howe asked MacMillan to become steel controller. MacMillan, who knew nothing about the steel industry, demurred, but a few days later he accepted an appointment as timber controller.[83] With 80 per cent of Canada's lumber production already geared to defence work, MacMillan was a natural choice. A.F.W. Plumptre, a senior official in the Department of Finance, was very impressed with MacMillan's performance during the summer of 1940.[84] By October, MacMillan was worried about the situation at Ottawa and anticipated that the whole munitions program would run into a "most serious crisis" in about six months. Although he thought highly of Howe, MacMillan no longer believed the government could just place orders without careful planning and coordination, taking into consideration manpower and materials projections and equally important delivery schedules. No one, he thought, was standing back and viewing the war situation as a whole, especially regarding Canada's industrial capacity. He viewed the Department of Munitions and Supply as a series of improvisations.[85] The men involved, for example Ralph Bell, Philip Malkin, and William Woodward, had generally run small businesses and knew little about large-scale industry. He thought the department should be rebuilt on the basis of coordinating labour, materials, and finance.[86]

The War Requirements Board was not a success. During its five-month history, Canada's industrial production remained disorganized. The new board – comprised of Graham Towers, governor of the Bank of Canada, Dr Clark from Finance, R.A.C. Henry and Carl Goldenburg from Munitions and Supply, and three representatives from the armed services – had the appearance of a strong body.[87] But Howe, who may have seen the need to plan, prioritize, regulate, and oversee production, was also obsessed with retaining control. The board was given enormous powers to gather information but remained an advisory body. Clark had recommended that it advise the Cabinet War Committee, but Howe ensured that it did so only through the minister of munitions and supply, which in view of the principle of ministerial responsibility was undoubtedly correct. On the other hand, the armed services already had direct access to the Cabinet War Committee through their own ministers and had no interest in making the board function effectively.

Within days of his appointment, MacMillan began having doubts about the board's efficacy, but he continued to serve as asked.[88] For all of his business acumen, Harvey MacMillan was an anglophile and patriot who desperately wanted to play an important role in the war. By mid-December 1940, however, he thought both the Cabinet and the war effort were leaderless. He was unable to find either "our war purpose or a war programme."[89] During December and January, Howe was out of the country, and MacMillan directed the board's attention toward the growing chaos in the aircraft industry and in ship repairing at Halifax. But although reports were produced, little resulted.[90]

Howe's biographers have accused MacMillan of plotting against him to take over the minister's department, but little beyond the malicious gossip of Liberal Party members and their sycophants in the press exists to support them.[91] If MacMillan was guilty of anything, it was talking too much about his fears and frustrations to politicians and reporters who were delighted to misrepresent them to create a scandal.[92] Like Wallace R. Campbell before him, MacMillan was insufficiently guarded when talking to members of the press gallery in Ottawa, and his inclination to voice concerns about the shortcomings of Canada's war effort embarrassed the government during Howe's absence in England.[93]

Upon his return, Howe moved to get rid of MacMillan, who had become the focus of criticism of the government's mismanagement of the war effort. During the month of February, he reduced the War Requirements Board to complete ineffectiveness, discrediting MacMillan in the process. Following a review of the board in March 1941, MacMillan informed Howe that it could not function as suggested by the order-in-council creating it and objected to the government and public's perception of the board as possessing administrative and executive powers that it had been unable to assume. Moreover, deciding priorities had been moved to the Cabinet War Committee, where projects contemplated by the armed services were referred.[94]

Several times during this period, MacMillan gave serious thought to his future action.[95] He did not resign, go home, and open up on Howe despite the abuse he had received within the government because, he acknowledged, the government was so strongly entrenched that there was no chance of rearranging management of the war effort, and he had doubts about his own correct course of action. He decided to carry out whatever job he was given.[96] Howe, ever suave and gracious and no longer threatened by MacMillan, urged him to stay on because he was needed. But he left him with nothing to do despite his nominal title as chairman of the War Requirements Board. At the end of the month, Howe asked MacMillan to look into the situation of service and repair of ships but appeared to have no further use for him.[97]

With MacMillan out of the way, Howe blamed much of the confusion and delay in war production on Norman McLarty, the minister of labour, who, he claimed, failed to deal resolutely with labour. He singled out McLarty's recent action to defuse trouble on the Halifax docks by raising stevedores' wages, thereby creating much more serious trouble in shipbuilding yards.[98] Howe's solution to mounting problems proliferating around shipbuilding and ship repairing was to create a new Crown company to take charge of the new cargo shipbuilding program, which he saw as a solution to the dilemma posed by American lend-lease.

On 4 April 1941 the government incorporated Wartime Merchant Shipping Limited (WMSL) at Montreal and, three days later, appointed MacMillan as president.[99] It proved to be a brilliant decision. Both men were prepared to let bygones be bygones, at least for the time being. MacMillan resigned from the War Requirements Board and took up his new task at Montreal.[100] The new company's head office at 420 rue de la Gauchetière was away from the pressures and politics of Ottawa. MacMillan was anxious to remove himself from Ottawa and, as a dynamic businessman, was temperamentally more fitted for an action job than for an advisory one. The company was to negotiate contracts for building cargo ships and to build and operate shipyards and plants.[101]

New problems appeared that would ensnare naval shipbuilding until the end of the war. The insufficiency of naval dry-docking for escort vessels at Halifax had become very serious by the end of 1940. Existing repair facilities on the East Coast were inadequate and badly organized to meet demands being placed on them. This had initially led to David Carswell's being appointed controller of ship construction and repairs in November 1940. Already named director general of the DMS's shipbuilding branch, Carswell's new appointment added ship repairs, including responsibility for the full utilization of facilities in the Maritimes, to his already heavy duties concerning the navy's construction program.[102]

Although Engineer Captain George L. Stephens was appointed engineer-in-chief in February 1941, as yet, the navy had no idea that its shipbuilding program would require unimagined repair facilities to maintain and refit as well as repair the new ships coming off the ways and being delivered down the St Lawrence River to Halifax. The small peacetime navy had always relied on private industry for dry-docking its ships even though repairs were handled in house at HMC dockyards at Esquimalt and Halifax.[103]

In January 1941, about the time the initial merchant shipbuilding contracts were signed with the shipbuilding companies, President Franklin D. Roosevelt committed the United States to building 2 million tons of these emergency-type ships, and Canada's minister of munitions and supply was considering ordering similar ships for Canada's own account.[104] On 5 March 1941, fearing that present naval work would slacken in the fall, the Cabinet War Committee approved David Carswell's recommendation that ten medium-size, single-screw cargo ships be built in order to keep the merchant shipyards at full capacity.

Carswell had recommended that the ships burn oil rather than coal for postwar marketability, which was also why he recommended the 4,700-ton vessels over the larger ones recently ordered by the British Merchant Shipbuilding Mission. Beyond favourable depreciation, the shipyards would not require capital assistance, and, he estimated, the cost of each vessel would amount to about $1 million. The naval service initially objected to the proposal, preferring to see the BATM invited to consider using the Canadian shipyards, and the War Requirements Board's strong support for the proposal was overtaken by events.[105] On 11 March, President Roosevelt signed the lend-lease bill into law. The same day, Howe told members of the House of Commons that Canada was now "going to build as many ships as we can build by reasonably economic methods." The following week, he informed the House that the government had already placed orders for the ships that filled existing berths.[106] But American generosity undermined the Canadian war effort by threatening to end or severely limit British purchases in Canada.[107]

Britain's shortage of gold and US dollar reserves had always been the chief impediment to placing large war orders in Canada, and Canada's own shortage of US dollars limited purchases south of the border. The government refused to denude itself of Canadian-owned US assets in order to obtain lend-lease aid for itself, which made it increasingly unlikely that it would obtain further British orders for munitions. The solution, which was arrived at after a good deal of Anglo-American financial diplomacy, was the Hyde Park Agreement, a declaration made by the US president on 20 April 1941.[108]

The agreement opened the US market to Canadian war production, and Howe successfully promoted shipbuilding as a key sector in which Canada had a proven ability to produce beyond its own needs. Since the declaration of war eighteen months before, Howe claimed that 104 steel and 380 wooden hulls of less than 113 feet had already been laid down.[109] Canada could sell ships to the United States for transfer to the British under lend-lease and thereby earn vital US dollars to purchase essential war materials such as machine tools for its own war production. The impact was immediate. The US government began placing orders for 10,000-ton ships to be built in Canada initially on a one at a time basis.[110] Later, between February 1942 and March 1943, the United States purchased ninety Canadian-built 10,000-ton cargo ships and transferred them to Great Britain on bareboat charter on lend-lease terms under the Hyde Park Agreement.[111] During the summer of 1941, the BATM began ordering warships from Canadian yards under the same program. This new turn of events also provided a solution to a local political problem that, although not of any great size, might have grown into something more serious.

Wartime Merchant Shipping Limited immediately took over the contracts and files concerning the first twenty-six ships being built for the British.[112] Much of the staff for the new company came from the Department of Munitions and Supply. David Carswell was the loser in the new changes. He had hoped to be the senior technical advisor at Wartime Merchant Shipping Limited but was excluded from having any place in the organization, forced out as director general of the department's shipbuilding branch, and reduced to being in charge of ship repairs. On 9 April 1941 he and his office of controller of ship repairs moved to Montreal and were located in the same building as WMSL's head office.[113]

The Canadian merchant ship program increased British shipbuilding capacity enormously. Boosters like E.P. Taylor thought the new company could produce 75 to 100 ships a year and that over 90 per cent of their content would be Canadian. MacMillan was more cautious, saying that 60 ships annually was a safer prediction; 100 ships was possible but wishful.[114] Taylor was closer to the mark, but neither man dreamed that Canadian merchant shipbuilding alone would exceed 1 million dwt in 1943 and 1944.

MacMillan appointed Colonel Alfred Henry Cowie, vice president of Dominion Bridge Company, as general manager of the Crown corporation and immediately travelled to the West Coast, where he appointed Austin Taylor, a wealthy Vancouver financier, rancher, and horseman, who had presented the Dominion government

Looking aft on hull no. 104 at West Coast Shipbuilders Limited, showing floor plates, frames, and tween-deck beams, 20 February 1942. Photo by W.J. Moore. CVA, City of Vancouver Photo Collection, 195-24.

with a $2 million interest-free loan, as vice president.[115] MacMillan also met with Clarence Wallace, president of Burrard Dry Dock Company, to discuss the 10,000-ton merchant ship program already underway. Wallace had laid down the first keel that same month and committed his yard to building an additional thirty North Sands–type vessels.[116] MacMillan then called Wallace to Montreal and contracted for over $60 million worth of ships.

Upon returning to Vancouver, Wallace called his executives together and continued sending out orders and dispatching telegrams and cables across the country in conformance with his contract. The next day an angry MacMillan called Wallace accusing him of tying up the country and shutting out other shipbuilders. Wallace pointed to his guarantees; he had done what he had to do. Not to be brooked, MacMillan called him back to Montreal and at a conference organized the manufacturers of machinery and components throughout Canada. Eastern shipbuilders fell into line behind Wallace. Wartime Merchant Shipping Limited took over all of Wallace's orders and began placing them for all Canadian shipyards in the merchant ship program, thereby halting at the very beginning what might have become a hopeless mess.[117]

The cargo ship program was quickly going to become very much larger than the naval construction program. The shipbuilding industry would be transformed beyond anything imagined. According to the DMS's official history, Wartime Merchant Shipping Limited was fully organized within three months of its incorporation and had established working relations with the British Merchant Shipping and Shipbuilding Missions in New York and Washington, DC, with the US Maritime Commission and the US War Shipping Administration, and with Canadian shipbuilders and manufacturers of machinery, auxiliary equipment, and parts across the country.[118] It was Harvey MacMillan at his best. Six months later, he could boast that Wartime Merchant Shipping Limited was supervising construction of 10,000- and 4,700-ton vessels on forty berths. A year before, there had been only nine. For the year ending 31 March 1942, WMSL had authorized construction of 174 cargo vessels (well over 1.5 million dwt of shipping). During the subsequent year, production increased from one 10,000-ton cargo ship being launched every eight days to one speeding down the ways every two days (see chapter 11).[119]

Growing Pains

Shipbuilding now involved at least three programs – naval, repairing, and merchant – that required still greater coordination and cooperation. The small-boat program initiated in 1939 may be counted as a fourth. Although related to the others, it operated separately without serious difficulty under the director general of the shipbuilding branch. The creation of Wartime Merchant Shipping Limited gave rise to confusion that further reveals Howe's casual approach to administration. David Carswell was not the only one to leave Ottawa. The navy seemed to pursue its own goals oblivious to anything else, and the BATM sought to educate Canadian shipbuilders about the need to adopt rigorous Admiralty specifications if they were to construct warships. The new cargo shipbuilding program, however, forced a sudden major expansion on the industry. Yet, with three major programs absorbing allocations of materials, finances, and manpower, planning remained virtually nonexistent.

F.A. Willsher, a career civil servant, briefly succeeded Carswell as director general of shipbuilding in April 1941, and Howe permitted MacMillan to raid the shipbuilding branch for staff for Wartime Merchant Shipping Limited at Montreal. Carswell at ship-repair control had a small staff of fewer than ten. Willsher had recently been appointed technical advisor to the shipbuilding branch while continuing his regular position as chairman of the board of steamship inspection, Department of Transport. Like Carswell, he was a native of Scotland and trained in the old country. He had immigrated to Canada in 1910 and worked in the shipbuilding industry in Toronto, Wilmington, Delaware, and Quebec City until 1913, when he joined the federal marine department. During the First World War, he assisted C.F. M. Duguid, who supervised wartime shipbuilding, and afterward remained in government, becoming responsible for the design of icebreakers and other craft. In 1931 he was appointed chief inspector of hulls and equipment for the Board of Steamship Inspection and in 1940 became its head.[120] Despite his experience and in keeping with Howe's aversion to civil servants, in June, Howe replaced Willsher with a businessman, Desmond A. Clarke, president of Clarke Steamship Company Limited.

When Clarke arrived in Ottawa, he found just thirteen people staffing the shipbuilding branch, which was wholly inadequate in view of the new shipbuilding programs. Clarke also found ship production bogged down, as plants were unable to secure delivery of materials and parts. Prior to this time, the shipbuilding branch had not included procurement of and follow-up on materials, machinery, and parts to go into ships. But with the expansion of both the naval and merchant programs in August, these became bottlenecks to be unplugged.[121] Willsher appears to have returned to full-time duty with the Department of Transport because about this time W. Harold Milne joined the branch and replaced him as technical advisor to the new director general.

W. Harold Milne (1898–1974) was a distinguished naval architect and partner in the successful firm of German and Milne at Montreal. He had served a thorough apprenticeship in the British shipbuilding industry with Fairfield Shipbuilding and Engineering Company at Glasgow and with Vickers Limited's naval construction works at Barrow-in-Furness, England. He attended technical schools in both locations and worked in the patent department before immigrating to Canada in 1917. He served for two years in the drawing office and as a hull surveyor in the marine department of the Imperial Munitions Board at Ottawa. During the early 1920s, he acted as a naval draughtsman and assumed executive positions with H.E. McClelland and Company, Canadian Allis-Chalmers Limited, and Wallace Shipyard (later Burrard Dry Dock Company). He was manager of Montreal Dry Dock Limited for a year before assuming the position of operating manager and later general superintendent at St John Dry Dock and Shipbuilding Company for eleven years. In 1936, not yet forty years old, he joined Lambert and German, perhaps the leading firm of naval architects in Canada, and three years later he became a partner.[122] W. Harold Milne was the ideal man to act as advisor to the new director of shipbuilding, for like many of C.D. Howe's dollar-a-year men, Clarke was a businessman rather than an industrialist and knew little about shipbuilding.

The creation of Wartime Merchant Shipping Limited and subsequent rebuilding and reorganization of the DMS's shipbuilding branch had detrimental effects on the naval shipbuilding program, especially after difficulties that occurred in the spring with fitting out corvettes and Bangor-class minesweepers. Under Carswell's traditional style of management, the shipbuilding branch had left procurement of boilers, engines, generators, pumps, valves, piping, electrical equipment, and many other items to the shipbuilding firms, which ignored the absence of procurement facilities in many plants. In June 1941 the deputy minister of the Department of National Defence was so concerned that he advised the DMS to follow the example of Wartime Merchant Shipping Limited and set up a strong procurement organization to centralize orders, carry out purchasing, and coordinate deliveries. In response, the shipbuilding branch adopted what appeared to be a ready solution, turning a large portion of the new naval program over to MacMillan's new Crown corporation.[123] MacMillan was only too happy to oblige, but the move was precipitate and unwise.

It was MacMillan who recommended to the minister in July 1941 that twelve Western Isles trawler minesweepers be approved for immediate construction "to utilize berths now vacant and becoming vacant on the Great Lakes" and because the plans for Algerine-class minesweepers might not arrive for two or three months. "Unless work is speedily arranged the men will drift away from the yards."[124] About the same time, Clarke, who was investigating the shipbuilding branch's purchasing procedures, found among several recommendations a way to reduce the branch's dependence on the naval service both for inspectors in shipbuilding plants and for information as to the suitability of contractors to accept contracts and monitor progress in the yards. The recommendations ignored the need to separate contract negotiations from production oversight. Clarke's expanding staff was carrying out duties that had not been initially contemplated, including procurement of and follow-up on materials. It became much more necessary after August, when the naval program was enlarged and the cargo shipbuilding program began to take off, to order machinery and parts to go into ships. Shipyards were not securing materials and parts as planned; yet expanding the shipbuilding branch was necessary to eliminate the bottlenecks of the past and to secure a steady flow of goods to the yards.

During the summer of 1941, reports flowed into Naval Service Headquarters and the BATM, which had just placed ship contracts for new corvettes and trawler minesweepers with the DMS, that procurement officers with the cargo ship program were approving equipment that failed to meet Admiralty specifications. Even worse, they were attempting to negotiate contracts for new, more sophisticated types of antisubmarine vessels, frigates, and Algerine-class minesweepers in the absence of complete specifications, thus undoing ten months of effort by the BATM's technical officers to educate selected firms to meet Admiralty standards of manufacture. Rear Admiral Sheridan was more than a little vexed when he realized what was happening.[125] Clarke, who was busy expanding and organizing the shipbuilding branch, had neglected to inform the BATM about his arrangement with Wartime Merchant Shipping Limited or about the reorganizations of his branch.

Early in September 1941, during an interview with Howard Mitchell, Howe dropped several remarks indicating his displeasure with WMSL and MacMillan. Mitchell, who was the latter's personal assistant, vigorously defended his boss, "causing Howe to give me some long hard unsmiling looks, and the others to raise their eyebrows."[126] MacMillan was finding Clarke impossible to deal with: suspicious, jealous, and non-cooperative. He refused to have anything further to do with the director general of naval shipbuilding.[127] The confusion was not resolved until the autumn, when the president of WMSL denied to Rear Admiral Sheridan that any restrictions on inspection or supervision by representatives of the Admiralty or the Royal Canadian Navy had been contemplated in the modus operandi that he had earlier proposed. Henceforth, naval ship construction was to be carried on by the director general of the shipbuilding branch; WMSL "shall have nothing to do with them."[128]

About 1 October 1941 the shipbuilding branch assumed responsibilities for all vessels for the army and air force as well as the navy. Clarke established three divisions in the shipbuilding branch: administration under R.E. Lawson, his executive assistant, technical under W. Harold Milne, and production under Douglas W. Ambridge. It was only in December that he set up a fourth division under M.G. Farquhar to manage negotiations, which divorced these duties from production.[129] Although Howe and the naval service should not be absolved for their contributions to the muddle, the initial lack of staff and considerable delay in reorganizing the branch's purchasing procedures undoubtedly contributed to the problems encountered in naval shipbuilding during the summer of 1941.

In October, probably in response to the preceding confusion, Howe rearranged the senior management of the shipbuilding branch, appointing Douglas W. Ambridge, assistant general manager of the Ontario Paper Company, director of the shipbuilding branch under director general Clarke. Ambridge, a rather bombastic, pugnacious engineer, was educated in Quebec and had served overseas with the Canadian field artillery during the First World War. In 1923 he graduated from McGill University in chemical engineering and was appointed general superintendent of Anglo-Canadian Pulp and Paper Mills Limited at Quebec City in 1928. He became assistant general manager of Anglo Newfoundland Development Company in 1933 before assuming a similar position with Ontario Paper at a later date.[130] Ambridge served under Clarke for only four months before Howe also appointed him a director of Polymer Corporation. On 3 May 1943 Ambridge succeeded Clarke as director general of shipbuilding until 15 October 1944, when he left to become president of Abitibi Power and Paper Company Limited.[131]

In response to the American lend-lease and the Hyde Park Agreement, on 13 May 1941 Howe also incorporated War Supplies Limited to obtain orders from departments of the United States government and appointed the young E.P. Taylor as president. The Crown company sold ships to the United States for transfer to the United Kingdom under lend-lease. Following creation of the US Priorities Board in May, shipbuilding companies found themselves unable to negotiate the difficult American procedures to establish their priority to acquire materials, and on 7 August the minister set up yet another Crown corporation, Trafalgar Shipbuilding Company Limited, to arrange priorities for materials required in the naval shipbuilding program. But it was quickly seen to be unnecessary and was dissolved. Its incorporation, however, was part of the muddle during the hectic summer of 1941.[132]

By the fall, the shipbuilding programs were assuming the shapes they would have for the remainder of the war. Much learning still lay ahead, but the cargo ship program very quickly expanded beyond the naval program. By early 1942 forty berths were available to handle 10,000-ton freighters, and nine more were capable of constructing 4,700-tonners in twelve shipyards, which represented about a 50 per cent increase above the previous fall.[133] In the third quarter of 1941, merchant shipbuilding employed just over 5,000 workers, compared to 15,000 working on naval construction, but the tables turned almost immediately thereafter, and the number of workers employed on warship construction actually declined during the next two quarters. Afterward, it grew slowly until it reached about 27,000 workers in the third quarter of 1943. The number of workers employed on cargo ships passed those employed on naval construction early in 1942, doubling to 32,000 by the middle of the year. It reached a peak of about 50,000 in the first quarter of 1943 before declining (see figure 6.1).[134]

As part of its continuing reorganization, the shipbuilding branch ceased to be directly responsible for Dufferin Shipbuilding Company in October 1941, when the government purchased all of the company's assets and incorporated Toronto Shipbuilding Company Limited to run the shipbuilding plant (see chapter 4).[135] At the same time, the shipbuilding branch staff grew steadily, from thirty-five in September to sixty-five at the end of the year; by March 1942 the Ottawa staff numbered eighty, divided among administration, technical, negotiations, production, and priorities divisions.[136] Wartime Merchant Shipping Limited was larger, with 106 officers and senior employees, including eight on loan from private companies.[137]

In April 1942 Colonel Cowie resigned as vice president of WMSL and was succeeded by Charles Redfern, a prominent Toronto engineer and building contractor. This change appeared to mark an attempt to oust MacMillan from the presidency.[138] What motivated and who was behind the attempted coup is unclear, but MacMillan weathered the challenge. According to Howard Mitchell, a meeting of the corporation's board of directors was called in late June, with Howe to attend, but the directors must have stood by MacMillan, for regardless of Howe's wishes the former's departure would have thrown the whole onus of the ouster directly on the minister's head.[139] Redfern departed WMSL on 10 July and only resurfaced a year later when he took control of Toronto Shipbuilding Company. A recommendation to consolidate Wartime Merchant Shipping Limited, the shipbuilding branch, and ship-repair control was ignored until 1944, when the major construction progams were coming to an end.[140]

By 1942 Wartime Merchant Shipping Limited had evolved into a tight organization. Working directly under president MacMillan were the vice president in change of Pacific Coast operations, two assistants to the president in charge of two major departments, operations and construction, and two managers of procurement and shipyard organization and personnel.[141] Due to the increased number of firms manufacturing parts in the Vancouver area for both East and West Coast shipbuilders, in July 1943 members of the production division left Ottawa to assist vice president Austin Taylor, who also represented the director general of shipbuilding and the controller of ship repairs.[142]

Events in 1941 had overwhelmed Halifax and the navy's recent reorganization of the dockyard. In response to additional responsibilities, the navy reorganized the dockyard administration yet again in the spring of 1942. The position of commander-in-chief of the dockyard was abolished, and all naval technical and repair services at Halifax, other than those operating under the emergency-repair agreement, were amalgamated under the engineer superintendent in the dockyard. Repair work handled under the emergency-repair agreement or undertaken at other East Coast naval bases became the responsibility of the supervising naval engineer for the Maritimes.[143]

Until the beginning of 1942, the BATM provided all advice on building warships for the Royal Canadian Navy. Constructor Captain A.G.W. Stantan, of the prestigious Royal Corps of Naval Constructors, was the senior constructor officer. Engineer Captain George L. Stephens wanted to form a constructor branch, and the Royal Navy loaned the deputy director of the Royal Corps of Naval Constructors. Commander A.N. Harrison, RCN, arrived in Canada at Naval Service Headquarters as Constructor Captain RCN (Temporary) and on 6 January 1942 was appointed director of naval construction. Later, he was appointed constructor-in-chief of the RCN.[144] In the summer, Engineer Captain Stephens was appointed chief of naval engineering and construction and was directing an enlarged staff divided among an engineer-in-chief, concerned mainly with ship repairing and repair bases, and three directorates, who dealt with naval construction, shipbuilding, and electrical engineering. Despite this growth, the staff remained wholly inadequate, and Rear Admiral Sheridan's technical staff at the BATM continued to exceed the number of Stephens's staff at NSHQ. A year later, responding to continuing pressure on Halifax, an executive officer was appointed commodore superintendent and placed in charge of repairing, refitting, and storing all HMC ships on the East Coast and outports; placed nominally under the commander-in-chief of the Canadian Northwest Atlantic, he was responsible directly to NSHQ at Ottawa.[145]

In April 1942 Vice Admiral Nelles did not propose to make any changes to the naval shipbuilding program, although he had been advised that the British Admiralty delegation in Washington had received an official request from the United States Navy that it be allowed to acquire frigates and Revised corvettes being built in Canada for

British account under lend-lease appropriations.[146] Authority to build the first ten frigates had appeared in July 1941, and in November the Cabinet War Committee had authorized an additional twenty frigates and ten Algerine-class minesweepers to be built for the RCN. On 28 January 1942 it authorized building two additional Tribal-class destroyers at a total cost of nearly $77 million, exclusive of armament and stores.[147] On 28 July 1942, however, the War Committee approved construction of thirty-five additional warships, seven frigates, six Algerine-class minesweepers, and twenty-two Revised corvettes, for which no provision had been made in the 1942–43 estimates. These unexpected ships came from the rate of Allied losses to submarines and the need to remove the menace in view of the anticipated shipments to various war theatres, especially the Mediterranean.[148] To obtain these ships, the DMS planned to assign Davie Shipbuilding and Repairing Company to frigate construction, hoping thereby to ensure delivery to the RCN of fifty-nine frigates by June 1945 if delivery of machinery and parts could be speeded up.[149] By 1 December 1942 the DMS had eighty-two frigates, forty-three Algerines, and fifty-three Revised corvettes on order for delivery in 1942, 1943, and 1944.[150]

A survey of the naval shipbuilding branch during the summer of 1942 attributed delays in naval construction to lack of working drawings, revisions to drawings after they had been issued to shipbuilders, and delays in manufacture and delivery of components.[151] Delays were frequent and sometimes bizarre, such as those associated with building the Algerine-class minesweeper. The original dual design created no end of problems. One firm in Great Britain designed the ship's forward end, while design of the aft end was the responsibility of a second British firm. This arrangement resulted in discrepancies in respect to tying the two sections together. Discovery in the Toronto shipyard required redesign work, which had of necessity to be submitted to the BATM for approval, causing additional delays.[152]

Circumstances combined with questionable policy in 1942 to create a major crisis that delayed the modernization of the Canadian fleet.[153] First, following the American withdrawal of destroyers from the North Atlantic early in 1942, there was no possibility of upgrading the first Canadian-built corvettes that had been rushed to sea in 1940 and 1941. These vessels were woefully ill equipped with respect to navigation aids and antisubmarine detection devices. Corvettes completed in 1942 had to be similarly rushed to sea without the latest equipment and with poorly trained crews to meet the gap. Second, on 6 August the Combined Munitions Assignment Board, of which Canada was not a member, transferred to the United States Navy (USN) from the British shipbuilding program in Canada fifteen Revised corvettes and eight Fairmile motor launches, thereby reducing the number that could be expected to remain available.[154] Third, in September the chief of the naval staff committed sixteen corvettes from the convoys to Operation Torch in the Mediterranean, further straining naval resources. Fourth, the USN's refusal to institute convoys along the eastern coast of America and the loss of four of twelve tankers assigned to Canada forced the CNS to assign eight escorts to convoy tankers en route to the West Indies.[155] Finally, successful U-boat attacks in the St Lawrence River and the Gulf of

St Lawrence forced additional scarce resources to be removed from the convoys and assigned to the St Lawrence River.[156] Existing conditions would not permit the naval staff to send ships into dry dock for modernization.

The need to modernize, an equipment crisis, and inadequate repair facilities led to curtailment of the naval shipbuilding program and the removal of Vice Admiral Nelles as CNS in 1943. The naval problems and labour shortages for both merchant shipbuilding and ship crews also led to a sharp cut in the cargo ship program. During a thorough discussion of shipbuilding in the Cabinet on 28 July 1943, Howe recommended continuance of the existing cargo program, but several ministers opposed him on the grounds of manpower shortages and competing interests. The Cabinet War Committee ordered a 50 per cent cut in the rate of construction for the merchant ship program.[157] The naval service had strongly influenced this decision. Two weeks earlier Captain Eric Brand had addressed a memorandum to the naval minister, secretary of the naval board, and assistant chief of the naval staff strongly recommending curtailment of the program.[158]

Contingent events continued to influence the programs. German mine-laying off Halifax in May and June 1943 had a powerful impact. Accordingly, in August the naval staff and naval board approved construction of sixteen 126-foot, wooden minesweepers, twelve for the East Coast and four for the West Coast. But as the BATM had already ordered twenty-four of these motorized vessels from three of Nova Scotia's largest wooden shipbuilders in December 1942, the navy's orders, made only in December, were placed a year later wherever a yard could be found.[159] Only ten of these minesweepers were ever built. In August 1944 slow progress in Ontario boatyards and events in Europe led to six contracts being cancelled, and of the ten remaining vessels, none was completed before the war in the Pacific ended. Most were commissioned into the RCN and turned over to the Soviet navy under Canada's mutual-aid agreement.[160] This was the last RCN wartime shipbuilding program, but orders for ships for the Royal Navy continued to be placed.

Conclusion

Canada's labour pool had dried up and a manpower shortage on the East Coast was severely affecting the ship-repair industry despite its priority over new construction. At a meeting at Ottawa on 12 August 1943, the combined Canada-UK-US committee to examine repair problems for warships and merchant vessels on the East Coast of Canada and Newfoundland acknowledged the existence of a shortage of between 4,000 and 5,000 men.[161] Although the rate of merchant ship production had been cut in July, on 8 September DMS officials obtained approval to reduce the actual number of large cargo ships still to be built from eighty-four ships to forty-two. Nine medium-size ships, inexpensive and needed for Canadian use, continued to be included.[162]

By September 1943 it was clear that shipbuilding had taken on a new complexion. In a letter to the president of Wartime Merchant Shipping Limited, Howe proposed amalgamating the corporation's divisional offices and the naval shipbuilding branch.[163] MacMillan replied that either WMSL should be wound up and placed under the director general of naval shipbuilding and both staffs amalgamated or the company should continue independently under C.L. Dewar as president, with a reduced staff to supervise and terminate contracts.[164] Maintenance of ships already built had become increasingly important, and the naval staff indicated that modernization of escorts and refits now took priority over any new warship construction. In December the naval staff cancelled the last forty-one frigates and eleven corvettes on order for the RCN.[165]

Harvey R. MacMillan retired as president of Wartime Merchant Shipping Limited on 16 December and returned to private business, and the corporation was reduced, renamed, and reorganized to manage both naval and merchant ship construction. Also in December, the minister of munitions and supply announced establishment of a shipbuilding coordination committee to deal with common problems of building and repairing naval and merchant ships. Chaired by David Carswell, the committee had two other members, Douglas Ambridge, who had replaced Desmond Clarke in October as director general of the shipbuilding branch, and C.L. Dewar, newly appointed president of Wartime Merchant Shipping Limited. The committee's aim was to ensure the fullest possible use of all existing facilities whether building or repairing ships.[166] Engineer Captain A.C.M. Davy, RCN, director of naval engineering development, was added to the committee in January to represent the naval service, but it appears that no other meeting was ever held.[167] Fullest use of all facilities, whether building or repairing ships, was already in hand, and no further purpose could be served. Although it took four years to weed out incompetence and reorganize repeatedly the structures of governance, Canada had become a well-oiled industrial-production machine.

Some functions of the shipbuilding branch were formally transferred on 15 January 1944 to Wartime Merchant Shipping Limited, recently renamed Wartime Shipbuilding Limited.[168] C.L. Dewar and Austin Taylor remained president and vice president, respectively, of the new company, which assumed responsibility for the naval escort program (i.e., frigates and corvettes) in addition to the cargo ship program. Douglas Ambridge continued as director general of the new shipbuilding branch, to which Wartime Shipbuilding Limited would report. The Toronto Shipbuilding Company was also wound up and placed under the direction of Wartime Shipbuilding Limited.[169] The merger of staffs from WMSL and the naval shipbuilding branch to form Wartime Shipbuilding Limited initially gave rise to some serious difficulties. The BATM found the men from the former cargo ship program "by no means" the same quality as those on the naval shipbuilding staff. They knew next to nothing about warships, so the process of educating had to be commenced all over again. A routine was gradually worked out whereby British naval officers settled all technical matters, and "good relations" were eventually established.

Fortunately, Wartime Shipbuilding Limited undertook only three new projects: maintenance ship conversions, construction of transport ferries (LST 3s), and amenities ship conversions.[170] Nevertheless, some confusion occurred in handling British orders. In May 1944 some negotiations were being carried out by the British Ministry of War Transport's representatives in Montreal and some through the DMS's representatives in London.[171] In mid-October, Douglas Ambridge returned to private business, and David Carswell once more became director general of the shipbuilding branch, the same post he had occupied between April 1940 and April 1941.[172] Ships continued to be launched, but during the remainder of 1944 and in 1945, no further reorganizations appeared necessary. The government had brought together all aspects of shipbuilding to be wound down.

The changes during 1944 resulted in a slight decrease in the output of cargo ships, but the decline was more than offset by the greater number of warships delivered in spite of contract cancellations. The fighting ship schedule for 1944 both in tonnage and dollar value exceeded that of the previous year. In addition, the naval yards began producing for the Royal Navy large landing ships, each costing in the neighbourhood of $1.5 million.[173]

Constantly changing demands in response to contingent events and the government's reluctance to plan had not prepared it for the challenges of war production. Throughout nearly six years, between 1939 and 1945, the government's response to events was a combination of casual, chaotic, and confused. Considering the size of the challenge facing a small nation with few human and material resources, there probably could have been no other response.

Organization of Canada's shipbuilding programs was haphazard, driven mostly by contingent events. Largely attributed to C.D. Howe and the Department of Munitions and Supply, Canada's ability to build ships during the Second World War was due to much more and many more. Howe's huge department with thousands of personnel who manned twenty-six branches and nineteen controls, not to mention twenty-eight Crown corporations with thousands more employees, had all the powers to plan, fund, and direct operations, but it did not build a single ship or anything else for that matter. Three programs, four if small auxiliary vessels and boats are included, does not speak well of government planning and management. It seems to be a function of Canadian historiography to make too much of the administrative dimensions of Canada's war production, which took more than four years to get straightened out, and not enough of the builders. Indeed, this traditional emphasis has been at the expense of the companies, the owners, and the workers who constructed the ships, to which the remaining chapters are devoted.

Shipyards and Their Owners

Introduction

Despite the number and widespread location of Canada's shipyards, their ownership was in surprisingly few hands. No one type of ownership prevailed over another. Single families privately owned some yards. Some were held in private partnerships or limited companies. Others were subsidiaries of large, publicly owned holding companies. Finally, during the war the government created several yards, including one of the largest. The press of circumstances also forced the government to assume ownership of other yards; some were Crown corporations with their own management and boards of directors, and the management of others was privately contracted out. Nevertheless, examination of shipyard ownership indicates that private industry played the most crucial role in wartime shipbuilding. This was as might be expected, for the government was unable to marshal and manage the necessary materials and resources alone. The great task facing owners was to ready their moribund yards – equipped with old, outdated, worn-out machinery and tools – in order to respond to the greatest challenge in their history.

Maritime Provinces

Men had built ships along Canada's East Coast for nearly three centuries and continued to practise their ancient crafts during the war, building slightly more than 2,000 vessels of many shapes and sizes. Almost all were of wooden construction, products of age-old skills for which Canada's East Coast shipwrights were justly famous. At first sight, it may seem surprising that only three corvettes, thirty-two medium-size cargo ships, and a few tugs were built of steel in the maritime provinces. East Coast ports were Canada's only ice-free ports giving access to the Atlantic, and it seems they should have been the location of a large modern shipbuilding industry. Yet the opposite occurred. The only warships built at Halifax were commissioned after the war was over.

Current historiography holds that the wartime shipbuilding industry in the maritime provinces was underdeveloped owing to a deliberate policy of the Dominion government to favour the nation's industrial heartland stretching between Quebec

City and Windsor, Ontario, and that this policy was detrimental to Canada's war effort as well as to the Maritimes.[1] Despite the good argument, no production figures have ever been presented to support this view, and the claim overemphasizes the significance of the delayed reopening of the Sydney plate mill. In addition to a lack of skilled labour and raw materials for modern ship construction in the region, the proximity of East Coast ports to the Battle of the Atlantic and the need to employ scarce human and material resources to repair ships damaged by war and peril of the sea were much more important considerations. One does not build ships on the frontline, which is where the maritime provinces were. Moreover, repair work was far more profitable than new construction and urgently needed.[2] Far from ignoring the Maritimes, the government acquiesced to unrelenting pressure from the Nova Scotia government and the minister of national defence for naval services, Angus L. Macdonald, to build a shipyard in the small town of Pictou exclusively for the construction of steel-hulled cargo ships.

Two shipbuilding yards dominated the maritime provinces, one at St John, New Brunswick, and the other at Halifax, Nova Scotia. Frank M. Ross was owner and president of St John Dry Dock and Shipbuilding Company.[3] Originally a subsidiary of Canadian Dredge and Dock Company of Midland, Ontario, the company had been established in 1916 to take up contracts formerly entered into by Norton Griffith and Company of London, England. In 1912 the Dominion government had contracted with that company to build a first-class dry dock at East St John, including a breakwater protecting Courtney Bay, and to dredge a channel and a turning basin. The project halted in 1915 when the company went into liquidation. Canadian Dredge and Dock began operations in 1918, and five years later Governor General Lord Byng officially opened the finished dry dock, but the world shipbuilding boom had gone bust. The company was struggling, and Ross acquired it relatively easily from Canadian Dredge and Dock in 1926.

Frank Mackenzie Ross was born in 1897 and immigrated to Canada as a youth from Glasgow, Scotland. In 1910 he joined the Canadian Bank of Commerce at Montreal. He enlisted in 1915, was severely wounded in France, and was decorated for bravery. After four years in the army, he may have found it difficult to settle down and left banking to pursue a career in business. He moved to St John, New Brunswick, where he secured a position with the St John Dry Dock and Shipbuilding Company. He soon became general manager.[4]

Ross's rise in business was meteoric. Within a year and a half, he acquired principal ownership of St John Dry Dock and Shipbuilding Company. In 1926 the company was getting by on government subsidies, which Ross used to acquire two more profitable companies, St John Iron Works, a ship repair company, and St John Towing Company. Ross also became vice president and director of Lindsay Swan Hunter, ship repairers, tugboat owners, and marine salvors, and he represented the English shipbuilding firm of Swan Hunter and Wigham Richardson. A man of imagination as well as business acuity, in 1926 he also founded Bristol Aero Engines Limited in Canada and Canadian Wright Limited in conjunction with Wright Engine Company of the

United States. He became president of International Paints Limited. Late that same year, Ross, who was already president of Montreal Dry Dock Limited, and Victor M. Drury, an investment dealer, acquired Canadian Vickers Limited at Montreal.[5]

Ross was credited with rebuilding St John's port facilities after a disastrous fire in 1931, and during the war's early years he, more than anyone else, was responsible for the great development of the dry dock, East St John, and Courtney Bay. In June 1943, when the City of St John granted him the freedom of the city in recognition of his activities, a local newspaper reported, "No individual has contributed more … to the growth of the port and its facilities."[6] Ross was also vice president of Sincennes-McNaughton Lines, Eastern Canada Coastal Steamships Limited, and Hamilton Bridge Company and a director of Canadian Dredge and Dock Company. These appointments connected him with Joseph A. Simard, president of Marine Industries Limited, and with Victor Drury, who was also a vice president of Hamilton Bridge.

During the war, while Ross was in Ottawa as a dollar-a-year man, his St John business associates, Frank G. Wilson, vice president and secretary treasurer, and his brother Charles N. Wilson, general manager, looked after the operation of St John Dry Dock and Shipbuilding Company. J.M.H. Fraser served as general superintendent. In September 1940 C.D. Howe appointed Ross director general of naval armament in the Department of Munitions and Supply. Ross, perhaps more than any other man, succeeded in convincing Vice Admiral Sir Alfred Evans, RN, and officers of the British Admiralty Technical Mission that Canadians could produce the necessary material, leading them to accept that the Royal Navy could acquire ships and arms from outside Great Britain for the first time since the eighteenth century. Ross and Evans became firm friends. Both men made many perilous crossings of the Atlantic by bomber, but only Ross survived. Admiral Evans was lost at sea in 1944.

Under Ross's direction, the Canadian Pacific Railway's Ogden shops in Calgary were taken over, along with 80 per cent of the Angus shops in Montreal, and Nova Scotia Steel and Iron Company at Trenton, Nova Scotia, and Dominion Engineering Works at Longeuil, Quebec, were commandeered to manufacture naval guns, gun mounts, depth charges, torpedo parts, asdic gear, and other naval equipment and munitions.

Early in 1944 Ross joined Colonel Victor Spencer, scion of a wealthy Vancouver business family, to buy full control of Western Bridge and Steel Fabricators, a subsidiary of Hamilton Bridge Company, of which he was already vice president, and together, in March 1945, they acquired controlling interest in West Coast Shipbuilders Limited. The two firms, which adjoined each other on False Creek and had cooperated since 1941 to build fifty 10,000-ton freighters, then amalgamated.[7] Ross sold his interests in St John Dry Dock and Shipbuilding to the Wilson brothers, and British Columbia henceforth became his field of endeavour.

The other major shipyard in the Maritimes was Halifax Shipyards Limited, formed in 1918 after C.C. Ballantyne, minister of marine and fisheries and of the naval service in Robert Borden's Union government, invited Joseph W. Norcross and Roy Wolvin, president and director, respectively, of Canada Steamship Lines (CSL), to establish a

Fairmile motor launch, Q084, built by John H. Leblanc Company, Weymouth, Nova Scotia, and commissioned 25 May 1942. LAC, PA-134191.

new shipyard to replace the Halifax graving-dock facility destroyed in the 1917 explosion. Both men were also involved in Collingwood Shipbuilding Company and Canadian Vickers Limited. Norcross and Wolvin demanded and received the expropriated Halifax Graving Dock Company, sufficient adjacent land to establish a large shipyard, and a contract to build four government ships.[8]

Wolvin was primarily a financial promoter, and in 1919, acting for a syndicate of British investors, he negotiated a takeover of Dominion Steel Corporation from J.H. Plummer of Toronto that allowed him to become its president. In 1921 the directors of Halifax Shipyards traded the $8 million in company assets for shares of the ill-fated British Empire Steel and Coal Company (Besco), characterized by historian Michael Bliss as "the single most troubled Canadian corporation in the 1920s."[9] Besco was a product of Wolvin and Norcross's collaboration with English financiers' postwar imperialist dream of becoming shipbuilders to the British Empire by creating a $500 million merger of Canada's principal shipbuilding and shipping companies and Nova Scotia's steel and coal companies. Dominion Steel, Dominion Coal, Dominion Iron and Steel, Nova Scotia Steel and Coal, Eastern Car, and Halifax Shipyards were involved in the merger. But it was all quite mad. World shipbuilding was drowning in excess capacity.[10]

Besco collapsed in 1925, and financial problems dogged Halifax Shipyards Limited until 1928, when a group of Toronto financiers backed by the Royal Bank of Canada created a new company. Dominion Steel and Coal Company (Dosco) arose out of the shambles of Besco, and although the parent company could not make any money during the 1930s, Halifax Shipyards, under general manager Robert J.R. Nelson, survived on repair work.[11] Indeed, during the Second World War, Halifax Shipyards and other yards in the Halifax area, including HMC Dockyard, were completely occupied with repair work, which put them on a different footing than other shipyards in Canada. From the owners' point of view, Halifax Shipyards became a very profitable company, for there was virtually no way to control the company's earnings (i.e., by placing work on a cost-plus-fixed-fee basis). Repairs varied enormously and were labour intensive and paid for on a time-plus-materials basis.

Small shipyards abounded in the Maritimes. Besides those at St Andrews, Buctouche, and Gagetown in New Brunswick and at Summerside on Prince Edward Island, there were many more in Nova Scotia.[12] In the spring of 1940 a new firm known as Clare Shipbuilding Company Limited took over the business assets of Meteghan Shipbuilding Company. It did not assume any liabilities of the old concern; instead, John F. Deveau, former business agent of Meteghan Shipbuilding became president of the new firm, and it was presumed at the time that creditors agreed he would personally assume the liabilities of the old firm.[13] Clare Shipbuilding went on to build twenty-seven wooden minesweepers during the war. By August 1943, when the company employed about 340 men, ownership of the company may have changed, for the president was then W.G. Clarke of Montreal.[14]

Acadians employed at Leblanc Shipbuilding Company Limited at Weymouth, Nova Scotia, built two wooden minesweepers and fifteen Fairmile motor launches, while men at Smith and Rhuland at Lunenburg, builders of the famous *Bluenose*, constructed twelve 65-foot, wooden tugboats for the British Ministry of War Transport. At Wagstaff and Hatfield at Port Greville and at Shelburne Shipbuilders Limited, workers built eleven 126-foot, wooden minesweepers. Those at Industrial Shipping Company Limited at Halifax constructed twenty-three 65-foot tugs and 435 MINCA ("Made in Canada") barges at its plant on Mahone Bay.[15] But it bears repeating that the great role played by maritime shipyards and led by Halifax Shipyards was ship repairing. During the Second World War, Halifax Shipyards carried out more than 6,700 ship repairs.

St Lawrence River

The heartland of Canada's shipbuilding industry, such as it was in 1939, lay along the St Lawrence River between Montreal and Quebec City, where three large and two small yards quickly moved into high gear at the outbreak of war. Davie Shipbuilding and Repairing Company Limited at Lévis was the oldest surviving shipyard in Canada. Founded in 1825 by Allison Davie, an English ship captain, the shipyard moved to its south-shore location seven years later, where it prospered until shortly before the First World War.[16] Between 1914 and 1917 the Davie shipyard at Lauzon ceased to be a family-owned business and through acquisition by British Maritime

Trust Limited, a great armaments conglomerate, became a minor subsidiary of Vickers Sons and Maxim Limited.

In 1914, to refinance his undercapitalized company, George Davie and his brother, Allison, who headed the firm, desperately needed working capital. They sold the company to Charles A. Barnard, KC, a Montreal barrister turned entrepreneur, who transferred four-fifths of his shares to British Maritime Trust Limited, thereby reducing the once-independent firm to an insignificant subsidiary.[17] In 1920 the company was controlled by Canada Steamship Lines, also a product of English financiers, and after going into liquidation three years later, it was purchased outright by CSL in January 1925, transforming Davie Shipbuilding and Repairing Company into a wholly owned subsidiary.

The company survived the last half of the 1920s and the 1930s owing to its position within the CSL organization, building several small ships for its parent company and filling a few orders for the Canadian government and private firms. Between mid-1931 and mid-1937 its slipways remained empty for all but eleven months. Business picked up late in 1937. In 1938 and in May 1939 the company contracted with the government to build an icebreaker and to service the vessel. By then, its workforce had been reduced to between 200 and 250 men.[18]

Situated at Lauzon on the south shore of the St Lawrence River about two miles east of Lévis, the shipyard covered an area of 42 acres and had waterfront of three-quarters of a mile, which during the war was made available for building berths. The Champlain Graving Dock lay at the east end of the property and the Lorne Dry Dock was at the western end. Although they were federally owned, Davie carried out work in both. In 1941, for example, the company docked as many as 104 vessels for various types of bottom repairs, inspections, drawing of tail shafts, and painting.[19]

The president of Canada Steamship Lines, William H. Coverdale (1871–1949), was president of Davie Shipbuilding and Repairing Company, but closer supervision was left in the hands of R. Brock Thompson, CSL's vice president. The small management team was comprised of David Craig, connected with the company for over thirty years as works manager, ably assisted by J.-C. "Charlie" Sauvageau. Owing to the location of CSL's head office at Montreal, Sauvageau's official position as assistant treasurer and the shipyard's subordinate position within the larger organization belied his true role as second-in-command at Lauzon. Alec C. Campbell was the company's British-trained naval architect, and Kenneth M. Wears was yard superintendent, assisted by Jérémie "Jerry" Gagnon, who was closer to the men than were any of the others.[20]

Canadian Vickers Limited at Montreal, the premier shipbuilding company in Canada, had been incorporated in 1911, but its first full year of operation was 1914. Controlled by Vickers Sons and Maxim Limited of England, it had been formed by its English owners to provide repair facilities for ocean shipping entering Montreal, thereby reducing marine insurance rates on vessels entering the port.[21] It was very active in shipbuilding during the First World War, but the same conditions during the 1920s that saw consolidation of shipyards in Quebec, Nova Scotia, and Ontario also affected the parent company in the United Kingdom. During its merger with another arms manufacturer, Armstrong's, Vickers discarded its Canadian subsidiary.

In March 1926 two prominent Montreal businessmen, Frank Ross, already president of Montreal Dry Dock Limited and of the newly formed St John Dry Dock and Shipbuilding Company, and Victor M. Drury, former vice president of Royal Securities under financier Izaak Walton Killam, approached Canadian Vickers Limited. Drury appears to have been an agent for James Playfair, a wealthy Great Lakes ship owner, shipbuilder, and chairman of Hamilton Bridge Company and of Canadian Dredge and Dock Company, from which Ross had previously acquired St John Dry Dock and Shipbuilding Company.[22] After three difficult years, Vickers was prepared to let its Canadian subsidiary go, and serious negotiations commenced in November. The two men took an option to purchase the company, including the physical assets and first-refusal rights to any Vickers patents and licences in Canada for $4.5 million. Vickers agreed to redeem its outstanding debentures of $3.6 million and to write off Canadian Vickers' debts to the parent firm, which totalled $2.8 million. Ross and Drury placed bonds for very large sums on the open market.[23] In 1928 Ross merged Montreal Dry Dock Limited with Canadian Vickers, which carried on with a heavy load of bonded indebtedness. Montreal's largest shipyard survived the Depression by fabricating structural steel and manufacturing turbines and by the increase in the ship-repair business in the late 1930s.

At the outbreak of the Second World War, Canadian Vickers had five covered building slips and was the most completely equipped, self-sufficient yard in Canada. Only it could build complete ships from keel to masthead, including the engines, boilers, windlasses, and auxiliary machinery. Company officers were J. Edouard Labelle, KC, president; J.McL. Stephen, first vice president; N.A. Timmins Jr, second vice president; and J.W. Savidant, comptroller and secretary-treasurer. Victor Drury remained a director, together with René Labelle, John I. Rankin, and Avila Raymond.[24]

J. Edouard Labelle remains a mysterious figure. He became a director of Canadian Vickers in 1931 and was elected president in 1938, but as the senior partner of the law firm of Labelle, Dupuis and Lafortune, as *administrateur*, or senior legal advisor, of the Séminaire de St Sulpice since 1919, and as a director of the Canadian National Railway since 1930, he seems a curious choice to head up the largest shipbuilding company in the country.[25] Frank Ross had moved on. Drury was elected president of Canadian Car and Foundry Company in 1937 and became chairman of the executive committee and vice president of Foundation Company of Canada.[26] In 1941 T. Rodgie McLagan replaced William Wardle as general manager of Vickers and became an officer of the company.

Controlling interest in Canadian Vickers changed hands during August 1944 when Roy Wolvin and his associates acquired close to 30 per cent of the stock from Losonac Limited, which in Canada represented the Hugh Solvay interests, originally of Belgium. Losonac had obtained its large stake in Canadian Vickers early the previous year through acquisition of the Timmins and Richardson estate holdings. Wolvin confirmed that he and his associates had working control of the company but did not anticipate any change in the management or the directorate.[27]

The machine shop at Canadian Vickers Limited, c. 1941. LAC, C-032665.

Situated midway between Montreal and Trois Rivières at the confluence of the Richelieu and St Lawrence Rivers, Sorel was ideally located for marine industrial development. Marine Industries Limited, founded in 1937 by Joseph A. Simard, was the product of twenty years of growth and consolidation. The son and namesake of a Baie St Paul riverboat captain, Simard began his career thirty-five years before when he entered Richelieu and Ontario Navigation Company at fourteen years of age. His real start occurred in 1908 when he became accountant of the City of Sorel. Two years later, he moved to Sorel Light, Heat and Power Company, becoming manager in 1927. Simard had a genius for business. In 1917 he and two partners, the notary J.B.T. Lafrenière and Alcine Beaudet, purchased Les Chantiers Manseau, a small shipyard on the left bank of the Richelieu River on the site of the future Marine Industries Limited. Founded in 1898 by Messrs Robidoux and Manseau, it employed about twenty men. The government shipyard, which built larger dredges, tugs, and barges, was located on the west point at the mouth of the Richelieu.[28]

Under Simard, Chantiers Manseau focused on dredging and on maintenance and repair of dredges and medium-size ships. After obtaining a dredging contract in 1926, Joseph induced his brother J. Edouard Simard to join the firm and become general manager (*directeur général*), a post he occupied until 1937. In 1928 Joseph sold his interest in Sorel Light, Heat and Power Company to devote himself to developing his shipyard. He formed a new company, General Dredging Contractors Limited, and Chantiers Manseau acquired three associated companies: Sorel Mechanical Shops Company Limited, Sorel Iron Foundries Limited, and Beauchemain et Fils, also known as Sorel Steel Foundries Limited. Simard's industrial interests had expanded to include dredging, foundry work, boiler making, shipbuilding, and ship repairing.

In 1929 Alcine Beaudet died, and the notary Lafrenière withdrew his interest from the firm. Joseph Simard became the principal shareholder of five companies, which he reorganized into Consolidated Marine Companies Limited as a holding company. In 1931 a third Simard brother, Ludger, came to Sorel and joined the firm.[29] Joseph acquired the bankrupt Sincennes-McNaughton Company in 1934 and formed Sincennes-McNaughton Tugs Limited to acquire the old firm's assets. He thereby gained control over 90 per cent of the general towing and harbour-tug towing business on the Canadian side of the Great Lakes from Fort William (today Thunder Bay) to the sea.[30] Following acquisition of the government shipyard at Sorel on 6 January 1937, Joseph incorporated Marine Industries Limited with authorized capital of $500,000 of no-par-value common shares.[31]

Joseph Simard's position atop Liberal Party patronage lists allowed him to buy the Dominion government's shipyard and large dredging fleet for $1.7 million. At the same time, the company obtained a government contract to strike a channel in the St Lawrence from Montreal to Lachine; its estimated value was approximately $11,500,000.[32]

During the years leading up to the outbreak of war, Marine Industries Limited began building small tankers and tugs for the larger market. MV *Beeceelite*, the first all-welded, steel ship built in Canada, was a foretaste of things to come. The *Oakbranch* and *Petrolite* quickly followed in 1938 and 1939. The shipyard also built four large tugboats. The *Radium King* and *Radium Queen* were disassembled after construction and shipped some 6,500 kilometres from Sorel to Great Slave Lake in the Northwest Territories, and the *Orient Bay* and *Nipigon* were delivered to a client on Lake Superior.[33] In 1938 Marine Industries manufactured three of the four main engines for the navy's Basset-class minesweepers. Early in the war, the company manufactured the engines and boilers for the icebreaker *Ernest Lapointe*, built at Lauzon. The shipyard also began converting small bulk carriers into tankers. All this activity, together with adoption of new technology, electric welding, and new customers, revealed Marine Industries as a shipyard with ambition.

Finally, on 11 October 1939 Joseph Simard formed Sorel Steel Industries Limited with himself as president to assume a contract awarded by the British War Office for manufacturing munitions. Schneider-Creusot, French munitions manufacturers, would supply the technical advice. Joseph Simard was president of Marine Industries

Limited, J. Edouard Simard was vice president, and A. Luger Simard was managing director. Other directors were E. de G. Power, general manager; Colonel H.S. Tobin, a Vancouver attorney who managed the company's western office; P.-A. Lavallée, comptroller; and later Walter Lambert, a well-respected naval architect.

Lambert's position with Marine Industries gave the company professional heft. He was among the most senior naval architects in Canada. Born in England, apprenticed as a draftsman at Thames Iron Works, and subsequently employed by Londonderry Shipbuilding and Engineering Company Limited of Ireland, Armstrong and Whitworth Company Limited at Newcastle, and J.I. Thornycroft and Company at Southampton, Walter Lambert immigrated to Canada in 1913 as office manager of John Reid and Company, consulting naval architects. He began practice on his own in 1917, almost immediately becoming assistant director of shipbuilding and technical officer in charge of British government shipbuilding in Canada. After three years with the Imperial Munitions Board, he resumed private practice. In 1932 he joined Horace German, who had been technical director and naval architect for Canadian Vickers, and together they continued private practice in Montreal as Lambert and German.[34] But in 1936 he severed his relations with German and retired to England, where he shortly became European representative of the Simard interests. Just prior to the war, the Canadian Manufacturer's Association co-opted Lambert to its war industries mission, appointing him to the gun committee and chairman of the shipbuilding committee. Upon his return to Canada in 1939, Lambert became technical director to Marine Industries Limited. In 1942 he was elected to the board of directors.[35]

Morton Engineering and Dry Dock Company and George T. Davie and Sons were two small shipbuilding firms in the Quebec City region. Both were family-owned and too small and inadequate for the tasks soon to be demanded of them. Their small professional staffs, the sudden pressure of unexpected construction demands, and their inability to respond to growing labour difficulties forced the government to take them over in 1943. Described as an "up-and-coming company," Morton Engineering and Dry Dock was located at the mouth of the St Charles River in Quebec City's Lower Town.[36] Robert W. Morton founded the company in 1919 and had a 2,500-ton marine railway installed. The firm was incorporated in 1927 and afterward survived by engaging in ship repairing, boiler making, and general engineering and repair work. Surprising to some, in 1936 Morton obtained a contract to build one of the navy's four Basset-class minesweepers. In 1939 Robert Morton was president of the company, D.S. Scott was general manager, and W.O. Henderson was naval architect.[37]

The location of Morton's yard was a major limitation; only the possession of the marine railway permitted it to launch ships. They were pulled sideways from launching ways on the west side of the St Charles River onto a railway cradle for lowering into the water. A 19-foot tide and constantly moving ice during winter months prevented any ships from being launched between December and March.[38]

Despite its ancient name, George T. Davie and Sons was founded in 1927 when George Duncan Davie and his brother bought the land immediately west of the Lorne Dry Dock on the south shore and set up a branch of the original family shipyard. It

HMCS *Shawinigan*, Flower-class corvette, under construction at George T. Davie and Sons, Lauzon, Quebec, 1941. The photo emphasizes the smallness of both the ship and the shipyard. Photo by Gosselin Studios, Lévis, Quebec. LAC, C-6571.

became known as the Lauzon Yard. Intended primarily to carry on ship repairs next door to the CSL subsidiary, its creation probably reflected the true feelings of the owner of a once-great shipyard who was now reduced to being one of several directors and general manager of a shipping company's subsidiary. The new yard opened for business in 1929 under management of Charles "Charlie" Davie, whose father and uncle sold him the yard for $195,859. Later, during the 1930s, they forgave the debt. For four years after 1929, the yard remained a branch of the family yard at Lévis, but in 1933 it was separated and retained the old name of George T. Davie and Sons. The yard, incorporated in 1941, became known as "*le petit Davie*" or "*chez Charlie*" (Charlie's place).[39]

Charles Gordon Davie was born in 1902 at Lauzon, Quebec. Educated locally, he trained as a shipbuilder at Lauzon and then for five years in New York and at Lorain, Ohio, in the yard of American Ship Building Company. During the Second World War, Maurice Paquet assisted Charlie Davie as assistant manager and secretary treasurer. J.B. Lemlin was hull superintendent, and J.A.D. Sampson was marine superintendent.[40]

Both companies' drafting offices, patternmaking facilities, and lofting sheds were inadequate, and they quickly encountered difficulties meeting Admiralty standards of production. Management did not keep up with the needs of the ever-growing labour force. Government antilabour policies on the one hand and poor wages, non-existent union representation, and working-class pride on the other hand made for a volatile situation that came to a head in 1943.

Little has been found about small shipyards and boat works in Quebec, but one that performed sterling service was Le Chantier Maritime de Saint Laurent on Ile d'Orleáns. Founded by Ovide Filion in 1910, it specialized in building wooden schooners. His son Gustave had succeeded him by the time war broke out in 1939. Gustave employed about 100 workers during the Second World War, when his small company built four wooden minesweepers, a gate vessel, and a wooden tug for the Royal Canadian Navy.[41] Another firm was Davie Brothers, located at the original Davie patent slip, or marine railway, at Lévis. It turned out ships' boats for the naval vessels built in the larger Quebec City yards. It had been legally separated from George T. Davie and Sons in 1933 and remained under George and Allison Davie's ownership. During the war, it was owned and operated by Allison and was kept busy with maintenance and repairs of local river ships.[42]

Great Lakes

Between 1940 and 1945 Great Lakes shipyards and boat works turned out 50 original and Revised Flower-class corvettes, 101 minesweepers of various types and sizes, and 59 Fairmile motor launches, a total of 210 warships in all. Of these, 134 were built for the RCN and 72 for the RN, including 4 taken into the United States Navy, and 5 were transferred to the Soviet navy after the war. All this took place in five shipyards and seven boat works (see table 11.4a). This shipbuilding assumed an importance out of all proportion to its total production because almost all of it comprised warships. The situation in Ontario is also interesting because one man, Roy Wolvin, owned controlling interest in four of the five Canadian yards and because the fifth and largest yard became a Crown company under unusual circumstances.

During the Second World War, Roy Mitchell Wolvin, the Montreal financier who had earlier been involved with Canada Steamship Lines, Halifax Shipyards, and the collapse of Besco, held controlling interest in the four Great Lakes shipyards. He was born on 21 January 1880 in St Clair, Michigan, and was educated at local schools. In 1896, at sixteen years of age, he joined the office of his uncle, Augustus B. Wolvin, ship captain and ship owner, in Duluth, Minnesota. He spent his days witnessing vessel transfers and assisting in the management of his uncle's fleets.[43] From 1903 to 1910 he was general manager of Great Lakes and St Lawrence Transportation Company, which his uncle owned and which operated the largest fleet of full canal-size steel ships between the Great Lakes and Quebec. He was also assistant general manager of three lines operating on the upper Great Lakes.[44]

In 1909 or 1910 he moved to Canada, and from then until 1916 he engaged in Great Lakes transportation, contracting, and vessel-agency business under the name of Standard Shipping Company at Winnipeg.[45] During these years, Wolvin became associated with Grant Morden and Joseph W. Norcross in founding Canada Steamship Lines. Morden, who was primarily responsible for creating the steamship company, had a limited capacity for handling practical details and depended on Wolvin.[46] Between 1916 and 1919 Wolvin served as president of Canada West Coast Navigation Company and president of Montreal Transportation Company, which had been absorbed by CSL. His closeness to Norcross's mismanagement between 1916 and 1922 and his widespread shipping connections and business dealings were "disturbingly entangled," which led to severance of relations with CSL in 1922.[47]

Port Arthur Shipbuilding Company Limited began life as Western Ship Building and Dry Dock Company in 1910, a subsidiary of American Ship Building Company of Cleveland, Ohio. In 1908, after Canada's Parliament imposed a duty of 25 per cent on all repairs of Canadian vessels in the United States, the owners of American Ship Building Company decided to build a subsidiary company at Port Arthur. They had learned that the Canadian government would grant them an annual bounty of 3 per cent for twenty years on the machinery, dry dock, buildings, and real estate and that property would be exempt from all but school tax. Augustus Wolvin was a member of the six-man committee that undertook to establish the subsidiary company.[48] James Walen of Port Arthur headed the Canadian minority shareholders. The dry dock was completed on 1 January 1911.[49]

By early 1916 Western Ship Building and Dry Dock Company had built only five ships. Its parent company had lost over half a million dollars and decided to sell. Roy Wolvin and Joseph Norcross, claiming to represent Canada Steamship Lines, purchased about $350,000 worth of Western Ship Building stock and expressed interest in purchasing the remainder. To consummate the deal, the parent company accepted 900 shares of CSL stock and credited the buyers with $60,000 to obtain a more suitable cash settlement.[50]

Although the company, renamed Port Arthur Shipbuilding Company, built only a few more ships to 1924, it required very little in the way of new facilities when war broke out because of the multitude of different jobs undertaken during the intervening sixteen years. In addition to extensive ship-repair work, the yard had carried on with the manufacture of pulp and paper machinery, with mill work and wood working of all kinds, and with general machine shop work, producing heating and power boilers, tanks, mining equipment, railway bridges and structural steel, and iron, brass, and bronze castings. Its pulp and paper machinery, manufactured under the name of "Pascal," was well known and used extensively across the country.[51] During the Second World War, Gordon F. McDougall managed the Port Arthur shipyard, which constructed thirty warships in four years.

Ships had been built at Collingwood on Georgian Bay since the middle of the nineteenth century, and during the First World War 1,700 workers had been employed there.[52] In November 1916, about the same time as they were acquiring Port Arthur Shipbuilding Company, Wolvin and Norcross joined Horace Bruce Smith of Owen Sound, a wealthy solicitor, industrialist, and president of the Northern Navigation Company division of CSL, to purchase the property, assets, and undertakings from the trustee of Collingwood Shipbuilding Company and sell them to a newly incorporated company of the same name. The financiers incorporated the company with an authorized capital of $2.6 million.[53] In January 1917 they distributed 1,000 shares to several directors of Canada Steamship Lines, including 500 shares to Sir Trevor Dawson of British Maritime Trust Limited (i.e., Vickers Sons and Maxim Limited), which probably indicates one source of funds for purchasing the shipyard.

Toward the end of the war, the three men also acquired Kingston Shipbuilding Company, which carried on business as Collingwood Shipbuilding Company at Kingston. Horace Smith became a president.[54] John S. Leitch was managing director at Collingwood, and H.C. Welch served as general manager of the Kingston yard.[55] It was Wolvin and Norcross's involvement in shipbuilding that prompted C.C. Ballantyne to invite them to re-establish the Halifax shipyard destroyed in the great explosion of 1917.

But the postwar bust affected Collingwood, as everywhere else in Canada, and in 1926 Wolvin and Smith reorganized the shipbuilding companies. On 1 December 1917 Collingwood Shipyards Limited purchased Collingwood Shipbuilding Company Limited, which had been carrying on business at both Collingwood and Kingston. The sale discharged all the vendor's debts and liabilities. Smith remained president of the new company, but reorganization did not build ships. By June 1932 the preferred shares of Collingwood Shipyards Limited were declared valueless. Four years later, however, dividends were still being paid on Kingston Shipbuilding Company shares, whereas Collingwood Shipyards Limited continued to pay no dividends on either its preferred or common stocks.[56] On 13 March 1937 the directors reincorporated Collingwood Shipyards Limited as a private company to take over the old one. The new company was formed in accordance with the offer of Kingston Shipbuilding Company to purchase the property and assets of the Collingwood shipyard. John S. Leitch was appointed vice president of Collingwood Shipyards Limited.[57]

By this arrangement, Kingston Shipbuilding Company became the owner of all of the issued shares of Collingwood Shipyards Limited and, except for 242 shares, the owner of all of the capital stock of Port Arthur Shipbuilding Company.[58] The new company's head office was at Collingwood, and the executive committee comprised Horace Smith, president; Roy Wolvin, vice president; and John S. Leitch, vice president and managing director.[59] Sanford Lindsay, secretary of Collingwood Shipyards and associated with the company for more than twenty years, died on 5 March 1938, and a year later to the day, Horace Smith passed away in his seventy-fifth year. Two days later, the directors elected Wolvin president of Kingston Shipbuilding Company Limited.[60]

Long associated with the Collingwood shipyard, John Shearer Leitch, born in New York City in 1880, learned his profession in Great Britain, having been educated in Glasgow and Newcastle-on-Tyne. He graduated with honours in naval architecture from South Kensington (today Imperial College), London, and apprenticed as a shipbuilder with Robert Napier and Sons. He subsequently spent four years as a draughtsman at Swan Hunter and Wigham Richardson's Neptune Works at Wallsend and had charge of the drawing office of Workman, Clark and Company at Belfast before being appointed assistant manager in 1911. He immigrated to Canada the following year and became managing director of Collingwood Shipyards Limited, where he remained until after the Second World War.

Wolvin prospered throughout the war. Kingston Shipbuilding Company's earnings permitted him to make two astute business decisions. Recognizing that the war was drawing to a close, he began restructuring his shipbuilding companies in August 1944. First, he arranged to buy controlling interest in Canadian Vickers Limited.[61] Second, in November he restructured his holdings in the Great Lakes shipyards by exchanging Kingston Shipbuilding Company shares for class-A shares of Canadian Shipbuilding and Engineering Limited and posting the new corporation's outstanding shares on the Toronto Stock Exchange for public trading.[62]

Roy Wolvin died suddenly on 7 April 1945 in his hotel suite while on a business trip in Toronto. He was sixty-five. At the time of his death, in addition to owning controlling interest in four shipyards on the Great Lakes, he was vice president of Canadian Vickers Limited and chairman of its executive committee.[63] Six months later, after consulting C.D. Howe, William Coverdale, president of Canada Steamship Lines, bought Canadian Shipbuilding and Engineering Limited from Wolvin's estate.[64] Already the owner of a shipbuilding firm on the lower St Lawrence River, CSL had no interest in acquiring Canadian Vickers. Acquisition of Wolvin's prize was left to others.

West Coast

British Columbia was a land of rugged individualists where shipyards were concerned. Shipbuilders were among the founders of the province's industries. British Columbia had no tradition of wooden shipbuilding, unlike the East Coast. Shipyards developed from repair work. During the First World War, the Imperial Munitions Board contracted for ships, and although the province possessed few manufacturing resources, it was able to import engines, large castings, and steel from eastern Canada and the United States sufficient to build forty-five steel-hulled freighters, each over 8,000 tons, between 1917 and 1921.[65] In the mid-1920s large dry docks were opened first at North Vancouver and then at Esquimalt, but no vessel was built for ocean trading between 1922 and 1940.[66] Nevertheless, BC shipyards enjoyed three advantages over eastern yards during the war. The mild winters made year-round construction and launching possible. There was little competition from other war industries for labour, and the high wages attracted many skilled tradesmen and unskilled workers from western Canada to work in British Columbia's shipyards.[67]

Victoria Machinery Depot traced its origins to 1858, when Captain Joseph Spratt, a native of London, England, arrived at Victoria, but it was 1882 before he built a machine shop and foundry on Bay Street and named it Victoria Machinery Depot, which repaired machinery and manufactured cast fittings, machinery parts, and finished goods. His son, Charles James Vancouver Spratt, succeeded him and incorporated the firm in 1898.[68] Spratt built a 3,000-ton marine railway in 1907. After a disastrous fire the following year, the shops around the marine railway were rebuilt and went into production. Before the war, half of all the work, including boilers, was for sawmills and other land operations.[69] During the First World War, the company built two 8,800-ton, steel freighters.[70]

In 1940 Victoria Machinery Depot, or VMD, as it was locally known, contracted to build five Flower-class corvettes but completed only four before switching to construction of 10,000-ton freighters. Charles Spratt died early in 1941, and his wife, Marguerite, assisted by a board of directors and general manager Herbert S. Hammill, carried on. At peak employment (1943), the company employed 2,900 men and women. Hammill became president of the company during the war. By 1945 the plant possessed half a mile of wharfage able to dock five 10,000-ton freighters at a time.[71]

The unofficial opening of the Panama Canal along with the Canadian government's assurances that it would build a large graving dock at Lang Cove, adjacent to British Columbia Marine Railway Company Limited, drew Sir Alfred Yarrow to Esquimalt at the end of 1913. Yarrow bought the company for $300,000, renamed it Yarrows Limited, and installed his son Norman to run it.[72] In 1921 he transferred his 68.75 per cent interest in the company to Norman A. Yarrow, who became the sole owner. The new president of Yarrows Limited had served a five-year apprenticeship with D. Napier and Sons at London and with W.H. Allen Sons and Company Limited at Bedford before entering the family firm.[73]

The promised dry dock opened on 1 July 1927. Completed at a cost of $6 million, it was 1,186 feet long and 135 feet wide and had a depth over the sill of 40 feet. It stood on the north side of Constance Cove, and the Yarrows shipyard stood on the south side, separated by Lang Cove. HMC Dockyard lay west of Yarrows. For taxation reasons, in 1930 the original company was wound up and re-emerged as Yarrows (1930) Limited with Norman as the sole director. Later the same year, it was incorporated as Yarrows Limited.[74]

Although Yarrows Limited built one of the Basset-class minesweepers for the Royal Canadian Navy in 1938 and obtained a contract to build three of the original sixty-four corvettes in 1940, naval repair remained the dominant activity until December 1941, when Norman Yarrow returned from Ottawa with a contract to build frigates and news that Yarrows was to be one of four Canadian yards to concentrate on naval construction.[75] Yarrows completed two more corvettes in the 1940–41 program and two 10,000-ton freighters in 1942, but its greatest single job that year was dry-docking and refitting the 83,000-ton *Queen Elizabeth*, the largest ship in the world. Later, Yarrows men and women built seventeen frigates and seven transport ferries, or LST3s, during which time the number of employees grew to over 3,000 and the twelve-month payroll between July 1943 and June 1944 totalled $2.75 million.[76]

Only one shipyard in Vancouver worked in steel at the beginning of the war, Burrard Dry Dock Company Limited, owned by the Wallace family. The much smaller firm with the grandiose name of British Columbia Engineers and Shipbuilders Limited was a foundry and repair shop. Three wartime shipyards that were started up –

North Van Ship Repairs Limited, South Burrard Dry Dock Company Limited, and West Coast Shipbuilders Limited – are dealt with in the next chapter. Together these .companies formed the largest concentration of shipbuilding in the country.

Burrard Dry Dock Company Limited, the largest shipbuilding firm in Canada during the Second World War, traced its origins to 1894, when Alfred Wallace established a shipyard on the shore of False Creek, Vancouver. In 1904 he moved across Burrard Inlet to North Vancouver and incorporated Wallace Shipyards Company the following year. Four years later, he had transferred all his operations there and began experimenting with steel-hull construction. Expansion occurred during the First World War. Wallace began building ocean-going vessels: three steel-hulled ships during 1917 and 1918 and several more for the Canadian Government Merchant Marine. In 1921 Wallace Shipyards became Burrard Dry Dock. Although a floating dry dock was finally completed in 1925, shipbuilding came to a halt for the next eighteen years.[77] Alfred Wallace died on New Year's Day, 1929, and was succeeded by his son Clarence, who proved his ability to run the company by successfully guiding it through the Depression years.[78]

In February 1940 Burrard Dry Dock obtained contracts to build four corvettes for the first program and immediately afterward received an order to construct six Bangor-class minesweepers. It was the only shipyard in the country to obtain orders to build both classes of warship, which boosted employment to 750.[79]

During discussions with Harvey MacMillan in April 1941, concerning Canada's ability to build merchant ships, Clarence Wallace, who had already contracted to build fourteen North Sands ships for the British, committed the company to building thirty more.[80] The commitment led to severe growing pains, and in February 1942 Wallace hired William J. Wardle from Canadian Vickers to be general manager of Burrard North Yard. The position should logically have gone to Hubert Wallace, Clarence's younger brother, but he was notoriously unreliable, and even though he had been trained in all aspects of shipyard work, he was often befuddled by drink.[81] Bill Wardle was an ideal choice, for he had been in charge of shipbuilding at Canadian Vickers for seventeen years, prior to which time he had been with Vickers Sons and Maxim at Barrow-in-Furness, England.[82] Toward the end of the war, Wallace began to buy out other yards, remaining the largest shipbuilding company on the West Coast.

Prince Rupert Dry Dock and Shipbuilding Company operated the only other yard on the West Coast at the beginning of the war. Originally conceived by the London directors of Grand Trunk Pacific Railway Company in 1911, the complete repair facility, equipped with two launching berths, foundry, pattern shop and machine shop, and a floating dry dock to accommodate vessels up to 20,000 tons, was opened at Prince Rupert in 1916. It failed to attract business and was used briefly as a ship-repair centre during the First World War; the high cost of materials and labour proved to be its downfall. Following a disastrous attempt to build ships at Prince Rupert at the war's end, the shipbuilding facilities and the dry dock reverted to the Canadian National Railway (CNR).[83]

Seeking to profit from the government's call for shipbuilding facilities, in 1939 the CNR incorporated Grand Trunk Pacific Development Company Limited with its head office in British Columbia. The company's president was S.J. Hungerford, chairman of the CNR, and all but one of the directors were located in eastern Canada, chiefly at Montreal.[84] C.D. Howe had appointed Hungerford the new president of the railway and of Trans-Canada Airlines. Among the directors were two other Howe appointees: Howe's old friend Herbert J. Symington, a western lawyer with whom he had worked for many years during the 1920s and whom he appointed power controller in September 1941; and Wilfrid Gagnon, a Montreal boot and shoe manufacturer. Howe had already appointed both men directors of the CNR and Trans-Canada Air Lines.[85] The Prince Rupert shipyard was the nearest thing to a government shipyard in Canada. The close ties to the government were revealed in the speed with which the new company obtained contracts and steel to build four Bangor-class minesweepers. The keels of the first two ships were laid down on 20 January 1940, and in September 1941 the company was authorized to build four North Sands–type cargo ships.[86] Thirteen 10,000-ton cargo ships were built at Prince Rupert. SS *Gaspesian Park*, completed in July 1945, was the last freighter to be delivered under the wartime emergency program.[87]

The entry of the United States into the war and the United States Army's discovery that it could ship troops to Alaska via Prince Rupert and the CNR faster than by sea from Seattle transformed the town and the importance of its shipyard. Prince Rupert's population tripled to 20,000, and docks, warehouses, an air base, and barracks for 3,500 US soldiers sprang up. Ship repairs exceeded shipbuilding in importance, growing until more than 3,000 had been carried out before the war's end.

Several smaller yards also operated in British Columbia. Chief among them was Star Shipyard (Mercer's) Limited of New Westminster, incorporated on 31 July 1928 with a capital of $30,000 divided into 300 shares. Edward Mercer was president and his son William E.A. "Art" Mercer was secretary-treasurer.[88] During the war, Mercer's constructed fifty-three marine craft, from 25-foot unpowered cutters to 126-foot minesweepers, for the RCN, Royal Canadian Air Force, and Canadian army.[89] Vancouver Shipyards Limited built twenty-five vessels, including five Fairmile motor launches and three wooden minesweepers, for the armed services, and A.C. Benson Shipyards built twenty-one similar craft.[90]

The most interesting West Coast company building small boats was Falconer Marine Industries Limited of Victoria. Robert Armstrong founded the plant, originally called Armstrong Brothers, in 1908. Its prewar work consisted primarily of building commercial fishing boats and yachts as well as repairs. Before the war, the company had employed twenty-five men, of whom only five were first-class boat builders. After war broke out, company policy was to stay with smaller craft and seek sufficiently large orders that multiple production and prefabrication methods could be introduced. As the wartime labour force grew, work was carefully planned and specialized so that it could be done with little training. Many women were hired; twenty-five were taken on as riveters. In July 1943, when the company employed about seventy-five men and women, Robert Armstrong sold his company to John Falconer, who reorganized it as Falconer Marine Industries Limited.[91]

The company built a variety of craft for all three armed services, but its greatest success was constructing 377 lifeboats, chiefly 26-foot Victory types for Wartime Merchant Shipping Limited, and obtaining large orders from the British Admiralty Technical Mission on the strength of building sixteen 32-foot diesel-powered cutters for the aircraft carriers being converted in Vancouver. By May 1945 the company had 216 employees, and production had reached one and a half 25-foot cutters a day. It had built or had on order 238 diesel cutters and fast motor dinghies for aircraft carriers and for maintenance and victualling ships.[92] The quality of work had improved as a result of multiple production techniques. Each piece of wood was sawn and made ready separately in large numbers, and the boats were built on an assembly line. The company did its own machine-shop work, pipefitting, and electrical work, but castings were bought from local sources. Falconer also designed and supplied to eastern firms many special boat fixtures.

Conclusion

At the beginning of the Second World War, shipbuilding plants, especially in the eastern half of the country, had fallen into the hands of financiers and businessmen who acquired them during the preceding two decades for a variety of reasons that had little to do with shipbuilding. Roy Wolvin, who had been involved in some of the most unsavoury financial promotion in the first half of the twentieth century, is the most pronounced example. Frank Ross and Victor Drury had sharp eyes for business opportunities and saw value in owning shipbuilding companies. Although some yards engaged in limited heavy industry, general engineering, and manufacturing, their chief attraction may have lain in the federal government subsidies for which they were eligible. With the exception of Robert Morton and members of the Davie family at Quebec City, most eastern owners resided in Montreal and were often connected to one another by membership on the boards of various companies. Thus Frank Ross was vice president of Joseph Simard's Sincennes-McNaughton Tugs, he and Victor Drury were both vice presidents of Hamilton Bridge Company, and Joseph Labelle was a director of Sun Trust Company, owned by Joseph Simard. The crucial exception was Marine Industries Limited, which was the creation of a brilliant businessman, Joseph A. Simard.

On the West Coast, with the exception of Prince Rupert Dry Dock and Shipbuilding Company, shipyard owners were men with long experience building and repairing ships. They were pioneers of industrial development in British Columbia and well equipped to expand their yards rapidly in response to new demands of government. How they all fared during the expansion of the ship construction programs is the subject of the next chapter.

Expanding Shipbuilding Capacity

Capital Assistance

Expanding Canada's shipbuilding capacity fit the government's policy of encouraging private industry rather than intervening directly. The first wave of shipbuilding expansion was relatively modest, for the industry possessed considerable unused capacity. The government moved quickly to place contracts for the navy's first ninety-ship program, and the country's eleven shipyards quickly filled with orders for corvettes. But after only twelve of twenty-six minesweepers were placed, new yards had to be found. After the cargo shipbuilding program was introduced the following year, it became obvious that the government would have to display much greater initiative. The Crown began directly to finance construction of new shipyards. The same sequence occurred when it became necessary to expand ship-repair and conversion facilities. Few companies had survived the Depression with any savings or ability to finance capital expansion out of earnings, and the government stepped in with two major programs to provide assistance. As shipyards expanded, firms manufacturing machinery and parts also had to be enlarged and better equipped.

Between September 1939 and August 1945, new business investment in buildings, structures, machinery, and equipment in Canada is estimated to have exceeded $4.5 billon, of which some $3.5 billion was directly or indirectly associated with the war effort.[1] About half of the latter sum was either directly financed or assisted by the government, which committed more than $750 million to industrial investment and encouraged private industry to spend another $800 million through special-depreciation allowances. An additional $500 million was available through special write-off provisions for tools and other small equipment, items that were used up rapidly during the war.[2] The other half of the $3.5-billion investment went to expanding the national transportation system, electric power, warehousing facilities, and other industries, particularly those in the primary sector producing basic materials.[3]

Late in August 1940 the government set up the War Contracts Depreciation Board to encourage expansion of war-production facilities in respect of capital disbursements that appeared to "have no reasonable post-war value" and "capital expenditure incurred under a war contract."[4] Accelerated depreciation permitted a company to write off new investment quickly so as not to be left with a potentially useless burden

Table 4.1 | Government-financed expansion of shipbuilding capacity as of 31 December 1943

Program	Shipbuilders	Commitment* Manufacturers	Total
Naval shipbuilding	13.314	4.467	*17.781*
Cargo shipbuilding	10.692	7.353	*18.045*
Ship repairing	3.448	1.315	*4.763*
Total	*27.454*	*13.135*	*40.589*

* Millions of dollars.

Note: Amounts shown are commitments, of which approximately four-fifths had been spent as of 31 December 1943.

Sources: Canada, DMS, *Report on the Government-Financed Expansion of Industrial Capacity in Canada as of 31 December 1943*; LAC, RG 28, box 7, "A Brief History of Wartime Merchant Shipping Ltd., Montreal, December 31, 1943, with an Addendum on Wartime Shipbuilding Ltd., January 1944–February 1947," typescript, 72–4.

at the end of the war.[5] Only the cost of land was not allowed. The special-depreciation allowance was to be 25 per cent written off in the year ending 1940 and 75 per cent at the end of the following year. Later, write-offs extended over three years. This proved to be the major stimulus private business sought as a means to invest in plant expansion and new equipment. Between 1940 and the end of 1943, North Van Ship Repairs, for example, wrote off more than $3 million.[6]

After eleven years of depression, industrial plants and equipment had become run-down, poorly equipped, and shabby. Between 1940 and 1945 the government authorized special-depreciation privileges totalling $514 million. Over $300 million was spent on machinery and equipment and the rest on building construction.[7] The proportion of accelerated depreciation that was allowed for the shipbuilding industry remains unknown, but in the total wartime context, it was probably small. Introduced in November 1944 to aid enterprises to make capital expenditures when costs were rising and levels of taxation were high, write-offs totalled only $5 million in the shipbuilding sector, less than 0.5 per cent of the $1.4 billion applied for nationally.[8]

Capital assistance was much more important to shipbuilding than accelerated depreciation. Often, only a single firm possessed sufficient experience and skill in manufacturing, which precluded setting up a new company. Title to plant extensions and equipment paid for in this manner (i.e., by the tax payer) was vested in the Crown to serve as security for the capital advanced.[9] Shipbuilding received 5.4 per cent of all government-financed expansion of Canada's industrial capacity, which speaks to the industry's unused capacity. The smaller aircraft industry, by comparison, received more than 11.7 per cent of total government finance.

Table 4.2 | Capital assistance authorized to shipbuilders and manufacturers, 1940–45

Category	Naval	Programs* Cargo ship	Total
Shipbuilders	8,574.4	10,361.6	18,936.0
Manufacturers	5,181.5	3,910.9	9,092.4
Special conversion	35.5	660.0	695.5
Total	13,791.4	14,932.5	28,723.9

* Thousands of dollars.

Note: Numbers are rounded to nearest $1,000; somewhat less than these authorized amounts was actually spent.

Source: LAC, RG 28, box 7, "Addendum on Wartime Shipbuilding Ltd., January 1944–February 1947," typescript.

Table 4.1 shows that total government-financed expansion of shipbuilding amounted to $40.6 million, of which more than four-fifths ($33 million) had been spent by the end of 1943. About $12 million was committed to government-owned facilities and new works such as the Princess Louise Basin at Quebec City ($2.4 million), a new tidal graving dock, repair berths, wharves, and wharf extensions at St John ($2.7 million), and new government-owned shipyards ($6 million). Naval and cargo shipbuilding programs received roughly equal amounts of government-financed assistance, and more than 10 per cent of the total was allotted to the ship-repair program.

Table 4.2 shows the remainder, approximately $28.7 million, which was authorized for private industry. It separates assistance to ship repairing from the two larger programs. Slightly more than two-thirds of the total amount went to shipbuilding facilities if the $660,000 approved for special conversion work is included. It was naval in character and was assigned to Burrard Dry Dock Company for plant and equipment to modify carrier-vessel escorts (CVEs) for the Royal Navy. The work was carried out under the authority of Wartime Merchant Shipping Limited and its successor agency, Wartime Shipbuilding Limited; hence the amount is listed under the cargo program. The need for capital assistance diminished rapidly as shipbuilders and manufacturers expanded their plants and improved production methods. Less than half a million dollars, 1.7 per cent of total capital assistance, was authorized after 31 December 1943. All projects were completed before the end of 1945.[10]

Of the nearly $7.6 million authorized for naval shipbuilding, $2.0 million went to Canadian Vickers Limited, $1.2 million to Yarrows Limited, and $3.3 million to twelve other yards, chiefly Halifax Shipyards and Burrard Dry Dock Company. Of more than $10 million paid to merchant shipbuilders, more than three-quarters, $2.6 mil-

Table 4.3 | Major manufacturing companies receiving capital assistance for naval and cargo shipbuilding programs as of 31 December 1943

Company	Program	Amount ($)
Trenton Steel Works Ltd	Both	2,948,026
William Kennedy and Sons	Both	1,549,621
Page-Hersey Tubes Ltd	Navy	1,251,404
Dominion Bridge Co. Ltd	Cargo	1,042,618
Canada Foundries and Forgings Ltd	Cargo	670,500
Montreal Locomotive Works Ltd	Navy	651,705
Canadian Car and Foundry Co.	Navy	487,080
James Morrison Brass Mfg. Co.	Navy	455,374
Peacock Brothers Ltd	Navy	351,596
Canadian Pacific Railway Co.	Navy	298,394
Subtotal		*9,706,318*
Twenty-six additional manufacturers	Both	2,114,303
Total		*11,820,621*

Sources: Canada, Department of Munitions and Supply, *Report on the Government-Financed Expansion of Industrial Capacity in Canada as of 31 December 1943*; LAC, RG 28, box 7, "A Brief History of Wartime Merchant Shipping Ltd., Montreal, December 31, 1943, with an Addendum on Wartime Shipbuilding Ltd., January 1944–February 1947," typescript, 72–4.

lion and $5.4 million, was committed to Foundation Maritime Limited and United Shipyards, respectively, to build two emergency yards. George T. Davie and Sons received $1.2 million for a three-berth extension to the existing yard in order to build 4,700-ton cargo ships, and Davie Shipbuilding and Repairing Company received $1.9 million, of which half went to expand yard facilities in order to permit accelerated construction of 10,000-ton cargo ships on five existing ways.

Over $13 million (see table 4.1) was paid to thirty-six manufacturers directly involved in producing main and auxiliary machinery and parts for both shipbuilding programs. Commitments ranging from nearly $3 million down to $7,150 were normally intended to expand existing machine-shop, forge, and foundry-shop facilities and to purchase machine tools. Table 4.3 lists the names of ten manufacturers that received more than four-fifths of the authorized total.

In view of accusations that the Dominion government ignored Nova Scotia, it is important to point out that in addition to expending approximately $5.5 million on a shipyard at Pictou and expanding existing plant facilities at Trenton, the government directed additional millions to other manufacturers in the Maritimes. With the exception of $43,614 authorized for Montreal shipyards, all $4.7 million of capital assistance to the ship-repair program was committed to the East Coast. Nearly half of the total amount was expended at St John for improvements to St John Dry Dock and Shipbuilding Company, St John Iron Works, and St John Machine Shop and for construction of a tidal graving dock. The remainder was spent chiefly in Nova Scotia. The provision of more than $10 million in capital assistance to shipbuilding and ship repairing industries in the maritime provinces contrasts sharply with British Columbia, where private business financed nearly all expansion of the shipbuilding industry, especially the portion devoted to the cargo ship program.

The overall effect of the government's financial assistance, including advanced depreciation, was the rebuilding of Canada's shipbuilding and ancillary industries. In general, these programs rebuilt the nation's industrial infrastructure, protected industries from losses due to plant expansion, and left them well endowed for the postwar years.

Naval Expansion

The Canadian Cabinet's approval of the Royal Canadian Navy's (RCN) first shipbuilding program in February 1940 led to a modest expansion of Canada's shipbuilding capacity on the West Coast, Great Lakes, and St Lawrence River. With government providing the financing, the chief problem lay in finding experienced, capable shipbuilders as well as businessmen and industrialists to manage the plants.

Toward the end of 1939, North Van Ship Repairs Limited built three small berths in North Vancouver in preparation to bid for a minesweeper contract.[11] The company belonged to Arthur C. Burdick of Vancouver, president of Island Tug and Barge Company. Founded in 1931 as a subsidiary of Pacific Salvage Company Limited, North Van Ship Repairs Limited handled only repair work and wooden shipbuilding until 1939. In February 1940 Burdick's company contracted to build six steel minesweepers for the RCN, and on 30 November it agreed to build six more for the Royal Navy.[12]

In 1940 Burrard Dry Dock Company constructed one new berth for corvette and minesweeper contracts as well as joiner and pipe shops and a pattern loft.[13] But little else was built before 1941. Whether the Canadian National Railway kept Prince Rupert Dry Dock and Shipbuilding Company sufficiently well equipped to allow construction of two minesweepers contracted for in 1940 without difficulty is moot, but the plant's main expansion came the following year after the shipyard began building 10,000-ton freighters.[14]

The greatest shipyard expansion arising from the naval program occurred on the Great Lakes, where conditions during the interwar years had devastated shipbuilding. Only Collingwood Shipbuilding Company still constructed ships, building three vessels during the 1930s.[15] The first expansion occurred in February 1940 when Roy Wolvin, who always had a sharp eye for business and whose three shipbuilding companies had contracted to build nineteen corvettes, purchased the old Midland Shipbuilding Company properties from Canada Steamship Lines to lay down additional hulls.[16] In April, amid calls to reopen the yard in order to ease serious unemployment in the Midland region, Wolvin purchased the shipyard as it stood for $160,000.[17] The new company was to be called Midland Shipyards Limited.

By this time, Kingston Shipbuilding Company, with its head office at Collingwood, was the parent company of Wolvin's shipbuilding operations, holding the other three shipbuilding companies, each of which, for all intents and purposes, did business as separate firms. The company's officers were Roy Wolvin, president; John S. Leitch, vice president; Melville F. Thompson, treasurer; and George L. Cole, secretary.[18] Thompson was a long-time employee and general manager of the Kingston plant, and Cole was an employee of Canada Steamship Lines.

Midland Shipyards experienced difficulties negotiating its first and second contracts. Its earliest tenders were so out of line that the Department of Munitions and Supply (DMS) refused to consider them, and in September a new bid failed because the navy had changed the specifications.[19] This hid the fact that Wolvin had asked to be exempted from excess-profits taxes and to receive a government bonus and a loan of $30,000.[20] Much precious time was lost. Operations commenced only in February 1941 with the laying of the keels for two Flower-class corvettes from the navy's second building program.[21] In keeping with the government's new policy of building minesweepers in Great Lakes yards, later that year Wolvin signed a second agreement with the DMS to build five Western Isles–type antisubmarine, minesweeping trawlers for the Royal Navy. He also contracted to construct five of these vessels at Collingwood and two at Kingston at a cost of $410,000 each.[22]

Herbert J. Whitmill was a retired shipbuilder from Cammel Laird living in the West Indies when he got in touch with David Carswell, who sent him to Kingston, where he was serving as superintendent in October 1941. Shortly afterward, he took over as manager of the Midland yard, where he remained for the duration of the war.[23] By the war's conclusion, in addition to the five Western Isles minesweepers, Midland Shipyards had built eleven corvettes. Peak employment reached 600 in 1944, when six corvettes were got away between May and November. Numbers were limited by supply; shortages of pipefitters and electricians created a real bottleneck.[24] Whereas Midland was the smallest yard on the Canadian side of the Great Lakes, the other new yard became the largest. It's origin and fate are among the most unusual of any shipyard during the war.

The second new yard was opened in 1940 in Toronto, where James Franceschini, a wealthy highway contractor and principal owner of Dufferin Paving and Crushed Stone Limited, incorporated Dufferin Shipbuilding Company Limited on 29 March. It was the first wartime shipyard to be established anywhere in the country. Located on the site of the derelict Dominion Shipbuilding Company, the new company obtained its first contract for four minesweepers on 1 April.[25] The first keel was laid down on 4 July. Three weeks earlier, the Royal Canadian Mounted Police had interned Franceschini, along with about 600 other Italian Canadians.

James (baptized Vincenzo) Franceschini was one of the few Italian-born, Toronto residents who prospered during the period before the war. Born in Pescara, Italy, in 1890, he came to Canada as a youth in 1906 and organized Dufferin Construction Company when he was just twenty-eight years old.[26] His firm grew into a large paving, concrete, crushed-stone, and building-supply business on Fleet Street.[27] Franceschini married an English Canadian woman named Annie and raised a family. He resided at Myrtle Villa, a fifty-acre estate named after his only daughter, at 415 Lakeshore Road at Mimico Beach. He became a British subject by naturalization in 1916 and by imperial certificate in 1927.[28] A man of many parts, he joined the Eglington Hunt Club and the Ontario Jockey Club and enjoyed exhibiting hackney show horses.[29] A proud Italian and, quite probably, a naive supporter of Benito Mussolini, Franceschini was interned on 17 June 1940, just seven days after Italy attacked France. His brother Leonard was interned late in August.[30]

Previously involved in local Italian cultural activities, such as financing Italy Week at the Canadian National Exhibition before the war, Franceschini appears to have been the dupe of Italian consular officials who had long controlled fascist activities in Toronto's Italian community. He became a victim of the anti-Italian, fifth-column hysteria that gripped the country in the wake of the invasion of western Europe and the fall of France during the spring of 1940 and, no doubt, a victim of the social snobbery of Toronto's Anglo-Canadian upper crust, which resented his success.[31] Political enemies and business rivals may also have had a hand in his arrest and incarceration, for Franceschini was a good friend and supporter of Ontario's premier, Mitchell Hepburn. During the Dominion election of March 1940, when the Ontario Liberal Party played no part in the campaign, Franceschini and other Hepburn friends threw their support to the federal Tories.[32] Whatever the case, Franceschini's internment ruined him.[33]

The government moved swiftly to take control of his new shipbuilding company. Within days, it was placed under the authority of David Carswell, director general of the shipbuilding branch of the new Department of Munitions and Supply, who was appointed controller of the company. J.H. Ratcliffe was appointed president, Colonel James Mess was Carswell's nominee on the board of directors, and the custodian of enemy property, who had seized Franceschini's holdings, appointed James W. Taylor of Price Waterhouse and Company a director. Robert M. Scrivener continued as the shipyard's general manager. The shipbuilding branch ran Dufferin Shipbuilding Company directly for more than a year, during which four minesweepers were completed and commissioned, construction was begun on two more, and contracts were signed to build ten additional vessels.[34] Although construction proceeded well during the first year of operation, the emphasis on ordering ships and the lack of planning at Ottawa as well as a paucity of management skills impacted operations by the spring of 1941.

The government released James and Leonard Franceschini from internment in June 1941.[35] In January, Judge James Duncan Hyndman, appointed special commissioner to hear the appeals of Franceschini and other internees, had declared that he was not disloyal to Canada, but Justice Minister Ernest Lapointe refused to release him. Only five months later, after doctors declared Franceschini suffered from cancer and was unfit for the rigours of camp life was the fifty-two year old released on compassionate grounds.[36] Prior to this, he had been transferred to Christie Street Military Hospital at Toronto, where he had undergone surgery.[37] Because of the conditions

Men and cranes in the Toronto Shipbuilding Company yard. AO, C5, Gordon W. Powley Fonds, 10011362.

of his release – Judge Hyndman's report was not made public – Franceschini was unable to clear his name or obtain the return of his property. Like so many others, he became a needless victim of the war.

Franceschini's release confronted the government with serious problems. First, it had grounds for fearing that if control of the company reverted to him, the workers would strike and refuse to work for him. Appointment of a controller was not a solution because it would not prevent profits derived from the yard's operation accruing to Franceschini. Second, with the cargo shipbuilding program getting underway elsewhere in the country and deep-water yards already expanding, the only yards available to build additional small, steel naval vessels were on the Great Lakes, where expansion was daily growing more necessary. The other yards were in the hands of one man. Dufferin Shipbuilding Company lent itself very readily to expansion, having the physical conditions, land, wharfage, buildings, railway facilities, and more important, available labour supply. The required expansion also needed substantial capital expenditure that could not be financed privately. The two alternatives of government financial assistance or takeover of the enterprise were really one, as the public interest did not permit advancing money to Franceschini. Finally, the government wanted its own industrial shipbuilding plant as a basis for comparison of production and price with the other four Canadian Great Lakes yards.[38]

On 20 October 1941, after four months of foot-dragging and after "discussions" with Dufferin Paving and Crushed Stone Limited and with Franceschini, the Canadian government purchased all of Dufferin Shipbuilding Company's issued and outstanding shares and certain of the paving company's freeholds and leases amounting to about 4.5 acres on the Toronto waterfront for $975,000.[39] This amount does not appear to be included in the capital assistance for the naval shipbuilding program. The company's name was changed to Toronto Shipbuilding Company Limited, and it became a Crown corporation.

In the hectic days of 1941 as the minister of munitions and supply struggled to whip Canada's chaotic war-production organization into shape and give it substance, the Crown corporation appeared to be an excellent device by which to get out from under the government's own stifling patchwork of regulations and controls designed chiefly to avoid political embarrassment and by which to mobilize war production quickly and effectively by creating government companies that would resemble private firms where none had been available before. Like private companies, Crown corporations issued shares and were managed by boards of directors rather than civil servants. The minister of munitions and supply held the shares for the king in right of Canada.[40] In spite of the name change, no alterations occurred to either the company's capital or its corporate structure. By bringing private businessmen and their organizations directly into the government, C.D. Howe hoped to cut through the clogging separation between government and industry. Whether he succeeded is another matter.

The new company held contracts to build sixteen minesweepers: six for the Royal Navy and ten for the RCN. In view of the properties, leaseholds, a soundly operating company, and existing contracts worth $9.5 million, the government had acquired a bargain, but Franceschini was not allowed to walk away with the purchase price. As a condition of the forced sale of his company, the government required his paving company to redeem all its outstanding Series A debentures, which had a par value of $795,515 and were held by the public with interest at 5 per cent, by 30 November.[41]

The minister appointed Desmond A. Clarke, director general of the shipbuilding branch, as president of the company and a group of distinguished businessmen and a labour representative as directors. Perhaps, reflecting civil-service influence, a management committee of three directors and a financial committee of two initially ran Toronto Shipbuilding Company Limited, but there is a suggestion that from October 1941 to January 1942 Fraser Brace, an engineering firm from Montreal, directed the company.[42] In any case, liaison between management and directors proved to be more convenient in the hands of one director, and on 1 March 1942 Howe appointed Gordon C. Leitch as the company's managing director.[43]

The government expanded the plant's facilities through acquisition of property adjoining both sides of the existing establishment, including land belonging to the government. With the launching of the last Bangor-class minesweeper, HMCS *West-*

mount, on 14 March 1942, the company began construction of Algerine-class vessels, and new ways were laid down to the west in order to allow simultaneous construction of five minesweepers.[44] Robert Scrivener remained general manager until the end of 1942, but it deserves notice that neither the director general of the shipbuilding branch nor the directors of Toronto Shipbuilding Company were practical shipbuilders.[45] Not surprisingly, problems arose. The yard had been started on a bit of waterfront undeveloped for shipbuilding. The equipment was not a patch on a regular shipyard. There were no boiler-making facilities, and only the crudest type of steel-fabricating facilities existed.[46] Changes in management, confusion over the company's organization, and too great an emphasis on multiple production of hulls in 1941 and 1942 without creating the necessary fitting-out facilities all led to difficulties.[47] On 13 August 1942, in an attempt to improve the existing situation, including new problems arising from attempts to organize labour in the shipyard, Leitch replaced Clarke as president.

Born in 1890 at Ridgeway, Ontario, Gordon Leitch was a grain shipper and ship owner. President of both Toronto Elevators Limited and Upper Lakes and St Lawrence Transportation Company at Toronto and director of several well-known companies, he brought much needed business experience, organizational talent, and management skills to the company.[48] In an effort to relieve delays fitting out the new Algerines at Toronto, Leitch set up a fitting-out yard at St John, New Brunswick, in November, subcontracting its management to Canadian Comstock Company Limited, an electrical engineering firm. The idea behind the move was to get the ships to tidewater as quickly as possible and to avoid limitations imposed on ship movements by freeze-up in the St Lawrence River. But the experiment was not a success.

Whether general manager Scrivener's departure at the end of 1942 was part of a continuing shake-up of management is unclear. Hal R. Carlson replaced him three months later on 8 April 1943. A native of the United States, Carlson had come to Canada in the spring of 1942 to accept a position with the company as works manager. Educated in California in naval architecture and marine engineering and possessing long experience in US West Coast shipyards, he was one of very few Americans in Canada's wartime shipbuilding industry.[49] In July, Leitch established a second fitting-out yard at Hamilton to hasten the fitting out of Toronto-built ships. Using a large warehouse taken over from the Hamilton Harbour Commission, he subcontracted the management to Carter-Halls-Aldinger Limited, a construction company.[50] On 12 August 1943, after one year as president, Leitch withdrew, returning to full-time management of his own business affairs, which had been growing during his absence. The government transferred management of the company to Redfern Construction Company.

Charles Redfern, a well-known construction engineer and president of a long-established Toronto firm, had earlier appeared briefly as executive vice president of Wartime Merchant Shipping Limited. He immediately set up Redfern Construction Company (Shipbuilding Division) Limited to manage Toronto Shipbuilding Company, which he reorganized in response to repeated complaints by the British Admiralty Technical Mission (BATM) and other interested parties of interminable delays and failures to keep promises. Under Redfern's management, the government authorized the shipbuilding company to incur capital expenses of up to $2.2 million, in addition to $1.1 million already approved, in order to cover additions to the yards, including those set up at St John and Hamilton.[51] Subsequently, the company incurred additional expenses, bringing the total to $2.4 million.[52] At peak employment, numbers reached 5,000, with 500 each at St John and Hamilton.[53]

Toronto Shipbuilding Company briefly kept up appearances as a Crown corporation, but its management had been subcontracted to Redfern on a cost-plus-fixed-fee basis, and on 31 December 1943 the company surrendered its charter as part of the changes in the administration of the government's shipbuilding program and thereafter operated as a government plant under the general supervision of Wartime Shipbuilding Limited.[54] In effect, the government abandoned direct management through a Crown corporation in favour of subcontracting it to private industry.

Although Toronto Shipbuilding Company's contribution to the war effort is indubitable, the question remains whether creation of a Crown corporation contributed to or hindered production.[55] Although production delays may have been due as much to failures in the delivery of materials over which the company had no control as to flawed organization, in the opinion of production manager Russ Cornell, the labour force at Toronto had been overexpanded and the yard overdeveloped using mass-production methods.[56] The several changes in organization and management suggest that Toronto Shipbuilding Company, originally created to save the government embarrassment, was a flawed vehicle for war production. Like another Crown company, Quebec Shipyards Limited, it was designed chiefly as a political expedient rather than to increase production.

Although Port Arthur Shipbuilding Company was in relatively good condition at the war's outbreak, capable of building anything required, a fire and explosion in the mould loft in December 1940 encouraged major expansion. In 1943 the company installed an electric annealing furnace adjoining the pipe-welding shop, which contained a galvanizing plant. This saved sending out many items requiring treatment and saved transportation costs. A new "Clyde" electrically powered crane with an 80-foot boom was installed to service better the building berths and the graving docks. By the summer of that year, Port Arthur Shipbuilding employed about 1,950 persons. The shipyard employed about 1,650, including technical and office staff. A large woodworking department had grown to about 250 workers, including 100 women, in order to produce parts that were delivered to a nearby aircraft factory.[57]

Expansion was relatively modest at Kingston. The company built a new machine shop to relieve congestion in the plant's production of marine engines and erected two overhead cranes across Ontario Street, but the most important development occurred in 1940 when Wolvin recruited Thomas G. Bishop, a mechanical engineer, to come out of retirement and become the company's general manager.

Expansion of the St Lawrence River yards to accommodate both naval and cargo shipbuilding programs was nearly continuous. Canadian Vickers Limited, already Canada's premier shipyard with five covered berths, Marine Industries Limited, and

Davie Shipbuilding and Ship Repairing Company were active, growing enterprises. The naval shipbuilding program filled up their berths, leading the government to authorize $2 million for expansion of the Canadian Vickers plant and about $1.8 million to expand two small Quebec City yards, George T. Davie and Sons and Morton Engineering and Dry Dock Company, in order to build warships.

At Davie Shipbuilding and Repairing, as Eileen Marcil has written, "four new building berths, several new buildings, and greatly improved cranage transformed a yard which, like most Canadian shipyards, had seen little change since the end of the previous war."[58] But most of this came after the yard began to build large cargo ships.

One further small expansion occurred in response to the naval program when Hubert Scott-Paine established Canadian Power Boat Company in 1940 at Montreal to build 70-foot high-speed launches (HSLs) and motor torpedo boats (MTBs) for the Royal Canadian Air Force (RCAF) and the Royal Canadian Navy, respectively, and to mass-produce hulls fitted with Packard marine engines for shipment to the United Kingdom to be armed.

Considered a genius by his admirers and a pain in the neck by others, Scott-Paine was a speed enthusiast and industrialist whose obsessive secrecy, mistrust, and refusal to cooperate with the British Admiralty led to his brilliance being largely ignored in official circles. On 20 September 1939, during a trip to the United States to negotiate an agreement to produce motor torpedo boats with the Elco Naval Division of Electric Boat Company (Elco) at Bayonne, New Jersey, Scott-Paine travelled to Montreal to discuss building high-speed boats suitable for aircraft rescue and harbour defence under licence for the Canadian government. More serious discussions occurred one month later when he visited Rear Admiral Percy W. Nelles at Ottawa and officials of Canadian Vickers at Montreal.[59] Now he proposed to manufacture an armoured target boat and sought to produce them at Canadian Vickers under licence.[60]

Scott-Paine's negotiations with Canadian authorities and Canadian Vickers stalled, resuming only in February 1940 after David Carswell indicated some interest in the armoured target-towing vessel and a new 70-foot, high-speed boat. In April the RCN and the RCAF indicated sufficient interest in the 70-foot boat to place orders, but Canadian Vickers bowed out, telling Scott-Paine that the company was unable to build his boats under licence because of existing war work. Scott-Paine then proposed to finance and build his own plant in Montreal.[61]

Canadian Power Boat Company was registered on 11 May 1940, and a small design office was opened in Montreal.[62] Construction of the new plant had begun only when Scott-Paine signed a contract on 18 July to build twelve MTBs, six HSLs, and six armoured target-towing boats. Two days earlier, his prototype 70-foot boat, PV-70, arrived in Montreal via the United States. PV stood for "Private Venture." This boat was completed to RCN specifications in November, and after trials on the St Lawrence River it was driven to Halifax, where it became Canadian Motor Torpedo Boat No. 1.[63] On 22 July the Dutch government placed an order for eight MTBs, to be shipped directly to the East Indies.[64]

Mechanics preparing to install a Packard 4M-2500 V-12 gasoline marine engine in a motor torpedo boat at Canadian Power Boat Company, Montreal, 24 April 1941. Canada, DND/ LAC, PA-132177.

The project had depended on being able to secure American Packard's 1,200-horse-power, 4M-2500 marine engines. As early as 18 May 1940, before any contract was signed, Scott-Paine had succeeded in persuading Carswell to purchase seventy-two engines.[65] With two in each boat, speeds of up to 48 knots were achieved.[66] In August, Captain W.E.G. Beaufort-Greenwood and A.L. Hill arrived from England as factory superintendent and works manager, respectively, and set about recruiting labour. After working from August to December to complete the factory, which involved reclaiming the silted-up side basin, and after recruiting and training a workforce, Beaufort-Greenwood and Hill saw the keel of the first boat laid on 16 December. Three more were begun before the year's end. About 210 employees were on the pay-roll.[67] On 28 December the Dutch ordered an additional eight boats for the Royal Netherlands Navy (RNN).

The wooden hulls were built upside down on moulds and then turned upright for installation of bulkheads, engines, and internal fittings. The first hull was turned over during January 1941; five hulls were turned over during February, and three 70-foot and one 40-foot hull were turned over in March. The first boat was finished and on trial on 16 May.[68]

Boat builders were hard to find in Montreal, and Scott-Paine's encounter with the first fifty brought from Nova Scotia fishing ports was a shock. The men carried the tools of their trade with them, heavy axes, adzes, augers, and caulking mallets. Writing to his brother, he described them as men

> who knew wooden ships and fishing vessels and dory building, smelt of the sea, and chewed 'bacca – couldn't have asked for much more, but are heavy handed. Well, how anything ever survived being sawn in half, how any screw wasn't twisted double, how anything anywhere survived their first shock assault can never be explained – it took me the first week clearing up and only a detailed elevation of my soul kept me from buying a revolver and calmly and deliberately shooting the whole 50. It ironed itself out, I took all their tools away, the same gear as old Brackly had or any of Stow's shipbuilders of our youth – same men – same gear, looked and smelt the same – same thumbs, square, wide and very strong, steel rules marked in ⅛" finest reading with brass joints, and the ends all worn away where they had been used to scratch suspected places to uncover hidden sorrows. With a few new tools, no saw, no hammers we've started them into a new and troublesome existence.[69]

Scott-Paine's changes worked well. By 28 July 1941, with his workforce clad in clean white coveralls, nineteen hulls had been turned over in the spotless plant. During the summer, employment grew to 450. By 1 October thirty-nine hulls had been almost completed: six 70-foot, high-speed rescue launches and six 40-foot target-towing boats for the RCAF, eleven MTBs for the RCN, and sixteen MTBs for the RNN. The target-towing boats were no longer armoured, and operational experience with Elco boats had led to several modifications to the Canadian ones. A shortage of aluminum led to the rotating gun turrets being built of laminated wood.[70]

Canadian Power Boat Company's main concern during the summer of 1941 was to secure additional orders from UK and Canadian authorities, but Scott-Paine's longstanding resistance to Admiralty procedures and concern for secrecy infected his relations with the RCN, which found no use for the MTBs in the new antisubmarine war into which it had been plunged. Scott-Paine openly accused RN officials of turning the Canadians against him. Following the fall of Crete in June, Canadian naval staff agreed to an Admiralty request to transfer all twelve Canadian MTBs to the Royal Navy for operation in the Mediterranean theatre, and the Dutch agreed to transfer their first six boats to the West Indies. Owing to delays in deliveries of components and modifications demanded by the British Admiralty Technical Mission, to whom the boats had been transferred, Scott-Paine obtained permission to move the unfinished Montreal boats to a boatyard at Greenwich, Connecticut. Beginning on 23 October, seventeen boats motored up the Richelieu River, crossed the American border into Lake Champlain, and via the Hudson River reach Greenwich. Four boats were towed. The entire transfer was completed within a month.[71]

Although the company's Montreal plant surpassed any other facility in the country for building coastal-force vessels, no further order for boats was ever placed with the company. The MTBs of the second Dutch order and any left from the first order were completed in the summer of 1942 and shipped south to Fyff's Shipyard at New York for completion.[72] Most of the company's employees were laid off, and the factory was extensively retooled to manufacture fuselages and wing flaps for the all-wood Mosquito fighter-bomber during the remainder of the war. Scott-Paine continued to own the company, which retained its name. He sold the plant in November 1946.[73]

On 11 March 1942 Harold Milne advised the director general of the shipbuilding branch that naval construction had reached the saturation point at least until the fall

Princess Juliana of the Netherlands inspecting motor torpedo boats being built for the Royal Netherlands Navy by the Canadian Power Boat Company, Montreal, September 1941. In the left foreground is an RCAF air-sea rescue launch. Another one (M-233) can be seen tied up on the far side of the basin. A 70-foot MTB, identified by its twin machinegun turrets and torpedo tubes, is moored at the near side; behind lies the Lachine Canal, hundreds of miles from the sea. City of Southampton Museum.

of 1943. If the RCN or the BATM required additional vessels, the DMS was not in a position to build them, nor had it any plans whereby the department could quickly increase production. Milne proposed Trois Rivières as the only location where further expansion might occur.[74] But one final expansion of the naval shipbuilding program occurred following the sudden approval in July of construction of thirty-five additional warships not in the 1942–43 war appropriations.

The decision to build fifteen frigates at Morton Engineering and Dry Dock and at George T. Davie and Sons led to the setting-up of a central fitting-out yard in order to speed deliveries from the two small Quebec City firms.[75] The yard was necessary because, as would be the case in Toronto a month later, hull construction had outrun fitting-out.[76] Searching for always scarce management talent, the government invited Anglo-Canadian Pulp and Paper Mills Limited to establish a shipbuilding division under the direction of vice president Walter J. Clarke. He would manage the government-owned yard, to be located in the inner Louise Basin, across the St Charles River from the main papermaking plant. The plant's machine shop could aid with work in the yard.[77] William E. Soles was appointed general manager with a staff of 150, including 12 draftsmen. The Anglo-Canadian Shipbuilding Division eventually employed 2,000 men in three shifts daily.[78]

The attempt to consolidate management and ease the burden on the two small yards had limited success. By 1943, with 3,000 to 4,000 workers employed on the two sites, labour strife had become unmanageable. A two-week strike by 7,000 shipyard workers at Quebec City and Lauzon from the 15 to 28 June forced the government to act. On 16 June it incorporated Quebec Shipyards Limited ostensibly to coordinate naval construction in the Quebec region but really to end labour strife and to lower costs and increase production.[79] The government expropriated the yards owned by Robert Morton and Charlie Davie and placed them under Quebec Shipyards Limited. C.D. Howe appointed his friend Wilfrid Gagnon as president. A French Canadian businessman from Montreal, Gagnon had been director general of the purchasing branch of the DMS since December 1940 and had served as Howe's appointee as a director of Canadian National Railway Company, Trans Canada Air Lines, and Grand Trunk Pacific Development Company.[80] Gagnon was given a board of directors that included J. Edouard Simard, vice president of Marine Industries Limited. Officers of the company were all French Canadians. The new management gave rise to at least one editorial protest that nonshipbuilders were now in charge of the new shipyard and were appearing elsewhere in the country; the lack of managerial talent in the industry was glaringly obvious.[81]

Within two weeks, Gagnon settled the strike and signed a contract with an industrial trade union agreeing to increased wages, and on 26 July 1943 he entered into an agreement with the government to supervise management of the two shipyards owned by the Crown and the outfitting yard operated by Anglo-Canadian Pulp and Paper Mills.[82]

Quebec Shipyards Limited kept a close watch on all three companies. Mould-loft templates were exchanged, information, purchasing, and stock records were centralized, and a school was set up in the yards to train French Canadian workmen for more responsible positions and to become foremen. The first ship finished at the fitting-out yard, HMCS *Dunver*, took ten months from its arrival to completion. The last ship would take just ten weeks.[83] During the thirty months of its existence to December 1945, Quebec Shipyards Limited delivered thirty-eight ships: eighteen frigates, twelve corvettes, and eight 4,700-ton dry-cargo ships.[84]

Cargo Ship Expansion

The cargo ship program provided the major incentive to expand Canada's wartime shipbuilding industry. It was a direct consequence of the US Lend-Lease Act, which became law on 27 March 1941, and of the Hyde Park Agreement, which followed less than a month later on 20 April. In contrast to naval construction, which had done little to provoke expansion on the West Coast, the new freighter program unleashed a wave of private investment that saw shipbuilding become the major wartime industrial activity in British Columbia, where the number of berths able to build 10,000-ton cargo ships grew from four in April 1941 to twenty-two a year later.[85]

In the spring of 1941 a group of Vancouver businessmen invited W.D. McLaren, a consultant naval architect, to set up a shipyard in conjunction with bridge-building and boiler-making firms located at False Creek on the site of the former J. Coughlan and Sons shipyard. This was the precursor of the largest expansion of shipbuilding facilities in the country; none of it required government capital assistance. McLaren engaged his son Arthur, a newly minted mechanical engineer from the University of British Columbia, to do the drawings for a four-berth shipyard. The new company, known as West Coast Shipbuilders Limited, received orders to build 10,000-ton merchant ships. At no time did this enterprise receive any capital assistance, but accelerated depreciation played a key role in the yard's financial success.

Major George Alexander Walkem, prime mover among the businessmen and president of West Coast Shipbuilders, had lived for forty-five years in Vancouver, where he had been active in the machinery and engineering business. He was born at Kingston, Ontario, and served an apprenticeship at Canadian Locomotive Works and at Kingston Foundry Company. After graduating with a bachelor's degree in sciences from McGill University, he went west. He served with the Royal Engineers in Palestine during the First World War and later became president of the Engineering Institute of Canada. Formerly manager of Vancouver Engineering Works Limited, Major Walkem was connected to Vancouver Machinery Depot Limited, Vancouver Iron Works Limited, Gulf of Georgia Towing Limited, and West Coast Salvage and Contracting Company.[86] His associates in West Coast Shipbuilders were his son, Knox, who was made managing director and later general manager; Philip William Burbidge, who was also on the board of West Coast Salvage and Contracting; and William Thomas Fraser. The four men each owned 500 shares. Richard Knox Walkem, KC, who probably did the legal paperwork, and William McLaren each held one share.[87] Colonel Victor Spencer and his associates at Western Bridge and Steel

A wooden shipyard to build steel ships. West Coast Shipbuilders Limited, showing the completed timber derricks and booms built of Douglas fir, 18 November 1941. In the background, the staging around hull no. 103 is in place, while on the right the double bottom of hull no. 104 is taking shape. Photo by W.J. Moore. CVA, City of Vancouver Photo Collection, 195-27.2.

Fabricating Limited, adjacent to the new shipyard, were closely connected with the Walkem interests.[88] This company, which had been in the hands of Hamilton Bridge Company since 1929, fabricated all the steel used in the shipyard.

The most astonishing feature of the shipyard was that it was constructed of local timber. No steel was available. McLaren designed two wooden buildings each running the length of a pair of berths. Each was 300 feet long, about 50 feet wide, and two storeys high and constructed to hold the workshops. He then placed enormous Douglas Fir timbers, each 12 by 24 inches, that were bolted together to form a row of double posts stretching into the sky. These were placed at each corner and at 100-foot intervals along the buildings' sides. From these were rigged great wooden booms that swung over the hulls, providing access to any part of each berth. In this unique setup, construction began on the first four freighters during the summer of 1941 while the shipyard was still being built. SS *Fort Chilcotin* was delivered in June 1942. During the next two and a half years, West Coast Shipbuilders Limited constructed over half a million deadweight tons of cargo ships.

In January 1944 Colonel Spencer and Frank Ross purchased Hamilton Bridge (Western) Limited, intending to operate it as an independent unit.[89] After acquiring full control of Western Bridge and Steel Fabricators, Spencer announced on 31 March 1945 that he and his associates, including Ross, had acquired controlling interest in West Coast Shipbuilders Limited and were amalgamating the two companies.[90] Ross became chairman of Western Bridge and Steel Fabrication and president of West Coast Shipbuilders.[91]

The switch from minesweepers to cargo ships led North Van Ship Repairs to replace its three small berths erected in 1939 with four large berths for 10,000-ton freighters, and in January 1942, well before the company completed its last minesweeper, the first 10,000-ton freighter was launched. The change in ship type led to a major reorganization of the yard. In addition to constructing the larger berths, the company increased the outfitting wharves and in August placed a 12,000-ton floating dry dock, built at a cost of $700,000, in service alongside the building berths. Colonel Alfred Henry Cowie, vice president of Wartime Merchant Shipping Limited, had visited the yard the previous autumn and reported that North Van's performance was unsatisfactory. He claimed management had taken on too much and was paying insufficient attention to organization by planning a four-berth yard while attempting to plan and build a floating dry dock. In Cowie's opinion, attempting too much before developing an organization was a recipe for failure. Harvey R. MacMillan concurred, recommending to C.D. Howe that he withhold materials for the dry dock until the company's performance improved.[92]

Improve it did, for during the next three years, North Van Ship Repairs constructed fifty-one 10,000-ton dry-cargo ships, five Victory-type maintenance ships, and four transport ferries (LST3s). A shipyard capable of only wooden-ship construction in 1939 built seventy-six steel ships before the war was over.[93]

The greatest expansion occurred at Burrard Dry Dock Company. Clary Wallace purchased additional properties in North Vancouver and installed four new berths with four long piers complete with air, water, electrical, oxygen, and acetylene-gas services. Four fixed, 5-ton cranes were installed between each of two pairs of berths, and two 5-ton travelling cranes were installed on three of the piers. The company also filled in the site of the recently built corvette and minesweeper berth, and many shops were expanded or rebuilt over it, including a new copper and sheet-metal shop and a new pipe shop; the marine machine shop was also extended. A new plate shop with a mould loft was built on the site of the old joiner shop; also, a second plate shop and a 345-foot-long steel-fabricating shop were built, complete with 5-ton bridge cranes. The new construction and many additions tripled the size of the yard from what had existed in 1939. The total cost amounted to approximately $3.5 million.[94]

After obtaining the contract to build thirty 10,000-ton cargo ships from Wartime Merchant Shipping Limited, Burrard Dry Dock Company began construction of a new site on the south shore of Burrard Inlet in the spring of 1941. Wallace pur-

Aerial view of Burrard Dry Dock Company's four-berth South Yard. Note the lots filled with steel plates on the left. NVMA, no. 27-3740.

chased the old Couglan dock site from his own company for $325,914 and incorporated Burrard (Vancouver) Dry Dock Company Limited with an authorized capital of $250,000.[95] He appointed one of the directors, Hugh M. Lewis, an executive of Pacific Mills at Ocean Falls, British Columbia, to manage the new company. By 1 September four berths had been completed, with ten 5-ton derricks, two large fabricating shops, compressor houses, stores buildings, lunchrooms, canteens, and offices.[96] Commonly known as South Burrard, the yard was equipped to build four 10,000-ton ships at one time.[97] Lewis served as general manager for the next three years before being succeeded by John Dalrymple.[98]

John Lochart, a legendary figure in West Coast shipbuilding, directed the works at South Yard. Trained in Scotland with Workman Clark and Company and in Ireland with Harland and Wolff, he came to Vancouver via the United States in 1916 as general manager of J. Coughlan and Sons, where he supervised ship construction. After a brief time spent as a surveyor for Bureau Veritas, he joined Burrard in 1926. Seventy-five years old when war broke out and confined to a wheelchair by a stroke that had paralyzed his left arm and right leg, he celebrated his eighty-first birthday in 1945 working at his desk in the yard.[99] Burrard South Yard launched its first hull on 24 January 1942 and its last in 1946. Fifty-five 10,000-ton hulls were built, but all machinery in the ships was installed across the inlet at Burrard North Yard. Strictly a wartime emergency plant, South Yard closed after the war and its equipment was transferred to North Yard or was sold.[100]

Taken *in toto*, Vancouver's capacity to build 10,000-ton cargo ships was expanded from two to sixteen berths in a single year, during which the keels of sixteen hulls were laid down. Only four hulls were launched, and none was completed in 1941, but the next year Vancouver yards delivered 540,000 deadweight tons to Wartime Merchant Shipping Limited.

Less dramatic expansion occurred at Esquimalt and Victoria at the south end of Vancouver Island. Although Yarrows Limited had contracted to build three of the original Flower-class corvettes early in 1940 and two more in 1941, significant expansion occurred only after Harvey MacMillan arranged with Norman Yarrow to put in two new berths for immediate construction of large cargo ships.[101]

With negotiations to construct four large cargo ships in hand, plans to build a new yard immediately north of the government graving dock began with blasting and levelling of the site. Approximately half a million cubic yards of rock were removed and used as fill, and contracts were let for new buildings.[102] Yarrows laid the keel for the first freighter in the new yard on 14 August 1941, just ten weeks after ground was first broken; the second keel was laid on 10 September.[103] Yarrows built only two cargo ships. The contract was partially cancelled in mid-November following a decision to transfer the final two ships to Burrard Dry Dock so that Yarrows might concentrate its attention on the new frigate program. Yarrows went on to complete seventeen frigates and seven LST3s.[104]

Additional expansion occurred after Yarrows switched back to naval construction. "B" Wharf was built in December 1942, along with a building for stores and outfitting. Fire had destroyed the joiner and pattern shops in 1941, so the workers moved into new quarters in the new stores building.[105] The government ultimately committed more than $1.2 million in financial assistance to the expansion. A new 45-ton derrick scow entered service in February 1943, and in March the air compressor plant was enlarged. In June 1944 work commenced to repair and renew Yarrows' marine railway.[106] Approval of the project came so late in the war because the absence of a haul-out meant the navy would have to rely on the slipway at Victoria Machinery Depot (VMD) for docking intermediate-size vessels. Dismantling the old dock began in August, and the new 3,000-ton railway was completed and in operation by March 1945. The old Esquimalt graving dock was also restored, and on 22 September HMCS *Coaticock*, a 1,800-ton frigate, was docked there, the first vessel to use it in twenty-five years.[107]

After Victoria Machinery Depot obtained contracts to build ten 10,000-ton freighters, the plant's site on Victoria's outer harbour proved to be too small. In April 1941 the company purchased the old Rithet Piers as well as seventeen acres of adjacent city property. VMD rebuilt the piers and constructed two launch ways, erecting six cranes, including three 20-ton locomotive types. The first hulls took shape while hard surfacing was being applied to the surrounding roadway. This extension became known as Plant No. 2.[108] A new pattern shop was also built.

The company purchased Victoria Brass and Iron Works at Esquimalt and moved the business and equipment to the shipyard, which enlarged operations at a cost of approximately $100,000.[109] This acquisition and a new foundry at its Dallas Road plant equipped with the latest electric steel, oil-fired brass, and pyrometer-controlled annealing furnaces, as well as with moulding and sand-conditioning machinery for producing steel castings, enabled VMD to speed up operations considerably. The blacksmith shop was equipped with three forging hammers and three electric treating furnaces. As a consequence, VMD manufactured some castings for Yarrows and for Vancouver plants and parts for cranes. Expansion continued in 1942 when new machine and plate shops were erected with several overhead bridge cranes, one of 20-ton and two of ten-ton capacity. Plate-cutting machinery and two "Unionmelt" automatic welding machines were also installed.[110] Possessing the heaviest crane on the West Coast, the company was able to carry out more prefabrication, especially of bulkheads set up on a fabricating way, than was any other yard. But no all-welded ship was ever attempted because the surveyors at Lloyd's Register of Shipping were dead against it.[111]

Responding on 22 June 1942 to criticism of the government's shipbuilding program, C.D. Howe claimed that during the previous year the number of berths able to take 10,000-ton ships had increased from eight in April 1941 to forty. Five had been turned over to naval building. Eleven additional berths had been built or enlarged to construct 4,700-ton cargo ships, of which two had been turned over to naval construction. Nine were currently occupied with cargo ships.[112] To achieve these numbers, the minister had been forced to build a shipyard in Nova Scotia.

Howe had not wanted to build steel ships in Nova Scotia for the very good reason that the province lacked materials, skilled labour, and management talent. Moreover, it made little strategic sense. Canada's East Coast was on the frontline in the Battle of the Atlantic. Ship repairing facilities were scarce yet desperately needed to meet the demands of merchant shipping and of naval escorts returning from the deadly struggles far out at sea. North Atlantic winter storms and the enemy took their toll of little ships. Unfortunately, the naval staff in Ottawa took a long time coming to the realization that the RCN's own repair facilities were inadequate. Strong advocacy by the Nova Scotia government and the minister of national defence for the naval service and the need for a new emergency shipyard forced the issue.

Angus L. Macdonald was a political animal and did all in his power to obtain the new yard. Following negotiations between the Nova Scotia Department of Industry and the president of Wartime Merchant Shipping Limited, agreement was reached and order-in-council PC 8056, dated 22 October 1941, authorized construction of three 4,700-ton cargo ships at Pictou, Nova Scotia. On the same date, PC 8045 authorized capital assistance of $562,000 to build the new yard.[113] Construction began almost immediately after the parties signed a contract to build the three vessels. At the time, Pictou possessed a marine slip with refit and repair facilities belonging to Pictou Foundry and Machine Company Limited, owned and operated by Ferguson Brothers.

The firm was one of Nova Scotia's oldest companies. It traced its origins back to 1833. After it had gone through several transformations during the nineteenth century, Allan A. Ferguson became its sole owner in 1910. Following his death in 1932, the firm went to his eldest son, Robert A. Ferguson, who incorporated the company the next year.[114] On the outbreak of war, his three brothers, Allan Jr, Thomas, and James, became associated with him and early in 1940 began to convert and repair the first armed yachts acquired by the naval service.[115] The family firm began construction of the new shipyard, laid down the first keels, and struggled through the first heartbreaking winter to build the first ships while recruiting the original workforce.

Work began on the bleak waterfront in the last month of 1941. A few machines moved and levelled a sea of mud. An office was opened in an old hotel on Front Street, but despite good wages, few men applied. With a population of just 3,000 souls, Pictou was less than half the size of the next smallest shipbuilding town in the country.[116] Labour scouts scoured the outlying villages and hired farmers and fishermen to lay the launch ways and to drive the trucks and bulldozers. Battery Hill, a prominent local landmark, was pushed into the harbour to create a deepwater wharf. In January 1942 the government authorized payment of $800,000 for a fourth berth and increased construction facilities.[117] Finally, on 27 February, after the lone crane had been installed and the first steel had arrived, Bob Ferguson, under the direction of engineer James Childs and with the aid of a few workmen, laid the keel of the first ship in a blinding snowstorm; by noon the next day, they had lined up and bolted two more keel plates.[118]

The fourth keel went down on 15 April, but work did not proceed quickly or smoothly. Following an inspection trip to Pictou and a meeting with Premier A.S. Macmillan and members of his provincial government, Harvey MacMillan voiced his dissatisfaction, whereas the premier remained confident that a second yard building steel-hulled ships might be established in the province.[119] Shortly afterward, on 2 July, at MacMillan's urging, the Ferguson brothers relinquished management and capital assistance for the new yard to Foundation Maritime Limited, a wholly owned subsidiary of the Foundation Company of Canada with its head office in Montreal. The former contracts with Pictou Foundry and Machine Company were terminated, and a new contract for six additional 4,700-ton cargo ships was awarded to Foundation Maritime on a cost-plus-management-fee basis, the fee being set at $10,000 for each ship.[120] Government ownership of the yard made the management change relatively simple.[121]

Robert Ferguson and his brothers carried on repairing ships for the navy through Ferguson Industries Limited, which combined four of their companies: Pictou Marine Railway Limited, operating 1,000- and 2,000-ton marine dry docks; Pictou Foundry and Machine, which set up a new operation for steel boatbuilding in Trenton, Nova

Scotia; W.C. Wetmore Limited, specialists in plumbing, sheet metal, and electrical marine wiring; and Fullertons Limited, a wood-working factory manufacturing life-boats and life rafts as well as ship furniture. By 1943 the company employed approximately 1,000 men now skilled in all trades of ship repairing and ship construction.[122]

Expansion of St Lawrence River yards proceeded steadily rather than spectacularly, for they were already in fairly good condition when war broke out. At the end of 1941 Charlie Davie picked Charles Beaudoin, then employed by the Canadian Steamship Inspection Service, as a man with sufficient knowledge of the local labour situation to build his workforce up from 300 or 400 men to about 1,600 in order to construct cargo ships. Davie appealed to Harvey MacMillan to exert his influence in order to obtain Beaudoin's services.[123] In January 1942 MacMillan advised Howe that the British Purchasing Commission wanted to keep berths with 4,700-tonners occupied and that the Canadian Shipping Board wanted to secure some of these medium-size ships for the West Indies trade. As the three yards – Pictou, St John Shipbuilding, and George T. Davie and Sons – held contracts for only one ship per berth, steel had to be ordered immediately if they were to build continuously. MacMillan also recommended building nine more ships.[124] The government authorized nearly $1.1 million for a three-berth expansion to build 4,700-ton cargo ships at George T. Davie and Sons.[125]

The cargo ship program also forced major new improvements elsewhere. In August 1941 the St Charles River at Quebec City was dredged upriver from Morton Engineering and Dry Dock Company to enable 4,700-ton cargo ships to turn around when launched and also dredged downstream to connect with the navigable channel.[126] The government provided $980,000 in capital assistance to Davie Shipbuilding and Repairing Company to expand its yard facilities, including the plate shop, steel storage, and cranes, in order to accelerate construction of 10,000-ton vessels on five existing berths. By 1943 this expenditure exceeded the valuation of all the yard's assets at the end of 1940, and the company had also expended several hundred thousand dollars.[127] By 1944 Quebec City yards had fourteen berths plus a large fitting-out basin capable of finishing six frigates at once.[128]

The cargo shipbuilding program provided the stimulus for major expansion at Marine Industries Limited. After its first contract for twelve 10,000-ton cargo ships was increased to twenty-seven in May 1941, work began to erect a new plate shop, a machine shop, and a new joiner shop, where all ship's furniture was manufactured, from tables and chairs to hardwood rails and flooring. In July 1943 two large AC "Unionmelt" welding machines were added to shipyard equipment, and thereafter all hull plates on ships' bottoms were welded.[129]

Work on a new six-berth yard began on 16 July 1941 on farmland adjacent to the yard. During the course of construction, the company carried out one of the most challenging engineering feats in the entire wartime industry. The Richelieu River being too narrow to allow conventional launching, Marine Industries constructed a 5,000-ton marine railway to lower the finished hulls into the river. Each ship was built on level ground, with three berths on each side of the railway. As work progressed, the hulls were moved sideways toward the railway cradle for lowering into the river, and a new keel was laid on the berth farthest from the launch site. Launching took three hours to complete.

Building the machinery and cables to move the launch platform capable of handling 5,000 tons, or the hull of a North Sands–type freighter, into the river proved a challenge. The structure and machinery were straight forward, but American manufacturers could promise only one-year delivery of the enormous chain needed to move the platform into the river. Marine Industries turned to its sister industry, Sorel Steel Industries Limited, to manufacture the largest cast-steel chain ever produced in Canada. The chain had to be strong enough to pull the launching cradle up again with a ship resting on it if this ever become necessary. The chain, one and one-quarter miles long, each link weighing 38 pounds, was completed in two months; only 9 of the 8,400 links failed during testing.[130] The keel of the first vessel was laid

Aerial view of Marine Industries Limited, 15 April 1944, showing the six-berth yard and a 10,000-ton dry-cargo ship being launched from the marine railway into the Richelieu River. SHPS, P001, Fonds Sorel Industries, series 8, subseries 1, D2.

on 24 January 1942, and ss *Port Royal Park* was launched six months later, one year and two days after work had begun to convert farm fields into a shipyard. Nineteen additional ships were launched during the next eighteen months.[131]

As early as August 1941, Harvey MacMillan had considered expanding the country's shipbuilding capacity beyond the existing shipyards if sufficient supplies of steel and machinery were available. From the standpoint of management, labour supply, and economy, he thought the best location would be somewhere in Montreal harbour, where existing prefabricating facilities and skilled labour from bridge and structural-steel companies could be utilized. These firms had many employees and supervisory staff whose training qualified them to do skilled work in shipyards and who were likely to become unemployed as the volume of civilian construction work fell off. MacMillan suggested a site between the Bickerdike and McKay Piers and asked Howe whether authorities would permit the use of the site and whether existing concrete cribs on the north side of the Bickerdike Pier could be used for fitting out.[132] No recommendation was made at that time, and almost immediately afterward, political considerations meant the first new yard was constructed in Nova Scotia. The loss of Canadian Vickers to the naval program in November, the current supply of equipment and machinery, and the anticipated supply of steel all appeared to justify construction of a second emergency yard.

MacMillan quickly dusted off his August consideration, transforming it into a December proposal. He recommended Montreal as the best location for the new yard on the basis of labour supply, capital cost, management, and availability of skilled workmen and steel-working facilities now becoming idle that could be used for fabrication. He estimated that a four-berth yard capable of constructing ten 10,000-ton ships annually could be built at a cost of $2.5 million and be ready for use in six months. Ever the optimist, MacMillan also claimed that the ships could be built at a lower cost than in private yards, thus establishing new standards. The Crown owned all the land, and cost would be further reduced, he argued, by using Dominion Bridge Company shops at Lachine for prefabricating steel and by the existence of railways linking the Lachine plant to the Bickerdike Pier.[133]

Howe quickly approved the proposal, and work began almost immediately on 9 January following the signing of a contract for twelve 10,000-ton North Sands–type cargo ships with United Shipyards Limited. The new yard's specifications called for six berths rather than four, and cost estimates had grown to $3 million. The first tasks were to dredge the water part of the area, fill in the swamps, and construct the yard's foundation. The six building slips were 1,000 feet long and had a total width of 1,000 feet.[134] Nine months later, officials at Wartime Merchant Shipping Limited amended the cost estimate to just over $4 million, and by the time the yard was completed and in operation, overruns had driven authorized capital assistance to $5,353,300.[135]

Like the smaller Pictou shipyard, United Shipyards was conceived and built by Wartime Merchant Shipping Limited and then placed under a joint-management agreement with Fraser Brace Limited and Dominion Bridge Company Limited. Fraser Brace, a well-known Montreal heavy-engineering firm was responsible for

United Shipyards Limited viewed from the water, 21 September 1943. NFB/LAC, WRM 3575.

constructing the yard, whereas Dominion Bridge concentrated on structural-steel work for the ships. The cost-plus-management-fee arrangement was similar to the one with Foundation Maritime Limited, although the agreed upon fee was $30,000 for the first 10,000-ton ship launched from each of the slipways and $25,000 per ship for each subsequent vessel. According to Wartime Merchant Shipping Limited, this compared favourably with fees current in the United States and the United Kingdom of about $100,000 for large cargo ships.

Both companies jointly controlled operation of the yard, each having equal representation on the board.[136] W.F. Angus, president of Dominion Bridge, became president, and Major J.H. Brace was vice president. Other directors were W. Taylor-Bailey from Dominion Bridge, appointed general manager, and Gordon R. Stephen from Fraser Brace.[137] In April 1942 Colonel Cowie resigned as vice president of Wartime Merchant Shipping Limited to return to his former post as general manager of Dominion Bridge Company, where he continued to be closely involved in the cargo ship program through United Shipyards.[138]

The six new berths were certainly needed, as five existing ones had been turned over to the naval construction program. The last cargo ships built at Canadian Vickers and Yarrows Limited were launched in May and July 1942, respectively, and those yards became exclusively devoted to naval construction for the remainder of the war. At United Shipyards, three keels were laid in May and three more in July.[139] But initial progress was painfully slow. Although the contract called for the first three ships to be delivered on 1 December and the next three before the end of December, only five hulls were launched and only one vessel was delivered before the end of the year.[140] United Shipyards Limited was proving to be a challenge owing to the lack of good shipbuilding management.

In the spring of 1943 Wartime Merchant Shipping moved John Rannie and his family from Victoria to Montreal so that Rannie could assume the position of general manager of United Shipyards.[141] Rannie, an experienced British shipbuilder who began his North American career at the Richmond, California, yards of Henry Kaiser, had been instrumental in getting Victoria Machinery Depot up and running smoothly. He quickly gained control of the new yard, delivering the last of the first six ships on 31 May. Sixteen more North Sands freighters followed during the next twenty-eight weeks before freeze-up.[142] One of them, SS *Fort Romaine*, delivered on 8 September, fifty-eight days after the laying of her keel, established a record for speed of construction in a Canadian shipyard during the war. Twenty-eight days later, she arrived in the United Kingdom with a full cargo.[143]

Much of the speed achieved was because Dominion Bridge Company carried out more subassembly work than regular shipyards. The forepeak was just one of the larger subassemblies. Plates and floors were riveted and welded into position in the company's shops at Lachine and transported along seven miles of railway line to the shipyard and hoisted into position. The chief constraint on the size of these subassemblies was the 70-foot right of way on the track.[144] Before the yard was closed in 1945, workers built forty-five 10,000-ton freighters, including nine of the Canadian type and three naval stores-issuing ships.

Ship-Repair and Conversion Expansion

Until the summer of 1940, shipbuilding plants were almost exclusively engaged in naval construction. By that autumn, however, ship repairing had assumed greater importance than before, and it became necessary to regulate and coordinate the ship repairing industry, settle priorities between naval and merchant shipping, and consider expanding ship-repair facilities. Late in November an order-in-council appointed David Carswell controller of ship construction and repairs. Less than five months later, a new order-in-council relieved the controller of his responsibilities for new ship construction, relegating him to ship repairing.[145] During the interim, Harvey MacMillan had sent a memorandum, together with supporting data, to C.D. Howe outlining the serious delays to transatlantic shipping occurring at Halifax and St John because of inadequate repair facilities. Howe, whose relations with MacMillan were strained at the time, turned the memo over to Carswell for immediate examination; action quickly followed.[146]

During the winter of 1940–41, the large graving dock at St John had been unable to cope with demands for its services.[147] St John Dry Dock and Shipbuilding Company had been specializing in Royal Navy work, handling both armed merchant cruisers and regular warships of the Third Battle Squadron. In order to dry-dock merchant ships and ease the strain on its resources, the government contracted with Canadian Dredge and Dock Company to build a new 440-by-60-foot, concrete, tidal graving dock at the Atlantic terminal on land conveyed to the Crown by St John Dry Dock and Shipbuilding. When completed, it proved large enough to dry-dock most cargo ships trading into the Bay of Fundy and used the extremely high tide at St John to save the expense of pumping the dock, except for the final five feet at the bottom.[148] The initial cost estimate for the job was less than half a million dollars, but the final authorized payment amounted to $1,080,016.

At St John Dry Dock and Shipbuilding the north berth was extended half again to 725 feet to permit armed merchant cruisers to moor safely while fitting out. The tidal dry dock was extended 40 feet to allow standard American and Canadian 10,000-ton vessels to be handled, and a machine shop was fitted with lathes and drills at government expense. Plans were drawn up to retool the entire St John Iron Works plant before winter, and the controller of ship repairs arranged for Fred Williamson Company to extend its machine shop on a quick write-off basis and supplied rolls, punches, and shears to aid ship repairs.[149] In 1942 the government built a 900-foot-long repair pier in nearby Courtney Bay to permit vessels to move away from the loading piers, and a fuel-oil line was laid to it from the Imperial Oil storage plant.[150] By promising a quick write-off, the government also persuaded some private firms to purchase equipment for repairs at several other locations, including Halifax, Sydney, Liverpool, and Lunenburg.

With a navy of just thirteen ships in 1939, Halifax naval repair facilities were very limited and were quickly revealed to be entirely inadequate. HMC Dockyard, which experienced serious delays, occupied a narrow strip of land some 3,800 feet long and not more than 500 feet wide.[151] Halifax Shipyards Limited was wholly taken up with repairing merchant ships.[152] In November 1940 naval architectural consultants German and Milne advised the government to construct a floating dry dock for Halifax despite the British Admiralty's preference for graving docks for naval vessels. Several considerations overruled the Royal Navy's preference. Whereas three years would be needed to construct two graving docks of 600 and 400 feet, a floating dry dock of 600 feet with a 25,000-ton capacity could be built in Canada using existing facilities. A 400-foot dock could be built in eight months at an estimated cost of $1.75 million, and a 600-foot dock would cost $3 million. The consultants estimated the maintenance costs at 1 per cent of capital cost, and although labour costs to operate a floating dock might exceed those required for a graving dock, total operating costs would be about the same since less power would be needed for pumping the floating dock. The ability to sell the floating dry dock at the end of the war was another consideration.[153]

After weighing early suggestions to transfer the 25,000-ton floating dock, named the *Duke of Connaught*, from Montreal or tow the 20,000-ton Prince Rupert dock to Halifax, the government decided to build a new dock patterned after the one at

Montreal.[154] Dominion Bridge Company undertook the work at an anticipated cost of $3 million, retaining German and Milne as advisors. Construction moved ahead rapidly. The 25,000-ton dock was launched in 1941, put in operation in February 1942, and completed in June. Afterward, it was leased to Halifax Shipyards.[155]

Early in 1941 construction also began on piers on the east, or Dartmouth, side of Halifax Harbour. One pier, 1,275 feet long and capable of berthing nine ships at one time, was erected with a repair shop alongside measuring 100 feet by 150 feet. Two additional piers capable of docking three and two vessels each were built alongside existing repair shops. On the west side of the harbour, another pier, 550 feet long, was built to moor the new floating dry dock, and a sixty-foot submersion pool was dredged in front of the pier so that the dock could be sunk reasonably close to it.

The first of four large marine railways of 3,000-ton capacity also came into operation at Halifax about the same time, enabling destroyers to be hauled out without using either floating or graving docks. Prior to this, destroyers damaged in convoy-escort work in the North Atlantic had occupied the pre-existing graving dock for more than half the winter.

Halifax Shipyards spent $268,900 to improve storage capacity and install machine tools. Purdy Brothers of Halifax received capital assistance to purchase a large motor launch equipped with an electric welder and an air compressor in order to carry out repair work in the harbour. By mid-1941 nearly half a million dollars had been expended on purchasing and installing tools and on constructing machine shops, repairing berths, and fitting-out wharves and extending existing ones.[156] As was the case at St John, most of this expenditure had been initiated to meet the anticipated needs of the Royal Navy and the merchant service rather than those of the RCN.

At Sydney, in 1940, the available firms were Sydney Foundry, with a small marine railway for hauling out vessels, and Atlantic Spring and Machine Shop, which could handle minor repair work. Another small marine railway and repair shop existed at North Sydney. The naval dockyard was opened at the government wharf on 23 September, but the situation remained lamentable.[157] As practically all the public piers were in ruins, a 400-foot wharf was built at the principal ship-repair yard in 1941, but because of an uncooperative attitude and the desperate lack of wharfage, in 1942 a double 400-foot pier was projected into the harbour to permit merchant vessels to come alongside, where both government and privately owned repair shops could provide repairs.[158] The government also constructed a 3,000-ton marine railway.

In addition to large railway haul-outs constructed at Halifax, Sydney, and Shelburne, the government built smaller marine railways at Pictou, Lunenburg, Liverpool, and Gaspé. With the exception of the one at Shelburne, which remained under direct naval control, they were leased to private firms. At Pictou, Pictou Marine Railway Company operated the 2,000-ton railway, along with its own 1,000-ton haul-out to undertake repairs of naval vessels. In September 1941 the DMS contracted with Pictou Foundry and Machine Company to build the marine railway. Ice floes constantly threatened diving crews during construction, and reinforced concrete was poured in subzero temperatures, but in July 1942 it was ready for operation, months before the scheduled completion date.[159] A year later, the company built a service wharf alongside the railway.[160] The Lunenburg and Liverpool marine railways, each of 1,400-ton capacity, were authorized in February 1942 after naval staff realized the RCN needed more facilities for corvettes.[161] Later, three small 200-ton haul-outs were built at HMC Dockyard to service motor launches and small auxiliary craft. Initially estimated to cost under $2 million, the whole East Coast marine-railway program ran to several million.

In the spring of 1943, Burrard Dry Dock Company contracted to convert carrier-vessel escorts (CVEs).[162] Nineteen Smiter-class carrier escorts were to be brought to Vancouver and converted for use by the Royal Navy. Wartime Merchant Shipping Limited, assigned to supervise the job, leased the Lapointe Pier from the National Harbours Board and contracted to carry out extensions and to equip the site for $500,000, but authorized capital assistance eventually grew to $660,000.[163] Within a month, the former grain-handling terminal had been transformed into a working shipyard, with staff increasing at a rate of about 100 per week. At its peak, the yard employed about 2,200 workers.[164]

Conclusion

By December 1943 Canada's shipbuilding industry had grown beyond anyone's wildest imaginings four and a half years before. Nine shipyards with a total of thirty-four berths were constructing naval vessels, ten yards with thirty-eight berths were building cargo ships, and one yard was building both corvettes and Great Lakes tankers. The industry also maintained four fitting-out yards: two employed completing Algerine minesweepers, one for frigates, and one for modifying aircraft-carrier escorts. Canada's repair facilities also comprised fourteen graving docks, five floating docks, and twenty-two marine slips.[165]

Whereas the shipyards did everything asked of them in the way of building new ships, the same could not be said of the nation's ship-repair facilities. As there was little need for additional facilities on the West Coast, it is surprising that ship repairing always seemed so inadequate. This was mainly because the navy lacked adequate management talents and technical knowledge to foresee the problems and to plan ahead before being overwhelmed.

Repairs, Conversions, and Modernization

Introduction

Ship repairing is an integral part of shipbuilding. During the Second World War, Canadian shipyards completed more than 36,000 repairs to naval vessels and merchant ships from many nations.[1] Ship conversions were among the first and the last wartime activities carried out in Canadian shipyards, and the Royal Canadian Navy's (RCN) modernization crisis led ultimately to the dismissal of the chief of the naval staff. Yet the relative size of ship repairing and related activities to shipbuilding and to the war effort remains virtually unknown.[2] Acknowledging the importance of issues surrounding wartime ship repairing, few historians have ever examined the whole picture. They do not know how large this aspect of the industry became. Nor are they aware that one out of every six dollars spent on shipbuilding was for repairs during the war (see table 5.1). The aim of this chapter is to contextualize wartime ship repairing.

There is also some confusion about the origins of wartime ship-repair problems. The navy's first official historian viewed East Coast shipyards as reserved for ship repairing and refitting in order to explain why so few ships were ever built there.[3] But this was mistaken. First, East Coast shipyards built many ships during the war, and second, the navy had to develop its own repair yards. It has also been claimed that the policies of C.D. Howe and his officials at the Department of Munitions and Supply (DMS) were uniformly detrimental to Maritimes industries, particularly ship repairing, and to Canada's war effort in general.[4] Naval historian Marc Milner shrewdly attributes the inadequacy of Canada's ship-repair industry to the RCN's failure to anticipate its needs or to plan for ship repairs.[5] Although there is truth in these assertions, neither is entirely fair. How to measure the inadequacy of an industry that repaired 36,000 ships in six years is moot, and discussion of the navy's failure to plan requires a broader context than is currently available.

According to Ernest Forbes, the ship-repair industry received short shrift at the hands of the minister of munitions and supply.[6] On the one hand, Maritimes yards were reserved for repairs and service, but, on the other hand, the minister failed to develop them for repair purposes or for year-round operation. Although there is something to agree with in this interpretation, it ignores both the nature of Canada's

Table 5.1 | Value and proportion of ship repairs to shipbuilding in Canada, 1939–45[a]

Year	Value of new construction[b] ($000)	Value of ship repairs ($000)	Total value of shipbuilding ($000)	Ship repairs as a percentage of shipbuilding
1939	2,344	7,744	10,088	76.8
1940	29,196	13,079	42,275	30.9
1941	86,548	19,901	106,449	18.7
1942	208,713	27,734	236,447	11.7
1943	334,472	34,383	368,855	9.3
1944	244,970	63,104	308,074	20.5
1945	145,262	44,338	189,599	23.4
Total	1,051,505	210,283	1,261,787	16.7

[a] Numbers are rounded to the nearest 1,000.
[b] The sum of the value of ships delivered during the year, less the value of work done the previous year on ships delivered in the current year, plus the value of work done on ships not completed at year's end.

Source: Canada, DBS, *Iron and Steel and Their Products in Canada, 1943–1945*, table 208.

ship-repair industry and the role of the RCN in delaying attention to its need for repair services. Any claim that East Coast repair yards were not developed is quite simply false. Arguing that fleet maintenance was the very foundation of operational efficiency, Milner lays the failure to anticipate and solve the naval ship-repair, maintenance, and modernization problem firmly at the feet of the naval staff in Ottawa. Its poor planning led to the failure to arrange for sufficient refit and repair facilities and to settle priority of manpower and resources for the fleet until far too late in the war. In focusing on just one government department, whether the naval service or the DMS, critics fail to recognize that both played important roles in meeting ship-repair needs. Forbes correctly points out that the prewar ship-repair industry was centred in the St Lawrence River but fails to explain why or that the business was both cyclical and seasonal. A more important consideration is that the government had no intention of shifting the industry's focus to the Maritimes or altering its seasonal nature. Yet East Coast yards carried out the majority of repairs every year between 1941 and 1945. Milner correctly identifies the weakness of naval planning to meet the needs for ship repairing, but he mixes repair and modernization problems when they should be kept separate. The history of wartime ship repairing in Canada may be one of confusion, but it is also one of challenges and remarkable achievement rather than failure.

More than $210 million, excluding expenditure on capital assistance, was spent on ship repairs during the war. At the beginning, Canada's shipbuilding industry was little more than a repair industry, as ship repairs accounted for more than three-quarters of its total value. But although the value of ship repairing increased annually

A crane hoists a new, 8-ton, Canadian-manufactured ship's propeller into position as a Yugoslavian freighter is repaired in an East Coast shipyard, July 1943. NFB/LAC, WRM 3183.

until the last year of the war, it declined in proportion to the total value of shipbuilding until it accounted for less than one-tenth by 1943. The sudden growth in the value of ship repairs in 1943 and 1944 to more than half the wartime total reflects not only the delayed response to growing problems of maintenance and modernization, especially in the navy, but also the successful resolution of the crisis.

Beginnings, 1939–42

Even as war was being declared in September 1939, the fast passenger liner SS *Letitia*, sister ship of the *Athenia*, was being fitted out at Montreal as an armed merchant cruiser, and the Pacific and Orient liner SS *Rajputana* was being converted at Esquimalt.[7] The conversions were carried out using a small stock of equipment previously deposited in Canada by the British Admiralty. Both ships departed from Canada to begin escort work before the end of 1939. They were followed soon afterward by several more armed merchant cruisers: *Aurania, Jervis Bay, Ranpura, Ascania, Voltaire,* and *Malaja.*[8]

HMS *Jervis Bay*, a 14,000-ton passenger ship converted into an armed merchant cruiser with seven vintage 6-inch guns, provided the Royal Navy (RN) with one of its defining moments during the Second World War. In the waning daylight hours of 5 November 1940, while providing the sole escort to the thirty-six merchant ships of Convoy HX-84 out of Halifax, the *Jervis Bay* was intercepted by the German pocket battleship *Admiral Scheer.*[9] Undeterred by the German ship's main armament of six 11-inch guns, Captain E.S. Fogarty Fegan, RN, ordered the convoy to scatter under cover of smoke and set course straight at the enemy, and although the *Jervis Bay* was put out of action in less than half an hour, the *Admiral Scheer* continued to shell the blazing ship for two more hours, allowing the vessels in her charge to escape. The gallant sacrifice of captain and crew permitted thirty-one ships from the convoy and their badly needed cargos to reach Great Britain. Captain Fegan was awarded a posthumous Victoria Cross, and the incident heartened British and Canadian resolve during the most desperate months of the war. Especially affected were the people of St John and workers at St John Dry Dock and Shipbuilding Company, where the *Jervis Bay* had undergone her final refit only three months earlier.[10]

The Canadian government had already offered to purchase and convert three ships that had once belonged to Canadian National Steamship Company on condition that twelve 6-inch guns set aside by the Admiralty be used. Funds for the conversions had been included in the original $10 million approved for shipbuilding on 19 September 1939. The Admiralty was only too delighted with the offer, and after some foot-dragging, work began in February 1940 on SS *Prince Robert* and SS *Prince David* at Burrard Dry Dock Company and Halifax Shipyards Limited, respectively. A third ship, formerly the *Prince Henry*, entered Canadian Vickers Limited for conversion in mid-May. Each of the three ships had its two upper decks removed as well as one funnel; they were then fitted with a cruiser-style superstructure and bridge and were armed with four 6-inch and two 3-inch guns, some light anti-aircraft guns, and a number of depth charges.[11] Work on the *Prince Robert* was completed in less than six months, and she was commissioned at the end of July. The *Prince David* was not commissioned until the end of December, whereas the *Prince Henry* was completed and commissioned at the beginning of December.[12] The slowness of work at Halifax Shipyards did not auger well for the future.

Fifteen Canadian registered merchant ships, including the Canadian National Railway's passenger liners *Lady Nelson* and *Lady Somers*, were stiffened and defensively armed before continuing their runs.[13] Smaller vessels were also converted. In December 1939 a Canadian naval officer travelled incognito to New York and Boston, where he identified suitable private yachts to replace elderly patrol vessels, and between March and May 1940, in order to circumvent American neutrality law, patriotic Canadian yachtsmen travelled to the United States, purchased them, and brought them back to Canada. After being requisitioned by the government, the fourteen yachts were readied in East Coast and Montreal shipyards for naval service. The armed yachts, familiarly known as the "animals," went off to war as H M C S *Beaver, Caribou, Cougar, Elk, Grizzly, Husky, Lynx, Moose, Otter, Raccoon, Reindeer, Renard, Vison,* and *Wolf.*[14]

Procurement of supplies from Canadian and American sources was comparatively simple during the early days of the war. Stockpiles of materials for ship repair and from ship chandlers' warehouses were consumed without causing too much difficulty. Until the summer of 1940, shipbuilding plants were almost exclusively engaged in new naval construction. The number of ships using the dry dock at Halifax Shipyards actually declined by about one-sixth in 1940 compared to 1939.[15] By autumn, however, repairing ships had assumed increased importance. Although the naval staff largely ignored the issue, it became necessary to regulate and coordinate ship repairing industries and to settle priorities between new naval construction and ship repairing. On 27 November an order-in-council, PC 6797, gave the position of controller of ship construction and repairs to David Carswell, already controller of shipbuilding and director general of the shipbuilding branch of the DMS. Less than five months later, a new order-in-council, PC 2510, relieved Carswell of his responsibilities for new ship construction so that he might focus his entire attention on organizing and regulating the ship-repair industry to secure maximum use of available facilities, including the construction, maintenance, and use of dry docks. Carswell, who resigned as director general of the shipbuilding branch on 9 April 1941, remained responsible for destroyer construction – a telling comment on that project's relative importance to the current war effort. The new controller of ship repairs moved his head office to Montreal, where he and his small staff occupied a suite of offices at the same address as the newly created Wartime Merchant Shipping Limited, 420 rue de La Gauchetière.[16] In August the government appointed the controller an administrator of the Wartime Prices and Trade Board to control prices of goods and services in the ship-repair industry and in salvage work.[17]

Geography and climate shaped Canada's repair business. The centre lay in the St Lawrence River yards, which were busiest between May and November. Work in Maritimes ports increased between December and April after ice closed the St Lawrence. Carswell's move to Montreal was quite proper. Ships needing repairs had always made the long voyage up river from the sea because Montreal and Quebec possessed well-equipped commercial-repair facilities. Halifax Shipyards Limited, by comparison, was a midsize repair yard that employed about 350 men at the beginning of the war. Canadian Vickers at Montreal owned both Montreal Dry Dock Limited and the largest floating dry dock in the country, and the Dominion government owned two large graving docks at Lauzon, opposite Quebec.[18] Damage from fierce winter storms on the North Atlantic as well as war damage ensured that Maritimes ports remained active during their busy season. August was usually the low point in both regions.

Although repairing continued during 1941, the year was devoted chiefly to procuring facilities, materials, and equipment. Assisting repair companies occupied most of the controller's time and energy. New sources in the United States and existing stocks were found and acquired. Between March and August more than $700,000 was invested in tools for ship repairs in the Halifax district, half by the Dominion government and half by private repair firms. This was quite apart from over $200,000 in tools purchased for destroyer construction, all of which could be used for repair work when needed. Total expenses authorized for expansion of Maritimes repair industries came to $5,291,000 for machine shops, piers, and marine railways at Dartmouth, St John, Sydney, Liverpool, and Lunenburg.[19] A marine railway, also called a patent slip, was a multitracked railway angled into the water and bearing a large cradle capable of supporting a ship; it provided a cheaper alternative to a graving dock for drydocking ships of less than 3,000 tons lightweight.

Little could be done to relieve congestion in East Coast ports at first, as both warships and merchant ships sought to repair damage from war and the sea on the harsh North Atlantic run. Nova Scotia and New Brunswick yards were quickly overwhelmed. Between January and May 1941 the lowest number of vessels entering Halifax in any one month was 329 and the greatest 434. The greatest number of ships in port on any one day was 126. Ship repairs at Halifax reached their peak on 4 April, when 64 ships were undergoing "major" repairs.[20] The following month, the demand

A Bangor-class minesweeper resting on a marine railway for repairs at Halifax, April 1942. Photo by Harry Rowed. NFB/LAC, WRM 1483.

for repairs became so critical that the British requested Halifax be developed as a repair centre with "multiple graving docks to hold the Royal Navy's largest ships."[21] Angus L. Macdonald went so far as to propose to the Cabinet War Committee that a large graving dock sufficient to accommodate the largest British battleships be built at Halifax, but Howe demurred. Completion of such an undertaking would consume the better part of two years and place a great strain on scarce skilled labour. According to the controller of ship repairs, the scarcity of skilled mechanics in Halifax was due primarily to lack of housing for them in winter.[22] Howe strongly protested the Admiralty's request, and the Cabinet deferred any decision to a later date.[23]

Throughout 1941 the British Admiralty pursued a policy of placing St John, New Brunswick, in a condition to refit capital ships. With the United Kingdom subject to sustained air attack, the Admiralty sought a location on the west side of the Atlantic to carry out repairs on ships, particularly those of the Third Battle Squadron based at Halifax. The presence of the largest graving dock on Canada's East Coast made St John the logical location. During the winter of 1941, an additional graving dock was built. This involved deepening the channel approaching the port and providing machinery, labour, and skilled technicians capable of handling equipment of large naval vessels and developing the dry dock, including constructing new berthing arrangements. Considerable dredging also took place during the year.

At least one capital ship, HMS *Ramillies*, entered the St John dry dock in 1941. But the entry of the United States into the war on 7 December caused the British to abandon the program in favour of withdrawing the Third Battle Squadron from Halifax and using the well-equipped docking facilities of American ports.[24] The government's expenditures were not wasted. Thereafter, St John played an important role repairing merchant ships and Canadian naval vessels.

The RCN did not really need graving docks to repair its own ships, which, with the exception of armed merchant cruisers, were small enough to be hauled out on marine railways. Carrying out repairs to merchant ships in Bedford Basin, an anchorage some four miles away from repair plants in the lower harbour, however, was very slow and inefficient, and construction of piers on the eastern side of Halifax Harbour began early in 1941. In January 1941 the Cabinet War Committee had approved $2.7 million to build the floating dock. Approval was based on the need for haste and on estimates obtained from Dominion Bridge Company Limited.[25] Normally, it took two years to build a dry dock of this size, but in February 1942, thirteen months after the contract was let, it was towed from Montreal to Halifax and put into operation. The new floating dry dock completely changed ship-repair operations in Halifax. Of modern design, equipped with electric cranes, it speeded up ship movements enormously. The dock was actually capable of repairing itself; built in three sections, any two could lift the third one out of the water for overhaul.[26] During the war, two 10,000-ton merchant ships were often dry-docked simultaneously.

David Carswell's heavy burden was eased somewhat in March with the appointment of another experienced shipbuilder and fellow Scot, William Percival, as deputy controller of ship repairs. Born in Glasgow, he had studied engineering at the West of Scotland Technical College, serving his apprenticeship with Alley and MacLelland Limited. After serving in the British merchant marine during the First World War, he emigrated to Canada, becoming assistant superintendent engineer of the Canadian Government Merchant Marine; he became chief engineer in 1920, serving at Montreal, Halifax, and St John. In 1927 he joined Clarke Steamship Company as general superintendent until 1940, when he was recruited for government work. In March 1942 he joined the DMS, becoming deputy controller of ship production and repair for the remainder of the war.[27]

In June 1941 Angus L. Macdonald, with Howe's full agreement, called for five marine railways to be built at Halifax, Sydney, Shelburne, Pictou, and Gaspé for an estimated cost of just over $1.3 million.[28] The first of three large marine railways of 3,000-ton capacity became operational in October, enabling escort ships up to the size of destroyers to be hauled out at Dartmouth, which so relieved the graving dock that it could be used almost exclusively for large merchant ships.[29] By the war's end, the Dartmouth marine railway division of Halifax Shipyards Limited possessed five marine railways: two slipways built during the war and capable of hauling out vessels of up to 3,000 tons; and three others that handled ships of 2,500, 1,400, and 200 tons. Together, they handled 3,600 ships during the war.[30]

But the solution to effecting repairs to warships lay in taking escort vessels out of Halifax and establishing repair facilities elsewhere in Nova Scotia. Two additional 3,000-ton marine railways were built at Sydney and Shelburne, and smaller haul-outs were built at Pictou, Liverpool, and Lunenburg and leased to private firms under the Emergency Repairs Agreement.[31] Despite disagreement between Macdonald and Howe, who sought to defer building marine railways at Liverpool and Lunenburg until the spring, the Cabinet conditionally approved Macdonald's request to build the railways in order to relieve the pressure on Halifax and increase total East Coast repair facilities.[32] In July 1942 Pictou Marine Railway Limited began operating the new 2,000-ton marine railway it had built for the government, together with its own pre-existing 1,000-ton slip.[33] At Liverpool the government purchased and installed a $15,000 milling machine in the machine shop of Mersey Paper Company to assist in ship repairs, and at Louisburg it fitted L.H. Cann Machine Shop with lathes, planers, drills, and portable equipment in anticipation of the busy winter to come.[34] The navy appeared initially to undertake construction of the marine railways without consulting with the controller of ship repairs. This led to delays.[35]

As practically all the public piers in Sydney Harbour were in ruins, in 1941 the government constructed a 400-foot wharf at the principal ship-repair yard, that of Sydney Foundry and Machinery Company, near the site of the newly installed 3,000-ton marine railway. In addition, the government supplied Pushie Machine Shop and Atlantic Spring and Machine Shop, both at Sydney, with machine tools, including a vertical boring mill for engine repairs.[36] A second 400-foot pier was projected into the harbour in 1942 to permit merchant ships to come alongside, where both government and privately owned repair shops provided services.[37] The uncooperative attitudes of Dominion Steel and Coal Company and of Sydney Foundry and Machine

Company hindered Sydney's usefulness for some time to come, even though the British Ministry of War Transport had appointed an official of the former company as its representative and despite the fact that the 3,000-ton marine railway had been constructed for the use of the latter firm.[38]

The seasonal nature of ship repairing made holding large numbers of men when no work was available for several days a problem. No provision in the naval ship-repair agreement permitted repair companies to claim such idle time as an expense, and labour difficulties arose. The Department of Munitions and Supply confidently anticipated both Halifax Shipyards and St John Dry Dock and Shipbuilding would continue new ship construction in order to hold their men during slack repair periods, but a shortage of steel broke the expected continuity. Contracts signed with St John Dry Dock and Shipbuilding for medium-size cargo ships and with Halifax Shipyards for destroyers were expected to hold workers, but destroyer steel was not expected to reach Halifax before November. By the end of 1941, however, many of the projects begun during the summer were nearing completion, and the majority of purchased machine tools had been delivered when closure of the St Lawrence River put added pressure on Maritimes repair resources in December. All dry docks on the East Coast were occupied with ship damages, and anticipating extra demand for supervisory labour, the ship-repairs controller began to recruit marine engineers from the Great Lakes to work in the Maritimes as soon as their ships were laid up.[39]

During the winter of 1942, ship repairs in Maritimes ports increased threefold yet were carried out more expeditiously than the previous year. Money invested in repair facilities accounted for much of this, but so too did reorganization of the groups responsible for repairs (i.e., the repair shops and shipyards, the British Ministry of War Transport, ship-repair control, and the DMS). David Carswell also identified the resolution of wage disputes, which speeded up repairs out of all proportion to concessions made, as an important factor. Workmen also displayed a better spirit than before.[40]

Table 5.2 shows ships repaired at Halifax Shipyards Limited only, but it is useful to compare with data for the total East Coast in table 5.4. In January 1942 ship repairs on the East Coast reached an all-time high, being two times more numerous than a year earlier. There was no scarcity of unskilled and semiskilled labour in the region, and machinists, welders, pipefitters, and electricians were recruited from central Canada. Over eighty skilled mechanics, including forty marine engineers from the Great Lakes, travelled to the Maritimes to work on engine repairs.[41] In February, St John Dry Dock and Shipbuilding started a training school for riveters, and Halifax Shipyards began training lathe operators. Also, a floating repair shop for steel repairs to boilers and ships' hulls was built at St John. The new floating dry dock at Halifax reached its full capacity in April, and although practically all the men from central Canada returned to Montreal and the Great Lakes in May, Halifax remained busier with repairs during the summer than during either 1940 or 1941.

The total number of repairs declined nearly 5 per cent during the year, but steady repair work and destroyer building, which absorbed idle steelworkers during the summer, permitted Halifax Shipyards to retain workmen and train new employees

Table 5.2 | Ships repaired by Halifax Shipyards Limited, September 1939 to March 1945

Period	Halifax	Dartmouth	Total
1939[a]	110	184	294
1940	451	190	641
1941	1,020	773	1,793
1942	870	839	1,709
1943	562	558	1,120
1944	452	458	910
1945[b]	120	119	239
Total	3,585	3,121	6,706

[a] September to December.
[b] January to March.

Source: NSARM, MG 2, box 1500, no. 298(9), list of ships repaired, sent by R.J R. Nelson, general manager, Halifax Shipyards Ltd, to Angus L. Macdonald, 4 April 1945.

into a permanent workforce, thereby becoming much better prepared for repair operations the following winter.

Renewed repairing at Sydney in May, together with improved equipment and organization at St John, Halifax, and Liverpool, was "more than sufficient" to meet the anticipated demands of merchant and naval operations.[42] In view of the controller's optimism, the navy's concern for the availability of skilled labour for repairs first aired in May seems curious and may indicate how far out of the loop the naval staff was.[43] On the other hand, unbeknownst to anyone and without permission of any Canadian authority, the US War Shipping Administration had recently completed a survey of Halifax that was severely critical of repair, salvage, and other port facilities. Copies of the report were obtained only through the Canadian legation in Washington. The Cabinet War Committee learned that the Americans proposed to open an office in Halifax and recommended that the US government send salvage tugs to Halifax to rescue vessels of all nationalities detained in Canadian waters for unreasonable lengths of time awaiting repairs.[44]

After having expended several million dollars during the past year upgrading facilities in general, including adding fourteen repair berths at Halifax in particular, Howe was angered the Americans had undertaken the survey without his knowledge or permission, and he correctly advised the Cabinet War Committee that their survey was inaccurate.[45] Two of his Cabinet colleagues proposed taking formal exception to the American action, but calmer heads prevailed. Nevertheless, the American report stung, and it was probably not coincidental that on 1 May a new order-in-council revised the ship-repairs controller's responsibilities to include ship and cargo salvage and rescue.

The St Lawrence River ports opened in April, but with the great improvements made on the East Coast, some dry docks upriver remained vacant for several weeks except for intermittent use for small repairs and painting. Indeed, St Lawrence ports never obtained the expected work, which may have been just as well, for unexpected U-boat activity in the Gulf of St Lawrence and lower reaches of the river in September closed it to commercial traffic.[46] During the summer, salvage operations doubled the work of ship-repairs control. The additional duties resulted in the saving of several valuable cargos and in the refloating of grounded ships.

The situation at Sydney continued to disappoint during 1942. The controller had been too optimistic in hoping that the provision of two self-propelled repair barges and additional tools in two repair shops, the rebuilding of one plant, and the construction of a special repair wharf would improve conditions. The lack of repair business led to the loss of men, and repair services remained at a low ebb throughout the summer. Indeed, all smaller Maritimes ports experienced difficulties retaining men owing to the irregular nature of repair work.

Salvage

Ship and cargo salvage had remained exclusively under private enterprise until May 1942, by which time the Canadian situation had become acute. With more work available than they were capable of handling with the equipment at hand, salvage companies were picking and choosing their work.[47] But this was just a part of the problem. The Americans had been correct in identifying the inadequacy of rescue and salvage facilities on the East Coast. Only one large deep-sea tug seemed to be available, and no arrangements had been made to recover flotsam and jetsam or wreck. Fishermen who picked up cargo washed ashore or left floating in the sea after vessels had been wrecked or damaged by enemy action, collision, or stranding were frequently detained by the Royal Canadian Mounted Police (RCMP) for investigation and by customs officers who demanded that duties be paid before such material was landed. The government had not arranged to purchase any wreck. Under such conditions, even patriotic men became discouraged and ceased to salvage goods, except for goods taken for the men's own illegal use and for clandestine sale. Ships and cargo were being lost because owners were satisfied to be paid a "constructive total loss" claim and because insurance underwriters were prepared to take their loss and write it off.[48] Ships and cargo that might have been saved were lost in the short time needed to find out what money underwriters were prepared to risk in further salvage.[49]

Order-in-council PC 3599, dated 1 May 1942, changing Carswell's title to controller of ship repairs and salvage, conferred on him authority to employ emergency measures in connection with rescue work and with salvaging of ships and cargos.[50] These powers enabled him to abolish operating districts for salvage companies and to send immediately a salvage vessel anywhere a ship was in distress off the Canadian coast.

The new duties greatly increased Carswell's workload. In June he appealed for support to open a Halifax office and build up his Montreal office, where, in addition to

Rear half of SS *Joel R. Poinsett*, an American Liberty ship, which broke in half during a gale 400 miles southeast of St John's, Newfoundland, and was taken in tow 14 March 1944, resting in the floating dry dock at Halifax Shipyards Limited. Note the size of the workmen standing by the keel blocks. MMA, M2002.9.1b/3, Boyd A. Gibson Collection.

himself and William Percival, there were just two marine engineers and eight stenographers.[51] Although Foundation Maritime Limited, which handled all important salvage operations on the East Coast, had recently acquired a 145-foot, 1,000-horsepower tug suitable for deep-sea towing, the navy had requisitioned one of the company's two largest tugs. The company possessed nine harbour tugs, but several were unable to proceed beyond Halifax Harbour, and the large 1,200-horsepower tug *Foundation Franklin*, the principal deep-sea rescue boat of the East Coast, was due for a major overhaul.[52] In order to avoid further criticism by the War Shipping Administration, Carswell advised the minister to lend the government tug *Graham Bell* currently at Churchill, Manitoba, in order to replace the boat lost to the RCN, and he recommended rebuilding the old icebreaker *Lady Grey* with new boilers, as the *Montcalm* had been handed over to the Russians. Finally, he suggested Howe try to acquire one of the deep-sea tugs being built in the United States so that it could be used by Foundation Company of Canada in rescue work for the duration of the war.[53] Building up Foundation Maritime to render improved service was a necessary response to the American criticism. The government had neither the ability nor the resources to get into the salvage business and was content, perhaps for political reasons, to leave responsibility in the hands of private enterprise.[54]

Recovery of ships and cargos abandoned by owners and underwriters improved, although not without some difficulty. Carswell encountered resistance from several government agencies that were unwilling to remove assessments on salvaged goods and demanded customs duties, sales taxes, harbour dues, and wharfage fees. Attempting to keep abreast of these issues, Carswell asked the manager of Quebec Salvage and Wrecking Company to inform him of test cases and of any rulings from the Department of Finance concerning sales tax and from the National Harbours Board concerning dues.[55] He complained to the commissioner of customs, Hugh D. Scully, about the detention of fishermen in Lunenburg County by customs and RCMP officers when they brought flotsam ashore. Neither agency had any legitimate measures of disposal or means of payment for such services.[56]

The issue provides a good illustration of civil servants and police unable to adapt to wartime conditions. Both viewed the fishermen as thieves, which they may have been, whereas the controller wanted to transform them into productive helpers deserving of reward. Carswell asked that customs staff serve as appraisers of wreck rather than collectors of duties, believing this was a key to resolving disputes and detentions. Otherwise, fishermen would continue their age-old traditions of wreckers. Carswell succeeded in persuading Scully, and with the cooperation of the Department of Fisheries, notices were posted in fishing communities with instructions on new procedures for handling flotsam and jetsam. Fishermen would hand over all salvage to the nearest receiver of wreck for appraisal by a customs officer. Copies of appraisal notes were to be sent to the controller of ship repairs and cargo salvage, who would arrange for disposal and awards. Fishermen avoided detention and delay, and the government recovered valuable war material.

Salvage held many problems. The SS Clare Lilley, wrecked during the winter of 1942 at Portuguese Cove, Nova Scotia, created a lot of unfavourable publicity from disgruntled fishermen who did not receive what they believed to be their due for salvage and from the local press, which attacked the government for not seizing the cargo. The press did not know that the owner was the US government. Several weeks afterward, when officials received authority over the wreck, ship-repairs control found a free-for-all looting campaign going on. Only after the cargo's owner and the US lend-lease organization transferred responsibility for financing the recovery to the War Shipping Administration was the controller of ship repairs and salvage able to begin work.[57]

But salvaging ships and cargo proved a worthwhile task. Cargo recovered from the SS Trongate was especially noteworthy. This Norwegian freighter was loaded with explosives and in the middle of Halifax Harbour when fire broke out. With visions of the 1917 explosion still vivid, she was deliberately sunk where she was. In addition to 72,493 imperial gallons of toluol, a major ingredient of TNT, recovered and sent to Defence Industries Limited at Valleyfield, Quebec, the wreck yielded 2,000 bars of pig aluminum, which were delivered to the British Ministry of War Transport for reshipment to the United Kingdom, and 2,000 tons of critical metals: copper, cobalt, cadmium, and zinc.[58]

Salvage also involved rescue work. According to Farley Mowat, during the war the Foundation Franklin salvaged 132 vessels with an aggregate capacity in excess of 500,000 gross tons and rescued nearly 1,000 men. Between April 1941 and April 1942, the tug steamed more than 50,000 miles – a double circumnavigation of the globe – to rescue ships, crews, and cargo.[59]

In August 1942 Carswell arranged with two Montreal and Quebec salvage firms to move large rescue tugs and other equipment to strategic year-round ports in Nova Scotia for winter operations and, as it turned out, for the duration.[60] A collision between two American vessels about 700 miles off Halifax on 23 December 1943 led to one ship being assisted to an American port and the other more heavily damaged vessel being towed to Halifax, where she arrived safely on New Year's Eve.[61]

By the end of March 1944, the value of war goods salvaged ran into hundreds of thousands of dollars, everything from 326,935 imperial gallons of high-test gasoline to twelve miles of telephone wire, 530 cases of 40-mm ammunition, 488 drums of honey, 700 cases of ubiquitous pork loaf, twelve cases of buttons, five bales of horsehair, seven cases of antigas ointment, four cases of 3-inch mortars, thirty cases and four bales of army clothing, and 516 tires and inner tubes. Items recovered from the sea floor included road-grading equipment, an anchor, four diesel tractors weighing just over 53 tonnes, turret lathes, drill presses, aircraft parts, machine guns, and canvas hose. All this represented thousands of hours of labour expended by divers and crews of salvage vessels employing a variety of barges and cranes.

The appointment of the salvage controller also ended an unofficial war between fishermen and salvage crews over who was first on a site. The program was a grand success. The amounts paid to fishermen were relatively small, $42,000 to more than 200 fishermen in two years, and the result was a good working system that saved many lives and much war production.[62]

"A supplement to repair work" – Tribal-Class Destroyers

The decision to acquire Tribal-class destroyers need not concern us.[63] The threefold purpose of this section is to demonstrate that the plan to construct destroyers in Canada bore no relation to the wartime shipbuilding program, was separated from the concerns and responsibilities of the director of the naval shipbuilding branch in the Department of Munitions and Supply, and was placed under the authority of the controller of ship repairs and salvage for a good reason. This action guaranteed the project would never achieve any immediate priority.

The decision to construct the vessels at Halifax rather than elsewhere was because of the persistence of the minister of national defence for the naval service and was political rather than strategic or cost-effective. It involved constructing the most complicated warship ever undertaken in Canada in a repair yard, for, with the exception of a small ammunition lighter built in 1939, Halifax Shipyards Limited completed no ships during the war. If destroyers had been part of the war program, the logical place to build them would have been on the West Coast.[64]

Although the RCN may have been looking to the future and the composition of the postwar navy when it contemplated building Tribals in Canada, the Department of Munitions and Supply was not. The wartime ministry had no mandate nor any interest in building for the future. Its mandate was to maximize Canada's war production in the timeliest manner possible. By pressing to build destroyers in a midsize repair plant at Halifax, the navy and its minister as much as acknowledged the Cabinet War Committee's decision that the project had a very low priority. It was this decision taken at the highest level and the higher priorities attached to ship repairing and naval modernization rather than an alleged shortage of skilled labour and engineering personnel that accounted for the delays in Tribal construction.[65]

The initial steps to build Tribal-class destroyers were taken during the brief five-month period when David Carswell was both controller of ship construction and repairs and director general of the DMS's shipbuilding branch. It was at the end of February 1941 that Tribals were designated to be built in Canada, two at first and two more decided upon a year later.[66] As the project had little or nothing to do with current naval ship construction, it made sense to leave the program under Carswell's direction.[67]

From the very beginning, there were delays. Admiralty officials remained skeptical of the project, initially refusing to send any trained personnel to Canada and failing to send detailed drawings before early 1941.[68] The RCN's leading engineer officer, Engineer Captain George L. Stephens, questioned the correctness of the decision by recommending that the destroyers not be built in Canada, and in May he argued that frigate construction should precede the building of destroyers.[69] C.D. Howe was lukewarm, advising the Cabinet War Committee that "the project was of doubtful efficiency in view of other shipbuilding needs and the enormous requirements for repairs which were straining existing facilities."[70] Macdonald had not been present when Howe expressed his reservations, and on 6 May he requested that the Cabinet reconsider the navy's request in light of the decision to embark on a large merchant ship program. Howe repeated his concern about the heavy and constant pressure on repair facilities but admitted it would be possible to lay down a destroyer in Halifax to be completed in three rather than two and a half years.[71] Two weeks later, the war committee approved laying down one destroyer and another at a later date on the understanding that there would be inevitable interruptions for more essential ship repairs: "Construction could proceed as opportunity offered. Progress would be slow, and the project would constitute a supplement to repair work and a means to acquiring destroyer technique for Canadian yards."[72] From the beginning, it was clear that these vessels were being built on sufferance.

On 21 June, Carswell advised Halifax Shipyards to go ahead on the destroyers, but delays continued.[73] Skilled labour of the sort required for such sophisticated work was not available anywhere in Canada, and in mid-August, Halifax Shipyards requested that its new supervisor, still in Britain, arrange through Vickers Armstrong Limited or Yarrow and Company for a frame bender (or furnace man), twelve shipfitters (or platers), five hull draftsmen, and three engine draftsmen to come to Canada. Carswell noted presciently that they would be of value for repair work next winter, "as the tradesmen are the class of workers which are scarce in Canada due to the merchant shipbuilding programme having absorbed all the better men."[74]

Although the destroyers challenged Canadian engineering competence and industrial facilities, delays arose chiefly from the lack of priority for the project. John Inglis

Company promptly completed its arrangements to manufacture the main and auxiliary propulsion machinery so that all necessary technical staff were currently available or engaged building turbines and water-tube boilers. Major machinery parts had been ordered, and in August, Carswell reported, "the work is well in hand."[75] But additional delays appeared the same month.

The United States Navy (USN) blocked Canadian efforts to obtain resilience data on high-tensile steel plate from Bethlehem Steel Company. British and American steel specifications differed, and American steelmakers refused to manufacture such small orders of special steel. The chief delay was due to uncertainty about whether the RCN would accept USN specifications and the naval staff's referral of the data once obtained to the Admiralty. Provided the American high-tensile steel was acceptable, Halifax Shipyards planned to obtain it from Bethlehem Steel and have the D-quality sections made in Sydney. Dominion Steel and Coal Company (Dosco) undertook to roll this steel and asked Algoma Steel Corporation to roll other sections too large for its mills. Much of the destroyer steel had to be galvanized, and a plant costing $150,000 had to be built at Halifax Shipyards and $175,000 worth of additional tools purchased.[76]

Halifax Shipyards stood ready to lay keels two weeks after delivery of steel from the mills, but at the end of September, the US Office of Production Management had yet to allocate the order to a mill. Canada's steel controller exercised all the influence he had, but the principal cause of delay remained the continuing absence of plans from the Admiralty, which Canadian naval officials were endeavouring to procure.[77] As a result of these delays, which included adapting the hull design to US high-tensile steel, the keels of the first two Tribals were not laid until May 1942.[78]

Canadian-made steel went into the second pair of destroyers. Dosco manufactured the high-tensile steel at its Sydney steel plant, whence the billets were shipped to Trenton Steel Works, where special rolls were made to manufacture the intricate sections called for in the design.[79]

In September 1941 John Inglis Company had raised the question of whether a second pair of destroyers would be built. If only two vessels were ordered, the company wished to order auxiliary machinery and parts from Britain, except for a few that could be manufactured by Canadian firms already possessing licences. But the Cabinet War Committee deferred a decision until early 1942, when it considered the RCN's whole 1942–43 shipbuilding program and authorized the order of a third and a fourth destroyer from the same principal contractors.[80]

The situation deteriorated during 1942 and 1943. Inglis was set up to manufacture the 50,000-horsepower twin steam-turbine drives complete with reduction gear sets at a rate of four ships per year, and with the addition of a pinion-cutting machine, the company was confident it could produce drives for eight ships annually, but this never happened. Members of the naval engineering overseer's (NEO) office at the plant were quite critical of company organization. In the opinion of Lieutenant Scoble, RN, and the inspector of engine fitters, F.A. Wood, too many executives were businessmen rather than engineers, and the men sent to England lacked practical experience and were of limited usefulness on their return. Also, best use was not made of men sent from England. A turbine expert and a boiler specialist arrived as technical advisors on government payroll but operated as the firm's employees with no authority to enforce their wishes. They had to nag to get things done. Despite the presence in the plant of a very expensive gear-cutting machine, difficulties with its operation were never resolved, probably due to unskilled operators. Consequently, Parsons Marine Steam Turbine Company in the United Kingdom cut the gears for the first destroyer, and Falk Corporation at Milwaukee, which manufactured most gears for the United States Navy, cut all the others. At the same time, however, Lieutenant Scoble thought some of the blading machines made locally in Toronto were an improvement on anything in the United Kingdom. The chief problem seemed to be that priorities were never clear-cut, and orders for freighter and corvette engines and parts received greater importance.[81]

The worsening situation at Halifax appeared to lead to a change of heart in Toronto.[82] Canadian industry was not incapable of producing Tribals, but the Cabinet had tied its and the navy's hands, and with no priority, delay was systemic. In October 1942 the naval board assigned priority to the acquisition of escorts over destroyers.[83] Little wonder that production schedules for machinery and boiler construction fell behind. Following an inspection of the Inglis plant in February 1943, David Carswell painted a pessimistic picture. Referring to the propulsion machinery, Carswell wrote: "From my observations, I would say that all other work that Inglis is handling is being given preference over destroyers."[84]

HMCS *Micmac* was launched on 18 September 1943, but by then even Halifax Shipyards was criticizing the naval staff for its inattention to the destroyer project. This roused the ire of newly promoted Engineer Rear Admiral Stephens, chief of naval engineering and construction (CNEC), who accused the company management of "becoming singularly incompetent."[85] But this was unfair. Stephens had never been an advocate of destroyer construction, and delays in frigate construction only reinforced his views. His outburst may have reflected some truth in management's criticism.

Improved progress occurred during the winter of 1944. The large Yarrow water-tube boilers were installed on the first destroyer in January, and the pioneering work had been completed on the turbine units.[86] At the end of April the shipyard launched the second Tribal and laid the keel of the fourth one, and the boilers for the second ship arrived in Halifax.[87]

Responding to growing public criticism of delays to the project, David Carswell identified three programs in 1942 that had higher priorities than the destroyers: escort vessels for convoy duty, the cargo ship program, and the synthetic-rubber plant (a reference to constructing Polymer Corporation's plant at Sarnia). He also claimed that the ministry's coordinator of production had reduced priorities for destroyer machinery and boilers at John Inglis Company in favour of manufacturing marine engines and boilers for the merchant ship program, noting that the frigate program had won out over the Tribals in the matter of supplying large steel turbine castings from one of the nation's foundries.[88]

The first complete set of twin-screw turbines and gears arrived in Halifax during August. The turbines had passed steam tests in Toronto three months before, but a month-long strike delayed installation until September. The shipyard was in need of electricians and other mechanics, and ship-repairs control advised that unless the electrical work was subcontracted out, the first destroyer would not be delivered until the next summer.[89]

The National Selection Service had never been able to dent the lack of skilled labour at Halifax, but in November, under great pressure, it supplied the shipyard with 238 men.[90] Not until January, however, was Carswell able to report that the Department of Labour had located skilled men from the Quebec City area who were prepared to go to Halifax "provided reasonably comfortable accommodation and food is available," and it took another month and the coordinated cooperation of Ed Cousins, wartime administrator of Canadian Atlantic ports, Major General W.H.P. Elkins, Air Vice Marshall G.O. Johnson, Joseph Piggott, chairman of Wartime Housing Limited, and Gordon Sheils, deputy minister of the Department of Munitions and Supply, to consummate the arrangements for their accommodation.[91]

At the end of February, the ship-repairs controller was looking forward to having the first Tribal in trials within two and one-half months, and the vessel completed the majority of her routine trials alongside the dock in May.[92] Sea trials were anticipated to conclude before the end of June.[93] Finally, on 9 September 1945 the navy commissioned its first Canadian-built Tribal. Progress on the second hull had fallen far behind, and HMCS *Nootka*, launched on 26 April 1944, was commissioned only in August 1946, and although the keel of the third Tribal had been laid down the day *Micmac* was launched, she would not be commissioned until 1947.[94]

The failure to build destroyers before the end of the war was due to lack of priority and choice of location in the midst of a war effort that focused on quantity over quality. Building the most complicated ship in Canada in a midsize repair yard located on the frontline of battle devoted chiefly to repairing naval and merchant ships in a city suffering from the greatest housing crisis in the country just made no sense at all. The yard could not keep a large workforce on the destroyers because of the priority assigned to ship repairing from 1943 onward. Labour shortages were endemic at Halifax and not helped by the strike during the summer of 1944. Although the strike failed in face of the company's refusal to negotiate, the government's nonintervention was additional comment, if any were needed, on the unimportance of completing the destroyers.

Repairing on the West Coast

Repair work and conversions on Canada's West Coast, to say the least about them, were varied. Everything from the world's largest ship, the *Queen Elizabeth*, to old, broken-down clunkers belonging to the Soviet Union passed through British Columbia's shipyards and dry docks. The Department of Munitions and Supply contracted with Yarrows Limited for repair services to vessels.[95] Manufacturing a new caisson

The world's largest ship, His Majesty's Transport *Queen Elizabeth*, entering the government dry dock at Esquimault, British Columbia, for a refit, 2 March 1942. NVMA, no. 27-3873.

or gate for the government-owned dry dock in preparation proved another triumph for Dominion Bridge Company. The caisson, weighing 161 tons, was manufactured in sections by its subsidiary, Manitoba Bridge and Iron Works Limited of Winnipeg, and shipped by rail nearly 1,500 miles to the Pacific Coast.[96]

Yarrows Limited, adjacent to the government-owned graving dock, carried out 611 repairs and conversions, as well as building twenty-seven ships during the war.[97] In addition to converting SS *Rajputana* to an armed merchant cruiser, guns and gun platforms were fitted to the *Empress of Canada* and her sister ships, the *Empress of Japan*, *Empress of Russia*, and *Empress of Asia*. Nearly 2 million gross tons of shipping were repaired at Yarrows.[98] Converting His Majesty's Troopship *Queen Elizabeth* from passenger liner to troop transport was the biggest job.

Docking the world's largest ship was a challenge. On coming up to the dry dock and partly in, she broke some paravane chains, pulled some keel blocks up, and had to back out so the dock could be pumped out and the blocks reset. The next day, she successfully entered the dry dock.

Unfinished when war broke out, the *Queen Elizabeth* had dashed across the Atlantic to New York in great secrecy in February 1940, where she had some conversion work done before leaving for the Pacific to ferry Australian and New Zealand troops to the Middle East and Singapore. After nearly two years of hard usage, she was in need of dry-docking. At Esquimalt the job entailed stripping her of all peacetime furnishings and installing 3,000 extra berths in cabins and public areas, additional lavatories, and galley equipment, as well as putting some armament on board, applying new exterior paint, and repairing engines and boilers. Three hundred naval ratings were requisitioned to clean and paint the hull, and sixty local schoolboys were hired to clean the boilers. One thousand employees working in two ten-hour shifts completed the job in two weeks. On 10 March 1942 the *Queen Elizabeth* quietly slipped over to English Bay, Vancouver, for bunkers and then was gone.[99] During the next three and a half years, carrying between 10,000 and 15,000 troops on each crossing, she transported between 750,000 and 800,000 people.[100]

At about the same time at Vancouver, workers at Burrard Dry Dock Company converted the *Daylight*, the largest four-masted barque ever built, into a barquentine. Built at Port Glasgow in 1906, weighing 3,756 gross tons, and having a length of 351 feet and a beam of 49 feet, she carried 50,000 square feet of canvas.[101] Nor was she the only sailing ship to operate on the West Coast. The *City of Alberni*, a five-masted schooner, the largest sail-powered ship under British registry, completed voyages from Vancouver to Australia and Chile during the war.

Following the German invasion of the Soviet Union in June 1941, the Russians bought a number of old ships that had been tied up for years for their merchant fleet, and the following March some began arriving in Vancouver at Burrard Dry Dock for overhauling, reconditioning, deck stiffening, and the installation of gunwale bars.[102] This early work was funded under the American Lend-Lease Act under the direction of the US Maritime Commission and carried out in Canada in order not to interrupt the assembly-line approach to ship production at the Kaiser yards to the south.[103] Eventually, twenty-eight vessels, mainly Liberty ships, went from the United States to Russia after first stopping off at Vancouver, where, for about $200,000 worth of work per ship, Burrard Dry Dock stiffened each hull and installed gunwale bars to overcome unexpected stress build-up in the welded hulls through contraction and expansion in cold water. In February 1943 a Liberty ship, after having been stranded and sustaining severe damage, was repaired at Vancouver, where her all-welded bottom was completely renewed. Repair work in this instance was supervised by the engineer inspector from the Seattle maintenance and repair division of the US War Shipping Administration rather than by the controller of ship repairs and salvage.[104]

In September 1943 the Canadian Mutual Aid Board assumed all the costs previously borne by the United States and requested that the controller of ship repairs make services available to the Soviet ships. At least two ships were dry-docked that fall, and sixteen vessels loaded with Canadian cargos departed for Siberian ports before the year ended.[105] In the spring, repairs to Soviet vessels assumed such substantial proportions that the controller called on the Vancouver office of Wartime Shipbuilding

Table 5.3 | Number of West Coast ship repairs, 1940–45

Year	Dry-docked	Repaired afloat	Total
1940	537	904	1,441
1941	525	1,003	1,528
1942	594	1,085	1,679
1943	407	687	1,094
1944	580	1,309	1,889
1945*	307	548	855
Total	2,950	5,536	8,486

* To June.

Source: LAC, RG 28, box 332, file 196-39-11, Ship Repair Control, 24 January 1944 and 7 August 1945.

Limited to assist in allocating, supervising, and regulating maintenance work on the West Coast and to coordinate it with new construction.[106] The age of the Soviet vessels, often twenty to thirty-five years old, meant that frequently major operations had to be undertaken to make them seaworthy.[107] Work started on rebuilding a "very old" icebreaker for use in Vladivostok Harbour and district during the coming winter. At the end of 1944 several obsolete vessels were delivered to Vancouver for rebuilding rather than repair. Repairs at Vancouver and Victoria reached such a point during the first quarter of 1945 that the ship-repairs controller was unable to handle all the work. "Soviet authorities," Carswell complained, "seem to have an unlimited volume of ship repairs piled up waiting to be carried out, and the more we do in Vancouver, the greater the continuing demands."[108] At the end of March he moved a considerable portion of Soviet ship repair to Prince Rupert.

In June, after Mutual Aid officials no longer agreed to pay, repairs to Soviet ships declined substantially.[109] Between August 1943 and October 1945, 124 ships (about 4.6 per month) departed from Vancouver for the Soviet Far East carrying about $150 million worth of war supplies.[110] Additional ship repairing services worth nearly $11 million and a gift of ten 126-foot, wooden minesweepers worth $5.7 million were unique features of Canada's aid to the Soviet Union.[111]

America's development of the port of Prince Rupert to connect its forces with Alaska and the Aleutians led to a great surge in repair work. The dry dock received 914 vessels, and another 2,513 ships berthed locally for repairs.[112] Indeed, Prince Rupert accounted for 40 per cent of all West Coast repairs shown in table 5.3.

In 1943 the navy sent the three Princes to Burrard Dry Dock for a second conversion. The ships were no longer suitable as armed merchant cruisers against new, more powerful enemy vessels. They had proven to be poor gun platforms and lacked modern gunnery-control systems. Naval authorities decided to employ them to meet their commitment to combined operations. Taken out of service on 2 January,

US-built aircraft-carrier escort (CVE) being modified for the Royal Navy by Burrard Dry Dock Company at Vancouver's Lapointe Pier, May 1944. Photo by Ronny Jaques. NFB/LAC, WRM 4551.

HMCS *Prince Robert* was handed over to Burrard Dry Dock for modification as an auxiliary anti-aircraft cruiser. Recommissioned on 7 June, she was armed with ten 4-inch twin, high-angle/low-angle, dual-purpose guns, eight 2-pounder pom-poms, and twelve 20-mm Oerlikons; she also retained her four depth-charge throwers. The *Prince David* and the *Prince Henry* arrived at Burrard Dry Dock on 30 April and 1 May, respectively, for conversion to landing ships infantry (medium). Each vessel was equipped to carry eight Canadian-designed, 20-ton landing craft hung on quadrangular davits, four per side along the upper deck. The old 6-inch guns were removed and replaced with two 4-inch twin, high-angle/low-angle guns and with two single 40-mm Bofors and ten Oerlikon anti-aircraft guns. Accommodations were greatly increased to carry additional naval ratings, including landing-craft crews and 550 army personnel. The *Prince David*, recommissioned on 20 December, and the *Prince Henry*, on 6 January 1944, were rushed in order to get them to the United Kingdom by February. Both vessels entered John Brown and Company at Clydebank for final fittings of guns, radar, and communications equipment for the invasion of Europe, and they served off the coast of Normandy on D-Day.[113]

Also in 1943 the Department of Munitions and Supply, on behalf of the Royal Navy, contracted to carry out alterations to US-built carrier-vessel escorts (CVEs) at Vancouver. Also known as "baby flattops" or "Woolworth carriers" because of their size and economy of construction, these ships were already converted merchant ships. The work was done by Burrard Dry Dock at the Lapointe Pier. The final plan called for the conversion of twenty-three Smiter-class carriers from Seattle-Tacoma Shipbuilding Corporation at Tacoma, Washington. Initial work proceeded slowly since the plant was not ready when the first carriers arrived ahead of schedule in July and since electricians proved hard to find.[114] As a result, the first four carriers averaged ninety days, whereas the remaining ships were delivered on average in between forty-five and fifty-five days. Flight decks were lengthened, catapult machines were altered, new arrester gear, landing lights, and steam lines were installed, firefighting equipment was augmented, and a host of electrical changes were made.[115] In all, some nineteen carriers were completed. At peak operations, in November the Lapointe Pier yard employed 2,040 workers, not including subcontractors.[116] Workers completed the final conversion on 12 July 1944, and the yard was immediately closed.[117]

Modernization and Repairing, 1943–45

The naval staff at Ottawa had generally ignored the issue of repairs to the fleet until a modernization crisis had struck at the end of 1942. Until then the navy dealt with the issue of repairs by repeated changes to the administration of HMC Dockyard at Halifax.[118] To be fair, the desperate situation in the Atlantic during 1941 and 1942 had driven the staff to emphasize getting escorts – any escorts – to sea, but whether this approach was wise remains open to discussion.[119] The modernization of the majority of the RCN's corvettes was a separate and serious matter distinct from ships needing annual refits and repairs to damage incurred by collision, stranding, the sea, and enemy action. It added enormously, however, to the ever-growing pressure on Canada's East Coast repair facilities and, in the eyes of some historians, swamped them. It is argued here that this did not occur. Bad naval planning was chiefly responsible for the delays to modernization.

With 200 vessels requiring service because of wear and tear of convoy work, repairs and refits had become vital. The number of warships allocated to the East Coast and Newfoundland had also greatly increased. An often overlooked factor affecting the naval repair problem was that whereas merchant ships had to have repairs made to the requirements of Lloyd's Register of Shipping before sailing and hence remained in port continuously until they were seaworthy, warships sailed when required if competent to put to sea. Most RCN corvettes, minesweepers, and destroyers were at sea with uncompleted schedules of work to be done.[120]

Shortage of labour, interference with refit schedules to meet urgent operational necessities, lack of coordination between naval departments concerned with repairs and refits, incomplete warships arriving from Great Lakes yards prior to freeze-up requiring attention before they could go to sea, and new weapons and fighting equipment forced the naval staff to deal with repairs as never before.[121] At the same time, the demand for repairs to merchant ships also grew at Halifax and St John as pressure increased on resources and facilities in Great Britain and the United States.

Unsettled labour conditions at St John Shipbuilding and Dry Dock contributed significantly to falling ship-repair production at the end of 1942. Although the men adopted passive resistance, David Carswell blamed neither the men nor the company for the poor situation, pointing to the National War Labour Board's uneven treatment of one section of workers in the matter of retroactive pay. He appealed to officials at the War Industries Control Board for help to adjust the wage rates of "the most temperamental type of men: that is riveting gangs."[122] Severe weather also taxed repair equipment to the limit. Heavy gales, accompanied by exceptionally low temperatures, made shipping conditions very dangerous. Ships on the coast lost their reserve stability due to ice on their superstructures, making safe navigation next to impossible.

Corvettes were makeshift vessels built to meet the war emergency. They were underequipped, lacking gyrocompass, searchlights, or radio telephone, and were fitted with obsolete asdic. Their technical deficiencies grew ever more serious as they shifted from serving as coastal-patrol vessels to ocean escorts and as new submarine tactics and weapons appeared during the Battle of the Atlantic.[123] Marc Milner has identified four major problems: the ship's short forecastle, mercantile bridge, primitive electrical system, and inadequate weapons system. By 1942 these twelve- to eighteen-month-old ships required modernization to fit them for the current struggle, yet in the eyes of the naval staff, they could not be withdrawn from the battle.[124] According to Milner, although the naval staff in Ottawa knew the Royal Navy was improving its own corvettes' sea-keeping capacity and livability by extending their forecastles, enclosing the well deck to increase accommodation and make it drier, and installing breakwaters when all but a dozen corvettes remained in Canadian builders' hands, it remains a mystery whether the naval staff considered similar modifications.[125] Naval officials in Ottawa seem to have ignored the question for more than a year, until the spring of 1942, after all but a few of the first seventy corvettes were commissioned and in service.

That this had been allowed to happen speaks volumes about the lack of technical knowledge among senior officers of the RCN and the poor technical liaison between the RCN and the Admiralty. It also confirms that the British Admiralty Technical Mission's primary purpose was to promote war production in Canada for the Royal Navy rather than to provide technical assistance to the RCN. Failure to incorporate changes based on war experience into new ships being built in the shipyards owing to the RCN's reliance on the Royal Navy greatly increased the subsequent task when it eventually commenced.

The poor understanding of tactical issues and the link between equipment and operations in the RCN, especially at naval service headquarters (NSHQ), where the staff's would-be authorities misunderstood the function of shipboard high-frequency direction finding, is especially startling.[126] David Zimmerman also points to the technical deficiencies arising from the absence of low-voltage systems in the ships.[127] But it was the lack of technical understanding that led staff officers, and naval officers generally, to grasp the importance of re-equipping the obsolete corvettes too late for the RCN to participate in the Allied turning of the tide in the battle for the convoys in 1943. Although seventeen Canadian-built corvettes had extended forecastles in June 1942, nothing had been done to rewire the ships in order to install low-power systems for gyrocompasses and new, improved asdic and radar. The naval staff remained unwilling to consider modernization because of the importance still attached to new construction and to repairs.

The winter of 1943, when modernization was finally begun, proved to be the worst since the beginning of the war; indeed, it was the worst in thirty years. Severe weather prevailed without letup during the first quarter and presented the worst problem in ship repairing since the war started. One-third of the escort force was knocked out with weather damage, further delaying modernization. Nevertheless, 828 vessels, including 145 warships, received repairs worth approximately $5 million during the period.[128]

By the end of April, 156 escort refits, which included destroyers and minesweepers as well as corvettes, were on the current year's program. The opening of Sydney Harbour in May allowed the new 3,000-ton marine railway to be used for naval repairs, and with the arrival of their hauling chains from Cleveland, Ohio, and installation, two new 1,400-ton railways at Liverpool and Lunenburg went into operation in June.[129] The 3,000-ton marine railway at Shelburne was also completed in June and, in contrast to those leased to private firms at Halifax and Sydney, was operated by the RCN. But this contributed little to the pressing need. Although the navy had chosen the site near the southeast tip of Nova Scotia to serve as a base as early as 1940, its repair and refit functions developed slowly. It really hit its stride only after new repair shops were completed in 1944, when the number of personnel, including many skilled workers, reached over 2,000.[130]

Twenty-seven Canadian corvettes were fitted with extended forecastles, modified bridges, and hedgehogs and were rewired to power gyrocompasses, improved echo sounders, asdic, and radar in 1943. Work in Canadian yards progressed painfully slowly. Whereas the British modernized four Canadian corvettes in an average time of fifteen weeks and American yards turned five corvettes around in ten weeks, Canadian yards took an average of twenty-two weeks to modernize eighteen corvettes. The cost of bringing 1941-built corvettes up to 1943 standards was in the neighbourhood of $175,000 per ship.[131] Work was distributed over the Montreal and lower St Lawrence areas, including the Gulf of St Lawrence ports at Pictou and Charlottetown.

A substantial amount of this naval work was done at Montreal in order to offset the lack of cargo tonnage coming into the port. During August, Montreal was as busy with reconstruction as it had ever been during the war.[132] The naval shipbuilding program was also curtailed in favour of reconstruction and acquiring ships from the Royal Navy in order to create a balanced fleet.[133]

Provision of new facilities had gone only part way toward resolving the labour shortage. A survey of manpower requirements in 1943 showed that the Maritimes ship-repair industry required nearly 5,000 additional workers, more than half of them at HMC Dockyard, for the year ending 31 May 1944. Halifax and Dartmouth required 1,076 workers, and St John and eight lesser Nova Scotia ports needed 1,351.[134] By 1943 the manpower question on the East Coast had become more critical than the expansion of repair facilities. With the National Selective Service (NSS) possessing full authority over hiring men to work in the industry, neither the DMS nor the controller of ship repairs could contribute to a solution.[135] Carswell proposed a committee of representatives from the RCN, the British Ministry of War Transport, and ship-repair control be set up to present a united front to the NSS, but to no avail. He was advised that St John Dry Dock Company should attempt to recruit 100 unskilled workers in Newfoundland. The RCN decided jointly with the RN, on the other hand, to double the size of naval repair facilities at St John's.[136]

Turnover in the workforce and lack of skilled men continued to create delays and bottlenecks. Between 2 March and 29 May 1943, for example, Halifax Shipyards lost 135 men but gained only 18. After placing orders for 239 first-class tradesmen, general manager R.J.R. Nelson obtained only 56: 23 first-class and 33 second-class workers.[137] A new naval and merchant ship-maintenance committee failed to find a solution. The problem was well known; no housing for workers was available in Halifax. An exasperated Carswell recommend to C.D. Howe that new inhabitants of Halifax be evacuated to provide living quarters for essential workers, and after reviewing Carswell's letter, the Cabinet War Committee turned down a request from the Royal Canadian Air Force to construct living quarters for air force personnel.[138]

The repair problem continued to grow. Increased damage to shipping arose as more convoys, with more ships carrying more cargo, sought to cross the Atlantic during the year leading up to the invasion of Europe. The repairs situation grew so critical that the Allies established a combined Canada, United States, United Kingdom committee in August to examine the whole problem for warships and merchant vessels on the East Coast of Canada and Newfoundland. Under the chairmanship of Engineer Rear Admiral Stephens, fourteen other members from Canada, Newfoundland, the United Kingdom, and the United States met to identify bottlenecks and consider solutions.[139] But this committee accomplished nothing new.

Pressure on repair services continued as the large fleet of cargo ships produced during the past three years began to need routine servicing. Foreseeing that dry docks were going to be continuously in demand for painting, hull examination, and shaft and rudder inspection, the repairs controller set aside old ships having lists of heavy repairs until the following summer or possibly until after the war in order to speed the movement of new vessels with lists of small defects through the dry docks. Modernization of escort vessels continued to occupy most of the manpower in the repairs industry.[140]

On 31 December 1943 the Shipbuilding Coordination Committee agreed that naval repairs would henceforth have priority over new naval construction and asked for yards to be set aside for the purpose. But only Morton Engineering and Dry Dock Company would become available the next summer for additional naval reconstruction.[141]

Nevertheless, several factors provided some relief during 1944. Lack of skilled labour was not as serious as during the previous year. The repairs controller awoke to the fact that men who had started green on repair work four years before were now skilled tradesmen in fact as well as in name and rate per hour. There were also fewer "old crocks" to repair and more ships with lists of smaller defects. Also, the modern equipment installed with government assistance and under its supervision was complete and functioning smoothly, and with fewer U-boats visiting the western Atlantic, the heavy damage they caused was substantially reduced. The navy's tardy decision to give modernization of escorts and refits priority over new construction also helped.[142]

During 1944 ship-repair facilities in the St Lawrence and Maritimes areas continued modernizing corvettes. Twenty-three were modified in Canadian yards in 1944, but the expanded repair facilities were so overtaxed in the spring that it proved impossible to carry out all the work the navy demanded. Fifteen corvettes completed modernization in US yards and one in the United Kingdom. The Americans also modernized one vessel in their well-appointed yard at Londonderry.[143]

In light of a tendency among naval historians to cite the aforementioned as evidence of inadequate ship repairing facilities in Canada, it is worth noting that during the three months ending 31 January 1944, 102 US ships were repaired in Canadian yards.[144] During the first quarter of the year, over 900 ships, including 250 naval vessels, received repairs costing in the neighbourhood of $2 million on the East Coast. Repairs to merchant vessels during the same period cost approximately $3 million. Repairs continued at full capacity as 829 additional ships were repaired in April and May.[145] Operation Overlord accounted for the noticeable decline in repairs in June, but more than 3,500 ship repairs were completed on the East Coast in 1944 (see table 5.4).

But old problems lingered. Carswell complained in May that 10 per cent of the labour force at St John Dry Dock was slated to be called up for military duty. Aside from the bad effect this had on morale – already twenty-five men had left to get into units of their own choice – the shipbuilding company had spent four years and a good deal of money training some of these men, who could not be replaced. Carswell noted with some asperity that the National Selection Service proved "to be of the least assistance in this matter."[146] Additional repair work was initiated under Canada's mutual-aid program during 1944, and urgent requests from Dutch, Norwegian, French, and US shipping interests for repairs to their vessels increased pressure on Canadian facilities. The British Ministry of War Transport sent five new 10,000-ton ships to Canada during the summer for insulating and fitting of cold-air-circulating trunks for carrying cold-storage cargos, which was completed at Montreal in record time and at a cost that was less than the ministry estimates. The last of these ships departed downstream in mid-November before the close of navigation.[147] During the summer and fall, the former passenger liner–cum–armed merchant cruiser HMS *Letitia* returned to Montreal to be converted into a hospital ship.[148] Converted to accommodate 756 casualties in addition to 200 medical and nursing staff and 160 crew, she was delivered to the Royal Canadian Army Medical Corps on 2 November.[149]

Conversions continued. Late in 1944 British authorities sent four large merchant ships previously employed as minelayers to Canada for conversion to naval auxiliaries for the Royal Navy's fleet train for the war against Japan. The vessels arrived at

Torpedo damage to SS *Samtucky*, a British merchant ship, received while in convoy from New York to Liverpool, December 1944. Note how the explosion opened the ship's hull, buckling plates and leaving steel hanging in shreds. Photographed in Halifax Shipyard Limited's floating dry dock, 3 February 1945. MMA, M2002.9.1b/96, Boyd A. Gibson Collection.

Montreal, Vancouver, and Victoria to be converted into accommodation and amenities ships for the Ministry of War Transport. Work on two was cancelled late in 1945, and of the other two, the *Southern Prince* was accepted in October and the *Menetheus* in January 1946.[150] Each of the stores-issuing ships had 111,480 cubic feet of refrigerated space installed between decks.[151] Back on the East Coast under the mutual-aid program, fishing trawlers from Free France were repaired at yards in the Maritimes and along the St Lawrence River.[152] In light of this evidence, it is not very convincing that modernization of RCN corvettes was delayed by inadequate repair facilities.

Ship repairs in the Maritimes reached an all-time high during the winter of 1944–45 due to bad weather, several major damages caused by enemy action, and increased volumes of freight moving out of the Maritimes to Europe. The high volume of repairs on the West Coast, St Lawrence River, and East Coast continued right into the spring of 1945. Indeed, at the end of April the controller reported ship repairs to be at a higher peak "than they have been in the past two years."[153] Repairs began to decline, however, at the end of June. The controller closed his St John office in May. Cessation of hostilities in Europe brought an end to convoys, permitting better regulation of work, and as the St Lawrence season opened, work was quickly transferred to Quebec and Montreal, relieving the strain on Maritimes ports. Heavy demands by the RCN in preparation for the Pacific campaign continued. Frigates were "tropicalized" and supplied with additional anti-aircraft guns and radar equipment for anticipated Pacific battles. But in August it was over. The controller ceased to regulate dry docks, and the following month, the government lifted all controls on ship repairs. On 23

November ship-repairs and salvage control was revoked nearly five years to the day after PC 6797 had added repairs to the duties of the controller of ship construction.[154]

Conclusion

Historians have ignored the role of ship repairing during the Second World War at their peril. Failure to examine evidence of the industry has led to unwarranted judgments and erroneous conclusions. This is ironic because at the beginning of the war Canada's shipbuilding industry was little more than a repairing business. By 1943, when the value of ship repairing was nearly three and a half times the value of the entire shipbuilding industry of four years before, ship repairing accounted for less than 10 per cent of the industry's total value (see table 5.1). Only by ignoring the ship repairing industry and the millions of dollars spent on government assistance to repairing companies in the maritime provinces has Ernest Forbes been able to argue that C.D. Howe consolidated disparities between the East Coast and central Canada.[155] Similarly, only by ignoring the ship repairing industry have naval historians been able to draw attention away from the inadequacies of the naval service, absolve the naval staff at NSHQ of its failings, and point to the limitations of Canadian industry, engineering, and workmen to account for the crisis in modernization. To claim that "The small yards, upon which the navy relied for its rudimentary annual refits of small vessels, were never part of the government's industrial plan for war and were not seen by the RCN as important to its long-term maintenance requirements" is misleading in light of the millions of dollars spent on improving the yards at Pictou, Sidney, Lunenburg, and Liverpool and blind to the fact that modernization occurred elsewhere than at Halifax and St John.[156] The chief fact is that modernization began two years after the naval staff knew the Royal Navy had begun to modify its own corvettes, a delay for which only naval officers were responsible.

Concern for ship repairing grew only slowly and incompletely. Setting up repairs control at the same time as Wartime Merchant Shipping Limited added to the confusion during the summer of 1941. The government was also remarkably late putting salvage arrangements in place and probably did so only after receiving uninvited yet stinging criticism from US officials concerned with the lack of facilities at Halifax. Nevertheless, when all factors are taken into account, it remains the case that ship repairs control presided over a significant accomplishment.

Table 5.4 shows that the centre of the ship repairing industry shifted during the war from the St Lawrence River to the East Coast, where 45.7 per cent of all repairs were carried out, as compared to 30.8 per cent in the St Lawrence River and Great Lakes regions. Indeed, in 1942, 1943, and 1945 more than half of all repairs in the country were carried out in East Coast yards. The value of shipbuilding and ship repairing in Nova Scotia moved from twelfth place among leading industries in the province in 1940 to third place in 1941 and to number one in 1943 and 1944.[157] The gross number of repairs was also 30 per cent larger than the number given in the DMS's official history.[158] This is significant in itself, for it indicates that 8,475 ship repairs, or 30 per cent

Table 5.4 | Naval and merchant vessels repaired and dry-docked in Canada, 1940–45

	1940	1941	1942	1943	1944	1945*	Total
VESSELS REPAIRED AFLOAT							
East Coast	966	2,461	3,338	2,377	2,704	1,782	*13,628*
St Lawrence and Great Lakes	1,713	2,040	1,805	1,192	2,200	597	*9,547*
West Coast	904	1,003	1,085	687	1,309	548	*5,536*
Subtotal	*3,583*	*5,504*	*6,228*	*4,256*	*6,213*	*2,927*	*28,711*
VESSELS DRY-DOCKED							
East Coast	285	359	423	580	823	384	*2,854*
St Lawrence and Great Lakes	275	288	248	300	364	66	*1,541*
West Coast	537	525	594	407	580	307	*2,950*
Subtotal	*1,097*	*1,172*	*1,265*	*1,287*	*1,767*	*757*	*7,345*
Combined Total	*4,680*	*6,676*	*7,493*	*5,543*	*7,980*	*3,684*	*36,056*
Percentage	13.0	18.5	20.8	15.4	22.1	10.2	100

* To June.

Source: LAC, RG 28, box 332, file 196-39-11, Ship Repair Control, 24 Januatry 1944 and 7 August 1945.

of the wartime total, occurred after September 1943, when the industry was apparently inadequate to meet the navy's needs. The industry was quite capable of meeting the needs presented to it. The navy was entirely responsible for its own inadequacies.

The matter of building Tribal-class destroyers is also illuminating. Although historians have speculated from the beginning that the Cabinet approved the project as a supplement to repair work and as an educational process to acquire technique, no one to date has clearly stated that this was the case. It was easy for the public and later historians to rail at the slowness of construction in 1944 and 1945 but quite wrong to suggest that it was due to inadequacies of either Canadian workmen or Canadian engineering.

Labour Recruitment, Stability, and Morale

Introduction

The number of shipbuilding employees in Canada in 1939 averaged just 3,500, but few actually built any ships.[1] A year later, the annual average number had grown to 9,707, which provides a more realistic base from which to measure the future growth of employment because we can be assured that most of these workers were building ships. Three years later, when shipbuilding employment peaked in July 1943, approximately 85,000 were employed in the industry.[2] This increase of 8.7 times compares quite favourably with the United States, where the increase was 8.9 times during the same period.[3] Employment in Canadian shipyards subsequently declined owing to curtailment of war-production programs and completion of defence projects that occurred during 1944, and numbers fell off rapidly afterward. By December 1945 they had dropped to just under 22,000.[4] The rapid expansion and equally swift contraction of the workforce reveal well the emergency nature of Canada's wartime shipbuilding programs.

These raw data can be restated in order to attach some significance to them. At peak employment, shipbuilding accounted for 4.5 per cent of all industrial employment, including civilian production, in Canada, which translates into 12.8 per cent of all employment in direct war manufacturing, or 31.5 per cent of all those employed in vehicle production.[5] Almost half of the increased employment in war manufacturing occurred in vehicle production: railway rolling stock and repair shops, airplanes, automobiles, trucks, tanks, and ships. The shipbuilding and aircraft industries expanded their employment thirty and twenty times, respectively.[6] By mid-1943, shipbuilding accounted for more than one out of every eight men and women employed in direct war manufacturing.

Figure 6.1 shows the estimated average employment on naval and cargo ships between 1940 and 1944.[7] It excludes those employed on ship repairs and conversions (i.e., workers at Halifax Shipyards Limited and at the Lapointe Pier yard) and those employed at wooden-shipbuilding yards and auxiliary steel yards. The numbers of men and women involved in each type of construction, whether naval or cargo, is clear. From the end of the third quarter of 1941 to the end of the first quarter of 1942, the proportion of workers employed on naval shipbuilding fell from 75 per cent to 33

Figure 6.1 | Estimated average employment on naval and cargo vessels, by half years, 1940–44

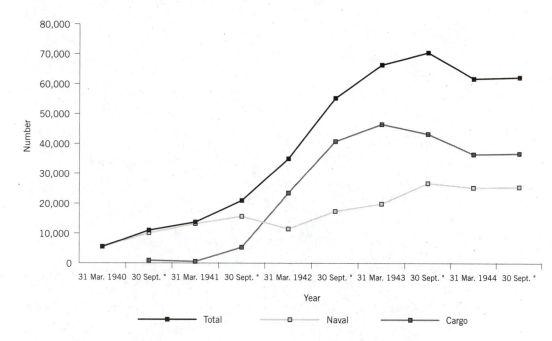

Source: Extrapolated from graphs in LAC, RG 28, box 29, Report on Canadian Shipbuilding, 6 July 1944, appendices 6 and 9.

per cent. Although it recovered slightly during the third quarter of 1943, the proportion devoted to naval shipbuilding did not rise above 41 per cent of the total during the remainder of the war.

Building steel cargo ships and small warships had become Canada's largest wartime industry. On 1 June 1943, when the 100th Canadian-built cargo ship went down the ways, over 6 per cent of all persons employed in wartime manufacturing were working in the cargo ship program, and in most centres where shipyards were located, they were the largest employers of wartime labour.[8] Toronto and Montreal were exceptions. Shipyard employment in the greater Montreal area rose from 800 at the beginning of the war to 13,000 on 1 July 1944 but accounted for just over 10 per cent of the 124,000 persons employed in direct war manufacturing in the city.[9] Although the 4,000 workers employed at Toronto Shipbuilding Company made it the largest shipyard in Ontario, this number represented a small but unknown percentage of direct wartime manufacturing in the city. In Vancouver, on the other hand – indeed, in British Columbia as a whole – shipbuilding became the largest form of wartime industrial production.

Men at United Shipyards Limited at work on the hatches of a 10,000-ton cargo ship, 21 September 1943. In the foreground, a welder wearing goggles operates an acetylene torch; behind him is a heater with his portable stove to heat rivets, and on the right a riveter and his team are at work. NFB/LAC, WRM 3583.

From the latter part of 1941 until the first half of 1943, the Dominion government struggled with the question of the best utilization of scarce national manpower resources in a nation of under 12 million involved in a global war. Meeting steadily increasing demands from the armed services was challenging under any circumstances and nearly impossible given the cross-purposes of contending parties and the fact that in different regions of the country citizens were becoming increasingly divided. Divisions within the Cabinet and among its advisors made the task even more difficult.[10] The rise and rapid fall of the shipbuilding labour force between 1939 and 1945 mirrored the general evolution of Canadians engaged in direct war manufacturing. But the rapidity of the industry's decline reflects the lack of official interest in preserving a shipbuilding industry in peacetime and confirms the notion that ships were simply another form of wartime munitions to be fired at the enemy. How the industry recruited so many men and women and the regional differences in the labour force are the first subjects of this chapter. After examining the numbers, the chapter looks at women workers, training, and factors that contributed to worker stability and that affected morale. Attempts to organize the workers, industrial relations, and strikes are treated in the next chapter.

Stabilizing labour may be defined as establishing conditions that made workers sufficiently contented with their jobs to make the effort to increase production.[11] Loafing, absenteeism, and turnover indicated low morale. Wages and collective status were major contributors to workers' high morale, but factors such as occupational health and safety and others, some intangible, also played a part. Adequate living conditions and social stimulation were as important as good working conditions. The chapter concludes by looking at efforts of government, shipbuilding companies, and the communities where workers lived to overcome low morale and to persuade shipyard workers that they and their contributions were important to winning the war. Explored in this context are wartime housing, national selective service, the impact of victory-bond campaigns, patriotism, and how communities responded to the thousands of newcomers in their midst.

Raising the Numbers

At first, numbers rose quickly and relatively easily as former workers returned to the old yards. Demands for soldiers and workers absorbed many unemployed.[12] The small shipyard at Kingston, Ontario, where perhaps two dozen men found casual employment in the 1930s, had on call between 100 and 120 men who were given a few days' work whenever it obtained a repair job.[13] These men quickly flowed into the yards as the naval building program got under way. By November 1940 at least 269 men were employed in the Kingston yard.[14] Across the country at Esquimalt, British Columbia, the labour force of Yarrows Limited grew the same way. Fewer than forty men were employed in August 1939. The workforce expanded quickly to about 320 in October during the conversion of ss *Rajputana* to an armed merchant cruiser, but the number fell back to about 50 at the end of the year after the job was completed. During the first half of 1940, numbers grew steadily to about 250. With the commencement of corvette construction in June, they continued to grow but never rose above 590 during the next fifteen months.[15]

Nationally, numbers grew quickly and then levelled off. Scant data for 1940 and 1941 permit only impressions. C.D. Howe reported to the House of Commons on 30 July that "some 14,000 men" were currently employed on ship construction; the number had trebled during the previous three months.[16] This sudden trebling of numbers reflected the navy's placement of contracts for ninety ships earlier in the year, the government's response to the German invasion of western Europe in April, and the recognition in the wake of the fall of France that Canada's war production would have to grow enormously. Despite enlistments in the armed services and in growing war industries, the great pool of unemployed workers, the chief legacy of the Depression, had not yet been absorbed. Government officials remained more concerned about shortages of power and machine tools than about labour.

At the year's end, the Department of Munitions and Supply's (DMS) statistician estimated that 16,000 workers were employed in shipbuilding. He thought this number represented about 11 per cent of employees in major war enterprises. In a revealing statement to the War Requirements Board, he did not anticipate any increase during the next three months.[17] At the end of 1940 the four largest shipyards and machine shops in the maritime provinces employed 2,435 men: Halifax Shipyards Limited and St John Dry Dock and Shipbuilding Company employed 943 and 798, respectively, and HMC Dockyard and Pictou Foundry and Machine Company employed 694, split roughly between them.[18] St John Dry Dock increased its workforce to over 1,100 during the first three months of 1941, yet in March the yard was still considerably below capacity.[19]

The optimism about manpower was misplaced. A lack of management, supervisory, and foreman talent had already affected some regions of the country. St John Dry Dock and Shipbuilding was operating at less than 60 per cent capacity, largely because of a "lack of skilled men, particularly foremen."[20] Howard T. Mitchell of the War Requirements Board noted that there was a conspicuous need in ship repair in the Maritimes for "competent directing talent." This was true even for one-shift operations and partly explains why double-shift work had not yet been attempted. The top men in the yards had no assistants to replace them. Robert Nelson, manager of Halifax Shipyards Limited, who rose through accounting, had no technical training and did not display unusual executive talent. David Scouter, superintendent, knew hulls but not engines and their repair. This was the sum total of executive talent at Halifax Shipyards.[21]

While training men occupied shipyards, three other related problems had to be overcome to allow more men to enter the yards. There was the need to secure an even flow of steel plate to the yards, machinery deliveries had to arrive on schedule, and fittings had to reach the yards as needed. Otherwise, men were laid off, recruiting became haphazard, and remaining workers were demoralized. Thirteen months after operations started at Dufferin Shipbuilding Company, the time for deliveries of raw materials for hulls and machinery had increased from four weeks to five months. By May 1941 producers were so far behind in deliveries as to threaten the entire current year's program.[22]

After cargo ship construction was added to the navy shipbuilding program, the situation changed considerably. As old yards began expanding and new emergency yards appeared at Vancouver, Montreal, and Pictou, workers became increasingly scarce. The average number of shipbuilding employees in 1941 grew to 21,240.[23] According to the royal commissioners examining the Ontario and Quebec shipbuilding industries, "more than 20,000 men" were employed nationwide in November.[24]

Men came from all over. On the West Coast many had been farmers, loggers, and miners. At Midland many men were drawn from the bush. Although many men returning to Kingston's shipyard were experienced Geordies and Clydesiders from the old country, most new entrants had been pitching hay on hardscrabble farms north of the city the summer before. They were willing and intelligent but needed training.[25]

Table 6.1 | Average annual number of shipbuilding employees, by year and region, 1939–45

Year	No. of employees	Maritimes	Quebec	Ontario	British Columbia
1939	3,491	642	1,379	502	968
1940	9,707		No data available		
1941	21,240				
1942	50,132	5,404	14,084	6,804	23,840
1943	75,847	10,285	24,716	9,578	31,268
1944	67,076	10,763	22,162	9,504	24,647
1945	48,118	7,946	15,496	5,549	19,127
PERCENTAGES					
1939	100	18.4	39.5	14.4	27.7
1940	100		No data available		
1941	100				
1942	100	10.8	28.1	13.6	47.6
1943	100	13.6	32.6	12.6	41.2
1944	100	16.0	33.0	14.2	36.7
1945	100	16.5	32.2	11.5	39.8
4-yr avg. (1942–45)		14.2	31.5	13.0	41.3

Source: Canada, DBS, *Annual Industry Report: Iron, Steel and Their Products Group: The Shipbuilding Industry* (1939–45), tables 1 and 2; no data other than the national averages were published for 1940 and 1941.

Pictou union leader George MacEachern was an optimist when he claimed that no more than 10 per cent of the employees in the yard were experienced skilled workers. Of more than 2,000 workers at Pictou, only 50 were experienced shipbuilders.[26] But he was correct when he wrote, "Mainly, we had farmers and bush workers and coal miners."[27]

Table 6.1 shows average annual numbers of shipbuilding employees. The national figures for 1940 and 1941 have limited value. The regional data are of some help, especially for the last four years of the war, when cargo shipbuilding and naval shipbuilding and ship-repair programs were all up and running. They show that the four-year average of the annual number of employees was spread very unequally across the country. Approximately three-quarters of the shipbuilding labour force was located in Quebec and British Columbia. Roughly one in seven employees worked on the East Coast, and nearly three in seven workers laboured on the West Coast. Fewer than one in seven worked in Great Lakes yards, whereas more than two in seven worked in yards along the St Lawrence River between Montreal and Quebec City.

The following map shows the distribution of approximately 75,000 workers across the country in March 1944, nine months after the industry had reached peak employment.[28] About 40 per cent of the total continued to be employed on the West Coast;

Figure 6.2 | Shipbuilding and ship repairing industries in Canada, geographical labour distribution, March 1944

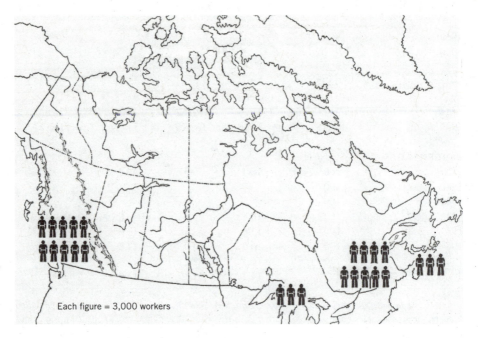

Each figure = 3,000 workers

Source: From a submission by the Canadian Shipbuilding and Ship Repairing Association to the Canadian Government, March 1944, reproduced from *Canadian Transportation* 47 (December 1944): 679.

approximately 36 per cent worked in St Lawrence River yards between Montreal and Quebec City, and 12 per cent each laboured in Great Lakes yards and on the East Coast, chiefly in Nova Scotia.

Labour recruitment grew from 33,115 wage earners in January 1942 to 55,089 in December, an increase of 66.4 per cent. The annual average number of wage earners was 47,264, which, when added to the average number of salaried employees, 2,868, brought the year's total average to 50,132. The highest annual rate of growth during the war occurred in 1942, when the average number of shipbuilding employees was up 136 per cent from the previous year.

Table 6.2 shows that a month after war was declared, one-fifth fewer workers were employed in Canada's shipyards than is indicated by the average annual number for 1939. The table also contains the only detailed picture of shipbuilding labour for any time during 1942 and shows that during the thirteen months following 1 June 1942, the workforce grew by 84.4 per cent. The data also confirm other evidence indicating that employment peaked in July 1943 and remained relatively high during the subsequent twelve months. Finally, they confirm that during the final years of the war, shipyard employment in the Maritimes was better than has been previously claimed.[29]

Table 6.2 | Employment in shipbuilding, by region and selected dates, 1939–44

Region	30 Sept. 1939	1 June 1942	1 July 1943	1 July 1944
NO. EMPLOYEES				
West Coast	414	20,987	31,917	27,430
Great Lakes	580	6,240	10,019	10,158
St Lawrence	1,227	12,762	28,502	20,372
Maritimes	506	4,290	11,664	13,894
Total	*2,727*	*44,279*	*82,102*	*71,854*
PERCENTAGES				
West Coast	15.2	47.4	38.9	38.2
Great Lakes	21.3	14.1	12.2	14.1
St Lawrence	45.0	28.8	34.7	28.4
Maritimes	18.6	9.7	14.2	19.3
Total	*100.0*	*100.0*	*100.0*	*100.0*

Note: Table 6.2 is constructed from detailed charts of wartime industrial employment using selected dates and is based on analysis of the reports of employers with fifteen or more employees to the employment and payroll statistics branch of the Dominion Bureau of Statistics.

Source: Canada, Department of Reconstruction and Supply, *Location and Effects of Wartime Industrial Expansion in Canada, 1939–1944.*

The new importance given to ship repairs added to already serious manpower difficulties in the Maritimes. High turnover and inadequate housing were contributing factors, but a lack of skilled workers was the greatest challenge. In April 1943 labour turnover at St John Dry Dock and Shipbuilding was 8.9 per cent, compared to 7.4 per cent in March; moreover, less than one-quarter of the 133 employees lost were classed as skilled or semiskilled. Sixteen per cent each of these employees were fired or went on active service, 15 per cent left for better jobs, and 23 per cent, the largest group, left to farm. During the same period, 122 men were hired, but only 3 were skilled or semiskilled. The net loss of 11 employees hid the departure of 28 skilled and semiskilled men.[30]

St John Dry Dock and Shipbuilding Company looked to Newfoundland for additional men but experienced only limited success. By the summer of 1942 the demand for labour in Newfoundland outstripped the local supply, and the Newfoundland government initially resisted Canadian recruitment efforts. But the government relented in June 1943, and some ninety Newfoundlanders eventually went to work in the New Brunswick yard.[31]

Table 6.3 provides a uniquely detailed breakdown of shipbuilding employees on Canada's West Coast. On 1 May 1943 more than 21,000 men and women were em-

Table 6.3 | Number of employees in West Coast shipyards on 1 May 1943

Yard	No. employees	Percentage
Burrard Dry Dock Ltd	9,892	36.2
North Van Ship Repairs	6,080	22.3
West Coast Shipbuilders	5,211	19.1
Victoria Machinery Depot	2,020	7.4
Prince Rupert Dry Dock and Shipbuilding Co.	1,650	6.0
Yarrows Ltd	2,470	9.0
Total	*27,323*	*100.0*

Sources: LAC, RG 28, box 257, file 196-13-8, memorandum, H.R. MacMillan to C.D. Howe, 15 May 1943; EMA, Yarrows Ltd Fonds, extrapolation from graph of number of employees, January 1939 to December 1945.

ployed in Vancouver, and like those at Victoria Machinery Depot and at Prince Rupert Dry Dock and Shipbuilding Company, all worked on 10,000-ton cargo ships and ship repairing. Only 9 per cent of British Columbia's shipbuilders were employed on naval construction.

Women Workers

In December 1942 women accounted for just 1.6 per cent of all wage earners employed in Canada's shipyards. Although a relatively small proportion compared with some other war industries, the number of women employed in shipyards had more than doubled from September to December.[32] Women worked in all Canadian shipyards, but "Rosie the riveter" did not appear. "Rosie" was an American creation widely applied and admired in Canada. Her popularity stemmed from the image projected of women voluntarily and temporarily entering the labour force owing to their patriotism and their acceptance of the predominant view that women did not work in industrial production. The image came from the aircraft industry, where women riveted small aluminum fasteners into lightweight aluminum aircraft hulls. Despite photographs of female shipbuilders wielding rivet guns on ships' hulls and although the Pictou yard boasted at least one gang of female riveters, they were unusual. Few women possessed sufficient upper-body strength to work hour after hour through an eight-hour shift with heavy pneumatic rivet guns in order to fasten large steel rivets up to seven-eighths of an inch in diameter and nearly three-quarters of a pound each.[33] Riveting destroyed men's shoulders and elbows; riveter burnout was a serious, hidden problem in wartime yards. Women worked on rivet gangs as heaters, passersboys, and even bolters-up but chiefly as "helpers," worker-trainees whose primary task was to help journeymen perform their jobs. They were new and largely unskilled.[34]

Unidentified heater draws a red-hot rivet from the coals of her portable heater in order to throw it to a "sticker" at the Pictou shipyard. NFB/LAC, COO-3895278.

Women came to play a significant role in some parts of the country and in particular shipyards, but they never played as large a role in Canadian wartime shipbuilding as women did in Great Britain and the United States or in some other wartime industries. During 1941 the number employed in British shipyards doubled to 4,000, comprising 2 per cent of the workforce.[35] In November 1944, when an estimated 150,000 women wage earners worked in America's shipyards, only 2,123 were employed in Canada's.[36] By 1944, when the number of full-time, working women in Canada had doubled since 1939 to 1.2 million, fewer than 4,000 were employed in shipbuilding, compared to 50,000 in the armed services.[37]

Canada was far less industrialized than the United Kingdom and the United States and was a much more conservative society than either. Shipbuilding work was also less attractive than other available well-paid war work that could be found elsewhere. Shipbuilding in Canada was heavy, dirty, and frequently carried on outdoors in nasty weather. Women also paid social and psychological costs to work in the shipyards. Shipbuilding was a traditional industry where prejudices against them were more firmly rooted than in newer industries. Trade unionists were often no more welcoming than the other workmen. After one disgruntled business agent of a union local

Table 6.4 | Average annual number of female employees in Canadian shipbuilding industries, by year and wage class, 1939–45

Year	Salaried		Waged		Total	
	No.	%	No.	%	No.	%
1939	47	10.2	1	0.03	48	1.4
1940						
1941			No data available			
1942	900	31.4	342	0.72	1,242	2.5
1943	1,776	33.3	2,350	3.33	4,126	5.4
1944	1,452	31.4	2,497	4.00	3,949	5.9
1945	1,157	30.2	1,269	2.87	2,426	5.0

Note: Percentages are of females in each category of employment. For example, in 1943, 1,776 salaried women represented one-third of all salaried employees, and 4,126 women represented 5.4 per cent of all employees.

Source: Canada, DBS, *Annual Industry Report: Iron, Steel and Their Products Group: The Shipbuilding Industry* (1939–45).

attempted to explain his opposition to a female welder taken on at Yarrows Limited, the national secretary of the Canadian Congress of Labour refused to respond to his abuse, advising him to get used to the idea of women in the industry.[38]

In 1939, when Canadian shipyards employed an average of 3,491 workers, only 48 were women; all but one were salaried. Table 6.4 shows the annual average number of female employees in the shipbuilding industry during the war. The Dominion government's statistics distinguished between salaried and hourly wage earners rather than between clerical staff or office workers and industrial-production workers, but it is reasonable to assume that a strong correlation existed between wage earners and industrial workers and that salaried employees worked in stenographic, secretarial, and clerical jobs or in food services and at other nonindustrial jobs in the yards.

Most women entering the industry before 1942 were salaried. Their numbers grew from one-tenth to just under one-third of the total salaried labour force. Indeed, in 1942 nearly three-quarters of all female employees in the industry were salaried. The number of salaried women in the industry increased sharply along with total numbers in 1943 and thereafter declined steadily. It is important to remember these women, for they tend to be forgotten as the spotlight on women's work shifts to the waged category, where most women were employed as production workers. In 1943 and 1944, the years of the greatest number of women employees, between 37 and 43 per cent of women remained salaried employees. Table 6.4 shows that between 1943 and 1945 women in the shipbuilding industry comprised 3.4 per cent of all waged workers and 5.4 per cent of all employees.

Average annual numbers disguise a great deal. During the first six months of 1942, for example, Canada's shipyards employed on average only 164 female wage earn-

One of the youngest shipyard workers in the country, sixteen-year-old Rosina Vanier, is strapped to a crane wire preparing to ride the hoist and guide the crane operator at Pictou, Nova Scotia, January 1943. NFB/LAC, WRM 2728.

ers a month. But during the summer, women began entering the yards in growing numbers. After increasing 15.6 per cent during the first six months, numbers rose by 69.1 per cent in July and August to 296, and as male teachers and boys returned to school from summer employment, the number of women entrants increased to 388 in September and to 872 by the end of the year.[39] Announcing the arrival of the first eleven "girls" at Burrard Dry Dock Company, general manager Bill Wardle spoke of a new policy of employing women to release men for more skilled employment. These first women employees worked as derrick signallers, template makers, truck drivers, bolt threaders, and stores help. A women's supervisor had been hired and a women's building with hot canteen, reading room, and showers was being built. The women were also to have their own infirmary with a registered nurse on duty.[40]

Canada had reached full employment, yet manpower remained far short of war-production requirements. Nationally, the average number of women shipbuilders grew steadily during the first eleven months of 1943, finally reaching a peak of 3,113 in November. The number of women workers declined slightly thereafter but remained fairly steady, averaging 2,724 wage earners over the next eight months. Between August 1944 and August 1945 numbers declined by more than half to 1,175, and by December only 268 women remained in Canada's shipyards.[41]

Table 6.5 | Women employed in Canadian shipbuilding, by region, 1939–45

Year	British Columbia	Ontario	Quebec	Maritimes	Total
1939	6	11	23	8	48
1940			No data available		
1941					
1942	360	234	501	147	1,242
1943	2,122	578	679	747	4,126
1944	1,923	645	714	667	3,949
1945	1,314	323	461	328	2,426

Source: Canada, DBS, *Annual Industry Report: Iron and Steel and Their Products Group: The Shipbuilding Industry* (1939–45).

Women were spread unevenly throughout the nation's shipyards. Table 6.5 presents a closer reflection of wartime reality. In Ontario and Quebec, for example, females accounted for 6.4 and 3.9 per cent, respectively, of the total labour force (see table 6.1). In Ontario women were almost equally divided between salaried and hourly wage earners in 1943, but the ratio more closely resembled that of the rest of the country in 1944, when 394 wage earners outnumbered 251 salaried women. Salaried females always outnumbered hourly wage earners in Quebec, a reflection of cultural pressures on French Canadian women not to work in heavy industry.

Early in 1943 officials at the Department of Labour informed the prime minister they had received over 7,000 letters, 100 telegrams, and 250 petitions protesting women's work outside the home. The St Jean-Baptiste Society of Quebec sent one petition bearing more than 120,000 signatures protesting "la conscription feminine," objecting to the moral hazards to women working in factories, the dangers to families when mothers engaged in factory work, and the injuries to women's health from fatigue.[42] Like Ontario, Quebec provided greater opportunities to find well-paid war work in other, cleaner industries than were available on either coast.

A major exception to the lack of women in Quebec shipyards occurred at Montreal, where as much as 40 per cent of the workforce of Canadian Power Boat Company may have been female. During the last four months of 1941, as the company recruited and trained its workers, women were employed almost everywhere in the plant. The clerical force was female, and more than 300 girls and women operated 30 per cent of the drafting room and 90 per cent of the electrical machines and equipment. In addition, 280 females were employed directly in the construction of boats. Women were taught to do practically everything, from making frames to laying decks, painting, cleaning the boats and shops, and installing all of the electrical equipment, including the elaborate radio apparatus.[43] Unlike traditional shipbuilding yards, Canadian Power Boat Company provided a clean working environment.

Women bolting steel girders into place over the hold of a new 4,700-ton cargo ship under construction at Pictou, Nova Scotia, January 1943. NFB/LAC, WRM 2498.

In the Maritimes in 1943, 747 women made up 7.3 per cent of the total shipbuilding labour force (table 6.1). Nearly three-quarters of them were wage earners. The following year, when the number had declined somewhat to 667, women still comprised 6.2 per cent of the shipyard workforce, of whom 70.8 per cent remained wage earners. Most were employed in the wartime emergency yard at Pictou. They began to enter the yard in August 1942, and at the end of the year officials at Foundation Maritime Limited claimed to have the largest number of women shipbuilders in the country, 137.[44] In January the number exceeded 300. At peak activity, when more than 2,000 people were employed, women formed more than one-third of the total workforce, a unique situation in Canada.[45]

Halifax Shipyards Limited stood in sharp contrast to Pictou. Only five women appear to have been employed briefly as welders in 1943. The women at Halifax Shipyards called themselves the "Electric Five" and loved their jobs, but they did not last long. The nature of the work, chiefly repairing old, damaged ships, required a large proportion of skilled workers who could not be easily trained. This may have been

left | Daycare was a problem for some women. Mrs Martin Malti of the Micmac nation and her child working at the Pictou shipyard, January 1943. LAC, PA-116154; *right* | Margaret McLean operates a semi-automatic radiograph steel-cutting torch at the Pictou shipyard. LAC, C-51716.

one reason for the low number of women. Lack of accommodation in Halifax was certainly another, but prejudice was probably just as important.

As many as fifty women may have been employed at St John Dry Dock and Shipbuilding Company, but few were production workers, perhaps for the same reasons as at Halifax. The Pictou shipyard, in contrast, was devoted to building a single type of ship rather than to repairing. Although women in the Maritimes made up a larger proportion of regional shipyard workers than the national average, they resembled other women in being the last hired and the first fired.

The greatest concentration of women in the industry occurred on the West Coast. In 1939, when just over one-quarter, or 27.7 per cent, of the nation's shipbuilding labour was located there, six women worked in shipyards. By mid-1943, when the number of employees had exploded to over 31,000, representing 47.6 per cent of Canada's total shipbuilding labour force, women made up about 6.8 per cent of British Columbia's shipbuilders.

In June 1943 women accounted for nearly 8 per cent of approximately 10,000 employees at the two shipyards operated by Burrard Dry Dock Company, but only 40 or 50 women were employed at North Van Ship Repairs Limited. None at all worked at West Coast Shipbuilders Limited, although about 100 were employed next door at the Hamilton Bridge Company plant, where all the machine work was done.[46] Sheila Anderson claims that near the peak of employment at Victoria Machinery Depot, about 200 women worked with 2,000 men.[47] An anonymous slip of paper in the uncatalogued archives of Yarrows Limited indicates that 401 women were employed there during the winter of 1943–44, comprising as much as 13.3 per cent, or nearly one in seven, of the shipyard's total workforce.[48] Table 6.5 shows that from 1943 to 1945 half of all female shipbuilding employees in the country worked on the West Coast, and between 62 and 74 per cent were wage earners, but all this was very temporary. By December 1945 only eighty-four women remained.[49]

Women worked at virtually every task in the yards, as sweepers, bottom cleaners, mould-loft and pattern-loft workers, truck drivers, crane operators, painters, tackle riggers, riggers' helpers, bench workers, drill press and lathe operators, plate makers, bolt threaders, chain makers, shaft greasers, burners, electricians' helpers, and tool-room and store-room assistants. They also worked at jobs more commonly seen as suitable for women, namely as secretaries, checking and recording clerks, cleaners, and food-service employees. But women were also trained for two jobs that could lead to journeyman status: electrician and welder.[50] Each trade required several months of intense training in schools off the jobsite.

Training

Training the thousands of workers needed to staff the yards became a never-ending task. A nucleus of skilled men, many of whom came out of retirement, existed in both the East and the West. Large numbers in the Great Lakes and St Lawrence River regions possessed industrial experience, but in the West the population was smaller, and few had industrial experience. Many new workers reached British Columbia from the prairie provinces. Between June 1941 and April 1944 a shift between provinces of approximately 50,000 persons per year occurred generally from the prairie provinces to Ontario and British Columbia. Quebec contributed only slightly to interprovincial migration. In the maritime provinces, the situation was mixed. War industries drew men to Nova Scotia from Prince Edward Island and New Brunswick. There were pockets of skilled workmen with industrial experience at St John, Halifax, and Sydney and in some smaller communities in Nova Scotia. During the war, the Prairies lost over 125,000 persons, British Columbia gained 90,000 and Ontario 58,000, and Quebec exported workers to Ontario and Nova Scotia. Despite claims to the contrary, Nova Scotia lost no industrial workers to Ontario or Quebec.[51]

To have simply manned the shipyards with untrained personnel would have so diluted the nucleus as to render it ineffective, but to take just enough new men into the yards to allow a proper training would have led to unacceptable delays in production. The solution was to have some men trained in the yards and some in schools established by the Department of Labour. The fact that many yards were building only one type of ship lightened the task considerably. Many learned only one job and became specialists but were less useful than fully trained mechanics, as they could not be moved from one job to another. Welders could be employed after 150 hours of training and riveters after three to six weeks. After about six months in a shipyard, these men and women could be classified as first-class workers. Shipfitters (platers), pipefitters, and electricians required six to eight weeks of pre-employment training before entering the yards and then would be allocated a specific job.[52]

Emergency training classes were offered wherever shipyards appeared. In December 1940 officials at the Department of Labour completed cooperative arrangements to establish wartime emergency training programs in each province in anticipation of greatly increased war production in the new year.[53] At Pictou, where the workforce had been largely recruited from women, fishermen, and farmers, a shipbuilding school was established in cooperation with the Nova Scotia Technical College in the Canadian National Railway roundhouse, and classes of forty students each were soon being taught. The chief instructor and a number of skilled men gave classes in riveting, welding, plating, and caulking.[54] Foremen and chargehands were selected from the few trained men available and from the more promising students attending classes. At Prince Rupert in 1942 classes were started at the local high school for ship lofting, steam engineering, machine-shop practice, electrical fitting, draughting, and marine pipefitting and were offered free to anyone who wanted to learn. The chief drawback was that after long hours in the shipyards, few workers had the inclination to attend.[55]

On the first day of actual construction at Pictou, rivet squads managed to drive an average of eighty rivets on a ten-hour shift. Later, Pictou attained 2,000 rivets per squad for the same working hours. The first ship took 237 days to launch; later on, the yard completed a ship each month.[56] An innovation occurred at St John Dry Dock and Shipbuilding Company in September 1942 when the machine shop took on seven machinist trainees rather than apprentices. Despite considerable skepticism, fifteen months later the undertaking was declared a success; trainees also entered the shop from schools at Moncton and Campbellton.[57]

At Lauzon a school of arts and crafts gave daytime instruction in industrial design, mechanics, and joinery, and at Quebec the technical school successfully graduated gangs of riveters, caulkers, chippers, oxy-acetylene burners, electric-arc and oxy-acetylene welders, joiners, carpenters, machinists, mechanics, electricians, and pipefitters. The school expanded from 400 students at the beginning of the war to over 1,000 in training at one time, including about 200 in special classes for war-industry training. Philippe Methe, civil engineer and principal of the school, and Louis Letarte, head plater at Morton Engineering and Dry Dock Company, began a practical shipbuilding course. After three months' instruction, students graduated as skilled steelworkers in bolting-up, punching, shearing, riveting, chipping, caulking, burning, and both types of welding. All were paid through the wartime emergency training plan. Riveters were trained in gangs of three: a riveter, a holder-on, and a heater; they were usually hired as improvers and found jobs as far away as Halifax and Collingwood.[58] In February 1942 the technical school inaugurated a new course for loftsman and draughtsman. Entrance requirements called for a tenth- or eleventh-grade education and preferably some shipbuilding experience. Twenty-five hours per week were devoted to classes: engineering drawing (15 hours), practical elementary mathematics (8 hours), and English (2 hours).[59]

The shipyards needed far more men than the schools could provide, and many workers received rough and ready training on the job. Roland Aubert was just seventeen when he went to work at Davie Shipbuilding and Repairing Company in May 1942. He was immediately assigned to the welding department. The next day, the foreman placed him alongside a welder whom he followed all day, watching through a mask. After three days, he was given an electrode and welding rod and shown the movements. Two weeks later, the foreman assigned him his own welding job making 6-inch tack welds to hold plates onto the hull for the riveters. The responsibility suddenly hit him; temporary welds that failed could lead to the death or serious injury of fellow workers.[60]

Founded in February 1943, the Marine Industries Limited welding department had trained 307 welders by September 1944. Although the company did not employ the largest group of welders in the country, the number employed during the twenty months following the school's establishment varied from 580 to 530.[61]

Sheila Anderson was a helper when she started working at Victoria Machinery Depot in September 1942. During the next six months, she attended 58 hours of school training in the evenings before receiving her certificate in "Marine wiring, freighter."[62] At Halifax, Dorothy Hendsbee, one of five women selected for training as a welder, received 420 hours of shop practice and 60 hours of theory at Nova Scotia Technical College during ten and a half weeks in the spring of 1943. Halifax Shipyards was not a very enthusiastic employer of women, for after contracting pneumonia in December and taking three months to recuperate, Hendsbee returned to the yard only to learn that her job no longer existed.[63]

Wartime Merchant Shipping Limited cooperated closely with the wartime emergency training program. At Vancouver an advisory council representing management, organized labour, and the technical high school assisted the government in training. Union-trades committees nominated trainees and instructors, the former largely selected from those already employed in the shipyards. Marine pipefitting classes, which stressed blueprint reading, began in July 1941, and by May 1943 classes had been organized to train coppersmiths, engine and machine fitters, marine electricians, platers, sheet-metal workers, shipwrights, and welders.[64]

These newly trained men and women were encouraged to attend part-time classes or evening classes to further their studies and broaden their training so that they could be promoted to higher grades of work and in time become leadermen or foremen. Men who became proficient in lesser-skilled trades could volunteer for training in more-skilled trades and were transferred inside the yards as they passed the neces-

Workmen guide cranes lifting steel plates and girders into place on a 10,000-ton freighter under construction at United Shipyards Limited, Montreal, 21 September 1943. NFB/LAC, WRM 3574.

sary tests. St John Dry Dock and Shipbuilding Company introduced a study incentive by reimbursing men the full cost of the International Correspondence School courses in shipbuilding or related trades upon successful completion of a course, and although there were few takers, men were given opportunities for advancement.[65]

The Pictou shipyard introduced a job instructor to help employees learn more about their work. Combining lectures with question papers and discussions seemed a good way to reinforce rudimentary training.[66] Classes in supervision were also held, as it was quickly realized that although chargehands and foremen might be thoroughly competent tradesmen, they might have little ability or experience in teaching others. After Quebec Shipyards Limited was incorporated in July 1943, French Canadian management set up a school almost immediately to train men in the yards for more responsible positions and to be foremen, thereby removing a serious grievance among workers whose advancement had been previously blocked by their lack of English.[67]

Some trades proved more attractive than others; welders were easier to recruit than riveters, as welding offered much-less-backbreaking work for the same pay. The amount of welding steadily increased during the war. By 1945 Burrard Dry Dock employed 1,200 welders.[68] This proved a happy solution to many problems, allowing greater scope for prefabrication. As many workers, particularly in Quebec, had prior experience in structural-steel work, building ships to the launching stage reached a high degree of efficiency. Nowhere was this more apparent than at United Ship-yards Limited, which employed hundreds of steelworkers from Dominion Bridge Company. A great deal of hull steel was prefabricated at the company's Lachine plant and sent along seven miles of railway track to the Bickerdike Pier. Steel bulkheads were completely fabricated in one or two pieces ready for fitting when required; deck-houses and large sections of hull material were too.[69]

The problem of adequate technical and drawing staffs for the yards was never really solved, although ways and means were found to get the work done. Draughtsmen were always in short supply. Outside of one naval architect, an assistant, and five lead-ing foremen, Port Arthur Shipbuilding Company had no technical experts to read drawings.[70] In 1939 naval architect Harold Milne estimated there were fewer than two dozen, including hull, engine, and electrical draughtsmen in the entire country, and in anticipation of war his firm, German and Milne, established a central draw-ing office, which produced much of the work for the Royal Canadian Navy (RCN) and the DMS from 1940 to 1945.[71] Several men came from the British Admiralty and old-country shipyards to assist the naval program, especially with the Tribal-class destroyers, but the British had no surplus of draughting room personnel and really could not spare them; only about a half-dozen men were obtained for the merchant ship program.[72] Other skilled men arrived from the United States and elsewhere, some quite circuitously.

Emil Dinkla, a loftsman in an Oslo shipyard, arrived at Pictou in 1942 after fighting the Nazis in his homeland, escaping to Sweden, where he was interned, and escap-ing again on orders of the Norwegian government-in-exile, which packed him off to America, but not before he got word to his wife, a Norwegian women's cross-country ski champion, who donned her skis, crossed the Swedish border at an appropriately lonely spot, rejoined her husband, and accompanied him to the United States and then to Canada.[73] Dinkla's story did not end there. As the Pictou shipyard had no skilled men and no mould loft, he created both while producing templates for the first ships built in the new yard. The mould loft quickly gained a reputation as one of the most efficient departments in the shipyard, and Dinkla was placed in charge of steel fabrication, bending slabs, and the blacksmith's shop, as well as the mould loft. In October 1943 he was made hull superintendent. His firing of an English workman a few months later proved too much for some workers, who shut down the yard to protest an alleged German firing an Englishman![74] This appears to be the only work stoppage at Pictou during the war, yet George MacEachearn, president of the union local, has recounted how hard it was to get the men back to work after this bigoted tempest in a teapot.[75] At the end of 1944 Dinkla was promoted to shipyard superintendent in charge of shipbuilding, as well as maintenance, draughting, planning, and production.

All shipyards in the naval construction program had resident naval overseers (RNOs), who ensured that rigorous Admiralty specifications were met. Some of these men were retired veterans from the Royal Navy or the Royal Canadian Navy Reserve who had returned to service at the outbreak of the war, and others were newly graduated electrical and mechanical engineers from Canadian universities who had joined the Royal Canadian Navy Volunteer Reserve. All were charged with ensuring that newly built warships met the demands of the service.

Throughout the war, classification-society surveyors from Lloyd's Register of Shipping and from British Corporation Register of Shipping and Aircraft were in constant attendance in all shipyards. This was possible because first-class mercantile building standards, rather than Admiralty standards, were initially applied to the hull, propulsion, and auxiliary machinery of Flower-class corvettes, and it was necessary because workmen were unfamiliar with the fundamental rules of marine construction.[76] The first seven corvettes built for the Royal Navy and rushed overseas late in 1941 were filled with builders' defects and examples of incomplete work.[77] In early ships, the integrity of watertight bulkheads was constantly in danger. Marine surveyors in the cargo ship program also acted as owners' (i.e., the government's) representatives, remaining in touch with all phases of work.[78] All ships in British Columbia were under the inspection of Lloyd's, which increased the number of its surveyors from two in 1939 to twenty-five before the end of the war. It also stationed surveyors at Winnipeg and Calgary as well as at Prince Rupert, Victoria, and Vancouver.[79] After the war, Sir Amos Ayre, director general of Britain's merchant shipbuilding, who had kept in close touch with Canada's program, testified that the rapid training of unskilled labour was "an outstanding feature" of the Canadian program, which delivered workmanship of "a high order."[80]

Stability

The many and varied factors affecting labour morale do not permit a close-knit narrative. Strikes and work stoppages may or may not be indicators of low morale, whereas loafing, petty theft, absenteeism, and turnover can be. Deliberate loafing, theft, and malicious damage occurred in the shipyards – of that there can be no doubt – but they cannot be measured and are difficult to consider as factors in slowing production, unlike absenteeism, accidents, and turnover.[81]

Turnover was a serious but often ignored problem. In a brief to the National War Labour Board in June 1943, the Prince Rupert Allied Trades Council, representing all shipyard unions, warned that "so many workers leave each year that on average an entire new shipyard personnel is being trained annually."[82] Victoria Machinery Depot, which employed 2,900 men and women in 1943, lost 1,380 workers to the armed services during the war. Port Arthur Shipbuilding Company, which employed 2,200 workers at its peak, lost about 700.[83] In 1944, across Canada, 17 employees per 1,000 were leaving each week, which meant that the entire personnel of any yard in Canada would be completely renewed once every fifty-nine weeks. To keep the labour force up to strength, the yards continually hired workers, virtually all of whom had to be trained. Keeping key people in the yards remained an urgent necessity throughout the war. John Robson, who ended the war as manager of the construction department of Wartime Shipbuilding Limited, listed three reasons for the high separation rate: workers being called for active service, workers being discharged after being found unsatisfactory, and workers leaving voluntarily for other jobs, the latter being the chief reason for departure.[84]

Michael Stevenson has effectively dealt with the reasons why these conditions were allowed to continue despite the critical nature of shipbuilding to the country's industrial war effort. The Department of Labour's mobilization of human resources was a failure owing to competition from three other government departments responsible for manpower, each of which insisted that voluntary enlistment in the armed services must have highest priority. Moreover, lax and permissive regulating strategies allowed tens of thousands of war workers to shop continuously for jobs paying higher wages.[85]

Absenteeism generally averaged about 10 per cent of the payroll and was fairly evenly spread across the country.[86] This was the same rate as in the larger US shipyards.[87] Weekly data compiled by Davie Shipbuilding and Repairing for thirty-six of forty-five weeks between 1 February and mid-December 1943, when the number of men on the payroll grew from 3,408 to 4,333, or 27 per cent, indicate that week-day absenteeism varied between 9 and 15 per cent and on Saturdays could reach 17 per cent. During periods of extreme cold or heavy rain, absenteeism rose as high as 22 and even 39 per cent.[88] But harsh weather was only an intermittent cause of absenteeism, which was attributable chiefly to sickness and accident.

At Prince Rupert daily absenteeism in 1943 was 9 per cent and estimated to cost $16,000 per ship.[89] At St John Dry Dock and Shipbuilding the daily average absentee rate was 11 or 12 per cent but averaged 15 per cent the day after payday.[90] Daily absenteeism in the six West Coast yards varied between 9 and 12.5 per cent; during the week it varied between 8.1 and 10.6 per cent and on Saturday from 11.5 to 17 per cent.[91] In brief, an estimated 5,000 men were absent daily from Canada's shipyards during 1943, enough workers to man another five-berth yard.[92] Although some of this was unavoidable, "well over half of the absentees ... just don't feel like working."[93] The total effect was that Canada had a ghost shipyard whose employees stayed off the job every day of the year. They could have built ten 10,000-ton cargo ships to add to the fleet their workmates completed.[94]

Absenteeism's causes shed some light on morale and conditions in the yards. Burrard Dry Dock's labour-management committee attributed absenteeism largely to failings of the government and of the company rather than to workers. Members listed five causes: taxation, including the difficulty filling out the tax forms; the employer's failure to "sell" the war to its employees; lax supervision of workers, some of whom stood around for twenty minutes "throwing pennies"; ignoring the viewpoint of younger workers; and the government's failure to make a clear statement concerning compulsory savings in order to counter the workers' belief that it would not pay back victory loans. The committee also expressed considerable doubt that young workers were the chief absentees.[95] This is not to say that the labour-management committee's assessment was correct. Management had its own views. At Vancouver, managers were generally convinced that closed shops led to much loss of productivity. Between April 1941 and June 1943, three local yards operating under closed-shop agreements accounted for 22,356 lost man-days, compared with only 1,085 lost man-days at West Coast Shipbuilders, which was an open shop.[96]

According to Peter McInnis, the government promoted labour-management committees to combat absenteeism and low productivity. Introduced initially in May 1942 in the aircraft industry, they grew fairly quickly, as major labour organizations called for their adoption.[97] Although they became one of the most successful and enduring cooperative experiments in Canadian industrial relations, no evidence exists that they reduced absenteeism or contributed to increased productivity in the workplace. Indeed, angry workers sometimes booed and walked out of the lectures and movies promoting teamwork that invariably accompanied labour-management committees in the workplace. They seemed to have had no function beyond the manipulative and exploitative, one more example of the government's ambition to control labour through management technique rather than to assuage it through negotiation.[98]

That taxation should contribute to absenteeism is at first glance puzzling, but as David Côté, a union organizer with the Canadian Congress of Labour, explained to an official of the National Selective Service after 300 men had been recently dismissed for absenteeism, workers felt they were working one or two days weekly to pay government taxes and believed they earned as much money in four days as in five. Côté advocated the government tax regular wages but leave overtime alone if it wanted to increase production.[99]

Taxation was the main instrument to pay for the war in Canada. Whereas 55 per cent of war expenditure in Canada came from taxes, the United Kingdom's and the United States' comparable proportions were 53 and 26 per cent, respectively.[100] Taxes became increasingly onerous. In 1939 a married workingman with two children paid no income tax unless he was in the upper income brackets; if he earned $3,000 dollars, his income tax was $10. Following the Dominion-provincial Taxation Agreement Act of 1942, workingmen began to feel the government's bite. Few understood what was happening, for the government gave little priority to explaining the income tax. In 1943, after incomes had been squeezed hard, the $3,000-a-year man was paying $334 in income tax while being forced to save $1,200 under a national campaign to prevent inflation. Ingenious it may have been from the Department of Finance's perspective, but workers reacted by absenting themselves from work.[101]

In June 1943, in a brief submitted to the National War Labour Board, both the president of the Dock and Shipyard Workers Union and the chairman of the Vancouver Shipyards Union Conference claimed wages were lower than two years previously owing to taxation and the inaccuracy of the index used to determine cost-of-living bonuses.[102] Morale seems to have been pretty low. Absenteeism was particularly high at Burrard Dry Dock during June and July 1943 owing to bitter disputes over continuous production. One Sunday in mid-July, when only two rivet gangs showed up for work, over 30 per cent of the dayshift was absent.[103]

Shutting down shipyards at Quebec City for Christmas in 1942 was occasioned by something other than absenteeism. It acknowledged a cultural difference between the English and the French and also represented an attempt to overcome low morale. Harold Milne, who had lived for many years in Quebec, advised the director general of shipbuilding to agree with suggestions from all three Quebec City shipyards that they be shut down for eleven days from 24 December for Christmas and New Year's celebrations. It had been a general practice before the war. The firms would gain an opportunity to catch up on plant maintenance and machine repairs, and, if not approved, loss of manpower would probably run as high as 60 per cent.[104]

The best absentee record in 1944 was one yard with 5 per cent, and the worst was another with 15 per cent. Size of yard, location, and climate bore little relation to a yard's attendance record. Whereas the highest absentee rate occurred in the smallest yard in the merchant ship program, the largest yard, Burrard Dry Dock, was also well above the general average. Absenteeism at Victoria Machinery Depot averaged around 11 per cent; in one Quebec City yard, the absentee rate was consistently 20 to 25 per cent higher than in another yard immediately adjacent. Absenteeism at Toronto Shipbuilding Company, which was easily accessible, was almost the same as at a Quebec yard where a large proportion of the workers had to travel a considerable distance and transportation was inadequate. Although the temperature seldom rose above the freezing point during December, January, and February at Quebec, average attendance was approximately the same as in the summer, when the temperature was often uncomfortably high and probably harder to withstand. During hot August days, the temperature inside ships being fitted out while in the water could soar in excess of forty-five degrees Celcius.

About 30 or 40 per cent of absenteeism was beyond employees' control. Sickness, excused absences, injuries, accidents, and the semi-rural character of much of the workforce, especially in the Maritimes, were all reasons for justified absenteeism. The remainder occurred among a restricted group of 15 to 20 per cent of the yard strength. Although most Canadians supported the cause of defeating the Nazis, poor morale quickly surfaced among the ranks of shipyard workers bound by wage freezes, compulsory conciliation, poorly explained taxation measures, and incomprehensible regulations. Various methods were employed to combat absenteeism, including cooperation with unions, posters designed to publicize comparative absentee rates, industrial health clinics, social organizations, and suspension or discharge of chronic cases. But few proved effective.

Full-time, professionally staffed, industrial health clinics proved a very effective means to combat absenteeism. Part-time doctors in West Coast yards attended to 1,465 cases in three months, and in three months at Pictou full-time doctors treated 5,714 cases, cutting absenteeism through feigned sickness by 80 per cent. Equally important, they discovered 150 cases of serious illness and arranged 265 changes of occupations to suit the physical strength of individuals in the yards, and they cut to zero the number of industrial diseases from exposure to welding, burning, and painting.[105] But such clinics were a long time coming and never arrived at several yards.

Health and Safety

Shipyards were dangerous industrial worksites. Like war itself, they sometimes exacted the ultimate sacrifice from workers. The numbers of permanent, partial, and temporary disabilities were very high. Injured workers were not new in Canada, but the enormous increase in industrial employment between 1940 and 1943 led to great increases in the number of industrial accidents.

In 1940 the number of industrial accidents in Canada jumped 29 per cent over the previous year, and it almost doubled in 1942. The figure of 82,568 accidents reported to the Quebec Workmen's Compensation Commission during 1941 was nearly double the average annual number in the 1930s.[106] Simply put, across the country there were about ten accidents in 1942 for every six in 1939.

More than 2 million Canadian workers sustained injuries in their factories, shops, and plants during the Second World War. These are very conservative numbers. Data concerning Canadian industrial accidents were gathered from provincial workmen's compensation boards, which existed in all provinces, except for Prince Edward Island. Not all firms were registered with compensation boards, which reported only accidents to employees; injuries incurred by employers and self-employed workmen were excluded. Nevertheless, these incomplete data reveal that wartime industrial accidents included 28,648 permanent and 669,039 temporary disabilities across the country; an additional 780,762 injuries required medical aid only. These figures should be increased by about 27 per cent to account for the missing number of non-fatal injuries in Quebec.[107]

Although the federal government gathered its own data concerning fatal industrial accidents, C.D. Howe assured the general manager of the Industrial Accidents Prevention Association that his department had no interest in interfering with the work of provincial organizations or in collecting other industrial accident data.[108] The data in table 6.7 show more than twice the number of fatalities recorded by provincial workmen's compensation boards, illustrating, yet again, the incomplete nature of Canada's industrial accident statistics.

Table 6.6 | Fatal and nonfatal industrial accidents, by number and as a proportion of the civilian nonagricultural labour force, 1939–45

Year*	Total accidents	Civilian nonagricultural labour force	Percentage
1939	180,979	2,741,000	6.6
1940	233,804	2,840,000	8.2
1941	295,582	3,047,000	9.7
1942	348,795	3,295,000	10.6
1943	349,291	3,373,000	10.4
1944	322,067	3,349,000	9.6
1945	310,141	3,303,000	9.4

* As of 1 June each year.

Source: Leacy, ed., Historical Statistics of Canada, 2nd ed., D130, E376.

Table 6.7 | Industrial and shipbuilding fatalities in Canada, 1939–45

Year	Industrial deaths	Shipbuilding deaths	Percentage
1939	1,031	2	0.2
1940	1,144	11	1.0
1941	1,509	23	1.5
1942	1,457	38	2.6
1943	1,412	60	4.2
1944	1,164	26	2.2
1945	1,309	24	1.8
Total	9,026	184	2.0

Source: Compiled from Canada, Department of Labour, Labour Gazette 39–47 (1939–47).

Table 6.7 further shows that the number of fatalities in the shipbuilding industry grew steadily until 1943, when they accounted for more than 4 per cent of all industrial deaths in the country. About 70 per cent of all shipbuilding fatalities resulted from persons falling or striking (or being struck by) objects. Edouard Genest and Gérard Mariage were killed on 17 February 1943 while transferring steel by crane at Davie Shipbuilding and Repairing. It was believed that the steel, being slick with ice, slipped from the chains holding the load, releasing 3,600 pounds that fell 40 feet and struck the men.[109] Four months later, Ferdinand Turgeon, crane operator, and Elzéar St Laurent, day labourer, were killed in the same yard when a crane arm collapsed with its 12,000-pound load.[110] The first fatality at the Pictou shipyard occurred after more than two years of operation when Edward Winn lost his life after falling from a ship's deck 45 feet to the ground.[111]

Falls from one level to another or on the same level were responsible for nearly 38 per cent of all deaths, moving vehicles accounted for about 17 per cent, falling objects gave rise to about 10 per cent, and more than 6 per cent happened after workers struck objects.[112] Another 14 per cent occurred after workers came into contact with dangerous substances, which included electricity and noxious fumes or gases. Shipyard cranes and other hoisting gear accounted for 6.5 per cent of fatalities, and a variety of causes, including prime movers (e.g., belts and motors), working machines, tools, and handling objects, were responsible for the remaining deaths. The greatest wartime disaster occurred in the ship-repair industry on 6 July 1943 when the Halifax Shipyards tug *Erg* was flipped over during a collision with a merchant ship leaving Bedford Basin. Nineteen of the twenty-four men on board lost their lives en route to a repair job on a ship anchored in the harbour.[113]

Safety in the shipyards was a critical problem owing both to the scarcity of experienced workers to teach workmen safe behaviour and to the large numbers of employees without any industrial experience at all. According to Wilfrid Beaulac, chief inspector of industrial plants for Quebec's Department of Labour, inexperience, lack of discipline, poor communications, and carelessness were the chief causes of the 2,000 accidents that occurred in Quebec shipyards between 1 January 1942 and 31 July 1943.[114] Following the recent deaths of Turgeon and St Laurent at Davie, Beaulac advised the company that seven fatalities had occurred during the previous fifteen months when the company employed between 3,000 and 3,500 men. This record, he stated, was "double and even triple the fatal accidents in other yards," and, he concluded, "the workers in your shipyard work in the worst possible conditions still existing."[115]

From 1940 to 1943, workers were hired at a rate that made real safety education impossible even if competent staff had been available. Moreover, worker safety was not a priority in the eyes of the federal government or of owners struggling to expand their yards and increase production. In 1942 Beaulac complained to his superior of his helplessness in the face of shipyard companies' resistance to adoption of hard hats and safety boots.[116] George Pearson, British Columbia's minister of labour, blamed employers for not checking the age of boys employed in the yards following the death of a fourteen year old in a Vancouver shipyard. Despite charging the National Selection Service with ignoring the British Columbia Factories Act, he admitted it was difficult to prosecute employers who had been permitted to hire boys less than fifteen years of age.[117] Safety was not a prevalent concern in the masculine working-class culture even among trade unionists.

Workers and union leaders did not question management's right to establish safe working conditions; indeed, they believed it was management's responsibility. To suggest otherwise might force workers to admit, as management often charged, that industrial accidents were primarily due to worker carelessness. Although management claimed the right to establish working conditions, it placed little emphasis on safety and much on increased productivity. The first meeting of the safety committee at Davie Shipbuilding and Repairing occurred only in March 1943.[118] Efforts to improve worker safety and occupational health were chiefly owed to provincial workmen's compensation boards, which assumed no-fault compensation. Their concern stemmed from growing anxiety about the rising costs of compensation claims and medical treatment rather than from an interest in the relief of pain and suffering or in worker health.[119]

The number of nonfatal accidents and permanent, partial, and temporary disabilities in Canada's shipyards remains largely unknown except for some anecdotal evidence, but data from American shipyards encouraged an attempt to estimate these numbers. During 1943 there were 102,500 disabling work injuries in US private shipyards. Of these, 0.5 per cent were fatal and 1.2 per cent resulted in permanent physical impairment. Also, twenty days were lost on average for every disabling injury incurred.[120] In brief, for every shipyard fatality, there were 199 nonfatal injuries, of which nearly 3 resulted in permanent disability. The twelve-month average injury-frequency rate in US shipyards in 1943 was 31.2.[121] This means that there were 31.2 fatal and nonfatal injuries for every 1 million employee-hours worked.

Assuming that Canadian shipyard-accident rates were similar to or higher than American ones and that the Canadian industry employed about one-eighteenth of the number employed in the United States, I multiplied by 200 the average annual number of shipbuilding deaths during the period 1940–45 taken from table 6.7 (30.3), which yielded 6,060 permanent and temporary physical-impairment injuries annually. These injuries do not include the much larger number that required medical aid only. Multiplying this estimated number of injuries by twenty days lost for recovery suggests that in 1943 about 121,200 employee-days were lost because of injuries sustained in Canadian shipyards. This is a very conservative estimate.

Twenty-eight accidents occurred at George T. Davie and Sons during the first eight months of 1941. Although none was fatal or led to permanent disability, they resulted in 843 working days lost, which yielded an accident-frequency rate of 54.4.[122] In 1942, the 1,090 accidents at Davie Shipbuilding and Repairing that were reported to the Commission des accidents du travail for compensation resulted in 18,064 man-days lost, equivalent to sixty workers absent every day of the year, or 16.6 man-days lost for each reported accident. This actually represented an improvement compared to 1941, when 1,092 accidents occurred, although fewer workers were employed in the yard. Evidence from Marine Industries Limited for the first nine months of 1944 indicates that 106 disabling accidents led to 4,670 days lost, averaging 44 man-days lost each.[123] The monetary cost of these injuries could be determined given sufficient data, but the suffering can never be evaluated, nor can future economic losses arising from deaths and permanent disability.[124]

After hearing representations concerning the prevention of accidents and establishment of sanitary conditions to safeguard employee health, the royal commission on shipbuilding in Quebec and Ontario reported in November 1941 that "in various yards the provisions so far made for these purposes [leave] much to be desired."[125] A one-day strike by welders at Collingwood Shipyards Limited in July 1942 over management's treatment of one of their number who attempted to seek treatment for an

A riveter proud of his work, probably taken at Victoria Machinery Depot. City of Victoria Archives, Photographic Archives, no. PR 264.

injury led to a full-scale inspection of conditions there by officials of the Ontario Department of Health and the Workmen's Compensation Board. In addition to inadequate toilet facilities and a poorly supplied first-aid shack, inspectors found several health hazards and instructed vice president and general manager John S. Leitch to attend to them immediately. Insufficient supplies of fresh air to ship compartments where welders were at work left them breathing carbon monoxide and nitrous fumes and susceptible to lead poisoning. In the pipe-bending shop, workers were susceptible to silicosis. Along with more detailed instructions, Leitch was ordered to bring the shipyard into accord with the Ontario Factory Act.[126]

Even after shipbuilding programs were well advanced and yards were approaching peak strength, first-aid departments were understaffed and facilities remained inadequate. In March 1942, at Burrard Dry Dock North Yard, which employed about 3,000 workers, the first-aid station treated an average of 1,300 workers per month. Chief medical attendant J.F. Livesy treated about 40 workers daily, chiefly for small cuts, bruised fingers, burned forearms, and tiny steel slivers in their eyes.[127] The Vancouver Metal Trades Council advised the National War Labour Board in May 1943 that recommendations made the previous August in the report of the royal commission chaired by Mr Justice Stephen E. Richards concerning improvements in sanitary working conditions in BC shipyards had not been implemented.[128]

Although the combination of accelerated production and employment of inexperienced workers resulted in an increased incidence of work injuries in the yards, the failure of federal agencies such as the Department of Labour, the DMS, Wartime Merchant Shipping Limited, and the RCN to insist on the establishment and maintenance of safety organizations adequate to cope with occupational health also contributed to the bloodletting. The slow growth of safety awareness among management and the need to create a safe work environment to prevent accidents and injuries contributed to the relatively high incidence of work injuries in Canadian yards.

The number of shipyard injuries may have been far higher during the early years, before any safety programs were implemented and when there was less appreciation of the effect of accidents on production and productivity. A safety program introduced at St John Dry Dock and Shipbuilding in October 1942 immediately reduced the number of monthly compensation cases from 127 to 79, of which 34 were lost-time cases and 45 were doctors' cases. A year later, the total number of compensation cases had fallen to 49, of which only 24 were of the lost-time category.[129]

Shipyard injury rates were far higher in Canadian than in US yards. The average accident-frequency rate in American yards during the first eight months of 1943 held fairly constant at about 33 disabling injuries for every 1 million employee-hours worked, whereas the rate for eight shipyards on Canada's West Coast was an appalling 119.7 during the first six months of the same year. Individual yard rates ranged from a low of 70.5 (more than twice the average rate in American yards) to a high of 144.1. By contrast, the frequency rate for St John Dry Dock and Shipbuilding, which was chiefly engaged in repairing ships during the same six-month period, was a poor 56.1. Huge manufacturing plants in the United States had six-month accident-frequency rates raging from 0 to 22.[130]

Riveters frequently suffered injuries to elbow and shoulder joints owing to continuous vibration and repeated impacts, during which these joints received maximum stresses and strains. Little investigation of these injuries was ever carried out in Canada, but a purloined document that survives in the archives of the Trade Union Research Bureau reveals that during 1943 and the first half of 1944 at Yarrows Limited, approximately 50 per cent of riveters employed at No. 2 Yard suffered burnout, while 22 per cent were played out at No. 1 Yard.[131]

Welders suffered from two kinds of injuries: flash burns to eyes and inhalation of poisonous gases. Flash burns caused to the white, or conjunctiva, of the eye from exposure to the welding arc's ultraviolet light also injured workers nearby. Testifying before the Richards royal commission in July 1942, welder Clifford A. Knight from Burrard Dry Dock South Yard condemned the hazardous breathing conditions in the yard and the poor ventilation system. Using compressed air to blow fumes away stirred up dust and rust, which workers inhaled.[132] Welding fumes were of two or three kinds. First, zinc oxide fumes from welding galvanized steel in warships produced metal-fume fever, or the zinc "shakes." Air masks were required. Second, ferric

Woman shipyard workers eating lunch in a lifeboat on a Victory ship under construction at Burrard Dry Dock Company, May 1943. Gentility had not entirely disappeared, as shown by the one woman who has brought a teacup to work. Photo by Joseph Gibson. NFB/LAC, WRM 5203.

oxide given off by boiled iron in electric arc welding if breathed in sufficient quantities in close spaces, such as in double bottoms, could cause a cough producing blood traces. Treatment was removal from the environment.[133] Third, although painters were supposed to leave bare metal for welders, errors occurred. Welders normally burned off any paint in order to clear welding surfaces. Lead poisoning from burning red lead priming off metal to be welded was possible, although the reported incidence was low.[134]

No data have been discovered about women's injuries in Canadian shipyards, but in US yards women experienced relatively more disabling injuries than did men in nearly every department. Unaccustomed to strenuous work involving larger body muscles, women suffered proportionately more strains and sprains, particularly of the back. They also injured legs and feet through falls much more frequently than did men. Analysts in the American Labor Bureau's industrial-hazards division attributed this higher accident rate among females to the need to climb about ships' hulls and frequently to work in strained and awkward positions. Women were entirely without industrial experience, and unsure footing seemed to be one of their greatest difficulties.[135]

Well-organized safety programs were not in effect throughout the country before the spring of 1943. Provincial jurisdictions ensured that no standard organization ever appeared. Some small yards that did not have a safety director assisted by a staff of safety inspectors relied upon the ability or conscientiousness of the company's personnel director. In some cases, safety committees whose members were drawn from among workers and unions supplemented company organizations, making weekly tours under the direction of inspectors and identifying and dealing with hazards.

Larger yards employed doctors who were in charge of well-equipped first-aid departments assisted by registered nurses. In the summer of 1943, the Pictou shipyard established the first industrial health clinic of its kind in the Maritimes, staffed by a physician and four nurses. During May 1944 an intensive campaign against eye accidents reduced the monthly incidence by one-quarter. But even so, the number of eye injuries was 494![136] During a three-week period later the same year, 723 accidents still occurred at Pictou, resulting in 28,424 man-days lost; 348 eye injuries accounted for nearly half of all the injuries.[137] In this example, more than 39 man-days were lost for each disabling injury in the yard.

Safety programs promoted, encouraged, and stressed the use of personal equipment. Helmets, safety boots, eye-protection equipment, and gloves were made available but were not always supplied gratis. Some companies required workers to pay for them. In July 1943 Davie Shipbuilding and Repairing procured 100 hard hats and charged workers $3.70 each.[138] Workers were also notoriously at fault for removing guards from machinery, and only conscientious foremen had them replaced. Nevertheless, eye-protection equipment, hard hats, safety boots, masks, and goggles were well received. By 1944 flash burns had ceased to be a problem among welders. Steel-toed safety boots had also become fairly common, greatly minimizing the effect of many accidents, although it must be admitted that women, if they were provided boots at all, had to wear men's small sizes because the Safety Shoe Company of Canada had no lasts for female boots. Curiously, men were reluctant to wear protective headgear, first called crash helmets, so foreign was it to shipyards. Adoption in Canada was disappointing compared to in the United States, and the frequency of head injuries remained high in Canadian yards.[139] One possible reason for this behaviour may have been the strong influence of British workers, who wore cloth caps on the job.

On 8 April 1943 the BC Workmen's Compensation Board published *Ship-Construction Accident Prevention Regulations* in an effort to stem the tide of injuries. The regulations made employers responsible for informing workers of the hazards of their employment and for seeing that safety rules were observed. Employers were to provide first-aid equipment, and workers were required to use all safety devices provided and to comply with the 136 regulations, which covered a host of dangerous conditions dealing with staging, stairways, ladders, runways, openings, cranes, derricks, materials handling, forges, clothing, ventilation, air and gas lines, and other items.[140] Company and government actions almost halved the number of accidents by the spring of 1945. The BC Workmen's Compensation Board claimed the shipyard accident rate fell from 5 per cent to 3.4 per cent, resulting in a savings to the yards from this reduction alone of $540,000.[141]

Safe working conditions might have improved worker morale in the shipyards, but accident-frequency rates suggest that safety engineers fought a losing battle during most of the war. In May 1945 management at Davie Shipbuilding and Repairing, now convinced of the merits of industrial safety measures, pleaded with workmen to wear goggles and safety boots and complained that too many injured men left the yard without reporting their injury.[142] Rather than insisting that management provide a safe work environment, the federal government made efforts to combat low morale among war workers that were generally crude and patronizing, varying from attempts to shame workers into higher production (by stressing that each small sacrifice or act of patriotism would lead to eventual victory over tyranny) to coercing workers to remain at their workplaces or face immediate call-up.[143] Manipulation of worker opinion through screening specially made movies in the yards, poster campaigns, and other devices was thought sufficient to maintain an acquiescent workforce in the face of a rising wave of strikes that swept the country in 1942 and 1943. At no time did federal government officials and politicians consider that increased worker safety and improved labour relations might increase production.

Housing, Victory Bonds, and Patriotism

The sudden expansion of industry for wartime production put impossible pressures on municipalities across the country for extra housing for the migrating workers who flooded in. This proved especially true for communities where shipyards were located. Whether in large cities like Vancouver or small towns like Pictou, private industry failed to meet the wartime demand for housing. It could not have been otherwise in view of the government's control of banking and finance and of the construction industry. Prewar conditions compounded the rapidly worsening situation. The Depression had seen a serious deterioration of the existing stock of dwellings and a major decline in new house construction. Overcrowding and doubling-up of families already existed. Thus, at the beginning of the war, deferred residential construction, substandard accommodation, and overcrowding were already in place, to be made worse by the pressures from migrating workers.[144]

In the autumn of 1940 the Economic Advisory Committee, which had direct access to the Cabinet War Committee, recognized that the housing shortage was impeding war production, that private industry could not meet the need for accommodation, and that the government would have to provide housing for war workers. In November rumours reached the timber controller, Harvey R. MacMillan, that between 3,000 and 5,000 houses might be required to accommodate workmen at new wartime industrial plants being established in remoter places and that as recently as three weeks prior, the DMS had given no consideration to the problem.[145] Early the next year, however, the DMS began to restrict civilian building in order to divert materials and labour into wartime housing and on 24 February 1941 ordered the incorporation of Wartime Housing Limited to build temporary housing for war-production workers. In a marked change from the recent past, the new program came under the Department of Munitions and Supply, but bowing to pressure from the Department of Finance and from business interests, the government retreated from its initial plan to terminate its prewar housing program and emphasized the temporary nature of the new housing.[146]

The problem of housing war workers already existed in urban areas. In April 1940 the Halifax District Trades and Labour Council had protested the rising rents that accompanied the housing shortage to Premier Angus L. Macdonald and the City Council, but nothing was done.[147] By January 1941 Halifax, normally with a population of 60,000 people, was swollen to 100,000 permanent and transient residents without any significant increase in housing. Owing to the impermanence of the population and to rent controls, no private construction was going on, nor was there likely to be any in the future. Recently arrived shipyard workers were living in substandard accommodations in basements and attics.

There was no room for housing at the naval dockyard, but on inspection, Howard T. Mitchell, special representative to MacMillan, who was also chairman of the War Requirements Board, found good space at the north end of the Halifax Shipyards property adjoining the dockyard to lodge approximately 1,000 shipbuilding workers. In an attempt to keep spending as low as possible, government policy was to house workers in barracks; Mitchell recommended building bunkhouse-type accommodation and setting up a dining concession.[148] Wartime Housing Limited was awarded its first contract to house Halifax Shipyard workers on 27 March 1941. It called for construction of 225 houses and 4 bunkhouses worth a half-million dollars and was completed in two and a half months.[149] At St John, where the population had not increased, the housing shortage remained manageable. Mitchell thought 200 or 300 men could find rooming-house accommodation, but he saw an advantage in concentrating the labour pool at St John Dry Dock and Shipbuilding in a similar bunkhouse scheme and employing trucks to transport men to the St John Iron Works plant.[150] The bunkhouses, soon to be called "staff houses," were quickly constructed.

C.D. Howe hired Joseph M. Piggott, a Hamilton contractor and president of Piggott Construction Limited, as president and appointed a board of directors comprised of architects, businessmen, and a labour representative. Between 1941 and 1945 Wartime Housing Limited built 16,869 temporary houses for war workers as well as staff houses, schools, fire halls, pump houses, garages, community centres, and office buildings.[151] But this number could not begin to accommodate the thousands of workers who poured into Canada's cities and towns. Moreover, the government's policy of leaving the Department of Finance free to administer its prewar housing policy while authorizing expenditure of $50 million under Wartime Housing Limited on workers' housing encouraged rivalry between civil servants and businessmen over the issue of whether to provide temporary or social housing that continually muddied the waters throughout the war.[152]

Between September 1941 and September 1942, Wartime Housing Limited reached agreements with both the city and district of North Vancouver respecting land transfers, payments in lieu of taxes, services, and postwar disposal and supervised construction of 683 houses in the home of Burrard Dry Dock Company and of North Van Ship Repairs. The Crown corporation also assisted in building an eight-room school and adding to another.[153]

As hundreds of workers poured into Pictou, nearly trebling the small town's peacetime population of 3,000, the struggle for accommodation became a weary daily chore for workmen moving from house to house seeking a place to stay after finishing an eight-hour shift in the shipyard.[154] Board and lodging were at a premium; rents rose rapidly. Men with cars drove miles into the countryside to find lodging. Large houses were converted to apartments. Shacks, tents, and trailers blossomed on vacant lots. Buildings vacant for years were swiftly tarted up for rent. At the same time, new stores and new restaurants opened. Housewives competed with workers for groceries, and after a large contingent of Cape Bretoners arrived and began working, the post office was daily challenged to deliver mail to the correct "Macdonald." The lack of accommodation became so severe that the shipyard refused to hire men who did not already have lodging of some sort.[155]

In April 1942 MacMillan strongly criticized the refusal of Wartime Housing Limited officials to pay attention to recommendations from Wartime Merchant Shipping Limited as to the number of men who should be accommodated in a certain district, claiming serious delays to shipbuilding had occurred in Prince Rupert, North Vancouver, Pictou, and Sorel.[156] The large number of ship sinkings in February and March undoubtedly lay behind MacMillan's criticism, but there was some basis for it. Testifying before the Richard's royal commission on continuous production nearly six months later, management and union officials blamed inadequate housing as being chiefly responsible for the lack of manpower in British Columbia's shipyards, especially for the 1,400 shipyard workers at Prince Rupert.[157]

Wartime Housing Limited provided some temporary housing at Lévis and Sorel, where thousands of workers were toiling at Davie Shipbuilding and Repairing and at Marine Industries Limited. About 150 houses were constructed to the east of the big Davie yard at Lauzon, but the number was inadequate.[158] It is doubtful whether the Crown corporation alleviated any of the housing shortage at Sorel. Of 15,802 wartime houses built before 11 June 1943, only 2,232, or 14.1 per cent, were located in Quebec.[159]

In the spring of 1942 Wartime Housing Limited began erecting 400 prefabricated bungalows at Pictou, creating Victory Heights at the east end of the town. The houses were prefabricated at New Glasgow and trucked to Pictou. A new school was built, as well as a staff house for single men. This grew to three bunkhouses with a large commissary. Two additional staff houses were completed later, and finally, a large recreational hall equipped with bowling alleys, a basketball court, which could be used as a gymnasium and auditorium, and several small meeting rooms was erected. Such a building went a long way to making the shipyard more of a community, uniting workers from many Nova Scotia towns, villages, and farms.[160] Similar situations occurred at St John, where housing and at least three staff houses offering room and board to single workers for $8.50 per week were erected in East St John near the dry dock.[161] But whatever occurred in the rest of Canada, Wartime Housing Limited failed to relieve the housing situation at Halifax. Although the Crown corporation eventually constructed 1,472 prefabricated houses in the area and all but 220 were occupied by war workers, conditions deteriorated steadily during five years of war, doubtless contributing to the notorious riots on VE Day.[162]

Along with raising taxes to pay for the war and the government's compulsory savings program, the victory-bond program was designed primarily to take money out of the economy in order to restrict civilian demand for goods and prevent inflation. According to Wendy Cuthbertson, the government's policy to borrow from the

A crowd gathers on 21 October 1944 (Trafalgar Day) in anticipation of the launch of SS *Ashby Park*, the 20th 4,700-ton cargo ship built by Foundation Maritime Limited at Pictou, Nova Scotia, and the 993rd ship built in Canada. The sign on the ship's side reads "Invest in Victory" to mark the opening of the seventh victory-loan campaign. Photo by Waisman. NFB/LAC, WRM 5207.

people was "almost unbelievably successful," and with strict wage and price controls, the program virtually eliminated inflation after 1941.[163] By the end of that year, the initial weaknesses of the programs to promote war savings certificates and war savings stamps had been recognized and merged with the victory-bond program under the new War Finance Committee. From the second victory-loan campaign in the spring of 1942 to the ninth victory loan in the fall of 1945, Canadian men, women, and children, who numbered only 11.5 million, loaned their government more than $11.5 billion.[164]

The National War Finance Committee marketed victory bonds according to the latest techniques, including public-opinion polling, sophisticated propaganda, appeals to local pride and self-interest, saturation marketing (including on-the-job canvassing), and pressure selling. Resistance was minimal and market penetration was close to 100 per cent. Nevertheless, some evidence suggests that Canadians, especially those in receipt of low wages, were not as enamoured with the government's demands as authorities would have liked. Some bonds were purchased under coercion, and some workers quickly cashed in bonds after campaigns concluded.[165] Shipyard workers provided one of the few examples of this resistance, although a threat to their beer supply was the immediate cause. In March 1943, as the fourth victory-loan campaign got under way, Vancouver shipyard workers set up signs and donned lapel pins warning "No beer, no bonds." The move, a response to the federal government's attempt to cut back alcohol consumption by introducing rationing, was followed by other workers across the country. The government took seriously the threat to the loan campaign, moderated its rationing program, and returned responsibility for the cutback to the provinces, which traditionally controlled liquour sales.[166]

Unions and companies were enthusiastic participants in victory-loan campaigns, building floats for parades and encouraging employees to buy bonds. At Victoria Machinery Depot, Pat Campbell of the plate shop rode the company float in the seventh victory-loan parade gowned in white satin as Britannia escorted by four men representing a soldier, sailor, airman, and shipyard worker (a riveter, of course).[167] But workers themselves may have been less enthusiastic. During the fifth victory-loan campaign in the fall of 1943, speakers at Davie Shipbuilding and Repairing implored workers to keep their bonds and not to cash them. Although the shipyard exceeded its objective by 20 per cent, several groups of workers – stagers, riveters, bolters-up, carpenters, labourers, pipefitters, rivet passers, and coppersmiths – contributed just 40 to 80 per cent of their targets. Resistance to the hard sell may also have been present at St John Dry Dock and Shipbuilding.

St John employees bought only $23,000 worth of bonds during the third victory-loan campaign, but with an improved sales organization set up under the personnel department with one sales person for every ten employees during the fourth and fifth campaigns, they purchased $85,000 and $106,000 in bonds, respectively. But the company never won the coveted three-star victory-loan pennant to fly over the firm's premises. The pennant indicated 90 per cent coverage had been achieved. The high mark, achieved during the fifth victory loan, attracted only three-quarters of the workers.[168] The growing transient nature of the workforce after 1943 as men left to farm and fish or to join the armed services may partially account for the lack of saturation coverage.

Shipyards encouraged the social life of all their employees in many ways. They fostered formation of sports associations, organized teams, and sponsored tournaments, hobby meetings, and choirs. Employees formed dance bands and orchestras. North Van Ship Repairs even had a pipe band. At Prince Rupert, with a prewar population of less than 6,700, dances were held every second Saturday, when a dry-dock orchestra played for as many as 700 in attendance. The companies also published journals and in-house newspapers that warrant close examination not only for the historical information often found nowhere else but also because they reveal much about life in the yards and something about management's concerns and fears. Pages are filled with in-house news and gossip, health hints and morale-boosting messages for wartime employees, jokes, cartoons, patriotic poems, movie reviews, and pictures of ship launchings and personnel. They contain informative articles about work going on in the various departments of the yards and, let it be acknowledged, repeatedly stress safety. Above all, they were clearly intended to deliver management's point of view to workers, to persuade them of their importance to the larger picture of the war effort, and to compete with union organizers.

One clear aim was to connect workers to the ships they were building and to the men at sea. Honour rolls of former workers currently in the armed services were quickly introduced in several journals to raise patriotic sentiment and connect workers to the war. West Coast Shipbuilders Limited had a servicemen's union that counted more than 700 veterans of the First World War on the payroll. The presence of a Victoria Cross holder among them did not go unannounced or unnoticed.[169] These men undoubtedly exerted a strong steadying influence on younger men and checked the activities of radical labour organizers in some of the yards. At St John Dry Dock and Shipbuilding the connection was made through a "Penny-a-Day" cigarette fund to buy smokes for former employees currently overseas; the bimonthly *Dry Dock Bulletin*, which began to appear in September 1943, gave a regular accounting of the fund's status.

The *Wallace Shipbuilder*, house organ of Burrard Dry Dock Company, began publication in July 1942; during its peak period, it reached 13,000 employees and included technical articles on shipbuilding as well as the usual social and recreational features.[170] The *Compass*, published by Toronto Shipbuilding Company, printed a monthly news column about the Yard Council, a labour-management committee set up in 1941.[171]

L'Écho maritime appeared at Davie Shipbuilding and Repairing as early as February 1943. Less substantial than some other journals, it tended to hector and admonish employees about safety, carefully recording monthly accident statistics, lost man-days, and workers' attendance. The misnamed *L'Écho de la marine* of Marine Industries Limited appeared on 16 March 1944, replacing an earlier paper that had been published during the previous two years. Its first issue was labelled volume 3 to acknowledge this earlier journal, of which only one number has survived. Initially inserted in *Le Courrier de Sorel* two Thursdays a month, by July it took the form of a tabloid distributed to workers leaving the plant on Friday afternoons; on 1 September it became a weekly.[172] Its content differed little from other shipyard newspapers across the country. Page 1 was devoted to a photo essay and biographies of a particular department and its foreman, as well as to news of contracts, victory-bond campaigns, and other events affecting all employees. Page 2 was reserved for official opinions from management, while the remaining two pages were devoted to professional matters, social news, and sports events. During its existence, *L'Écho de la marine* regularly highlighted work accidents, training, blood donation, and suggestions to increase productivity. "Nos Marinettes" was a weekly photo of a young female employee – a modest head-and-shoulders portrait – no bathing beauties at Sorel. And in a lighter vein, the paper also published marriage and birth announcements.

Thousands of shipyard workers were often in their first, full-time jobs. Most were unskilled, new employees, frequently from farms or small towns, strangers to Canada's largest cities, and far from home. Like ship launchings, victory-bond campaigns, ceremonies, and visits to the yards by American movie stars, high-ranking military officers, politicians, and often quiet shy young war heroes, shipyard journals were carefully designed to combat loneliness and encourage a sense of belonging and participation. How much they helped to overcome hostility and alienation brought on by wage freezes and incomprehensible regulations remains moot. Shipyard journals attempted to meet management's need to get workers on their side, but too often editorials chivvied workers to participate by sending news for the journals to publish, to buy victory bonds, to shun absenteeism, to work hard and safely, and to get involved. But such injunctions had their limits, especially in view of the government's appalling industrial-relations policy. Most Canadian shipyard workers wanted to contribute to the fight against the Nazis, but many did not know for whom they were working, or why, or for what. Alone, many workers had only the unions to turn to, but many remained as suspicious of them as of the bosses. The government probably had the greatest impact on worker morale. Wage rates and disputes over wage differentials were important causes of unrest, although foot-dragging by companies over job classifications was also a major cause of job dissatisfaction. The message that fair treatment might yield large results never reached the policymakers, and government labour-relations policy remained behind most worker unrest and undermined all efforts to raise morale.

Organizing Shipyard Labour

Introduction

Canada was still experiencing large-scale unemployment when war broke out, and during the next eighteen months, men responded positively to new work opportunities, happy to have a job. As men entered the armed services in growing numbers, further shrinking the pool of unemployed men, better wages and improved working conditions were negotiable. Craft unions allied with the Trades and Labour Congress of Canada, which was affiliated with the American Federation of Labor (AFL), had signed agreements in several shipyards across the country. Workers in British Columbia were relatively well organized in Locals 1 and 2 of the Boilermakers and Iron Shipbuilders Union of Canada (BISUC), located in Vancouver and Victoria, respectively. Late in 1939 the secretary of Local 1 asked Norman Dowd, secretary of the All Canadian Congress of Labour (ACCL), whether something could be done to organize the shipbuilding industry in the rest of the country, as wages paid in the East were way below those paid in the West: "[This] creates a bogey between us and the employer whenever wages were discussed."[1] Dowd replied that the congress had recently increased its levy on members in order to "extend very considerably" its organizing activities: "we will endeavour to do something with the shipbuilding industry in the east."[2] With the exception of British Columbia, small AFL-affiliated, craft-based union locals generally dominated shipyards in Canada. One of these was the International Brotherhood of Boilermakers, Iron Shipbuilders, Welders and Helpers of America (hereafter International Brotherhood of Boilermakers).

Unlike the International Association of Machinists, an AFL affiliate that quickly organized new wartime aircraft-industry workers, the International Brotherhood of Boilermakers was slow to organize workers in the shipbuilding industry. The Vancouver local was not well adapted to the war situation, which may have been true of others around the country. Its sickness insurance and pension schemes involved the membership in high initiation fees, and high monthly dues did not appeal to young people entering the yards. Moreover, the great majority of union members were employed in railway locomotive shops. Local leaders soon found the new situation intolerable and quit.[3] Subsequently, the BISUC came to play a prominent role there and in many other yards. But the war years were chaotic, and labour organizers had not

Riveter Lorenzo Periard trimming rivets while helper André Chausée bucks them from inside the bottom section of a water-tube boiler at Canadian Vickers Limited, September 1943. Photo by Ronny Jaques. NFB/LAC, WRM 4169.

achieved unity before the war ended: far from it. The reasons for this labour unrest are explored in this chapter, and an assessment of organized labour's role among shipyard workers is attempted.

Only after the merchant shipbuilding program in Quebec and British Columbia and other war industries had taken up most available skilled labour across the country did industrial relations in the shipbuilding industry begin to deteriorate. This unrest was largely due to the government's stubborn adherence to obsolete labour policies, to the savage hostility toward labour of businessmen, industrialists, and major social institutions, including most churches and the press, and to competition within the labour movement itself.

Some historians consider the war years to have ended a decade-long watershed during which Canadian labour had achieved a breakthrough that gave unions a place, however constricted, in Canada's economy.[4] Although this may hold true generally, the evidence from the shipbuilding industry provides a contrary interpretation that stresses confusion, betrayal, and conflict rather than unity and breakthrough. During the Depression and early war years, the Canadian labour movement was in disarray. Religion, language, the nature of work, and labour relations deeply divided Canadian workers. By 1939 no less than four central organizations sought to represent working-men. All were present to a greater or lesser degree in the nation's shipyards.

The Trades and Labour Congress of Canada (TLC), affiliated with the American Federation of Labor, was the first and oldest. It was also the largest labour central in Canada. During the war, its membership grew more than two and a half times.[5] Forces within the AFL during the 1930s, however, had given rise to a strong indus-trial-union movement, known as the Congress of Industrial Organizations (CIO), that greatly increased conflict in the labour movement.

The second central was the All Canadian Congress of Labour, founded in 1927 by communists and nationalist unions expelled from the TLC for advocating national and industrial unionism. Led by the Canadian Brotherhood of Railway Employees, the ACCL was committed to industrial unionism. In 1939 the AFL ordered the TLC, which it treated as just another US state labour federation, to expel Canadian locals of the CIO, and in September the following year, most of these isolated unions joined the ACCL to form a new central, the Canadian Congress of Labour (CCL).[6] During the founding convention, social-democratic trade unionists, many of them allied to a political party, the Co-operative Commonwealth Federation (CCF), gained control after a fierce struggle with communist union leaders, but the seeds of continuing conflict between some unions and the central were firmly planted.[7] Membership in the two main labour centrals, which accounted for less than two-thirds of all trade unionists in 1939, grew to include over four-fifths by 1946.[8]

The Confédération des travailleurs catholique du Canada/Canadian and Cath-olic Confederation of Labour (CTCC/CCCL), founded in 1921 under the auspices of the Roman Catholic Church, was the third central. Fearing that its social doctrines concerning relations between capital and labour were not being heard in Quebec, the church had initiated the labour organization. Although an anomaly in the North American labour movement, the CTCC represented nearly one-third of all organ-ized workers in the province of Quebec in 1940.[9] During the 1930s Catholic trade unions adopted a corporatist view of social relations.[10] Corporatism was fiercely antidemocratic and anti-individualistic, professing a collectivist view of society that called for the integration of labour and capital into the state. Corporatists believed that incorporating competing economic interests would resolve conflict and achieve social harmony. In 1942 the CTCC adopted a corporatist platform, opposing strikes and abuses of capitalism and enjoining collaboration between workers and manage-ment.[11] During the war the Catholic syndicates generally remained passive in the face of government labour policy but did play a minor role among the employees of Marine Industries Limited.[12]

In 1936 a split occurred in the executive of the ACCL over its amalgamation with some CIO unions, resulting in the re-establishment of a new, emasculated Canadian Federation of Labour (CFL). Its directorate was fiercely pro-British, pro-government, anticommunist, and anti-American. It had few members, who were chiefly left over from the One Big Union and from some local building-trades unions in Toronto, Winnipeg, and Vancouver. This fourth central would scarcely deserve mention if members of the Amalgamated Building Workers Union had not been active in BC shipyards: unit 1, pattern-makers union; unit 2, shipwrights, caulkers, and joiners union; and unit 4, welders and burners union.[13]

Finally, there was the Communist Party of Canada, which linked radical nationalism and communist leadership. Although the Workers' Unity League, the party's labour voice and instrument for organizing labour, had been abolished in 1935 on orders from Moscow and the government had abolished the party shortly after the outbreak of war, communist union organizers infiltrated union locals everywhere. Their dedication, hard work, and organizing skill led them to gain influential leadership positions in several unions and locals by the time war began.[14]

The four central labour organizations reflected a host of confusing, contradictory ideas, thus undermining the achievement of unity in the Canadian labour movement. Nowhere was this more apparent than among the thousands of shipyard workers who found themselves toiling in different labour traditions across the country.

Against this chaotic situation stood industrial employers, well organized by the Canadian Manufacturers Association, which in turn exerted a strong influence on the press and in the corridors of power on individual members of Parliament, the government, and its major institutions. Although the federal government continually denied it, little evidence can be adduced that it was anything but hostile to labour.[15] In contrast to both Great Britain and the United States, where labour played important roles in central administrative planning of war production, the Canadian government excluded worker representatives from wartime decision making.[16] Any representation Canadian trade unionists found on the National Labour Supply Council, on national and regional wartime labour boards set up to handle wage controls, or on the boards of directors of Crown corporations was ineffectual and powerless.[17] The federal government sought to restrict further the power of labour unions by introducing the Wartime Prices and Trade Board in 1939, which was in charge of a sweeping system of wage controls, and the National War Labour Board in 1941. The latter, especially by its partisan nature and failure to act quickly to render decisions on applications put before it, promoted strife. Although it may be extreme to assert that government officials and politicians were in complete support of employers in war industries who refused to deal with worker representatives, it is nearly true.[18]

Wartime labour ministers were weak. Norman McLarty, KC, appointed in September 1939, was an unknown corporate lawyer and party man who drank too much. With personal ties to Wallace Campbell, president of Ford of Canada, he enjoyed socializing with the rich. In 1940 he declined to enforce a new provision in the criminal code designed to protect workers from dismissal for trade-union activity at John Inglis Company.[19] Beyond the fact that McLarty sat for Windsor, Ontario, he had little sympathy for and less understanding of the workingman.[20] Humphrey Mitchell, appointed his successor on 15 December 1941, was an old-line trade unionist from the ranks of the TLC. Although he had served the government on several boards and commissions, he was ill equipped – indeed, it might be said, utterly incompetent – to speak for labour in the rapidly changing times of growing industrial unionism and war production.[21] Mitchell's equivocating rendered him ineffectual in Cabinet, and he was significantly not a member of the Cabinet War Committee. Far from being labour's advocate in the government, some shipyard unions denounced Mitchell as constituting "a major obstacle to national unity and harmonious labour relations."[22] The relative weakness of the Department of Labour vis-à-vis three strong departments – Finance, Munitions and Supply, and National Defence – effectively undermined attempts to mobilize Canada's human resources during the war. With weak ministers, labour officials could approach industrial relations only on an ad hoc basis largely devoid of policy.[23]

C.D. Howe's biographers claim he was not antilabour but, indeed, was more enlightened than the Canadian industrialists around him.[24] But this is a biased view; just because Howe said he was not against labour does not make it so. Howe's behaviour during the Arvida strike in July 1941, when he willingly accepted dishonest reports from corporate executives and blackmailed the Cabinet into giving him power to call out troops (bypassing the attorney general of the province), was not

Workers guide a crane and fix deck bolts during construction of a frigate at Canadian Vickers Limited, September 1943. Photo by Ronny Jaques. NFB/LAC, WRM 4180.

the conduct of a moderate man.[25] Howe's appointment of Howard Chase, an old-line railway-union official, as his labour advisor was a provocation to the organizers of new industrial unions. Howe's views were very old-fashioned, which is the best that can be said about them. He never thought labour's voice had any place in war-production policy.

Shipyard workers, often embarked on their first jobs, faced a bewildering situation in which employers were hostile, craft unions shut them out, and internecine strife characterized the labour movement, while the government delayed, prevaricated, and obfuscated. It was quite likely that the vast body of workers did not understand the orders-in-council, the new income taxes on their wages, or interpretations of new laws that froze wages.

Compulsory conciliation was the government's chief tool to avoid strikes during the war. According to Jeremy Webber, compulsory conciliation was a malaise that lay in the government's preoccupation with strike prevention and reluctance to grapple with the substance of labour issues. Its refusal to give direction to boards of concilia-tion or to establish standards and a policy of appointing judges in order to appear impartial led to the adjudication of disputes by lawyers rather than attempts to find workable settlements. Above all, compulsory conciliation was flexible, promoted mediation of disputes, and delayed and postponed work stoppages. Direct interven-tion was rare. Conciliation boards could only recommend solutions to the minister and later to the National War Labour Board, which often took months to reach a par-ticular decision. Owing to such behaviour, the government weakened the boards and undermined its own authority.[26] Because the government refused to legalize union recognition, collective bargaining, and the right to strike, unions refused to sign "no strike" agreements. Whereas government increasingly surrounded workers in a con-stricting net of hostile law, it left owners free to deny workers union recognition or the right to bargain collectively. At least one historian sees the war years as a period when government activists experimented with plans to manage both society and the economy, with labour and management participating in a kind of tripartite corpora-tism versus free enterprise.[27]

The anticommunist fears of the commissioner of the Royal Canadian Mounted Police (RCMP) overly influenced the minister of justice, who supported his repressive antisubversion measures without question. In November 1939 the government issued an order-in-council greatly expanding police power and outlawing the Communist Party of Canada. The employment of police spies to infiltrate the labour movement became a normal part of the government's approach to labour relations.[28] Coward-ice, weakness, indecision, bullying, and absence of planning – in stark contrast to boldness, foresight, and initiative displayed in war finance, Allied cooperation, and industrial mobilization – characterized the Canadian government's handling of in-dustrial relations. Labour troubles mounted steadily for four years as the government sought to force workers to remain at their workplaces. The question that continues to bedevil Canadian labour historians is whether or not mounting labour strife actually influenced the government to change its industrial-relations policy in February 1944.

In 1939 Canada experienced 120 strikes at a cost of 224,588 lost man-days. By 1941 the numbers had soared to 231 strikes and 433,914 lost man-days, and the following year, 354 strikes resulted in 450,202 lost man-days. Still, the government pursued the same policies, and in 1943 there were 401 strikes and 1,041,198 man-days lost, many in war industries.[29] Seventy-one strikes, or 11.3 per cent of all major strikes in the country, racked the shipbuilding industry in 1942 and 1943. Thirty-nine of the largest strikes in the country, or 14.2 per cent, occurred in shipbuilding in 1942, and the industry accounted for 32 of the country's major strikes, or 9 per cent, in 1943.[30]

Wages and Working Conditions

Although most Canadian shipyards were open shops and workers were not well paid, craft unions negotiated wage increases relatively easily for their own members directly with owners and management during the first eighteen months of the war.[31] In June 1940, in response to a TLC delegation that had met with Prime Minister Mackenzie King nine months earlier, the government issued order-in-council PC 2685, which recommended that "fair and reasonable" wage standards be observed and that workers' rights to form their own unions be recognized. But as the legislation was merely advisory, the order-in-council was at best meaningless and at worst a cynical exercise in public relations.[32] The same month, a board of conciliation recommended increases for workers at Davie Shipbuilding and Repairing Company, and another board recommended revised hourly wage rates and quarterly cost-of-living reviews for members of three AFL-affiliated unions at Burrard Dry Dock Company.[33] Wages paid at Burrard, which signed at least ten agreements with different AFL-affiliated unions in 1940 and 1941, became the industry standard at all West Coast yards.[34] Employees at Collingwood Shipyards Limited obtained major increases in their wages prior to July 1940.[35] After a brief two-day strike at Canadian Vickers Limited, the International Brotherhood of Boilermakers, an AFL affiliate, won a wage increase averaging 10 per cent for its 150 members.[36] But members of these craft-based trade unions made no attempt to organize semiskilled and unskilled workers anywhere.

In the spring of 1937 a union organizer in Vancouver sought help directly from the new American CIO-affiliated Industrial Union of Marine and Shipyard Workers of America (IUMSWA) owing to the lack of organizing effort by the International Brotherhood of Boilermakers, spontaneous meetings of small groups of men to discuss wages and hours, and the failure of any other AFL locals to organize workers in the shipyards.[37] But nothing came of this effort. The IUMSWA's first success would come a little later, on the East Coast.

Brief strikes over wages, working conditions, and union recognition at Collingwood, Kingston, and Montreal in the fall of 1940 showed which way the wind was blowing. On 24 October members of Local 343 of the International Brotherhood of Boilermakers struck at Collingwood Shipyards, demanding a further 29 per cent wage increase, from 58 cents to 75 cents an hour, after refusing to accept a majority report of a board of conciliation.[38] After the minister personally intervened, a settlement was reached on 5 November.[39] That month, members of the same union ceased work at Kingston to enforce demands for higher wages. They had applied for a board of conciliation in September but had agreed to allow their application to remain in abeyance pending the findings of the board established to look into wages and conditions at Collingwood. When the board's report became known, the men gave notice of their intention to strike and ceased work on 28 November. The Department of Labour declared the strike illegal and refused to appoint a chairman of the board until the men returned to work; this occurred on 2 December.[40]

On 25 October, 150 to 200 unorganized riveters, reamers, riggers, and painters at Canadian Vickers staged a "sit down" to protest alleged discrimination and excessive overtime and demanded recognition of their Independent Industrial Union of Shipyard Workers. The following day, some 300 workers were allegedly locked out after attempting to return to work. A Department of Labour conciliation officer got the men back to work on the understanding that all strikers would be taken back and that employees would be able to discuss their grievances with management. But after a few hours back on the job, the men again ceased work, alleging that four men had been refused employment. Again, the conciliation officer intervened with the company; but the strike continued. The dispute was settled on 31 October after an officer from the Department of Munitions and Supply (DMS) supervised a representational vote, which showed the majority of striking workers favoured recognition of an unaffiliated shop committee rather than the union.[41] The strike is interesting for several reasons. First, the strikers did not belong to a union, nor did one appear to represent them. Second, despite the existence of PC 2685, the company refused to meet or negotiate with workers' representatives or to comply with their legal right to organize. Third, government intervention made life easy for recalcitrant management by doing its job; and fourth, the success of the DMS official highlighted both the ineffectiveness of the Department of Labour and confusion within the civil service.

Members of Local 1 of the BISUC who had moved north from Vancouver to Prince Rupert in search of work encountered difficulties keeping informed by their local, and the ACCL quickly chartered Local 4 of the BISUC in December 1940 to meet their needs and to counter the recruiting efforts of both AFL and CFL organizers.[42]

Union recognition and wage rates for stagers were the principal points in dispute in June 1940 between certain semiskilled and unskilled employees of Victoria Machinery Depot (VMD) and Yarrows Limited. Mediation in December by a labour department official obtained an agreement signed between the companies and the Dock and Shipyard Workers Union, a CCL affiliate, but in June 1942 distinctions between stagers and stagers' helpers and the question of whether men erecting stages were classified as stagers continued to cause bitterness at VMD.[43] Wage scales in the Vancouver district provided the basis of these agreements.[44] In this instance, the government's willing interference excused companies from any obligation to negotiate with workers, and success came at the cost of a six-month delay.

Nor was this isolated. In June 1940 a board of conciliation had presented a unanimous report concerning a dispute between Davie Shipbuilding and Repairing and

Workers on the frame-bending floor in a shipyard foundry at Burrard Dry Dock Company. NVMA, no. 27-3546.

its mechanics, helpers, and labourers, members of Local 3 of the BISUC, which was accepted by both parties.[45] But union members alleged afterward that certain workers were not being paid in accordance with the board's findings. A Department of Labour officer failed to resolve the matter, and on 30 December, six months after the report had been delivered, a meeting held in Ottawa of all parties to the dispute, the mayor of Lauzon, and an official from the DMS succeeded only in agreeing to meet again in February to try to solve the dispute.[46] Compulsory conciliation was a euphemism for delay.

In December 1940 severe inflationary pressures from government spending, rapidly growing output, full employment, and labour shortages drove the government to introduce its first attempt at a comprehensive policy to control wages in war industries. Under the extended Industrial Disputes Investigation Act (IDIA), order-in-council PC 7440 dictated that prevailing wage rates between 1926 and 1929 or higher rates established during the 1930s would be considered "generally fair and reasonable" limits for wages during the war, and payment of cost-of-living bonuses would protect workers from inflationary pressures.[47]

Problems quickly appeared that, combined with the enormous expansion of Canadian shipyards for the cargo ship program, led to more boards of conciliation, new strikes, and the first of two wartime royal commissions into wages and working conditions in the shipyards. The first dispute of 1941 was a strike by approximately 250 passerboys, labourers, and steelworkers, about one-quarter of the workforce, at Halifax Shipyards Limited for increased wages. The men demanded the same wages as were paid at HMC Dockyard for similar work. After two days, the men returned to work, and a conciliation board was set up that led the new Industrial Union of Marine and Shipyard Workers of America to secure its first wage contract, covering about 700 men, with the company in August.[48]

The number of shipyard strikes grew during the spring of 1941, which saw strikes by riveters in Quebec City, platers and fitters in North Vancouver, and general shipyard workers in Halifax.[49] In Kingston, where the labour situation had been "precarious and unsettled for sometime past," Roy Wolvin established a company union, or shop committee, in which over 80 per cent of the employees signed the agreement.[50] At a small shipyard in New Westminster, British Columbia, employees of Star Shipyards (Mercer's) Limited signed a similar agreement.[51]

In June the government established the Industrial Disputes Inquiry Commission, replacing the useless, recently abolished National Labour Supply Council, to supplement the appointment of formal boards of conciliation. The council's mandate to resolve disputes without conciliation appeared confused, to say the least, as compulsory conciliation was the government's alternative to collective bargaining.[52] By the summer of 1941 it was apparent to all clear-sighted observers that Canadian labour's position was "subordinate and servile." Labour was to be ordered about rather than consulted.[53]

The year's second dispute over wages and working conditions occurred between Dufferin Shipbuilding Company and members of Local 128 of the International Brotherhood of Boilermakers. On 31 May the Department of Labour established a board of conciliation and subsequently enlarged the scope of the inquiry to cover disputes involving three other AFL-affiliated unions in the shipyard: the United Brotherhood of Carpenters and Joiners of America, the International Brotherhood of Electrical Workers, and the International Union of Operating Engineers.[54] These workers were already the highest-paid employees in the yard; the fate of the majority was of little interest to them or to anyone else.

The board was unable to make a satisfactory comparison between present wage rates and those in effect from 1926 to 1939 as set out in PC 7440 because from 1922 to 1939 the Great Lakes shipbuilding industry had been moribund. It remained for the board to recommend such rates of pay as might be considered "fair and reasonable." Taking into consideration wages paid in comparable trades in the Toronto zone, the prices of life's necessaries, and the nature of the work actually performed in the shipyard, the board recommended minimum hourly rates of pay ranging from 82.5 cents to 95 cents for operating engineers, carpenters, shipwrights, joiners, and electricians and rates of 50 cents for inexperienced helpers of all types. The recommendations contained a full range of intermediate wage rates for workers not covered by any union agreement: riveters, platers, fitters, caulkers, chippers, welders, drillers, burners, holders-on, punch and shear operators, electrical improvers, rivet heaters, bolters-up, reamers, and counter sinkers. The highest wages were to be paid to members of the four craft unions that had applied for the board of conciliation, and lower rates were assigned to the vast majority of nonunionized employees who worked on the ships' hulls. Two points are worth noting. The conciliation boards recommended minimum wage rates, and the shipbuilding industry was characterized by a multitude of job classifications, sixty to seventy in each yard, which remained a sore point with workers.

The board recommended these rates become effective from 1 June 1941 for the duration of the war and that workers' wages be supplemented by payment of cost-of-living bonuses. It recommended against establishing variable workweeks, thereby disposing of the carpenters' demand for a forty-four-hour week. The board recommended that overtime be set at time and a half on all public holidays, except for New Year's Day, Labour Day, and Christmas Day, when work should be paid for at double the regular rate of pay. On the delicate matter of training and apprenticeships, the board recommended only that unskilled and semiskilled workers receiving specialized training for war production be permitted opportunities to extend their technical training in order to ensure their future occupational adaptability.[55] This recommendation did not sit well with tradesmen who sought to preserve their rigorous four-year (12,000-hour) apprenticeship programs. In point of fact, apprenticeship in the shipbuilding trades was normally suspended for the duration of the war, and categories of "improver" and "specialist," job classifications somewhere between helper and journeyman, were substituted throughout the industry. The board's report was unanimous, and following receipt of its recommendations in December, the parties settled all disputes by negotiation.

But despite its unanimity, the report quickly became a dead letter, for on 2 September 1941, in the midst of the board's deliberations and in response to continuing difficulties over wage differentials at various shipyards, the government had appointed a royal commission to inquire whether wages or other labour conditions should be the same at seven yards in Ontario and Quebec: Canadian Vickers, Davie Shipbuilding and Repairing, George T. Davie and Sons, Marine Industries, Midland Shipbuilding, Collingwood Shipyards, and Kingston Shipbuilding.[56] Like Dufferin Shipbuilding, Morton Engineering and Dry Dock Company was omitted because a board of conciliation and inquiry was already sitting to investigate a dispute between the company and its employees.[57]

The government appointed Senator Leon Gouin, KC, chairman of the royal commission, and the two other commissioners were Vincent C. Macdonald, KC, dean of the law faculty at Dalhousie University, and F.H. Marlow, KC, master of the Ontario Supreme Court. Establishing the royal commission under the Inquiries Act enabled the government to deny both shipbuilding companies and workers any representation, which confirms Webber's claim that the government was reluctant to grapple with the substance of labour issues. During eleven weeks, between 16 September and 22 November, the commissioners met in seven cities, heard from over one hundred

USS *Natchez*, a
Canadian-built frigate
under construction in a
covered berth at Canadian
Vickers Limited, 1942.
LAC, C-032833.

persons, and received more than eighty exhibits before retiring to write their report,
which they completed in a week.[58] After acknowledging that wages in the industry
were based on minimum rates of pay for men in specific classes, the commissioners turned to the different situations in which the shipyards found themselves. The
proximity of the two largest firms, Canadian Vickers and Marine Industries, to a
large aircraft plant and an armaments factory, respectively, both of which employed
many men of similar classes, affected both companies' ability to secure and retain
men. Canadian Vickers enjoyed a large advantage in having available a large pool
of trained shipyard workers and skilled labour in other industries. The problem of
training men in other yards, especially in the small Ontario plants, was much greater
than in the big cities, which had relatively large pools of skilled workers who needed

to be adapted to new work rather than trained. The commissioners found basic wage rates in each of the companies to be low "as compared with rates generally prevailing for the same, or substantially similar occupations in the locality, or in a locality which … is comparable."[59]

After much consideration and deliberation, the commissioners concluded that the period 1926–39 could not be used to establish "fair and reasonable" wage rates. Reports of boards of conciliation could not be taken as conclusions of what was "fair and reasonable," and actual cost-of-living data for specific localities provided very uncertain (and sometimes illusory) guides to precise conclusions. The commissioners gave qualified support for uniform wage rates in spite of differences between yards and localities, but they opted for uniformity of regions. Ontario companies outside Toronto that relied on local sources of labour should have uniform wages and job classifications, whereas the Quebec shipyards should be treated as being in two regions, Montreal and Quebec-Sorel. The latter drew labour from local manpower resources, which were largely unskilled. These yards also required different job classifications, from helper, learner-improver, and specialist to journeyman. The commissioners recommended establishing three schedules of basic minimum rates. Despite the thoroughness of the commissioners' report, the government negated the whole thing.

On 26 January 1942 the government issued order-in-council PC 629, which fixed lower rates than the commissioners recommended for mechanics in designated Quebec and Ontario shipyards and authorized the minister of labour to adjust basic wages for other job classifications that, "having regard to all the circumstances, are fair and reasonable." The new wage rates also applied to employees of the new Toronto Shipbuilding Company and of Morton Engineering and Dry Dock. PC 629 preserved the commissioners' recommendation that three schedules of basic minimum rates be established. The new rates for Quebec yards outside Montreal were the lowest, Canadian Vickers received the highest, and wages in Ontario were in-between.[60] Aside from being arbitrary, the settlement of wages by orders-in-council eliminated any worker's right to bargain collectively, or indeed, any form of negotiating at all. The government continued undermining its credibility among shipyard workers, and the establishment of regional wage differentials contributed to labour unrest during the next two years.

The situation worsened. In July 1942 the government issued order-in-council PC 5963, which charged national and regional war labour boards with adjudicating wage demands, thereby removing all applications for boards of conciliation in the matter of wages from the ambit of the IDIA.[61] It also removed wages from issues that employees and employers could "bargain" and extended the definition of wages to include work rules and regulations, further enmeshing workers in red tape.[62] W.J. Coyle, international vice president of the AFL-affiliated International Brotherhood of Boilermakers, called for a new royal commission in September to investigate existing wage differentials in lower St Lawrence shipyards and demanded the appointment of labour and management representatives.[63] But the royal commission was not appointed, and wage differentials among different shipyards continued to plague the industry until the end of the war.

After Collingwood shipyard workers failed to back Kingston and Midland workers' strike action early in 1942, industrial unionists in the plant began to reorganize themselves. Late in the year, they obtained a union charter as Local 4 of the Industrial Union of Shipyard and Marine Workers of Canada from the CCL. This was a confused response to both the international unions' exclusivity and general manager John S. Leitch's effort to organize a company union for the remainder of the workers.[64] Membership in the new CCL local grew swiftly and reached a high of 439 paid-up members in October 1943.[65] In December the industrial union obtained an overwhelming vote (95.6 per cent of the ballots cast) to represent the workers in contract negotiations.[66] But by 1943 Canadian shipbuilding workers were thoroughly enmeshed in a confusing net of differential wages, high taxation, and incomprehensible regulations that only undermined their morale and left them relatively helpless in the face of social and political hostility.

Organizing in the Maritimes

During the early days of the war, coal and steel industries predominated in Nova Scotia. Local shipyard workers were relatively unimportant in the eyes of Canadian labour and faced a long struggle to organize. In December 1939 an estimated 600 men were employed in several Halifax repair yards. A few men, led by James O'Connell, had turned to the recently founded Industrial Union of Marine and Shipyard Workers of America, a CIO affiliate located at Camden, New Jersey, and on 17 November, the IUMSWA chartered Halifax Local 34.[67] During the next seventeen months, the new local struggled with scant success to organize workers and to negotiate an agreement with owners. But the environment was discouraging. Men were hired as repair jobs appeared and then were laid off. An estimated average of 765 shipyard workers were employed during the period. A high occurred in June 1940 when an estimated 1,100 men obtained employment, but numbers fell to 700 during the summer and grew only slowly to 900 during the first quarter of 1941.

With men spread across three repair plants, namely Halifax Shipyards, the marine slip at Dartmouth, and HMC Dockyard, as well as across several smaller firms, such as Purdy Brothers, T. Hogan Company, Collins and Sons, and Nova Scotia Boiler Scalers and Tank Cleaners, organization proved very challenging.[68] The union never succeeded in signing up more than one-quarter of the workforce and failed to obtain an agreement with any employer. AFL organizers were also applying pressure. The executive of Local 34 pleaded for support.[69] Unable to service their Canadian members, the general executive asked CIO organizers from central Canada to assist, but to no avail.[70] In September 1940 the local executive applied for affiliation with the new Canadian Congress of Labour, but more than half a year passed before the central chartered Local 1 of the Industrial Union of Marine and Shipbuilding Workers of Canada (IUMSWC).[71]

Members of the Halifax local were confused. They had been all but abandoned by both American and Canadian industrial-union movements. Finally, on 3 April 1941 the IUMSWA formally transferred Local 34 to the CCL under terms set out by president Aaron Mosher and agreed to by the CIO's national office in January.[72] The Halifax local was rechartered as Local 1 of the Industrial Union of Marine and Shipbuilding Workers of Canada. By May the new local reported membership included nearly 70 per cent of the shipyard workers "and [was] growing stronger every day."[73]

The new union plunged almost immediately into a threatened illegal walkout by 150 men over parity of rates of pay with HMC Dockyard.[74] This marked the beginning of a three-and-a-half-month struggle that led the union to sign its first collective agreement with Halifax Shipyards.[75] Local 1 signed an agreement with T. Hogan Company, a small ship-repair firm in July.[76] The agreement signed with Halifax Shipyards in August included a wage increase of more than 8.6 per cent and a new cost-of-living bonus. Membership declined as the union failed to obtain dues check-off, the automatic deduction of union dues from paycheques. Early in February 1942 CCL organizers claimed there were approximately 3,000 potential members at Halifax Shipyards, but it was doubtful whether Local 1, with 1,100 members, had a majority. The union was strongest at Dartmouth marine slips, where 400 of 500 employees were union members. The union made no headway at all at HMC Dockyard, where workers enjoyed higher rates of pay thanks to labour minister Humphrey Mitchell.[77]

Interunion rivalry increased tension during the following summer.[78] With the expiry of the union's first contract, representatives of two international craft unions – machinists and boilermakers – claimed jurisdiction in Halifax Shipyards. The company ignored all attempts by Local 1 of the IUMSWC to negotiate a new agreement. Low membership lent strength to the craft unions' attempts to become bargaining agents. But on 28 August a heavy representational vote favoured a union shop. Of 1,406 votes cast (or 76 per cent of those eligible), 1,382 fought off the AFL challenge.[79] Although the government was always hostile, labour in the Maritimes was sometimes its own worst enemy.

The turbulent, bitter history of the province's coalmines in District 26 of the United Mine Workers of America profoundly affected industrial relations in Nova Scotia. During the interwar years, decades of confrontation between proud, ragged coalminers and poor, nearly bankrupt coal companies and their government lackeys shaped labour militancy into diamond hardness unequalled anywhere else in the country.[80]

Lack of organization among the growing number of new employees being taken on at St John Dry Dock and Shipbuilding Company led to a disturbing situation that further illustrates how internecine feuding among workers and trade unions made it relatively easy for business and government to pay little attention to workers' demands. Local 2 of the Canadian Steel Workers Union, a directly chartered local of the ACCL, came into being in May 1940. It appeared to owe its origins to a steelworkers social club whose members had gone on strike six months before.[81] Lack of organization in the shipyard had led to a poor settlement, and the new local had arisen in response. The failure of the union was probably inevitable owing to its origins and lack of leadership. Ostensibly an industrial union, it closed its ranks to journeymen steelworkers and members of related trades. At St John Iron Works, a subsidiary of the shipbuilding company, Local 3 of the same union remained open to unskilled labourers, whereas membership in Local 2 became by invitation only. As the labour force grew at the dry dock, many union members were promoted to supervisory chargehands, leading to new tensions.

Trouble followed the formation of the Canadian Congress of Labour in September 1940. The new union central adopted the CIO policy of one union, one industry, which had not been rigorously enforced in the old ACCL. In January 1941 the CCL, which was reluctant to enforce its own policy on the existing Local 2 of the Canadian Steel Workers Union, directly chartered Local 1 of the Canadian Dry Dock and General Workers Union. The leader of the new local was James K. Bell, a fierce left-wing radical.

The situation festered throughout 1941 and 1942 as the two industrial locals competed to represent the majority of unskilled workers at St John Dry Dock and Shipbuilding. Labour relations there worsened after wage agreements expired on 1 March 1942. New wage rates were referred to the National War Labour Board (NWLB), but workers were not helped by the presence of four AFL-affiliated unions and two industrial unions claiming to represent them in whole or in part. During the summer of 1942, dissatisfaction with the board's finding and direction gave rise to refusals to work overtime, or more than forty-four hours per week. In September the four international unions signed agreements with the company accepting the board's approved wage adjustments. The industrial unions rejected the terms and continued to refuse to work overtime. This led to serious problems dry-docking naval vessels and making urgent repairs over weekends. Following threats and mediation by the Department of Labour, the men resumed working overtime, or fifty-six hours weekly, on 29 October, but a new finding of the NWLB providing for wage increases in certain job classifications retroactive to 8 September was rejected.[82]

During the fall of 1942, a new CCL union, Local 3 of the Industrial Union of Marine and Shipbuilding Workers of Canada, united Local 2 of the Steel Workers Union and Local 1 of the Dry Dock Workers Union, and on 7 December the company indicated a willingness to reach an agreement with the new union.[83] Unlike many new industrial locals, the one at St John Dry Dock and Shipbuilding achieved recognition and bargained successfully with management. That month, however, its leader, the fiery James Bell, who inveighed against the centralizing policies of CCL organizers trying to bring directly chartered locals to heel, persuaded his members to leave the CCL and seek a broader alliance of shipyard workers in the maritime provinces through the Eastern Maritime Workers Council. In 1943 this alliance incorporated Local 3 of the Canadian Steel Workers Union at St John Iron Works, finally bringing all the workers at St John into one industrial union, but it remained independent of the CCL.

The IUMSWC was especially active in 1943 organizing shipyard workers at Halifax, Meteghan, and Louisburg into new locals. In August, after a long struggle even to

Workmen checking the fit of a 4,700-ton merchant ship's rudder against the screw's torque axis to prevent vibration of the ship when sailing, Pictou, Nova Scotia, January 1943. NFB/LAC, WRM 2493.

enter HMC Dockyard, CCL organizers chartered Local 7 of the union for workers there, but paid-up membership never exceeded 100 before November 1944, nor did the union ever succeed in negotiating an agreement with the navy yard.[84]

Some 1,100 to 1,200 workers were affected when Clare Shipbuilding Company locked out its employees for trying to form a union. On his arrival at Meteghan early in August 1943, H.A. "Pat" Shea signed up 305 members immediately, and the next day elections were held and the union formed. Subsequently, 336 of 340 men employed took out memberships. Immediately on formation of the union, chartered as Local 6, management began "dirty means and methods using threats and by firing some of the workers."[85] Shea met with general manager T.R. Grant and concluded, "He was a very obstinate and bull-headed person who would stop at nothing to gain his point."[86] On Monday, 16 August, Grant called all the committees of the union together with chargehands to inform them that if they insisted upon a union, "he would leave a scar upon the people of Meteghan that they would never forget … he did not care if ever a ship left the ways and would in defiance of anyone in the world stop production and close down the yard completely." Shea added, "I did not realize a man could be so insane as to make such statements and then carry out such a threat."[87] Unlike anywhere else in Canada, the employees at Clare Shipbuilding worked ten hours daily and nine on Saturday, a fifty-nine-hour week, for between 50 cents and 60 cents an hour.[88]

Shea went to the Selective Service officials in Yarmouth, and after lengthy discussions, they ruled that seven days' notice was necessary to lay off the men, but at noon the following day the men were laid off. Selective Service officials enforced their ruling that the men be paid for the seven-day period. Shea had won the first round. To the Acadian workforce, he was a saint; the town was his. Management flatly denied there was a problem, as well it might, for it had a contract to build twelve minesweepers.

Department of Labour officials moved quickly. Following acrimonious hearings and negotiations before Judge M.B. Archibald during the next month, agreement was reached with Local 6 settling all matters regarding the suspension of work from 16 to 19 August as well as suspension of work from 6 to 8 September.[89] But the reactionary management of the shipbuilding company ensured strong support for the union. Between September 1943 and March 1945, nearly three-quarters of the workforce, or 73.3 per cent, remained paid-up union members.[90]

Greater contrast with Meteghan could not have occurred at Louisburg on Cape Breton Island, where the CCL issued a charter to Local 8 of the IUMSWC in October 1943. L.H. Cann, the owner-manager of Cann's Marine Repairs, "heartily approved of his men organizing." Louisburg was a year-round port, and during the winter the number of employees was anticipated to increase to about 250, this being the busiest time of the year. Cann's Marine Repairs signed an agreement with the union the following month recognizing Local 8 as sole bargaining agent and agreeing to dues check-off.[91] Thus it was that in the Maritimes each shipyard had its own traditions and problems. They had to be organized one at a time.

Early union organization at Pictou was equally independent. Although miners employed at the new shipyard were familiar with trade unions and the unique traditions of the Cape Breton labour movement, farmers, fishermen, and women were not likely to welcome either. James Bell once admitted that new war workers often thought unions were illegal conspiracies, and employers tried to overwhelm them, often saying it was illegal to join one.[92] Organizers had to be educators. George MacEachern, a machinist, communist, and union president, has recounted how Danny Rankin, an employee in the coppersmith's shop, began to organize at Pictou. First, he was by himself, but then he and George rented a covered-in alley in town between the Stanley Hotel and the building next door. At a second-hand store, they bought a desk, a swivel chair, a kitchen chair, and a briefcase for $10 and began to publish their own paper, the *Marine Worker*, which had a powerful effect. The *Pictou Advocate* printed the union paper, and the publisher used its contents as boilerplate to fill the pages of the local weekly.[93] Nevertheless, it was G.M. Dick, the Steel Workers Organizing Committee representative from Trenton, who collected the dues and sent them to Ottawa to obtain the charter for Local 2 of the IUMSWC in April 1942.[94] George MacEachern became secretary of the union, and Rankin was elected president. Later, MacEachern succeeded him.

Unrest was growing in the shipyard over rates of pay set for Pictou. The situation came to a head in August 1942 when W.J. Coyle, international vice president of Local 565 of the International Brotherhood of Boilermakers at Pictou, denounced the previous year's agreement signed between the IUMSWC and Halifax Shipyards Limited and applied to the Department of Labour for a board of conciliation. The CCL quickly sent in Donald MacDonald, member of Parliament for Cape Breton, and a congress organizer to assist the officers of Local 2. MacDonald claimed the IUMSWC represented the majority of some "752 employees" in the plant, in contrast to the boilermakers, with less than 100, and met with officials of Foundation Maritime Limited to discuss a plant-wide vote.[95] A recent influx of experienced trade unionists from the industrial area of Cape Breton had added new life to Local 2. By August 1943 the number of employees at Pictou had grown to nearly 2,900, and two AFL affiliates and Local 2 of the IUMSWC were contending for recognition and the right to bargain. In a representational vote conducted by the Department of Labour, the industrial union overwhelmingly won the contest.[96]

Changes in the pace of the war effort and new priorities in 1944 led to a change in CCL policy. The union central began to advocate formation of a broad alliance of shipyard workers. Competition between various labour bodies had marked the early years at Halifax and St John, but by 1943 the chief unions in both yards were Locals 1 and 3 of the IUMSWC. On 26 July 1944 the Halifax local overreached itself when it led 3,000 workers out on strike over the issue of the check-off. The shipyard workers fell victims to their leaders' lack of judgment and poor timing. The industry was winding down, and repair work had fallen off. The strike had minimal impact on convoy sailings and the port's ability to perform repairs since naval ratings continued to dock smaller vessels on marine railways and since Quebec and Montreal were available to take on a larger portion of work. Finally, ship repairs during the summer were at a lower level than in previous years.[97]

Halifax Shipyards Limited refused to negotiate, and with production no longer a priority, the government's policy was not to intervene. Nor did the CCL sanction the Halifax strike. The congress had successfully worked to have the National War Labour Board investigate shipyard wages across the country and believed "no good will come out of your strike, and in fact may do some harm."[98] The congress believed that the NWLB's decisions, although not perfect, had led to a distinct improvement in the shipbuilding industry and did not want to jeopardize its two-year struggle to standardize wages and working conditions. The strike ended one month after it began, the workers having gained nothing. Minimal assistance from other labour groups and a financial crisis partially brought on by theft of dues by local union leaders forced the strikers to accept a provincially brokered settlement. Local 1 of the IUMSWC lost credibility, and the AFL-affiliated Halifax District Trades and Labour Council began signing up members and turned in defence to the Marine Workers Federation.

Employees of Halifax Shipyards Limited at Dartmouth had always been stronger union supporters than those on the Halifax side. Earlier in July they had waived their proposal for a separate local in order to negotiate the new contract. But in light of the strike's failure, Dartmouth union members demanded their own local, which was chartered as Local 13 of the IUMSWC in October after local organizers had recruited nearly 88 per cent of a possible 630 employees.[99]

The Regional War Labour Board was unable to reach a decision and sent the matter to Nova Scotia's Supreme Court. Judgment was rendered in February 1945. The union was denied a closed shop at a sharp cost of increased labour disunity. In March the CCL formed the National Marine Workers Federation, incorporating both new locals and the former outlaw St John Local 3 as constituent members. Locals 1, 2, 3, and 6 of the new union were recognized at St John, Pictou, Halifax, and Metaghan, respectively. The war years had been very challenging to the labour movement in the maritime provinces. Not before 1945 were shipyard workers unified for the struggles that lay ahead. The story of wartime labour organizing in eastern Canadian shipyards well illustrates the exhausting, unprofitable impact of interunion conflict – not only between AFL and CIO affiliates but also between moderate social-democratic trade unionists and radical left-wing organizers – which absorbed so much energy and effort when the true opponents of union recognition and collective bargaining remained business and government.

Continuous Production in British Columbia

Although wages were higher on the West Coast, the situation in Victoria and Vancouver was not much better than in the East. The trades and labour councils in both cities had split in 1919 when western delegates withdrew support from the AFL-affiliated Trades and Labour Congress of Canada over the formation of the One Big Union. Victoria and Vancouver labour councils were set up as a result. After the Winnipeg General Strike, the trades and labour councils were reconstituted as less radical organizations, but two labour councils remained in each city, becoming almost moribund during the 1930s. Following the revival of wartime economic activity, the Victoria Labour Council and the Victoria Trades and Labour Council re-established ties by forming a joint committee in 1942.[100] This was good for the city since the West Coast shipbuilding industry was about to be wracked by the most serious quarrels in the wartime Canadian labour movement as the government moved to impose continuous production on the shipyards and as communist and social-democratic labour organizers fought for the soul of industrial trade unionism in British Columbia's shipyards. Through it all, ships continued to flow almost daily from the province's shipyards.

The Department of Labour's struggle to impose continuous production in West Coast shipyards was the main cause of labour's grievances. In the United States the actual working-out of continuous production was left to the shipbuilding companies and the unions and proved very successful. In Canada the attempt failed owing to a dispute between the government and labour.[101]

Continuous production, or operating the shipyards twenty-four hours a day, seven days a week, had its origins in complaints from Wartime Merchant Shipping Limited that it took twenty-five days longer to build a cargo ship in British Columbia than on the St Lawrence River or in the United States. This led to fourteen rivet gangs being placed on piecework for ten days early in January 1942 in Burrard Dry Dock South Yard at Vancouver. The average gang's production increased from 228 to 425 rivets per eight-hour shift, and one group drove 686 rivets.[102] This was not a patch on Quebec riveters, who normally drove over 750 rivets in a similar shift. The Vancouver riveters opposed piecework. Low production, they claimed, was due to low wages, poor equipment, green hands, and constantly changing personnel.[103] At South Yard they voted overwhelmingly against piecework and were supported by their union, Local 1 of the Boilermakers and Iron Shipbuilders Union of Canada. On 15 January the riveters returned to hourly pay.

After the experiment, the number of rivets per gang dropped to 203 per eight-hour shift. But as veteran riveter Walter Haydon said, defending fellow workers from Austin Taylor's charges that in refusing piecework riveters were slowing ship production, "you can't do piecework when you have to wait for tools, look for hose, wait for bolting up men and staging." Haydon, who had worked for Burrard Dry Dock during the First World War, claimed the yards had been better organized then.[104] At Burrard North Yard and at North Van Ship Repairs, riveters continued on piecework in defiance of the union.[105]

On 30 January the president of Wartime Merchant Shipping Limited complained to C.D. Howe about lost shipbuilding capacity. US yards building cargo ships were working 168 hours per week (i.e., twenty-four hours per day). Typically, an employee worked five eight-hour days per week on straight time, plus eight hours per week at time and a half. Sunday work in the United States was the same rate as every other day. MacMillan charged that in Canada shipyards were losing from fourteen and a half to fifty-eight and a half hours per week depending on where they were located. Sunday work was paid at double time. MacMillan recommended the NWLB study the matter with a view to setting a policy of having the yards work continuously, with the men working forty-eight hours straight time before being paid overtime.[106] This became the origin of the continuous-production policy that the government imposed on West Coast yards building 10,000-ton cargo ships. The poorly conceived policy, formed with insufficient consultation with either shipbuilding companies or trade unions, ultimately led to appointment of the second royal commission to inquire into Canada's wartime shipbuilding industry.

Only the large size of British Columbia's shipbuilding program and its emphasis on one type of ship allowed consideration of continuous production. On 1 June 1942 nearly 21,000 workers were employed in West Coast shipyards (see table 6.2), 17,000 of them in Vancouver. For other yards that drew on a small pool of labour and an even smaller group of skilled workers, staffing the dayshift was a challenge. There were too few skilled workers to consider a second shift. Shortage of skilled labour and high demand led to longer than normal working days. Single shifts in the maritime provinces totalled sixty-eight hours per week at Halifax and fifty-six hours at St John. There can be little wonder why men demanded Sunday off and why absenteeism was much more prevalent at the former yard than at the latter.[107] At Pictou, with less than 50 of more than 2,000 workers on four berths being experienced shipbuilders, 90 per cent worked the dayshift.[108] The same shortage of skilled workers prevailed at Prince Rupert. Some shipyards came close, but continuous production did not exist in Canada's shipyards. Quebec City yards worked 109.5 hours per week.[109] Canadian Vickers Limited at Montreal worked 153.5 hours per week, but even there, during July and August 1941, the weighted average of overtime hours was only 8.7 per cent of straight-time hours worked.[110]

Following MacMillan's memorandum to Howe, Gordon Sheils, deputy minister of the DMS, and Henry Borden, the department's general counsel, visited Vancouver and consulted Austin Taylor, vice president of Wartime Merchant Shipping Limited and head of the Crown corporation's Vancouver office, to discuss the proposal to increase shipbuilding production.[111] In light of a 50 per cent increase in the number of berths since the previous fall, MacMillan thought Canada ought to be able to build nearly 3 million tons of merchant shipping during 1942 and 1943. His object was to achieve 1,250,000 tons for the current year.[112]

To achieve this goal, MacMillan turned to the minister of labour, Humphrey Mitchell, rather than to the companies or shipbuilding unions, which by January 1942 were gaining power and becoming radicalized. Labour department officials sent a group of "experts," none of whom was a shipbuilder, to Vancouver, where they viewed the situation and proposed continuous production of three eight-hour shifts daily to be achieved by men working six eight-hour staggered shifts weekly.[113] During a visit to the West Coast in March, Mitchell proposed that shipyard employees work six full eight-hour shifts per week and requested voluntary compliance. No better illustration could be found of the labour minister's paternalistic attitude. It apparently never occurred to this old trade unionist that consultation with the unions might be useful, let alone necessary. A few days later, management at Burrard Dry Dock and at North Van Ship Repairs posted notices in their respective plants that continuous production was to go into effect immediately.

Trade-union officials were livid. Frank Carlisle of the plumbers and steamfitters local at Burrard Dry Dock fired off a telegram to the prime minister protesting such arbitrary action, and a few days later, union delegates met to record their opposition to setting aside existing agreements between their members and the shipbuilding companies.[114] Representatives of the companies informed Mitchell's western representative several times that the men would not accept the proposed new hours and reduced rates of pay, as these were inferior to terms contained in American arrangements for continuous production. Officials flatly turned down a union proposal for five shifts per week with one day off and no overtime, except for on Sunday, when workers, as was the case across the country, would be paid at double time. Continuous production was a product of ministerial and civil-service arrogance. Alex

Pipefitters' shop at Burrard Dry Dock Company. NVMA, no. 27-175.

McAuslane, national vice president of the CCL, complained publicly about the minister's lack of negotiation.

On 4 April 1942 Harvey R. MacMillan visited Vancouver and, after finding shipbuilding routine in the yards unchanged, telegraphed Mitchell advising him to impose the plan by decree. To support his demand, MacMillan used a bogus threat of US denial of ship plate if continuous production was not imposed.[115] MacMillan was undoubtedly sincere in his concern. He was in a position to know that shipping losses from German submarines during early 1942 were growing at an appalling rate; this appeared to lie behind his increased pressure on Mitchell.[116] A week later, the DMS increased pressure on the labour minister, repeating the canard about the United States withholding ship steel if continuous production was not adopted.[117] Not only was there no evidence for this claim, but continuous production was not being considered anywhere else in Canada.

Despite cajoling and threats by labour department representatives, some ship-building unions remained adamantly opposed, and on 1 May the government issued order-in-council PC 3636, which ordered continuous production into operation in West Coast shipyards. Men were to work dayshifts of 48 hours a week for 50 hours' pay; the second, or nightshift, would be 46 hours for 54 paid; and the third, or grave-yard shift, was to be 43 hours for 54 paid.[118]

The effect in Vancouver was to be expected. The joint conference of shipyard unions protested the order-in-council to Prime Minister Mackenzie King, reminding the author of *Industry and Humanity* that its coercive character had created a "status of forced labour when free labour must be the standard bearer in every democracy."[119] Machinists and blacksmiths refused to work Saturday evening and Sunday for less than double time, and the companies refused to enforce the new law on more than 17,000 shipyard workers in the Vancouver area.

The joint conference of shipyard unions, representing 15,000 workers employed in six BC shipyards, proposed a six-day week of eighteen shifts and a clear Sunday, but this was rejected.[120] MacMillan demanded Mitchell enforce the law. Mitchell equivo-cated, hoping moral suasion, patriotism, and pressure from AFL union headquar-ters in Washington would force the recalcitrant machinists and blacksmiths into the yards on Sundays. In mid-June notices were posted in all shipyards that work-ers not appearing for work on Sundays would face disciplinary measures, but Clar-ence Wallace refused to suspend workers until so ordered by government regulation. Blacksmiths and machinists began strike action on 23 June. The following day, 400 pipefitters walked out in sympathy at Burrard North Yard.[121] The next day, Mitchell rushed a second order-in-council through Cabinet threatening individual workers with imprisonment of not less than three months or fines of between $50 and $500 for failing to appear for scheduled shifts.[122] The blacksmiths and machinists remained off work, implicitly calling on the minister to jail or fine nearly 800 men. Production was at a standstill in three of Vancouver's four shipyards; morale had been destroyed. Other unions considered whether to join the strikers. Mitchell, who did not want to act directly, found a uniquely Canadian solution to the problem. He appointed a royal commission to get himself out of the hole into which he had dug himself.

The Royal Commission to Examine into and Report as to the Most Effective Means of Securing Maximum Production in the Shipyards in the Province of British Colum-bia was formally established on 13 July 1942 by order-in-council PC 5964, which also mandated a board of inquiry and investigation under the IDIA.[123] Mr Justice Stephen E. Richards of the Manitoba Court of Appeal was appointed chairman. Other com-missioners were, on behalf of the employers, Don Service, general manager of North Van Ship Repairs, and Hugh M. Lewis, general manager of Burrard South Yard, and on behalf of the employees, Chris Pritchard, of the United Plumbers and Steamfit-ters Union and also president of the Vancouver Metal Trades Council, and Alex A. McAuslane, CCL vice president.

As Mr Justice Richards and the commissioners listened to the conflicting testi-mony of civil servants, executives of Crown corporations and shipbuilding companies, and trade-union representatives, it became clear that the unions had never refused to work 168 hours a week. If they had been allowed to keep their old agreements, with provisions for overtime and double time on Sundays and holidays, continuous production would have been adopted months before. But smug civil servants, seeing a chance to reduce wages while increasing production by dictatorial methods, had come a cropper.[124] The parties directly involved might well have fashioned an agreement for continuous production in short order if they had been left to themselves.

During the six weeks between 20 July and 28 August, when it completed its work, the commissioners heard evidence, reviewed exhibits, and visited Vancouver, Seattle, and Victoria. But the preparation of majority and minority reports meant the issues were not resolved. The labour minister had gained only a summer respite. In September, with the prospect of renewed labour strife, the initiative was back in Mitchell's hands.

On 22 September he sent Mr Justice Richards back to British Columbia to confer with shipbuilders and worker representatives. During negotiations, Richards came to accept that only a modified version of the seven-day plan recommended in his majority report would fly. He favoured incorporating into the plan a few of the provisions employed in American West Coast shipyards, such as paid vacations and increased weekly paid hours for second and third shifts. The unions, including previous holdouts, signed on, and in January 1943 the revised proposals were sent to the NWLB for approval.[125] At this point, they ran afoul of a three-month-long battle for control of Local 1 of the Boilermakers and Iron Shipbuilders Union of Canada. Although the NWLB approved the revised proposals, Mitchell delayed implementing continuous production until the dispute between the BISUC local and the CCL was resolved.[126]

Talks at Vancouver dragged on into April. Nevertheless, the *Vancouver Province* reported that 80 per cent of nearly 7,200 workers who voted favoured the scheme.[127] At Victoria continuous production commenced in April.[128] Finally, on 2 May 1943, nearly fifteen months after it had been proposed, the Vancouver shipyards signed supplementary agreements with the unions to bring the terms of continuous production into effect.

The undertaking rapidly fell apart. In Victoria continuous production failed within a month of its adoption, although getting rid of it would take much longer. Rather than accept the government's three shifts as agreed, the navy dockyard instituted two twelve-hour shifts despite the men's objections. The workers believed that since they were now working a full six-day week, their pay was cut down to about half straight time with the steeply graded taxation, whereas when they were working overtime, they had been receiving time and a half or double time. A great deal of the trouble also arose from the Department of Labour being "completely understaffed," with two men trying to carry on the job of at least a dozen.[129] Although workers in Vancouver now enthusiastically favoured the plan, interpreting its terms swiftly became the subject of controversy that undermined morale. The promised improvements, especially paid vacation time, were not forthcoming quickly enough. High levels of absenteeism on Sundays created shortages that made continuous production questionable, and soon companies wanted to revert to the old arrangements. Finally, changes in shipbuilding priorities made the entire plan of continuous production irrelevant to production.

C.D. Howe's 50 per cent reduction in the rate of production of cargo ships nullified the program's raison d'être. This led Wartime Merchant Shipping Limited to agree to transfers of workers out of the shipyards in order to meet shortages in the mining and logging industries. Management became indifferent to continuous production as it began laying off workers. On 23 September 1942 Wartime Merchant Shipping instructed all companies to revert to a workweek of five and a half days as formerly agreed. In Victoria the shipbuilding companies set aside continuous production a month later.[130]

Continuous production failed for many reasons. Obstacles to efficient production such as shortages of worker housing, inadequate transportation for workers, and absenteeism were only mentioned rather than resolved.[131] Indeed, after continuous production was adopted, absenteeism proved to be the major factor accounting for its failure. The urgency for continuous production subsided. The large number of sinkings in 1942 declined as the Allies turned the tide of battle in the Atlantic in 1943 and American shipyard production surpassed lost tonnage.[132] Harvey R. MacMillan's forcefulness and Humphrey Mitchell's weakness and equivocating also contributed to failure. Neither man appeared to understand that workers were not opposed to continuous production but had to be negotiated with to get them there. Negotiation is what free collective bargaining was all about. Mitchell's paternalism is what made him so hopeless. Mr Justice Richards appeared to be one of the few nonunion men who understood the problems and also grasped the means to achieve a solution, as his successful negotiation of an acceptable plan so ably demonstrated. Once the crisis of maximum ship production passed in July 1943, Ottawa reverted to its normal policy of indifference toward labour for another six months. When the government did change its attitude, the reasons were political rather than economic or strategic. Ironically, technology may have made a greater contribution to improved production than continuous production ever would have. At the end of 1942 it was reported that the introduction of a "Unionmelt" machine in Burrard South Yard had done more to speed up production than any other factor thus far during the war.[133]

Struggling for Labour's Soul

The key issue surrounding shipyard labour in 1943 was political. Nowhere was this more obvious than on Canada's West Coast. During the first three months of the year, communists and social democrats in the labour movement struggled for control of the largest union local in the Canadian shipbuilding industry, Vancouver Local 1 of the Boilermakers and Iron Shipbuilders Union of Canada (BISUC). During the previous year, communist organizers had taken over the local, which had grown from perhaps 200 members in 1939 to more than 13,000 by early 1942. Most of these new members knew little about either politics or the labour movement. It was pos-

Woman drill-press operator in a Vancouver shipyard, September 1943. Photo by Claude P. Dettloff. Canada, DND/LAC, PA-108051.

sible for a small group of politically motivated persons to capture the leadership of a union local. It was quite likely that the vast body of shipyard workers did not understand the orders-in-council, freezing of wages, and interpretations of new labour laws being handed down by obscure government boards. CCL officials alleged that the attraction of the local was its large treasury and the inexperienced trade unionists currently in charge.

The takeover began with one member, Malcolm Macleod, a long-time communist labour organizer who entered the shipyards at the outbreak of war, joined the union, became a shop steward, and was elected secretary. Others followed from communist-controlled trade unions such as the International Woodworkers of America (IWA), the United Mine, Mill and Smelter Workers of America, and the Communist Party of Canada itself.[134] William Stewart, who became president in 1943, did not know a davit from a rivet. A former business agent of the Hotel and Restaurant Employees Union and an organizer for the IWA, he had joined in the spring of 1942. The AFL-affiliated Vancouver Trades and Labour Council had suspended him for his communist leanings.[135] Not all members of the boilermakers acquiesced to these developments. Some older members left.

In December 1941 a group of welders broke away to take cards in an independent union, forming the Welders and Burners Unit No. 4 of the Amalgamated Building

Workers of Canada (ABWC), affiliated with the Canadian Federation of Labour. The new organization claimed to represent 98 per cent of the welders employed at Burrard Dry Dock South Yard and opened negotiations with the company for a working agreement. By 2 January 1942, however, Burrard North Yard had signed a closed-shop agreement with Local 1 of the BISUC, and on 16 March, South Yard management signed a similar agreement. North Van Ship Repairs followed soon after. Through development of a powerful shop stewards' committee, the boilermakers obtained closed-shop agreements in three of Vancouver's shipyards. Only W.D. McLaren managed to keep West Coast Shipbuilders Limited as an open shop.

The Amalgamated Building Workers of Canada applied for conciliation and arbitration, but the Department of Labour refused to intervene in this interunion dispute. In mid-June, in the midst of the imposition of continuous production in the shipyards, the welders and members of the CCL-affiliated Dockyard and Shipyard Workers Union began a series of short-lived strikes at the Burrard Dry Dock yards and at North Van Ship Repairs.[136] When 1,500 boilermakers downed their tools on 19 June, Clarence Wallace gave the ABWC welders thirty days to join the boilermakers or face dismissal.[137] Later the same month, pipefitters walked out in sympathy with the welders, and in July the welders went out again, but these isolated efforts failed.[138] By mid-1942 the power of the boilermakers in Vancouver's shipyards was obvious to all.

The communist takeover of Canada's largest union local deeply disturbed officials of the CCL. President Aaron Mosher moved to discipline the local but failed owing to the crudeness of a process that eventually proved to be illegal. At the beginning of 1942 vice president Alex McAuslane charged the boilermakers with twenty-one violations of their constitution, singling out its officers for failing to hold properly constituted meetings during the previous year, paying scrutineers during union elections, taking ballot boxes into the shipyards, and disqualifying paid-up union members who were without their union cards.[139] CCL officials later charged the boilermakers with physically intimidating and terrorizing members, but such allegations were never proved. Bill White, a communist union official, denied the allegations.[140] Organized labour increasingly divided against itself. In April the Vancouver Metal Trades Council resolved not to attend any further meetings or conferences in collaboration with non-AFL-affiliated unions, and in May it dissociated itself from the joint conference of shipyard unions and from any AFL-affiliated unions, such as the carpenters and electricians, that were involved.[141]

A 120-member shop stewards' working committee supported the communist executive of the boilermakers local, which successfully resisted the CCL's clumsy attempts to place the union under its central administration. On 30 December Alex McAuslane, appointed administrator of the local by the CCL's Ottawa headquarters, declared all the local's executive offices vacant and named a twenty-member administrative board. The ousted executives occupied the union offices and threatened to expel members of the administrative board from the union if they did not resign; the Vancouver Labour Council supported the ousted executives.[142] In February the expelled union executives sought remedy in the courts, where Mr Justice Sidney Smith completely vindicated them. The CCL had acted arbitrarily and illegally.[143] After continuing the struggle for another month, the CCL withdrew in defeat from attempting to control the local and expelled it and its members from the central organization. There was little else the CCL could do. It had no allies in the province. By the spring of 1943, the leadership of the Dock and Shipyard Workers Union, the Vancouver Labour Council, the International Union of Mine, Mill and Smelter Workers, and the IWA, which represented the vast majority of the industrial union membership in British Columbia, was largely communist.[144]

The CCL surrendered in November 1943 after the BC Supreme Court set aside an injunction obtained by the CCL against the boilermakers and declared the union local's executive legally elected. It lifted its suspension of the boilermakers, recognized the executive, and in January 1944 acquiesced in setting up the BC Federation of Shipyard Workers, which comprised the boilermakers, the ship and dockyard workers, and several smaller CCL locals. Malcolm MacLeod became the federation's first president.[145] It was a major defeat for the social democrats in the Canadian labour movement. The Federation of Shipyard Workers was a communist fiefdom, as was almost all of British Columbia's organized labour for the remainder of the war and beyond.[146]

Political changes on the left in 1942 and 1943 rather than the growing number of strikes undoubtedly influenced the government finally to recognize workers' rights to free collective bargaining employing representatives of their own choosing.[147] The defeat in 1942 of a national Conservative Party leader by an unknown member of the Cooperative Commonwealth Federation, the near victories of social democrats in 1943's British Columbia and Ontario provincial elections, a national opinion poll showing the CCF ahead of both the Liberal and Conservative Parties, the CCL's declaration in 1943 that the CCF was labour's political arm, the presence of local union leaders as elected members of provincial legislatures, and the electoral victories of two communists in Ontario and one in Ottawa led to a change in government attitudes toward labour at the highest level.[148] It is a significant reflection of the conservative nature of Canadian society that nothing that occurred in the labour movement itself appeared to influence the forthcoming changes. Prime Minister Mackenzie King always viewed himself as a friend of the workingman, and perhaps he was considering the hostility of some in his Cabinet, but he was a consummate political animal with extremely sensitive antennae attuned to shifting attitudes among the Canadian electorate.

Changes in government policy did not come without some struggle. In a meeting of the Cabinet on 1 September 1943, the prime minister appeared disturbed over criticism from the Trades and Labour Congress of Canada in Ontario and opined that labour should be represented on all government boards. Labour minister Mitchell, of all people, joined C.D. Howe in arguing against the idea.[149] Early in November the prime minister met for two hours with Mitchell, Howe, two other ministers, and a large TLC delegation come to outline grievances, including alleged discrimination against the AFL. Mackenzie King acknowledged labour's bitterness against Mitchell "and his methods of handling labour and their problems." But whatever he thought of Humphrey Mitchell, King kept him in his Cabinet as minister of labour for many more years. It remains moot whether the greatest number of strikes, involving the greatest number of workers in Canadian history, or recent political changes led the government, however reluctantly, to reverse its bankrupt four-year-old policies and issue PC 1003 in January 1944.

The new order-in-council superceded the thirty-seven-year-old Industrial Disputes Investigation Act and supplementary wartime orders-in-council. It introduced a national labour code more in line with US labour law. It contained protection of workers' rights to organize, certification of bargaining units, and compulsory collective bargaining, together with enforcement provisions, and it retained from older legislation the compulsory two-stage conciliation of disputes and the delay of strikes or lockouts pending investigation.[150] Regardless of one's interpretation of the significance of PC 1003 for later developments within the Canadian labour movement, it brought an immediate reduction in the number of strikes until the end of the war.[151] During the next year and a half, only seventeen strikes occurred in all of Canada's shipyards, compared to sixty-eight in 1942 and 1943.

Quebec's Long Angry Summer

Labour conflict in Quebec shipyards resembled the unrest across the rest of the country in several respects, including strikes, loss of production, especially during 1942 and 1943, and anger over wages, working conditions, and the application of wage controls. Like the rest of the country, labour strife largely ceased after PC 1003 appeared in February 1944, but there were significant differences. Strikes were proportionally more numerous than elsewhere; few were for union recognition. Indeed, less than one-fifth were even union-led.[152] The largest shipbuilders' strike in the province was union-led, but unions were sometimes quick to assure labour department officials they had nothing to do with the unrest and often urged workers back to work. Many strikes were spontaneous and arose over wages and working conditions. Consequently, despite the important role of trade unions, militant unorganized workers were significant agents of disruption in Quebec shipbuilding plants. The BC story of big labour confronting big business and big government was not replicated in Quebec, where unions often struggled to control the workers they wanted to represent. The spontaneity of worker struggle in Quebec yards, however, was due less to union weakness than to conflict between craft- and industrial-based trade unionism.[153]

Although AFL-affiliated craft-based unions dominated Quebec's organized labour, except for the International Association of Machinists in Montreal, they displayed no interest in organizing semiskilled and unskilled workers in the shipbuilding industry.[154] Its rival, the CCL, was not afraid of strike action and was anxious to organize workers on an industrial basis, but it appeared to have few French-speaking organizers and greater priorities than shipbuilding.[155] Thousands of shipyard workers remained unorganized for a long time yet were as militant as others elsewhere. Thirty-seven strikes, about 40 per cent of all those in the country's shipyards, occurred in Quebec between October 1940 and June 1945.

At the beginning of the summer of 1943, the number of shipyard workers had more than doubled during the previous year to 28,502, or more than one-third of the national shipbuilding labour force. Owing to the establishment of United Shipyards Limited at Montreal, numbers had nearly tripled there, and in the Quebec City area and Sorel they had increased by 94 and 66 per cent, respectively.[156] Many of these new workers were not only unskilled but also young, often in their first jobs, bewildered, and as suspicious of trade-union organizers as of the bosses.

The largest and longest strike in Quebec's wartime shipbuilding industry was fought primarily to improve wages and working conditions and to enforce terms of the closed shop that a conciliation board's majority report had rejected. It totalled 77,000 man-hours of the more than 1 million hours lost in 1943. Its consequences were unique to Quebec, for they led directly to the government's seizure of two of the three shipyards involved and their incorporation into a Crown company established by the Department of Munitions and Supply. This is even more surprising because unlike most strikes in Canada, this one was legal, having followed a vote supervised by officials of the Department of Labour.

Davie Shipbuilding and Repairing Company tugs *Chateau* and *Manoir* tow a just-launched 4,700-ton cargo ship from Morton Engineering and Dry Dock Limited at the mouth of the St Charles River, Quebec, c. 1945. Photo Moderne, Quebec. Reproduced by permission of Eileen Reid Marcil.

Two months earlier, a board of conciliation held its first formal meeting to deal with disputes between Davie Shipbuilding and Repairing Company, Morton Engineering and Dry Dock Company, and George T. Davie and Sons and their respective locals, 3, 6, and 7, of the CCL-affiliated Boilermakers and Iron Shipbuilders Union of Canada. Two weeks later, a majority report recommended acceptance of two of the union's demands: the establishment of union-management joint-production committees and an increase in wage rates corresponding to those for similar work at Canadian Vickers at Montreal.[157] The majority report rejected company arguments for a partial adjustment in the wage differential and accepted the union's claim that zonal or area differentials as recommended in the Gouin royal commission report of 1941 and later adopted by PC 629 no longer applied, especially when companies received the same payments for the ships they were building. Although the majority report recommended acceptance of the union's demand for overtime, it and the minority report recommended against demands for check-off and closed shops.[158]

The labour minister received the conciliation board's reports on 12 May 1943 but failed to act, so on 14 June, following a supervised vote in which more than 90 per cent of 6,400 workers in the three yards favoured a strike, the men ceased work.[159] The government's response was immediate. The next day, C.D. Howe seized Morton Engineering and Dry Dock and George T. Davie and Sons from their owners and appointed Wilfrid Gagnon as federal controller. Gagnon resigned his position as director general of the purchasing branch of the DMS and travelled immediately to Quebec City to confer with the striking workers. The next day, Howe incorporated the two yards, along with the shipbuilding division of Anglo-Canadian Pulp and Paper Mills, whose workers were not on strike, into a new Crown corporation to be known as Quebec Shipyards Limited.[160]

The government denied vigorously that creation of the new company had anything to do with the strike, stating that it had been contemplated for some time as a means to increase the efficiency of these yards.[161] But in response to a question in the House of Commons, Howe acknowledged the existence of labour unrest in the area and expressed the hope that labour would take no action (i.e., would return to work) "until after the government plans have been announced."[162]

The new company contained less than half the strikers, the majority of whom were at Davie Shipbuilding and Repairing, which belonged to Canada Steamship Lines. The stated reason for the new company's creation was to coordinate the work of the shipyards in the Quebec district, but no explanation was ever given for the exemption of the big Davie yard from government control, even though all three yards were beginning to build frigates and workers in all three were on strike. The political influence of Canada Steamship Lines probably saved Davie Shipbuilding and Repairing from becoming part of Quebec Shipyards Limited. The fact that 10,000 men were on strike elsewhere in Ontario and Quebec – including 1,500 workers at Dominion Engineering Works at Lachine, the largest manufacturer of marine engines for the cargo ship program, and workers at Hamilton, Galt, and Kitchener – may have moved Howe to act the way he did.[163] At Galt a strike of eight war plants by 1,400 workers represented by the United Steel Workers of America was in its twenty-sixth day.[164] Given the reduction of the rate of ship production that occurred less than a month later, the sudden concern for efficiency and coordination in Quebec City shipyards nearly four years into the war seems precious.

Wilfrid Gagnon arrived in Quebec City on the same day as Alex McAuslane and immediately conferred with the CCL's vice president and provincial director, Paul Marquette. Federal labour conciliators also converged on the city to attempt to find a settlement. The chief obstacle was the absence of any representative of Davie Shipbuilding and Repairing. According to Marquette, "il faut que l'on règle la grève simultanément dans les trois chantiers, sans quoi, il n'y aura pas de possibilité de règlement."[165] McAuslane repeated the same argument the next day.[166] The strikers repeated their demand for a closed shop.

Gagnon very quickly concluded a new collective agreement at the Anglo-Canadian Pulp and Paper Mills plant, where the workers had not gone out, in order to demonstrate the new company's willingness to negotiate within the terms of the conciliation board's recommendations made more than a month earlier.[167] But its greatest effect may have been on "le grand chantier" (the big yard), as it was locally known, for at the beginning of the strike's second week, representatives of Davie Shipbuilding and Repairing Company met with Quebec Shipyards Limited and representatives of the CCL and the BISUC locals. "For the sake of the war effort," the latter allowed naval authorities to move three nearly completed ships from the big Davie yard and from Morton's to the Anglo-Canadian fitting-out yard, together with naval materiel and equipment.[168] Negotiations continued at a swift pace, and on Saturday, 26 June, representatives of both companies and CCL officials signed a new collective agreement. Signing the collective agreement may have been the price Davie Shipbuilding and Repairing paid for not being taken into the new Crown corporation.

Although they did not gain a closed shop, the unions won sole bargaining rights in all three plants, plus assurance that superintendents would no longer attempt to dissuade men from joining the union. The companies also agreed to bring before the National War Labour Board the workers' subsidiary demands for wage-rate parity with Montreal shipyards retroactive to 16 April 1943, a boost in the weekly cost-of-living bonus, permission to institute a plan of paid holidays, formation of joint-production committees, and time and a half for hours worked after completion of an eight-hour day.[169] The CCL's victory was a most unexpected consequence of Howe's precipitate action.

The June 1943 strike at Quebec City was the most significant in the province's wartime shipyards, but another important strike broke out at Canadian Vickers less than a month later. Although initiated by AFL-affiliated craft unions, it soon turned into a nasty interunion slanging match that left a great deal of bitterness in the yard. On 14 July about fifty employees in the Vickers boiler shop ceased work to protest not having received the full cost-of-living bonus that had been the subject of a joint application made a fortnight earlier by the company and union to the National War Labour Board. Union members blamed the labour department's provocation, stating the department had "callously turned a deaf ear to their earlier demands for improved conditions over a long time."[170] During the next two days, 310 other workers joined them, and about sixty welders walked off the job in sympathy. By Saturday, 17 July, the strike, involving 3,500 men demanding the full cost-of-living bonus, had spread to all sectors of the shipyard. All operations ceased.[171]

Unusually, the strike originated with AFL unions and was joined by the CCL industrial union only later. By agreeing to receive a workers' delegation in Ottawa the next morning, labour department conciliators successfully persuaded members of Local 373 of the International Brotherhood of Boilermakers and three other AFL locals to return to work on Monday, 19 July, in order to allow the NWLB to deal with the matter in the ordinary way. After company representatives agreed to join the unions in applying to the board for paid holidays, the AFL strike was over; members wanted to return to work. But CCL picketers prevented them from doing so.

That afternoon, the labour department's director of industrial relations, Murdock M. Maclean, met officers from the CCL, who claimed to represent employees covered by the previous year's agreement negotiated by the United Steel Workers of America. The CCL had handed jurisdiction over to the newly chartered Local 5 of the Industrial Union of Marine and Shipbuilding Workers of Canada, subsequently changed to Local 15 of the BISUC. Although this union was not responsible for the strike and had not called it, CCL officials saw little hope of getting the men back to work before company representatives met them regarding the bonus question and other grievances.

Although a federal industrial-relations officer arranged a conference between management and CCL representatives on 21 July, David Côté, the chief CCL organizer at the Vickers yard, urged employees from one or more craft unions not to return to work, calling them "scabs, saboteurs and strikebreakers."[172] But interunion tension increased. In an open letter to Prime Minister King, AFL representatives alleged that the Department of Labour favoured the CCL and sought to drive international unions from the shipyard. They demanded Murdock Maclean's resignation and threatened a general strike. The AFL unions and their local organization, the Montreal Metal Trades Council, also alleged the labour department had forced the company to recognize the CCL union.[173]

The RCMP took David Côté into custody on 25 July for allegedly inciting workers to continue their strike at Vickers's Viau Street yard.[174] The minister of labour invited the signatories of the open letter and the president of the TLC to meet him for a frank discussion and the next day issued a statement defending himself and his officials against the allegations of recent days, but to what effect? The interunion damage had been done.

In August the National War Labour Board announced, effective immediately, that vacations with pay would prevail in all shipyards under its jurisdiction but that existing wage structures were still under consideration.[175] Vickers's general manager, T.R. "Rodgie" McLagan, complained that the NWLB must handle these matters more expeditiously or risk a general strike.[176] AFL union leaders still rankled at the labour department's favouritism toward "demagogic agitators of the Canadian Labour Congress."[177] David Côté was found guilty as charged and fined $500, but Quebec's long angry summer was not over.[178]

In the midst of the strike at Canadian Vickers, unrest spread to Marine Industries Limited at Sorel. On the same day that the Montreal strike spread to the entire plant, 250 unorganized burners and closers at Sorel brought Marine Industries Limited to a halt, affecting 5,400 shipyard workers.[179] Mostly young men, they struck for the same reasons as elsewhere: wage increases already applied for by the company, full cost-of-living bonuses, increased wages for improvers (a classification omitted from a recent application to the NWLB), and approved wages not yet paid to be retroactive to 2 May. Work resumed three days later after a federal industrial conciliator reached an agreement with the company to implement immediately the last NWLB finding and direction and an agreement with the men to await the board's decision on the bonus question.[180] The company made some adjustments to job classifications, the NWLB approved an increase of 5 cents an hour for improvers, and the strike appeared settled.[181] But there were some disturbing features.

According managing director Luger Simard, "no union questions [were] involved whatsoever," and an RCMP telegram reported the strike was "spontaneous" and "unorganized."[182] More significant, members of the RCMP sent to Sorel to maintain order had been pelted by strikers with rocks and stones. It was probably not the first time that police had been attacked while on guard duty at a struck plant. According to the young strikers, the stone throwing was "just fun," although a few Mounties suffered bruises about the head and shoulders. None of the strikers, mostly improver types or apprentices, would accept responsibility for the strike. Hiding their identities, the strikers claimed "city officials and other big shots" were discussing their case for them,[183] but labour conciliators had no one to negotiate with.

Another interunion struggle next door at Sorel Industries Limited, the large gun-manufacturing plant, had just been concluded. On 16 July the Confédération des travailleurs catholique du Canada won a supervised vote over the AFL-affiliated Sorel Metal Trades Council concerning which union central would represent some 2,000 workers, but the Catholic syndicate in the shipyard had made no effort to intervene.[184] The Sorel Metal Trades Council stepped in to represent the young shipyard workers.

This was very curious because the Catholic union (Syndicat national catholique des chantiers maritime de Sorel) had experienced a hard struggle with Martine Industries in 1937 and was present in the yard. Following a vote taken on 9 December 1942, 55 per cent of those who cast ballots (1,933 men) had voted in favour of the union, and the company had almost immediately signed a contract recognizing the union, although no salary increases or changed conditions of work occurred.[185] Marine Industries also signed an agreement with the union a month later. But members may have faded away. Six months later, it was the Sorel Metal Trades Council (Conseil des métiers de la métallurgie de Sorel) that acted for the young shipyard workers, but with little lasting effect.[186]

Across the province, shipyard workers' morale remained low. At Quebec City in mid-July 1943 lack of enthusiasm among workers continued to thwart the new Crown company.[187] Although management kept all three yards in close contact in order to increase efficiency, "loafing in the yards" remained prevalent well into September and would continue, added the managing director in a letter to C.D. Howe, until the NWLB approved the labour settlement negotiated in June; loss of production had to be expected.[188] Dismissal of a worker who was also the business agent for the union's grievance committee at Davie Shipbuilding and Repairing led to a brief strike by 900 men on 24 July. Four days later at Canadian Vickers, 100 unorganized testers briefly struck to obtain restoration of their 5-cent wage differential above the basic rate paid to labourers.[189] In mid-December workers at Morton Engineering and Dry Dock, now part of Quebec Shipyards Limited, complained that subscription lists to provide Christmas and New Year's gifts to foremen and superintendents were circulating and that those who opposed them had been dismissed. Management did not halt "la pratique reprehensible" until mid-January.[190]

NWLB delays in announcing wage adjustments caused constant brief walkouts, sometimes affecting thousands of employees, as workers protested alleged mistakes in one department or another. Overly officious company police writing down employees' badge numbers for allegedly breaking company rules led to a spontaneous strike by 1,800 workers at Marine Industries. Rather than face an indefinite work stoppage, managing director Luger Simard ignored government conciliators and used the company's public address system to announce the indefinite withdrawal of "labour supervisors" until further notice; in future, company police would confine their activities to police work.[191]

Organizing workers in Quebec shipyards was difficult and remained unfinished at the end of the war. Rather than big unions leading the way, as much labour historiography suggests was the norm, militant workers often struggled without the leadership they had a right to expect, while union centrals often ignored workers and quarrelled among themselves. Most work stoppages and strikes in the industry were small affairs. Before 1943 they had been largely spontaneous protests against job classifications and working conditions. Government conciliators intervened to delay strikes rather than solve problems, and labour boards delayed making important decisions, undermining the efforts of officials at the Department of Munitions and Supply to increase production through achieving greater efficiency. The behaviour of AFL-affiliated craft unions, which ignored semiskilled and unskilled workers during the early years, and the drive of the CCL industrial-union organizers are to be expected, but the absence of Quebec's Catholic trade unions from the shipyards in all but one case is more puzzling. Whereas trade unions were normally the focus of organizing workers in Quebec's shipyards, during 1943 workers themselves appeared to be the most important agents of change.

Conclusion

Canadian shipyard workers won few victories during the war, and they were ill prepared to confront the postwar world. Unlike President Franklin D. Roosevelt's

Democrats in the United States, neither major Canadian political party recognized organized labour as a political constituency before late 1943. Although PC 1003 granted workers the right to bargain collectively, the order-in-council was not a parliamentary statute; it remained in effect only until the war's end. In June 1945 trade unionists at Midland Shipbuilding were still attempting to have clauses inserted into their proposed collective agreement providing for vacation pay, a grievance procedure, seniority, maintenance of union membership, and dues check-off even after the conciliation board established to deal with their dispute with the company had unanimously recommended them.[192] As the 1944 strike for the check-off at Halifax Shipyards indicated, PC 1003 did not guarantee victory by any means.

Shipyard workers were not well paid. Those on the West Coast, who earned about 30 per cent more than the men in Quebec plants, were not much better off because the cost of living was higher in British Columbia. Charles Saunders, business agent for the Vancouver local of the Dock and Shipyard Workers Union, testified before the Richards royal commission that 1,000 of his 2,300 members, whom he called "the lowest paid workers in [British Columbia's] shipyards," with basic wages of 50 cents to 55 cents an hour, earned less than $25 weekly.[193] Differentials remained as much a problem as low wages during the war. No serious effort was ever made to apply the wage policy embodied in PC 7440. As Peter McInnis has concluded, "at best a muddled administration of the order prevailed, and expediency alone directed whether reports of wage disparities were to be heard." Significant wage variation for men engaged in equivalent jobs existed between shipyard workers across the country and within regions.[194] In January 1942 PC 629 set aside the recommendations of the Gouin royal commission by fixing lower wage rates than were proposed and by giving the minister of labour the power to set basic wages in the shipbuilding industry at whatever amount he, in his opinion, judged "fair and reasonable."

From the beginning of the war, the government had rejected free collective bargaining in favour of compulsory conciliation. Government bureaucracy and various boards prevented negotiations between employers and workers. The story of continuous production on the West Coast makes clear that the government was committed to coerced labour if necessary. Government interfered between business and workers, was comfortable ignoring workers' needs, and preferred to hinder union development rather than to increase ship production. Police spies and informants operated wherever men and women were employed in war production.

With the exception of Toronto, shipyards on the Great Lakes were located in remote, conservative communities where the opportunity to work was more precious than resisting exploitation. No culture of militancy existed. Indeed, working-class culture had almost ceased to exist during the Depression. In these small Ontario towns, virtually the entire community, including religious and local business leaders, the press, and above all the government, opposed trade unionism.

Labour department officials were among shipyard workers' worst enemies. They thought employing sophisticated management techniques rather than negotiation was the best way to deal with employees. It is astonishing, but not surprising, that after the chairman of the National War Labour Board recommended family allowances as an alternative to loosening wage controls and the minister of finance and the governor of the Bank of Canada concurred, Department of Labour officials opposed the proposal on the grounds that it would be too difficult to administer.[195]

Some historians of the working class emphasize the importance of union recognition in the great wave of strikes that swept the country in 1943, but evidence from the shipbuilding industry does not completely bear this out.[196] The AFL-affiliated International Brotherhood of Boilermakers, Iron Shipbuilders, Welders and Helpers of America was never interested in organizing shipyard workers.[197] In part, this was due to direct competition from the CCL-affiliated Boilermakers and Iron Shipbuilders Union of Canada. In Vancouver there was no contest. Local 1 of the BISUC, chartered by the ACCL as long ago as 1928, became the largest shipbuilding local in Canada. Local labour traditions prevailed. In Toronto, for example, the United Steel Workers of America proved unable to organize Toronto Shipbuilding Company in the face of concerted opposition from craft unions within the plant. In Ontario and Quebec the International Brotherhood of Boilermakers at Canadian Vickers, Collingwood, and Kingston was not interested in organizing the new workers. Labour in the maritime provinces had its own traditions. At Halifax, Local 580 of the International Brotherhood of Boilermakers quickly lost whatever influence it had enjoyed in the shipyard.

In Quebec shipyards, most work stoppages were spontaneous owing to perceived unfairness arising from wage differentials in the province, payment of partial cost-of-living bonuses, and especially, lengthy delays between joint company-worker applications to the NWLB for wage increases and final decisions. Reasons for strikes were often trifling. Lack of a place to hang coats, congestion around time clocks, an English-speaking naval architect placed to supervise French-speaking workers, dismissal of an employee, and failure to explain first-time income-tax deductions from pay packets were all causes of strikes.

During 1943 in Quebec, union recognition was the major issue in only the biggest strike and may have contributed nearly 10 per cent of all the man-days lost to industrial action across the country. Yet any benefits were very short-term. Labour organizers still had their work cut out for themselves at the war's end. Although the urgent demand for war production ought to have presented a massive shift of power in favour of workers, it did not. The freeze on wages, compulsory conciliation, disorganization and interunion rivalry, ethnic tensions, cultural misunderstanding, and political struggle left shipbuilding workers often betrayed and ill prepared to struggle for increased wages and improved working conditions.

8 | The Struggle for Steel

Introduction

No commodity is more essential to modern warfare than steel. Without steel, Canadians could have had no ships, no tanks, no guns, no armour, no shells, no automotive transport, nor any of the machines and tools necessary to produce these weapons. Steel was the key to the success of Canada's war production, yet for a long time, few people grasped this, and the industry was slow to begin tooling up for the war effort. In view of the dismal economic performance of the steel industry before the war, mill owners were reluctant to expand, while the government's tradition of noninterference in the industry led it to approach intervention only after questions of finding financial resources were answered. The slowness was also due to early indications that the British did not intend to call for support from Canada's industries.

The value of iron and steel used in the shipbuilding industry in 1940 was just $44.7 million, or less than 5 per cent of the total value of Canada's steel production at factory prices.[1] Later, shipbuilding came to consume nearly half of all the steel assigned to Canada's war production. Despite a commonly held belief that Canadian-built merchant ships were 95 per cent manufactured from Canadian materials, this was true only if steel is excluded.[2] The wartime shipbuilding industry relied on the United States for a substantial, if declining, portion of the steel it consumed. This chapter describes the intimate relation between the production of ever more steel and the ever-growing demand for ships. But some understanding of what steel is and how it is made, where it was produced, and its influence on Canadian-American relations is also required.[3]

Steel is a hard blue-grey alloy of iron, carbon, and other elements used as a structural or fabricating material, but steel makers disagreed in their definitions.[4] Steel codes varied between Great Britain and Canada, which forced a marriage of the two for shipbuilding. The British Admiralty used Vickers Limited's standard code of materials, in which metals were designated by physical characteristics (whether it was soft, brittle, etc.), whereas Canadians had adopted the American Society of Automotive Engineers standard of denoting the metal by its chemical properties, chiefly its carbon content but also the presence of other elements: phosphorous, manganese, tungsten, molybdenum, vanadium, nickel, and so on. Phosphorous and manganese increase steel's tensile strength, but one tends to make the metal brittle, whereas the other, depending on the amount of carbon present, makes it hard and therefore difficult to machine.[5] The coordination of the British and Canadian classification systems occurred in actual experiments conducted by firms and in government laboratories, chiefly at the Department of Mines and Resources, where the physical was married to the chemical.[6]

Pig iron, the chief constituent of steel, is produced in blast furnaces for use with coke and scrap in the production of steel in open-hearth furnaces. Thus Canadian war production called for millions of tons of scrap iron and steel for use with basic pig iron in open-hearth furnace charges. Before the war, Canada's primary steel industry was unbalanced and teetered on the brink of collapse.[7] Steel production in 1939 remained below the level established twenty-two years earlier.[8] Canada had produced an annual average of 1.7 million tons of steel during the years 1917–20, but steel production declined by 35 per cent during the next five years before recovering to previous levels during the second half of the 1920s. Production fell again during the early 1930s before beginning a modest recovery after 1935.

Steel is not simply a generic term encompassing the aggregate tonnage of transforming pig iron, coke, and scrap. Steel had to be rolled, drawn, pressed, forged, and cast into useful products. Table 8.5 below lists more than twenty different varieties of steel used in shipbuilding. In 1939 Canadian steel mills rolled sheet, drew rods and bars, pressed angles and shapes, and cast pieces, and although they manufactured 75,650 net tons of plate, they did not roll the sort used for shipbuilding.[9] This task required considerable investment in equipment, but the steel industry was old and worn out and had not received much capital for many years.

Ships required a lot of steel, although it made up less than 10 per cent of their cost.[10] Millions of pounds of nonferrous metals, especially brass and bronze, as well as copper, lead, zinc, aluminum, tin, and babbit, were used, but shipbuilding overwhelmingly consumed steel.[11] A Revised Flower-class corvette required nearly 927 tons, including 752 tons of hull steel. The total figure includes a surprising 15 tons of steel rivets, but not the 5 tons of welding rod also needed to construct the hull.[12] Marine forgings and engines demanded additional steel. Algerine-class minesweepers and frigates called for 940 and 1,151 tons of steel, respectively.[13] With the commencement of the cargo ship program, shipbuilding consumed far more steel than before. Whereas a 4,700-ton cargo ship needed 1,650 tons, a 10,000-ton vessel consumed about 3,350 tons of steel, of which 2,500 tons were plate.[14] Victory and Canadian types required more than 4,000 tons of hull steel, together with 510 additional tons per unit.[15]

Using the figure of 3,400 tons of steel to build a North Sands cargo ship, the Combined Shipping Adjustment Board determined that by completing three voyages annually, such a ship could transport 30,000 tons, which, after full allowance for losses and repairs were considered, was seven times as many tons of military stores as the steel itself.[16] Putting steel into cargo ships was a very worthwhile way to contribute to the war effort. The remarkable feature of steel's development during the war was

Woman bolter-up at work in a ship's bow, 1 November 1942. The bolts used to pull steel pieces together prior to riveting are clearly visible. NFB/LAC, WRM 2302.

that although the shipbuilding programs relied on a steady stream of domestic and imported steel, the amount of US steel declined, especially from late 1943 onward, whereas domestic production not only grew but became more technically sophisticated to meet the demand. Indeed, Canada's modern steel industry was an important legacy of the Second World War.

Expanding Production, 1939–41

Three large steel mills, Dominion Steel and Coal Company (Dosco), Steel Company of Canada (Stelco), and Algoma Steel Corporation (Algoma), operated blast furnaces in Canada and produced basic iron for their own use in open-hearth furnaces. Although its head office was at Montreal, Dosco's primary manufacturing plant was at Sydney, Nova Scotia. Stelco was located at Hamilton and Algoma at Sault Ste Marie, Ontario. Several other critically important companies, such as Atlas Steels Limited at Welland and Dominion Foundries and Steel Corporation (Dofasco) at Hamilton, Ontario, also manufactured steel, but only the first three companies made primary steel.[17]

During the first two years of the war, the number of blast furnaces operating in Canada grew from seven to twelve as of 1 September 1941, and by the year's end their

Table 8.1 | Pig iron, coke, and steel manufactured in Canada, 1939–45*

Year	Pig Iron	Coke	Steel
1939	846,418	2,410,095	2,345,199
1940	1,309,099	3,015,394	3,457,101
1941	1,528,053	3,145,715	3,977,292
1942	1,975,014	3,265,549	4,425,914
1943	1,758,269	3,551,773	4,336,032
1944	1,852,628	4,017,696	4,370,155
1945	1,777,945	3,912,390	4,310,606

* Short tons.

Note: The steel figures were obtained by adding together the quantities of steel ingots and castings, hot rolled iron and steel bars, structural steel shapes, steel rails, pipes and tubing, and steel wire. No statistics on steel plate, sheet, or strip are given for the war years, hence the significance of table 8.4.

Sources: Canada, DBS, *Iron and Steel and Their Products in Canada, 1943–1945*, table 24 for pig iron; Leacy, ed., *Historical Statistics of Canada*, 2nd ed., R756, R692, R693–704.

daily capacity had increased by 89 per cent.[18] Twelve more furnaces were planned for 1942. Pig iron production grew from 846,418 gross tons to 1,309,099 tons in 1940 and to 1,528,053 tons in 1941 (table 8.1). Pig iron production, normally reported in gross, or long, tons, is given in short tons in order to compare it more easily with coke and steel production, which are reported in short, or net, tons. In 1939 thirty-three open-hearth furnaces operated in Canada and forty-four in 1941. As the number of electric steel furnaces grew from nine to eleven, ingot production nearly doubled from 58,280 to 110,000 tons. Atlas Steels Limited increased its electric steel furnaces from two to four and ingot production from 12,937 to 70,000 gross tons. As of 1 September 1941 the number of operating plate mills had grown from two to three, and by year's end production, which included armour plate, had increased over two and a half times from 75,655 to 194,647 net tons.[19]

The government began to think seriously about becoming involved in steel production ten months after the war began. On 24 June 1940, one week after the capitulation of France, the government imposed steel control under the War Measures Act by order-in-council PC 2742. The order created the Office of Steel Controller (hereafter Steel Control), conferred broad powers, and appointed Hugh D. Scully steel controller. Toronto-born and a graduate of the University of Toronto, Scully had had a long career in business, first as secretary of the Canadian Manufacturers Association and then as secretary and assistant general manager of Russell Motor Company. In 1932 he entered government service as commissioner of excise and was commissioner of customs at the outbreak of war. Scully was already a member of the Foreign Exchange Control Board and the Economic Advisory Committee, which reflected how few senior civil servants had any familiarity with either business or industry. As steel controller, Scully spent only half of each working day outside the customs department. During the next fourteen months, Steel Control was concerned chiefly with surveying, organizing, and expanding Canadian production.[20]

In August 1941 Fredrick B. Kilbourn replaced Scully. A native of Owen Sound, Ontario, he graduated in engineering from McGill University. In 1939 he was appointed vice president and assistant general manager of Canada Cement Company. One month later, Martin A. Hoey, also employed at Canada Cement, was appointed deputy steel controller. Kilbourn was named general manager of Canada Cement in 1942, and on 1 October Hoey became associate steel controller. A few days before Christmas, Kilbourn suffered a serious heart attack that imposed a long period of hospital care and convalescence, and Hoey assumed leadership of Steel Control for nearly a year and a half until July 1944.[21]

The steel controller's job was to bring together men in the industry to coordinate and regulate resources and make efficient use of the substantial unused capacity in Canada's steel mills. Despite its draconian powers, Steel Control asserted its authority over producers by persuasion to achieve consensus through compromise and cooperation. On 4 July 1940 C.D. Howe summoned the presidents of the four principal steel companies – Stelco, Algoma, Dosco, and Dofasco.[22] Howe introduced the steel men to Scully and informed them he wanted cooperation, not regulation. Expediency ruled the day. Steel prices were frozen at prewar levels for rolled steel products, and competition between producers was abolished. Steel Control streamlined production by forbidding sales of raw materials and paying for intercompany transfers to balance slack rolling capacity with ingot supply, thereby ensuring that excess finishing capacities of some mills were matched with excess capacity of others to produce pig iron and steel billets.

Government officials hoped appointment of a steel controller would permit increased production with only modest improvements in equipment and techniques. No knowledgeable person wanted to build new steel-making facilities if it could be avoided. The industry was fragile, and a new steel-making plant would create grave problems after the war. Although P C 2742 provided authority, the steel controller had to work out how to ensure steel for the three basic sectors of wartime industry: war production, direct and indirect industries contributing to war industry, and essential civilian requirements. This task occupied the controller and his small staff for most of the first year.

Steel Control was thrust into a world of uncertainties. Pending clarification of supply and demand, little could be done except to encourage informally steel manufacturers to meet the demands of war contractors who were ready to use the available supplies. This was the procedure followed during the first year as a staff was assembled from among steel company executives and engineers. Questionnaires were prepared, and data concerning the number of coke ovens, blast furnaces, open-hearth furnaces operating, and estimates of output of coke, pig iron, and steel ingots were gathered and analyzed and reports commissioned and prepared. Although Canada's steel mills had capacity in excess of peacetime production (one reason for the industry's fragility), increasing demands, new projects mooted, and mounting backorders revealed that the nation's iron and steel capacity was quite inadequate to meet demand. On the other hand, US mills gave assurances that plentiful supplies of steel were available. US mills were meeting approximately one-third of Canada's steel requirement, and as the United States was not in the war, imports grew rapidly. US mills were running at capacity, and few problems appeared before January 1941, when the American government placed steel exports under licence.

British Iron and Steel Corporation, the purchasing agent for steel in the United States for the United Kingdom, endeavoured to place all steel exports to Canada under a blanket empire licence. This would have seriously impeded the flow of steel to Canada. The head of the agency, Ian Elliott, believed Canadian steel requirements should be incorporated with the British and secured only through itself. An empire steel committee set up in London attempted to obtain Canadian production-data and requirements information, but requests for such information ceased, and the inclusion of Canadian data in the empire picture was apparently dropped. No doubt the Department of Munitions and Supply's (DMS) representative in London had something to do with this.[23] But the case illustrates well that British agencies in North America remained largely uninterested in Canadian industrial production and sought to arrogate all US supplies for themselves. The British concern over possible Canadian competition was unwarranted. US steel exports to the United Kingdom in 1941 increased 64.3 per cent over the previous year and were worth half again as much as exports to Canada.[24]

In January 1941 Arthur G. McKee and Company at Cleveland, Ohio, a firm of steel engineers and contractors, submitted a preliminary report to the DMS on Canada's steel shortage.[25] This formed the basis for a much more ambitious report issued by the DMS in March of the country's requirement for the coming year. The revised report estimated Canada's total steel needs for the year at 3,390,000 long tons, of which one-third was required for war production. The report estimated that Canadian capacity would grow to 2,100,000 tons, leaving a balance of 1,140,000 tons to be imported. Shipbuilding would require a modest estimated 148,000 tons. In brief, in 1941 shipbuilding would require 4.4 per cent of Canada's total need, or 13 per cent of all steel required for war production.[26] This estimate, made before the decision to expand the cargo shipbuilding program was taken, proved to be far off the mark.

A shortage in the available supply of pig iron for use by foundries developed early in 1941, and some expansion of steel capacity was undertaken. The plate mill at Stelco opened in April, and a new blast furnace and open-hearth furnaces were authorized and begun. A more serious situation threatened at Algoma, where the older blooming and billet mills were insufficient to handle the full capacity of the steel-making furnaces and threatened to give out, which would have resulted in closing down the finishing mills and a loss of production for war purposes. American authorities made available a new blooming mill and billet mill being built for Japan and not released. Also in 1941, the first actions were taken to remedy Canada's wholly inadequate capacity to produce tool steel and special high-alloy steels. The only producer of stainless steel in Canada, Atlas Steels Limited at Welland, had two small electric furnaces of 10 and 5 tons with an annual capacity of about 20,000 tons. A new company, Atlas Plant Extension Limited, was formed, and the government authorized two 30-ton electric furnaces, forging presses, and the building to house them. Atlas later installed two additional 30-ton furnaces. Elsewhere, open-hearth and electric furnaces, some idle for ten to twenty years, were rehabilitated and put into operation.[27]

Shipbuilding's demand on the steel industry was for plate, which Canada's mills produced in limited amount and form. Only one large plate mill, located at Dominion Foundry and Steel Corporation at Hamilton, operated at the outbreak of war. It produced plate to a maximum width of 78 inches. It was adaptable and used for manufacturing cold-reducing sheet steel for tin-plate production, but being Canada's only source of armour plate, its availability for manufacturing ship plate was limited. Eastern Car Company, a Dosco subsidiary at Trenton, Nova Scotia, had a small mill capable of producing 48-inch plate, which was used in the manufacture of railway cars, but it was of no use for shipbuilding plate.

In March 1940 the directors of Steel Company of Canada had approved erection of a plate mill with a practical width capacity of up to 100 inches, and this came into operation on 30 March 1941.[28] At Sydney, Dosco had installed a similar plate mill twenty years before, but it had been unused for many years, was steam-powered, and had been largely dismantled; there was no plan to rehabilitate it.[29] Moreover, in May 1940 Dosco's ingots were fully committed for export to Great Britain. None were available to be rolled into plate. The minister and his steel officials still had no clear idea of the future expansion of shipbuilding. Howe had recently taken this matter up in England, and British officials were "extremely anxious that there should be no reduction in the shipments of ingots from that mill to Britain."[30] Also, Howe was confident that 40 or 50 per cent of Stelco's new plate-mill capacity would "amply provide" for the shipbuilding industry's total anticipated requirement.[31]

Dosco executives, including president Arthur Cross, had been attempting to obtain government support for rehabilitating the old plate mill since the summer of 1940, but nearly a year later, Steel Control and the minister continued to refuse their application for capital assistance, believing that Stelco's new mill was sufficient to meet the shipbuilding industry's needs.[32] With commencement of the cargo shipbuilding program, however, the situation changed. Harvey R. MacMillan's strong recommendation that the plate mill be rehabilitated won Howe's support, and in July 1941 the US Office of Production Management assigned ratings to two projects connected to expanding the Sydney steel plant, including rehabilitation of the mill for manufacturing 110-inch plate.[33]

By this time, the steel controller's duties were proving too heavy to be exercised within a dual capacity by the commissioner of customs. Recalling the summer of 1941 from the vantage point of early 1943, Martin Hoey wrote that "things were almost chaotic."[34] There was a great danger of the whole shipbuilding program collapsing into confusion. Hugh Scully relinquished his duties and on 12 August, and Fred

Kilbourn replaced him. The new steel controller moved to institute more comprehensive and closer control and to build a larger organization by securing more men from Canada's steel industry. Kilbourn also gave immediate orders to Stelco to run its plate mill at maximum capacity as quickly as could be done without injuring the plant. He knew that putting 20,000 to 25,000 tons of plate through the mill would divert an equal tonnage of other products necessary for the maintenance of Canada's entire munitions program, and he dreaded what would happen. He was not disappointed: a shortage of bars, rivets, bolts, wire, and wire products "that almost drove him insane" developed immediately. But there was no alternative, as the DMS was unable to procure sufficient plate in the United States to maintain the shipbuilding program in Canada.[35] Unable to obtain the sizes and quantities of steel from domestic mills, Canadian shipyards had initially imported supplies from the United States. But steel mills there, in order to increase supply, began to standardize their production, with the result that some sizes and thicknesses of plate called for in Canada's naval program became unavailable. This led Stelco to produce the bulk of the steel used in naval shipbuilding, which was just as well, for in September the United States adopted formal mandatory priorities.[36]

Unloading steel plate from a railway gondola car at a Burrard Dry Dock Company yard. NVMA, no. 27-268.

In October MacMillan summarized the impact of steel shortages on the shipbuilding programs in a memorandum to Kilbourn copied to Howe. Keel laying had been delayed one or two months at various berths, work on twelve keels already laid had been suspended or delayed, and nine berths were currently idle awaiting steel. The steel shortage at the first of the month was 30,000 tons, and monthly plate deliveries from the United States were not yet firm. The programs required 89,300 tons of plate during the next five months.[37] Ship-repairs controller David Carswell reported that steel shortages on the East Coast had broken the plan to institute new ship construction at Halifax and St John as a means to keep men during slack repair periods, and on the West Coast ocean-going vessels ready to load for the United Kingdom were being held up for want of steel to make their hulls seaworthy.[38]

At a meeting of representatives of Steel Control, of the steel companies, and of the cargo and naval shipbuilding programs, discussion centred on demand for and supply of carbon-steel plate. The estimated shortage would be reduced if 5,400 tons per month could be obtained from the United States from December through to the end of 1942. There was also a possibility of Stelco stepping up plate output by 4,000 tons monthly in April or May 1942, but it would require steel for a plant extension. At the end of the month, Howe and Kilbourn were scheduled to go to Washington, DC, to plead for at least 4,500 tons of ship plate. Until adequate supplies of steel became available, the meeting agreed that all supplies would be prorated between the naval and cargo ship programs. Clifton Sherman, president of Dofasco, pointed out that considerable time could be saved if shipyards could side-shear plates themselves rather than have it done at steel plants. A week later, officials asked Stelco to put in a third shift to increase output by 4,000 to 5,000 tons in January rather than in April or May as previously planned.[39]

Despite near chaos, order was being imposed. By the end of 1941 Canada's steel-ingot production had been boosted nearly 75 per cent over 1939 output.[40] Special alloy-steel production was nearly five times as great, and it would be eight times greater in 1942.[41] Steel-plate production was two and a half times larger than it had been in 1939 and would be five times greater in 1942.[42] Production for war work had been met by increased domestic production, curtailment of civilian demand, and increased imports from the United States. Although no acute shortage had arisen, mild-steel plate used in shipbuilding and for mechanized transport was in tightest supply, as were steel scrap and cast-iron scrap.[43]

Imports

Canada had always depended upon imported steel. The limited domestic market rendered uneconomical the installation of equipment to produce efficiently many forms of steel. Canadian manufacturers imported large quantities of steel from the United States, which were supplemented by imports from the United Kingdom and Europe. When European supplies were cut off early in the war, Canada had to rely on the United States for a greater supply. Imports were largely of types or sizes not produced by Canadian steel mills as well as flat rolled steel in quantities exceeding the capacity of local finishing mills.[44] Deficiencies in Canadian steel manufacture affected ship-building particularly severely, as very few steel ships had been built in the country during the previous twenty years.[45] As Canadian mills could not supply plates before June 1940, these were imported from American mills in time to allow ten keels for corvettes to be laid down during the spring at Canadian Vickers, Marine Industries Limited, and Davie Shipbuilding and Repairing Company.[46] At the same time, 75 to 80 per cent of the output from Dosco's Sydney plant was being shipped to Great Britain to fulfil orders secured before the war.[47]

Until the United States entered the war, it was the practice of Canadian Steel Control officials when confronted with requirements that could not be met immediately from domestic resources to instruct purchasers to obtain the material in the United States. American producers were quick to respond to Canada's wartime needs. Steel imports grew quickly, more than doubling in 1940 and increasing to 1,001,831 tons in 1941 (see table 8.2). Plate comprised only small portions of these totals, 7.1 and 11 per cent, respectively. About one-third of all the steel going into early Canadian-built ships came from the United States.[48]

Steel plates required for shipbuilding had been added to a priorities critical list in mid-March and were not freely available.[49] The principle acknowledged in Washington under the terms of the Hyde Park Agreement of 20 April 1941 that Canadian purchases should receive treatment in the United States equal to American purchases was not easily effected. Implementation of the agreement fell to the US Office of Production Management, and the practical machinery for equal treatment of the Canadian requirement took time to create. Not everyone was equally enthusiastic, and the flow of steel to Canada was somewhat curtailed.[50] Nothing existed in Canada to issue American preference ratings, whereas at least two independent, competing agencies existed in the United States. The steel controller hoped to have the Office of Production Management establish a quota of steel for export to Canada against which withdrawals would be made by means of purchase orders originating in Canada and approved by the steel controller. But this took several months to arrange, and when adopted the system created further difficulties.

In the interim, MacMillan reported his frustration to Howe in July after returning from a trip to Washington to try to free the clogged channels of communication. Although the steel controller had allocated to American mills 478 tons of shapes and 700 tons of plates that could not be currently manufactured in Canada for each 10,000-ton ship and although US mills possessed detailed specifications of the steel and had reserved the tonnage since May, no action could be taken until word was given from the highest authority in Washington. Although the monthly requirement was for 8,000 to 9,000 tons, work could not begin without American steel. So the Canadian yards waited. If supplied with $55,000 worth of steel, concluded a frustrated MacMillan, Canada could manufacture a ship worth $1.8 million; "This represents the best use of the Canadian share of North American shipyards, engineering shops and labour."[51] The situation was about to become more difficult.

On 1 September 1941 the American government introduced preference ratings, and in October, Steel Control issued the first Canadian steel budget estimating Canada's requirements in 1942 to meet this new challenge.[52] American authorities were not in a position, nor were they willing, to allocate resources in the manner the Canadians desired. The highly centralized control and command of the steel industry in Canada was not replicated in the United States, which proved extremely frustrating to Canadians seeking to know with whom to deal.[53]

Establishment of the Canada-US Joint War Production Committee in November, co-chaired by two General Motors executives, Harry J. Carmichael of Canada and C.E. Wilson of the United States, may have hastened the integration of the US Production Requirements Plan's priorities system with Canadian Steel Control's administration by maximizing labour, raw materials, and technical resources in all forms of industrial production.[54] But it also became apparent that the Office of Production Management and the Army and Navy Munitions Board were issuing competitive preference ratings that gave rise to much rerating and confusion. Nevertheless, by the end of 1941 the value of US steel exports to Canada amounted to US$853.5 million, almost double the 1939 value, and represented one-fifth of total US worldwide steel exports.[55]

Steel Control struggled to make Canadian orders attractive to US steel makers. Kilbourn insisted that Canadian mills take "all bits and pieces" of plate required for a multiplicity of purposes, whereas plate orders placed in the United States were mostly for the shipbuilding program and were all of very attractive thicknesses and widths.[56] His insistence on Canadian mills taking small orders led to such dissatisfaction among rollers in Hamilton that C.H. Millard, executive director of the Canadian section of the Steel Workers Organizing Committee (after May 1942 the United Steel Workers of America), led a delegation of twenty workers to meet Martin Hoey in order to complain that continued roller changes were affecting workers' earnings and would lead to trouble if not eradicated.[57]

The Production Requirements Plan, which was mandated in Canada in July 1942, remained unsatisfactory. In response to growing steel shortages in the United States, the US War Production Board (WPB) developed a system of allocations called the Controlled Materials Plan, made obligatory for Canadian industry, that largely solved the earlier confusion.[58] During the fourth quarter, the first allocation of 367,500 tons of American steel was established. In effect, the steel controller finally obtained what he had tried to get eighteen months before (see table 8.2). But now he feared the effect of this abrupt halt to Canada's hereto free access to the American steel market.[59] The allocation system established a ceiling on tonnage granted; it did not guarantee delivery. Canadian importers were given preference ratings to purchase steel in the United States if they could find it, but this did not appear to affect actual imports. In 1942, for example, Canadian imports of 1,580,749 tons of carbon and alloy steel, on average 395,187 tons per quarter, were higher than the fourth-quarter allocation (table 8.2).[60] Steel plates comprised 19.4 per cent of total US imports, compared to 7 and 11 per cent in 1940 and 1941, respectively.

Table 8.2 | Allotted and actual steel imports from the United States, 1939–45[a]

Period	Quarterly allotments	Actual quarterly imports	Annual imports
1939			402,294
1940			839,588
1941			1,001,831[b]
4th qtr 1942	367,500	379,834	
1942			1,580,749
1st qtr 1943	359,000	327,355	
2nd qtr 1943	380,000	311,784	
3rd qtr 1943	335,000	314,009	
4th qtr 1943	321,000	204,012	
1943			1,157,160
1st qtr 1944		178,360	
2nd qtr 1944	508,000	200,453	
3rd qtr 1944		226,425	
4th qtr 1944		229,295	
1944			834,533
1st qtr 1945		215,430	
2nd qtr 1945		230,305	
3rd qtr 1945		209,658	
4th qtr 1945			
1945			655,443
Total			*6,471,598*

[a] Net tons.
[b] Records for 1941 are incomplete; this figure is 1.5 times the actual imports in the first eight months. The total for 1945 is for only the first three quarters.

Sources: LAC, RG 28, box 22, "History of Steel Control, October 1st, 1943, to October 31st, 1945," 60; LAC, RG 28, box 261, file 196-14-13, "Report on the Activities of the Steel Control ... to October 1st, 1943," 64; LAC, RG 28, box 332, file 196-39-12, Minister's desk book – Steel Control – steel mill products; NARA, RG 179, CPRB, file 76, Steel Canada – Canada Fourth Quarter 1944.

Membership on the Combined Production and Resources Board (CPRB), which Canada gained on 7 November 1942, proved of little value. The board never worked satisfactorily owing to its failure to develop good relations with US military authorities. E.P. Taylor, C.D. Howe's deputy on the board, identified loose organizational arrangements on the US side and shifting relations with the War Production Board as additional weaknesses.[61] It is a mistake to think that the CPRB handled Canada's steel requirement.[62] It continued to remain under the WPB's steel division, which had been set up to deal with foreign allotments.[63]

The true solution to Canadian difficulties was not far away. Effective 1 January 1943, the War Production Board set up a Canadian division with a branch in Ottawa to process Canadian quarterly applications for steel that had been screened beforehand by both the steel controller and the priorities branch of the DMS. This did much to assuage Martin Hoey's fears that Americans did not understand Canadian difficulties.[64] Although the WPB dealt fairly with Canadian quota submissions, these had to be fully explained and defended. Canadian officials sometimes found it difficult to refrain from reminding their American counterparts of the large shipments of nickel, copper, zinc, asbestos, and so on for which no such strict accounting as to use was required.[65]

The problems surrounding steel imports largely disappeared six months later when the government severely curtailed both shipbuilding programs in favour of ship re-

A workman puts finishing touches to a frigate propeller at Yarrows Limited, 29 April 1943. The lines of rivets show well the complexity (and the beauty) of the compound curves at the ship's stern. Canada, DND/LAC, PA-150151.

pairing and modernization. Canadian imports declined rapidly from the high of nearly 1.6 million tons in 1942. Steel imports fell by 26.4 per cent in 1943 and a further 28.1 per cent in 1944. In 1945 they were down 80 per cent from the 1940 amount (table 8.2). Nevertheless, despite the decline in imports, table 8.4 below shows that over 35 per cent of carbon-steel plate used in the shipbuilding programs came from the United States.[66] Before this chapter examines the record of domestic steel production during the last four years of the war, a brief look at the role of iron and steel scrap and salvage in Canadian wartime steel production is needed.

Steel Scrap and Salvage

Scrap was the scarcest of all the steel industry's raw materials. It is the richest and therefore the most economical of the materials that can be charged into an open-hearth furnace to manufacture new steel.[67] In 1942, 72 per cent of all scrap iron and scrap steel was used in steel-making furnaces.[68] Steel makers require it in vast quantities. The ratio of iron and steel scrap to pig iron varied considerably, ranging from 30 per cent scrap and 70 per cent pig iron to 60 per cent scrap and 40 per cent pig iron in various Canadian steel mills.[69] On average, scrap comprised between 52 and 55 per cent of the material used in Canada's wartime steel furnaces. Electric furnaces used 100 per cent scrap to make new steel. Steel makers with their own rolling and finishing mills could count on large supplies of mill scrap, but one estimate claimed they might supply only about 37 per cent of Canada's needs.[70] The remainder, between 1.2 and 1.6 million tons annually, had to be found elsewhere.[71]

Not surprisingly, as Canada's steel production grew, prices of iron and steel scrap increased and, after the freezing of steel prices in July 1940, drew immediate attention from Steel Control. Nearly half of the steel controller's formal orders during the war concerned local scrap iron and steel prices across the country.[72] This reflected the local character and structure of the scrap metal business, which was largely in the hands of Jewish dealers. In August 1941 Steel Control established a scrap section to supervise and control distribution of scrap iron and steel.

Canada had been a net exporter of iron and steel scrap from 1935 to 1939, when nearly 8,000 net tons annually left the country.[73] Although Canada became a net importer in 1939, more than 93,000 tons of scrap iron and steel were exported to Japan, the United States, the United Kingdom, the Netherlands, and Germany.[74] In 1940 and 1941 Canada imported 30,429 tons of scrap from the United Kingdom, British Guiana, Jamaica, Trinidad, the British West Indies, and Newfoundland. But this quantity paled beside the 681,542 tons imported from the United States (see table 8.3).[75]

Public collection of scrap within Canada proved of limited value. The Department of National War Services established a salvage branch, which encouraged the public through radio, billboard, and magazine advertising to collect scrap, but people confused scrap with discarded household items. Local salvage campaigns encouraged boy scouts and school children to gather old pipes, metal fixtures, and tin cans. These items were virtually useless as scrap steel, and the costs of collecting, sorting,

Table 8.3 | Iron and steel scrap imports from the United States, 1939–45*

Year	Iron and steel imports	Iron and steel exports	Net total
1939	177,564	93,837	83,727
1940	415,981	3,261	412,720
1941	295,990	28,089	267,901
1942	114,017	57,348	56,669
1943	37,018	105,737	- 68,719
1944	71,440	68,304	3,136
1945	58,795	28,459	30,336
Total	1,170,805	385,035	785,770

* Net tons.

Source: Canada, DBS, *Iron and Steel and Their Products in Canada, 1943–1945*, tables 331 and 332.

discarding, storing, and shipping these public collections of scrap proved very expensive. During two and a half years, about 55,000 tons were privately collected; the morale boosting qualities of collecting them far surpassed whatever limited usefulness they may have been to the steel industry.[76]

Scrap became so scarce in eastern Canada during the spring of 1942 that David Carswell sought to salvage wrecked ships for scrap. Salvors usually dealt with the recovery of cargo and refloating ships, not with cutting them up under water for scrap. Carswell sought the steel controller's legal advice in dealing with marine insurance agents (i.e., Lloyd's Register of Shipping), as their delays often led to ships being lost. Preliminary reports indicated "large numbers of steel hulls resting on our beaches."[77] During the summer, he undertook a test of ship cutting in Belle Isle Strait, where the SS *Empire Kudu* with a cargo of steel billets had been wrecked. Although Steel Control opined that less expensive scrap than wrecked ships existed at abandoned mine sites and in the form of paved-over streetcar rails in the nation's cities, which should be salvaged before turning to ship breaking, Carswell gained approval for his salvage project.[78] Some 6,300 tons of steel, copper, and aluminum scrap and 900 tons of phosphates were recovered from the *Empire Kudu*.[79]

The greatest source of domestic scrap came from discarded agricultural implements on western Canadian farms. In the spring of 1942 the United States requested that Canada stop importing steel scrap, as several US steel mills in the East had had to be shut down intermittently for lack of it. Canadian authorities turned to the West. Estimates had already been made in anticipation of the American request, and work began quickly to organize, collect, and ship scrap from the Prairies to eastern steel mills. Grain elevators along railway lines became collecting points, and scrap was gathered in, paid for by the elevator companies, and shipped east to Winnipeg from Saskatchewan and Manitoba. Alberta scrap flowed to Edmonton and Calgary, where sharp-eyed citizens complained that Calgary Rolling Mills was not operating at capacity for lack of scrap. Its principal activity was manufacturing steel shapes for West Coast shipbuilders. In the summer of 1942 the steel subcommittee recommended installing a 20- or 25-ton open-hearth furnace and ancillary equipment to convert scrap. Calgary Rolling Mills was the only plant west of Winnipeg capable of resmelting the wrought-iron scrap scattered over the Prairies to whatever specification was required.[80] Ontario mills received about 200,000 tons from western Canada in 1943 and 1944 and perhaps 50,000 tons in 1945. Not ordinarily an economical transfer, this was made possible by the activities and financial assistance of the Wartime Salvage Company. Some scrap also moved from Montreal and the Maritimes to Ontario. Dosco had sufficiently large supplies of mill scrap to stay out of the market.[81]

The scrap steel situation in British Columbia was exceptional. The province had no use for scrap steel, yet all export of scrap was prohibited except for under licence. In September 1939 and for nearly two years, some 20,000 tons of steel scrap destined for Japan sat on Vancouver docks, keeping BC prices low. But until the United States imposed similar export restrictions, Canadian authorities were loath to allow it to go to the United States, where it might be exported, or to release US scrap for export. The United States finally imposed restrictions in the spring of 1941, and Canada allowed 25,000 tons of BC scrap to be exported to Bethlehem Steel Company at Seattle.

During 1941 a Greek freighter loaded with 7,400 tons of scrap destined for Japan was held at Victoria at the request of the British Ministry of Shipping, which wanted the ship. Disposition of the cargo required long, complicated negotiations involving the Japanese minister at Ottawa and the ship owner, and an order-in-council authorized its purchase by the Crown less than three weeks before the Japanese attacked Pearl Harbor. The cargo was subsequently sold to Bethlehem Steel.[82] About 10,000 tons of BC scrap were also exported to the United States in reciprocity for a similar amount being allowed to cross the border and enter eastern Canada from the United States. Twice that amount was shipped by special arrangement from British Columbia to Algoma between 15 June 1942 and 31 March 1943 in order to replace lost sources of scrap from northern Michigan and Minnesota. Approximately 3,000 tons a month had been shipped from British Columbia in 1941, and another 18,000 tons were ready to move in May 1942.[83] At the end of 1943, 25,000 tons of machinery scrap were gathered in British Columbia and exported to San Francisco.[84]

The great struggle to find scrap was not over, but by 1943 the system for drawing it from the farthest reaches of the country was in place and operating effectively. Whereas some smelters had previously possessed over a year's supply of scrap iron and steel even as other smelters had been working hand to mouth, by March 1943 all smelters had three to four month's supply, with no plant carrying less than enough for one month.[85]

The large imports of scrap from the United States in 1940 and 1941 are understandable in light of that country's nonbelligerent status, and so too is the tapering-off of imports in 1942 and the movement of scrap in the opposite direction in 1943. During the first six months of the year, Canada imported just over 10,000 tons of scrap and exported over 42,000 tons to the United States. For the whole year, Canada experienced a net loss of 68,717 tons (table 8.3). More important, the United States preferred to employ requests to Canadian Steel Control concerning the movement of scrap rather than issue formal restrictions. Even though steel production in Canada failed to surpass the figure for 1942 before the end of the war, the struggle to find sufficient scrap continued.

Domestic Production, 1942–45

Steel production reached a peak of 4.43 million tons in 1942, an amount nearly double Canada's steel production in 1939 and not exceeded until 1948.[86] Between 1943 and 1945 Canadian steel makers produced 11,301,793 tons, just over 4.34 millions tons annually (see table 8.1). Canadian steel consumption also peaked during 1942. Not to be confused with production, consumption is determined by adding the quantities of Canada's production and imports and deducting exports. The 4.3 million tons used was more than two and three-quarters times the 1939 level of consumption.[87] C.D. Howe's policy to expand production within the existing industry was paying off and endowing Canada with minimal excess capacity to plague the industry in peacetime.

The budgets drawn up by Steel Control for 1942 and quarterly thereafter proved to be remarkably accurate in their forecasts. This was due to the cooperation of the companies and the exigencies of wartime but also because the small number of producers, fewer than a dozen in the entire country, allowed government to obtain a clear picture of each facility's capabilities and to treat all facilities as a single entity.[88]

In response to government demands, Stelco officials initiated a third shift at their plate mill in October 1941, and by February 1942 the mill was producing between 16,000 and 17,000 tons monthly, well above its rated capacity of 180,000 tons per annum.[89] A 500-ton, unused blast furnace belonging to a Dosco subsidiary was transported from Ojibway, Ontario, to Sydney, where it was rehabilitated and brought into production. Scrap had become so scarce that Docso's plans to construct an open-hearth furnace had to be postponed in favour of making more pig iron.[90] A blast furnace with a capacity of 150 tons per day installed at Canadian Furnace at Port Colburne, Ontario, came into production on 1 March and began easing the foundry's pig iron shortage. Manitoba Rolling Mills built a 20-ton open-hearth furnace at Selkirk. Algoma also began a $17-million expansion program to step up production to 500,000 tons annually. Completion was expected in the spring of 1943. The extension and rehabilitation of facilities (additional coke ovens and open hearths) were to be completed by August to allow production to begin. Dosco's rehabilitated plate mill was broken in two months ahead of schedule on 17 March, and within a few weeks substantial tonnages of plates began to relieve shortages of one of the scarcest items under Steel Control due to the urgent demand for shipbuilding steel.[91]

By 1942 the quantity of steel castings of all sizes in Canada had more than doubled 1939 production, which had been approximately 5,000 tons per month. Production increased slightly in 1941, and with the expansion of foundries largely completed,

DMS officials anticipated average monthly production would grow to 8,300 tons. Average shipments beginning in March had already reached 6,000 tons monthly.[92]

Steel production was not without difficulties and challenges. A breakdown in communications within the DMS in February led to failure to coordinate steel orders. Divisions inside the ministry were ordering castings from producers without informing the steel controller. In one example, Wartime Merchant Shipping Limited approached Canada Iron Foundries for seventy-five sets of marine engine castings, which could not be obtained because the naval service required certain ones for its trawler minesweepers and corvettes.[93] Technical problems sometimes appeared unexpectedly. Only in early 1942, for example, did high sulphur and high phosphorous content in Canadian steel come to light in the United Kingdom, and only then was any move taken to exclude such steel from use in any part of ship machinery and its systems. This was an example of the relatively poor standard and inexperience of Canadian marine engineering.[94] The government also had its critics, such as the pro-labour publication *Canadian Forum*, which unfairly charged the steel industry and government with business-as-usual attitudes leading to failure to achieve full capacity in 1940 and 1941. The publication chastised management for excessive concern with earnings, competition between large and small companies, and postwar positioning and accused the government of reluctance to use its authority, lack of planning, and antilabour policy, all of which may have been true but were beside the point.[95]

In February, Harvey R. MacMillan claimed the shortage of ship plate was slowing the cargo shipbuilding program, which was currently using between 15,000 and

One of ten maintenance ships built for the Royal Navy's fleet train by Burrard Dry Dock Company in 1945. NVMA, no. 27-2311.

20,000 tons monthly. A month later, he loosed a blast at the steel controller, attacking three steel manufacturers for delayed shipments. Dofasco had received orders for 700 tons of plates from October to January but was two months in arrears, and about 500 tons per month would be required from April onward. Manitoba Rolling Mills, which supplied angles to five BC shipyards, "for months have been behind with their obligation." According to MacMillan, the cargo program could not be maintained unless 2,500 tons of angles and bars already on order were shipped in March and 1,300 tons monthly thereafter. He found the situation at Dosco even worse. Pictou Foundry and Machine Company, George T. Davie and Sons, and Marine Industries Limited could not hire any more men unless deliveries were made on time. Dosco needed to ship in March 2,000 tons currently on order and in April 2,000 additional tons.[96] MacMillan also accused the steel controller of ignoring the fact that in Canada shipbuilding carried a higher priority than was carried by "almost all other munitions efforts," which, he claimed, was also the case in the United States. He assumed that when Canadian mills failed to produce on shipbuilding orders, personnel in the controller's office had not set or had disregarded priorities. Neither was true.

Clearly stung by MacMillan's letter, Fred Kilbourn correctly denied that any formal system of priority rating existed in Canada; this absence permitted needed flexibility in deliveries in view of the numerous current projects for war manufactures.[97] Writing to the minister two days later, he denied he had abandoned the shipbuilding program, a charge MacMillan had not made, and accused him of not understanding that priority ratings were established in Washington.[98] This may have been a minor tempest, but more serious challenges to the shipbuilding program were never far off.

A case in point was the Aluminum Company of Canada's request to Steel Control for an increase in its steel allotment for April. The War Production Board's assignment to the aluminum industry of an A-1-a rating directly challenged both shipbuilding programs.[99] The armed services' manpower demands also threatened the steel industry. Howe claimed in September that steel output was down 15 per cent because more than 1,400 men had enlisted or been drafted. The minister favoured an order freezing men in their occupations, but defence minister Layton Ralston was opposed.[100]

During the summer of 1942, Wartime Merchant Shipping Limited (WMSL) consumed plate faster than it was being delivered to the shipyards. During June, July, and August, WMSL received 58,300 tons of plate and delivered twenty-seven 10,000-ton cargo ships containing 67,500 tons of hull plates. The deficit did not bode well for the final four months of the year, for which Steel Control allotted only 22,000 tons of plate monthly: 10,000 tons from Canada and 12,000 from the United States. WMSL planned to deliver forty-three ships containing 107,500 tons of plate, which would create an even greater deficit. Consuming steel inventory could not last.[101]

Insecurity of iron ore supply was a great weakness of the Dosco steel plant. In 1942 two loaded vessels carrying iron ore from Brazil to Sydney were sunk by enemy action, resulting in a loss, including the ships, of $3.5 million.[102] In September and November, German U-boats sank four ore ships with severe loss of life at the com-

Table 8.4 | Domestic production and imports of steel plate, 1939–45

Period		Domestic production	Imports	Total steel plates available
1939		75,655	28,721	104,376
1940		82,481	92,486[a]	174,967
1941	1st half	59,833	ndf[b]	ndf
	3rd qtr	60,653	ndf	ndf
	4th qtr	110,836	ndf	ndf
1942	1st qtr	71,289	56,937	128,226
	2nd qtr	89,180	92,292	181,472
	3rd qtr	83,820	71,379	155,199
	4th qtr	89,001	86,129	175,230
1943	1st qtr	93,460	95,522	188,982
	2nd qtr	99,098	84,635	183,733
	3rd qtr	95,737	83,988	179,725
	4th qtr	73,707	29,726	103,433
1944	1st qtr	95,856	14,727	110,583
	2nd qtr	96,686	14,152	110,837
	3rd qtr	91,377	20,393	111,770
	4th qtr	85,488	27,034	112,522
1945	1st qtr	80,397	16,383	96,780
	2nd qtr	76,590	9,727	86,317
	3rd qtr	60,001	8,501	68,502
	4th qtr	19,710	1,362	21,072
Total		1,690,855	834,094	2,014,383

[a] Records for 1940 are incomplete; this number is 1.2 times the actual imports in the first ten months.
[b] No data found.

Sources: NSARM, MG 2, box 1523, file 1.157, "Imports of Steel Plate into Canada," in J.D. Gray to W F. Drysdale, director general of munitions, 24 December 1940; LAC, RG 28, box 261, file 196-14-13, "Report on the Activities of the Steel Control … to October 1st, 1943," 51; and LAC, RG 28, box 22, "History of Steel Control, October 1st, 1943, to October 31st, 1945," 51; Canada, DBS, *Iron and Steel and Their Products in Canada, 1943–1945*, table 61.

pany's Wabana anchorage at Bell Island, Newfoundland.[103] These attacks forced temporary abandonment of the anchorage, occasioned construction of antitorpedo nets to protect the ore-loading wharves, and revealed how insecure iron ore supplies were for the Sydney mill. Scarcity of shipping for transporting ore from Wabana to Sydney and the submarine attacks led the Department of Munitions and Supply to arrange to reopen an old mine near Bathurst, New Brunswick.[104] Iron ore from Bathurst was never used; alternative supplies of superior ore were found in the United States, and the mine was closed in 1944.[105]

Supplies remained tight in the face of continuing new consumption by new military projects. In October the steel controller advised David Carswell that his steel inventories would have to be reduced from 7,000 to 2,000 tons of plate for all of Canada. Thirty repair yards could clearly not continue in business with such a small inventory, and Carswell refused to accept any further responsibility for delays to vessels being prepared for convoy work if the reductions were implemented.[106] The extreme steel shortage was soon relieved. In 1944 ship repairs received allotments of 1,000 tons of ship plate per month and obtained surplus stock at various yards left over from the shipbuilding cutback. Ship repairs used only 5,000 tons during the year, and the US's allocation of alloy steel was reduced to 3,000 tons per month.[107]

By the end of 1942 the Canadian steel-expansion program was complete. In November, Howe cancelled proposed further expansions at both of Dosco's Sydney mills and at Stelco in Hamilton.[108] At the beginning of 1943 the output of alloy steel was five times greater than it had been in 1939.[109] In three short years, Canada's steel-making industry had evolved from a run-down, incomplete, underdeveloped, unbalanced collection of coke ovens, blast and open-hearth furnaces, and rolling and finishing mills scattered across the country to become a single national industry integrated into the larger continental structure. Howe had never been interested in seeing a self-sufficient industry emerge, and when Washington's War Production Board denied priority assistance for further expansion, he did not object. Steel ingots and billets accumulated from US seaboard mills were offered to fill Canada's excess rolling capacity.[110]

Steel consumption declined from a high of nearly 4.3 million tons in 1942 to 3.6 million and 3.4 million tons in 1943 and 1944, respectively.[111] The steel budget for 1943 called for more than 5 million tons, leaving a shortage of 1.6 million tons beyond total estimated production. Table 8.5, showing estimated steel requirements of 775,000 tons for shipbuilding, indicates that the industry needed 15.5 per cent of the nation's total steel, a far cry from 1940, when the industry had consumed less than 5 per cent of the year's production. The naval and ship-repairs programs required just over one-fifth of the shipbuilding steel, and the merchant program needed the remainder.[112] This large figure is not a reflection of actual consumption, as the merchant shipbuilding program was sharply curtailed in mid-1943, but it does indicate the enormous place that shipbuilding was playing in the nation's war production. Plate and structural steel occupied the greatest place in shipbuilding needs, but the role of alloy and stainless steels should not be ignored. Despite comprising small amounts, they were vital to both programs.

Labour problems came to the fore in 1943 and accounted for a considerable loss of production. About 13,000 employees at Algoma and at Dosco's Trenton Steel Works went on strike during the latter part of January for about two weeks, resulting in a loss of about 65,000 tons of steel production. Steel Control also lost about 35,000 tons of steel imports during the first quarter owing to the application of US Production Requirements Plan regulations. Military service had drawn off robust mill workers,

Table 8.5 | Shipbuilding steel requirement for 1943[a]

Item	Shipbuilding programs			
	Naval	Merchant	Repairs	*Total*
Ingots, billets, and tube rounds	324	9,323		*9,647*
Structural shapes and piling	12,670	123,160	2,400	*138,230*
Plates (universal and sheared)	74,235	412,140	12,000	*498,375*
Hot rolled bars	13,550	22,730	1,500	*37,780*
Alloy wire and wire products	338	30	96	*464*
Alloy sheet, strip, pipes, tubes, and castings	104	858	962	
Cold finished bars	2,198	2,004	250	*4,452*
Pipe and tubing	10,912	18,588	1,600	*31,100*
Wire rods	695	3,292		*3,987*
Sheets and strip	16,100	6,960	1,500	*24,560*
Steel castings	5,662	10,980	2,000	*18,642*
Stainless bars[b]	96	110		*206*
Stainless sheets and strip	23	16		*39*
Stainless castings	28			*28*
Alloy ingots and billets		1,020		*1,020*
Alloy structural shapes	120			*120*
Alloy armour plate	3,670			*3,670*
Other alloy plates	1,224			*1,224*
Alloy hot rolled bars	398	169		*567*
Alloy cold finished bars	20	36		*56*
Total	*142,367*	*611,416*	*21,346*	*775,129*

[a] Short tons.
[b] Stainless steel bars, sheets and strip, and castings, in pounds in original, have been reduced to nearest ton to preserve consistency.

Source: LAC, RG 28, box 171, "Steel Budget for ... 1943," 15 February 1943.

and female and juvenile replacements were less productive. During the spring, deterioration of labour relations in steel mills across the country was so great that the union feared losing control of the situation. By June a monthly loss of production of about 10 per cent had occurred. Steel Control thought an estimated 1,600 men were needed to man the industry and to staff new equipment being installed at Algoma.[113]

In August 1943 the British made a second attempt to gain control of Canadian steel production when Sir John Ducanson, iron and steel controller in the British Ministry of Supply, co-authored a report with a US representative of the Combined Raw Materials Board criticizing the Canadian steel-control system and recommending it be amended so that all claimant agencies (i.e., UK-US combined boards) secured full information in order to control allocation for future use. It also recommended relieving the steel controller of responsibility for decisions over priorities, predetermining allocations (i.e., removing Canadian flexibility), and instituting quarterly returns to all consumers (i.e., the British).[114] Whatever its merits, the report had no hope of succeeding. Duncanson had ignored a report that Steel Control had presented to him in March, written a report filled with errors, and could not be bothered to send a copy to Steel Control.[115] It was little more than a crude display of imperial condescension. Regardless of whether it made good sense, the British high commissioner advised London that Canadians had no intention of accepting Duncanson's proposed centralized control.[116] Moreover, although the report claimed Canadians allocated too much steel to nonmilitary purposes, Steel Control claimed that considerably less steel went to civilian supply than in either Great Britain or the United States.[117]

Despite the labour problems and the effects of the Production Requirements Plan on US imports, plate production and plate importation in April was sufficient to maintain the shipbuilding program without interruption or curtailment and enabled Steel Control to build up fairly substantial inventories that had not existed eighteen months earlier. Two of Canada's three plate mills were running at full capacity, and Dosco's was producing at about two-thirds capacity.[118] The sharp curtailment of the merchant shipbuilding program during the second half of the year allowed Steel Control to return 30,000 tons of allotted carbon steel for the fourth quarter to the US War Production Board. This tonnage represented plates, structural sections, and bar-size structural shapes no longer required for cargo shipbuilding.[119]

This was just as well, for steel requirements in the United States remained very tight throughout 1944 and 1945, and the requirements of new Victory and Canadian types of cargo ships led to a resurgence in demand for plate.[120] Imports, which had comprised nearly one-third of the nation's steel consumption in 1943, made up less than one-quarter of Canadian consumption in 1944.[121] Further reduction of war programs led Canadian authorities to return another 30,000 tons allocated for the fourth quarter of 1944 (see table 8.2).[122] The cut in the merchant shipbuilding program temporarily eased the tightness in the supply of plate, but the demand for ship structurals and bar stock used to make bolts and rivets meant the programs continued to consume large quantities of steel. Orders for plate for the new types came in a flood.

Table 8.6 shows that from 1 July 1943 to 30 June 1944, the first twelve-month period of operations of the WPB's modified Controlled Materials Plan and of Steel Control's classification system, the combined Canadian shipbuilding programs consumed half a million net tons of steel. This included Canadian producers' shipments plus Steel Control's authorizations to import steel. These did not normally agree because American producers could ship steel fifteen days in advance or thirty days in arrears of the authorized month. This caveat notwithstanding, the distribution list reveals clearly the enormous impact the curtailment of the merchant shipbuilding program had in the final quarter of 1943.

What is missing here is a comparable table showing tons of ships built during the same quarters. Readers may find it useful to consult tables 11.1, 11.2, and 11.6, which show numbers of naval and merchant ships and displacement and deadweight ton-

Table 8.6 | Steel distribution in Canada for shipbuilding, 1 July 1943 to 30 June 1945*

Period		Shipbuilding programs			Net distribution
		Naval	Merchant	*Total*	
1943	3rd qtr	42,822	187,634	*230,456*	841,512
	4th qtr	27,929	46,307	*74,236*	729,449
1944	1st qtr	23,933	62,151	*86,084*	735,159
	2nd qtr	29,974	78,356	*108,330*	782,205
12-month total		*124,658*	*374,448*	*499,106*	*3,098,325*
Percentage of total		*4.02*	*12.08*	*16.10*	*100.00*
1944	3rd qtr	33,656	88,740	*122,396*	785,240
	4th qtr	37,400	49,598	*86,998*	810,878
1945	1st qtr	44,626	23,830	*68,456*	804,934
	2nd qtr	41,306	22,620	*63,926*	819,239
12-month total		*156,988*	*184,788*	*341,776*	*3,220,291*
Percentage of total		*4.87*	*5.73*	*10.60*	*100.00*

* Net tons, carbon and alloy steels combined.

Source: LAC, RG 28, box 22, "History of Steel Control, October 1st, 1943, to October 31st, 1945."

nage constructed by year for 1944 and 1945, in order to obtain a rough idea of production alongside steel distribution. The reduced distribution in the naval program is surprising in view of the number of warships launched during 1944 (see table 11.1), but table 8.6 shows increased steel consumption thereafter. During the year after the industry peaked, shipbuilding still consumed 16.1 per cent (nearly one of every six tons) of the steel available in the country, accounting for more than one-third, or 36.1 per cent, of all the steel directly employed in war production.[123]

During the first above-mentioned twelve-month period, Canadian steel makers produced 2,754,820 tons, or 75.4 per cent, of the total amount distributed, which meant that the 896,834 tons of imported steel had declined to 24.6 per cent of the total.[124] Between 1 July 1944 and 30 June 1945, Canadian steel production increased again, accounting for 76.2 per cent of total net distribution, and 903,505 tons of imported steel represented just 23.8 per cent of the total.[125] In March 1944 Canadian steel makers produced 233,070 gross tons of ingots – a wartime record. Labour availability remained the chief constraint on increasing production. The steel budget's call for 480,016 tons for the naval and merchant shipbuilding programs represented more than one-third less than the previous year's requirement (table 8.5).[126] In response to American appeals for relief under their lend-lease during the second quarter, Canada undertook to supply Great Britain, India, and the Soviet Union with 130,000 tons of steel rails, ingots, wire, and even ship plate under its own mutual-aid program.[127] Yet this apparent surfeit of steel hid continuing tight supply and low productivity. In July, Steel Control anticipated shipbuilding would require 377,509 tons for the first half of 1945, which on an annualized basis represented over 97 per cent of the 1943 requirement (see table 8.5).[128] Responding to a request for 22,500 net tons of ship plate for the month of August, the deputy steel controller could promise only 17,500 tons owing to demands from other producers and to overscheduling by the three steel mills.[129]

Dosco's production never met expectations. The opening of its rehabilitated plate mill at Sydney in March 1942 had been greeted with much public enthusiasm. Actual output of the mill, if working to capacity, would be 180,000 tons of plate annually.[130] But no such production level was ever achieved. During the opening phase, the mill not unexpectedly produced approximately 8,000 tons monthly.[131] But a year later, the mill continued to operate at two-thirds capacity.[132] During the first half of 1944, Dosco manufactured only 35,996 tons of ship plate, or about 6,000 tons monthly. Just over half was for Canadian shipbuilders. Dosco's costs were also far higher than those of Ontario mills. Nor was the situation likely to change. Steel Control concluded that Stelco at Hamilton was producing approximately double the tonnage of steel ingots with 1,000 fewer employees than Dosco.[133]

High costs were to be expected, but low productivity was not. Late in February 1944 Arthur Cross, president of Dosco, promised total steel production would reach 50,000 tons per month in May, but from April to June monthly averages declined 10 per cent to 43,825 tons despite the fact that the steel plant had a monthly rated capacity of 53,000 tons.[134] By June, Howe had become fed up with continual unfulfilled promises and the constant drain of subsidies. Also, Steel Control did not expect the plate mill, a rebuild of an old plant put into operation as a matter of war emergency, to be useful after the war.[135]

The basic cause of the company's difficulties was uneconomical iron ore. Before the war, small profits had been achieved at the expense of unduly low wages.[136] Dosco delivered less than 32,000 tons of plate during the first ten months of the year to Wartime Shipbuilding Limited. In view of the large subsidies, the minister unofficially directed Steel Control to use Dosco "to the minimum extant possible even if we have to buy steel in the United States."[137] In September, Wartime Shipbuilding Limited ceased placing orders for ship plate and cancelled all outstanding orders beyond the end of October.[138] To reduce the size of the subsidies, Howe instructed Wartime Shipbuilding to pay $11 per ton extra for all the ship plate delivered during the first eight months of 1944 and ordered the Crown corporation to pay $75 per ton (50 per cent greater than was paid to Ontario mills) for 7,762 tons to be shipped in September and October.[139]

Not surprisingly, plate supplies remained tight until the end of the war. Steel Control endeavoured to obtain 19,000 tons of plate in the United States, but none was available.[140] Consequently, in February 1945 the controller's office requested that Wartime Shipbuilding Limited place the largest possible tonnage with Dosco to relieve the situation at the Ontario mills. President C.L. Dewar followed instructions, ordering as much as possible for February and nearly 43 per cent of a total of 13,705 tons of plate for March and April from the Cape Breton mill. Rolling schedules were full until May, and the war ended so quickly that there was no full schedule at any of the three steel companies in June.[141] Acquiring sufficient ship plate had remained a struggle until the end.

Late in August 1945 the US War Production Board announced that the Controlled Materials Plan, under which Canada secured its steel quota, was being discontinued and that steel would be released on a selective priority basis. Canadian officials thought Steel Control should also be dissolved, leaving the DMS's priorities branch to handle any steel requirements from the United States. Orders for steel plates and mill scheduling for imported steel were withdrawn in mid-October. The Canadian government obtained title to Dosco's plate mill in return for assuming the $2.4 million liability the company still owed and closed it before the end of September.[142] The only control orders remaining were those affecting iron and steel scrap and the one limiting steel inventories. These were rescinded and re-enacted as orders-in-council of the Wartime Prices and Trade Board, and on 1 November, Steel Control was terminated.[143]

Conclusion

By the end of 1942 Canada's steel-making plants had become fully integrated in a single continental industry. It was on the whole productive, efficient, and prosperous. The Second World War wrought a major change to the Canadian steel industry, transforming it from one marked by technical deficiency and low productivity to one that was relatively advanced and able to produce a broad range of steel products never before manufactured in Canada. Moreover, to the satisfaction of the Americans, this had been done by virtually eliminating Canadian dependence on imported scrap. Paraphrasing historian Duncan McDowall, the mixture of anxiety and resentment with which steel owners and management greeted government intrusion into every aspect of their affairs in 1940 gave way to a "consensus of expediency" that shifted gradually into a lasting basis of understanding, consultation, and accommodation as both partners sought an orderly return to a prosperous, peacetime economy.[144] This was not a product of laissez-faire capitalism but rather a joint work of private management and government investment, direction, and consumption.

Among the wartime industry's greatest achievements was manufacturing steel in all the many types required by the shipbuilding industry. Little that was consumed in such large quantities for the naval and merchant programs had ever before been made in this country. At the same time, Steel Control's greatest achievement was to negotiate successfully with American authorities for ship plate and to keep the supply coming even if it was reduced. The cooperation over the use of steel that ultimately developed between Canadians and Americans may have owed much to the fact that many officials were businessmen engaged in getting things done rather than civil servants managing files.

9 | Machinery, Manufacturers, and Auxiliary Equipment

Introduction

Although ships were being launched almost daily somewhere in Canada between 1942 and 1945, shipyards would have failed if manufacturers and subcontractors across the country had not made regular, scheduled, on-time deliveries of an enormous variety of machinery, parts, and equipment. In addition to 700 tons of steel plates and shapes, each Canadian-built corvette required 39 tons of copper wiring, 14 tons of anchor chain, 1,500 brass valves weighing from 8 ounces to 700 pounds, and 600 light bulbs.[1] A 10,000-ton freighter needed 110 tons of piping and tubing, 600 valves, 25 tons of copper wire, and 7,000 yards of wire rope.[2] A single minesweeper consumed 1,100 valves, 2.5 miles of piping, 32 miles of electrical wiring, 26 tons of copper, and 350,000 to 375,000 man-hours of labour.[3] Every corvette, frigate, and transport ferry (LST3), most minesweepers, and each medium and large merchant ship were supplied with one or two triple-expansion, steam-driven reciprocating engines. They also received two or more propellers (some were spares), shafts, two or three coal-fired Scotch marine boilers or two oil-fired water-tube boilers, a condenser, a steering engine, and two or more anchors. When it came to marine forgings, the finished rudderstock for a 10,000-ton freighter weighed 48.8 tons, and its rudder main pieces weighed 163.7 tons; the tail nut alone weighed 440 pounds.[4]

All ships required a steam-powered anchor windlass, and merchant ships were equipped with twelve pumps, three generators, twelve booms, eleven winches, ventilators, hatch covers, life rafts and life boats, lockers, gauges, miles of electrical wiring and pipe from 0.25 inch to 12 inches in diameter, and a storeroom full of spare parts and fittings. Indeed, a 10,000-ton cargo ship required about 7,000 separate items, ranging from galley equipment to medical stores.[5] By 1943 it also carried nearly as much armament as a frigate.

Canada was not a highly industrialized country. At the beginning of the war, the country's engineering industries had limited capacity. Capability in engineering design and innovation was very circumscribed. Although significant progress in industrialization occurred during the war, the level of technology was considerably behind the major belligerent powers. Unlike in the United States, where prodigious examples of industrial production became the norm and where the fraction of na-

SS *Laurentide Park*, North Sands–type dry-cargo ship completed at Marine Industries Limited, 29 April 1943, with a 60-foot harbour tug, CT-74, built for the British Ministry of War Transport, stowed on the starboard side aft as deck cargo. SHPS, P006, Fonds de Marine Industries Ltd, series 2, subseries 2, subsubseries 1, D19.

tional output constituted by the thousands of items flowing into shipyards caused few problems, the small industrial base and limited manufacturing facilities in Canada required the government to take the greatest care to coordinate the nation's industrial war production.

Despite these limitations, the volume of manufacturing increased. After 1940, for the first time, Canada's net value of manufacturing exceeded that of primary production, and by 1943 it was over 50 per cent higher.[6] In 1944 the annual gross value of manufacturing in Canada exceeded the average gross value for the period 1935–39 by 182 per cent.[7] With the exception of steel plate, 95 per cent of all the material going into Canadian-built ships was domestic in origin.[8] How that occurred and who contributed are the focus of this chapter. Not every item needs to be mentioned or discussed; the aim is to provide a general idea of the breadth of industrial activity and the human initiative that was often displayed.

The government had no alternative but to utilize the whole engineering industry of Canada to manufacture machinery and component parts and to relieve shipyards of a great deal of auxiliary-equipment production. Only Canadian Vickers Limited was capable of building a ship from keel to masthead, providing engines and boilers, condensers, steering gear, winches, and windlasses. Shipyards had never provided everything required for a ship. Thousands of separate items, ranging from navigational instruments to temperature and pressure gauges, were demanded. The naval service was charged with scheduling production of warships, but this was accomplished only by working through the shipbuilding branch of the Department of Munitions and Supply (DMS), which worked as both a regulator and a procuring body. Other branches of the DMS played important roles in scheduling materials going into the ships. The steel controller was of critical importance, and negotiations and production branches were vital in arranging and scheduling the manufacture, delivery, and flow of machinery and auxiliary equipment. Naval armament and equipment was another vitally important branch.

The branch was crucial to the British Admiralty Technical Mission's (BATM) success. In September 1940 C.D. Howe appointed Frank Ross as director general of naval armament to place contracts and supervise production of stores and equipment for both the Royal Navy (RN) and the Royal Canadian Navy (RCN), which created a naval equipment branch only in 1942.[9] Ross's immediate task was to coordinate the demands of both services and to locate suitable production facilities. The branch faced two difficulties. First, the best engineering firms in the country were already heavily engaged in war work, and second, the naval service's orders were rarely large enough to adopt multiple production methods for manufacture.[10] The strain on Canada's manufacturing capacity became very much greater in the spring of 1941 after the introduction of the cargo shipbuilding program.

Authorities at the Department of Munitions and Supply quickly realized that the nation's capacity to build ships depended upon its ability to manufacture components for the shipyards to assemble. Great Britain could not be relied upon for delivery of components because its own requirements were increasing and because shipments across the Atlantic were daily growing more precarious. In March 1941 German U-boats sank 489,299 tons of shipping. In April almost 800,000 tons went down.[11] The continually expanding US shipbuilding program also made it inadvisable to rely upon American sources of supply. Consequently, in the spring and early summer of 1941, department officials conducted a rapid but extensive study of Canada's manufacturing capacity. The country's industrial capacity already appeared to be filled by war contracts. Industry was then asked to produce components that were new for Canada. For example, engines, propellers of the size required for large ships, and other items had never been built in this country.

By June the survey of the country's capacity made clear that in order to maintain control of production of components, some central authority had to be created. Until that time, shipyards had been ordering their own machinery and auxiliary equipment. Any new building program would place intolerable pressure on them. Shipyards would be buying in competition with one another in a seller's market, and results would be chaotic. A central plan was adopted for shipyards to receive components according to their capacity to use them, which enabled the DMS to keep a more effective check on shortages and to approve the use of substitutes where necessary.[12]

On 27 June 1941, on the recommendation of Wartime Merchant Shipping Limited (WMSL), order-in-council PC 4737 authorized the Crown company to purchase all major components directly and to supply them to the shipbuilders as government issue.[13] Shipbuilders would reduce the prices established for the ships by the amount it normally cost them for these components. In this way, WMSL bought large quantities and effected considerable savings, eventually purchasing more than sixty major components, including main engines, boilers, condensers, superheaters, pumps, shafting, windlasses, winches, booms, steering gear, stern frames, propellers, and electrical generators and generating sets. WMSL carried out and completed all of its own negotiations for these parts. Contracts were normally let on a fixed-price basis, with escalator clauses covering changes in labour and material costs if the period was extended over a long time or if the contract was for a large amount. Speaking on 15 October at the launching of the West Coast's first 10,000-ton freighter, Harvey Mac-Millan claimed that over 150 engineering firms, of which more than one-third were located in British Columbia and Alberta, were already contributing to the shipbuilding programs on a daily basis.[14] Later, the number for all manufacturers associated with shipbuilding rose to nearly 500.

After numerous objections from manufacturers to the necessity of perusing and signing lengthy formal contracts when the supplies ordered were only of moderate value, in April 1942 the minister gave Wartime Merchant Shipping Limited its own authority to place orders for amounts up to $100,000. Also, early in 1942 the US Maritime Commission faced a shortage in its own supplies of some components, and WMSL placed orders for them with Canadian manufacturers.[15] Although this put a heavy burden on Canadian production schedules as units originally destined for Canadian shipbuilders were diverted to American shipyards, this caused no delays in the delivery of Canadian ships. By the end of 1943 twenty-three marine engines, sixty-five stern frames, and six winches had been shipped south, and thirty-four sets of anchor-chain cable were on order. Before 1942 Canada had not manufactured anchor chain.

Several plants manufacturing machinery and auxiliary equipment were enlarged and more completely equipped to meet both navy and cargo shipbuilding programs as shipyards expanded. This was accomplished by substantial capital assistance, and as already noted (see chapter 4), in order to reduce risk, the government allowed manufacturers accelerated depreciation on machinery and machine tools bought for war production and guaranteed them against losses by allowing them cost-plus contracts. Manufacturers were paid certain guaranteed amounts over whatever it cost to produce an item rather than determining a final price beforehand. Eighteen companies in the cargo ship program and seventeen in the naval program received assistance. Two examples, steering engines and anchor cable, illustrate both expansion problems and the responses to them.

George W. Allan, president of Canadian Sumner Iron Works at Vancouver, displayed outstanding initiative in contributing to Canada's emergency shipbuilding programs. His thirty-year-old company had manufactured steering engines, pumps, and other equipment during the First World War and had continued on a greatly reduced scale afterward. Allan modernized and redesigned much equipment during the interwar years, anticipating the needs of an expanded shipbuilding program in Canada. He also sought, but failed to obtain, permissions from four British firms to manufacture their patented steering engines.[16] Upon their refusals, the company, led by chief engineer Percy Bland, designed its own equipment, obtained approval from government authorities, and began delivering steering engines and other auxiliary machinery to shipyards in British Columbia, Ontario, Quebec, and the Maritimes far ahead of anticipated schedules.[17] Sumner designed an 8-by-8-inch steering engine for the cargo ships, and manufactured 70 per cent of the steering engines used in the cargo program.[18] William Kennedy and Sons and Stephens Adamson Manufacturing made some under licence, but the experience of Canadian Sumner Iron Works illustrates the private entrepreneurial drive behind much wartime production, which is often attributed solely to government departments. Successful completion of earlier projects led Canadian Sumner to be chosen to manufacture the steam-driven, hydraulic, steering-gear unit for the 1942–43 frigate program.[19] At peak production in 1944, the company employed 240 people, including 40 women, who manufactured ten cargo and three frigate steering engines per month. By the war's end, the firm had manufactured 389 steering engines, including 258 for the cargo ship program.[20]

Until early 1943 all anchor chain was purchased in the United States from Baldt Anchor, Chain and Forge Company at Chester, Pennsylvania. In a single press release in 1942 the Department of Munitions and Supply reported buying 25 miles of anchor chain of various types and lengths for Canadian naval use. Even this purchase was sufficient to supply only a small number of warships currently under construction.[21] So much anchor chain was needed that the wartime requirement for each freighter was reduced by 45 fathoms (83.2 m).[22]

Anchor cables required time to manufacture. Sixteen sets ordered from Baldt's in January 1942 were to be delivered at a rate of only one to three per month between the following July and February 1943. Further reduction of the wartime requirement for each cargo ship to 180 fathoms (329 m) in response to the growing expansion of the American shipbuilding program led to a decision to create a Canadian source of supply. A government-owned plant was set up on Granville Island, Vancouver, and Wartime Merchant Shipping Limited contracted with Electro-Weld Metal Products Limited to manufacture and supply 144 sets of anchor-chain cable for the cargo ship program.[23] The Crown company purchased the process outright from Pacific Chain and Manufacturing Company at Portland, Oregon.[24] "Electro-weld" cable was manufactured according to the same process employed in the US firm's Seattle plant. Bar stock was cut to the exact length required to make individual links, heated in a furnace, and formed by pressure around a mandrel, the stud was inserted, and the joint was "Unionmelt" welded. The plant was soon turning out 15 fathoms (27.4 m) per shift, or fifteen sets of chain per month. The venture was so successful that Canadian-type 10,000-tonners were supplied with a full prewar quantity of 270 fathoms (494 m) of anchor cable, which was also exported to the United States.[25]

Propulsion Machinery

Propulsion machinery includes everything necessary to drive a ship through the water: engines, boilers, and related equipment. Engines include marine versions of steam-turbine, diesel, and gasoline types, but the chief propulsion unit in Canada's wartime shipbuilding industry was the triple-expansion, steam-driven reciprocating engine. It was a simple piece of machinery. Machinery for the Flower-class corvette was based on a 1936 whale-catcher design by Smith's Dock Company near Middlesborough, Yorkshire, but it was up rated from the indicated 2,300 horsepower (hp) to 2,750 indicated horsepower (ihp) with higher rotations per minute (rpm).[26] A complete corvette engine set included throttle valve, condenser, thrust block and shaft, intermediate shaft and plummer block, stern tube, tail shaft, bronze propeller, tools, and spares.[27] Twin versions of the same engine powered the frigates and transport ferries (LST3s) built in Canada. To get a more powerful engine without a low-pressure cylinder of unmanageably large diameter, two identical low-pressure cylinders of smaller dimensions were substituted. This was the largest marine engine built in Canada. It stood 15.5 feet high, was 22.5 feet in length, and including the condenser, weighed 78 tons.[28] About 331 were manufactured and installed in Canadian-built warships.

This was antiquated marine propulsion technology. Indeed, marine triple-expansion, steam-driven engines were no longer manufactured in the United States, and in 1941 their use was revived to build the North Sands–type ships for the British Merchant Shipbuilding Mission and for the Liberty ship program because they were less complicated than either diesels or turbines.[29] They cost much less to manufacture and could be quickly produced. Slow production of steam turbines in the United States may have been a factor, and the underdeveloped state of British diesel technology may also have affected the decision. John Harland has suggested that this is why LST3s, ordered late in the war, continued to rely on the same engine that powered the original corvettes.[30] Canadians' ability to build steam-powered reciprocating engines based on First World War experience was an added bonus. Finally, no difficulty was met in obtaining marine engineers with operating experience to man merchant ships equipped with these units, which could also be repaired virtually anywhere in the world.[31]

Canadian Vickers built all of its own marine engines and boilers from the beginning until the end of the war and also delivered others to Morton Engineering and Dry Dock Company at Quebec City. On the Great Lakes, Collingwood Shipyards Limited and Port Arthur Shipbuilding Company built their own engines. After switching to Algerine-class minesweepers in 1942, Port Arthur Shipbuilding shipped its engines elsewhere. The twin engines for the new Algerines were the same as for the Bangor class and were delivered ready for installation from Canadian Allis-Chalmers Limited. Because all of the patterns and castings for corvette engines were available, the company continued to build them in its machine shops, whence they were

Clockwise from top left: Workman machining a crankshaft for a corvette steam engine at Canadian Vickers Limited, c. 1940. LAC, C-032681; Workmen assembling the columns for a corvette engine at Canadian Vickers Limited, c. 1940. LAC, C-032679; Fitting a crankshaft into a steam engine under construction at Canadian Vickers Limited, c. 1940. LAC, C-032783; Possibly the first of more than 330 2,750-ihp triple-expansion, steam-driven reciprocating engines manufactured in Canada for the naval shipbuilding program. Built at Canadian Vickers Limited, 25 July 1940. LAC, C-032839.

shipped to Midland, Collingwood, Kingston, Quebec City, and even Esquimalt.[32] The boiler shop continued to build boilers for all its ships, successfully switching over to manufacture the intricately constructed water-tube boilers for Algerines.[33]

Other manufacturers of these large steam engines were John Inglis Company at Toronto, Dominion Engineering Works at Montreal, and Dominion Bridge Company at Lachine.[34] In 1943 the Canadian Pacific Railway retooled part of its Angus shops in Montreal and began manufacturing these engines and main condensers. Seventy-five were produced at a rate of one per week.[35] British Admiralty specifications called for special high-pressure, nickel-steel engine-cylinder castings for steam engines mounted in corvettes and frigates. These were cast by Warden King Limited at Montreal and rough machined before being shipped to Canadian Vickers and Dominion Engineering Company for finishing and final assembly.[36]

Bangor-class minesweepers were fitted with two much smaller triple-expansion reciprocating engines, which together gave 2,400 ihp. Canadian Allis-Chalmers Limited built them at its Rockfield plant outside Montreal. The company began manufacturing marine steam engines from the beginning, in 1940; the first version, for the Bangor, was followed in 1941 by a larger version (2,500 ihp), for the North Sands–type cargo ship. Like other manufacturers of marine engines, Canadian Allis-Chalmers was able to fall back on First World War experience and its long-term, skilled workforce. Many employees had served the company for over twenty-five years. By December 1941 the company had completed sixty Bangor engines, including condensers and shafting, and had delivered them to Toronto, Port Arthur, and Vancouver.

Suppliers of main engines for cargo ships were hard to find owing to lateness in introducing the program. North-Eastern Marine Engineering Company at Wallsend-on-Tyne developed the 2,500-hp, steam-driven reciprocating engine, which produced speeds of 11 knots. In July, Canadian Allis-Chalmers contracted for seventy-three sets of main engines for 10,000-tonners. Deliveries began in December, and by November 1943 forty-seven had been produced and shipped.[37] Other manufacturers of this engine were Dominion Engineering Company at Montreal and John Inglis Company at Toronto. Collingwood Shipyards Limited built some of the smaller 850-ihp engines that powered the Western Isles trawler minesweepers built there and at Midland, Kingston, and Quebec City. Consolidated Mining and Smelter Company at Trail, British Columbia, built others.[38]

Following the introduction of more powerful depth charges, corvettes, frigates, and Algerines experienced cracked engine bedplates owing to the violent concussions of underwater explosions. At the BATM's request, Dominion Bridge Company undertook to solve the problem and developed an entirely new bedplate acceptable to British and Canadian naval authorities and to the classification-society surveyors from Lloyd's Register of Shipping and from British Corporation Register of Shipping and Aircraft. Welded steel plates replaced iron castings in the new design, and special fabricating methods and welding procedures were developed to secure the necessary accuracy. The bedplates were stress-relieved before machining so that they would possess the required strength and ductility to absorb the shocks from underwater

Table 9.1 | Engines and boilers manufactured for merchant shipbuilding, 1939–45

Location and company	Engines 10,000 tons	Engines 4,700 tons	Boilers (ship sets)* 10,000 tons Scotch	Boilers (ship sets)* 10,000 tons Water-tube	Boilers (ship sets)* 4,700 tons
British Columbia					
Dominion Bridge Co.			68		
Vancouver Iron Works Ltd			62	123	
Ontario					
John Inglis Co.	58		34		
Quebec					
Canadian Allis-Chalmers Ltd	89				
Canada Iron Foundries Ltd		33	13		
Canadian Vickers Ltd	6				
Dominion Bridge Co.		10	45		43
Dominion Engineering Works	197				
United States					
American Locomotive Works			9		
General Machinery Corp.	4				
Total	*354*	*43*	*231*	*123*	*43*

* Three Scotch boilers and two water-tube boilers comprised a ship set for 10,000-tonners, and two Scotch boilers constituted a ship set for 4,700-tonners.

Source: Robson, "Merchant Shipbuilding in Canada," 284.

explosions. There was no recurrence of the problem, and the information was made available to other producers.[39]

A smaller engine that developed 1,176 ihp drove the medium-size Gray-type freighter. Central Marine Engine Works at West Hartlepool, England, supplied all specifications and drawings. Early in 1942 Wartime Merchant Shipping Limited contracted with Dominion Bridge Company for eighteen sets of main engines and marine boilers for the 4,700-ton vessels. Delivery was to commence with five engines in July 1942, with the remainder to be delivered thereafter until February 1943.[40] In 1943 Canada Iron Foundries Limited contracted to manufacture twenty-six additional sets of main engines at its Trois Rivières plant. Deliveries, one or two per month, were to begin in June and continue until September 1944.[41] Some orders were switched from Dominion Bridge to Canada Iron Foundries, and only forty-three engines were built for this class of vessel (see table 9.1).

After construction of minesweepers was concluded at Prince Rupert Dry Dock and Shipbuilding Company and Burrard Dry Dock Company in the fall of 1941 and at North Van Ship Repairs Limited the following winter, concentration on building 10,000-ton cargo ships made the situation on the West Coast much simpler. Thereafter, with the exception of Yarrows Limited, BC yards built only the North Sands type and its variants.

Vancouver workers had protested after Burrard Dry Dock ordered six engines from eastern Canada for the first minesweepers, and the Vancouver Trades and Labour Council passed a resolution demanding all future BC-built ships be fitted with locally built engines.[42] But table 9.1 shows that all engines installed in BC-built ships were constructed in eastern Canada. Only boilers were manufactured on the West Coast.

No comprehensive statistics for Canadian marine-engineering output during the Second World War seem to have been kept. Between 1940 and 1945 an estimated 571 reciprocating engines totalling 1,147,850 ihp were manufactured for the naval ship-building program, and 403 units amounting to 950,568 ihp were produced for the cargo ship program. This may bear no comparison with UK or US production, but as Canada had not possessed a marine-engineering industry for many years prior to the war, it represented a magnificent, if wholly derivative, effort.[43]

A condenser is an apparatus that collects used steam from the main engines, converts it into water, and returns it warm to the boilers, thus conserving energy and fresh water. The main condenser on a 10,000-ton freighter used about 3 miles of brass tubing cut into 1,584 10-foot lengths and mounted inside a steel body. A corvette condenser contained about 1 mile of similar tubing cut into 788 pieces.[44] Condensers posed a big challenge to manufacturers. Materials and parts had to be procured from many cities because they were manufactured from iron, steel, bronze, and copper. Condensers made by Dominion Bridge Company involved assembling castings, billets, gauges, tubing, and valves gathered from Montreal, St John, Sault Ste Marie, Sherbrooke, Toronto, Trois Rivières, and Welland, as well as from Carbondale and Chicago in the United States.[45]

Boiler technology was limited when war began. The corvette's designer had intended to fit the vessel with water-tube boilers, but with hostilities imminent, this relatively sophisticated equipment was reserved for "real" warships, so corvettes in the first program received a pair of oil-fired Scotch boilers. The Scotch boiler was the ideal other half of the unit comprising the steam-driven reciprocating engine; its maximum design pressure coincided with the cargo ship's triple-expansion engine of 220 pounds, sometimes put up to 250 pounds. It was still a medium-pressure boiler not suitable for higher pressures necessary for turbine machinery. It was also a very slow boiler requiring twelve to twenty-four hours to get a ship under way. Many favoured it because of its simplicity and lower capital cost. Apart from minor differences in furnace design and shape, the Scotch boiler of the 1940s was similar to one of sixty years before.[46] Three-drum, water-tube boilers replaced these fire-tube boilers in later "Revised" corvettes and frigates.[47]

Although the earliest true water-tube boilers appeared in the 1860s, they came into their own only in the mid-1890s when Babcock and Wilcox brought out their version of a straight-tube header boiler. A completely different type appeared shortly after the turn of the century: the Yarrow three-drum, small-tube boiler. Water-tube boilers represented a significant advance over the older Scotch boilers. Their most distinctive feature is that the water from which steam is generated is inside the tubes, with the flame and hot gases outside.[48] In cylindrical and locomotive boilers, this is reversed, with the hot gases passing through the tubes to heat the water outside. Yarrow boilers had nearly 3,000 water tubes of small diameter and demanded great care and precision in their manufacture. They also cost nearly three times as much as a Scotch boiler.[49]

Page-Hersey Tubes Limited at Welland, Ontario, manufactured the vital tubes necessary for the boilers. In 1941 the company purchased thirty-five acres of property adjoining its plant from Canadian Car and Foundry and built a cold-draw plant to manufacture small-diameter pipe within close tolerances. The federal government provided more than $1.2 million for the facility to produce tubing for the boilers for corvettes, frigates, and Tribal-class destroyers.[50]

Minesweepers, corvettes, frigates, and LST3s each required two Scotch marine boilers, and the North Sands–type and Gray-type merchant ships required three and two, respectively. A "ship set" refers to all the boilers in a particular ship. Canadian Vickers Limited, Babcock-Wilcox and Goldie-McCullough at Galt, Foster-Wheeler Limited at St Catharines, and John Inglis Company all manufactured both Scotch marine and water-tube boilers for the naval construction program; Dominion Bridge Company and John Inglis produced them for the cargo ship program (see table 9.1).[51] Foster-Wheeler, which also manufactured evaporators for corvettes, received $200,000 in capital assistance partly to cover the cost of an annealing furnace and x-ray equipment.[52]

Babcock-Wilcox and Goldie-McCulloch manufactured water-tube boilers for minesweepers being built at Toronto. The company produced 132 marine boilers for the naval program between 1940 and 1944. These comprised 32 three-drum, bent-tube boilers (2 per set) for Bangor-class minesweepers for Dufferin (later Toronto) Shipbuilding Company, 18 cross-drum, marine boilers (2 per set) for corvettes built at Midland, Collingwood, Kingston, Yarrows, and Victoria Machinery Depot, and 78 three-drum Admiralty boilers (2 per set) for Algerine-class minesweepers for Toronto Shipbuilding and 4 three-drum Admiralty boilers shipped to Marine Industries Limited for LST3s.[53]

By April 1943 the five eastern boiler manufacturers were cooperating closely with one another and producing 37.5 units per month. Although they had excess manufacturing capacity, tube delivery was a constant problem. To manufacture boilers for four corvettes, four Algerines, and four frigates, the companies required more than half a million feet of 1- to 1.5-inch tubes each month.[54]

Vancouver Iron Works Limited and Dominion Bridge Company's Vancouver plant manufactured all the marine boilers fitted on the West Coast. Vancouver Iron Works manufactured 516 marine boilers for 227 ships built in British Columbia. The company's first job was constructing 44 Yarrow-type boilers for the 22 minesweepers built in the province. Later, it built all of the water-tube boilers for frigates and LST3s. Development of new methods and special machinery built in-house greatly aided production. A high degree of accuracy in the drilling of tube holes in the drum

A Scotch marine boiler manufactured for a 10,000-ton freighter by John Inglis Company, Toronto, en route to Marine Industries Limited, Sorel, Quebec. LAC, CNR 4373-6.

was required; Vancouver Iron Works adopted the use of multiple drills to make and ream the hundreds of thousands of tube holes.

Machinery invented by A.E. House, mechanical superintendent at Vancouver Iron Works, allowed hundreds of marine boilers to be electrically welded, enabling even the irregularly shaped combustion chambers to be automatically welded. The process quite amazed members of the British shipbuilding trade-union delegation that toured the United States and Canada during the winter of 1942–43. The chambers were wholly welded by a "Unionmelt" machine mounted on an ingenious device of local design for revolving the chambers slowly so that the welding machine remained horizontal while travelling along a parallel rail track that completely encompassed the chamber. Every inch of the weld was subsequently examined by radiography (x-ray photography) and invariably found to be perfect. Under the right conditions, the "Unionmelt" machines could produce a thoroughly reliable weld to resist steam pressure as well as join metal plates together.[55] Lloyd's Register of Shipping approved the company's methods for class-A pressure work. All welded drums were stress-relieved, being heated to a temperature of 1,250 degrees Fahrenheit in specially built furnaces.[56]

Some 428 boilers were built for 183 of the largest cargo ships. Sixty-two North Sands and Canadian types required 3 Scotch boilers each; Vancouver Iron Works built half of them and Dominion Bridge built the other half. The former company also constructed all 242 water-tube boilers required on the West Coast for Victory ships, which were fitted with 2 each (see table 9.1).[57] Under the press of wartime orders, Dominion Bridge Company departed from accepted methods of manufacture to increase production. Standardized boiler parts were made. Boiler heads made at Lachine were shipped to Vancouver and elsewhere, and combustion-chamber heads were supplied to every boiler manufacturer in Canada. The company also developed, over some opposition, a completely welded Scotch marine boiler, and with the assistance of Wartime Merchant Shipping Limited and the classification societies, the company's innovations were accepted. By 1944 the Lachine and Vancouver plants of Dominion Bridge were producing seventeen Scotch marine boilers per month, and all 4,700-ton cargo ships were being fitted with the all-welded version.[58] Canadian innovation was a major contributor to successful production.

Although marine diesel technology was not entirely absent from Canadian ship-building during the war, it proved uneconomical to build large marine diesel engines. The RCN ordered ten Bangors to be powered by 1,000-hp 9RS29 Sulzer diesel engines, but the experiment was not a success. The second largest of the Dominion-Sulzer type of marine engines, this one of 9 cylinders, was cast in blocks of three and bolted together to produce one unit; it had a one-piece forged crankshaft. The twin-screw minesweepers employed two engines each. Suzler Brothers Limited at Winterthur, Switzerland, designed the engines, and a major problem facing Dominion Engineering Works, where the engines were manufactured under licence, was to convert all the metric dimensions on hundreds of drawings. The engineering department finally had to make a whole new set.[59] Although the drawings were produced, the time taken to manufacture the engines proved uneconomical. A 2,750-ihp steam engine required 3.6 hours of labour per horsepower to manufacture, whereas the two 1,000-ihp diesel engines required 14 hours of labour per horsepower. Moreover, unlike machine shops, boiler shops were not congested with work orders.[60]

Several interesting experiments were introduced during the war, but generally speaking, Canadian-designed and -built marine diesel engines were confined to tugs and auxiliary craft. Will Vivian, sole owner of Vivian Engine Works Limited at Vancouver, enjoyed the greatest success manufacturing diesel engines. A brilliant tinkerer, Vivian designed all of his own engines. He founded the company thirty years before the war and had established a reputation on the West Coast and overseas. Production skyrocketed during the war, when the company manufactured over 690 engines totalling more than 190,000 hp.[61]

Over 100 different types of Vivian engines were fitted into many small craft. A 10-cylinder, 400-hp marine diesel powered a 94-foot, target-towing tug launched in January 1941.[62] The company's 500-hp diesel engines powered 105-foot, wooden minesweepers, and its 10-cylinder, 625-hp engines went into nine 126-foot mine-sweepers built on the West Coast for the RCN.[63] By 31 October 1942 the company was manufacturing 87 diesel engines, with a total horsepower of 31,821, for Australian, Brazilian, New Zealand, Newfoundland, and US governments as well as for all three Canadian armed services, the United States Army, and the local logging and fishing industries.[64] Two years later, the company had shipped 137 6-cylinder, 240-hp engines east for 60-foot tugboats being constructed for the British Ministry of War Transport at Trenton, Walkerville, and Owen Sound, Ontario.[65] That year, 1944, claimed Vivian, his company manufactured 52 per cent of all diesels made in Canada. Earlier, it had shipped some of its larger 320-hp models to Ontario and Nova Scotia to be fitted in 65-foot tugs being built at Lunenburg and Mahone Bay, Nova Scotia, for the RCN and the British Ministry of War Transport.[66] Vivian marine diesels were fitted into boats ranging from the 60-hp engine for army service boats to the 250-hp, 6-cylinder engine for 84-foot Seine packer boats employed on offshore patrols. Eight-cylinder, supercharged, 200-hp Vivian diesels powered the Royal Canadian Air Force's (RCAF) salvage and supply vessels *Siwash* and *Haida*.[67] By the end of the war, Vivian Engine Works Limited had 950 employees, used over 100 subcontractors, and per day turned out a diesel engine weighing 22,500 pounds. Total annual production had reached 71,804 hp.[68]

Imported marine diesel engines were generally fitted into vessels built on the East Coast. Two engines of 165 brake horsepower (bhp) from Gray Company powered an RCAF 114-foot supply and salvage vessel. All fifty-three 105- and 126-foot, wooden minesweepers that the BATM ordered on the East Coast for the Royal Navy appear to have been fitted with Fairbanks Morse engines imported from the United States.[69] Two Fairbanks Morse diesel engines also powered each of the Fairmile depot ships, HMCS *Provider* and HMCS *Preserver*, built at Sorel in 1942.[70] Late in the war, Dominion Engineering Works manufactured the 6-cylinder diesel engines that powered the 3,600-ton, Canadian-designed tankers built at Collingwood and Sorel (see chapter 10).[71]

All marine gasoline engines were imported. Hubert Scott-Paine's success, in February 1940, in persuading David Carswell, then director of shipbuilding for the Defence Purchasing Board, to import seventy-two newly developed M4-2500 marine engines from Packard Motor Car Company at Detroit made possible the interesting, but disappointing, motor torpedo boat (MTB) program.[72]

Whatever their potential for blowing up, gasoline engines offered such enormous promise by reducing weight and increasing power that marine engineers willingly accepted the risk. Marine gasoline engines in war virtually eliminated smoke, making boats less visible to the enemy, and reduced the number of men handling the engine, leaving more personnel to handle weapons, while efficient fuel consumption extended endurance.[73] Although aircraft engines modified for marine use were lightweight for the power produced, they lacked sufficient stamina for heavy-duty use. Hall-Scott Motor Car Company at Alameda, California, and Packard Motor Company at Detroit, the same two companies that during 1917 had created the Liberty aircraft engine, collaborated on a new marine engine. Troublesome difficulties with ignition, carburetors, and cylinders led to important modifications, and the 4M-2500 was ready for testing in March 1940. The big V-12 was rated at 1,250 hp at 2,500 rpm. Later, supercharged versions were rated at 1,500 hp.[74] Two of these inclined engines installed in each motor torpedo boat gave them speeds in excess of 40 knots.

Several types of Hall-Scott engines were also imported. The 225-hp "Invader" engine powered 38-foot RCAF crash boats, giving them a speed of 18 knots, while the same engine moved 60-foot target-towing vessels along at a more sedate 11 knots. Twin 630-hp "Defender" engines, a V-12, 2,200-cubic-inch engine produced for the United States Navy, were fitted into Fairmile motor launches.[75] Considered the outstanding engine of its class, more than 8,000 were built during the war.[76] Later, larger 700-hp engines made by Sterling Motor Company at Buffalo, New York, were fitted in the last eighteen Fairmiles built. Two 630-hp Kermath engines produced 18 knots for 48-foot harbour-patrol boats. Kermath Manufacturing Company at Detroit also manufactured a small, 27-hp diesel engine, which was fitted into each of the 100 25- and 32-foot cutters built by Falconer Marine Industries at Victoria.[77]

Marine Forgings

Marine forgings encompass some of the largest steel pieces used in any ship: stern frames, rudderstocks, rudder main pieces, shafts, and propellers. A description of the manufacture of stern frames will help to show the contributions of foundry men and patternmakers to shipbuilding and how companies not often associated with the industry became crucial to the entire manufacturing process. Stern frames comprise two steel castings of a total weight of 30,000 pounds in the case of a 10,000-ton freighter; their purpose is self-explanatory. Their manufacture requires a foundry-pouring capacity of approximately 10 tons per "heat." A further requirement is a double overhead crane arrangement to permit pouring a large casting from both ends. Dominion Bridge Company manufactured stern frames for 10,000-ton cargo ships at its Lachine plant, and Canadian Car and Foundry Company Limited at Montreal manufactured them for the 4,700-ton Gray-type freighter.[78] On the West Coast, Vancouver Engineering Works set up a production schedule to turn out the necessary stern frames using plate scrap from the shipyards.[79]

The initial step was the making by skilled patternmakers of large wooden patterns for forming sand moulds. As the stern frame was made in two sections, great care had to be taken to ensure perfect alignment of the assembled frame. Fabricated steel boxes, partly buried in pits in the foundry floor, formed the "drag," or lower part of the mould. A similar box, weighing many tons, was constructed to form the "cope," or upper part. For both the drag and the cope, the pattern is surrounded with foundry sand, which is rammed into place, and then the wooden pattern is carefully withdrawn using the overhead crane. Sand cores are made up in special core boxes to leave holes for the propeller shaft and rudderstock and to provide a hollow V-section in order to facilitate riveting the ship's plates. After treating the surface of the mould, these cores are inserted. Later, the cope is turned over and lowered over the drag, and the joint is sealed with sand and heavily clamped to avoid run-out of molten steel.

Foundrymen poured molten steel into the mould, controlling two ladles that each weighed from six to eight tons and that moved on overhead cranes. At the same time as the pouring of the stern frame, test bars were poured to determine the quality of each heat, which had to meet Lloyd's approval. In addition, Lloyd's representatives carefully inspected each complete stern frame. Large reservoirs of steel, called "risers," were used to compensate for shrinkage during cooling. As soon as solidification occurred, the mould was opened to allow cooling, which took several days. But before the cooling was complete, the casting was transported to the hydro-blast room, where cores were washed out and foundry sand was removed by a water jet that contained sand and was delivered at 1,200 pounds of pressure. Afterward, in the chipping department, the risers were burnt off by oxy-acetylene equipment and various stiffening webs removed. The risers were shipped in 80-ton lots to eastern steel mills for conversion to steel plate. Grinders removed any excess metal, and the casting was then ready for annealing.

Annealing is a critical operation in the manufacture of marine forgings. The process is intended to remove internal stresses in castings that arise as they cool. They must be removed before machining, or distortion can occur. Annealing occurs when a casting is inserted into an oil-fired furnace that has been brought to a predetermined temperature. After holding the casting at the correct temperature until it is "soaked," it is left to cool and is ready for machining. Large lathes, shapers, and special tools are used to bore out the cores and shape the pads for the assembly of the two separate castings. Afterward, they are set on a frame and aligned, and rivet holes are bored. The stern frame is then dismantled and shipped for reassembly at the shipyard when laying the keel of the next 10,000-ton freighter. At Lachine, Dominion Bridge Company produced the largest subassembly around the stern frames for the 10,000-ton freighters being built at United Shipyards Limited at Montreal, attaching the propeller-shaft bearing and the top and bottom rudder-post bearings at the plant before shipping the 29-ton assembly along a railway track to the shipyard.[80]

Rudders and rudder main pieces were manufactured in much the same way. Molten steel was poured into moulds, the rough castings were removed and annealed and later machined before being transported to the shipyard. The amount of steel lost during machining is startling. At Trenton Steel Works, machining reduced a rough forged rudderstock weighing 91.75 tons to 43 tons; and rudder main pieces weighing 301.8 tons were machined down to 163.7 tons.[81]

Shafts were initially forged in several sections called variously intermediate, thrust, and tail and propeller shafts. When finally assembled, they connected a ship's engine to its propeller, which was also forged and machined. They required tons of steel. One "ship set" of marine forgings, including shafts, connecting rods, crank journals, rudderstock, and rudder main piece for a 10,000-ton cargo vessel, required 160,233 pounds of steel ingots. A ship set for the medium Gray-type called for 63,866 pounds of ingots.[82]

Canadian manufacturers required considerable capital assistance in order to expand their foundries to meet the tremendous demand. Trenton Steel Works and

Canada Foundries and Forgings at Welland received together nearly $1.6 million to expand their existing forges and machine shops. The two manufacturers of rough shafts and Kennedy and Sons Limited, which produced propellers, consumed nearly two-thirds, or 65.7 per cent, of the entire cargo ship program's authorized capital-assistance expenditure.[83]

Forging shafts was only the beginning of the process. Afterward, the rough shafts were shipped to other companies for machining and finishing. Dominion Engineering Works carried out the work for 4,700-ton cargo ships, and Hydraulic Machinery Company, also at Montreal, machined the same equipment for all 10,000-ton cargo ships built in eastern yards. After taking delivery of rough-turned shafts, these firms carefully machined them to given sizes, flanges were bored, and coupling bolts were fitted to give a "driving fit." All work was done so that when shafts were delivered to shipyards, no further machining was necessary. Tail-end shafts arrived in rough state accompanied with a continuous bronze liner, which was carefully heated and shrunk onto the shaft. The skill lay in the care and precision with which the liner was heated and shrunk to become part and parcel of the shaft when cooled. Afterward, the complete shaft was machined to specifications. The propeller shaft, in its bronze sleeve, rotated in the stern tube, which supported the shaft where it emerged from the ship. The stern tube was fitted with brass or cast-iron bushings lined with white metal to reduce rotational friction.

The manufacture of ships' propellers was special. Most, if not all, bronze and cast-iron types produced during the war came from one firm, William Kennedy and Sons at Owen Sound. William Kennedy had immigrated to Canada from Scotland in 1831. He established a millwright and foundry business at Owen Sound in 1857. During the Second World War, members of the third generation carried on the business: T. Dowsley Kennedy was president and managing director, and Mathew Kennedy was vice president; one of the founder's great-grandsons was also a vice president.

Designing ships' propellers requires much scientific and technical knowledge. The lines of the vessel, horsepower, revolutions of the engine, and minimum and maximum depth of the hull's immersion in water, along with other important factors, are taken into consideration so that the best design can be developed and the correct number, pitch, and area established for the blades. Although plans and specifications were supplied to the manufacturer, only specially trained workmen with years of experience could produce the finished product. In the case of a bronze propeller, raw materials consisting of copper, iron, aluminum, zinc, and manganese had to be ordered, tested, and mixed according to given specifications. Even the sand used in the forming moulds was tested before use so that nothing would be left to chance in turning out the finished article.[84] The materials were then melted in crucible and reverberatory furnaces and poured into propeller moulds. The rough casting was machined and polished; holes were drilled and tapped to take the propeller cone studs, and the finished propellers were prepared for shipment to West Coast, Great Lakes, and East Coast shipyards. The large 18.5-foot propellers, weighing approximately 14 tons for 10,000-ton cargo ships, were the largest bronze castings ever poured in Canada.

Manufacturing ships' propellers at William Kennedy and Sons, Owen Sound, Ontario. LAC, e000761670.

Special stowage on railway flatcars had to be worked out, as they were too high to pass under railway bridges if shipped vertically and too wide to remain within railway track limits to be shipped horizontally. Each cargo ship constructed in Canada between 1941 and 1945 was equipped with one bronze propeller and one cast-iron spare.

Smaller propellers for naval vessels were planed-to-pitch on machines designed and built by the Kennedy firm and had to meet Admiralty standards on inspection. The entire driving surface of the propeller blade was machined to an exact specified pitch from tip to root of each blade to provide a higher overall efficiency for the propeller and to provide the ship on which it was installed the maximum speed possible in response to the engine's driving power.

To achieve these results, Kennedy and Sons maintained a metallurgical staff and a laboratory for testing raw materials, in addition to the more obvious modern foundry and machine shop and equipment to handle the weight and size of these castings. The prewar foundry had been able to manufacture propellers for the navy's first program, but a new foundry and a machinery and erection shop were added in 1941 as soon as the cargo ship program began. The foundry was equipped with an electric furnace of 8 tons capacity and two reverberatory furnaces. To provide the extra electric power for such expanded activity, a special line was installed from the hydroelectric generating plant and substation at Eugenia, Ontario. The machine shop, approximately 400 feet long and over 50 feet high, was equipped with large-size lathes, milling machines, boring mills, planers, and polishing tools. By the spring of 1943 Kennedy and Sons employed about 900 people, including a largely female office staff.

Kennedy and Sons also manufactured centrifugally cast bronze liners weighing over 2 tons each to be shrunk onto tail shafts of the largest cargo ships and Hastie-type steam-driven, hydraulic steering engines and windlasses for frigates being built for the RCN. The firm had obtained manufacturing rights for this equipment from John Hastie and Company and from Thomas Reid and Sons, both of Scotland.

Pumps, Valves, and Fittings

Marine pumps, valves, and fittings were manufactured throughout Canada in unprecedented numbers. Wartime Merchant Shipping Limited ordered directly from manufacturers at least thirteen kinds of pumps for issue to shipbuilders. Some of them were auxiliary and circulating air pumps, ballast and general service pumps, fuel-oil service and transfer pumps, main feed pumps, fire and bilge pumps, salt-water service pumps, and boiler feed and circulating pumps.[85] These pumps were not cheap. Canadian Allis-Chalmers Limited, for example, contracted to manufacture and deliver eighteen sets of circulating-pump units for delivery at a rate of one per week from 7 August 1942 onward for a price of $2,830 each.[86]

Manufacturers also produced marine valves weighing from a few ounces to several hundred pounds each. A 12-inch, cast-alloy, steel-flanged gate valve stood over 5 feet high and weighed 600 pounds. All had to be manufactured to marine standards established by the British Admiralty for warships and by Lloyd's or British Corporation for cargo ships. Whether employed in the boiler system, plumbing, pumping, or other systems, valves had countless uses. A single contract with Jenkins Brothers at Montreal in 1942 called for nearly 3,000 valves for 10,000-ton freighters, even though a similar contract one week before had called for 1,092 valves.[87] Canadian Fairbanks Morse Company's contract to manufacture eighteen sets of elbows and pipefittings for 4,700-ton cargo ships included ninety-one items per set.[88] Crane Limited's contract for eighteen sets of valves and fittings for the same type of freighter included 134 items per set.[89]

Major valve manufacturers were Crane Limited and Jenkins Brothers, both at Montreal, and T. McCavity and Sons at St John, New Brunswick. Not even the addition of new companies, including Garth Company Limited, Mason Regulator Company at Montreal, Empire Brass Manufacturing Company, and George White and Sons at London, Ontario, could meet the insatiable demand for ships' valves. In New Westminster, British Columbia, Wartime Merchant Shipping Limited authorized $52,300 in capital assistance in order to permit Webb and Gifford Limited to acquire machine tools for manufacturing valves and fittings and boiler mountings on the West Coast.[90]

New manufacturers appeared from the pulp and paper and mining industries. In 1941 the executive committee of the Pulp and Paper Association of Canada organized the War Time Machine Shop Board, and the industry's machine shops successfully undertook certain subcontracts, which led to a steadily expanding volume of production.[91] The idea originated with James O'Halloran, chief engineer of Anglo-Canadian Pulp and Paper Mills since 1928.[92] When war broke out, the industry was suffering from a lack of skilled men, ranging from executives and engineers to skilled tradesmen. In distant locations, companies arranged with International Correspondence Schools Canadian Limited for courses to be given at virtually all eighty-three pulp and paper mills in the country in machine-shop work, pipefitting, welding, mill working, tinsmithing, blacksmithing, and electrical work. Machine shops in the industry normally worked eight hours daily on a forty-eight-hour week. Adding a shift meant that war work could be done for ninety-six hours weekly and that the workforce could be preserved. By September 1941 over $1.25 million worth of orders was being handled, and expectation was that $4 million annually could be taken on. The War Time Machine Shop Board had already manufactured thirty items for the naval and cargo ship programs, ranging from tunnel and tail-shaft bearings to stop throttles and fuel-oil pumps.[93]

Mine machine shops were initially unsuccessful in securing subcontracts largely due to misunderstanding. The operators of Porcupine Mines and G.C. Kemsley of Dome Mines Limited, acting as coordinators and working through the War Time Machine Shop Board, finally began work on a subcontract obtained through the latter.[94] Work was shared among all the mines in the Porcupine district. Kirkland Lake mines had also been unsuccessful in securing subcontracts until the operators formed the Wartime Mine Shops Association and obtained a subcontract through the Porcupine Mines operations. In 1942 and 1943 the mine machine shops worked on

Kingston Shipbuilding Company workers stand beside the propeller of HMCS *Belleville* on launch day, 17 July 1944. The rudder is turned 90 degrees in preparation for side launching. Photo by Francis MacLachlan. MMGLK, Francis MacLachlan Collection, 1984.0006.0061.

two large projects, chiefly ships' pumps in the Porcupine area and generating sets at Kirkland Lake. An early contract between Wartime Merchant Shipping Limited and Dome Mines at South Porcupine, Ontario, was for eighteen sets (including spares) of 12-by-12-by-10-inch Vertical Dupuy Ballast Pumps, Carruthers type.[95]

Faced with a continuing shortage of valves, the Department of Munitions and Supply ultimately arranged with thirty-two pulp and paper and sixteen mining companies to employ their machine shops for the duration of the war. Located far from urban, industrial areas, these self-contained companies had well-equipped machine shops staffed with skilled workers.[96] The DMS allocated each company a sufficient quantity of the total requirement to enable it to tool up and produce rapidly.[97] Collectively, these companies manufactured annually in excess of $3 million worth of marine valves.[98]

Problems arising from the destroyer valve program in 1943 well illustrated the challenges created by the existence of two competing shipbuilding programs. Each Tribal-class destroyer required 1,233 valves, exclusive of bulkhead pieces and branches. These items were small and required a high degree of technical ability to be manufactured to Admiralty standards, which placed the program at a serious disadvantage in the face of the large production requirements of Wartime Merchant Shipping Limited.

John Inglis Company, the principal machinery contractor, had found it necessary to make its own shop drawings in order to manufacture these valves, none being available from England. Drawings were made and released by June 1943 for 1,084 valves, and of these, 887 were ordered from fourteen different Canadian suppliers; 170 were ordered from English sources and naval stores. By then, however, John Inglis was encountering serious difficulties with the three major suppliers, which together were responsible for 568 valves: Mulcott Company at Montreal, Canadian Gauge Company at Merrickville, and Guelph Stove Company. The first two companies were the sole manufacturers of the only type of patented Klinger asbestos-packed cocks approved for naval service. Both companies were overloaded with orders for the corvette and frigate programs, and although John Inglis was seeking approval from Ottawa of a substitute cock, nothing had been agreed.

The situation at Guelph Stove was more serious. The company was reluctant to proceed with the valve order due to quality-control problems that had arisen early in 1943. Also, greatly increased volumes of orders from WMSL allowed the company to focus on quantity production for the cargo ship program rather than on the small number of very exacting items required for the destroyer program.[99] The valves were vital to progress on the destroyers, and the prime contractor had been unable to locate an additional suitable supplier. Officials at John Inglis believed that transferring the program to any other source at the current time "would be disastrous" and requested that David Carswell secure recognition of the importance of the orders and assist the subcontractors in acquiring needed tools to complete the work.[100]

Deck Equipment

Deck equipment includes a variety of stationary fixtures and steam-driven machinery such as derricks, booms, Samson posts, davits, blocks, pulleys, wire rope, anchor windlasses, and winches. Guns, depth charges, and other weapons might also be considered deck equipment but are dealt with separately under naval armament. Deck equipment is confined chiefly to cargo ships or to gear that would be found on both naval and merchant vessels. Its manufacture reflects well on Canadian engineering inventiveness, initiative, and entrepreneurial ability. The Canadian railway system also played a crucial role in delivering components and auxiliary equipment to shipyards across the country. Taking one example, Vulcan Iron Works at Winnipeg, Manitoba, manufactured heavy derrick posts, roughly 2,500 miles away from Pictou, Nova Scotia, where they were installed in 4,700-ton cargo ships.[101]

It was estimated that during the winter of 1940–41 (i.e., before the introduction of cargo shipbuilding), British Columbia machine shops employed 10,000 to 15,000 men on subcontracts for the shipbuilding industry. The experiences of several companies in the Vancouver area reveal an interesting story.[102] Progressive Engineering Works Limited employed 40 men prior to the war, manufacturing mining and transmission machinery. By January 1943 the plant operated twenty-four hours a day and employed about 200 men producing winches and windlasses for all classes of vessels, both naval and merchant. In the early days, the owner, R.E. Samson, travelled to Ottawa and secured approval from naval authorities of his design for a suitable windlass for minesweepers, corvettes, and naval tankers.[103] Shipbuilders supplied the orders, and the firm launched itself as windlass builders. During the first three years, it built more than 130 units, supplying nearly every shipyard in Canada. Although not very large, these windlasses were very powerful and were built of nonshattering steel to be able to withstand shocks from gunfire and depth charge.

Windlasses on the decks of a 10,000-ton ship were very much larger, being designed to handle 270 fathoms (493.8 m) of $2^1/_{16}$-inch anchor chain weighing 30 tons. Cargo winches were of many styles and subject to abuse and hard service. Eleven cargo-handling winches were fitted on board each 10,000-ton freighter: six of the 7-by-10-inch type, two 50-ton heavy-duty types at the main hatch, two 30-ton heavy-duty types at number 4 hatch aft, and one 7-by-10-inch warping winch. A full set of double-cylinder, single-drum, steam-driven winches for the smaller Gray-type cargo ship consisted of three right-hand and two left-hand 7-by-10-inch winches and one warping winch. These two types of cargo vessels required more than 4,100 winches.

During 1940 Samson designed winches and windlasses for the cargo ship program and at year's end secured contracts for the first ships placed by the British Merchant Shipbuilding Mission. Early in 1941 the cargo ship program expanded so rapidly that orders soon outstripped the Vancouver plant's capacity. Undaunted, Samson organized a groups of six plants to cooperate, and he presented a clear plan to Wartime Merchant Shipping Limited, which authorized $50,600 in capital assistance largely to secure machine tools.[104] The group was capable of handling 100 ships annually, although at the time only 73 contracts for 10,000-tonners had been let.

The principals in this group comprised Heaps Engineering (1940) Company, Westminster Iron Works at New Westminster, Tyee Machinery Company, Letson and Burpee Limited, Progressive Engineering Works at Vancouver, and Consolidated Engineering at Victoria. John Reid founded Westminster Iron Works in 1874, and his two sons continued the business. William J. Reid was president and general manager, and John A. Reid was superintendent of works. A grandson of the founder, W.J. Reid, was secretary-treasurer of the company. Owing to the scarcity of machine tools, the company designed its own machines to manufacture the winches.[105]

Heaps Engineering Limited had been a well-established firm owned since 1912 by E.M. Heaps. In 1940 a farsighted group of Vancouver businessmen in the shipping and shipbuilding industries took over the firm and reorganized it, replacing older machinery and greatly increasing the manufacturing capacity of its site on Lulu Island near New Westminster. The president of the new company was Frederick H. Clendenning, president of Empire Shipping Company and representative of the British Ministry of War Transport at Vancouver.[106] The managing director was J. MacInnes, also managing director of North Pacific Shipping Company Limited. Other directors were Captain W.M. Crawford, president of Empire Stevedoring Company Limited; A.C. Burdick, president of North Van Ship Repairs Limited; A.B. Graham, president of Anglo-Canadian Shipping Company Limited; the lawyer H.J. Sullivan, KC; and

Workers splicing an eye into a steel wire at Canadian Vickers Limited, c. 1941. LAC, C-03267.

E.M. Heaps, the former owner. By September 1941 the company was employing 200 men, including 60 in the foundry and 15 in the pattern shop. In addition to winches, the firm manufactured rudder stocks and other marine equipment.[107]

Heaps Engineering and Progressive Engineering produced the large, heavy-duty windlasses for 10,000-ton merchant ships. Each weighed 10 tons. Progressive Engineering also built an extension to its existing plant and installed new machinery. Many windlasses and winches were built in Ontario under licence. Four such firms included Stephens Adamson Manufacturing Company of Canada at Belleville, United Steel Corporation at Welland, E. Leonard and Sons Limited at London, and Link Belt Company at Toronto.[108] The contract with E. Leonard and Sons for eighteen sets of winches for 4,700-ton cargo ships specified that Progressive Engineering at Vancouver would provide the drawings.[109] Stephens Adamson also manufactured steering gears for 4,700-ton ships.[110] A group of Quebec papermaking plants built cargo winches under supervision of the Canadian Pulp and Paper Association's War Time Machine Shop Board.

Steel pulley blocks were not manufactured in Canada before the war. All blocks and pulleys were imported from the United States and the United Kingdom. Early in

1940 Keating and Sons Limited at Montreal consisted of an engineer, a blacksmith, and W.J. Keating. By March 1943 the firm employed 325 workers, including office staff. After the plant extension was completed later that year, employment was expected to rise to 1,000.[111] Keating and Sons was producing every kind of pulley block required for war purposes, from tiny, bronze, single-sheave blocks to quintuple-sheave blocks weighing 2,800 pounds for the 50-ton derricks on board 10,000-ton cargo ships and every intermediate size block needed for lifeboat falls, rope guys, cargo runners, engine-room pulley blocks, and armament tackle blocks. The company also manu-factured 250-pound turnbuckles for 2¼-inch heavy stays; each 10,000-ton freighter required eight of them plus fourteen more for 2-inch wire rope and rigging screws weighing up to 350 pounds each. Drop-forged shackles for boom heads weighing 175 pounds were produced, as were the 200-pound shackles in the head of quintuple-sheave blocks.[112]

Electrical Equipment

Providing electrical equipment to the Canadian shipbuilding industry was a difficult business for several reasons.[113] As a moribund industry prior to 1940, shipbuilding had very limited technical resources for carrying out electrical work. In addition to shortages of suitable equipment and skilled labour to install electrical wiring, ma-chinery, and fittings at the beginning of the war, different electrical standards and voltages used in British and North American warships and the nature of the Can-adian electrical manufacturing industry created unique problems. Thus merchant ships were built to commercial marine standards, which required that electrical com-ponents be built to North American specifications, whereas warships built for British account were constructed to British Admiralty specifications. These generally called for more robust construction and for greater reliability. Compounding this difficulty was the Royal Canadian Navy's preference for North American voltages for its war-ships. Electrical manufacturers were sometimes producing the same piece of equip-ment for the same type of ship, minesweeper, or corvette according to two separate specifications.

The principal problem was that the different specifications and voltage require-ments called for in British ships and electrical plans often required considerable re-working and redesign by the companies involved. It might have been possible to save time and effort by adopting American wiring standards and equipment, but no Brit-ish staff was available to experiment with and test equipment, nor was there any one to train British naval personnel overseas in the operational use, maintenance, and repair of such machinery and equipment. Moreover, the Admiralty was a very con-servative organization, unlikely to change its ways, and mistrustful of foreign equip-ment and mass-production techniques.

When the naval shipbuilding program began, shipyards had responded by recruit-ing electricians from local industries. With one or two exceptions, none recruited electrical engineers or organized electrical departments. Those few that set up departments headed by electrical engineers quickly grasped the basic principles of naval electrical work and after building two or three ships worked up satisfactory standards and maintained them. Electrical workers had to be closely supervised, and classification-society surveyors, who were primarily mechanical engineers, did not possess either the knowledge of or the interest in naval electrical work required to oversee it and to educate shipbuilders. At some point, electrical overseeing was taken out of the hands of the societies, and Admiralty overseers were introduced. These men, in some cases, had to act as foremen advising shipbuilding firms on the layout of components, sequence of work, purchase of cable and fittings, and other activities normally outside their province. By the end of 1942, however, all yards employed on naval construction were working to a satisfactory standard.[114]

Commercial marine fittings were not manufactured in Canada before the war, and claims that Canada boasted an advanced electrical manufacturing industry need qualification.[115] Canada's electrical manufacturers were chiefly branch plants of American and British parent companies established to circumvent Canadian protective tariffs and to take advantage of imperial preference. Many firms were not fully staffed on the engineering side. They tended to be manufacturing units dependent on their parents for engineering, design, and in some cases components. Most engineers were employed in sales. Moreover, new manufacturing facilities were not easily found. In 1942–43 Lake Shore Mines Limited at Kirkland Lake was subcontracted to manufacture 114 steam-driven generator sets, and this was followed by a second contract for 243 sets.[116]

On arrival in Canada in the summer of 1940, members of the British Admiralty Technical Mission could find only four companies that were able to handle the whole manufacturing process within their own organizations (i.e., development, design, engineering, and manufacturing). These were Canadian General Electric, English Electric, Cemco Electrical Manufacturing, and Electric Tamper and Equipment. The others were dependent on their principals in some way or another.

The chief engineer of Canadian Westinghouse admitted he did not have a staff of engineers qualified to design a direct-current small motor for fans. Policies of parent companies also influenced behaviour. In 1943, for example, Canadian General Electric undertook to manufacture the metadyne, a British electrical machine designed to allow for remote-control firing of navy guns. By this time, however, the parent company in the United States was manufacturing another version of this invention and produced a similar machine called an "amplidyne." The American parent provided little encouragement to its Canadian subsidiary, and only after some struggle did Canadian General Electric win enough independence to complete the project. Despite its name, English Electric Company at St Catharines, Ontario, was the only independent electrical manufacturing company in Canada, although it was under the financial control of John Inglis Company. English Electric manufactured machines, switchgear, fittings, switchboards, and transformers for the naval program.

In the beginning, the BATM modified standard electrical fittings to develop a range of makeshift ones, and although they were clumsy and heavy, they proved satisfactory in service. Admiralty fittings individually cost from three to ten times the price of the makeshift equivalents, but the BATM successfully persuaded the Department of Munitions and Supply that manufacturing fully interchangeable equivalents to British made fittings was essential to the Canadian naval shipbuilding program. The changeover started early in 1942 and was completed in a surprisingly short time. The last Western Isles minesweepers were supplied with the new interchangeable fittings. At least thirty companies took part in manufacturing more than $8.5 million worth of Admiralty-pattern electrical fittings for the Canadian shipbuilding program and for shipment to the United Kingdom. No complaint of noninterchangeability was ever received.[117]

In the summer of 1941 the government established a committee on naval electrical equipment with D.W. Ambridge, deputy director of shipbuilding, as chairman and with representatives from the BATM, the RCN, and electrical manufacturers. The committee's aim was to centralize and control all purchases of marine electrical fittings and to smooth out orders, production, and delivery by estimating quantities of each pattern of fitting, allocating production, and instructing shipbuilders regarding from whom to purchase. The committee obtained authority to instruct firms to proceed with work and authority to guarantee them against loss, and its work proceeded until Wartime Shipbuilding Limited took over control of naval shipbuilding at the end of 1943. At no time during its operation did the production of electrical fittings cause anxiety or delay to the shipbuilding program.

After initial difficulties and the decision to adopt Admiralty specifications for electrical cable early in 1941, six Canadian wire-cable manufacturers produced several million yards of degaussing cable and electrical cable for shipbuilding and for Royal Navy bases abroad, both of which were shipped until the end of the war. These were Canadian General Electric Company at Peterborough, Canadian Telephone and Supplies at Toronto, Automatic Electric (Canada) Limited at Toronto, Northern Electric Company at Montreal, Canada Wire and Cable Company at Montreal, Boston Insulated Wire and Cable Company at Hamilton, and Federal Wire and Cable Company at Guelph. The major initial problem lay in abandoning the extrusion processes of rubber-insulation wire cables and adopting the strip process normally used by the Admiralty for high-quality rubber-insulation cables. Canadian manufacturers had previously concentrated on producing cheap, low-end, commercial insulated cable for telephone lines and house wiring.

The electrical section of the BATM initially comprised six men. Two more were soon added, and late in 1941 two naval officers from another section within the BATM and a third from the Caribbean were added, which, with two more from Britain, increased the staff to thirteen. Before the war was over, the electrical-staff section rose to seventy-three, including eight engineers, fifteen overseers, and fifty women examiners mostly recruited locally. Two of the electrical engineers were officers with the Royal Canadian Navy Volunteer Reserve (RCNVR). During the first two years (i.e., until August 1942), members of the section had a most difficult row to hoe as they struggled to convince disbelieving Canadian electrical engineers to change their normal practices and manufacture goods "the hard way," the BATM way. Canadians were deeply suspicious of British naval officers, whom they accused of "trying to run the whole show," and it required much tact, patience, and perseverance on both sides to achieve cooperation and to maximize production.

During the summer of 1941 twenty women recruited locally enrolled in a drafting course begun at Ottawa Technical High School; sixty more were enrolled in two classes that autumn, and by the end of the year, women entirely staffed the BATM's drafting offices. Employment of these women was so successful that the RCN, the Canadian army, and manufacturers asked Ottawa Tech to continue the training scheme. The BATM also replaced male inspectors with women, who were required to have a reading knowledge of blueprints and the ability to use precision instruments. Recruitment of women inspectors was agreed to only with reluctance, partly because examiners were normally recruited from machinists. But it proved to be another success. Qualifications were initially severe. Two years of college work in mathematics and physics were demanded. During the first eighteen months, all women were university graduates; some had earned a master's degree in science. They received a one-month course in reading blueprints and use of precision instruments, followed by a one-month course for special students in fire control and optical instruments.

The production of small motors for ship fans and auxiliary drives proved a challenging problem. Practically no direct-current motors were made in Canada, and the quantities required in the early naval shipbuilding program were too small to interest large manufacturers in producing a machine to Admiralty standards. The cost of special designs, tools, jigs, and fixtures was prohibitive. Consequently, the work fell to two smaller firms whose peacetime production was inexpensive small motors for washing machines, pumps, fans, and small machine tools. Competition was intense, quality and workmanship were low, and quality production to meet naval-service standards was beyond achievement without very careful supervision and inspection. One firm, Robbins and Meyers, improved its methods sufficiently to produce machines of an acceptable standard, but Leland Electrical Company did not. The BATM eventually persuaded the Department of Munitions and Supply to eliminate the company from naval production in 1942. Only toward the end of 1943 did Canadian Westinghouse Company and Electric Tamper and Equipment Company begin producing motors of a satisfactory standard.

In 1942 the Royal Canadian Navy formed an electrical engineering department under Electrical Commander A.G. Cullwick, RCNVR. This served the navy and provided the BATM with a comprehensive overseeing organization without the trouble of further expanding its staff. Through close working arrangements in the manufacturing districts, young naval electrical officers felt free in most cases to call on the expertise of local Admiralty overseers. The navy's electrical branch was established in April 1943.[118]

By 1943 the Canadian electrical industry had made enormous strides in its ability to manufacture marine electrical equipment and fittings. The better firms were producing equipment of such good design and workmanship that it became possible to undertake more exacting projects than before. In the spring of 1943 Canadian General Electric began to manufacture the electric portion of remote-controlled gun mountings with complete success. Canadian Westinghouse Company at Hamilton was tasked with building fuse-keeping clocks, part of a complex fire-control apparatus comprising about 5,000 separate parts, many machined to very fine tolerances and demanding 25,000 to 30,000 man-hours to manufacture. Although not entirely successful, by 1944 it was producing three a month in two different versions.[119] Cemco Electrical Manufacturing Company, a small Vancouver firm, completed the design and manufacture of a shockproof, hand-operated circuit breaker. The industry was tackling all types of electrical equipment used by the Royal Navy. This makes the failure to develop and manufacture an effective radar set in Canada all the more tragic. Radar was so secret that private electrical manufacturers were not asked to take part in its production, which may partially account for the failure. Radar was the

Electrical shop where armature winding and motor repairs were carried out, Burrard Dry Dock Company, July 1945. NVMA, no. 27-75.

only electrical device whose manufacture remained completely in the government's hands.[120]

Proof of the industry's evolution appeared in 1944 when the Canadian electrical industry completely engineered and built the electrical equipment for the Royal Navy's maintenance ships being built on the West Coast. The decision in 1944 to order construction of these ships presented a considerable challenge to the industry, which was fully occupied producing equipment for minesweepers and LST3s. These new ships were 10,000-ton depot ships with a great deal of electrically driven auxiliary machinery, machine tools, compressors, pumps, and fans. The only solution was to build these maintenance ships to commercial rather than naval standards. The ships were fitted with an alternating-current supply system instead of the direct-current system specified in the British-built ships of the same class, which threw open the entire production resources of the domestic and industrial equipment manufacturers in Canada and the United States. In addition to being fitted for alternating-current systems, these ships were the first to be completely engineered in Canada. All twenty-one ships were ordered on 1 May 1944 from four Vancouver yards, and fifteen were completed and accepted before the RN cancelled the remainder in August 1945.

Naval Armament

A detailed history of the wartime manufacture of naval armament in Canada awaits its own historian. This is perforce a brief overview of the weapons and equipment that were manufactured for and employed in Canadian-built ships. Thus, although some sixteen firms located across the country produced more than $11 million worth of components for both 18-inch and 21-inch torpedoes, no complete weapon was manufactured here.[121] Similarly, ahead-thrown weapons such as hedgehog and squid were not developed in Canada. Canadian-built warships did not receive hedgehog before 1943 and were not equipped with squid before the end of the war.[122] This section deals chiefly with guns, gun mountings, and depth charges as weapons and with antisubmarine equipment such as plots, echo sounders, depth recorders, and asdic and navigation instruments.

Canada's antisubmarine navy used a lot of depth charges; not surprisingly, a great many were manufactured in Canada. But as historian William Rawling has shown, such a relatively simple weapon, which consisted of only four parts – container, explosive, primer or detonator, and pressure-sensitive pistol – proved to be a great challenge. Each device required great care in manufacture, but this was not beyond the abilities of Canadian engineers and workmen. It was the coordination of production that proved to be the challenge.[123] Part of the problem lay with the government rather than with private industry. Depth charges were all filled with explosive by Defence Industries Limited at the Dominion Arsenal filling plant at Cherrier, Quebec, and pistols were manufactured by the Department of Transport at government workshops at Prescott, Ontario. A total of 116,000 pistols were produced during the war.

Table 9.2 | Naval guns and gun-wharf stores manufactured in Canada, 1940–45

Item	Type	Mark	Quantity
GUNS			
1	QF 4-inch	XVI*	396
	QF 4-inch	XIX	932
	QF 4-inch	XXI	121
Subtotal			*1,449*
2	QF 12-pounder	V	1,000
3	QF 2-pounder	VIII	754
4	QF 40-mm Bofors	I	500
5	0.5-inch Vickers machine gun		1,000
Total guns			*4,703*
GUN-WHARF STORES			
1	4-inch breech block assemblies	XVI*	80
2	4-inch lever breech mechanisms	XVI*	120
3	2-pounder gun barrels	VIII	750
4	40-mm spare barrel assemblies	I	1,000
5	40-mm spare barrel assemblies	XI	100
6	40-mm spare barrels	IX	500
Total gun-wharf stores	*2,550*		

* Indicates a change within a mark insufficient to designate a new mark.

Source: Smith et al., "History of the British Admiralty Technical Mission in Canada," 140.

This device had thirty-four parts, some of rubber and others of forged steel machined to extremely fine tolerances.[124] Delays in supplying the navy's needs throughout the war appeared to lie with confused communications between the navy and its government suppliers rather than with the actual production.

Naval guns had never been produced in Canada, and no provision to manufacture them had been considered before the war. The government reached a decision to manufacture naval guns only in June 1940 after it became clear that it was the only way to arm the minesweepers and corvettes it had recently contracted to build. Five kinds of guns were manufactured in Canada for naval use: the quick-firing 4-inch gun, the 12-pounder "A" quick-firing gun, the 2-pounder pom-pom, the 40-mm Bofors, and the 0.5-inch Vickers machine-gun. "Quick-firing" was a British term applied to guns that fired ammunition incorporating a shell and a cartridge case containing a propellant fixed together. Table 9.2 shows the models or marks and quantities manufactured during the war.

The quick-firing 4-inch gun was the basic weapon used on all corvettes and frigates and on some Canadian-built minesweepers during the war. Early corvettes had the Mark IX gun with its box-like shield, which was not manufactured in Canada, but Revised corvettes were fitted with the Mark XIX in an HA/LA mounting and had a smaller shield.[125] Some early corvettes were armed with a 12-pounder gun in place of a second 4-inch gun, but the majority of the former were mounted on merchant ships.[126] According to Max Reid, half of all the 4-inch and 12-pounder guns manufactured in Canada were installed on Canadian-built merchant ships. Normally, the 4 inch gun was mounted aft and the 12-pounder forward. On 4,700-tonners, only a 12-pounder was mounted aft; 20-mm Oerlikons were twin-mounted. From 1943 on, merchantmen were also armed with a Pillar Box, an anti-aircraft weapon fitted forward and above the main gun aft, which fired a ten to twelve salvo of 2-pound rockets. Like Oerlikons, these were not manufactured in Canada.[127]

The 2-pounder pom-pom and the 40-mm Bofors were light and medium anti-aircraft weapons, respectively, and the machine guns provided secondary armament for minesweepers, corvettes, and frigates. They were also mounted on Fairmile motor launches and other small coastal craft. National Railways Munitions Limited at Montreal manufactured 932 Mark XIX guns, nearly two-thirds of all the 4-inch naval guns in Canada. Sorel Industries Limited, which produced both Mark XVI* and XXI guns and Mark XVI* breechblock assemblies and lever-breech mechanisms, is better known for having produced 25-pounder guns for the Canadian army.

Production of 12-pounder A Mark V naval guns was begun at the beginning of 1942 by National Railways Munitions. This subsidiary of the Canadian National Railway started construction of a 260,000-square-foot plant on 26 December 1940. The plant, which manufactured 500 of these guns, was designed to be converted to a railway-car repair shop at the end of the war.[128] Canadian Pacific Railways manufactured another 500 of these guns at its Ogden workshops at Calgary, while Sawyer-Massey Limited at Hamilton produced the gun mounts.[129] In September 1942 the Cabinet War Committee approved the naval minister's recommendation that all Canadian-flagged vessels over 500 tons be armed with 12-pounders. This requirement was chiefly to obtain crews. Provision of guns would encourage recruitment. Some 200 vessels would be involved, and the cost of providing guns, ammunition, and accommodation for gun crews was estimated at just under $5 million.[130]

Dominion Bridge Company produced 754 Vickers Mark VIII, 2-pounder anti-aircraft guns at a new plant outside Vancouver, and Otis-Fensom Elevator Company at Hamilton produced an additional 750 barrels for the same gun. Late in 1940 the Canadian government, acting on behalf of the British government, instructed Dominion Bridge to design, erect, and equip a plant on its property at Burnaby, British Columbia. A company representative travelled to the United Kingdom in search of information about equipment, tools, and jigs and techniques, and as quickly as information was received, company engineers laid out the plant. Modern guns like the 2-pounder pom-pom, which was employed singly or in multiples of two, four, and even eight and which fired 120 2-pound shells per minute, bore little relation to older products. A single gun of this type required 4,000 separate operations to manufacture. Company engineers prepared 4,000 working sketches, 1,500 gauges, and 1,000 jigs and fixtures. The initial contract meant machining, heat treating, assembling, and inspecting about 300,000 individual parts involving about 2 million separate operations. Engineers continually sought to increase production without additional machine-tool outlay, and their revision of drawings, jigs, fixtures, and gauges meant that after less than a year, manufacturing time on some components, of which there were more than 600 per gun, was reduced by 20 per cent.[131]

The Allies adopted the Swedish-designed 40-mm Bofors as its medium anti-aircraft gun in 1941, and the Department of Munitions and Supply authorized capital assistance of $14 million to Otis-Fensom to build a special plant to produce them in large numbers. Naval versions of the gun differed little if at all from the army model and were produced in relatively small numbers. Otis-Fensom also produced spare barrels and spare-barrel assemblies in addition to the Mark I gun and Mark III mounting.[132]

Naval gun mountings were specifically designed for warships. Bata Shoe Company at Batawa, Ontario, produced the first naval gun mounting for Vickers machine guns.[133] In all, twenty-one different gun mountings, including single, twin, and quadruple mounts for 20-mm Oerlikon light anti-aircraft guns were manufactured in Canada.[134] About 14,000 gun mountings in all were produced. The large number was due to the British Admiralty's desire for full production of selected marks and models in Canada in order to release British manufacturers for other purposes and to reduce reliance upon American suppliers who were reluctant to accept British designs and specifications.[135] Up to the end of 1943, the naval armament and equipment branch of the DMS placed orders to the value of just over $100 million for guns and gun mountings, which represented 50.6 per cent of the total value of all orders placed.[136]

Early in 1941 Vivian Engine Works Limited contracted with the Department of Munitions and Supply to manufacture fire-control equipment, gun sights for twin 4-inch guns (Mark XIX) and for single guns (Mark III**), fuse-setting machines (Mark V), ammunition trays, and auto grips. This led eighteen months later to an agreement to set up a new company, to be called Vivian Diesels and Munitions Limited, in order to manage new buildings and equipment worth nearly half a million dollars, paid for by both the Canadian and British governments, to manufacture the equipment. The new company would also undertake such fine precision work as crankshafts for 18-inch torpedoes and manage the war contracts for diesel engines being produced.[137]

The successful manufacture of asdic stands in such marked contrast to Canada's failure to manufacture radar sets as to leave the historian to wonder whether the failure lay in the government organization itself.[138] Unlike radar, the manufacture, if not the development, of asdic was left largely in the hands of Canadian industry.

Asdic appeared in the 1920s, and the most basic set, Type 123A, was obsolete in 1940 when it was fitted to the first Canadian-built corvettes.[139] The government intended to purchase asdic sets from the British at the beginning of the war, but this proved impossible due to the lack of funds in the 1938–39 departmental appropriations. Four unfitted sets bought for the Basset-class minesweepers were all the naval service had, apart from those installed or about to be installed in Canada's six destroyers.[140]

Canadian production of this indispensable piece of submarine-detection equipment was left until the last minute. Only during the fall of France, when losses of shipments from the United Kingdom made it doubtful whether sufficient equipment would be available to fit in the new minesweepers and corvettes being built, and after the British saw a need for a supplementary source of supply, was a decision taken to build asdic in Canada. In June 1940, at the same time as the decision to manufacture naval guns in Canada was taken, the Admiralty and the naval service reached an agreement to build 100 sets for the RN and 144 sets for the RCN.[141] In July, A.E.H. Pew, one of the original designers of asdic, and A.W. Mathew, a technical officer with long experience, arrived in Canada with 8 tons of equipment and were attached to the BATM. The RCN's equipment division was charged with finding sources of supply, obtaining raw materials, guiding manufacturers, inspecting the sets as they were produced, and fitting them in the ships.[142]

Production commenced immediately on three types, and by keeping in touch with developments in the United Kingdom, Canadian officials were able to change these as quickly as technical progress required. In all, twenty-one different types of asdic were manufactured.[143] A critically important piece of any asdic set was its quartz crystal. These were mined, cut, and polished, not created in a laboratory. The quartz came from Brazil and was cut into disks for storing and shipping. It was in short supply. By February 1941 only 6,400 pounds of quartz were in hand, almost 4,000 pounds short of minimum requirements; 10,400 pounds of ore translated into 840 quartz disks, cut and polished by the industrial minerals division of the Department of Mines and Resources' Renfrew plant. By January 1942 the plant had nothing left, and two-thirds of its quartz-cutting saws were idle. Division members complained bitterly about the navy's inability to provide a regular supply and its demand for double-shift work when the raw material arrived.[144]

The complexity of asdic as well as secrecy was reflected in the creation in Toronto of Admiralty Store, which accepted deliveries of components and subassemblies numbering 600 and 700 per set produced by fifty to sixty contractors. Admiralty Store then "plan packed" and issued sets on demand to BATM and RCN fitting-out parties in the shipyards.[145]

The first workable Canadian-built asdic appeared in July 1941, a reflection of co-operation by the BATM, the RCN, the naval armament and equipment branch, and the manufacturers. By the end of 1943 approximately 2,600 complete sets with a value of some $70 million had been manufactured. From this supply, all RN and RCN warships built in Canada and a large number loan-leased to the United Kingdom from the United States were equipped. Sets were also shipped to the United Kingdom, to British naval establishments around the world, and to the United States, Russia, and Mexico. In Canada 175 firms were involved. Up to the end of 1943, the naval armament and equipment branch placed orders for antisubmarine equipment worth in

The corvette HMCS *Belleville* in mid-launch. Ships were side launched on the Great Lakes because lake levels changed continually throughout the building season and could not be controlled. Photo by Francis MacLachlan. MMGLK, Francis MacLachlan Collection, 1984.0006.0063.

excess of $59 million, an amount representing 29.7 per cent of the total value of orders placed.[146] Asdic was a triumph of Canadian manufacturing. In all this vast production effort, there was "no record of a single Canadian-built set having been found unserviceable on issue" – high praise, indeed, from the demanding and exacting personnel of the BATM.[147] But it must be acknowledged that this triumph was primarily due to the care with which the British supervised the entire manufacturing process.

Like so much else, magnetic compasses were not manufactured in Canada before the war. They were initially imported from the United Kingdom until after the BATM arrived in Canada in July 1940. Owing to a lack of trained personnel, the BATM inspected and tested all magnetic compasses and binnacles manufactured in Canada, and Admiralty overseers in shipbuilding yards ensured correct installation of binnacles, compass corrector coils, and other accessories.[148] Young Canadian electrical engineers entering the RCNVR assisted materially in the shipyards, particularly in gyro work later on. Commercial compass adjusters were employed in the Great Lakes and St Lawrence shipyards and in the merchant shipbuilding yards, but standards were not reliable and in certain instances instructions were not obeyed, so the work of the BATM's compass section remained heavy.

The BATM's terms of reference included immediately commencing the manufacture of magnetic compasses, binnacles, and accessories, and after a detailed search, it settled on Hughes-Owens Company at Ottawa as the only possible supplier. A great many difficulties had to be overcome, including magnesium found in the metal for compass bowls and cloudy liquid caused by the chemical reaction of strong alcohol on metals as well as conditions in the plant due to dirt and unskilled workers, lack of air conditioning, and the scarcity of capable supervisors. Particularly difficult challenges arose from changes in the magnetic meridian in the direction-testing room and the great pressure from the DMS on the company for other war production. These factors combined as late as 1944 to cause a "very low" rate of production and an "unusually high" percentage of rejections. Nevertheless, by the war's end, Hughes-Owens had manufactured 5,264 magnetic compasses of eight types.

More than a half-dozen other firms were also involved manufacturing binnacles and accessories. Along with Hughes-Owens, Northern Electric Company and Ideal Upholstering Company, both at Montreal, produced 1,624 binnacles. The three companies also manufactured the following accessories: 1,100 electric-light fittings, 732 sets of Flinders bars, 1,264 corrector spheres, 800 corrector boxes, 2,404 corrector coils and terminal boxes, and 47,557 corrector magnets. Chadwick Carroll Brass and Fixtures Limited at Hamilton manufactured an additional 2,650 electric-light fittings. Other manufacturers were Hiram L. Piper Company, Sagamo Company, Electrolux (Canada) Limited, and Bepco Canada Limited, all at Montreal, Canfield Electrical Works Limited at Toronto, and Small Electric Motors (Canada) Limited at Leaside, Ontario.[149]

Gyrocompasses were not manufactured in Canada, nor were any installed in Canadian warships before 1943, which seriously affected the combat performance of the RCN during the fierce battles of the convoys in 1941 and 1942.[150] In this case, the British were uninterested in manufacturing the instruments in Canada, and consequently Canadian minesweepers and corvettes waited until quite late in the war before receiving this equipment. Gyrocompasses were finally obtained from the United Kingdom and fitted in all frigates and some Algerine minesweepers, but the earlier failure to equip the navy with this essential device in the antisubmarine war was a significant failure in Canada's war effort and a good illustration of Canadian dependency on the British for advanced engineering and technology.[151]

Conclusion

According to Harry J. Carmichael, the DMS's coordinator of production, the most outstanding manufacturing accomplishment by the end of 1942 was the hundreds of medium-size firms whose normal business never exceeded $400,000 or $500,000 a year who were currently producing war materials to the value of $5 million to $7 million per year.[152] Although this was propaganda, it was probably correct. First and foremost, the shipbuilding industry involved far more than building ships. Tens of thousands of workers, engineers, and managers employed in hundreds of manufacturing plants across Canada contributed directly to Canada's shipbuilding effort. The degree to which Canadian manufacturers went to war along with the nation's sailors, soldiers, airmen, and women can be seen in great factories but more so in these middling companies identified by Carmichael. Nowhere was this more apparent than in the vital contribution of a company that in peacetime manufactured doll carriages and wheels for junior tricycles. During the war, this modest firm in Orillia, Ontario, turned out copper nails to build the delicate, but sturdy, hulls of Fairmile motor launches. That such a small company was involved in war production was a telling illustration of just how completely Canadian industry, from Halifax to Victoria, had become co-opted into ship production.

Much of this success would not have been possible without the almost unheard of work of members of the British Admiralty Technical Mission. The expertise of these British naval officers, together with their tact, patience, and perseverance, contributed in no small way to the success of the shipbuilding effort. Canadian manufacturers displayed a surprising amount of entrepreneurial initiative and creative enterprise in solving production bottlenecks. Those who have placed a great deal of emphasis on the activities of dollar-a-year men working in the ever growing bureaucracies in Ottawa to organize Canada's war production ought to reconsider whether much of their vaunted success might better be attributed to manufacturers, both great and small, and their employees: managers, engineers, and working men and women who dealt with the day-to-day realities of industrial production with a "can do" spirit. Naval historians who have been quick to point to the inadequacies of Canadian engineers and manufacturers as sources of production bottlenecks might do well to re-examine their own briefs for evidence of naval dithering, lack of planning, and poor management talent before casting stones.

10 | Small Types and New Designs

Introduction

Canada's small-boat program quickly became an important part of wartime marine construction. Shortly after war was declared, the navy began to gather a fleet of small craft from other government departments, from patriotic citizens, and through charter and purchase. Hundreds of small craft and even large steamships were acquired, but the navy quickly learned that few such vessels met its many specific needs. The army and air force also needed boats. Despite chartering and purchasing more than 250 vessels, by November 1940 the three armed services had ordered an additional 350 small craft, of which half had been completed and delivered.[1]

The Canadian army required service vessels and special craft, including more than 2,300 assault boats and pontoons for use in river crossings in Europe. The Royal Canadian Air Force (RCAF) had more than 250 small boats built: service and bomb-loading dinghies, refuelling launches, aircraft tenders, crash boats, and supply and salvage vessels up to 147 feet in length. Before the end of the war, more than 100 small shipyards and boatbuilding yards delivered over 8,300 assorted craft to the armed services and to the British Ministry of War Transport.

Most vessels were not ships and might be excluded from a history of the shipbuilding industry, but many were steel-hulled and some were ocean-going. Their manufacture deserves notice, if only to record their existence. Many played important roles during the war. Some production centres were neither boatbuilding yards nor shipyards but structural-steel plants that built all-welded, steel-hulled barges, ammunition lighters, tugboats, and auxiliary oil tankers. More than 1,000 craft – chiefly pulling boats, sailing dinghies, whalers, and 10-oared cutters – were without power, but a wide variety of gasoline and diesel engines of various makes and sizes powered the remainder.

The number of small craft built across the country shown in table 10.1 provides an approximate idea of the total size of the small-boat program. Ontario boat builders surprisingly constructed more than half of all the small craft in the country, followed by Nova Scotians, who manufactured nearly one-quarter. The following account is marred by the absence of information about all but a few of the 1,223 craft shown to have been built in the St Lawrence River region. François Xavier Lachance,

Table 10.1 | Total marine craft built in Canada, by region, 1939–45*

Region	Marine craft (all types)	Naval and cargo ships	Small craft
West Coast	1,268	363	905
Great Lakes	4,501	214	4,287
St Lawrence	1,467	244	1,223
East Coast	1,996	84	1,912
Total	*9,232*	*905*	*8,327*

* Thirteen of eighteen Warrior-class tugs included.

Source: LAC, RG 28, box 29, "Contracts for Ships and Boats – contracts, purchases, and construction."

owner of a boatyard in the village of Saint Laurent, on Ile d'Orléans, built *grandes chaloupes*, or whalers, for the Royal Canadian Navy (RCN) at a rate of two per week on a production-line basis. He also built 21-, 15-, and 11-foot boats. His semi-industrial yard, known as a *chalouperie*, employed as many as twenty workers.[2] Davie Brothers, located on the site of the original patent slip in front of the family homestead at Lévis, kept busy with repairs and built beautiful mahogany boats for ships during the war, but how many remains unknown.[3]

A few fishing boats on the West Coast and canallers and tugboats on the Great Lakes and St Lawrence River continued to be built for private industry and for government nonmilitary use. The Department of Transport awarded a contract to build an icebreaker to Davie Shipbuilding and Repairing Company in 1939, and although the vessel's keel was laid before the outbreak of the war and she was launched in November, she had to wait until February 1941 to be completed because of priority granted to corvettes.[4] Christened *Ernest Lapointe* in honour of the recently deceased minister of justice and the prime minister's closest political colleague, the icebreaker left immediately and began performing her vital services, namely clearing ice jams and preventing flooding in the St Lawrence River and the Gulf of St Lawrence.[5] In 1940 Marine Industries Limited constructed a Great Lakes tanker for Shell Oil Company of Canada. In the meantime, the small-boat program grew by leaps and bounds. The increase in the number of warships operating from Canadian naval bases on the East Coast forced rapid expansion of harbour facilities requiring ammunition and stores lighters, self-propelled barges, motor boats, auxiliary oilers, water barges, tugboats, and various special-purpose craft connected to such passive harbour defences as minefields and antisubmarine nets.

The navy initially assigned names to many of the vessels acquired from others, but in 1941 it officially began to use the designation HC, standing for Harbour Craft, when it decided to allot numbers to some of the 200 vessels then in service whose original civilian purposes were not recorded and whose names led to confusion. Effective January 1942 all harbour craft ceased using names and were numbered.[6] By 1944 the RCN had three distinct classes of purpose-built harbour craft in service: a 46- and a 72-foot harbour craft designated HC and a 48.5-foot harbour-patrol craft.[7] By the war's end, 112 of the 46-foot launches and 31 of the 48.5-foot craft had been built, chiefly in Nova Scotia and Prince Edward Island, with some built in British Columbia and Ontario.[8] Over 300 small craft, including 88 16-foot, fast motor dinghies and 168 25-foot and 57 32-foot diesel-powered cutters, also entered the navy's harbour service. Eighty-eight more of these three types were built for the British Admiralty Technical Mission (BATM), and another 140 were under construction in May 1945.[9] But some of the more interesting craft may be found among the larger noncombatant support vessels. The purpose of this chapter is to describe five sections of the large program in order to capture most of the craft constructed and to highlight several significant features.

Auxiliary Oilers, Tenders, and Canadian-Designed Tankers

The 10,000-ton tankers built for the cargo ship program are relatively well known, but the navy's auxiliary oilers and noncombatant vessels of several sorts, usually omitted from the wartime shipbuilding story, were crucial to the success of military operations and the domestic economy. Ensuring access to fuel oil quickly became a pressing concern. In 1940 Marine Industries Limited converted four old steam-powered canallers – hulks really – into small diesel tankers of less than 2,000 gross registered tons (grt) each and set up Branch Lines Limited to operate them. All four tankers entered service by the end of the year transporting oil from St Lawrence River ports to the Great Lakes.[10] The same year, Upper Lakes and St Lawrence Transportation Company had Muir Brothers Dry Dock at Port Dalhousie, at the entrance to the Welland Canal on Lake Ontario, convert the small bulk-carrier barge MV *Blue Cross* into a tanker and chartered her to Shell Canada Limited.[11]

Rapid expansion placed severe pressure on the navy's tiny inadequate infrastructure. The RCN acquired two Department of Transport hopper barges in 1940, converted them to fuel-oil carriers, and commissioned them in Halifax as HMCS *Moonbeam* and HMCS *Sunbeam*.[12] Other strange conversions followed. A former Department of Public Works dredge (*No. 306*) was transferred to the RCN, converted on the West Coast to an auxiliary tanker, and delivered to Imperial Oil Company for operation in the South American oil trade transporting fuel to naval storage tanks. She was commissioned as HMCS *Mastodon* on 9 December 1942.[13]

In 1942 Marine Industries Limited set up a barges division within its recently established Branch Lines Limited to operate four former steam-powered cargo ships that once belonged to Canada Steamship Lines after converting them to diesel-powered coal barges. The first two, *Ashleaf* and *Bayleaf*, departed immediately for the East Coast and began operating for the American government. The second pair of barges, *Aspenleaf* and *Palmleaf*, operated under the control of the Department of Munitions and Supply (DMS) transporting coal. All four later operated together between Shediac, Montreal, Pictou, and Sydney.[14]

HMCS *Preserver*, Fairmile depot ship, 4,670 displacement tons, built by Marine Industries Limited, during trials off Sorel, Quebec, 27 June 1942. Canada, DND/LAC, PA-134525.

The naval board authorized construction of two auxiliary oilers in 1942, but as no building berth was available in the wake of the rapidly expanding cargo ship program, Canadian Bridge Company at Walkerville, Ontario, a firm that fabricated structural steel, undertook construction of the 168-foot vessels. The twin-screw oilers were of all-steel, all-welded construction, propelled by two Vivian diesel engines providing 700 horsepower (hp) at 400 rotations per minute (rpm), and displaced about 1,500 tons.[15] Designed by German and Milne to transport both bunker "C" fuel oil and diesel fuel, the tankers were equipped with two cargo pumps with a capacity of 75 tons per hour for the former and 30 tons per hour for the latter.[16]

Canadian Bridge Company was already building welded tugboats for the British Ministry of War Transport. Various parts of the new oilers, stern section, engine base, tanks, and funnels were constructed at the company's Walkerville plant and transported to its shipyard at Ojibway for assembly.[17] Where possible, the company constructed completely welded subassemblies for bulkheads, decks, and tank tops. The first tanker, launched on 14 July 1943 and christened HMCS *Dundalk*, was followed soon afterward by HMCS *Dundurn*.[18] Both ships were commissioned on 25 November and rushed to Halifax before the closure of St Lawrence River navigation.[19]

The need for small tankers continued. SS *Riding Mountain Park* was one of the weirder conversions carried out during the war. In 1943 Wartime Merchant Shipping Limited had St John Dry Dock and Shipbuilding Company convert this former Department of Public Works ladder dredge (ex-*PWD No. 1*, ex-*W.S. Fielding*), built in 1905, into a diesel-powered tanker of 1,854 gross tons. She measured 245 feet between perpendiculars and was 43 feet abeam.[20] Owing to the age of the vessel, this became a reconstruction job, and more work had to be done than had been contemplated. She was completed during the summer and handed over to Park Steamship Company. After her first voyage to Africa for a cargo of palm oil, the company sold her to the British Ministry of War Transport in November 1944.[21] Also in 1943, Muir Brothers Dry Dock at Port Dalhousie rebuilt the thirty-one-year-old ss *Transbay* into an auxiliary oiler. It took longer but cost less to tear down and rebuild the vessel and install a used engine than to build a new ship. General manager Charles A. Ansell directed the work, and in August the completed ship was ready to sail to Sarnia to pick up her first cargo.[22]

The navy ordered the first of two base-supply vessels from Marine Industries Limited in 1941. Designed as a mother ship for Fairmile motor launches, she was essentially a small oil tanker fitted with a machine shop, sickbay, spare accommodation, and space for stores. Laid down in July 1941, she was launched in December and commissioned as HMCS *Preserver* in July 1942. Both the *Preserver* and her sister ship, HMCS *Provider*, commissioned on 1 December, were 269 feet long and 44 feet amidships, with a maximum draft of 18 feet. Each ship displaced 4,670 tons, and two imported Fairbanks Morse diesel engines developing 944 hp moved them along at 10 knots. Armament consisted of one 12-pounder or one 4-inch gun and two 20-mm Oerlikon guns.[23]

Six small tankers ordered in November 1942 and designed by German and Milne were the most original vessels built during the cargo ship program. At 3,600 deadweight tons, they were intended to transit the St Lawrence River canals. Their overall length of 259 feet was 1 foot less than the shortest lock in the canal system; each ship's breadth was 44 feet. The origin of these ships was a similar tanker, MV *Lakeshell*, built by Marine Industries Limited in 1940. Designed by German and Milne for Shell Oil Company to carry bulk petroleum products on the Great Lakes and St Lawrence River, her antecedent may have even been earlier, for her lines were similar to those of MV *Franquelin*, designed by the same firm and built in 1936 at Wallsend-on-Tyne for Quebec and Ontario Transportation Company Limited. German and Milne also supervised construction of the *Lakeshell*, which was launched on 1 June 1940; she entered service before the end of July. The largest tanker built in Canada to date, she was also all-welded and equipped with double rudders. The major innovation was her framing, incorporating German and Milne's patented "conduit bilge" system for canallers, which offered special protection against damage in locks and canals.[24] Two sets of diesel engines of Sulzer design delivering a total of 960 brake horsepower (bhp) at 430 rpm gave the new tanker a speed of 9.5 miles per hour on a loaded draft of 14 feet freshwater.[25] She was the largest tanker capable of passing through the Lachine Canal with a full cargo.

Laid down in 1943 and completed in 1944, the six tankers were the largest all-welded, steel ships built in Canada during the war and were fitted with Suzler diesel motors manufactured by Dominion Engineering Works at Montreal, which were similar to the ones in the *Lakeshell*.[26] The DMS assigned the building of three each to Marine Industries Limited and Collingwood Shipyards Limited and granted capital assistance in the amount of $148,000 to the latter yard so that it could acquire the machine tools and welding equipment, including electric transformers, needed to build these vessels.[27] Two tankers, the *Nipiwan Park* and *Norwood Park*, were completed at Collingwood in November 1943 and hastened to the sea before the navigation season closed. Marine Industries completed the *Otterburn Park*, *Eglington Park*, and *Millican Park* at Sorel in May, June, and August 1944, respectively. The final Great Lakes tanker, the *Springbank Park*, was completed at Collingwood in September.[28] All were delivered to Park Steamship Company, which nominated Imperial Oil Company of Toronto to manage them. These tankers went on to transport high-octane aviation gasoline, particularly to Newfoundland, to meet the needs of streams of bombers being ferried to the United Kingdom.[29]

Ontario's Fairmile Builders

Canada's boat builders produced eighty-eight Fairmile B-type motor launches. Fourteen were built on the West Coast, fifteen at Weymouth, Nova Scotia, and fifty-nine in Ontario. The government authorized construction of the first twenty-four for the Royal Canadian Navy as early as May 1940, but delays in receiving complete drawings, specifications, and performance data from Great Britain meant the first contract was not let until January 1941.[30] Twelve more launches were ordered in July, and the BATM ordered eight more in August. The naval staff ordered eighteen additional launches in February 1942 to supplement corvettes assigned to antisubmarine work in the St Lawrence River and off Canada's East Coast.[31] Following the sinking of the Newfoundland ferry SS *Caribou* in Cabot Strait in October, the navy added eight more to another eighteen to serve as fast ferry escorts and to ensure employment during the winter.[32]

Designed as an antisubmarine vessel, Fairmiles were 112-foot, wooden craft with a standard displacement of 79 tons. The first seventy motor launches were powered by twin V-12, 640-hp, American Hall-Scott "Defender" gasoline engines. They had an emergency speed of 20 knots and a maximum continuous speed of 16.5 knots. Their economical endurance was 1,455 nautical miles at 7.5 knots. Twin V-12, 700-hp, Sterling "Admiral" gasoline engines manufactured at Buffalo, New York, powered the last eighteen launches, increasing their full speed to 22 knots and adding nearly one-third more distance to the endurance range.[33] Armed with machine guns and depth charges, a Fairmile was no match for a German U-boat on the surface. Depth charges were the principal armament. The Fairmile's task was to detect attacking U-boats and keep them submerged, pinned with asdic, while other motor launches and larger warships went into action. Ill suited as escorts, they were intended to operate in flotillas of six or eight. Although the boat was an ideal candidate for mass production to achieve savings, Canada's limited, dispersed labour force prevented this from occurring.[34]

Test trials in Britain proved disappointing, and consideration was given to cancelling the whole program. Lack of an alternative vessel and the urgent need for more antisubmarine patrol vessels in the St Lawrence River led to the construction of these motor launches despite their limitations.[35] Subsequent operations revealed all of the Fairmile's problems. The vessels were less manoeuvrable than expected; fixed oscillators on the sonar (asdic) sets meant that the whole vessel had to be turned in order to scan ahead and that operations had to be conducted at slower speeds than originally planned.[36] That eighty-eight of these craft were built reflects the desperate nature of the times. Indeed, eight were immediately transferred to the United States Navy to meet a critical shortage.

The government sought to have as many boats as possible built in Nova Scotia. But despite the help of the provincial government, just three of twelve bids came from the province; only one contained prices comparable to those from Ontario.[37] Aside from charges made in Parliament that Nova Scotia builders lacked initiative, owners of small yards had neither the organization nor the facilities to handle heavy gasoline engines and were not accustomed to working on a sufficiently large scale. They were certainly unaccustomed to bidding on Dominion government contracts. East Coast builders also lacked the necessary capital to invest in marine hardwoods like mahogany, and they had limited experience building light craft.[38] Nevertheless, the largest number of Fairmiles constructed in Canada at any one site was completed by John H. LeBlanc Shipbuilding Company at Weymouth, which produced all fifteen built in Nova Scotia. On the West Coast, six launches were built for the first program in 1942 and eight more in 1944 as part of the last program (see table 10.2).

Ontario's pleasure-craft builders had considerable expertise constructing boats like the motor launches, and the early war years had seen a revival of boatbuilding in Muskoka because a number of Americans who could no longer visit many parts of Europe came to Canada for their holidays and spent their dollars on new boats.[39] As boatbuilding in Ontario became a wartime industry, it employed workers at places as far from the sea as Bracebridge, Gravenhurst, Orillia, Penetanguishene, Port Carling, Honey Harbour, and Sarnia, as well as Toronto.

Of the first twenty-four Fairmiles ordered, the government placed contracts for two boats each with one East Coast, three West Coast, and five Ontario firms. Two additional Ontario builders each obtained contracts for three boats. Ontario builders constructed all but three of the thirty-five boats in the second, third, and fourth programs.

In 1935 Port Carling Boat Works established a branch operation at Honey Harbour at the request of boat owners on Georgian Bay wishing to have their boats serviced. The company was controlled by E. Douglas Milner, vice president, designer, engineer, and supervisor of operations at Port Carling, and by his brother J. Cameron Milner, who managed business at Honey Harbour. In December 1940 they formed a joint venture with Minett-Shields Limited at Bracebridge and built a plant at Honey Harbour that enabled them to contract to build three Fairmiles the next spring. Although as much work as possible was carried out at Port Carling and Bracebridge, from half frames to bunks, and trucked to Orillia and up the Coldwater Road to Honey Harbour for fabrication, all nine boats were launched into Georgian Bay. At peak operation, the Georgian Bay plant employed between 300 and 350 men.[40]

Table 10.2 | Fairmile B-type motor launches built in Canada, by builder and year, 1941–44

Boat builder	1941	1942	1943	1944	Total
Greavette Boats, Gravenhurst, ON	3	4	2		9
Grew Boats, Penetanguishene, ON	2	3	3		8
Hunter Boats, Orillia, ON	2	3	1	1	7
Mac-Craft, Sarnia, ON		5	3		8
Midland Boat Works, Midland, ON	2	3	3		8
Minett-Shields, Bracebridge, ON	2	6	1		9
Port Carling Boat Works, Port Carling, ON			1		1
J.J. Taylor and Sons, Toronto, ON	2	4	3		9
LeBlanc Shipbuilding, Weymouth, NS		12*	1	2	15
A.C. Benson Shipyards, Vancouver, BC		2		2	4
Star Shipyards (Mercer's), New Westminister, BC		2		3	5
Vancouver Shipyards, Vancouver, BC		2		3	5
Total	13	46	18	11	88

* Eight of these motor launches ordered for the Royal Navy were assigned to the United States Navy.

Sources: Tucker, Naval Service of Canada, vol. 2, 509–11; Smith et al., "History of the British Admiralty Technical Mission in Canada," 81.

Bryson W. Shields was president and general manager of Minett-Shields, and Douglas Van Patten, a naval architect, designer, and engineer, was vice president.[41] The navy listed Minett-Shields as the sole contractor for convenience only.[42] By their own accounts, Minett-Shields built at Bracebridge twenty-one 10-foot dinghies, five 25-foot motor-launch hulls, two 40-foot range boats, and two 46-foot harbour craft, and Port Carling Boat Works at its plant on Lake Rosseau built 107 boats for the RCN, chiefly small utility craft, service dinghies, whalers, and cutters, nine range boats for the RCAF, and 390 12-foot (Mk IIc) assault boats for the Canadian army. Two smaller Port Carling firms, W.J. Johnson and Duke Boats, constructed eighty-one pulling boats and forty-seven motor cutters.[43]

Several companies were formed to handle government contracts. Two on Georgian Bay owed their origins to the old pre-First World War Gidley Boat Company. Following the First World War, J.G. Gidley and Son at Midland was sold and became Midland Boat Works, owned and operated by Honey Harbour Navigation Company Limited. In 1939 Thomas McCullough was president and general manager. In addition to the eight Fairmiles, the company constructed fifty-five pulling boats and two 46-foot harbour craft for the RCN, two 40-foot range boats for the RCAF, and 100 pontoons for the Canadian army. The second company was located at Penetanguishene.

Early in 1939 wealthy Toronto businessman Clarence A. Kemp partnered with Eric Osborne to purchase controlling interest in the Penetanguishene plant and assets of Gidley Boat Company and merged the two with Grew Boats Company Limited. Prior to the merger, Grew Boats had been a small boatbuilding firm owned by Kemp located at Jackson's Point on Lake Simcoe. In 1932 he had stepped in to save Art Grew's boatbuilding business and became owner and general manager. After 1939 Penetanguishene became the centre of Grew Boats Company's operations.[44] The company built eight Fairmiles, one 126-foot minesweeper, and 201 pontoons for the army, together with forty-seven small pulling boats and motor cutters for the navy and aircraft tenders for the air force.

Mac-Craft Company Limited at Sarnia, Ontario, was a new company set up largely to engage in war work. The first two Fairmiles built by Mac-Craft were commissioned into the RCN at Sarnia on 18 April 1942. Shortly before, Mac-Craft had agreed to construct 178 bridge pontoons for the army and on 1 April had assigned the entire business to William Gourlay Webster, a well-to-do London industrialist, member of the provincial Parliament of Ontario, and president of Webster Air Equipment Limited, who set up Mac-Craft Company Limited to receive the assets to build both pontoons and three more motor launches.[45] Mac-Craft, which built eight Fairmiles, launched the last of them in November 1943 in only sixty-seven days. The first boat had taken seven months to build.[46] The firm also constructed 216 pontoons for the army.

Alestair Peter Hunter incorporated Hunter Boats Limited in 1941 with himself as president, his son, Donald A. Hunter, as vice president, and I. Stopps as secretary-treasurer. Hunter senior (1892–1965) was a brilliant mechanic with a flair for design. During the 1920s he had worked in Gravenhurst for Ditchburn Boats Limited, becoming supervisor of marine motors and electrical installations in 1927 and moving to Orillia to carry on the same work at Herbert Ditchburn's new plant, which was established to build larger yachts for the Great Lakes, to which access was gained through the Trent-Severn canal system. Ditchburn Boats went into receivership in 1931, and the following year, Hunter purchased the abandoned Orillia plant on the shore of Lake Couchiching. After hiring a naval architect, he began designing and building boats and servicing and storing yachts with considerable success. The onset of war found him well placed and equipped to begin production for the government.

In 1939 Hunter converted a 58-foot pleasure yacht donated to the government to train naval personnel, and at about the same time, he received a contract to build thirteen 18-foot bomb-loading dinghies powered by Buchanan motors for the RCAF.[47] During 1941 his newly incorporated company grew from about a half-dozen employees to over 125.[48] On 13 October 1943 an explosion on board Q116, while she was undergoing final finishing at dockside, blew the engine-room superstructure through the side of the Hunter plant, killing one employee, Stanley Peacock, and severely injuring several others. This last Fairmile was rebuilt during the winter and commissioned the following summer.[49] Hunter eventually built seven Fairmiles and also constructed nine drop-keel dinghies, thirteen 18-foot bomb-loading dinghies, two 46-foot harbour craft, and two 75-foot passenger launches for the navy as well as 187 20-foot, steel pontoons (Mk V) for the Canadian army.[50]

Fairmile motor launches were constructed at two sites at Toronto, one at the foot of Bathurst Street and the other at Humber Bay on the site of Sachau Marine Construction Limited. William "Bill" Taylor, son of James J. Taylor, president of the firm, headed the well-established firm of J.J. Taylor and Sons. The senior Taylor was almost seventy years old and stood back to allow his four sons and a daughter to operate the firm during the war. The challenge of constructing 112-foot vessels after a lifetime of working on much smaller craft demanded a lot of organization and energy. Taylor's daughter, Dorothy, managed the business side of the family's activities.[51]

As in all yards, lack of materials and slow deliveries from American, British, and Canadian sources delayed early construction. The navy did not designate Fairmiles as ships. Hence they were not christened or given the designation "HMCS." Instead, they were assigned commissioning numbers. The first two Taylor-built Fairmiles, 052 and 053, were commissioned on 31 October and 17 November 1941, respectively. As a result of priorities given to Ontario boat works, thirteen motor launches were commissioned that year, but only nine reached Halifax. The last four ran into winter storms after sailing late from Georgian Bay and had to be laid up at Sarnia and Toronto.[52] J.J. Taylor and Sons built four Fairmiles (079, 080, 086, and 087) in 1942 and three more (088, 112, and 113) in 1943. The larger American Sterling engines powered the last two. J.J Taylor and Sons also completed one 126-foot minesweeper and eighteen 25-foot motor cutters for the navy.

Thomas Greavette (1881–1958) grew up in Muskoka, where he began working at the Ditchburn agency beside W.J. Johnson's boat livery near the locks in Port Carling as early as 1903. Following Ditchburn's business failure, he incorporated Greavette Boats Limited in 1931 at Gravenhurst and after finding backers initiated production of "runabouts" the following year. To gain access to the Great Lakes, a requirement of the Department of Munitions and Supply, Greavette leased the site of Sachau Marine Construction Limited at Humber Bay, Mimico, and hired Hans Sachau as works superintendent.[53]

During the 1930s Sachau, a German-immigrant yacht builder who arrived in Canada in 1928, gained an enviable reputation for building quality yachts. His boatyard west of the Humber River, at 227 Lakeshore Road, possessed a 600-foot marine railway that allowed him to launch directly into Lake Ontario. During 1939 and 1940, while building one of the largest yachts ever launched on the lake, he added a "Y" branch to the railway, which allowed him to build two boats at once, both under cover. Sachau's friendship with Thomas Greavette, and perhaps the government's reluctance to deal with a German immigrant, led to Greavette's arrangement. The contrast between the Dominion government's treatment of Hans Sachau and James Franceschini (discussed in chapter 4), could not have been greater. Three boats (054, 055 and 056) were commissioned at Humber Bay in the fall of 1941, two more (077 and 078) on 2 June 1942, and two more (089 and 090) in the fall of 1942. The final motor launches (091 and 114) were commissioned in May and November 1943.

Greavette's Gravenhurst plant remained busy during the war. Some parts of the motor launches, probably superstructures, were built there and shipped to Toronto for final assembly.[54] In addition to fifteen sailing dinghies and five range boats built for the RCAF, Gravenhurst employees constructed 150 12-foot assault boats (Mk IIc) and seventy-seven folding boats (Mk III) for the army. In September 1944 Greavette secured a contract to build forty 36-foot harbour launches for the transport ferries (LST3s) being built for the BATM.[55]

By April 1942 the Ontario builders were facing problems. The navy's custom of demanding extras based on war experience and on the appearance of new products added many difficulties. Production problems, prices for extras, and the formation of an association brought the builders together on 18 July at a site near Penetangui-shene.[56] The main items of business were to agree on a list of items to be charged to the DMS and accepted as standard for extras on the current program and to agree on another list of extras actually installed during the previous program. In response to a fire at Midland Boat Works five days earlier, which damaged two Fairmiles, members also agreed unanimously to assist Tom McCullough to complete the damaged boats before freeze-up. Finally, Stan McNabb of Grew Boats Company obtained everyone's agreement to form the Ontario Fairmile Association (OFA) in order to deal with the government. Those present elected Bill Taylor president and Don Hunter secretary-treasurer, and each member deposited a $25 entry fee.[57] A week later, OFA members invited the only other Fairmile builder in the East, John H. LeBlanc of Weymouth, Nova Scotia, to join. The survival of the association's minutes provides a rare glimpse into the challenges facing small boatbuilding firms in their dealings with the government.

The substance of the next meeting a week later dealt with the headaches caused by filling out forms for the government and whether the builders came under the government's Production Requirements Plan. The solution was to have the secretary invite Mr Stewart of the priorities division of the shipbuilding branch to attend a meeting of the builders to assist in correctly filling out the wretched forms.[58] The completion of forms appeared again ten months later, but then the government suggested the association file one complete set to cover all members.[59]

The irregular timing of contracts adversely affected the builders, who daily lost key men because of uncertainty about future Fairmile construction. Members called for a year-round program. It never happened. The need for the OFA became more apparent in January 1943 when members met with Richard Pearson of the naval service in Toronto to discuss the introduction of complete changes in construction methods for the new Fairmiles. These involved relocating throttle controls, installing tachometers in the wheelhouse, removing coalbunkers, and installing oil-burning stoves and boilers. Mounting the new Sterling engines – which required removing the funnel and taking exhaust ports out through the side of the hull and dispensing with previous shaft logs and stern tubes in favour of standard bronze tubes with cutlass bearings to deal with cracked manifolds and valves resulting from undersized, poorly designed scoops – proved especially challenging, as did the switch from Philippine to Honduran mahogany planking. With no new Fairmiles to build, the members were also anxious to pool materials.

The OFA discussed production costs for the new program in March, seeking clarification on the meaning of telegrams sent to members from the negotiation division

HMCS *Cedar Lake*, a 126-foot, wooden motor minesweeper built by J.J. Taylor and Sons at Toronto, on launch day. Commissioned 4 November 1945, it was one of ten transferred to the Soviet navy for mine clearance in Arctic waters and the Black Sea. Private Archive, James Taylor Collection, no. 49.

of the DMS. New financial arrangements requiring builders to purchase equipment valued at nearly $13,000 per vessel and to pay freight or express and insurance proved burdensome. Builders demanded a handling charge. Finally, responding to rumours, members agreed not to accept future contracts on a cost-plus-5-per-cent basis. The first year of the Ontario Fairmile Association had been busy; indeed, members reimbursed the secretary $300 for his efforts and re-elected him and the president to their offices for a second term.

Following the introduction of the wooden minesweeper program in 1944, the OFA was divided into two sections. The minesweeper division comprised J.J. Taylor and Sons, Mac-Craft Company, Port Carling Boat Works, Grew Boats Company, and Midland Boat Works. An aircraft marine division included Greavette Boats, Minett-Shields, and Hunter Boats.[60] While the first five firms turned to building wooden minesweepers, the three remaining companies began constructing range boats and aircraft tenders for the RCAF.

The successful campaign by German U-boats to lay mines off Canada's East Coast gave rise to this last shipbuilding program of the RCN. British orders for twenty-four 126-foot motor minesweepers had absorbed the whole capacity of the three largest builders of wooden boats in Nova Scotia, which accounts for the RCN orders being placed with Ontario firms. Although naval staff approval occurred in August 1943, the contracts were not placed until December.

This was an entirely new type of vessel for Ontario's Fairmile builders. With an overall length of 140 feet and displacing 360 tons, they were a major challenge. Two boats each were awarded to the five builders of the minesweeping division, but following optimistic projections of the successful European campaign, the government cancelled five of the minesweepers. Port Carling Boat Works launched its minesweeper, christened *Pine Lake*, on Trafalgar Day of 1944. Like the other minesweepers, it was not completed or commissioned before VJ Day, and shortly afterward, together with nine similar vessels, she was turned over to the Soviet navy under Canada's mutual-aid program.[61]

At the end of 1944 production was being wound down. Members of the OFA turned their attention to the postwar period. At the urging of the Canadian Manufacturers' Association, they agreed to form the nucleus of an all-Ontario boat-builders association to link up with other boat builders on the East and West Coasts in a Canada-wide organization.[62] At the same time, they sought government assistance to export boats and permission to purchase materials for postwar production and reconversion. Members opposed any lowering of tariffs on imported pleasure boats from the United States and rejected a request from the United Kingdom that Ontario boat builders represent an English line of boats.

On 28 October 1945 members renamed the OFA the Ontario Boatbuilders' Association, which had a president, three vice presidents, and a secretary-treasurer, in order to present a broader picture of the Ontario boatbuilding industry. Entry was confined to builders of wooden boats, and new members would be approved by a majority of old members. Tom McCullough was elected acting president and Don Hunter acting secretary. After building 1,750 boats and marine craft during the previous five years, Ontario's Fairmile builders had gained great experience, but the postwar period would prove more challenging than wartime.

Tugs and Towing Vessels

The manufacture of more than 330 tug boats and towing vessels, ranging in size from small 40-foot tugs called "pups" to medium ocean-going vessels more than 100 feet long, is another forgotten yet important feature of Canada's wartime shipbuilding program. Gate vessels, boom-attendant vessels, and 25-ton derrick scows were associated with passive harbour defences, usually single or double steel-wire, antisubmarine or antitorpedo nets suspended from steel buoys at harbour entrances. They normally had an opening operated by two gate vessels, which opened and closed the net to permit ships to enter and exit the harbour. The earliest gate vessels had been requisitioned from among existing craft, but new ones were built as passive harbour defences spread from Halifax and Esquimalt to St John, Gaspé, Prince Rupert, Sydney, and Shelburne, as well as to Newfoundland.[63] In 1942 the navy purchased four hopper barges from Canadian Dredge and Dock Company at Midland, Ontario, and sent them to Kingston to be converted into gate vessels. They were 102 and 108 feet long and 28 feet wide.[64] Commencing in 1942, the same company also built at Kingston six 25-ton, steel derrick scows for boom-defence maintenance. They were 120 feet long and 42 feet wide, drew 9 feet, and cost from $136,000 to $195,000.[65] Star Shipyards (Mercer's) Limited at New Westminster, British Columbia, built four large wooden gate vessels for the RCN on the West Coast, and Le Chantier Maritime de Saint Laurent, on Ile d'Orléans, built a similar one for Halifax. The Quebec builder also constructed a 60-foot wooden tug, HMCS *Listowell*, and delivered four wooden,

Table 10.3 | Tugs and towing craft built in Canada, 1939–45

40-foot, steel gate-attendant vessel	14
46-foot boom-attendant vessel	3
100-foot, wooden gate-attendant vessel	5
60-foot, antisubmarine target-towing vessel	9
95-foot target-towing vessel	1
40-foot, steel tug	25
60-foot, wooden tug	1
60-foot, steel, diesel tug	198
65-foot, wooden, diesel tug	35
80-foot, steel, diesel tug	16
80-foot, wooden, diesel tug	4
105-foot Warrior-class tug	13
106-foot, 1,000-hp tug	6
Total towing vessels and tugs	*330*

Sources: LAC, RG 28, box 29, file 5 of 6, Shipbuilding, ship and small-boat contracts; Canada, Wartime Information Board, *Canada at War*, no. 45, "Recapitulation Issue" (July 1945): table 57.

105-foot minesweepers to the RCN and the RN. Additional 90-foot, wooden derrick scows were built on both the East and West Coasts.[66]

Target-towing vessels were connected to army and navy training. The nine shown in table 10.3 were commissioned into the RCN as antisubmarine towing vessels. They were 60-foot, wooden tugboats given the suffix "wood," as in *Brentwood*, and were employed training antisubmarine crews.[67] All nine were built on the East and West Coasts: LeBlanc Shipbuilding Company at Weymouth, Nova Scotia, and Palmer and Williams Company at Summerside, Prince Edward Island, built four and two, respectively; and Armstrong Brothers (later Falconer Marine Industries Limited) at Victoria, British Columbia, built three.[68] The latter were powered by 225-hp, Hall-Scott "Invader" gasoline engines, which gave a top speed of 11 knots.

The greatest demand was for tugboats. The Royal Canadian Navy had no tugs at the beginning of the war, and the needs of the service and of shipping in general grew quickly.[69] Early in the war, the British withdrew three large British-built and British-subsidized tugboats from Halifax, St John, and Victoria and returned them to the United Kingdom. This deprived the country of tugs when they were most needed; yet construction of tugs began in earnest only in 1942.[70] During the interim, the RCN chartered at least eight tugboats and purchased five more, including two from an American owner.[71]

Table 10.3 shows the twelve kinds of tugs built in Canada. There may not have been any difference between 40-foot, gate-attendant vessels and the small harbour tugs of the same length. Russel Brothers Limited at Owen Sound, Ontario, built all thirty-nine vessels for the RCN. The all-steel, welded vessels were a prewar design accepted by the navy. Later, they were designated Ville-class tugs, and their names all ended in "ville." Russel Brothers' wartime tugs were "Steelcraft" electric-welded boats powered by a Cummins 6-cylinder marine diesel engine rated at 150 hp at 1,800 rpm.[72]

Ottawa-born brothers Colin and Robert Jardine Russel were working as machinists in the Grand Trunk Railway shops in Winnipeg when, in 1907, they decided to go into business for themselves and opened a small shop to do general machinery repairs at Fort Frances, Ontario. A few years later, they began building small winching boats and warping tugs for the Canadian logging industry. The company was incorporated in 1927 and, two years later, constructed a small, electric-welded, steel boat believed to be the first of its type in North America. The company survived the Depression by working at general machinery repairs and whatever came to hand, but the need to expand and respond to changes in the forest industry led the brothers to relocate in 1937 to Owen Sound, which was closer to both materials and their markets. By October they were operating in their new premises under the mark of "Steelcraft." Russel Brothers' first war work was manufacturing British-designed, 25-kilowatt, diesel-powered generator sets that employed Cummins diesels produced in Columbus, Indiana. The company was the sole Ontario distributor.[73]

The navy also ordered 80-foot tugs in both steel and wooden versions. In 1942 the navy ordered five at $56,000 each from Russel Brothers, to be delivered the following spring and summer.[74] Designated Glen-class, they displaced 170 tons and had a length of 80.5 feet, a breadth of 20 feet, and a draft of 10 feet. An 8-cylinder, Vivian diesel

HMC Tug *Glenkeen*, one of five 80-foot, Glen-class, all-welded, steel tugboats built in 1944 by Canadian Dredge and Dock Company at Kingston, Ontario. Photo by D.B. Thorndick. DND/ LAC, PA-152045.

engine rated at 320 hp at 500 rpm (400 hp with supercharger) powered the first tugs, which were also fitted with Russel hydraulic steering gear.[75] HMCS *Glendower*, commissioned 18 June 1943 at Owen Sound, was the first of these all-steel, diesel-powered tugs. The second, HMCS *Glenlea*, left Owen Sound in August for the East Coast, and the final three, launched during the next three months, were sent on their way to the sea before the close of the navigation season.[76] Russel Brothers built six more of these tugs in 1944 and 1945. These and other later tugs had a shorter main deckhouse than did the earlier versions in order to accommodate larger diesel engines rated at 400 hp at 400 rpm manufactured by Enterprise Engine and Foundry Company at San Francisco, California.[77] Both versions were suitable only for harbour work, as they had very low freeboards and were not noted for their stability.[78]

The navy ordered twenty Glen-class tugs during the war. Russel Brothers built eleven. Canadian Dredge and Dock Company constructed five at Kingston, and McKenzie Barge and Derrick Company constructed three wooden versions in Vancouver.[79] The first Kingston-built tug was laid down in July 1943; all were commissioned between November 1944 and May 1945.[80] The West Coast tugs, built mainly of Douglas fir and yellow pine, were powered by Vivian diesel engines. HMC Tug *Glendevon*, commissioned at the end of January 1945, was the first tug built for the RCN in British Columbia.[81] The last tug built on the West Coast was not commissioned into the navy. The only wooden tug built on the East Coast, by LeBlanc Shipbuilding Company, was unfinished when the war ended. It was sold to, and completed by, St John Dry Dock and Shipbuilding Company.[82]

Russel Brothers Limited constructed more than 20 per cent of all the tugs built in Canada during the war: two 30-foot, steel launches for the army, twenty-five 40-foot tugs, fourteen similar gate-attendant vessels, and fifteen 60-foot and eleven 80-foot tugs, sixty-seven in all.[83] Not included are three more 60-foot tugs, one built for Minas Shipping Company at Hantsport, Nova Scotia, and two constructed for the Canadian National Railway.[84]

Six larger 1,000-hp tugs, able to handle the large passenger liners converted to troop ships and capital ships calling at Halifax with increasing frequency, were also constructed for the navy in 1943 but entered service only in 1944. Canadian Bridge Company at Walkerville and Montreal Dry Dock Limited built three each.[85] Designed by German and Milne, they were ice-strengthened and equipped for coastal salvage. One such tug constructed by Montreal Dry Dock was 106 feet long overall and had a moulded breadth of 26.5 feet and a mean draft of 9.5 feet. When fully loaded and equipped, her riveted hull displaced 462 tons.[86] Two Suzler-Dominion, 8-cylinder diesel engines delivering 1,000 hp at 330 rpm gave her a speed of 10 knots.[87] The navy designated these large tugs Norton class, and all six had names with "ton" in the suffix, as in *Beaverton* and *Clifton*.

Late in the war, the British Ministry of War Transport became the largest purchaser of Canadian-built tugs. In addition to ordering 195 60-foot, steel tugs from three Ontario builders, it ordered thirty-five 65-foot, wooden tugs from Nova Scotia builders, as well as eighteen larger ocean-going Warrior-class tugs from Kingston

Shipbuilding Company and Midland Shipyards Limited. Russel Brothers Limited was responsible for fifteen of the smaller tugs. The largest manufacturers were two Ontario steel-fabricating firms: Central Bridge Company at Trenton and Canadian Bridge Company at Walkerville. Construction of tugboats by structural-steel fabricators was additional evidence of the total harnessing of Canadian industry to war production. Uninhibited by any shipbuilding customs or traditions, both companies, employing unique building and launching techniques, performed an excellent job producing 111 and 69 tugboats, respectively.

Canadian Bridge Company Limited was a subsidiary of Dominion Steel and Coal Company. It launched CT-1, the first of twenty tugs, at Ojibway, Ontario, in February 1943. Fifteen more were completed by July. The keels were laid in one of the company's main shops at Walkerville, where all framing was carried out. Side plating was then fitted and tack welded. At that point, the hull was moved into another shop and placed in a specially designed jig, which, after being clamped into position, allowed it to be rotated about its longitudinal axis so that welding could be carried out in the most convenient position. Afterward, a railway flatcar transported the welded hull to the company's shipyard berths at Ojibway, where workers fitted and welded the preassembled deckhouse, installed machinery, and completed final fitting. A large crane then lifted the complete tug into the waters of the Detroit River for trials. The Fairbanks-Morse diesel engines in these first tugs developed 200 bhp at 400 rpm.[88]

Central Bridge Company was the child of William A. Fraser, a prominent Trenton, Ontario, businessman, promoter of local business development in the Bay of Quinte region, and since 1930, Liberal member of Parliament for Northumberland. A former mayor of Trenton from 1924 to 1930, Fraser had been a strong advocate for the establishment of the Trenton air force station. He was president and virtual owner of Trenton Cooperage Mills Limited and Trenton Amusement Company and director of a number of industrial firms whose undertakings included canning, lumber, and can manufacturing.[89] During the 1930s Fraser became "boss" of a political machine whose sway extended over much of east-central Ontario. Ambitious, aggressive, and bold, he ruled with an iron hand, earning the sobriquet "Little Caesar."[90] It was no mere coincidence that in 1939 Fraser was appointed to chair the Public Accounts Committee of the House of Commons, which investigated the Hahn contract for machine guns let by the amiable, bibulous minister of national defence, Ian Mackenzie.[91]

Sometime during the 1930s Fraser encouraged Alexander Hill, a steel fabricator from Hamilton, to set up in Trenton.[92] Hill Steel Construction Company Limited, incorporated in Hamilton in 1936, remained inactive until the following year when Fraser incorporated Central Bridge Company. Alexander Hill became plant manager and his son, Alex B. Hill, was secretary-treasurer of both Hill Steel Construction Company and Central Bridge Company, whose president in 1939 was William H. Cunningham of Toronto. Central Bridge remained a structural-steel company during 1941, erecting several buildings for the government's expanding aircraft-production program.

At least twelve 60-foot, all-welded, steel tugboats under construction by steelworkers of Central Bridge Company, Trenton, Ontario, April 1944. Photo by Pace Toles. NFB/LAC, WRM 5148.

It obtained its first shipbuilding contract for two 79-foot, diesel-powered ammunition lighters in June 1942.[93] Later, the order was expanded to include six additional lighters and two water barges, all for the Canadian navy.[94] They were completed without a hitch, and the company moved on to build 60-foot tugs for the British Ministry of War Transport. Fraser arranged for Herbert Ditchburn, who had recently completed a contract in Trenton to build high-speed, rescue launches for the Royal Air Force, to organize production of the tugboats on an assembly-line basis.

Hulls were prefabricated in five sections and constructed upside down in an old munitions factory located inland and owned by Fraser. Later, they were moved outside and completed with the addition of engines, fittings, and deck housing that had been fabricated on a subassembly line. Engine-room piping and electrical harnessing were also prefabricated under Ditchburn's direction, although Alexander Hill remained general manager. Each tug fitted out for firefighting and harbour duties displaced 74 tons. By January 1944 one tug was being completed every week, and by August a monthly production rate of eight completely fitted tugs had been attained.[95]

Of all-welded steel construction, insulated, and air-conditioned for operation in tropical climates, these tugs were shipped around the world. The plant was connected directly to the Trent River, and hence to the Bay of Quinte, by a railway line. Workers loaded each finished tug onto the company's own specially built flatcars and moved them two miles over Canadian Pacific Railway tracks to the water. During launch operations, the flatcar was run down a standard gauge spur directly into the river, and after the car was sufficiently submerged, the tug was floated off. At the time of launching the fiftieth tug, on 5 August 1944, the company had 260 employees. General manager Hill's boast was that his employees were not shipbuilders but bridge builders who were launching a completed tug every four days.[96]

Following a trial run on the Bay of Quinte, the tugs were formed into flotillas and driven under their own power across Lake Ontario to Oswego, New York, whence they travelled via the Oswego and Erie Canals to New York and Baltimore. There, they were hoisted up by a large crane and loaded as deck cargo onto newly built merchant ships for dispatch to all parts of the British Empire.[97] Others travelled down the Mississippi River via Chicago to US Gulf of Mexico ports for shipment overseas.[98]

The majority of these tugboats nearly missed being built in Canada. The initial order for sixty-five tugs was announced in February 1943, but in August, C.D. Howe refused the British ministry's request for 100 additional boats.[99] The minister had already cut the cargo ship program's rate of production by 50 per cent and was concerned that the shipbuilding branch had too much uncompleted work on hand.[100] Strong representations by ministry officials in Canada persuaded Howe to relent, and in October 1944 the DMS contracted with Central Bridge and with Russel Brothers to build fifty of these craft; final contracts for thirty-five more were signed as late as May 1945.[101]

The 261 vessels, including 250 tugboats, built by Russel Brothers, Canadian Bridge, and Central Bridge were worth $20.1 million, which, compared to the value of production of Ontario's five shipbuilding yards, ranked them collectively third in value of wartime production after Toronto Shipbuilding Company and Port Arthur Shipbuilding Company.

Wooden versions of these tugs were built in Nova Scotia, twenty-three by Industrial Shipping Company at its yard on Mahone Bay, and twelve by the famous wooden shipbuilding firm of Smith and Rhuland at Lunenberg. Each tug was 65 feet long, and most were powered by Vivian diesel engines. Construction began in 1943 and continued after the war. Smith and Rhuland completed five before the end of 1945.[102] Nova Scotia builders contracted as late as May 1945 to build fifteen more wooden versions of these tugs.[103] Like all Canadian-built tugs produced for the British Ministry of War Transport after 1943, these were called TANAC tugs. The reverse acronym stood for "CANAda Tug"; when V followed the acronym, it indicated the propulsion unit was a Vivian diesel engine, although anyone could be forgiven for believing the letter stood for "Victory."

In May 1944 the United Kingdom placed an order for twelve large ocean-going tugs of the modified Warrior-class. The order was divided between the Midland and Kingston shipyards, which built eight and four respectively. The tugs, displacing 233 tons, were 105 feet long and steel-hulled but were of outdated British design. Unlike any others built here during the war, they were powered by triple-expansion, steam-driven reciprocating engines that produced 1,000 indicated horsepower (ihp) at 110 rpm.[104] The first tug was delivered in April 1945. The British ministry then ordered six more, which were distributed equally between the two shipyards.[105] The last tug was delivered in October 1946, but as the war had ended long before, the British accepted only thirteen. The others were transferred to War Assets Corporation for disposal.

RCAF Marine Craft

The Royal Canadian Air Force operated a large fleet of vessels during the war. These ranged from 15- and 16-foot rowboats and motorized dinghies through various sizes of chartered, purchased, and confiscated boats to large, high-speed crash tenders and rescue launches and even larger supply and service vessels. For as long as Canada's air force had been in existence, small boats and barges had been employed to facilitate flying operations, which involved seaplanes, flying boats, and amphibious aircraft. In 1935 the RCAF formed a marine-section training program at Trenton, Ontario, and the same year imported two 38-foot seaplane tenders manufactured by British Power Boat Company of the United Kingdom.[106] Larger and more varied craft were acquired as war approached, and as RCAF operations expanded, the number, locations, and assigned tasks of marine craft grew. New seaplane stations and bombing ranges were set up on both coasts, and the introduction of the British Commonwealth Air Training Plan greatly increased the need for small boats to service ranges set up at bombing and gunnery schools inland, whether near shallow bodies of water on the Prairies or beside the Great Lakes and St Lawrence River in Ontario and Quebec.[107] These required boats to service and repair targets, to rescue crews of crashed aircraft, and to carry out a range of operations, including refuelling and salvage.

By October 1940 western air command on the West Coast had 111 marine craft, ranging from 18-foot, bomb-loading dinghies to 84-foot, offshore patrol boats, on establishment.[108] Air force marine-craft manufacturers were located right across the country. On the West Coast, Victoria Motor Boat and Repair Works, A.C. Benson Shipyards, A.C. Linton and Company, Greenwood Canoe Company, McKenzie Barge and Derrick, Newcastle Shipbuilding Company, Star Shipyards (Mercer's), Vancouver Shipyards, and West Coast Salvage and Contracting Company manufactured more than 100 boats for the RCAF. These builders also produced twelve 38-foot, aircraft-crash tenders patterned after the one imported from British Power Boat Company. They built twenty supply and service vessels ranging in length from 60 to 147 feet and three 65-foot pinnaces, employed as torpedo-recovery vessels.

The first two 84-foot, Seine-type fish-packer boats, launched in September 1940 and christened *Siwash* and *Haida*, were capable of transporting a Bolingbroke bomber or

Thirty-eight-foot RCAF aircraft tenders built by Grew Boats Limited at Penetanguishene, Ontario, loaded on railway cars for shipment, 1940. Private Archive, Joe Fossey Collection, no. 5.

a Stranraer flying boat on their aft deck from any one of several air stations along British Columbia's rugged coast to the repair depot in the Vancouver area.[109] Of rugged wooden construction, powered by 8-cylinder, supercharged, Vivian diesel engines delivering 200 hp at 700 rpm, they displaced 150 tons fully loaded. Eight of these serviceable boats, including four for the RCN, were eventually built on the West Coast.

Fifteen refuelling launches and thirteen flat and derrick scows were manufactured on the West Coast.[110] A.C. Linton and Compnay at Vancouver built eleven 18-foot aircraft tenders. Greenwood Canoe Company at Vancouver manufactured 18-foot bomb-loading dinghies, and A.J. Jones at Kelowna produced eleven 16-foot scows and one 41-foot refuelling launch designed to transport 2,000 gallons of aviation gasoline.[111]

Fifteen small-boat builders located around the East Coast – from St Andrews, New Brunswick, to Summerside, Prince Edward Island, and Shelburne, Nova Scotia – provided the air force with more than fifty boats ranging from 18-foot aircraft tenders to 60-, 84-, and 114-foot supply and service vessels. The largest displaced 235 tons and were powered by two Gray-type, 165-bhp diesel engines.[112] Other boats included refuelling launches and barges, harbour utility craft, and flat and derrick scows. The smaller number of purpose-built vessels on the East Coast may have been due to the number of craft that were purchased, leased, and requisitioned from government departments and private owners. Some made strange bedfellows. The *Arresteur* (M-305) and the *Detector* (M-306) were former patrol boats of the Royal Canadian Mounted Police, whereas the *OK Service* (M-361) and the *Aristocrat* (M-302) were former rumrunners. The capacities of the latter, which had allowed them to carry plenty of booze to the Boston States in prewar days, enabled them to transport easily construction materials, stores, and personnel to radio and radar stations being built along the Labrador coast.[113] Although commercial carriers transported the bulk of the equipment, nearly 37 per cent of all freight shipments, or 3,168 tons, was carried from Halifax to Newfoundland and Labrador in RCAF marine craft during the first eleven months of 1943.[114]

Most marine craft required inland for the British Commonwealth Air Training Plan were manufactured in Ontario. The familiar Muskoka and Georgian Bay names of Greavette Boats, Grew Boats, Port Carling Boat Works, and Hunter Boats, along with Peterborough Canoe Company, Cliff Richardson Boat Works at Meaford, and Shepherd Boats and Equipment at Niagara-on-the-Lake, built some seventy marine craft. Many were quite similar to the rowboats, aircraft tenders, bomb-loading dinghies, utility boats, and crash boats built on the West and East Coasts, but where bombing and gunnery ranges were on bodies of water open to the public, range safety boats were needed, as were high-speed target-towing boats used for air-to-surface gunnery training. Greavette Boats Limited at Gravenhurst constructed three 30-foot and three 40-foot range boats, and Shepherd Boats built eight 30-foot and two 32-foot range patrol boats for the air force.[115]

High-speed rescue launches (HSRLs), or crash boats, were among the fastest air force marine craft. As early as February 1940, David Carswell announced the War Supply Board's intention to order ten examples of a proven design for "crash boats" and four experimental types from Canadian manufacturers in response to the air force's demand for nine air/sea rescue craft. To no one's surprise, the navy was not interested even after Carswell proposed ordering one prototype each from the British firms of Vosper and British Power Boat Company.[116] On 22 August 1940 C.D. Howe announced that a contract worth $600,000 for six HSRLs for the Royal Air Force had been awarded to Aero-Marine Crafts Limited.[117] Canada's most famous boat designer and builder, Herbert Ditchburn, had set up the company in association with Gar Wood and Phil Wood, of speedboat-racing fame, with the assistance of William Fraser, who persuaded Ditchburn to move to Trenton and build the launches there. Ditchburn, known for his beautiful Muskoka launches, designed the 65.5-foot boats to the same high standards as before the war, and the Wood brothers supplied modified American Liberty aircraft engines, which had been successfully used for unlimited speedboat racing during the prewar years. With three engines in each boat, the launches achieved a speed of 35 knots during trials on the Bay of Quinte.[118]

Another design for high-speed rescue boats arose out of the PV-70, a variation of Hubert Scott Paine's design of a 70-foot motor torpedo boat (MTB) from the British Power Boat Company; "PV" stood for private venture. In May 1940, when Scott Paine's Canadian Power Boat Company contracted to build twelve MTBs for the Canadian navy, he also bid successfully to construct for the RCAF six deep-sea, high-speed air-rescue launches and six 40-foot, armoured target boats.[119] The rescue launches were less complex than the MTBs being built for the RCN. Designed to accompany convoys several hundred miles offshore in order to rescue any escorting aircraft that had to ditch in the sea, they lacked torpedo tubes, but some mounted a single aircraft-type machine-gun turret. Pattern examples for both boats were shipped from Britain, and work on the air force launches was well underway by May 1941. The Canadian boats were to be powered by a single Packard M4-2500, V-12 gasoline engine. A speed of 41 knots could be obtained. By 1 August official trials on the first high-speed rescue launch, M-208 *Nootka*, were under way. In the intervening period, the air force revised its needs so that the 40-foot target boats were completed as unarmoured towing boats. As well as adapting the design in order to take the American engines in place of the original British units, there was the need to change the electrical and mechanical specifications in order to meet Canadian standards. Eventually, all six HSRLs were built, but they appear to have met with limited success.[120] In April 1942 four of the 70-foot HSRLs were transferred to the West Coast, and in August the RCAF acquired five PT-type boats from the United States for use on the East Coast.[121]

By June 1943 the RCAF had an established strength of 590 marine craft, nearly half of which had been built during the war. The air force acquired its two largest ships shortly afterward, following a decision to move the equipment and supplies of 162 (Bombing Reconnaissance) Squadron to Iceland. In September, Canadian authorities expropriated a 164-foot, wooden motor vessel, *Lawrence K. Sweeny*, then being privately built at Yarmouth, Nova Scotia. They also acquired a second ship of 170 feet still under construction from Smith and Rhuland at Lunenburg.[122] The ships were given their air force names, *Eskimo* (M-456) and *Beaver* (M-522), respectively, and in January 1944 they successfully completed the hazardous 4,000-mile return voyage through U-boat- and iceberg-infested and gale-prone waters with the squadron's heavy equipment, including 50 tons of depth charges.[123]

Landing Craft, Pontoons, and Assault Boats

The Second World War forced the Allies to design, develop, and mass produce a wide variety of landing craft and other specialized craft such as barges, bridging pontoons, and small assault craft for riverine operations in Europe. Although the British pioneered some developments such as the tank-landing ship (LST) and the tank-landing craft (LCT), the Americans modified the original designs and undertook production for all.[124] No acknowledgment of the more than 3,000 landing craft built in Canada appeared in the United States Navy's official guide to Allied landing craft. Although not all Canadian developments were successful, they made a significant contribution to the Allied assault on Europe and provide interesting examples of resourcefulness.[125]

When C.D. Howe reported to the House of Commons that total deliveries of landing craft produced in Canada at the end of February 1944 had reached 925, he identified three types: the 51-foot landing craft, the 52-foot ramped cargo lighter, and the 72-foot MINCA barge.[126] MINCA stood for "Made in Canada." Late engine deliveries contributed to major production delays of ramped cargo lighters, and a lack of labour in the Maritimes hampered production of the MINCA barges.[127]

Early in 1942, during a visit to Canada and the Department of Munitions and Supply, General A.G.L. McNaughton suggested that Canada build and man 1,000 landing craft to transport the Canadian army in the event of an invasion of Europe, and the Cabinet War Committee authorized purchase of 200 of these wooden landing craft, or LCM(W), at a cost of $7,000 or $8,000 each.[128] During the summer, the director of naval construction prepared a design in association with Ernest F. Cribb, managing director of West Coast Salvage and Contracting Company at Vancouver. Three models were produced, and orders were placed to build 116. An engine shortage made it impossible to build more, and the navy displayed no interest in the project.[129] This first experimental craft was a failure, but others proved to be a grand success.[130]

The second craft, really a powered lighter, was designed to carry ordnance and men and to perform general lighterage duties. Built of plywood to save time and critical materials, it was 52 feet long, 18 feet wide, and equipped with twin rudders and 24-inch propellers. The landing craft had watertight compartments and was prefabricated in sections for easy disassembly, shipment, and simple reassembly overseas. Twin 6-cylinder, 330-cubic-inch engines, each of 100 hp, delivered a speed of 9 knots. Two winches raised and lowered the plywood ramp, which was faced with steel and hinged. It weighed 26 tons and had a carrying capacity of 35 tons. More than 1,600 were built for the British Ministry of War Transport. At least three contractors carried out construction. Dominion Construction Company Limited at Vancouver and Howard Furnace and Foundries Limited at Toronto built 453 and 435 lighters, respectively, for a total cost of $6,256,581. The Vancouver firm built a special plant, employing about 200 men.[131] A Quebec firm or firms probably built many more, for an estimated 1,616 were completed by the end of 1944.[132]

On the West Coast, 100 lighters had been completed by late August 1943. Production had reached 18 per week, and the estimated time to completion was mid-March 1944. The hold-up was nondelivery of the engines manufactured by Gray Marine Motors at Detroit, Michigan. The British Admiralty Delegation in Washington, DC, had purchased the engines under lend-lease, but the United States Navy (USN) controlled production and refused to release them. By late August the company was two and a half months behind its promised delivery of 300 engines. It had shipped only 38 starting in mid-July and was promising 48 per week, and Canada wanted 75 per week. The Canadians had no influence, and the director of naval shipbuilding could only advise C.D. Howe to have the British Admiralty Delegation apply pressure to get the USN to release the engines.[133]

In October 1942 the Montreal office of the British Ministry of War Transport received an order for 1,800 prefabricated Thames River–type barges, to be built in small enough sections that they could be transported as deck cargo and to be sufficiently narrow that they could be carried on English railways. Their design had to allow for rapid assembly anywhere along a seacoast, whether ashore or in the water. The project was entrusted to Will F. Fleicher, an English naval architect, technical director of the Ministry of War Transport's Montreal office, and a forty-year resident

Six Mark V pontoons, built by Grew Boats Limited for the Canadian army, loaded onto railway cars for shipment from Penetanguishene to the East Coast, c. 1942. Private Archive, Joe Fossey Collection, no. 37.

of the city. Fleicher designed a wooden barge in six sections. Each consisted of four rectangular midship sections, weighing 5 tons each, and two peak ends. Coamings, hatches, and fenders were also prefabricated. Before being bolted together, the sections were interleaved with felt gaskets and a bituminous compound to ensure watertight joints. Ninety steel bolts fastened each section. Designed to carry 150 tons of cargo, the barges were 72 feet long, 21.5 feet in beam, and 7 feet, 8 inches, deep.[134] They drew 6 feet of water fully loaded. The steel plates used in manufacture were rolled at New Glasgow, and the wood was produced in the Maritimes.[135]

The barge was essentially a wooden, modular floating dock propelled by an outboard motor. The engine, weighing 2.5 tons, had propellers capable of operating 360 degrees, thus obviating any need for a rudder, and it had a tail section that could be elevated out of the water for maintenance. Murray and Tregurtha Incorporated, American pioneers in the manufacture of marine gasoline engines, designed the propulsion unit for the United States Navy in 1940. Manufactured in Quebec by Sherbrooke Machineries Limited, the giant outboard engines pushed the barges along at 4 knots, providing a welcome independence of movement.[136] The barges were carried overseas and used extensively to carry supplies to Allied armies via Europe's rivers and canals.[137]

Initially, the British ordered 450 barges, but lack of manpower in the Maritimes hampered early production. In July 1943 five New Brunswick and Nova Scotia boatyards were employing 718 men but needed an additional 370.[138] Authorities hoped production could be increased from six to thirteen barges per week, but this could happen only after the current harvest and fishing seasons ended and if farmers and fishermen could be found to enter the yards.[139] To Howe's request for more labour, the minister of labour replied that none was available. Humphrey Mitchell was seeking close to 5,000 additional workers for ship repairing in the Maritimes and advised

Howe that the contractors ought to search for women to work in the yards.[140] Labour was found, and 924 barges were completed by 31 October 1944. The contractors eventually built 1,400 for a total cost of $19,783,034.[141]

In addition to more than 3,000 lighters and barges for use during the invasion of Europe, Ontario boat builders manufactured approximately 2,560 nesting barges, pontoons, and assault boats intended for the Canadian army's use for river crossings. The wooden nesting barges built by Grew Boats Company at Penetanguishene were experimental and abandoned after only four were produced. Hamilton Bridge Company Limited constructed 190 60-foot, steel, sectional nesting barges for the British Ministry of War Transport. Grew Boats, Hunter Boats, Mac-Craft Company, and Midland Boat Works also constructed at least 704 pontoons for the Canadian army. These Mark V models were 20 feet long and steel-hulled. A special inspection tank was positioned at the end of Hunter's production line to test each pontoon under pressure to assure water tightness.[142] Upon completion, they were stacked two deep, four each to a railway flatcar, for the long journey from Ontario to the sea and eventual use in Europe.[143]

In the absence of new contracts for motor launches, in August 1943 Greavette Boats at Gravenhurst and Port Carling Boat Works turned their hands to building light assault boats. Together with Morris Boat Works at Hamilton and Peterborough Canoe Company, they manufactured 1,259 12-foot (Mark IIc), 200 17-foot (Mark III), and 204 collapsible or folding boats, 1,663 in all.[144] By then, Canada had truly become a "land of little ships." At the end of 1943 approximately 85 builders of small craft had delivered over 6,000 boats to naval, army, and air services, and two years later, more than 100 builders had constructed over 8,300 (see table 10.1).[145]

11 | Production and Productivity

Introduction

This chapter presents estimates of national, regional, and annual ship production, outlines the changing nature of ships constructed, and presents some notions of shipbuilding costs, the value of production, and labour productivity. The intention is to make the data comprehensible and comprehensive. It is common knowledge that Canada ranked third among Allied shipbuilding countries, launching about 1,000 merchant and fighting ships, 3,300 landing craft, and more than 5,000 other marine craft both with and without power during the Second World War, but it is important to note that shipbuilders also completed over 36,000 ship repairs, including approximately 7,300 dry-dockings. At peak production, Canada's shipbuilding, marine-engineering, and ship-repair industries employed 126,000 men and women, or nearly 15 per cent of the nation's labour force engaged in war production.[1] The $1.2 billion spent on shipbuilding and ship repairing represented over 12 per cent of Canada's total expenditure on war production.[2] Less well known is when, where, and by whom all these vessels were constructed. Before proceeding further, I gratefully acknowledge the work of many predecessors who counted ships in order to prepare the following tables. Errors have undoubtedly crept in, and suggested corrections are welcome.

Production

Table 11.1 presents a useful picture of total national ship production. The numbers may differ slightly from those given elsewhere because ships begun before VJ Day but completed after 31 December 1945 have been excluded. Thus thirty-five China coasters begun in 1945 are not included because none was completed before 1946.[3] Similarly, one stores-issuing ship and thirteen maintenance ships ordered for the British Admiralty and not completed until after 1945 are excluded. The number of warships differs from those in several general histories because they exclude warships built for the Admiralty. In a history of the shipbuilding industry, the final user is less important than total production. The number of 10,000-ton and 4,700-ton cargo ships, which stands at 391, agrees with the official history of the Department of Munitions

Table 11.1 | Canadian ships built, by year and type, 1940–45

Type	1940	1941	1942	1943	1944	1945	Total
NAVAL							
Corvette, Flower class	12	52	6				70
Corvette, Revised Flower class		4	10	11			25
Corvette, Revised Increased Endurance				9	18		27
Frigate, River class			2	24	44		70
Fairmile B-type motor launch		16	43	18	11		88
Motor torpedo boat		19	8				27
Transport ferry (LST3)					1	25	26
Minesweepers:							
Bangor, steam		30	20				50
Bangor, diesel		1	9				10
Western Isles trawler			14	2			16
Algerine class				15	28	19	62
105-foot, wooden		11	22	1	8		42
126-foot, wooden					13	17	30
Total naval vessels	*12*	*133*	*134*	*80*	*123*	*61*	*543*
CARGO							
10,000-tonners:							
North Sands type		1	81	100	18		*200*
Victory type				33	48		*81*
Victory tankers				4	8		*12*
Canadian type					13	15	*28*
Stores-issuing					8	4	*12*
Maintenance						15	*15*
Subtotal		*1*	*81*	*137*	*95*	*34*	*348*
4,700-tonners:							
Gray				13	14		27
Revised					4	6	10
Dominion						6	6
Subtotal				*13*	*18*	*12*	*43*
3,600-ton tanker					6		6
Total cargo vessels		*1*	*81*	*150*	*119*	*46*	*397*
Grand total all ships	*12*	*134*	*215*	*230*	*242*	*107*	*940*

Sources: Tucker, *Naval Service of Canada*, vol. 2, 504–14; Smith et al., "History of the British Admiralty Technical Mission in Canada," 77–90; LAC, RG 28, box 7, "A Brief History of Wartime Merchant Shipping Ltd., Montreal, December 31, 1943, with an Addendum on Wartime Shipbuilding Ltd., January 1944–February 1947," typescript; Canada, Department of External Affairs, *Canadian War Data*; Sawyer and Mitchell, *Oceans, the Forts and the Parks*; Milner and MacPherson, *Corvettes of the Royal Canadian Navy, 1939–1945*, 124.

Frigates at various stages of completion at Canadian Vickers Limited's fitting-out dock, Montreal, September 1943. Photo by Ronny Jaques. NFB/LAC, WRM 5243.

and Supply (DMS) and has been accepted by Robert Halford and Francis Mansbridge.[4] It differs from the number offered by S.C. Heal, who claims 402 vessels built.[5] Table 11.1's chief feature is that it presents national wartime ship production by type and year. It also shows the dramatic rise in cargo ship output during 1943, which was and remains one of the outstanding achievements of Canada's wartime industrial production.

The number and type of ships show how desperate the situation was in 1940, 1941, and 1942 as the industry struggled to get warships to sea. They also indicate the impact of the cargo ship program on naval construction. Merchant shipbuilding quite literally took off and began competing fiercely with the naval program for resources. Although only one 10,000-ton ship was completed and sent to sea in 1941, similar ships soon began pouring off the ways. From 1942 to 1944 one cargo ship was delivered to Wartime Merchant Shipping Limited on average less than every four days. For all intents and purposes, however, the differences between naval and cargo

Table 11.2 | Displacement tonnage of Canadian-built warships, by year, 1940–45

Naval vessels	1940*	1941	1942	1943	1944	1945	Total
Corvette, Flower class	11,400	49,400	5,700				66,500
Corvette, Revised Flower class		4,060	10,150	11,165			25,375
Corvette, Revised Increased Endurance				8,730	17,460		26,190
Frigate, River class			2,890	34,680	63,580		101,150
Minesweeper, Bangor, steam		20,160	13,440				33,600
Minesweeper, Bangor, diesel		590	5,310				5,900
Minesweeper, Western Isles trawler			7,630	1,090			8,720
Minesweeper, Algerine class				14,850	27,720	18,810	61,380
Transport ferry (LST3)					4,290	107,250	111,540
Subtotal steel	*11,400*	*74,210*	*45,120*	*70,515*	*113,050*	*126,060*	*440,355*
Motor torpedo boat		836	352				1,188
Fairmile B-type motor launch		1,264	3,397	1,422	869		6,952
Minesweeper, 105-foot, wooden		2,508	5,016	228	1,824		9,576
Minesweeper, 126-foot, wooden					4,680	6,120	10,800
Subtotal wooden		*4,608*	*8,765*	*1,650*	*7,373*	*6,120*	*28,516*
Grand total tons	*11,400*	*78,818*	*53,885*	*72,165*	*120,423*	*132,180*	*468,871*
Grand total percentage	*2.4*	*16.8*	*11.3*	*15.4*	*25.7*	*28.2*	*100*

* Includes last four months of 1939.

Sources: See table 11.1.

shipbuilding were so great as to be separate enterprises, and this should be kept in mind as the data are examined.

The data in table 11.2 transform the number of naval vessels in table 11.1 into an estimate of displacement tons produced annually during the war. Tonnage reveals more than numbers of ships, showing that more than half of all warship tonnage was produced in 1944 and 1945 when the Battle of the Atlantic was all but over.

Although the 133 ships commissioned in 1942 were probably the industry's most important contribution to the war, they represented less than 12 per cent of all warship displacement tonnage. In 1942 two more complex vessels, the frigate and the Algerine-class minesweeper, were introduced, which led to a marked decline in tonnage delivered (see also figure 11.3). This decline was not checked until more yards, more manpower, and in some cases better management were brought to bear on the naval program.[6] Table 11.2 also reveals clearly the effect of competition from the cargo ship program and the effect of the steel-supply bottleneck. The eighty warships delivered the following year actually represented a 34 per cent overall increase in tonnage (57 per cent if only steel-hulled vessels are considered), and the steel bottleneck had clearly been broken, for that year witnessed delivery of 150 cargo ships.

Table 11.3a | Ships built in Canada for the Royal Navy, by year, 1940–45

Type	1940	1941	1942	1943	1944	1945	Total
Corvette, Flower class	8	2					10
Minesweeper, Bangor class			12				12
Minesweeper, Western Isles trawler			14	2			16
Corvette, Revised Flower class			4	11			15*
Frigate, River class			2*	8			10
Minesweeper, Algerine class				10	21	19	50
Transport ferry (LST3)					1	25	26
Maintenance						15	15
Subtotal, steel	8	2	32	31	22	59	154
Motor torpedo boat, 70-foot			12				12
Minesweeper, 105-foot, wooden			11	20	1		32
Fairmile B-type motor launch			8*				8
Minesweeper, 126-foot, wooden					13	8	21
Subtotal, wooden			31	20	14	8	73
Grand total	8	2	63	51	36	67	227

* Eight Revised corvettes, two frigates, and eight Fairmiles were commissioned into the United States Navy.

Source: Smith et al., "History of the British Admiralty Technical Mission in Canada," 77–91.

Table 11.3a summarizes an important, overlooked dimension of Canada's ship production made possible by orders from the British Admiralty Technical Mission (BATM). These orders on behalf of the Royal Navy (RN), placed largely in 1941, ensured that shipyards would be kept working to expanding capacity as the ships in the initial Canadian naval program neared completion. The first ten corvettes were actually ordered on 22 January 1940, two weeks before the Cabinet War Committee approved the first Canadian naval program and six months before the first members of the BATM arrived in Ottawa. Although all vessels reached the Atlantic before freeze-up in 1940, some were in dishevelled states; two were completed for sea in Nova Scotia at Liverpool and Halifax in January 1941 before being rushed overseas.

Twelve Bangor-class minesweepers were ordered on 30 November 1940. But although all were launched during the following spring and summer, none were accepted before February 1942 owing to delays in starting up the two yards where they were built and in deliveries of machinery and equipment.[7] The sixteen Western Isles trawler minesweepers and eight Fairmiles ordered in August 1941, especially the former, helped to keep production of Great Lakes yards at capacity, although their construction interrupted the flow of corvettes for the Royal Canadian Navy (RCN), which were beginning to come down the ways. Four of the minesweeping, antisubmarine trawlers were built at George T. Davie and Sons' small yard at Lauzon, Quebec, the last two being accepted in May 1943 just weeks before the June strike.

The BATM's orders for fifteen Revised corvettes, ten River-class frigates, and fifteen Algerine-class minesweepers, placed in October and December 1941, played a more important role than the previous ones. Not only did these forty ships ensure continuation of naval shipbuilding at an equivalent or greater pace than before, but they also initiated the construction of two classes, representing the second generation of antisubmarine vessels, that had not yet been built in Canada. The frigate was larger, faster, and better-armed and had twice the endurance of a corvette, and the Algerine-class minesweeper surpassed its predecessor, the Bangor, being nearly 50 per cent larger and possessing greater range and more antisubmarine equipment. Both ships had much-improved crew accommodations.[8]

Although these British programs delayed placement of contracts for the same vessels for the RCN, they were also educational orders on which shipbuilders developed manufacturing skill and yard capacity. More important, they were financed by American lend-lease, which paid the Canadian government for the ships, thus earn-

"Take Her Away USA." Urbain Martel, head of the launching crew, shakes hands with Commander Vincent H. Godfrey, USN, at the launch of the first Canadian-built frigate, USS *Danville*, 14 November 1942. NFB/LAC, WRM 2303.14.

ing valuable US dollars that allowed purchase of machine tools and other vital war materials. No ships were built in Canada for the United States Navy (USN), but in August 1942 the Combined Munitions and Assignment Board at Washington, DC, transferred these fifteen corvettes and eight Fairmiles to the United States from the British program in Canada.[9] Eight of the corvettes, the Fairmiles, and later in the fall the first two frigates built in Canada were commissioned into the USN to meet an acute shortage of American escorts.[10]

Fifty-six of the sixty-two Algerines built in Canada arose from two BATM orders and from one RCN order. The first fifteen vessels were ordered in 1941, the second order (for sixteen) was placed in September and November 1942, and the third order (for twenty-five) was made in March 1943.[11] All were to be built for escort work rather than for minesweeping and were chosen instead of Revised corvettes because they could be completed more rapidly. Shortly after signing its intention to order twenty-five Algerines in April 1943, the Admiralty and the RCN agreed to exchange one Algerine for one British-built corvette. All sixteen vessels in the Canadian order were traded for four Revised Increased Endurance corvettes and twelve newer Castle-class corvettes.[12] Thus the third-generation corvette, equipped with new advanced weaponry, was never built in Canada, as it could be acquired more quickly from Great Britain.

Except for motor torpedo boats built at Montreal, nearly all of the wooden-hulled boats for the Royal Navy were constructed in the maritime provinces. The sole exceptions were two 105-foot motor minesweepers built by Le Chantier Maritime de Saint Laurent, on Ile d'Orléans, and accepted in late 1943.[13] These small motor minesweepers, intended to hunt magnetic mines, were ordered between 14 January 1941 and 30 January 1942 and delivered during 1942 and 1943. The BATM ordered twelve larger 126-foot, wooden minesweepers on 18 December 1942 and twelve more two months later. Three were cancelled, and twenty-one were delivered between May 1944 and June 1945.[14] Early in 1944 the BATM ordered seventeen transport ferries and subsequently increased the order to seventy-one. Despite their inoffensive name, they were large tank-landing ships (LST3s) intended for the Pacific war. Fifteen were delivered before the war ended and are counted in table 11.1. Eleven were subsequently completed, and the British government cancelled forty-five.[15]

In addition to the 227 ships shown in table 11.3b, the British sent nineteen US-built aircraft carriers, one accommodation ship, and an amenities ship to Vancouver for conversion. Between 1941 and 1943 the BATM also acquired ten small minesweepers in Newfoundland and rushed them into the battle. In November 1940 the mission bought four partially completed fishing trawlers from a shipbuilding cooperative established by the Newfoundland government at Marystown in Placentia Bay. These were launched in January 1941 and taken to St John's to be fitted out as minesweepers. The previous March, the BATM had also contracted with Steers Limited for two trawlers, which left for the United Kingdom in January 1942, at which time the BATM ordered four more minesweepers. These appear to have been built at Clarenville by Henry Stone, backed by St John's businessman C.C. Pratt. The keels were laid in June

Table 11.3b | Displacement tons of warships built in Canada for the BATM, 1940–45

Type	Unit displacement	Number	Total displacement
Corvette, Flower class	950	10	9,500
Minesweeper, Bangor class	672	12	8,064
Minesweeper, Western Isles trawler	545	16	8,720
Corvette, Revised Flower class	1,015	15	15,225
Frigate, River class	1,445	10	14,450
Minesweeper, Algerine class	990	50	49,500
Transport ferry (LST3)	4,290	26	111,540
Total, steel		*139*	*216,999*
Motor torpedo boat, 70-foot	44	11	484
Minesweeper, 105-foot, wooden	228	32	7,296
Fairmile B-type motor launch	79	8	632
Minesweeper, 126-foot, wooden	360	21	7,560
Total, wooden		*72*	*15,972*
Grand total		*211*	*232,971*

Sources: Smith et al., "History of the British Admiralty Technical Mission in Canada," 77–91; Tucker, *Naval Service of Canada*, vol. 2, 504–14.

HMCS *Anticosti*, Western Isles minesweeping trawler underway, built at Collingwood Shipyards Limited and commissioned 8 August 1942. George Metcalf Archival Collection, acc. no. 19920085-1072, © Canadian War Museum.

Table 11.4a | Warships built in Ontario and Great Lakes Shipyards, 1940–45*

Type	1940	1941	1942	1943	1944	1945	Total
Corvette, Flower class	2	17	1				20
Corvette, Revised Flower class		2	5	7			14
Corvette, Revised Increased Endurance				5	11		16
Minesweeper, Bangor class		6	16				22
Minesweeper, Western Isles trawler			12				12
Minesweeper, Algerine class				15	28	19	62
Fairmile B-type motor launch		13	28	17	1		59
Minesweeper, 126-foot, wooden						5	5
Total	2	38	62	44	40	24	210

* As per date of commission.

Table 11.4b | Displacement tons of warships built in Great Lakes shipyards, 1940–45

Type	Displacement per vessel	Number built	Total displacement
Corvette, Flower class	950	20	19,000
Corvette, Revised Flower class	1,015	14	14,210
Corvette, Revised Increased Endurance	970	16	15,520
Minesweeper, Bangor class	672	22	14,784
Minesweeper, Western Isles trawler	545	12	6,540
Minesweeper, Algerine class	990	62	61,380
Fairmile B-type motor launch	79	59	4,667
Minesweeper, 126-foot, wooden	360	5	1,800
Total		210	137,901

Sources: Smith et al., "History of the British Admiralty Technical Mission in Canada," 78–86; Tucker, *Naval Service of Canada*, vol. 2, 505–14.

1942, but the BATM accepted the completed vessels only in November and December 1943.[16]

Finally, table 11.3b shows the total estimated displacement tonnage of Royal Navy warships built in Canada. Its significance is that the 232,971 displacement tons represent nearly half of all the warship tonnage constructed in Canada during the war. Although the twenty-six LST3s account for nearly half of all the tonnage, the critically important point is that alone the Canadian navy could not order sufficient ships to sustain the shipbuilding industry. The British orders were critical to industrial success. It is not clear whether the chief of the naval staff and his advisors ever appreciated this fact.

Table 11.5 | Ships built in Quebec and St Lawrence River shipyards, by year and type, 1940–45

Type	1940	1941	1942	1943	1944	1945	Total
NAVAL							
Corvette, Flower class	17	25					42
Corvette, Revised Flower class		2	4				6
Corvette, Revised Increased Endurance				4	7		11
Fairmile depot ship			2				2
Minesweeper, Bangor, steam		6					6
Minesweeper, Bangor, diesel		1	9				10
Minesweeper, Western Isles trawler			2	2			4
Frigate, River class			2	17	34		53
Transport ferry (LST3)						21	21
Motor torpedo boat		16	11				27
Minesweeper, 105-foot, wooden			2	2			4
Subtotal naval	*17*	*50*	*32*	*25*	*41*	*21*	*186*
CARGO							
North Sands 10,000-tonner		1	47	24	13		85
Canadian 10,000-tonner					9		9
Stores-issuing						3	3
Gray 4,700-tonner				3			3
Revised 4,700-tonner					2	2	4
Dominion 4,700-tonner						4	4
Great Lakes tanker					3		3
All others*		1				1	2
Subtotal cargo		*2*	*47*	*27*	*27*	*10*	*113*
Grand total		*52*	*79*	*52*	*68*	*31*	*299*

* Includes the icebreaker *Ernest Lapointe* and a pulpwood carrier.

Sources: Smith et al., "History of the British Admiralty Technical Mission in Canada," 77, 80–2, 87–8; Tucker, *Naval Service of Canada*, vol. 2, 505–14; Sawyer and Mitchell, *Oceans, the Forts and the Parks*, 12–16, 21, 24–6, 27.

With the exception of seasonal repairs carried out annually on Great Lakes ships, a few conversions, and three 3,600-ton tankers built at Collingwood in 1944, Ontario's shipyards were devoted to warship construction. Table 11.4a shows that more steel-hulled warships were built in 1942 than in 1944 and 1945 combined. It also indicates that more than two-thirds of all Fairmiles were built in Ontario. Table 11.4b shows just how much the Great Lakes yards contributed to warship construction. The 137,901 displacement tons produced represented nearly 30 per cent of the entire warship tonnage constructed in the country.

Table 11.6 | Canadian-built cargo ships, by deadweight tons and year, 1941–45*

Type	1941	1942	1943	1944	1945	Total
10,000-tonner						
North Sands	10.0	810.0	1,000.0	180.0		2,000.0
Victory			330.0	480.0		810.0
Victory tanker			40.0	80.0		120.0
Canadian				130.0	150.0	280.0
Stores-issuing				80.0	40.0	120.0
Maintenance					150.0	150.0
Subtotal	10.0	810.0	1,370.0	950.0	340.0	3,480.0
4,700-tonner						
Gray			61.1	65.8		126.9
Revised				18.8	28.2	47.0
Dominion					28.2	28.2
Subtotal			61.1	84.6	56.4	202.1
3,600-tonner						
Great Lakes tanker				21.6		21.6
Grand total	10.0	810.0	1,431.1	1,056.2	396.4	3,703.7

* Thousands of tons.

Note: Although the larger merchant ships displaced 10,350 tons when loaded to capacity, the table was prepared by multiplying the numbers given in table 11.1 by 10,000, 4,700 and 3,600, respectively, to obtain estimates of annual deadweight tonnage.

Nevertheless, Quebec shipyards lay at the heart of Canada's wartime shipbuilding industry, and a wide variety of ships were built along the St Lawrence River. Table 11.5 presents a quick summary of the number and types of ships as well as the year in which they were accepted or commissioned.

Frigates were the most sophisticated naval vessels completed in Canada during the war. Three-quarters of them were built in Quebec. Indeed, Quebec shipbuilders constructed more than half of all naval tonnage and together with Great Lakes yards accounted for more than 82 per cent of all warship tonnage built in Canada. The more than 1 million tons of cargo ships built in Quebec represented more than one-quarter, or 27.9 per cent, of all merchant ship construction.

Although impressive for an industry that had never built a warship to British Admiralty specifications, the total size of the naval shipbuilding program, less than half a million displacement tons, remained relatively small. Indeed, without the orders from the BATM, it would never have amounted to much. It is with the cargo ship program that the true size and remarkable nature of the industry's war production

Figure 11.1 | Naval and cargo vessels built in Canada, average monthly production, 1940–44

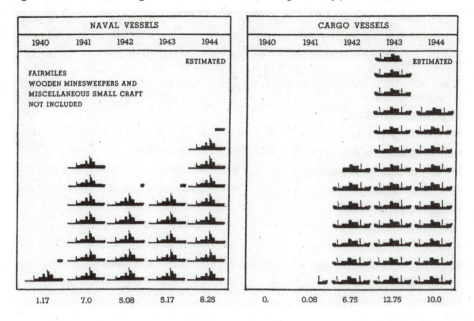

Source: From a submission by the Canadian Shipbuilding and Ship Repairing Association to the Canadian government, March 1944, reproduced from *Canadian Transportation* 47 (October 1944): 569.

become apparent. Table 11.6 presents estimates of the annual number of deadweight tons (dwt) produced in Canada during the war.

During the forty-four months from December 1941 to July 1945, inclusive, Wartime Merchant Shipping Limited and its successor, Wartime Shipbuilding Limited, accepted delivery of 3,703,700 tons of cargo shipping from Canadian shipyards. Just as American lend-lease paid for at least forty warships for the BATM, it also paid for ninety 10,000-ton cargo ships delivered between February 1942 and March 1943.[17] According to one estimate, by "1943 Canada's production of merchant ships was only fifteen per cent less than the United Kingdom, itself."[18] During that year, Canadian shipyards delivered an astonishing 150 cargo ships totalling 1,478,000 dwt (compared to 81 ships and 838,000 dwt in 1942), 80 naval and escort vessels (compared to 130 in 1942), and 3,600 small craft of 4,300 ordered.[19] It was an astonishing feat for a nation with a population of a little more than 11 million people, 1 million of whom were enlisted in the armed forces. One factor that made shipbuilding so successful, as table 11.6 shows, was that a single class of ship constituted 94 per cent of all the cargo tonnage built during the war.

Figure 11.1, showing the average annual monthly rates of ship production, indicates that although the rate of cargo vessels built peaked in 1943, the production rate of steel-hulled warships continued to increase until 1944, when nearly half of all Al-

Table 11.7 | Naval and cargo ships built on Canada's West Coast, by type and year, 1941–45

Type	1941	1942	1943	1944	1945	Total
NAVAL						
Corvette, Flower class	13	6				19
Minesweeper, Bangor class	7	15				22
Frigate, River class			7	10		17
Transport ferry (LST3)				1	4	5
Subtotal steel	20	21	7	11	4	63
Fairmile B-type motor launch		6		6		12
Minesweeper, 105-foot, wooden				12		12
Subtotal wood		6		18		24
Subtotal naval	20	27	7	29	4	87
CARGO						
North Sands		54	51	10		115
Victory			33	49		82
Victory tanker			4	8		12
Canadian				4	15	19
Stores-issuing				8	1	9
Maintenance					15	15
Subtotal cargo		54	88	79	31	252
Grand total	20	81	95	108	35	339

Sources: Tucker, *Naval Service of Canada*, vol. 2, 509–14; Smith et al., "History of the British Admiralty Technical Mission in Canada," 87–9; LAC, RG 28, box 7, "A Brief History of Wartime Merchant Shipping Ltd., Montreal, December 31, 1943, with an Addendum on Wartime Shipbuilding Ltd., January 1944–February 1947," typescript, 32–52; *Harbour and Shipping* [no. not available] (August 1945): 379–80.

gerines and more than 60 per cent of all frigates were commissioned (see table 11.1). The bar graph of figure 11.1, prepared in 1944, excludes data for 1945. The 1,050,200 deadweight tons (table 11.7) delivered during 1944, about 26 per cent less than in 1943, was the result of a deliberate decision to make the cargo program conform both to the need to increase naval production and to the decline in manpower available in the shipyards.

The rate of delivery of cargo ships reached about 10 per month at the end of 1942, and during the spring and summer of 1943, it increased to about 14 ships per month. But in July the Cabinet War Committee ordered a 50 per cent reduction in the rate of production of cargo ships, and in August it reduced by 42 the number of 10,000-ton ships on order while ordering that the program be thinned out and extended. The government imposed a further curtailment on 1 October, reducing the total number

A Victory-type cargo ship ready for delivery from Burrard Dry Dock Company. NVMA, no. 27-2320.

of cargo ships constructed and on order to 315. The number of 4,700-tonners remaining on order was reduced from 36 to 27, and shipbuilders were instructed to reduce their production rates from 14 to 9 ships per month. In December the RCN belatedly cancelled the last 41 frigates and 11 corvettes on order.[20] In brief, almost all warships and cargo vessels delivered in 1944 and 1945 were ordered before the end of 1943.

Two-thirds of all the cargo shipping constructed in Canada was built on the West Coast, together with 78,849 displacement tons of steel-hulled warships, which accounted for about 18 per cent of all naval tonnage in the country (see table 11.2). Burrard Dry Dock Company produced more than one-quarter of all the merchant tonnage built in Canada. Although half of the company's cargo hulls were built by Burrard South Yard at Vancouver, all engines were installed by Burrard North Yard at North Vancouver. During twenty-six months between April 1941 and June 1943, Burrard completed 50 North Sands ships, or 500,000 tons.[21] During the war, Burrard constructed 109 large cargo ships, North Van Ship Repairs and West Coast Shipbuilders each constructed 54, Victoria Machinery Depot and Prince Rupert Dry Dock built 19 and 13, respectively, and Yarrows Limited built 2 before being transferred to naval construction.

The estimated displacement and deadweight tonnage of ships built in the Maritimes (table 11.8) represented less than 4 per cent of the national totals. The three corvettes contracted with St John Shipbuilding and Dry Dock Company in February 1940 were the only steel-hulled warships completed on the East Coast during the war. All wooden-hulled naval vessels, with the exception of seven Fairmiles, were built to

Table 11.8 | Ships built in the maritime provinces, by type and year, 1941–45

Type	1941	1942	1943	1944	1945	Total
Corvette, Flower class	2	1				*3*
Fairmile B-type motor launch		12	1	2		*15*
Minesweeper, 105-foot, wooden		11	20	1		*32*
Minesweeper, 126-foot, wooden				13	8	*21*
Subtotal, naval	*2*	*24*	*21*	*16*	*8*	*71*
Gray, 4,700 tons			10	15		*25*
Revised, 4,700 tons			1		6	*7*
Subtotal, merchant			*11*	*15*	*6*	*32*
Grand total	*2*	*24*	*32*	*31*	*14*	*103*

Sources: Tucker, *Naval Service of Canada*, vol. 2, 505–6, 510–11; Smith et al., "History of the British Admiralty Technical Mission in Canada," 79–81, 84–5; Heal, *Great Fleet of Ships*, 228, 235, 238, 293, 298, 300, 302; Wallis, comp., *Story of Pictou's Park Ships*, 27–96.

British order and placed with five Nova Scotia boat builders at Meteghan, Shelburne, Port Greville, Mahone Bay, and Weymouth and with one New Brunswick firm at St Andrews. The eight medium-size cargo ships, including three Revised types, built by St John Shipbuilding and Dry Dock between 1943 and 1945 were intended to keep skilled men employed during slack periods of repair work. The remaining twenty-four cargo ships were constructed at Pictou, Nova Scotia.

By the beginning of 1944, the number of RCN ships had expanded fiftyfold. The 6 combat ships at the beginning of the war had grown to roughly 250 fighting ships. Auxiliary vessels and patrol craft, which numbered 7 in the early days of September 1939, stood at more than 450.[22] At the end of February, 234 10,000-ton and 15 4,700-ton cargo vessels, totalling 2.6 million dwt, had been delivered, and plans for 1944 included delivery of 120 cargo ships, making 1.1 million additional dwt.[23] When the naval and cargo ship programs were merged in January 1944, nine shipyards with a total of thirty-four berths were constructing naval vessels, ten yards with thirty-eight berths were building cargo ships, and one yard on the Great Lakes was building both corvettes and 3,600-ton tankers. The naval shipbuilding program also maintained four fitting-out yards, two employed making Algerine minesweepers, one working on frigates, and one modifying American-built carrier-vessel escorts (CVEs).

As West Coast shipbuilders completed Victory ships in 1944, they received orders to build twenty-one maintenance ships for the Royal Navy fleet train for the war in the Pacific. Although commissioned into the Royal Navy, these were basically Victory-types built to commercial marine standards, hence their exclusion from table 11.3b and inclusion in table 11.7. With extensive additions and alterations in the number of decks, internal configurations, auxiliary machinery, and accommodations, they required more time to build than previous cargo ships. At the beginning of 1944, West Coast builders also began to construct stores-issuing ships for the Royal Navy. Ordered by the British government in 1943, nine were of the Victory type built to commercial marine standards, eight of which were equipped with refrigeration machinery, while the other vessel was equipped to issue air stores. Another three ships, constructed at Montreal, were of the Canadian type and intended to carry ammunition and heavier stores. The refrigerator ships were all built at Burrard Dry Dock, but Carrier Corporation at Syracuse, New York, supplied the direct freon systems for the refrigerated spaces.[24] Eight ships were delivered by the end of 1944 and the remainder by 1 September 1945.

With shipbuilding contracts quickly running out, in May 1944 the British Ministry of War Transport ordered eighteen 105-foot, modified Warrior-class tugboats. Thirteen were delivered before the end of 1945 and the remainder declared surplus. The ministry also ordered thirty-five China coasters in 1945, but they are not included in the data. The same is true of three diesel-powered cargo ships, each of 7,500 gross tons, completed after 1945. Five maintenance ship contracts were also cancelled. For the second time in the twentieth century, the Canadian shipbuilding industry proved that it was an emergency product of war. Despite its accomplishments, it had no reason to exist in peacetime. An examination of the prices, costs, and value of ships built shows why this was so.

Prices, Costs, and Value

The cost of building ships in Canada was high. In 1920 the cost of sixty-three steel-hulled ships was determined to be about $192 per ton.[25] A decade later, Canadian costs were thought to be 30 per cent higher than in Britain. American costs were more than 50 per cent greater.[26] During the Second World War, market forces were not in play, and although several factors reduced the cost differential, Canadian-built ships remained more expensive than British ones. The experience, volume, and efficiency gained by building numerous ships of the same type enabled Canadian shipyards to turn out 10,000-ton cargo ships at a relatively low cost by American standards.

Table 11.9 indicates the value of shipbuilding and repairs between 1939 and 1945. It shows in some detail how the figure of $1.185 billion for the total value of wartime shipbuilding was obtained. The number includes the value of tugs and landing craft, about 11 per cent, and integrates shipbuilding and ship repairing values. The ratio of military to cargo ship values is roughly 2:3, which may be a bit surprising in view of traditional emphases on naval shipbuilding. Indeed, it is worth pointing out that the value of escort ships and minesweepers comprised less than three-quarters of the value of military shipbuilding, as shown in the table, and constituted only 30 per cent of the total value of shipbuilding. The value of large cargo ships in 1943 alone surpassed the total value of escort ships built during the war. Thirty-one per cent of the total value was produced that year, compared with less than 22 per cent during the three previous years. The countrywide average values for 4,700-ton and 10,000-ton

Table 11.9 | Value of shipbuilding and repairs, 1939–45[a]

Type	1940	1941	1942	1943	1944	1945	Total
10,000-tonner		2	138	234	177	81	632
4,700-tonner				16	22	14	52
All others[b]					6	2	8
Subtotal, cargo		2	138	250	205	97	692
Escorts	9	36	18	82	68	6	219
Minesweepers		21	28	25	40	28	142
Tugs				4	14	11	29
Landing craft		4	2	7	21	69	103
Subtotal, military	9	61	48	118	143	114	493
Total value	9	63	186	368	348	211	1,185

[a] Millions of dollars.
[b] Includes thirteen Warrior-class tugs constructed in 1945 in addition to six 3,600-ton tankers in table 11.1. Tugs and landing craft are dealt with in chapter 10.

Source: Kennedy, History of the Department of Munitions and Supply, vol. 1, 247, 505.

cargo ships of $1,209,302 and $1,816,092, respectively, derived from table 11.10, have limited bearing, as the value of commercial ship repairing is presumably included. But there are other ways to get at both regional and national values. Before these are considered, however, it is worth taking a brief glance at the changing value of the import and export content of shipbuilding, which is shown in figure 11.2.

Speaking in the House of Commons in March 1944, Angus L. Macdonald acknowledged that not more than 50 per cent of the first warships were Canadian in origin. Much of the material, steel for hulls, auxiliary machinery, and other apparatus for equipment and operation had been imported. But, he claimed, Canadian warships were currently about 95 per cent Canadian in material, machinery, guns, and other equipment.[27] Figure 11.2 shows how the value of imported content employed in both shipbuilding programs – chiefly steel plates and shapes, equipment, and other materials – declined by more than 50 per cent between 1940 and 1944, whereas the value of exports more than tripled by 1945. These two trends reflect the growth in the number of ships built for the British in 1942 and 1943 and again in the last year of the war. During 1943 and 1944 exports declined as a percentage of the total value of production because Canada consumed more, especially after the creation of Park Steamship Company.

The prices for the first sixty-four corvettes awarded by the War Supply Board were subject to adjustments to meet Canadian specifications on all but the ten built for the Royal Navy. They called for improvements in steam heating and electrical equip-

Figure 11.2 | Imports and exports as percentage of value of shipbuilding production, 1940–45

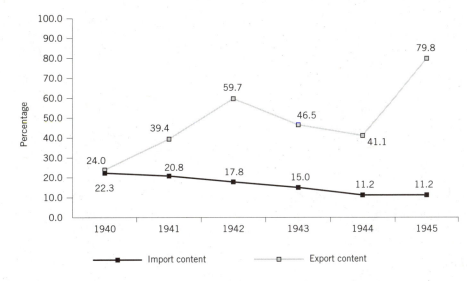

Source: Kennedy, *History of the Department of Munitions and Supply*, vol. 1, 247.

ment. Consequently, additional charges of between $15,000 and $27,000 accrued to the RCN ships.[28] After further adjustments to meet rising labour and material costs, the costs per vessel were substantially higher than the prices given in the official history. The cost per vessel shown in table 11.10 provides a more accurate amount.

The average cost of these first corvettes was $573,520 in eastern yards, $651,888 in western yards, and $585,765 for all yards. Increases in labour, materiel, and transportation accounted for the 13.7 per cent differential between the East and West Coasts. This differential meant that all ships built in eastern Canada were constructed for less than the national average cost. Thirty-three corvettes were built at established yards in Quebec and at Collingwood, Ontario, for seven-eighths of the cost of Pacific-built vessels.[29] The cost per vessel of the first eighteen Bangor-class minesweepers is surprising and may be due to the fact that, although smaller than corvettes, they were built to British Admiralty standards rather than to commercial marine standards, as were the first corvettes. The fourteen Bangors constructed on the West Coast were 14.4 per cent more expensive than the average cost of the first sixty-four corvettes.

As materials and labour prices mounted, so did ship costs. In April 1943 the following approximate costs of warships being built in Canada were published: corvette $950,000, Bangor minesweeper $700,000, trawler minesweeper $500,000, wooden (105-foot) minesweeper $175,000, motor torpedo boat $200,000, and Fairmile motor launch $125,000.[30] Although of limited bearing, these numbers provide a useful corrective to many others published during and after the war.

Table 11.10 | Prices and costs of the first sixty-four corvettes, 1 March 1940

No. ships	Builder	Price per vessel ($)	Cost per vessel ($)	Estimated cost ($)
CORVETTE, FLOWER CLASS				
3	St John Dry Dock and Shipbuilding Co.	540,000	583,200	1,749,600
10	Davie Shipbuilding and Repairing Co.	530,000	570,240	5,702,400
3	George T. Davie and Sons	532,000	574,560	1,723,680
4	Morton Engineering and Dry Dock Co.	530,000	572,400	2,289,600
7	Marine Industries Ltd	530,000	570,240	3,991,680
8	Canadian Vickers Ltd	530,000	570,240	4,561,920
3	Kingston Shipbuilding Co.	532,000	574,560	1,723,680
8	Collingwood Shipyards Ltd	528,000	570,240	4,561,920
8	Port Arthur Shipbuilding Co.	540,000	583,200	4,665,600
4	Burrard Dry Dock Ltd	605,000	651,240	2,604,960
3	Yarrows Ltd	606,000	652,320	1,956,960
3	Victoria Machinery Depot	606,000	652,320	1,956,960
64			585,765	37,488,960
MINESWEEPER, BANGOR CLASS				
6	North Van Ship Repairs	620,000	669,615	4,017,690
6	Burrard Dry Dock Ltd	620,000	669,615	4,017,690
2	Prince Rupert Dry Dock and Shipbuilding Co.	625,000	675,000	1,350,000
4	Dufferin Shipbuilding Co.	568,000	ndf*	ndf
18		609,000		9,385,380

* No data found.

Sources: Tucker, *Naval Service of Canada,* vol. 2, 43, 38; *Canadian Transportation* 43 (April 1940): 214; *Canadian Transportation* 43 (May 1940): 269.

Price evidence indicates that productivity increased considerably during the war. Canadian shipbuilders and manufacturers had no experience, and officials at the Department of Munitions and Supply had little information to guide them as to prices. British authorities had determined unit prices of $1,860,000 on the West Coast and $1,785,000 on the St Lawrence River for the twenty-six North Sands cargo ships ordered from established Canadian builders. Although the price difference acknowledged the high cost of labour and materials on the West Coast, these prices were rough estimates based on current prices in the United Kingdom and the United States. No independent experience in Canada permitted a more reliable estimate.[31] By May 1941 Burrard Dry Dock Company had reduced its estimated cost of construction to match the eastern price, which was confirmed in October (table 11.11).[32] Shipbuilders claimed materials and labour costs would inevitably increase in wartime,

Table 11.11 | Estimated cost of six West Coast–built North Sands cargo ships, October 1941

Charge	Material ($)	Labour ($)
Hull steel	247,710	309,960
Hull timber	12,900	15,300
Hull fittings	7,390	10,400
Mooring arrangements	25,800	3,500
Steering	21,500	7,100
Piping (e.g., engines and boilers)	19,500	25,000
Joiner work	18,700	19,000
Boats, etc.	9,800	2,500
Masts, cargo gear	35,500	11,300
Paint, cement, tiles	12,500	13,200
Canvas	5,200	2,500
Electrical (e.g., generators)	12,500	8,500
Launch	3,000	5,200
Cleaning	–	17,000
Outfitting and fees	23,500	2,540
Drawing office	500	5,000
Trials (e.g., dock)	3,500	2,000
Subtotal	*459,500*	*460,000*
Installation of engines, boilers, shafting, propeller, and generators	34,500	40,000
Total hull	*494,000*	*500,000*
Total hull, material and labour	*994,000*	
Main engines, boilers, auxiliaries	331,000	
Total	*1,325,000*	
Workmen's compensation (5% labour)	25,000	
Estimated allowance for overtime	35,000	
Overhead and margin	400,000	
Total price	*1,785,000*	

Source: NVMA, Fonds 27, box 364, estimated costs on basis of six ships, October 1941.

and price variation or escalation clauses were inserted into the early contracts to protect both parties.

After Wartime Merchant Shipping Limited took over management of the original contracts, the Department of Munitions and Supply decided that where possible the onus for improvements, expansion, and renovation in its yards must be placed on the builders. It was generally agreed that where a company expended its own capital, it

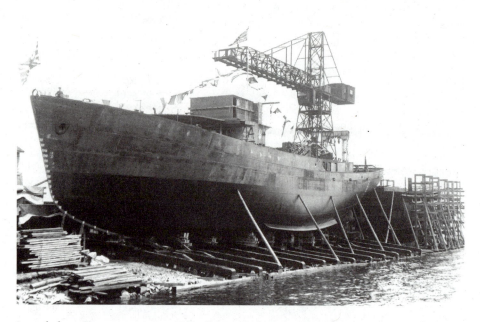

Launch day, 17 June 1944, HMCS *Belleville*, Revised Increased Endurance corvette, at Kingston Shipbuilding Company. Note the beginnings of a new hull aft of the ship. Later, it will be completed in situ and launched as HMCS *Smiths Falls*. Photo by Francis MacLachlan. MMGLK, Francis MacLachlan Collection, 1984.0006.0062.

would receive an enhanced price for the first ships completed. The enhanced price for 10,000-ton North Sands ships was to be the aforementioned price set by British authorities for the East and West Coasts. Roughly speaking, shipbuilders were awarded two ships at the enhanced price for each berth in their yard. The price was reduced for all subsequent ships to $1,775,000 on the West Coast and $1,700,000 in the East. Other factors caused this arrangement to vary. Table 11.11 shows that Burrard Dry Dock quickly got its estimated costs for these ships down to $1,785,000. It also indicates that every 10,000-ton cargo vessel built in Canada provided about half a million dollars in direct wage payments to workers in British Columbia and Quebec.

The price of the first two medium-size cargo ships built at St John Dry Dock and Shipbuilding Company was $1,064,000, which was acknowledged to be the enhanced price to assist expansion of the yard. The basic price was $973,000 per ship, later reduced to $955,666.[33] George T. Davie and Sons received $960,000 for each of its first three 4,700-ton ships, and since neither Davie yard at Lauzon was willing to finance expansion, the government authorized capital assistance through the usual channels.[34] The contract for the three ships originally let to Pictou Foundry and Machine Company was at a fixed price of $950,000, subject to the usual escalation clauses, but when operations were transferred to Foundation Maritime Limited, this contract was cancelled and a new one for six ships was awarded on a cost-plus-management-fee basis of $10,000 per ship. The second government-built yard also contracted on this new basis. The fee agreed upon at United Shipyards was $30,000 for the first ship launched from each slipway and $25,000 for each subsequent vessel. Similar fees current in the United States and Great Britain were about $100,000 for each large cargo ship.[35]

As cargo shipbuilding progressed, it became apparent that through standardization of output and volume of production, builders were achieving substantial cost reductions with corresponding increases in profit margins. The Excess Profits Tax Act introduced in 1942 did not deal adequately with the situation because the DMS and its Crown corporations were mandated to purchase war materials at prices containing profits. The situation became acute in the fall of 1942 when a House of Commons subcommittee of the War Expenditures Committee visited a number of shipyards, checked production and production costs, and found their profits "too substantial."[36] Consequently, in December the DMS reopened the shipbuilding contracts and commenced renegotiating them as well as contracts with several major suppliers.[37] With one or two exceptions, the response was favourable, and full cooperation was obtained. Chartered accountants who were auditors to eastern shipyards often conducted the work of reassessment under the supervision of the cost accounting division of the Treasury.[38] All fixed-price contracts with escalator clauses were changed to a cost-plus-management-fee basis, effective from the beginning of the program. A basic fee of $50,000 per ship was paid for each 10,000-ton ship subject to some additional allowances in particular cases.

The estimated average cost of 167 North Sands cargo ships on original fixed-price contracts had been $1,990,000 per vessel for West Coast yards and $1,950,000 for East Coast ones, averaging $1,977,000 for all yards. The estimated average cost of the same vessels on the renegotiated cost-plus-management-fee basis – inclusive of special depreciation, extras, increased labour and material costs, and management fee – was $1,676,000 for West Coast yards, $1,742,600 for East Coast yards, and $1,700,000 for all yards.[39] These figures exclude any consideration of United Shipyards Limited, where contracts originally awarded on a cost-plus-management-fee basis were considerably in excess of the above. On the basis of 115 West Coast and 52 East Coast North Sands–type ships, Wartime Merchant Shipping Limited anticipated savings in excess of $46 million, or 14.2 per cent of the original estimated cost of these vessels.[40] Generally speaking, commercial building costs had been reduced by this percentage by the end of 1943. These cost-plus-management-fee contracts appeared to put sufficient pressure on firms to reduce overall costs, although the same did not hold true in the United States.[41]

Old, established yards along the St Lawrence River such as Canadian Vickers Limited and Davie Shipbuilding and Repairing Company became increasingly productive, and West Coast shipyards working solely on large cargo ships achieved even greater reductions in costs. On the basis of the renegotiated cost-plus-management-

Table 11.12 | Average cost of large cargo ships built by Marine Industries Limited, Sorel

Charge	North Sands ($)	Canadian ($)
Material	490,561	597,948
Labour	528,625	552,588
Overhead	400,995	328,879
Total per ship	*1,420,181*	*1,279,414*

Source: SHPS, P006, series 2, subseries 2, subsubseries 1, file D16, Joseph La Rochelle, treasurer, to Senator John J. Kinley, 1 March 1951.

fee contracts, the relative cost of North Sands–type ships was completely reversed between East and West Coast yards. The 115 ships built on the West Coast were estimated to cost $1,676,000 each, compared with the $1,742,600 for each of the 52 St Lawrence–built ships. Indeed, by October 1943, at Burrard Dry Dock Company, the estimated cost of these ships had dropped to $1,447,000, only slightly more than the $1,432,000 average cost of the same ships at Davie Shipbuilding and Repairing.[42] The new Burrard cost represented a 19 per cent reduction in the company's estimated price to build the same ship just two years earlier (see table 11.11).

Contracts for the Victory-type cargo ships were arranged slightly differently based on cost plus a fixed minimum management fee plus a capped incentive bonus. The amount received by the West Coast yards where these vessels were constructed varied from $30,000 to $37,000 per ship; the maximum fee, including the bonus, was between $40,000 and $50,000 per ship. Victory tanker contracts were placed based on straight cost plus a management fee of $50,000, as insufficient data in regard to costs prevented the introduction of an incentive bonus.[43]

Fixed-price contracts originally placed for the medium-size cargo ships were left undisturbed. The price awarded to St John Dry Dock and Shipbuilding did not permit the company to charge its full overhead rate, indicating that any profits could not have been excessive. This was also true of George T. Davie and Sons. As previously mentioned, Foundation Maritime Limited operated the government yard at Pictou based on cost plus a management fee of $10,000 per ship. This was later changed to cost plus a minimum fee plus an incentive bonus.[44]

The first ship at Pictou, which cost $1,854,693 to build, was nearly double the contract price, but the actual price of the eighth ship was $1,422,440, a drop of 23.3 per cent, with an estimated price of $1,235,279 for the tenth ship.[45] Nevertheless, these improved prices, which do not include capital expenditures or special depreciation, remained well above those at established yards at Quebec and St John.

Production costs of thirty large cargo ships built by Marine Industries Limited reveal a considerable increase in productivity. Table 11.12 shows that the average cost of a Canadian-type vessel completed in 1944 was nearly 10 per cent less than

Table 11.13 | Added-value productivity of Canadian shipbuilding, 1935–46[a]

Year	WPI[b] 1935–39 (= 100)	Employees	Gross selling value or output ($000)	Materials ($000)	Fuel ($000)	Value added ($000)	Labour productivity ($/employee)
1935	94.10	2,967	7,124	2,021	259	4,844	1,734.99
1936	96.70	2,801	6,502	1,531	236	4,438	1,638.50
1937	108.40	3,502	10,361	3,205	280	6,876	1,811.30
1938	109.90	3,596	11,171	4,436	297	6,438	1,756.94
1939	99.00	3,491	11,235	3,814	299	7,122	2,060.71
1940	107.80	9,707	44,691	18,634	575	25,482	2,435.17
1941	116.20	21,240	109,326	41,472	1,112	66,742	2,704.20
1942	122.80	50,132	242,138	73,325	2,359	166,454	2,703.84
1943	127.80	75,847	376,561	123,317	3,429	249,815	2,577.21
1944	130.50	67,076	329,300	101,056	3,611	224,633	2,566.23
1945	132.00	48,118	204,595	60,294	2,654	141,646	2,230.09
1946	139.20	20,246	91,851	25,915	1,400	64,536	2,289.94

[a] Expressed as the dollar value of net output per employee.
[b] Wholesale Price Index.

Sources: Canada, DBS, *Annual Industry Report: Iron, Steel and Their Products Group: The Shipbuilding Industry* (1946), table 1; Leacy, ed., *Historical Statistics of Canada*, 2nd ed., K33.

the average cost of twenty-seven North Sands ships constructed between 1941 and 1944, even though material and labour costs had risen 22 and 4.5 per cent, respectively. Overheads had been substantially reduced from a shockingly high 76 per cent of the labour cost for the earlier North Sands ships to a more normal 60 per cent for the Canadian versions. The average cost of three 3,600-ton Great Lakes tankers built at Sorel in 1944 amounted to $1.1 million, and the overhead was reduced to 54 per cent of the average labour cost.[46] Although output increased and costs declined, the effectiveness of Canada's shipbuilding effort, the measure of combining capital and labour in a shipyard, remained in doubt. To examine the question, one must look at productivity.

Productivity

It has not been possible to obtain reliable measures of output per worker per ship or even per ton built over time, but labour productivity expressed in terms of annual net added value per employee is interesting. The limited annual data in table 11.13 suggest that labour productivity increased only modestly.[47] Labour productivity increased significantly between 1939 and 1942 as the industry rapidly expanded. Annual salaries and wages declined from 44.1 to 29.6 per cent of the gross selling value of the prod-

HMS *Rajah*, an American-built aircraft-carrier escort (CVE), in the Atlantic on 31 May 1944, after having been modified for the Royal Navy at Burrard Dry Dock Company between 1 January and 17 March 1944. LAC, PA-13818.

ucts of Canada's shipyards. But afterward, salaries and wages rose steadily from 38.1 to 48.6 per cent of the annual gross selling value of shipyard production.[48]

Table 11.13 uses a more accurate measure by deducting the cost of fuel and materials from the gross selling value so that the added value expressed in constant dollars may be compared directly to wages and salaries (i.e., labour costs). The most interesting fact appears to be that during 1940, even though the number of employees increased that year nearly five and a half times, added-value labour productivity increased from $2,060 to $2,435, or 18.2 per cent, and although the labour force grew again nearly two and a half times during 1941 and 1942, labour productivity increased by 11 per cent during the first year and remained steady through 1942. In economist-speak, extra inputs of labour were the major mechanism by which extra production was obtained. Thereafter, labour productivity declined slightly as the rate of production declined after July 1943, due to later types of ships requiring more work, and shipyards struggled to release workers as quickly as possible. The slight productivity increase in 1946 indicates the success of layoffs in 1945.

Although published statements of the number of man-hours required to construct a warship or cargo ship were common features of wartime propaganda, they are of little assistance in determining whether labour productivity increased as the war progressed.[49] Shipyards kept such data, but little has survived. More satisfactory data showing the relation between output and employment are presented in figures 11.3 and 11.4. The two curves are quite different from one another, indicating just how

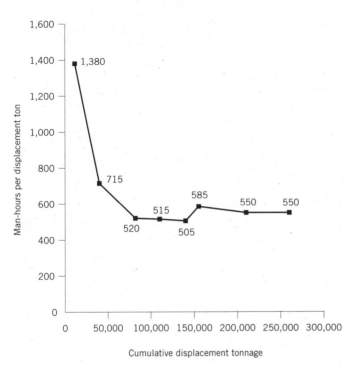

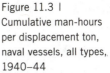

Figure 11.3 |
Cumulative man-hours
per displacement ton,
naval vessels, all types,
1940–44

Source: LAC, RG 28, box
29, Report on Canadian
Shipbuilding, 6 July 1944,
appendix 7.

different naval shipbuilding was from cargo shipbuilding. Yet they express the same
relationship between man-hours employed and cumulative tonnage produced. Economic planners at the DMS found the cumulative figures for both man-hours and
tonnage gave the most satisfactory results because of the industry characteristics,
such as the relatively few units delivered over time and the effects of seasonal change
on deliveries.

In the early stages of the naval program (see figure 11.3), the number of man-hours
per displacement ton dropped steeply and characteristically. The number of man-
hours per ton for the first twelve corvettes (i.e., 11,400 displacement tons) delivered in
1940 was 1,380, but the number declined to 520 during 1941 as shipbuilders gained experience through repetitively building only corvettes and Bangor-class minesweepers. After the yards had delivered approximately 85,000 displacement tons, which was
toward the end of 1941 (see table 11.2), the number of man-hours per ton continued
slowly to decline until the more complex frigates and Algerine minesweepers entered production, when man-hours increased once more.[50] Figure 11.3 was produced
in mid-1944 and does not show the effect of putting transport ferries (LST3s) into
production, but man-hours per ton would probably have remained low, as the tonnage of each ship was much larger than that of any other naval vessel built in Canada
and since the LST3s had the same engines as the frigates, meaning work was similar
in boiler rooms and in engine rooms. The armament and detection equipment was

Figure 11.4 | Cumulative man-hours per deadweight ton, cargo vessels, all types, 1941–44

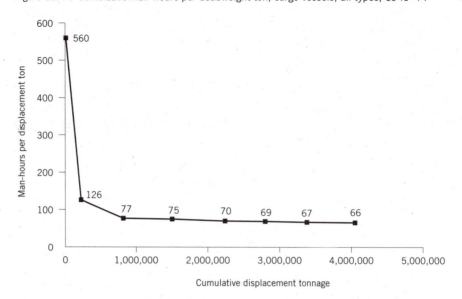

Source: LAC, RG 28, box 29, Report on Canadian Shipbuilding, 6 July 1944, appendix 8.

also less extensive; the larger ship probably allowed greater output per man, and the labour force's collective experience in 1944 had vastly improved since 1942.

The curve in figure 11.4, which also expresses the relation between output and employment, is much simpler than that in figure 11.3. It is entirely characteristic of any mass-production industry and repetitive manufacturing process. Cargo shipbuilding was not a mass-production industry in terms of the number of units delivered – hence the preferred phrase "multiple production" – but the repetitive nature of many shipyard tasks certainly led to many similar techniques being introduced. The first point to observe about figure 11.4 is the much lower number of man-hours required to produce a ton of cargo shipping compared to a ton of naval shipping. Even at its best, labour's performance on naval shipbuilding declined to approximately 505 man-hours per ton compared to less than 75 man-hours per deadweight ton for merchant shipbuilding. In brief, a ton of naval warship required more than six times the amount of labour needed to produce a ton of merchant shipping. Naval shipbuilding and cargo shipbuilding really were two separate kinds of activity. Amid calls to switch cargo shipbuilding yards to naval shipbuilding, it appears that no one in the navy was told about this difference, although Rear Admiral George Stephens may have known it intuitively.

The man-hours per ton for the first 10,000-ton ship, which began with 560 man-hours per deadweight ton, declined to 77 man-hours per ton by the end of 1942, when eighty-two ships, or 820,000 tons, had been delivered (see table 11.6). By the time Canadian shipbuilders had delivered 2 million tons during the fall of 1943, the number of man-hours per ton had dropped below 75. The continuing decline shown in figure 11.4 after 3 million tons had been built is an estimate. Another way of looking at this is to say that more than 5.5 million man-hours appeared to be required to build the first cargo ship, whereas from the beginning of 1943 onward, large cargo ships required 770,000 man-hours, a number that is not far off the average of 726,416 man-hours required to build a North Sands vessel at Sorel. After multiple production had fully developed at Marine Industries Limited, the average number of man-hours for the final eighteen North Sands ships declined to 631,881.[51] The simplicity of the curve in figure 11.4 allowed for very accurate planning of cuts to the labour force since the amount of future tonnage required could be expressed by allowing the number of deadweight tons per man-hour to rise or fall below 70 as the military and the economy required. The decline in employment in cargo shipbuilding during 1944 and 1945 was entirely manageable.

Improved technology (i.e., capital inputs) greatly increased the speed of production. New tools, machines, and construction methods, larger cranes with increased lift, welding in place of riveting, growing use of subassemblies, and large steel-working machinery contributed steadily to increases in gross tons per man-hour and per ton of steel worked. Modest changes could be very effective. With 190,000 rivets in each corvette, for example, a simple change such as new methods for heating rivets speeded up production. Seventeen specially designed portable gas furnaces installed in 1941 at one West Coast shipyard ensured better heating of the 2-inch rivets employed.[52]

Large cargo ships were initially 90 per cent riveted. Hulls required 383,000 rivets, and approximately 100,000 more were used in the superstructure. Although never adopted as completely as in the United States, welding increasingly replaced riveting as the war progressed. As early as October 1941, the knowledgeable American naval attaché in Canada, Commander Edmund W. Strother, reported that at Marine Industries Limited "in the double bottoms [of cargo ships] the transverse seams are welded and the longitudinal seams are riveted [which] gives a continuous two sea joint, standardizes the size of rivets, eliminates hundreds of liners, and the many joggle joints, thereby making for greater speed in production and for reduction in costs."[53] That same fall, a shipyard as small as the one at Kingston Shipbuilding Company on Lake Ontario arranged to weld the bulkheads of Western Isles antisubmarine minesweepers.[54] In February 1942 Vancouver shipbuilders announced steps were being taken to have all deck housing on new cargo ships welded instead of riveted, reducing by 20 per cent the number of rivets in each 10,000-ton freighter.[55] Six months later, two new automatic "Unionmelt" welding machines were installed at Burrard Dry Dock Company's South Yard.[56] At Marine Industries Limited, the number of men in the welding department grew to 580 in 1943. By 1944 a Sorel-built 10,000-tonner consumed 205 tons of welding rod, including 49 tons of electrode.[57] Burrard Dry Dock, the country's largest shipyard, employed 1,200 welders and burners in 1945. "Unionmelt" welding machines that could do two feet of half-inch weld per minute had been installed in several shipyards and were employed on all flat surfaces such as decks, bulkheads, and tank tops.[58]

Standardizing each yard to build one type of ship as in US yards was the single most important contributor to high labour productivity.[59] By the beginning of 1942, Canadian Vickers Limited at Montreal and Yarrows Limited at Victoria were building frigates exclusively. With the exception of three small tankers built in 1944, all five Canadian yards on the Great Lakes were producing corvettes and minesweepers. Indeed, Toronto Shipbuilding Company constructed only minesweepers.[60] Six yards on the West Coast built only large cargo vessels, accounting for two-thirds of all Canadian production. From 1942 Marine Industries Limited at Sorel and two government-built yards at Montreal and Pictou, respectively, constructed only one type of freighter. Quebec City yards were the only exception, building a wide variety of naval escorts, large and small cargo ships, and LST3s.[61]

Time on the ways declined substantially during the war. Data from one of the smallest shipyards in the country illustrate this very well. The first hulls in this four-berth yard took an agonizingly long 242 days from keel laying to launching, but to be fair, the inexperienced workers were building the shipyard at the same time. During the fourth round, the thirteenth through sixteenth hulls spent only 118 days on their berths. The improvement was even greater than indicated because all the steel work was erected and tanks tested in the shorter time period, whereas the first hulls had been launched only partially completed.[62] The time to outfit each hull from launch to sea trials was about 200 days each for the first four hulls, including completing unfinished steel work, but dropped to 62 days for the thirteenth through sixteenth hulls. By 1944 the sixty-day period was controlled by the twelve-ships-per-year program adopted after July 1943 when the government ordered a 50 per cent reduction in the rate of construction to allow more resources to be put into ship repairing. But the effect of standardization and growing experience is clear. Stated another way, by 1944 the women, farmers, and fishermen shipbuilders at Pictou were performing as well as any in the country. But speed of production must not be mistaken for productivity.

Productivity declined as Victory, Canadian, Revised, and Dominion versions of standard types began to be built (see table 11.2). The addition of the Royal Navy's stores-issuing ships and maintenance ships to the cargo ship program substantially reduced the speed of production. Hull work only slightly increased, but outfitting work more than doubled. The labour force was no longer balanced, and it proved impossible to recruit sufficient tradesmen (electricians, sheet-metal workers, and pipe-fitters) so late in the war to complete the ships in the same proportionate time of 70 percent for the hull and 30 percent for outfitting, as before. Outfitting time became greater than hull-building time, which congested the outfitting wharves.[63]

Labour costs were of most interest to the shipyards because these could be at least partially controlled. At Pictou, labour costs as a percentage of a theoretical target cost toward which the yard was working declined dramatically from about 206 per cent for the first four hulls to about 104 per cent for the thirteenth through sixteenth hulls. The target cost was reached for the first time on the fifteenth hull.[64] This meant that as the yard became more efficient, labour costs were cut in half and the yard was in a position to compete with the three other established yards building Gray-type cargo ships.

Another way to measure productivity is by calculating tonnage erection curves. At Pictou shipyard this was done for the first hull of each group of four hulls (i.e., the first, fifth, ninth, and thirteenth hulls) and projected against an ideal erection curve for twelve ships per year, or one per month. The ideal curve was constructed after studying the speed of erection of the first three groups of ships, analyzing what occurred and which steel plates were hung in what sequence during each week, and scheduling them for an annual twelve-ship program. Ironically, productivity had reached a point where the predetermined rate of production governed any further increase.

Many Canadian-built ships remained largely of riveted construction, although welding and employment of subassemblies increased during the war. Pictou shipyard measured productivity by the number of rivets driven per gang per eight-hour shift. From the days in 1941 when 250 rivets driven by a gang was only a dream, productivity grew to 400 rivets daily, reached by gangs in 1944. During 1943 and 1944, Pictou riveters more than doubled their production, increasing the number of rivets driven per hour from 22.5 to 50, and they reached an all time high of 54.3 rivets per hour for each riveter in the yard per eight-hour day at the end of 1944.[65]

That it took twenty-five days longer to build a ship on the West Coast than on the St Lawrence River or in the United States was attributable directly to low rivet production. In January 1942 at Burrard Dry Dock Company, the average number of rivets driven per gang per eight-hour shift was 228. During an experiment, workers put on piecework increased their production to 425 rivets per shift, and some groups drove 600 to 700 rivets per shift.[66] But when piecework was discontinued, the average number of rivets driven per gang per eight-hour shift dropped to 203, a figure that remained well behind the average production of French Canadian workers at Quebec City yards, who drove 750 to 900 per day, and Montreal workers, who drove 700 to 800 daily.[67]

Government officials expected a great increase in productivity after adopting continuous production in West Coast shipyards in 1942, but data in table 11.14 suggest that little was achieved. The table shows an increase in production after Burrard Dry Dock North Yard moved from two berths to four berths and coincidentally to continuous production during the summer of 1942. Fabrication (column 2) involved cutting, shaping, and drilling steel plate, and erection (column 3) involved putting steel on hulls. The overall increase in production was chiefly due to expansion of the yard. As measured by the change in the number of tons of steel worked per man per day during the three months between March and May and during a similar three-month period between July and September, productivity increased only from 5 to 5.5 tons per man per day, or 11 per cent.

Table 11.14 | Production at Burrard Dry Dock Company, North Yard, before and after introducing continuous production, March–September 1942

Month	Steel worked		Rivets driven	Average daily attendance
	Fabrication tons	Erection tons		
2 berths				
March	1,983	1,660	345,179	2,870
April	2,190	2,072	323,906	3,061
May	3,522	4,411	348,515	3,606
Total	*7,695*	*8,143*	*1,017,600*	*3,179*
4 berths, after introducing seven-day program				
July	4,615	3,828	434,083	4,459
August	4,449	5,102	571,676	4,086
September	3,584	5,076	625,197	4,980
Total	*12,648*	*14,006*	*1,630,956*	*4,508*
Increase				
Numbers	4,953	5,863	613,356	1,629
Per cent	64	72	60	51

Source: NVMA, Fonds 27, box 364, production records.

Transport ferry (LST3) no. 3504, built for the Royal Navy by Canadian Vickers Limited in 1945. LAC, C-032120.

One crucial factor affecting labour productivity that stood in stark contrast to the situation in the United States was the appalling state of labour relations in Canada's shipyards. For all of the government's publicly stated concern to increase war production, it did not moderate its hostility to labour until it legalized union recognition and the right to strike and to bargain collectively in February 1944. John Robson, manager of the construction department of both Wartime Merchant Shipping Limited and Wartime Shipbuilding Limited, estimated that from the beginning to the end of the cargo ship program, the reduction of man hours per ship was "something like 22 per cent," which compares very favourably with Frederick Lane's estimate of 24 per cent for the rise in productivity of the US Maritime Commission's shipbuilding during its best years, which were 1942 and 1943.[68]

Given that value-added labour productivity in Canada's wartime shipbuilding industry increased 31 per cent between 1939 and 1942 (table 11.13), it seems fair to quote from Peter Elliott's survey of Allied escort shipbuilding programs: "the shipbuilding effort made in Canada was probably the most remarkable of the three great naval powers, and delivery delays can take nothing away from the fantastic achievement."[69] Indeed, if Elliott had looked at the entire shipbuilding picture, he would have been even more impressed. The decline in labour productivity of Canada's shipbuilding industry after 1942 meant that it would not survive the peace. Although Canadian shipyards incorporated many technical changes, the industry was unable to adopt new financial, engineering, and managerial techniques to allow it to continue in the postwar era without heavy subsidies, which the government was not prepared to grant. Canada's wartime ships, it seems, were little more than large, rather complex shells fired at the enemy.

Conclusion

Canadian wartime shipbuilding contributed to the size of the Royal Navy and to Allied sea power. Considered alone it appears less significant than it really was. British warship construction, which had the highest priority during the war, totalled just less than 2 million displacement tons.[70] Canadian-built naval vessels, all of British design, represented additional tonnage of nearly 23 per cent. As British historians long ago pointed out, Canada's escort vessel construction was far more valuable than the tonnage figures suggest because it began two and a half years earlier than in the United States.[71] At times, these little ships were all that stood between victory and defeat during the darkest days of the war.

The contribution of Canadian-built merchant tonnage was equally important. Compared to combined Allied tonnage produced during the war as shown in table 11.15, Canada's total production appears so small as to be negligible. Its significance lay in the timing. During the 1930s British shipbuilders had sought to reduce shipbuilding capacity in the United Kingdom in order to bring supply into line with demand. By 1939 they had been so successful that British officials concluded the industry could produce only about 1 million gross registered tons (grt) (approximately

Table 11.15 | Comparison of Canadian and combined Allied (UK, US, Canada) merchant vessel construction, 1939–45*

Year	Tankers		Dry-cargo		Minor types		Total	
	Canada	Allied	Canada	Allied	Canada	Allied	Canada	Allied
1939				336				336
1940		200		1,048		27		1,275
1941		810	10	1,459		25	10	2,294
1942		1,498	810	9,059		126	810	10,683
1943	40	3,825	1,330	17,548	61	659	1,431	22,032
1944	80	4,277	870	12,520	85	429	1,056	17,226
1945		1,947	340	5,166	106	157	396	7,270
Total	120	12,557	3,360	47,136	252	1,423	3,703	61,116

* Thousands of deadweight tons.

Source: Hall, North American Supply, 425 and table 9.6.

1.4 million dwt) per annum, an amount far less than would be required in wartime. British shipbuilders had considerably less than 1 million grt on the stocks when war broke out, with just 801,000 grt being completed in 1940. Overall, from January 1940 to August 1945, 6 million grt (approximately 8.4 million dwt) of merchant shipping were completed in British shipyards.[72] Although more than 1 million grt were constructed in each of 1941, 1942, 1943, and 1944, the failure to meet demand was obvious. Viewed against this background, Canada's completion of nearly 3.8 million dwt of merchant shipping from 1942 to 1944 was equivalent to more than three-quarters, 77.1 per cent, of British merchant-shipping output during the same three-year period. Between 20 May 1943 and the end of 1945, Great Britain received $406 million worth of naval and cargo ships and repair services through Canada's own mutual-aid program. This amounted to 19 per cent of the $2.1 billion in mutual aid supplied gratis to Great Britain during the war.

12 | Conclusion

Canada's wartime shipbuilding industry left no lasting legacy. Several factors – historical, economic, technical, and political – account for shipbuilding's reversion to its prewar status. Shipyard expansions far exceeded the possibilities of domestic consumption. Not even war-torn economies abroad could keep the industry operating at levels approaching current capacity. Nor was there any possibility that the industry could survive unsupported, even if severely reduced. Peacetime shipbuilding would require large government subsidies.

Labour costs were too high and uncompetitive. Although Canadian labour costs compared quite favourably with those in American yards, the latter were around three times greater than in Great Britain.[1] Even the most optimistic comparison acknowledged that construction costs of a Canadian-built, 10,000-ton freighter were from 37 to 47 per cent higher than for a similar British-built ship, while operating costs were 35 per cent higher.[2]

Wartime shipbuilding had not required Canadian shipyards to develop an engineering design capacity. In the end, the typical Canadian yard was a large manufacturing concern without a design and development capability. The industry remained wholly dependent on what the British wanted built – the simplest ships possible – and on British naval architects and engineering talent. With few exceptions, wartime shipbuilding followed British plans and specifications. Little was conceptually new; in fact, the steam technology employed was more than a half-century old. Innovations and reorganization in the yards were limited to increased welding to replace riveting, often over the objections of British marine engineers and naval architects, and sometimes involved brilliant use of new machines such as "Unionmelt" welding on combustion chambers of Scotch boilers. Other improvements occurred outside shipyards among steel fabricators and machinery manufacturers.

The industry was hidebound. From beginning to end and from one side of the country to the other, men trained in Great Britain, often thirty or more years before the war began, managed Canadian shipyards. A few like John Rannie, general manager of United Shipyards, who later went on to head the great Scottish shipbuilding firm of John Brown and Company Limited, were brilliant managers, but others like John S. Leitch, vice president and general manager of Collingwood Shipyards Limited, had nothing but contempt for anything Canadian after thirty years in the country.[3] The greatest improvements in Canada's shipyards were probably in fixed capital invested and skilled industrial workers rather than in new developments or management. Shipbuilding's greatest legacy may well have been the thousands of trained industrial workers who became available for employment in other industries, especially in Montreal, Toronto, and Vancouver.

Warship production, like other armaments, required a relatively sophisticated engineering industry and a machine-tool industry. Canada lacked both. Little original engineering design was carried out in Canada, which remained wholly reliant upon the United States and the United Kingdom for machine tools until 1942. The development of electrical and mechanical engineering left a strong postwar legacy, and although Canada acquired high-speed-tool steel and developed a manufacturing capacity for machine tools, little of this arose from shipbuilding.[4] Canadian-trained naval architects did not exist. Most Canadian engineers had long been employed in American and British branch plants and were usually in sales. Canadian engineering, in general, lacked traditions of design and innovation, and wartime shipbuilding encouraged little domestic engineering development or technological advance. Canada was hard pressed to train sufficient marine draftsmen during the war. Although Canada developed and carried out a successful emergency program to construct escort vessels, it failed to develop a capacity to go beyond initial ship specifications. Much of the navy's modernization crisis was due to its failure to learn from combat to modify its own escort ships. All improvements had to wait until they were received from the British Admiralty.

Ironically, the Royal Canadian Navy (RCN), which had been technologically challenged throughout the war, proved to be better positioned for the future than the shipbuilding industry. Since 1943 the navy had been maturing plans for its postwar fleet. The acquisition of light aircraft carriers, cruisers, and fleet destroyers and expectation of a new form of naval warfare in the Pacific led to a major shift during 1944 and 1945 from a simple escort navy of emergency-built ships to a balanced fleet of modern warships with technically advanced weapon systems.[5] The four Tribal-class destroyers completed at Halifax from 1945 onward proved vital to more advanced capability in the future. Both the move to a balanced fleet and the construction of destroyers led to major changes and additions to the navy's technical personnel after Japan surrendered. Rapid demobilization forced the navy to make decisions quickly in order to preserve its small but growing technical cadre. Although the RCN still lacked a warship design capacity, at the end of the war it was swiftly acquiring one. These developments and the government's response to the Cold War, rather than any wartime legacy, kept Canadian postwar shipbuilding alive.[6]

In October 1943, at the same time as Harvey R. MacMillan was proposing a reorganization of Wartime Merchant Shipping Limited, the Cabinet War Committee established a broad-based interdepartmental committee on merchant-shipping policy with representatives from the Departments of Transport, Trade and Commerce, External Affairs, National Defence, Finance, and Munitions and Supply and from the Canadian Shipping Board, the National Harbours Board, and Park Steamship Company.[7] C.D. Howe, who was in London, approached Lord Leathers, minister of war transport, for assistance to build a modern ship of 15,000 gross tons and a speed of 17 to 18 knots with refrigerated space suitable for postwar Canada–West Indies and Canada–Far East trades.[8] But Leathers was distinctly unhelpful, informing Howe that no such vessel was currently contemplated for wartime purposes and that all ships of this type built before the war had plans whose owners had proprietary rights. Any agreements to use them must be negotiated with the owners or a naval architect hired to submit new proposals for the vessels.[9] The British, who had been building faster merchant ships since 1942, had no interest in encouraging development of an independent Canadian shipbuilding industry.[10]

As construction wound down during 1944, the future of shipbuilding and shipping was intensely studied. In March 1944 a special technical subcommittee on shipbuilding submitted its report to the interdepartmental committee on merchant-shipping policy, which approved it and passed it on to the Cabinet War Committee along with its own report.[11] The shipbuilding subcommittee had examined three questions: first, whether cargo ships currently under construction could be economically employed in postwar trades as they were, with minor or major modifications; second, whether these ships could meet specific or specialized requirements of ship-owning or ship-chartering companies; and third, whether and when special ships for special trades might be built given the current schedules of Wartime Shipbuilding Limited and the available facilities of Canadian machinery manufacturers. The general impression had grown in the ship-owning and shipping fraternity that the current cargo ships would have little or no value when the war ended. Apart from the bad experience with Canadian-built ships at the end of the First World War, the main reasons for this belief were that the United States was building large numbers of fast cargo vessels and that the tonnage of Liberty ships was decreasing. Authorities at the US Maritime Commission were placing great emphasis on speed in their desire to obtain the cream of postwar cargos in a world of expanding trade, leaving the slow-tramp trade to the prewar maritime nations.[12]

Turning to the standard products of Canadian shipyards, subcommittee members based their report on the fact that 80 per cent of Canada's exports were bulk cargos of lumber, grain, pulp, newsprint, and so on and that freight rates, rather than speed, would govern the business decisions of Canadian shippers. Canada would end the war with a surplus of slow vessels. Members concluded that it was impossible to discontinue current production and begin construction of other classes of ships without many months of preparation. Since it was believed that the current slow tramps being built could be employed after the war, the question became whether modifications could be built into the standard ships currently under construction.

After presenting the subcommittee's study of operating costs, the report recommended fitting the ships with diesel motors to replace the present steam-driven reciprocating engines. The discontinuation of new frigate and corvette construction had released capacity, and committee members thought that Canadian Vickers Limited and Dominion Engineering Works could devote resources to building diesel engines without interfering with the present construction programs. The relative economy of steam versus diesel was estimated to reduce the annual cost per cargo ton of these ships from $13.15 to $12.10, or by 8 per cent, chiefly owing to a diesel-powered vessel's ability to maintain a higher full speed in heavier seas with economical fuel consumption. Tank tests had shown that the present hull designs allowed the ships to be driven at 12.5 knots as compared with 10 knots in the current steam-powered configuration. The challenge to industry would be to increase the power from the present 2,500 indicated horsepower (ihp) to 3,660 ihp rated capacity. This was unlikely to occur.

Vivian Engine Works at Vancouver provides a good example of local limitations. Although the firm had been a grand success, ending the war with 850 employees manufacturing a 22,500-pound diesel engine a day, no technical improvements had occurred during the war. American diesel manufacturers had increased the number of rotations per minute (rpm) almost on an annual basis, getting up to 1,800 rpm, which left the heavy, slow-rotating Vivian motors far behind with basically the same engine as in 1939. Will Vivian had reached his limit. He was not interested in changing or in surrendering any control. Instead, after the war, he exported his engines successfully to South America, where fishing fleets were only then changing from sail to motor. He finally sold his business in 1950, unable to adapt to changing technology and the times.[13]

The subcommittee's report also recommended improving crew accommodation. This could be accomplished without any major modifications to the structure of the vessels. Requiring more thought were changes involving deadweight and lines of the 10,000-ton ships to increase speed and achieve more general-purpose vessels capable of carrying both bulk and package cargos with diesel engines. No thought was given to whether an entirely new cargo liner capable of 14 knots could be built cheaply enough to justify its operation in the Canadian export trades. The subcommittee did recommend that designs, tank tests, and cost estimates be initiated in order to build such a vessel with a tween deck and modern crew accommodations.

The subcommittee was less positive about the advantages of converting the medium-size freighters. While recommending that consideration be given to converting them to diesel engines placed aft in order to increase cargo capacity, it recommended that immediate design work be undertaken to install a tween deck in order to improve the postwar usefulness of the vessels. Following Cabinet approval in principle of the report in April, work began on the last recommendation, which appeared in the last six ships, the Dominion types.[14]

The chief challenges for the future lay in Canadian capacity to construct marine diesel engines of sufficient power for large special-purpose cargo ships, as no Canadian manufacturer had ever built either diesels or steam turbines large enough to power a large, fast ship. Furthermore, procurement of auxiliary equipment, generators, and refrigeration machinery would be difficult without recourse to American and British suppliers. If shipbuilding was ever to become a permanent industry on any considerable scale, it would be necessary for some company to lay the foundations and gain experience. The subcommittee's final recommendation was that steps be taken to encourage consultations between ship owners such as Canadian National Steamships and an individual yard or the newly formed Shipbuilders Association in order to set on foot the necessary studies preliminary to construction of special-purpose ships.

A year later, in April 1945, after Canadian Vickers had arranged to manufacture large Sun-Doxford marine diesel engines under licence, Wartime Shipbuilding Limited contracted with Canadian Vickers, Davie Shipbuilding and Repairing, and Burrard Dry Dock for three large motor cargo liners.[15] At 7,500 deadweight tons and more than 400 feet long, they would be the largest peacetime ships ever built in Canada. They were wholly foreign in design and engineering. Despite strong protest from German and Milne at Montreal, the naval architectural firm of Cox and Stevens at New York provided detailed plans and specifications.[16] The large 4-cylinder, 6,000-horsepower Sun-Doxford diesel engines to be built by Canadian Vickers were British in design.[17] No additional ships of this type were built. The chief intention in ordering these ships was to ease the transition from war to peacetime by providing employment for returning servicemen rather than to develop a peacetime shipbuilding industry. The same was true of other shipbuilding contracts let on behalf of foreign governments in 1945.

In the spring of 1944, shortly after the Cabinet War Committee had approved the recommendations of the interdepartmental committee on merchant-shipping policy, eighteen steel shipbuilders formed the Canadian Shipbuilders and Ship Repairing Association (CSSRA) in order to lobby the government to preserve, maintain, and develop the shipbuilding and ship repairing industry in Canada.[18] At its inaugural meeting at Vancouver on 10 May, newly elected president J. Edouard Simard of Marine Industries Limited affirmed the association's main objective: "to avoid a repetition of what happened to the shipbuilding industry between World War I and World War II." Simard struck an optimistic note, believing the government to be sympathetic to the industry and that members of the CSSRA would stick together. But this must have been for public consumption. Simard had to know that the government was not sympathetic to either shipbuilding or shipping. Both industries had commercial enemies as well.

The Montreal Board of Trade, for example, expressed opposition in July when its committee on postwar international trade called for a return to prewar shipping, expressing fear that any attempt to favour Canadian shipping might harm Canada's export trade.[19] J.E. Michaud, the minister of transport, saw no future in Canada going into the shipping business after the war.[20] Canada's export trades easily trumped shipping. Yet favouring Canadian shipping and shipbuilding was exactly what the CSSRA desired. In its brief to Ottawa on 30 August, the association outlined ten recommendations, including one to reserve coastal shipping for Canadian ships. Another asked that Canadian ship owners be encouraged to build and register their own ships engaged in foreign trade in Canada, and others called for all naval and fishing vessels to be built in Canada and for reduction of tariffs on certain imported marine machinery such as main engines and gearing. As historian Francis Mansbridge has pointed out, the government did not respond favourably.[21]

Douglas Ambridge, general director of the shipbuilding branch at the Department of Munitions and Supply, responded quickly to the CSSRA brief, recommending to C.D. Howe that the industry rationalize itself before asking for government assistance. He proposed the shipbuilding firms be reduced to four through a series of mergers. In the Maritimes, he favoured shutting down and disposing of the government-owned yard at Pictou and merging St John Dry Dock and Shipbuilding Company with Halifax Shipyards Limited. On the St Lawrence River, he called for a single company to be made out of the five established shipyards and the closing and disposal of United Shipyards Limited. On the Great Lakes, he recommended closing the small Midland and Kingston yards and merging Port Arthur Shipbuilding and Collingwood Shipyards with the Toronto shipyards. Ambridge knew that the four yards outside Toronto were under single ownership and probably knew that they were being merged into Canadian Shipbuilding and Engineering Limited as he wrote. Just why he thought the government-owned Toronto Shipbuilding Company should not be closed is unclear. On the West Coast, Ambridge assumed West Coast Shipbuilders Limited would disappear and that the Canadian National Railway would operate its Prince Rupert facility as a repair depot. He recommended shutting down Victoria Machinery Depot and that Burrard Dry Dock Company, North Van Ship Repairs, and Yarrows Limited be merged into a single shipbuilding company.[22]

Ambridge's recommendations came closest to realization on the West Coast. In 1946 the Wallaces, owners of Burrard Dry Dock, bought out Norman Yarrow's company at Esquimalt and five years later acquired Pacific Dry Dock (formerly North Van Ship Repairs) from seventy-six-year-old Arthur Burdick. But in neither case did the Wallace family close the shipyards.[23] In general, the shipyards entered peacetime without the support of assigned contracts, forced to compete with one another and ill equipped to do so. Failure to reduce the industry's capacity on the approach of peacetime reflects the lack of management talent among the owners.

Ambridge's memorandum was not the only government response to the shipbuilding industry's postwar ambitions. The Departments of Transport, Finance, and Trade and Commerce and the navy all submitted separate studies, generally endorsing some form of protection for shipping and shipbuilding, but such recommendations fell on deaf ears.[24] The report of the interdepartmental committee on merchant-shipping policy echoed Ambridge's earlier critical memorandum in its report to the Cabinet War Committee concerning the CSSRA's brief.[25]

C.D. Howe did not favour either Canadian shipping or the shipbuilding industry, nor did he foresee a promising future. Far from counting shipbuilding among the industries it wanted to save in the postwar years, as historian Marc Milner claims, the Canadian government was most anxious to dispose of its merchant fleet and saw no commercial future for shipbuilding.[26] As minister of transport in 1936, Howe had been responsible for disbanding and disposing of the last ships of the Canadian Government Merchant Marine. The total loss to Canadian taxpayers, exclusive of interest on capital and other charges, had been over $82 million.[27] This experience and his fondness for aviation must have heavily influenced his decision to dispose of Canada's wartime Crown-owned merchant fleet numbering more than 200 ships.

Howe, a firm believer in free enterprise, was anxious to get rid of controls over the economy and hostile to government support for Canadian shipping in general and shipbuilding in particular.[28] His decision to sell the vessels belonging to Park Steamship Company at bargain prices to Canadian shipping companies with the proviso that they be under Canadian registry and therefore with Canadian crews reflected his desire to dispose of the government-owned merchant marine while continuing employment for thousands of men who had joined the merchant marine during the war. Twenty vessels were sold in 1945 and 130 more in 1946, when an additional 45 were chartered and all spare gear from the company was delivered to War Assets Corporation for disposal. Finally, on 1 December 1946 an agreement was completed for the disposal of 91 ships (the so-called Forts) on bareboat charter to the British Ministry of War Transport.[29] With the decision to dispose of the government-owned merchant fleet, it is inconceivable that the minister had any sympathy for continuing such heavily subsidized industries.

Government-owned shipyards were all disposed of before the end of 1945. The naval fitting-out yards at Hamilton and Quebec were closed in November 1944, and the yard at St John was transferred to War Assets Corporation for disposal in September 1945. The government-financed expansion of Yarrows Limited, known as No. 2 Yard, was also delivered to War Assets Corporation. The emergency shipyard at Pictou delivered its final ship in July 1945 and was transferred to War Assets Corporation. Redfern Construction Company (Shipbuilding Division) Limited (formerly Toronto Shipbuilding Company) and United Shipyards Limited at Montreal completed their work and were transferred to the same agency on 29 and 30 November 1945, respectively.[30] Quebec Shipyards Limited surrendered its company charter to the secretary of state for cancellation on 31 October, after the yards of Morton Engineering and Dry Dock and George T. Davie and Sons had been returned to their owners.[31] During the next three years, the government retained only 0.4 per cent of nearly 2 million square feet of floor space owned in thirty-four shipbuilding plants. Seventy-seven per cent of all floor space was made available to private industry at bargain prices, 15 per cent was dismantled, and 4 per cent was declared available for disposal.[32]

Howe was not wholly unreceptive to the Canadian Shipbuilding and Ship Repairing Association. Two years after the war ended, he moved to aid the steel shipbuilding industry when it encountered severe difficulties as foreign shipyards began to recover and the American Marshall Plan shut Canadians out of building ships for war-torn European nations. Even then, his support was carefully qualified. In April 1946 Howe, by then minister of trade and commerce, announced the establishment of the Canadian Maritime Commission to salvage the Canadian shipping and shipbuilding industries, but the prime minister's appointment of J.V. Clyne as chairman signalled the future, for the new broom was opposed to any policies that would lead government to making a major financial commitment.[33]

The Second World War marked the beginning of a long-term cycle of Canadian prosperity and a major twofold sectoral change involving a shift from agricultural to manufacturing and a greatly increased development of the service sector that transformed the country. The government moved massively to increase its share of total output and remain permanently involved in Canada's economy as never before seen.[34] In contrast to the steel industry, shipbuilding was not an end in itself but an example of government involvement in the economy for war purposes. The fate of these two industries also reminds us that the war re-enforced the regional nature of Canada's economy. The government focused on the war rather than on regional issues such as transferring wealth from one part of the country to another, and consequently the war reinforced the existing wealth and economic power of the industrial heartland in Quebec and Ontario. The history of shipbuilding reminds us that despite its apparent wartime success, Canada's economy had a dark side. Steel shipbuilding was not feasible, except for under special conditions. The small locks on the St Lawrence River canals meant that commercial shipbuilding would survive on the Great Lakes. But naval shipbuilding would survive on a greatly reduced scale only because of massive government support forced on it by the Cold War.

Despite its magnificent achievement, Canada's wartime shipbuilding industry left no lasting legacy. The great volume of ship production that Canada achieved was not planned in advance. It was forced upon the country during 1940 and 1941 by the desperate needs of war. Canadian North Sands, Victory, and Canadian types were designed for the sole purpose of providing as many ships as possible in the shortest time possible to move essential war cargos and supplies across the Atlantic faster than the enemy could sink them. That was the task, and it was accomplished.

Notes

ACKNOWLEDGMENTS

1 I have been unable to locate an original copy, but for an illustration of this poster, see *Canadian Transportation* 45 (November 1941): 638; and *Canadian Machinery and Manufacturing News* 52 (December 1941): 310.

PREFACE

1 "Progress in Shipbuilding," *Canadian Transportation* 48 (November 1944): 627.
2 Lane, *Ships for Victory*; Corkhill, *Tonnage Measurement of Ships*.
3 Behrens, *Merchant Shipping and the Demands of War*, 466.
4 Smith, *Conflict over Convoys*, 240.
5 Lane, *Ships for Victory*, 640.

CHAPTER ONE

1 Donald, *Canadian Iron and Steel Industry*.
2 See Sager and Panting, *Maritime Capital*, for a partial discussion of the decline of East Coast marine industries at the end of the nineteenth century.
3 Stephen Salmon, review, *Northern Mariner* 15, no. 2 (April 2005): 5.
4 For three excellent histories of the Canadian steel industry, see Kilbourn, *Elements Combined*; McDowall, *Steel at the Sault*; and Heron, *Working in Steel*.
5 *Statutes of Canada*, 1882, 45 Vic., chap. 17, Act to Encourage the Construction of Dry Docks.
6 According to Ouderkirk and Gillham, *Ships of Kingston*, 3–7, the *Polana*, *Bellechase*, and *Dollard* were built for the Departments of Agriculture and Marine and Fisheries.
7 *Statutes of Canada*, 1910, 9–10 Edw. VII, chap. 17.
8 Except where used in the possessive (i.e., Great Britain's), the terms "Great Britain" and "United Kingdom" are used interchangeably throughout the text.
9 Tucker, *Naval Service of Canada*, vol. 2, 40; Taylor, *Shipyards of British Columbia*.
10 Hadley and Sarty, *Tin Pots and Pirate Ships*, 99–100, 114. See also Smith, *Britain's Clandestine Submarines*, for Canada's effort to secure a modern shipbuilding industry. Tucker, *Naval Service of Canada*, vol. 1, 234–6, says very little about shipbuilding; Smith is to be preferred.
11 Scott, *Vickers, a History*, 113.
12 Smith, *Britain's Clandestine Submarines*, 118–21. For more on the work of the Imperial Munitions Board, see Bliss, *Canadian Millionaire*, 257–388.

13 Wilson, *History of Shipbuilding and Naval Architecture in Canada*, 49.

14 Mansbridge, *Launching History*, 37–8.

15 Wilson, *History of Shipbuilding*, 50.

16 Ibid., 51; Harris, "Canadian Warship Construction," 149–58.

17 Gaul, "Canada's Shipbuilding Industry," 57.

18 Bliss, *Canadian Millionaire*, 387.

19 Wilson, *History of Shipbuilding*, 51–2; Settle, "Halifax Shipyards."

20 Wilson, *History of Shipbuilding*, 52; Mackenzie, "C.C. Ballantyne."

21 Johnman and Murphy, *British Shipbuilding and the State*, 8, 12.

22 Mansbridge, *Launching History*, 34.

23 Ibid., 54.

24 Bliss, *Northern Enterprise*, 388–9.

25 Salmon, "British Competition," 20–6.

26 Marcil, *Tall Ships and Tankers*, 97–9.

27 Anonymous, "Consolidation of Great Lakes Shipbuilding Companies."

28 Ibid.

29 MMGLK, Canada Steamship Lines Fonds, 1993.0002.0016, Midland Shipbuilding Company file, sale.

30 Ibid., 1993.0002.0010, Midland Shipbuilding Company file, "Statement of Operating Results, 1927 to 1938."

31 *SR&SB* 28, no. 3 (March 1945): 32–3; Gillham, *Ships of Collingwood*, 2.

32 Tucker, *Naval Service of Canada*, vol. 2, 32, 503; Mansbridge, *Launching History*, 62–3.

33 Settle, "Halifax Shipyards," 43–5.

34 Plumptre, *Mobilizing Canada's Resources for War*, 10. The author probably used the Dominion Bureau of Statistics (DBS) data for 1938, which reported forty-one shipyards in Canada: seventeen in British Columbia, seven in Nova Scotia, eight in Ontario, six in Quebec, and one each in New Brunswick, Manitoba, and the Yukon.

35 Canada, DBS, *Annual Industry Report: Iron, Steel and Their Products Group: The Shipbuilding Industry* (hereafter *Shipbuilding Industry*) (1939 and 1943); government naval dockyards were not included.

36 Glover, "The RCN: Royal Colonial or Royal Canadian Navy?" 74. On wartime Canadianization, see Douglas, "Conflict and Innovation," 210–32.

37 Buxton, "British Warship Building and Repair," 81. See also MacPherson and Milner, *Corvettes of the Royal Canadian Navy*.

38 MacPherson and Burgess, *Ships of Canada's Naval Forces, 1910–1993*, 68.

39 Tucker, *Naval Service of Canada*, vol. 2, 507, gives only five of these short-fo'c'sle corvettes. The error is repeated in Elliott, *Allied Escort Ships of World War II*. The missing one is HMCS *Dundas*.

40 Milner, *U-boat Hunters*, 272–3. There is some confusion about these ships in Douglas et al., *Blue Water Navy*, 43; the British Admiralty Technical Mission ordered fifteen (not fifty-one) Revised corvettes in 1941 rather than in 1942, and those completed in 1943 were Revised rather than Increased Endurance versions.

41 McKay and Harland, *Flower-Class Corvette Agassiz*, 18. The excellent brief text is accompanied by 14 pages of photographs and 126 pages of ship drawings; HMCS *Agassiz*, commissioned at Vancouver in January 1941, was one of the original short-fo'c'sle corvettes.

42 MacPherson and Burgess, *Ships of Canada's Naval Forces*, 44; LAC, RG 2 7c, vol. 5 (reel C-4654), Cabinet War Committee minutes, 10 July 1941.

43 Mansbridge, *Launching History*, 94; Halford, *Unknown Navy*, 144–5; Marcil, *Tall Ships and Tankers*, 239–40.

44 In May 1941 Prime Minister Churchill amalgamated the Ministries of Transport and Shipping into a single Ministry of War Transport. See Smith, *Conflict over Convoys*, 47.

45 See Elphick, *Liberty: The Ships That Won the War*, 23–33.

46 For details, see Rannie, "10,000 Tonner."

47 *CS&MEN* 14, no. 8 (March 1944): 39; Heal, *Great Fleet of Ships*, 44; Bunker, *Liberty Ships*, 7.

48 For details on comparative dimensions, speed, and engines, see *CS&MEN* 14, no. 11 (June 1944): 54. See also Lane, *Ships for Victory*, 574–607.

49 LAC, RG 2 7C, vol. 12 (reel C-4875), Cabinet War Committee minutes, 7 April 1943; Heal, *Great Fleet of Ships*, 37.

50 *CS&MEN* 15, no. 10 (May 1944): 30–1, and no. 13 (August 1944): 76; Kennedy, *History of the Department of Munitions and Supply*, vol. 1, 496; Mansbridge, *Launching History*, 77–9.

51 Ayre, "Merchant Shipbuilding during the War," 9.

52 Heal, *Great Fleet of Ships*, 38.

53 LAC, RG 28, box 7, "A Brief History of Wartime Merchant Shipping Ltd., Montreal, December 31, 1943, with an Addendum on Wartime Shipbuilding Ltd., January 1944–February 1947," 29.

54 LAC, MG 30 B121. Heal, *Great Fleet of Ships*, 46–7, attributes the design to Milne, Gilmore and German, a postwar name for the firm.

55 LAC, RG 117, box 1928, file 2861, pts 1–2, "Report of Operations of Dufferin Shipbuilding Company Limited," by R.M. Scrivener, general manager, Toronto, 9 June 1941.

56 Leacy, ed., *Historical Statistics of Canada*, D8–D85.

57 Canada, DBS, *Shipbuilding Industry* (1939), table 1; Canada, Department of External Affairs, "Estimated Value of War Production," table 63. These figures cover only war production and construction contracts placed by the Department of Munitions and Supply.

58 This dominant trend may be found in any general history of Canada during the Second World War, but see Pickersgill, *Mackenzie King Record*; Bothwell and Kilbourn, *C.D. Howe*; Bryce, *Canada and the Cost of World War II*; Fullerton, *Graham Towers and His Times*; Granatstein, *Ottawa Men*; and Schull, *Great Scot*.

CHAPTER TWO

1 Howe was rightly proud of his department's achievements and the primary force behind the writing of its official history by John de Navarre Kennedy, *History of the Department of Munitions and Supply* (hereafter *History of DMS*). But he assigned the task to a lawyer rather than a historian, and its narrative conveniently omits embarrassing episodes and eschews analysis in favour of self-praise. Hubris was a given among Howe's men. The army's official historian, Professor Charles Stacey, who read the manuscript too close to publication to affect the outcome, was not impressed and advised others to be on their guard. See Cook, *Clio's Warriors*, 174.

2 Stephens, "Reminiscences," 25.

3 See Scott and Hughes, *Administration of War Production*.

4 See Bliss, *Canadian Millionaire*, 257–388, for the best account of the work of the Imperial Munitions Board.

5 Nelles is a very controversial figure. German, *Sea Is at Our Gates*, 144, 148, presents a harsh assessment of Nelles's poor leadership based on his naive faith in the RN, poor decision making, and lack of originality. Milner, *North Atlantic Run*, 6–7, is more sympathetic, claiming Nelles

did a good job as CNS. Zimmerman, *Great Naval Battle of Ottawa*, 145–6, is less accommodating, seeing Nelles as "not the man for the job" (165). For a positive view, see Sarty, "Admiral Percy W. Nelles," 74–6, 80, who credits the CNS with attempting to develop naval shipbuilding during the mid and late 1930s and pressing for a substantial beginning during the early months of the war. Sarty also claims that Nelles lost his position as CNS "largely as a result of the shortcomings of Canadian industry" (91), but he offers no evidence. In the most complete examination of the admiral's removal from office, Mayne, *Betrayed*, presents Nelles as the victim of a clique of naval volunteer reserve officers and of politicians whose self-serving machinations rather than any faults of his own did in a decent man.

6 Douglas et al., *No Higher Purpose*, 33.

7 Tucker, *Naval Service of Canada*, vol. 2, 31–2.

8 Stacey, *Arms, Men and Governments*, 315; Zimmermann, *Great Naval Battle of Ottawa*, 131.

9 Tucker, *Naval Service of Canada*, vol. 2, 418–21.

10 Stephens, "Reminiscences," 24.

11 Tucker, *Naval Service of Canada*, vol. 2, 460.

12 Eayers, *In Defence of Canada*, 128–9.

13 MacPherson and Milner, *Corvettes of the Royal Canadian Navy*, 11.

14 Buxton, "British Warship Building and Repair," 86.

15 Beck, *Pendulum of Power*, 220, 228. For a detailed discussion, see Granatstein, *Politics of Survival*.

16 See Miller, "The 1940s: War and Rehabilitation"; Evans, *John Grierson and the National Film Board*; and Robinson, *Measure of Democracy*.

17 See McInnis, *Harnessing Labour Confrontation*, 20–8, for a brief outline of Canada's command economy.

18 Stacey, *Arms, Men and Governments*, 495–6.

19 The full name of the act establishing the Defence Purchasing Board makes this clear: The Defence Purchasing, Profits Control and Financing Act of 3 June 1939 (3 Geo. VI, 1939, ch. 42).

20 Stacey, *Arms, Men and Governments*, 102.

21 LAC, RG 28, box 346, file 1-1-1, Defence Purchasing Board minute book.

22 In an otherwise excellent article, Mackenzie, "Bren Gun Scandal and the Maclean Publishing Company's Investigation of Canadian Contracts, 1938–1940," argues that the "scandal" hindered development of an industrial defence policy, but this tentative hypothesis could just as easily be turned on its head. By clearing away the unsavory connections between the Department of National Defence and private contactors, Canada freed up the country's industrial war-production capabilities to reach maximum capacity more speedily than would have been the case if production had not been placed securely in the hands of civilian industrialists and businessmen who were neither civil servants nor soldiers.

23 Smith et al., "History of the British Admiralty Technical Mission in Canada" (hereafter "History of BATM"), 42.

24 LAC, MG 27 III B20, box 64, file S-26-2 (3), "History of the British Supply Organizations in the U.S.," January 1944; Hall, *North American Supply*, 68–9.

25 Pickersgill, *Mackenzie King Record*, 27.

26 LAC, RG 28, box 436, files 22 and 23, contracts between the War Supply Board and Halifax Shipyards and between the War Supply Board and Burrard Dry Dock, respectively, 21 October 1939.

27 LAC, RG 28, box 346, file 1-1-21-1, minute book of War Supply Board; *Canadian Transportation* 43 (March 1940): 158.

28 LAC, RG 2, registers, PC 3599, 1 May 1942.

29 Cox, *Canadian Strength*, sketch of Carswell, 17–19, originally published in the *Montreal Standard*, 28 December 1940; *Canadian Transportation* 46 (1942): 616; LAC, RG 28, box 256, file 196-13-4, press releases from the DMS, 12 October 1944 and 7 November 1945.

30 This paragraph summarizes Douglas et al., *No Higher Purpose*, 71–82, which presents a useful account of the evolution of the navy's first shipbuilding program from early 1939 to Cabinet approval on 7 February 1940.

31 Tucker, *Naval Service of Canada*, vol. 2, 34; *Canadian Transportation* 42 (December 1939): 633.

32 LAC, ArchiviaNet, *Diaries of William Lyon Mackenzie King, 1893–1950*, 8 December 1939.

33 *Canadian Transportation* 43 (February 1940): 103.

34 LAC, RG 24, box 3841, file 1017-10-22(1), copy of PC 511, 7 February 1940, authorizing and amending PC 337, 26 January 1940, and others to increase the shipbuilding program from twenty-five antisubmarine patrol vessels to an additional twenty-nine; ibid., copy of PC 438, 7 February 1940. See also Stacey, *Arms, Men and Governments*, 15–16; and Douglas et al., *No Higher Purpose*, 80. *Canadian Transportation* 43 (April 1940): 214, presents a breakdown of the costs by firm and ship type.

35 Smith et al., "History of BATM," 77.

36 Buxton, "British Warship Building and Repair," 86.

37 Tucker, *Naval Service of Canada*, vol. 2, 44; Douglas et al., *No Higher Purpose*, 82n237.

38 MMGLK, Canada Steamship Lines Fonds, 1993.002.011, 18.2, Edward Beatty to R.B. Thomson, 28 March 1940; Canada, House of Commons, *Debates*, 785, 14 June 1940, for Howe's speech regarding shipbuilding.

39 Tucker, *Naval Service of Canada*, vol. 2, 48–9.

40 Ibid., 47–8, 86; but see also Graves, "'Hell Boats' of the R.C.N."

41 LAC, MG 30 B121, box 2, files 2–5, "Notes by a naval architect, post-war shipbuilding, by W. Harold Milne, 1944."

42 LAC, MG 30 B121, box 1, files 1–6, memoranda describing the firm's history, "Prospects for 1949."

43 Donald Page's son, David, interview by author, Kingston, 22 July 2007.

44 Bothwell and Kilbourn, *C.D. Howe*, 123–4, 129. See also AO, F-4153, Floyd S. Chalmers Fonds, file 3-0-8, conversation with Wallace R. Campbell, 26 October 1939; ibid., file 2-0-50, clipping from *Financial Post*, 18 May 1940. Chalmers was the editor of the *Financial Post*, which had become the government's fiercest critic.

45 Granatstein, *Canada's War*, 82.

46 LAC, RG 28, box 29, file 48, "History of Naval Shipbuilding Branch."

47 Granatstein, *Canada's War*, 97–8.

48 See Bryce, *Canada and the Cost of World War II*, 52–83, for a full discussion of the problems involved.

49 Doughty, *Merchant Shipping and War*, 86–7, 113–14; Smith, *Conflict over Convoys*, 15–19.

50 Canada, House of Commons, *Debates*, 785–88, 14 June 1940.

51 Granatstein, *Canada's War*, 98; Bryce, *Canada and the Cost of World War II*, 63–4, 71–2.

52 Roberts, *C.D.*, 85, incorrectly attributes this survey to DMS officers.

53 For more on this, see Pritchard, "Fifty-Six Minesweepers and the Toronto Shipbuilding Company during the Second World War."

54 Roberts, *C.D.*, 105, cites NSARM, MG 2, [file 1503?], Angus L. Macdonald diary, 28 June and 17 July 1940.

55 Henderson, *Angus L. Macdonald*, 77, 85.

56 NSARM, MG 2, file 1503, Angus L. Macdonald diary, 17 July 1940; Granatstein, *Canada's War*, 105.

57 Pickersgill, *Mackenzie King Record*, 367; Henderson, *Angus L. Macdonald*, 90–149, provides a detailed study of the deteriorating relationship.

58 NSARM, MG 2, box 1520, file 867, lists of war orders placed in Nova Scotia, sent by Frank Ross to Macdonald over several dates (see, e.g., 23 November 1940); NSARM, MG 2, box 1524, file 1221, Macdonald to Premier A.S. Macmillan, 21 August and 25 September 1940, and Macdonald to D.B. Carswell, 7 September 1940; NSARM, MG 2, box 1524, file 1222(8), Macdonald to Macmillan, 24 March 1941, and no. 10A, Macdonald to Harold Connolly, 1 April 1941.

59 Milner, *North Atlantic Run*, 263 6; German, *Sea Is at Our Gates*, 147–8.

60 Milner, *U-boat Hunters*, 51.

61 Smith et al., "History of BATM," 42.

62 Ibid., 1.

63 Brief notices of the BATM are provided in Tucker, *Naval Service of Canada*, vol. 2, 53, 67–9; and Douglas and Greenhous, *Out of the Shadows*, 53–6.

64 *Canadian Transportation* 43 (July 1940): 390.

65 *Canadian Transportation* 43 (September 1940): 487, report on C.S. Power's review of naval construction for Macdonald.

66 Canada, House of Commons, *Debates*, 2114, 30 July 1940.

67 NSARM, MG 2, box 1524, file 1223(1), memorandum, Carswell to G.K. Sheils, deputy minister, DMS, 7 September 1940.

68 Douglas et al., *No Higher Purpose*, 144–5.

69 See LAC, RG 24, box 3841, file 1017-10-22(1), naval shipbuilding policy, with correspondence containing several illustrations of the British Admiralty attempting to change construction policies already agreed to and underway in Canada (e.g., A.L. Macdonald to O.D. Skelton, 3 October 1940). See also LAC, RG 28, box 77, file 1-1-166, ten 105-foot minesweepers for the BATM.

70 Smith et al., "History of BATM," 20.

71 QUA, Norman Lambert Papers, diary, September 1940.

72 LAC, RG 28, box 54, file 1-1-90, Frank Ross to Sheils, 20 December 1940, and Sheils to Heads of Branches, 28 December 1940.

73 Lane, *Ships for Victory*, figure 7, 64. For merchant shipping losses, see Tucker, *Naval Service of Canada*, vol. 2, 338–9, plate 9.

74 A valuable literature identifying the decline of British shipbuilding with domestic causes rather than with foreign competition may be found in Barnett, *Audit of War*, 107–24; and Johnman and Murphy, *British Shipbuilding and the State*. Smith, *Conflict over Convoys*, 5–27, offers a devastating, closely argued critique of British shipbuilding during the war.

75 Weir, "Truly Allied Undertaking"; Johnman and Murphy, "British Merchant Shipping Mission in the United States." The Liberty ship has given rise to a very extensive historical literature, some of it erroneous. For an accurate, detailed history of the British mission and the ship to which it gave birth, see Elphick, *Liberty: The Ships that Won the War*, 23–52.

76 Canada, House of Commons, *Debates*, 263, 20 November 1940. See also *Canadian Transportation* 43 (December 1940): 644.

77 Heal, *Great Fleet of Ships*, 38–9, erroneously gives twenty-six ships in the original contract and ignores the role of the DMS. Kennedy, *History of DMS*, vol. 2, 490, is the source of the figure twenty-six. In addition to the twenty ships contracted for in January and February, Clarence

Wallace signed a contract with the DMS for six more in April, just days before WMSL was incorporated.

78 Halford, *Unknown Navy*, 132.

79 Mansbridge, *Launching History*, 71; Marcil, *Tall Ships and Tankers*, 232.

80 See QUA, Norman Lambert Papers, Lambert diary, 19 and 23 November 1940, recording conversations with William Woodward and Harvey MacMillan, respectively; Lambert was president of the National Liberal Federation.

81 QUA, William Clifford Clark Papers, file N-2-5-4, memorandum by W.C. Clark, 31 October 1940.

82 Drushka, *H.R.: A Biography of H.R. MacMillan*.

83 Ibid., 101–2.

84 Plumptre, *Mobilizing Canada's Resources for War*, 33.

85 For a similar expression of opinion, see Hutchison, "Job Now Is to Make the War Effort Jell."

86 AO, F-4153, Floyd S. Chalmers Fonds, file 3-0-9, conversation with MacMillan, Toronto, 15 October 1940. MacMillan was not alone. According to Wallace Campbell (ibid., file 3-0-9, conversation, 21 June 1940), head of another large industrial enterprise, Howe's associates were second-raters; Woodward was nothing more than a ribbon-cutting clerk.

87 See LAC, RG 19, box 661, file 183-3, pt 1, for a copy of PC 6601 establishing the board.

88 AO, F-4153, Floyd S. Chalmers Fonds, file 3-0-9, conversation with MacMillan, 18 November 1940; QUA, Norman Lambert Papers, Lambert diary, 23 November 1940, records a conversation with MacMillan. See also, Hutchison, "Job Now Is to Make the War Effort Jell."

89 AO, F-4153, Floyd S. Chalmers Fonds, file 3-0-9, conversation with MacMillan, 15 December 1940. See also, QUA, Norman Lambert Papers, Lambert diary, 26 December 1940, regarding conversation with MacMillan.

90 See QUA, William Clifford Clark Papers, file 2-5-41, for agendas and minutes of the board's meetings, which reveal the impact of the East Coast problems on the board's activities.

91 For more on this, see the pro-Howe account in Bothwell and Kilbourn, *C.D. Howe*, 144–9.

92 Drushka, *H.R.: A Biography of H.R. MacMillan*, 211, denies MacMillan is the villain in the Howe-MacMillan contretemps. MacMillan later claimed not to understand many references to himself in Howe's speech to the House of Commons of 26 February 1941, nor had he seen Bruce Hutchison's recent article, which purported to be a copy of his recommendations to the government. He had heard rumours that he did not understand until about 7 or 8 March, when Hutchison came to him and apologized for the article. The reporter claimed he had tried and failed to get an interview with MacMillan and then cooked up some views purporting to be MacMillan's and written them for the *Vancouver Sun*. Someone at the *Sun* had "jazzed" the article by assigning the views more directly to MacMillan. MacMillan claimed he did not see the article with a two-column picture of himself until Hutchison showed it to him. AO, F-4153, Floyd S. Chalmers Fonds, file 3-0-10, memo: conversation with H.R. MacMillan, 5 April 1940.

93 Drushka, *H.R.: A Biography of H.R. MacMillan*, 211–20, provides the fullest account of the controversy, but he is less satisfactory concerning the remainder of MacMillan's wartime career. Mackay, *Empire of Wood*, 142, not only ignores MacMillan's wartime career but also manages to get wrong the name of the Crown corporation he ran.

94 QUA, William Clifford Clark Papers, file N-2-5-41, memorandum by Clark, 7 March 1941; draft, MacMillan to Howe, 10 March 1941, and minutes of the war requirements board, 20 March 1941.

95 QUA, Norman Lambert Papers, Lambert diary, 4 and 26 February 1940.

96 AO, F-4153, Floyd S. Chalmers Fonds, file 3-0-10, memorandum on MacMillan, 5 April 1941.

97 Ibid., file 3-0-11, memo to self regarding MacMillan, whom Chalmers interviewed on 24 March 1941.

98 Gibson and Robertson, eds, *Ottawa at War: The Grant Dexter Memoranda*, 138. Grant Dexter also reported T.A. Crerar's claim that McLarty had been so drunk twice the previous week that he was unable to rise in the House of Commons to answer questions.

99 LAC, RG 28, box 528, file 66-1, Letters Patent, 4 April 1941.

100 UBCSC, H.R. MacMillan Papers, box 100, file 16, MacMillan to Howe, 3 May 1941, acknowledging Howe's letter of 28 April accepting his resignation.

101 Gibson and Robertson, eds, *Ottawa at War*, 139.

102 Plumptre, *Mobilizing Canada's Resources for War*, 33–4. Seven controllers were established for seven industries: steel, oil, metals, timber, machine tools, power, and shipbuilding and repair. Their powers were very great and derived from the War Measures Act, on the books since the First World War, the Department of Munitions and Supply Act, and the National Resources Mobilization Act of June 1940 (4 Geo. VI, 1940, ch. 3).

103 Tucker, *Naval Service of Canada*, vol. 2, 126–7.

104 Lane, *Ships for Victory*, 43.

105 LAC, RG 2 7C, vol. 3 (reel 11789), Cabinet War Committee minutes, 5 March 1941, and accompanying documents; ibid., Carswell to Howe, 20 February 1941; ibid., K.S. MacLachlan, acting deputy minister for naval services, to secretary of the Wartime Requirements Board, 27 February 1941; and ibid., R.A.C. Henry, acting chairman, Wartime Requirements Board, to Howe, 27 February 1941.

106 Canada, House of Commons, *Debates*, 1451, 11 March 1941, and 1630, 18 March 1941.

107 Granatstein, *Canada's War*, 137–8.

108 See Cuff and Granatstein, *Ties that Bind*, 69–92, for an important revisionist view of the declaration and negotiations leading to it. See also Bryce, *Canada and the Cost of World War II*, 85–116.

109 Canada, House of Commons, *Debates*, 1356, 10 March 1940.

110 Halford, *Unknown Navy*, 134.

111 Behrens, *Merchant Shipping and the Demands of War*, 384. Sawyer and Mitchell, *Oceans, the Forts and the Parks*, 21–2, lists the names, the dates of delivery, and the fates of ninety ships; twenty-five were sunk during the war.

112 UBCSC, H.R. MacMillan Papers, box 100, file 17, MacMillan to Sheils, deputy minister, DMS, 24 April 1941.

113 H.T. Mitchell Papers, Mitchell to wife, 3 and 8 April 1941.

114 AO, F-4153, Floyd S. Chalmers Fonds, file 3-0-10, interview with E.P. Taylor, 5 April 1941, with penciled marginalia regarding MacMillan; ibid., conversation with MacMillan, 5 April 1941.

115 Newman, *Canadian Establishment*, 244, 423.

116 Mansbridge, *Launching History*, 72.

117 J.S. Marshall and Co. Ltd, *History of Burrard Dry Dock Company*, vol. 3, 163–4.

118 Kennedy, *History of DMS*, vol. 1, 491. See *CS&MEN* 13, no. 3 (October 1942): 34, for an organizational chart of Wartime Merchant Shipping Limited.

119 LAC, RG 58, series C-1, box 252, files 16 and 17, audit of Wartime Merchant Shipping Limited accounts.

120 *Canadian Transportation* 45 (April 1941): 219; (May 1941): 277; (June 1941): 355.

121 LAC, RG 28, box 77, file 1-1-166, D.A. Clarke to Howe, 13 March 1942.

122 MMGLK, German and Milne Papers, 1989.0044.0005.008, W.H. Milne to Montreal Board of Trade, 4 June 1941; LAC, MG 30 B121, notice of W. Harold Milne Fonds.

123 Douglas et al., *No Higher Purpose*, 315.

124 UBCSC, H.R. MacMillan Papers, box 100, file 16, memorandum, MacMillan to Howe, 5 July 1941.

125 Douglas et al., *No Higher Purpose*, 315–16. See also LAC, RG 28, box 3844, file 1017-10-38, for relations between the director general of shipbuilding and Wartime Merchant Shipping Limited regarding naval shipbuilding between July and September.

126 H.T. Mitchell Papers, Mitchell to wife, 7 September 1941.

127 Ibid., Mitchell to wife, 21 September 1941.

128 LAC, RG 24, box 3840, file NNS 1017-10-38(1), president, WMSL, to Admiral Sheridan, BATM, 29 September 1941. The official history of naval operations contains two useful sections on shipbuilding (Douglas et al., *No Higher Purpose*, 71–82, 307–19), but they were written without reference to the Canadian shipbuilding industry, the lack of technical expertise in the RCN, and the navy's dependence upon British officers with the BATM. Correctly identifying Wartime Merchant Shipping Limited in one place (309), the text refers mistakenly (315, 316) to a nonexistent company, Wartime Shipping Limited, which may be confused with Wartime Shipbuilding Limited, the 1944 successor Crown corporation to Wartime Merchant Shipping Limited. The same section also refers (309) mistakenly to the Defence Requirements Board rather than the War Requirements Board.

129 LAC, RG 28, box 77, file 1-1-166, John A. Marsh to D.A. Clarke, 15 July 1941.

130 *Canadian Transportation* 45 (December 1941): 697. See also Bellamy, *Profiting the Crown*, 50.

131 Newman, *Canadian Establishment*, 322n, 415, gives a misleading story about how Ambridge replaced Clarke in 1943, ignoring the fact that Ambridge served under Clarke for nearly two years before succeeding him. Bellamy, *Profiting the Crown*, 40, 69, claims Ambridge was replaced in February 1942 upon being named a director of Polymer Corporation, but there was no need for him to resign from the shipbuilding branch on being made a director of a Crown corporation. In 1945 Ambridge assumed the presidency of Polymer Corporation.

132 LAC, RG 28, box 540, file 77-1, letters patent of Trafalgar Shipbuilding Company Limited. See also LAC, RG 28, box 20, "History of Trafalgar Shipbuilding Company," 30 September 1943, which was not included in Kennedy, *History of DMS*.

133 AO, F-4153, Floyd S. Chalmers Fonds, file 2-0-89, memorandum regarding MacMillan, 5 February 1942.

134 LAC, RG 28, box 29, "Report on Canadian Shipbuilding, July 6 1944."

135 See Pritchard, "Fifty-Six Minesweepers," for details.

136 LAC, RG 28, box 77, file 1-1-166, Clark to Howe, 13 March 1942.

137 LAC, RG 58, series C-1, box 252, file 14, Wartime Merchant Shipping Ltd, Salaries of Officers and Senior Employees in force to 31 March 1943.

138 Kennedy, *History of DMS*, vol. 1, 504, is the soul of discretion, noting only that Redfern was a director and vice president of WMSL from 6 May to 10 July 1942. According to MacMillan (UBCSC, H.R. MacMillan Papers, box 100, file 17, MacMillan to J.P. Pettigrew, 2 April 1942), Redfern joined WMSL as chief executive assistant to carry on Cowie's work. For more on Redfern, see Greene, ed., *Who's Who in Canada, 1943–44*, 918.

139 H.T. Mitchell Papers, Mitchell to wife, 24 and 27 June and 11 July 1942.

140 LAC, RG 28, box 77, file 1-1-166, Shipbuilding branch organization by A.P. Low, 20 July 1942; LAC, RG 28, box 181, survey of shipbuilding branch, 22 July 1942, and Low to Sheils, deputy minister, DMS, 22 July 1942.

141 See Kennedy, *History of* DMS, vol. 1, 498–501, for more detailed description of the organization of the four departments.

142 LAC, RG 28, box 86, file 1-1-218, memorandum, Angus McGugan, director of production, and James Muirhead to Russell Yuill, 5 January 1944; ibid., J.O. Meyers to Muirhead, 1 November 1944.

143 Tucker, *Naval Service of Canada*, vol. 2, 134.

144 Stephens, "Reminiscences," 24; Brown, *Century of Naval Construction*, 350–1.

145 Tucker, *Naval Service of Canada*, vol. 2, 143.

146 LAC, RG 24, box 3842, file 1017-10-22(2), Engineer Captain G.L. Stephens, CNEC, to CNS, 15 April 1942; ibid., Clarke to secretary of the naval board, 13 April 1942; ibid., copy of E.P. Taylor, president, British Supply Council, to Thomas B. McCabe, deputy administrator, office of lend-lease administration, 21 March 1942.

147 LAC, RG 24, box 3841, file 1017-10-22(1), A.L. Macdonald to Treasury Board, 17 February 1942.

148 Ibid., A.L. Macdonald to Treasury Board, 19 August 1942.

149 LAC, RG 24, box 3842, file 1017-10-22(22), Clarke to Captain Stephens, 24 November 1942.

150 Ibid., target schedules from the DMS, technical division, 1 December 1942.

151 "Components" was a generic term used by administrators of the shipbuilding programs and appears frequently in government documents. Shipbuilders do not employ the term, referring normally to main engines, auxiliary machinery, and parts.

152 LAC, MG 30 B121, box 1, H.R. Carlson, works manager, Toronto Shipbuilding Limited, to Clarke, 9 May 1943; LAC, RG 28, box 181, survey of shipbuilding branch, DMS, 22 July 1942.

153 Sarty, "Admiral Percy W. Nelles," 87–8.

154 LAC, RG 24, box 3842, file 1017-10-22(2), naval message from British Admiralty Delegation to CNS, 7/8/1942.

155 Milner, *North Atlantic Run*, 98–9, 106, 168–9; Douglas et al., *No Higher Purpose*, 407–14; Fisher, "'We'll Get Our Own.'"

156 See Douglas et al., *No Higher Purpose*, 429–76, for a complete account of what has come to be called the Battle of the St Lawrence. See also Hadley, *U-Boats against Canada*, 112–43.

157 LAC, RG 2 7c, vol. 3 (reel C-4875), minutes of merchant shipbuilding program, additional construction, 21 and 28 July 1943. See also LAC, ArchiviaNet, *Diaries of William Lyon Mackenzie King, 1893–1950*, 28 July 1941; and Stacey, *Men, Arms and Governments*, 410.

158 LAC, RG 24, series D-1-b, box 3842, file 1017-10-22, pt 3, E.S. Brand to minister and others, 10 July 1943; LAC, RG 28, box 162, file 3-S-15, memorandum, Howe to H.J. Carmichael, 15 December 1943.

159 Hadley, *U-Boats against Canada*, 168, 185; Smith et al., "History of BATM," 84–5.

160 Tucker, *Naval Service of Canada*, vol. 2, 80–1.

161 LAC, RG 28, box 129, file 3-C-21, minutes of the combined Canada-UK-US committee, 12 August 1943.

162 LAC, RG 2 7c, vol. 13 (reel C-4875), Cabinet War Committee minutes, 8 September 1942; Stacey, *Arms, Men and Governments*, 410.

163 UBCSC, H.R. MacMillan Papers, box 100, file 16, C.L. Dewar, assistant to president of WMSL, to Howe, 22 September 1943.

164 LAC, RG 28, box 78, file 1-1-166, minutes of board of directors of WMSL, 28 October 1943.

165 Tucker, *Naval Service of Canada*, vol. 2, 84.

166 LAC, RG 28, box 162, file 3-S-15, memorandum from Howe to Carmichael, 15 December 1943; ibid., minutes of the first meeting of the shipbuilding coordination committee, 31 December 1943; *CS&MEN* 15, no. 5 (December 1943): 75.

167 LAC, RG 28, box 162, file 3-S-15.

168 LAC, RG 28, box 528, file 66-1, supplementary letters patent, 15 January 1944. Douglas et al., *No Higher Purpose*, 315, 316, confuses the two Crown corporations involved.

169 LAC, RG 28, box 256, file 196-13-4, DMS press release, 20 January 1944.

170 Smith et al., "History of BATM," 52.

171 LAC, MG 27 III B20, box 41, file S-9-25, A.C. McKim to Howe, 22 May 1944.

172 LAC, RG 28, box 29, file 98, "History of Naval Shipbuilding Branch."

173 Canada, DMS, *Industrial Front*, vol. 1, 154.

CHAPTER THREE

1 Forbes, "Consolidating Disparity," is the basis for most historical accounts of shipbuilding in the Maritimes during the war. See, for example, Miller, "The 1940s"; and Zimmerman, *Great Naval Battle of Ottawa*, 91.

2 NSARM, MG 2, vol. 1524, file 1222, no. 6, "Nova Scotia Shipbuilding," anonymous report (internal evidence indicates that the probable author was D.B. Carswell, who prepared it in March 1941).

3 New Brunswick Provincial Archives, corporate records of St John Dry Dock and Shipbuilding Company.

4 CVA, Add. Mss. 902, box 38, file 12, "Cover Story–Frank Ross," *Western Business and Industry*, December 1955, 24–6.

5 Taylor, "Merchant of Death in the Peaceable Kingdom," 234–5.

6 CVA, Add. Mss. 902, box 38, file 13, clippings.

7 Ibid., file 3, "The Life Story of Frank Mackenzie Ross by Ishbel Ross," typescript; ibid., "Anatomy of Success," *Business and Financial Chronicle*, December 1965, 39–41. See also ibid., clipping from *Vancouver News Herald*, 31 March 1945.

8 See Settle, "Halifax Shipyards, 1918–1978," 37–8.

9 Bliss, *Northern Enterprise*, 388.

10 See Johnman and Murphy, *British Shipbuilding and the State*.

11 Bliss, *Northern Enterprise*, 405.

12 These were W.E. Vaughan, later Vaughan Shipbuilding Company; J.D. Irving Limited, later Irving Shipyards Limited; and McMulkin and Son and Ashley Colter. E.A. Chappel and Palmer and Williams Company Limited were on Prince Edward Island.

13 CTA, John Inglis Company Fonds, box 107, Dun and Bradstreet report, 10 May 1940.

14 *Labour Gazette* 43 (September 1943): 1249; *Halifax Herald*, 20 August 1943.

15 LAC, RG 28, box 29, "Contracts for Ships, Purchases and Construction."

16 Marcil, *Tall Ships and Tankers*, 30–3, 44.

17 Ibid., 138–41.

18 Ibid., 187–200, 240.

19 *CS&MEN* 15, no. 6 (January 1944), reprinted in *L'Écho maritime* (February 1944): 9–10.

20 See Marcil, *Tall Ships and Tankers*, 245–50, for further details.

21 See Scott, *Vickers, a History*, 58–9, for further details.

22 This and the next paragraph are indebted to Taylor, "Merchant of Death in the Peaceable Kingdom," 234–5.

23 Scott, *Vickers, a History*, 168.

24 Canadian Vickers Limited, *Annual Report for Year Ending February 2, 1940*.

25 Roberts and Tunnel, eds, *Canadian Who's Who, 1936–1937*, 603; Boas, *Canada in World War II: Post-War Possibilities*, 507; *Canadian Transportation* 44 (April 1941): 215.

26 Roberts and Tunnel, eds, *Canadian Who's Who, 1938–1939*, 201; Greene, ed., *Who's Who in Canada, 1945–46*, 1077.

27 "Wolvin Buys Vickers Control," *Financial Post*, 19 August 1944.

28 SHPS, Objois, "Répertoire numérique du fonds Marine Industries Limited, série 2 division navale, sous-série 1, 1926–1939," typescript, 1.

29 "Historique de la famille Simard," *L'Écho de la marine* 3, no. 28 (1944): 1; Roberts and Tunnel, eds, *Canadian Who's Who, 1938–1939*, 615.

30 According to Walter Lewis and Rick Neilson, Simard acquired the bankrupt ship-salvage firm, whose assets were estimated to be worth more than $1 million in 1928, from Montreal Trust Company for a paltry $150,000 in cash. The firm had defaulted on its bond payments, and the trust company was desperate to salvage its investment.

31 CTA, John Inglis Company Fonds, box 107, Marine Industries Limited 1940, Dun and Bradstreet report, 24 January 1940; Roberts and Tunnel, eds, *Canadian Who's Who, 1938–1939*, 615.

32 QUA, Norman Lambert Papers, Lambert diary, 6 February 1937; Steven, "Canada's Shipyards Are Helping to 'Finish the Job'," 39–40; Newman, *Canadian Establishment*, 195.

33 For more, see Baird, *Under Tow*, 240, 243–6.

34 Some idea of the breadth of services they offered to the maritime business world may be found in Lambert and German, *Floating Equipment Designed by Lambert and German*.

35 *CS&MEN* 14, no. 3 (October 1942): 68.

36 Marcil, *Tall Ships and Tankers*, 221, 228.

37 Eileen Reid Marcil Papers, note of a conversation with Bruce Morton, 15 July 1990; "First Vessel Is Dry-Docked Here," *Quebec Telegraph*, 29 April 1929.

38 MacNeish, "Shipyard Layout at Morton's," 11–13.

39 Marcil, *Tall Ships and Tankers*, 201, 240.

40 Ibid., 283.

41 Bélanger, *La Construction navale à Saint Laurent, Ile d'Orléans*, 111–18.

42 Marcil, *Tall Ships and Tankers*, 203, 239, 242.

43 Miller, "Teeming with Enterprise," 25.

44 Wolvin's biography in *Canadian Transportation* 47 (October 1944): 571.

45 Roberts and Tunnel, eds, *Who's Who in Canada, 1936–1937*, 1198.

46 Collard, *Passage to the Sea*, 100.

47 Ibid., 111.

48 Miller, "Teeming with Enterprise," 25.

49 Wright, *Freshwater Whales*, 169–70.

50 Ibid., 177–8.

51 Steven, "Great Lakes Yard Produces Naval Craft," 47–8; *SR&SB* 28, no. 3 (March 1945): 32–3.

52 See Gillham, *Ships of Collingwood*, 1–2, for the early history of Collingwood shipbuilding.

53 QUA, Canada Steamship Lines Ltd, box 125, Collingwood Shipyards Ltd minute book, 16.

54 International Press, *Who's Who in Canada, 1917–1918*, 445, lists Smith as a director of Grey and Bruce Loan Company and of Canada Steamship Lines and as president of Collingwood Shipbuilding Company, Northern Navigation Company Limited, North American Furniture Company Limited, and Owen Sound Chair Company. The 1927 edition of the same book (page 1311) also lists him as president of Port Arthur Shipbuilding Company.

55 See *Kingston Daily Standard*, 24 March 1921.

56 MMGLK, Collingwood Shipbuilding Company Collection, 1992.0168.0026, G.M. Waite to Collingwood Shipyards, 10 June 1932; ibid., 1992.0168.0026, Shareholders return of Kingston Shipbuilding Co. Ltd, January 1936, which reveals that Horace Smith owned 11,074 shares and that his late wife's estate held 4,524 shares.

57 QUA, Canada Steamship Lines Ltd, box 125, Collingwood Shipyards Ltd minute book [1937], letters patent; ibid., pages 50, 59, 61, dated 13 March 1937.

58 QUA, Canada Steamship Lines Ltd, box 109, Kingston Shipbuilding Co. minute book no. 2, 89–91.

59 Ibid., 104.

60 Ibid., 121; QUA, Canada Steamship Lines Ltd, box 125, Collingwood Shipyards Ltd minute book, 54.

61 QUA, Canada Steamship Lines Ltd, box 109, Kingston Shipbuilding Co. minute book no. 2, 199. See also CS&MEN 15, no. 10 (May 1944): 64; and "Wolvin Buys Vickers Control," Financial Post, 19 August 1944.

62 MMGLK, Collingwood Shipbuilding Company Collection, 1992.0168.0026, share-transfer pages; Canadian Transportation 47 (December 1944): 682. This should correct the error in Collard, Passage to the Sea, 189, which states that the reorganized company appeared at the beginning rather than at the end of the war.

63 Wolvin obituary, Montreal Gazette, 9 April 1945; Canadian Transportation 48 (May 1945): 291.

64 QUA, Canada Steamship Lines Ltd, box 109, Kingston Shipbuilding Co. Ltd minute book no. 2, entry for 9 November 1944, contains the minutes of a meeting of the directors of Canadian Shipbuilding and Engineering Limited, who were the same as for Kingston Shipbuilding Company. Collard, Passage to the Sea, 189, is unreliable; he mistakenly has Wolvin acquiring all four yards during the 1930s and creating Canadian Shipbuilding and Engineering Limited at the beginning of the war.

65 NVMA, Fonds 27, Burrard Dry Dock Clippings, vol. 4, no. 487, J.H. Hamilton in Vancouver Daily Province, 28 September 1939.

66 For a brief history of early dry-dock construction in British Columbia, see Mansbridge, Launching History, 45–52; and Taylor, Shipyards of British Columbia, 10–11.

67 Mansbridge, Launching History, 86.

68 For shares, see UBCSC, Trade Union Research Bureau Records, box 15, file 5, F.H. Dyke, secretary-treasurer, BISUC, to G.S. Culane, 4 May 1944.

69 DHH, Series 30: 8000, 75/270, interview by Lt Kerr with [Herbert S.] Hammill, president, VMD, 22 May 1945.

70 MMBC, Miscellaneous re: Victoria Machinery Depot Ltd, "One hundred year history of Victoria Machinery Depot," typescript.

71 Ibid.; Victoria Machinery Depot, The Convoy 4, no. 2 (February 1945): 1–3.

72 Taylor, Shipyards of British Columbia, 68.

73 CS&MEN 15, no. 4 (November 1943): 78.

74 For the early history of Yarrows from 1921 to 1939, see J.S. Marshall and Co. Ltd, History of Yarrows Limited, vol. 2, chs 3 and 4.

75 Drent, "Labour and the Unions in a Wartime Essential Industry," 62n10, citing Victoria Times, 1 December 1941.

76 Tucker, Naval Service of Canada, vol. 2, 41, 504-5, 506-7; LAC, RG 28, box 21, "Contracts for ships and small boats."

77 See Mansbridge, Launching History, 1–40, for the brief history of Alfred Wallace's early years.

78 Ibid., 66–7.
79 PC 661, 20 February 1940; PC 842, 28 February 1940; Mansbridge, *Launching History*, 70.
80 Ibid., 72.
81 Ibid., 77.
82 *CS&MEN* 13, no. 11 (June 1942): 64.
83 Taylor, *Shipyards of British Columbia*, 99–100, 148–9.
84 BCARS, GR 1583, 986-41, incorporation no. 441.
85 Bothwell and Kilbourn, *C.D. Howe*, 96, 109.
86 MacPherson and Burgess, *Ships of Canada's Naval Forces, 1910–1993*, 217–18. See also PC 7361, 20 September 1941, amending PC 3590 and PC 4463 by changing the authorizing body from the CNR to Grand Truck Pacific Development Company Limited of Montreal.
87 Some confusion persists as to how many ships were built at Prince Rupert. Taylor, *Shipyards of British Columbia*, 107, 116, gives ten and twelve on different pages, and Mackay, *People's Railway*, 136, gives eleven. The correct number is thirteen.
88 BCARS, GR 1583, incorporation no. 10387.
89 LAC, RG 28, box 29, "Contracts for ships and small boats – British Columbia."
90 Ibid; DHH, Series 30: 8000, 75/270, interview by Lt Kerr with Mr Moran, superintendent and plant manager, Falconer Marine Industries Limited, 22 May 1945.
91 LAC, RG 28, box 536, file 75-A-3, agreement between the Department of Munitions and Supply and Armstrong and Falconer, 9 July 1943.
92 Vancouver Sun, *Industrial British Columbia, 1945*.

CHAPTER FOUR

1 Canada, Department of Reconstruction and Supply, *Encouragement to Industrial Expansion in Canada*, 13.
2 Canada, DMS, *Report on the Government-Financed Expansion of Industrial Capacity in Canada*, 2.
3 Canada, Department of Reconstruction and Supply, *Disposal and Peacetime Use of Crown Plant Buildings*, 11.
4 LAC, RG 2, PC 4217, 27 August 1940; NVMA, Fonds 27, box 329, War Contracts Depreciation Board file 1944.
5 Bothwell and Kilbourn, *C.D. Howe*, 161.
6 NVMA, Fonds 27, box 329, War Contracts Depreciation Board file, containing several certificates.
7 Bothwell and Kilbourn, *C.D. Howe*, 176, citing Canada, Department of Reconstruction and Supply, *Encouragement to Industrial Expansion*, 21.
8 Canada, Department of Reconstruction and Supply, *Encouragement to Industrial Expansion*, 22, 27–8, 43, 75.
9 Kennedy, *History of the Department of Munitions and Supply* (hereafter *History of DMS*), vol. 2, 493.
10 LAC, RG 28, box 7, "A Brief History of Wartime Merchant Shipping Ltd., Montreal, December 31, 1943, with an Addendum on Wartime Shipbuilding Ltd., January 1944–February 1947" (hereafter "Brief History of WMSL"), typescript, 71.
11 Carter, ed., *Who's Who in British Columbia (Registered), 1944-45-46*, 35; McLaren and Jensen, *Ships of Steel*, 50.

12 LAC, RG 2, PC 842, 28 February 1940; Tucker, *Naval Service of Canada*, vol. 2, 43; Smith et al., "History of the British Admiralty Technical Mission in Canada" (hereafter "History of BATM"), 78.

13 Mansbridge, *Launching History*, 76.

14 LAC, RG 2, PC 7361, 20 September 1940, amending the original contract, dated 21 May 1940, authorizing the work to be undertaken by Grand Truck Pacific Development Company Limited.

15 MMGLK, Canada Steamship Lines Fonds, 1993.0002.0016, letters patent, 30 August 1937, and secretary, CSL, to J.J. Ashworth, 14 February 1940; ibid., 1993.0002.0010, T.R. Enderby to H.A. Cresswell, 1939; Gillham, *Ships of Collingwood*, 60–2.

16 MMGLK, Canada Steamship Lines Fonds, 1993.0002.0016, Midland Shipbuilding Co., R.B. Thomson, secretary, CSL, to Cresswell, 14 February 1940; ibid., 1993.0002.0010, statement of operating results for 1927 to 1938.

17 Ibid., 1993.0002.0010, William Coverdale, president, CSL, to R.B. Thomson, 17 February 1940; QUA, Canada Steamship Lines Ltd, box 109, Kingston Shipbuilding Company Ltd, minute book no. 2, 136.

18 QUA, ibid., 142.

19 MMGKL, Canada Steamship Lines Fonds, 1993.0002.0016, [Midland] *Free Press* [*Herald*], 30 October 1940.

20 NSARM, MG 2, PC 1,524/1,223/4, 5, 6, and 19, R.M. Wolvin to A.L. Macdonald, 30 September and 18 October 1940; Macdonald to Wolvin, 7 October 1940; and Macdonald to Dr Alex Johnston, 4 October 1940.

21 Tucker, *Naval Service of Canada*, vol. 2, 507–8; Sweeting and Gillham, *Ships of Midland*, 56–8.

22 LAC, RG 28, box 317, file 4-4-218, formal agreement, 8 July 1941.

23 DHH, Series 30: 8000, 75/270, interview by Lt Kerr with Herbert Whitmill, manager, Midland Shipyard Ltd, 10 May 1945; MMGLK, German and Milne Papers, 1989.0044.0005.5, Herbert Whitmill, superintendent, to Walter Lambert, German and Milne, 28 October 1941.

24 DHH, Series 30: 8000, 75/270, interview by Lt Kerr with Herbert Whitmill, manager, Midland Shipyard Ltd, 10 May 1945; Sweeting and Gillham, *Ships of Midland*, 68–75.

25 Tucker, *Naval Service of Canada*, vol. 2, 43.

26 "He Won His Fortune by Pick and Shovel," *Toronto Star Weekly*, 31 August 1929.

27 Moir, "Toronto's Shipbuilding Industry," 95.

28 LAC, RG 117, box 589, file CZ 216, affidavit of claim, 25 January 1949.

29 Kluckner, *Toronto: The Way It Was*, 307 and accompanying photograph.

30 LAC, RG 18, box 3,563, file C11-19-2-3, vol. 1, internment orders for Vincenzo Franceschini, 10 June 1940, and his brother Leonard, 30 August 1940.

31 Cook, "Canadian Freedom in Wartime, 1935–1945," 37–53.

32 Saywell, *"Just Call Me Mitch,"* 174, 446; McKenty, *Mitch Hepburn*, 183.

33 Principe, "A Tangled Knot," 28.

34 LAC, RG 28, box 20, C.A. Geoffrion, "History of the Toronto Shipbuilding Company" (draft), 1; Smith et al., "History of BATM," 78.

35 LAC, RG 18, box 3,563, file C11-19-2-3, vol. 4; LAC, RG 18, box 3,569, record of internment hearings, 1939–45.

36 Editorial, *Toronto Globe and Mail*, 19 December 1945.

37 LAC, RG 117, box 1,928, file 2,861, pt 1.1, clipping from the *Montreal Gazette*, 24 June 1941.

38 In Kennedy, *History of DMS*, vol. 2, 454–5, the official history of Toronto Shipbuilding Company is two reticent pages. For more, see LAC, RG 28, box 20, Geoffrion, "History of Toronto

Shipbuilding Co." (draft), 2–3; and LAC, RG 28, box 256, file 196-13-14, press release, DMS, 21 October 1941.

39 LAC, RG 28, box 540, file 83-1, "Agreement to Purchase Dufferin Shipbuilding Co. from Dufferin Paving and Crushed Stone Ltd., 20 October 1941."

40 For more on wartime Crown corporations, see Borins, "World War II Crown Corporations," 447–75.

41 LAC, RG 28, box 20, Geoffrion, "History of Toronto Shipbuilding Co." (draft).

42 DHH, Series 30: 8000, 75/270, interview by Lt Kerr with Russ Cornell, production manager, Redfern Construction Co., Shipbuilding Branch, 4 May 1945.

43 Kennedy, *History of DMS*, vol. 1, 454–5.

44 *Canadian Transportation* 45 (1942): 237.

45 LAC, RG 28, box 20, Geoffrion, "History of Toronto Shipbuilding Co.," (draft), 5.

46 Canada, House of Commons, *Debates*, 760, C.D. Howe, 22 February 1944.

47 LAC, RG 28, box 29, file 5 of 12, Carswell to J.deN. Kennedy, 24 October 1947, in which Desmond Clarke is blamed for the "faux pas."

48 For more on Gordon Leitch, see Macht, *First 50 Years*, 15–49.

49 *CS&MEN* 14, no. 5 (December 1942): 70; *CS&MEN* 14, no. 9 (April 1943): 74.

50 *CS&MEN* 15, no. 10 (May 1944): 64; DHH, Series 30: 8000, 75/270, interview by Lt Kerr with Mr [Gordon F.] McDougall, general manager, Port Arthur Shipbuilding Co., 14 May 1945.

51 Canada, DMS, *Report on the Government-Financed Expansion of Industrial Capacity*, 18.

52 LAC, RG 28, box 521, file 51-T-11, correspondence and contracts authorizing capital expenditures by Toronto Shipbuilding Limited and Redfern Construction, 1943–44; Tucker, *Naval Service of Canada*, vol. 2, 74.

53 DHH, Series 30: 8000, 75/270, interview by Lt Kerr with Cornell, 4 May 1945.

54 Canada, House of Commons, *Debates*, 1698, C.D. Howe, 21 March 1944. In January 1944 Wartime Shipbuilding Limited came into existence as the successor to Wartime Merchant Shipping Limited; this, too, was part of the government's reorganization of the country's shipbuilding program.

55 For more on Toronto Shipbuilding Company, see Pritchard, "Fifty-Six Minesweepers and the Toronto Shipbuilding Company during the Second World War."

56 See note 54.

57 Steven, "Great Lakes Yard Produces Naval Craft," 47–8.

58 Marcil, *Tall Ships and Tankers*, 245. For additional details, see also ibid. 258–61; Steven, "Shipbuilders of the St. Lawrence"; and *L'Écho maritime* (February 1944): 10.

59 For details of the navy's developing interest in MTBs, see Graves, "'Hell Boats' of the R.C.N."

60 Rance, *Fast Boats and Flying Boats*, 110, 115.

61 Ibid., 120–1.

62 Ibid., 125–30.

63 Ibid., 40; Graves, "'Hell Boats,'" 40.

64 Rance, *Fast Boats and Flying Boats*, 127.

65 Ibid., 111.

66 See "TM-22-class MTB" at http://www.netherlandsnavy.nl.

67 Rance, *Fast Boats and Flying Boats*, 125–30.

68 Sutton Jr, "Scott-Paine's Canadian MTBs," 3.

69 Quoted in Rance, *Fast Boats and Flying Boats*, 127–8.

70 For details, see ibid., 154–55; and Graves, "'Hell Boats,'" 41–2.

71 Rance, *Fast Boats and Flying Boats*, 155–6.

72 http://www.netherlandnavy.nl. The Dutch motor topedo boats TM-32, TM-35, and TM-37 were commissioned as PT-368, PT-369, and PT-371.

73 Rance, *Fast Boats and Flying Boats*, 151, 162, 188.

74 LAC, MG 30 B121, box 1, W.H. Milne to D.A. Clarke, 11 March 1942.

75 LAC, RG 24, box 3,842, file 1017-10-22 (2), "Naval Construction Programme, 1942–1943–1944," prepared by the Technical Division, Shipbuilding Branch, DMS, 20 August 1942, sent to the Navy Board by Harold Milne, 16 September 1942; Tucker, *Naval Service of Canada*, vol. 2, 74.

76 DHH, Series 30: 8000, 75/270, interview at Esquimalt by Lt Kerr with Cdr Annandale, RCN, former resident naval overseer (RNO) at Quebec, 23 May 1945.

77 Eileen Reid Marcil Papers, Carl Whyte to Marcil, 17 May 1992.

78 Marcil, *Tall Ships and Tankers*, 241.

79 According to Commander Annandale, Quebec Shipbuilding Limited was created because the smaller companies found financing the subcontracts too heavy a burden; see DHH, Series 30: 8000, 75/270, interview by Lt Kerr with Cdr Annandale, 23 May 1945.

80 On Gagnon's connection to Howe, see Bothwell and Kilbourn, *C.D. Howe*, 109.

81 Editorial, *CS&MEN* 15, no. 6 (January 1944): 21.

82 LAC, RG 28, box 32, file 104, H.L. Clifford, general manager, to Howe, 14 September 1943.

83 Marcil, *Tall Ships and Tankers*, 241.

84 LAC, RG 28, box 32, "History of Quebec Shipyards" (draft), and Kennedy, *History of DMS*, vol. 1, 404–5, indicate that in addition, ten 500-ton C-type China coasters were built, but all of these were completed in 1946.

85 *Canadian Transportation* 45 (July 1942): 430; Kennedy, *History of DMS*, vol. 1, 491.

86 *Down Our Ways*, no. 15 (15 February 1943).

87 BCARS, GR 1583, box 84-35-356, incorporation no. 17,421, West Coast Shipbuilders Ltd, return of shares allotted, 28 May 1941.

88 Taylor, *Shipyards of British Columbia*, 112.

89 *Vancouver News Herald*, 7 January 1944.

90 *Vancouver News Herald*, 31 March 1945; BCARS, GR 1583, box 84-35-356, incorporation no. 17,421, West Coast Shipbuilders Ltd, notice to [new] directors, 23 March 1945, Frank Mackenzie Ross, James Hill Lawson, William D. McLaren, and Colonel Victor Spencer.

91 CVA, Add. Mss. 902, box 38, file 3; ibid., file 13; *Vancouver Daily Province*, 27 October 1945. Ross also became president of Red Barge Line Limited at Vancouver.

92 UBCSC, H.R. MacMillan Papers, box 100, file 16, memorandum, MacMillan to Howe, 14 December 1941.

93 Taylor, *Shipyards of British Columbia*, 110.

94 J.S. Marshall and Co. Ltd, *History of Burrard Dry Dock Company*, vol. 3, 151–2; Mansbridge, *Launching History*, 76.

95 Mansbridge, *Launching History*, 76.

96 Ibid., 72, 76–7.

97 Ibid., 76–7.

98 J.S. Marshall and Co. Ltd, *History of Burrard Dry Dock*, vol. 3, 148.

99 Mansbridge, *Launching History*, 76; *Harbour and Shipping* 28, no. 1 (January 1945): 29.

100 Mansbridge, *Launching History*, 77.

101 UBCSC, H.R. MacMillan Papers, box 100, file 16, MacMillan to Howe, 19 April 1941; LAC, MG 28, box 359, file 4-4-123, memorandum of agreement with Yarrows Ltd, 23 April 1941, which includes the cost of the two new berths in the price of the ships; Tucker, *Naval Service of Canada*, vol. 2, 41.

102 EMA, Yarrows Ltd Fonds, 997.10, lease with Department of Public Works of 10.22 acres for $200 per annum, dated 24 June 1941.

103 J.S. Marshall and Co. Ltd, *History of Burrard Dry Dock*, vol. 2, 104–5, 109.

104 LAC, MG 28, box 359, file 4-4-123, amendment no. 1, dated 23 December 1941, to the formal agreement of 23 April 1941.

105 MMBC, Historical Data 1, memoirs of Walter F. Jenkins, patternmaker at Yarrows Ltd.

106 LAC, RG 28, box 314, file 196-26Y-1, Carswell to J.G. Godsoe, coordinator of contracts, 15 June 1944; ibid., Martin Hollinger to C.L. Drury, 26 June 1944.

107 EMA, Yarrows Ltd Fonds, 997.10, contract N. 196 [n.d.] – specifications prepared by Codark Associates, Cambridge, Massachusetts.

108 CTA, John Inglis Company Fonds, box 107, Dunn and Bradstreet reports – VMD – received 6 May 1941; MMBC, "History of VMD."

109 *Canadian Machinery and Engineering News* 53 (April 1942): 132.

110 See advertisement in *Canadian Machinery and Engineering News* circa 1945.

111 DHH, Series 30: 8000, 75/270, interview by Lt Kerr with Herbert Hammill, president, VMD, 22 May 1945.

112 *Canadian Transportation* 45 (July 1942): 430.

113 Wallis, comp. *Story of Pictou's Park Ships*, 4, citing the *Pictou Advocate*, 9 October 1941.

114 NSARM, RG 73, box 25, registry of joint-stock companies, certificate no. 3,770, 4 January 1933.

115 "Birth and Growth of A.W.C. Wetmore Department," *The Refitter* 2, no. 5 (June 1945): 3.

116 According to Canada, DBS, *Census of Canada, 1941*, vol. 2, *Population*, table 7, Pictou's population in 1941 was 3,069; the population of the next largest shipbuilding town, Collingwood, Ontario, was 6,270.

117 LAC, RG 2, PC 53 and PC 2260 as amended by PC 2668 dated 2 April and PC 3698 dated 5 May 1942.

118 "Three Keel Plates Laid in Ferguson Yard," *Pictou Advocate*, 5 March 1942, in Wallis, comp., *Story of Pictou's Park Ships*, 14; Sherwood, *Pictou Parade*, 22–3, 31.

119 "Discusses Shipbuilding with Premier," *Halifax Herald*, 19 May 1942, in Wallis, comp., *Story of Pictou's Park Ships*, 18.

120 For a brief history of Ferguson Industries, see *The Refitter*, 1, no. 3 (July 1944), 1–2. See also LAC, RG 28, box 7, "Brief History of WMSL," typescript, 15.

121 LAC, RG 2, PC 5693 dated 2 July as amended by PC 7212 dated 14 August 1942 and PC 10689 dated 1 December 1942.

122 Sherwood, *Pictou Parade*, 12–13; *CS&MEN* 14, no. 9 (April 1943): 72

123 UBCSC, H.R. MacMillan Papers, box 100, file 16, memorandum MacMillan to Howe, 9 January 1942.

124 Ibid., memorandum MacMillan to Howe, 29 January 1942.

125 LAC, RG 28, box 7, "Brief History of WMSL," typescript, 71.

126 UBCSC, H.R. MacMillan Papers, box 100, file 16, memorandum, MacMillan to Howe, 8 August 1941.

127 LAC, RG 28, box 663, file 204-D-1, memorandum, F.H. Brown to Howe, 23 March 1943.

128 *SR&SB* 27, no. 7 (July 1944): 26.

129 Steven, "Canada's Shipyards Are Helping to 'Finish the Job.'"

130 *SR&SB* 26, no. 3 (March 1943): 58.

131 LAC, RG 28, box 7, "Brief History of WMSL," typescript, 47; *L'Écho de la marine* 3, no. 7 (8 June 1944): 2.

132 UBCSC, H.R. MacMillan Papers, box 100, file 16, letter, MacMillan to Howe, 9 August 1941.

133 Ibid., memorandum, MacMillan to Howe, 13 December 1941.

134 *CS&MEN* 13, no. 4 (November 1942): 31–6.

135 LAC, RG 28, box 378, file 4-5-185, contract with Fraser Brace Ltd, 14 January 1942, and amendment, dated 16 September 1942; LAC, RG 28, box 7, "Brief History of WMSL," typescript, 71.

136 Stephen, "United Effort in Cargo Ship Construction," 31–6.

137 LAC, RG 28, box 166, file 3-W-10, evidence placed before subcommittee for war expenditures, 13 October 1943.

138 *CS&MEN* 13, no. 10 (May 1942): 46.

139 LAC, RG 28, box 7, "Brief History of WMSL," typescript, 48.

140 LAC, RG 28, box 359, file 4-4-123, memorandum of agreement with United Shipyards Ltd, 2 March 1942.

141 LAC, RG 58, series C-1, box 252, file 14, Auditor General to G.K. Sheils, deputy minister, DMS, 26 November 1943. On John Rannie, see *CS&MEN* 15, no. 10 (May 1944): 31.

142 LAC, RG 28, box 7, "Brief History of WMSL," typescript, 48–9.

143 Kennedy, *History of DMS*, vol. 1, 496.

144 See Dominion Bridge Company, *Of Tasks Accomplished*, 13, 17, for photographs of a forepeak being welded onto a hull's keel in winter conditions.

145 LAC, RG 28, box 18, file OF7, "DMS: History of Ship Repairs and Salvage Control" (draft).

146 UBCSC, H.R. MacMillan Papers, box 100, file 14, memorandum, Howe to MacMillan, 17 March 1941.

147 QUA, William Clifford Clark Papers, file N-2-5-4-2, memorandum, H.T. Mitchell to MacMillan re: ship repairs at Port of St John, 6 January 1941.

148 LAC, MG 28, box 466, file 30-3-8, contract with Canadian Dredge and Dock Co. Ltd, 30 May 1941.

149 LAC, MG 28, box 256, file 196-3-13, Carswell to Howe, 8 July 1941.

150 LAC, MG 28, box 18, file OF7, "DMS: History of Ship Repairs and Salvage Control" (draft).

151 Tucker, *Naval Service of Canada*, vol. 2, 107.

152 NSARM, MG 3, box 1990-215, file 016, no. 11, "Operations of Dry Dock, 1940."

153 MMGLK, German and Milne Papers, 1989.0044.0005.7, "Comment on the Use of Drydocks on the Eastern Canadian Seaboard," by Walter Lambert, German and Milne, 29 November 1940.

154 Tucker, *Naval Service of Canada*, vol. 2, 127.

155 Ibid., 128; MMGLK, German and Milne Papers, 1989.0044.0005.7, floating dry dock file.

156 LAC, RG 28, box 256, file 196-3-13, Carswell to Howe, 8 July 1941.

157 Mitchell, "Sydney Harbour: The War Years," 44; MacNeill, "Development of Pictou Foundry and Machine Company Limited," 2.

158 LAC, RG 28, box 18, file OF7, "DMS: History of Ship Repairs and Salvage Control" (draft).

159 MacNeill, "Development of Pictou Foundry," 3.

160 LAC, RG 28, box 466, file 30-3-18, agreement with Pictou Foundry and Machine Co. Ltd, 27 August 1941, amendment no. 1 of 31 July 1942, and amendment no. 2 of 12 January 1943; LAC, RG 2 a-1-a, box 1720, PC 82/4417, 18 June 1941.

161 LAC, RG 2, PC 57/832, 4 February 1942; LAC, RG 28, box 256, file 196-13-3, quarterly report on ship repairs for period ending 30 June 1943.

162 NVMA, Fonds 97, box 48, series 3, contract for conversion of CVEs, 5 April 1943; Mansbridge, *Launching History*, 90.

163 NVMA, Fonds 27, box 48, series 3 A-116-6, contract of 31 August 1943 with DMS on capital expenditures of the CVE program, Lapointe Pier; UBCSC, H.R. MacMillan Papers, box 100, file 17, A.B. Graham, assistant to the president, WMSL, to A.J. Martin, executive assistant,

National Harbours Board, 29 September 1943, agreeing to pay rental of $3,000 per month for harbour-shed and wharf space.

164 J.S. Marshall and Co. Ltd, *History of Burrard Dry Dock*, vol. 3, 154.

165 LAC, MG 28, box 332, file 196-39-11, "Ship Repair Control," sent by Carswell to minister's secretary, 24 January 1944.

CHAPTER FIVE

1 LAC, RG 28, box 256, file 196 13 3, DMS press release, 2 November 1945. The estimate in Clarke, "Ship Construction and Repair," 37, is incorrect.

2 A few pages may be found in Kennedy, *History of the Department of Munitions and Supply* (hereafter *History of DMS*), vol. 2, 200–7.

3 Tucker, *Naval Service of Canada*, vol. 2, 39.

4 Forbes, "Consolidating Disparity."

5 Milner, *North Atlantic Run*, 168, 268.

6 Forbes, "Consolidating Disparity."

7 Stacey, *Arms, Men and Governments*, 537–8.

8 Tucker, *Naval Service of Canada*, vol. 2, 153.

9 The term "pocket battleship" was a mark of contempt inappropriately given by the British press to three heavily armoured cruisers built in Germany during the 1930s. Displacing only 10,000 tons, they were nevertheless armed battleship fashion with very heavy guns in triple turrets.

10 Duskin and Segman, *If the Gods Are Good*, 78–9. In an unusual effort to increase the ship's buoyancy, 24,000 empty steel drums were placed in the vessel's holds at St John.

11 Tucker, *Naval Service of Canada*, vol. 2, 10; Mansbridge, *Launching History*, 29; McKee, "Princes Three."

12 German, *Sea Is at Our Gates*, 75, incorrectly claims that due to "shaky technical organization," it took a whole year to convert the *Princes*, whereas work on two was completed in six months, and even Halifax Shipyards Limited got its *Prince* out in ten rather than twelve months.

13 Tucker, *Naval Service of Canada*, vol. 2, 11.

14 LAC, MG 30 B121, box 1, file 1.8, "World War II," German and Milne, Naval Architects, Montreal, [1948]. See also, Douglas et al., *No Higher Purpose*, 83; and McKee, *Armed Yachts of Canada*.

15 NSARM, MG 3, box 1990-215, file 016, no. 11, "Operations of Dry Dock, 1940."

16 LAC, RG 28, box 18, file OF7, "DMS: History of Ship Repairs and Salvage Control" (draft).

17 Kennedy, *History of DMS*, vol. 2, 205.

18 Marcil, *Tall Ships and Tankers*, 136–8.

19 LAC, RG 28, box 256, file 193-13-3, Carswell to Howe, 8 July and 4 September 1941.

20 Kennedy, *History of DMS*, vol. 2, 200.

21 LAC, RG 19, box 3984, file N-2-9-2, W.C. Hankinson, office of British high commissioner, to minister of external affairs, 15 May 1941; ibid., N.A. Robertson, external affairs, to British high commissioner, 26 May 1941; LAC, MG 27 III B20, box 42, file 5-9-36, Howe to Robertson, 26 May 1941.

22 MMGLK, German and Milne Papers, 1989.0044.0005.004, Carswell to German, 3 July 1941.

23 LAC, RG 2 7c, vol. 4 (reel C-11789), Cabinet War Committee minutes, 27 May 1941.

24 Tucker, *Naval Service of Canada*, vol. 2, 154.

25 LAC, RG 2 7C, vol. 4 (reel C-11789) copy of minutes of committee of Privy Council, 24 January 1941.

26 Dominion Bridge Company, *Of Tasks Accomplished*, 40–1.

27 *CS&MEN* 12, no. 4 (November 1942): 76; *Canadian Transportation* 45 (1942): 616.

28 LAC, RG 2 7C, vol. 4 (reel C-11789), Cabinet War Committee minutes, 3 June 1941.

29 LAC, RG 28, box 256, file 196-13-3, report on ship repairs for the period ending 31 October 1941. Graving docks were carved from rock and emptied by the tide or by pumping-out. The longest on the East Coast was at St John; another, built in the nineteenth century, existed at Halifax.

30 Halifax Shipyards Ltd, *Halship Saga*, 1–2.

31 Tucker, *Naval Service of Canada*, vol. 2, 128. See also LAC, RG 2, PC 82/4417 dated 18 June 1941 and PC 57-832 dated February 1942; and LAC, RG 28, box 521, file 51-T-9, contract for repairs to Thomson Brothers Machinery Co., Liverpool, Nova Scotia, 15 July 1941.

32 LAC, RG 2 7C, vol. 4 (reel C-4654), Cabinet War Committee minutes, 22 October and 12 November 1941; significantly, Cabinet deferred the project until Macdonald conferred with Howe.

33 MacNeill, "Development of Pictou Foundry and Machine Company Limited," 1–2; *CS&MEN* 15, no. 3 (October 1943): 71.

34 LAC, RG 28, box 256, file 196-3-13, Carswell to Howe, 8 July 1941.

35 LAC, MG 27 III B20, box 20, file S-19-2 (6), A. Heeny to Howe, 1 November 1941.

36 LAC, RG 28, box 256, file 196-3-13, Carswell to Howe, 8 July 1941.

37 Tennyson and Sarty, *Guardian of the Gulf*, 257 (see also the map at 289).

38 Mitchell, "Sydney Harbour: The War Years, 1939–1945," 47.

39 LAC, RG 28, box 256, file 196-13-3, quarterly summary, 31 December 1941; *CS&MEN* 13, no. 6 (January 1942): 102.

40 LAC, RG 28, box 256, file 196-13-3, ship repairs – revised quarterly summary, first quarter 1942.

41 Ibid. This and the next paragraph are based on a summary of nine monthly and two quarterly statements for 1942, but see also LAC, RG 28, box 256, file 196-13, advisory committee on ship repairs, minutes of fourth meeting, 23 February 1942.

42 Ibid., ship repairs – quarterly summary – second quarter 1942.

43 See, for example, Tucker, *Naval Service of Canada*, vol. 2, 134; and Milner, *North Atlantic Run*, 216–17.

44 LAC, RG 2 7C, vol. 9 (reel C-4874), Cabinet War Committee minutes, 8 May 1942; Forbes, "Consolidating Disparity," 16–17.

45 LAC, RG 2 7C, vol. 9 (reel C-4874), Cabinet War Committee minutes, 8 May 1942.

46 Hadley, *U-boats against Canada*, 112–43.

47 Canada, House of Commons, *Debates*, 1904, C.D. Howe, March 1944.

48 "Constructive total loss" is a marine insurance term indicating that the cost of repairing a ship will exceed its total value, and an insurance payment is the sum for which the vessel has been insured rather than the cost of repairs. See Kemp, ed., *Oxford Companion to Ships and the Sea*, 197.

49 LAC, RG 28, box 256, file 196-13-3-1, "Control of Ship Repairs and Cargo Salvage," 11 May 1943.

50 LAC, RG 28, box 18, file OF7, "DMS: History of Ship Repairs and Salvage Control" (draft); Kennedy, *History of DMS*, vol. 2, 203–4.

51 LAC, RG 28, box 257, file 196-13-0, Carswell to R.C. Berkinshaw, chairman, Wartime Industries Control Board, 2 June 1942.

52 Built for the Royal Navy as a Dainty-class tug in 1918, it was purchased, refitted, and operated by Foundation Maritime Limited. Its fame, many rescues, and salvage triumphs are vividly recounted in Mowat, *Grey Seas Under*.

53 LAC, RG 28, box 256, file 196-13, Carswell to Howe, 28 May 1942.

54 Baird, *Under Tow*, 95, 141, hints at this.

55 LAC, RG 28, box 256, file 196-13-0, Carswell to Quebec Salvage and Wrecking Co. Ltd, 28 August 1942.

56 Ibid., Carswell to Hugh Scully, 1 September 1942.

57 Ibid., file 196-13-3, ship-repairs controller's report for the period ending 28 February 1943.

58 Ibid., ship-repairs controller's reports for the periods ending 28 February, 30 June, and 31 August 1943.

59 Mowat, *Grey Seas Under*, 173, 203.

60 LAC, RG 28, box 256, file 196-13-3, report on ship repairs and salvage, periods ending 31 May, 31 August, and 30 September 1942.

61 Ibid., ship-repairs controller's quarterly report for the period ending 31 December 1943.

62 Ibid., ship-repairs controller's quarterly report for the period ending 31 March 1944; Young, "Cheating the Nazis through Salvage," 31–4.

63 See Milner, *North Atlantic Run*, 10, 20, 217; and German, *Sea Is at Our Gates*, 146. Whitby, "Instruments of Security," 1–15, provides a well-argued defence of the reasonableness of the naval staff's decision to obtain approval to build these vessels in wartime Halifax; Douglas et al., *No Higher Purpose*, 75–82, 307–8, reaches a similar conclusion.

64 At first sight, Canadian Vickers Limited might be thought a more logical choice, as it possessed five well-equipped, covered berths, together with manufacturing capabilities for whatever was required and the largest pool of skilled labour in the country. But if a ship was ready early in winter, Vickers's berths might be held up for as much as five months in launching, which would add seriously to the cost, as men could not be employed on other hulls. Working with light-hulled destroyers in a place where ice conditions might be encountered during launching was also not desirable; see DHH, Series 30: 8000, 75/270, interview by Lt Kerr with Engineer Capt. A.D.M. Curry, 22 May 1945.

65 Chappelle, "Building a Bigger Stick," 7.

66 Ibid. Chappelle incorrectly identifies Carswell as controller of naval shipbuilding, which was a nonexistent title. Carswell ceased to be director general of shipbuilding on 9 April 1941 and did not resume that position until late in 1944.

67 LAC, RG 28, box 18, file OF7, "DMS: History of Ship Repairs and Salvage Control" (draft).

68 Tucker, *Naval Service of Canada*, vol. 2, 54–7; Chappelle, "Building a Bigger Stick," 6. See also Douglas et al., *No Higher Purpose*, 308.

69 Tucker, *Naval Service of Canada*, vol. 2, 58–9; Milner, *North Atlantic Run*, 19–20; Knox, "An Engineer's Outline of RCN History," 108.

70 LAC, RG 2 7c, vol. 4 (reel C-11789), Cabinet War Committee minutes, 21 April 1941.

71 Ibid., Cabinet War Committee minutes, 6 May 1941.

72 Ibid., Cabinet War Committee minutes, 21 May 1941.

73 LAC, RG 28, box 256, file 196-3-13, Carswell to Howe, 15 August 1941.

74 NSARM, MG 2, box 1524, file 1222, no. 37, Howe to Macdonald, 28 June 1941; LAC, RG 28, box 256, file 196-3-13, Carswell to Howe, 11 August 1941.

75 LAC, RG 28, box 256, file 196-3-13, Carswell to Howe, 11 August 1941.

76 Ibid., Carswell to Howe, 15 and 25 August 1941.

77 NSARM, MG 2, box 1524, file 1122, no. 45, telegram Carswell to Macdonald, 29 September 1941.

78 Chappelle, "Building a Bigger Stick," 8; Milner, *North Atlantic Run*, 20, claims the keels were not laid until September.

79 Kennedy, *History of DMS*, vol. 2, 202–3.

80 LAC, RG 2 7c, vol. 8 (reel C-4874), Cabinet War Committee minutes, 28 January 1942; Tucher, *Naval Service of Canada*, vol. 2, 60.

81 DHH, Series 30: 8000, 75/270, interview by Lt Kerr with Lt Scoble, NEO, and F.A. Wood at John Inglis Company, 9 May 1945. Scoble had been a chief engine room artificer and had overseen the building of HMCS *Skeena* and HMCS *Saguenay* at Thornycroft's in 1930–31; Wood was from Vickers Armstrong in the United Kingdom.

82 CTA, John Inglis Company Fonds, box 16, DMS file, R.G. McLeish, general sales manager, to Desmond Clarke, director general of shipbuilding, DMS, 25 September 1942.

83 Milner, *North Atlantic Run*, 166.

84 CTA, John Inglis Company Fonds, box 16, DMS file, telegram, Carswell to R.J.R. Nelson, general manager, Halifax Shipyards, 7 February 1943.

85 Chappelle, "Building a Bigger Stick," 11.

86 LAC, RG 28, box 256, file 196-13-3, "1944: Report for staff meeting, January 17, 1943 [1944]."

87 Ibid., ship-repairs controller's report for the period ending 30 April 1944.

88 *CS&MEN* 15, no. 11 (June 1944): 46; LAC, RG 28, box 257, file 196-14(2), M.A. Hoey, associate steel controller, to J.B. "Jack" Carswell, director general, DMS, Washington office, 2 February 1943.

89 LAC, RG 28, box 257, file 196-14(2), ship-repairs controller's quarterly reports for the periods ending 30 June and 30 September 1944 and report for the period ending 31 August 1944.

90 Ibid., ship-repairs controller's report for the period ending 31 October and 30 November 1944.

91 LAC, RG 28, box 256, file 196-13-3, ship-repairs controller's report for the period ending 31 January 1945.

92 LAC, RG 28, box 460, file 30-1-45, subcontract of John Inglis Co. with Halifax Shipyards Ltd, 13 February 1945; LAC, RG 28, box 256, file 196-13-3, ship-repairs controller's report for the period ending 28 February 1945.

93 LAC, RG 28, box 256, file 196-13-3, ship-repairs controller's report for the period ending 31 May 1945.

94 *Canadian Transportation* 47 (May 1944): 278; Tucker, *Naval Service of Canada*, vol. 2, 503.

95 LAC, RG 28, box 540, file 75-Y-1, original agreement between the DMS and Yarrows Limited, dated 15 July 1941.

96 Dominion Bridge Company, *Of Tasks Accomplished*, 40.

97 J.S. Marshall and Co. Ltd, *History of Yarrows Limited*, vol. 2, 131.

98 DHH, Series 30: 8000, 75/270, interview by Lt Kerr with Mr Isard, general superintendent, Yarrows Ltd, 22 May 1945.

99 EMA, Arthur J. Daniels Fonds, 984.3, C2, 6, dock master's docking books; J.S. Marshall and Co. Ltd, *History of Yarrows Limited*, vol. 2, 117–18; *SR&SB* 28, no. 1 (January 1945): 22–3; Tucker, *Naval Service of Canada*, vol. 2, 217–18.

100 Konings, *"Queen Elizabeth" at War*, 30–3.

101 J.S. Marshall and Co. Ltd, *History of Burrard Dry Dock Company*, vol. 3, 193–5.

102 Gunwale bars were angles welded onto decks connecting deck and housing. See "Salvage Jobs for Russia," *CS&MEN* 14, no. 12 (July 1944): 47.

103 LAC, RG 28, box 256, file 196-13-3, report on ship repairs for the period ending 31 May 1942; Mansbridge, *Launching History*, 93.

104 LAC, RG 28, box 256, file 196-13-3, ship-repairs controller's report for the period ending 28 February 1943.

105 Ibid., monthly report of the controller of ship repairs and salvage for the period ending 30 September 1943.

106 Ibid., ship-repairs controller's report for the period ending 30 April 1944.

107 LAC, RG 28, box 18, file OF7, "DMS: History of Ship Repairs and Salvage Control" (draft). See also LAC, RG 28, box 540, file 75-W-10, amendment to contract for emergency ship repairs with West Coast Salvage and Contracting Co. Ltd, Vancouver, 14 February 1944.

108 LAC, RG 28, box 256, file 196-13-3, ship-repairs controller's report for the period ending 28 February 1945; ibid., ship-repairs controller's quarterly report for the period ending 31 March 1945.

109 Ibid., ship-repairs controller's quarterly report for the period ending 30 June 1945.

110 LAC, RG 36, box 17, vols 75 to 80, manifests listed from Canadian Mutual Aid Board files. In September and October 1945 two ships each departed from New Westminster and Victoria.

111 Canada, Mutual Aid Board, *Final Report*; Bryce, *Canada and the Cost of World War II*, 157.

112 Taylor, *Shipyards of British Columbia*, 149.

113 Tucker, *Naval Service of Canada*, vol. 2, 87–8; McKee, "Princes Three," 125–6, 128–9; Mansbridge, *Launching History*, 93.

114 This account varies considerably from Poolman, *Escort Carriers, 1941–1945*, 88–9, which identifies HMS *Khedive* as the first carrier escort converted at Burrard Dry Dock in August 1943 and claims HMS *Nabob* was the second converted in September, followed by twelve more. Smith et al., "History of the British Admiralty Technical Mission in Canada" (hereafter "History of BATM"), 86, which lists nineteen carriers completed with their acceptance dates, identifies HMS *Ameer* as the first, converted in October; HMS *Nabob*, the fifth ship, followed in December. See also Douglas et al., *Blue Water Navy*, 456n12.

115 Mason, "Flat Tops for Britain," 34–5, 47.

116 Mansbridge, *Launching History*, 89–90.

117 "1,000 Discharged at Lapointe as Carrier Repair Yard Closes," *Vancouver Province*, 5 July 1944; Smith et al., "History of BATM," 86. HMS *Ranee* was completed on 12 July 1944.

118 See Tucker, *Naval Service of Canada*, vol. 2, 132, 134.

119 Milner, *North Atlantic Run*, 216. See Douglas et al., *No Higher Purpose*, 531–2, for a strong defence of the RCN's decision to keep its ships at sea.

120 QUA, William Clifford Clark Papers, file N-2-5-4-2, memorandum Mitchell to Macmillan, 6 January 1941.

121 Tucker, *Naval Service of Canada*, vol. 2, 141–3.

122 LAC, RG 28, box 257, file 196-13-8, telegram Carswell to Gordon Fogo, 18 December 1942.

123 The following paragraphs are indebted for the facts to several historians who have dealt extensively with the modernization of the RCN's wartime corvettes. Douglas et al., *Blue Water Navy*, 44–55, 175–84, provides a recent summary of the problem as it emerged and its eventual solution, but see also Milner, *North Atlantic Run*, 123–4, 153, 216–18, and his *U-boat Hunters*, 260–79, appendix 1, "Escort Building and Modernization, 1942–1945." MacPherson and Milner, *Corvettes of the Royal Canadian Navy, 1939–1945*, chapter 4, "Modernization, 1942–1944," contains a more extended discussion, and Zimmerman, *Great Naval Battle of Ottawa*, 86–92, sheds further useful light on this complicated issue.

124 German, *Sea Is at Our Gates*, 89.

125 Milner, *U-boat Hunters*, 269.

126 Milner, *North Atlantic Run*, 123.

127 Zimmerman, *Great Naval Battle of Ottawa*, 86–92.

128 LAC, RG 28, box 256, file 196-13-3, quarterly report of the controller of ship repairs and salvage for the period ending 31 March 1943; German, *Sea Is at Our Gates*, 136.

129 LAC, RG 28, box 256, file 196-13-3, ship-repairs controller's report for the period ending 31 March 1942 and quarterly report for the period ending 30 June 1943.

130 Tucker, *Naval Service of Canada*, vol. 2, 173–80.

131 LAC, RG 28, box 256, file 196-13-3, ship-repairs controller's quarterly report for the period ending 31 December 1943.

132 Ibid., summary of eight monthly and three quarterly reports of the controller of ship repairs and salvage for 1943. The fact of this work at Montreal contrasts sharply with Tucker's dismissive statement in *Naval Service of Canada*, vol. 2, 151–2, that "some use was made of ship-repair firms at Montreal and Quebec for repairing and refitting Canadian warships after the shipbuilding programme began to taper off toward the end of the war."

133 Tucker, *Naval Service of Canada*, vol. 2, 85.

134 LAC, RG 28, box 150, file 3-N-5, "Survey of Manpower Requirements for Canadian Ship Repair Industry." HMC Dockyard required 2,445 workers.

135 LAC, RG 28, box 257, file 196-13-8, Carswell to deputy minister of the naval service, 5 April 1943; LAC, RG 28, box 150, file 3-N-5, Carswell to Henry Borden, coordinator of controls, DMS, 10 June 1943.

136 LAC, RG 28, box 257, file 196-13-8, Carswell to Fogo, 8 May 1943, and Allan Michell to Fogo, 19 May 1943; Neary, "Canada and the Newfoundland Labour Market, 1939–45." See also Tucker, *Naval Service of Canada*, vol. 2, 199–201; and Collins, "'First Line of Defence.'"

137 LAC, RG 28, box 150, file 3-N-5, minutes of second meeting of committee for naval and merchant ship maintenance, St John, 1 June 1943.

138 LAC, RG 2 7c, vol. 12 (reel C-4875), Cabinet War Committee minutes, 13 May 1943.

139 LAC, RG 28, box 129, file 3-C-21, minutes of the combined Canada-UK-US committee, Ottawa, 12 August 1943.

140 LAC, RG 28, box 256, file 196-13-3, ship-repairs controller's report for the period ending 31 October 1943.

141 LAC, RG 28, box 162, file 3-S-15, minutes of shipbuilding coordinating committee, 31 December 1943.

142 LAC, RG 28, box 256, file 196-13-3, "1944: Report for staff meeting, January 17, 1943 [1944]."

143 Milner, *North Atlantic Run*, 268; Douglas et al., *Blue Water Navy*, 180n113. MacPherson and Milner, *Corvettes of the Royal Canadian Navy, 1939–1945*, 61, note that twelve corvettes, including those lost in action, were never modernized.

144 LAC, RG 28, box 256, file 196-13-3, ship-repairs controller's reports for the periods ending 30 November 1943, 31 December 1943, and 31 January 1944.

145 Ibid., ship-repairs controller's quarterly report for the period ending 31 March 1944 and reports for the periods ending 30 April and 31 May 1944.

146 LAC, RG 28, box 257, file 196-13-8, Carswell to Fogo, 22 May 1944.

147 LAC, RG 28, box 256, file 196-13-3, ship-repairs controller's reports for the periods ending from June to October 1944.

148 Kennedy, *History of DMS*, vol. 1, 495.

149 *CS&MEN* 16, no. 1 (August 1944): 82; *CS&MEN* 16, no. 4 (November 1944): 61.

150 Smith et al., "History of BATM," 69–70, 91; LAC, RG 24, acc. no. 1983/84/167, box 3880, file NSC8260-500/923, memo for the director of naval stores, 6 February 1945.

151 Mansbridge, *Launching History*, 79.

152 LAC, RG 28, box 18, file OF7, "DMS: History of Ship Repairs and Salvage Control" (draft).

153 LAC, RG 28, box 256, file 196-13-3, ship-repairs controller's report for the period ending 30 April 1945.

154 Ibid., ship-repairs controller's reports for the periods ending from May to November 1945.

155 Forbes, "Consolidating Disparity."

156 MacPherson and Milner, *Corvettes of the Royal Canadian Navy*, 55.

157 Compiled from Canada, DBS, *Canada Year Book, 1941–1948/49*, "Statistics of Leading Industries of Nova Scotia, 1939–1945."

158 Kennedy, *History of DMS*, vol. 2, 200, gives 27,581 repairs to September 1943.

CHAPTER SIX

1 Canada, DBS, *Annual Industry Report: Iron, Steel and Their Products Group: The Shipbuilding Industry* (hereafter *Shipbuilding Industry*) (1939), table 1, gives 3,491 shipbuilding employees.

2 There is no agreed upon figure. At peak employment in July 1943, according to Canada, DBS, *Shipbuilding Industry* (1944), tables 1 and 4, there were 76,414 wage earners in the industry. A DMS press release, dated 20 January 1944, when employment was already declining, stated 50,000 employees were engaged in the naval shipbuilding program, including component production, and 30,000 were employed directly in nine cargo shipbuilding yards; see LAC, RG 28, box 256, file 196-13-4. Robson, "Merchant Shipbuilding in Canada," 293, claims that at peak employment 85,000 were employed in shipbuilding, of whom 57,000 were in the cargo ship program.

3 Lane, *Ships for Victory*, 236.

4 Canada, DBS, *Shipbuilding Industry* (1945), tables 1 and 2.

5 Canada, Department of Reconstruction and Supply, *Location and Effects of Wartime Industrial Expansion in Canada, 1939–1944*, 32, table 8.

6 Ibid., 29–30.

7 Extrapolated from graphs in LAC, RG 28, box 29, "Report on Canadian shipbuilding, July 6 1944," appendices 6 and 9.

8 Victoria Machinery Depot, *The Convoy* 14, no. 11 (June 1943): 1.

9 Canada, Department of Reconstruction and Supply, *Location and Effects of Wartime Industrial Expansion*, 41.

10 Stacey, *Arms, Men and Governments*, 403.

11 Lane, *Ships for Victory*, 411.

12 See Leacy, ed., *Historical Statistics of Canada*, D-125, D-262-63. Between 1939 and 1941 paid civilian employment in nonagricultural industry increased by 487,000 and in the armed services by 287,000.

13 Canada, Government of, "Royal Commission on Shipbuilding in the Provinces of Quebec and Ontario," 20.

14 LAC, RG 27, box 408, file 186.

15 EMA, Yarrows Ltd Fonds, "Graph showing number of employees, January 1939 to December 1945." Numbers have been extrapolated from the graph, wherein the thickness of the ink line represents about ten employees. Even so, this graph contains the most accurate, detailed record of employees of any shipyard in the country.

16 Canada, House of Commons, *Debates*, 2114, 2 April 1941.

17 QUA, William Clifford Clark Papers, file N-2-5-4-1, report of C. Goldenberg to members of the War Requirements Board, 28 December 1940.

18 Ibid., file N-2-5-4-2, "Total Number of Employees at Larger Individual Shipyards and Machine Shops in Nova Scotia and New Brunswick as at Nov./Dec. 1940," 8 January 1941.

19 UBCSC, H.R. MacMillan Papers, box 100, file 13, memorandum, MacMillan to Howe, 8 March 1941.

20 Ibid., file 14, Sir Edward Beatty, representative of the British Ministry of Shipping, to MacMillan, 22 January 1941.

21 QUA, William Clifford Clark Papers, file N-2-5-4-2, memorandum, H.T. Mitchell to MacMillan, 7 January 1941.

22 LAC, RG 117, box 1928, no. 2681, Franceschini file, pt 1.2, Robert Scrivener, general manager, Dufferin Shipbuilding Co., to Howe, 6 May 1941.

23 Canada, DBS, *Shipbuilding Industry* (1943), table 1.

24 Canada, Government of, "Royal Commission on Shipbuilding in the Provinces of Quebec and Ontario," 20.

25 DHH, Series 30: 8000, 75/270, interviews by Lt Kerr with Mr [Herbert J.] Whitmill, general manager, Midland Shipyards Ltd, 10 May 1945, and with Mr [Herbert S.] Hammill, president, VMD, 22 May 1945; Roy, *Kingston*, 337.

26 Daniels, "Progress at Pictou," 46–7.

27 MacEachern, *George MacEachern*, 11.

28 Figure 6.2, reproduced from *Canadian Transportation* 47 (1944): 679, accompanied the Canadian Shipbuilding and Ship Repairing Association's representation to the Dominion government.

29 Forbes, "Consolidating Disparity."

30 LAC, RG 28, box 150, file 3-N-5, Minutes of 2nd Meeting, Naval and Merchant Ship Maintenance Committee, St John, 1 June 1943.

31 See Neary, "Canada and the Newfoundland Labour Market, 1939–45," for a thorough discussion.

32 Canada, DBS, *Shipbuilding Industry* (1943), table 5.

33 Wallis, comp., *Story of Pictou's Park Ships*, 152, from the *Pictou Advocate*, 16 September 1943. On the weight of rivets, see NVMA, Fonds 97.

34 Thornton, "Women of the Victoria Shipyards, 1942–1945," 35.

35 Smith, *Conflict over Convoys*, 264n36. See also BANQ-CAQ, E 24, 1960-01-040, box 220, file L26-42-43, report of British trade-union delegation, appendix J, which notes that in January 1943 11,332 women employed in three Kaiser shipyards on the US West Coast constituted 13.7 per cent of the workforce.

36 Kossoris, "Work Injuries to Women in Shipyards, 1943–44," 552; Canada, DBS, *Shipbuilding Industry* (1944), table 4.

37 Pierson, *"They're Still Women after All,"* 9.

38 LAC, MG 28 I103, box 55, file 19, A. Clyde to P. Conroy, 10 May 1942, and Conroy to Clyde, 13 May 1942.

39 Canada, DBS, *Shipbuilding Industry* (1943), table 5.

40 *Canadian Machinery and Manufacturing News* 53 (November 1942): 84.

41 Canada, DBS, *Shipbuilding Industry* (1944 and 1945), table 4 in each volume.

42 LAC, RG 27, box 160, file 611.3: 4, "Mémoire sur la conscription du travail feminin"; ibid., memorandum, J.A.D [?] to the prime minister, 16 March 1943. See also BANQ-CAQ, E 24, 1960-01-040, box 219, file L18-42-43, "travail feminin" (1943) – three thick files containing letters from municipalities and Catholic organizations addressed to Quebec's minister of labour.

43 Sutton Jr, "Scott-Paine's Canadian MTBs," 4.

44 *Canadian Machinery and Manufacturing News* 53 (December 1942): 370.

45 Wallis, comp., *Story of Pictou's Park Ships*, 19, from *The Fo'c'sle*, 6 January 1943; LAC, RG 25, box 151, file 611.1: 16–2, Reference Papers, Canadian Wartime Information Board, no. 7, "Canadian Women in the War," 10 June 1943, 6; Sherwood, *Pictou Parade*, 32. The unsupported claim in Halford, *Unknown Navy*, 133–4, that 600 women worked at Pictou may be correct, but the unsupported assertion in Miller, "The 1940s: War and Rehabilitation," 313, that close to half of the 3,800 persons employed at Pictou were women is wrong on both accounts.

46 "Women 8 P.C. of Shipyards," *Vancouver Sun*, 18 June 1943, 28.

47 Sheila Anderson Papers, "Memoirs," 12.

48 EMA, Yarrows Ltd Fonds, unsigned note, "Figures for the boss – highest employment, men 2,624, women 401 [total] 3025, Nov. 43/March 44," cited in Thornton, "Women of the Victoria Shipyards," 32. Thornton claims that Anderson said over 250 women worked at Victoria Machinery Depot, but I have been unable to confirm the figure.

49 Diamond, *Women's Labour History in British Columbia*, 42.

50 Thornton, "Women of the Victoria Shipyards," 38; Dempsey, "Women Working on Ships and Aircraft," 82.

51 Canada, Department of Reconstruction and Supply, *Location and Effects of Wartime Industrial Expansion*, 35–9.

52 Robson, "Merchant Shipbuilding in Canada," 282. The author was manager of the construction department of Wartime Shipbuilding Limited.

53 LAC, RG 27, box 267, file 2, organization and administration of wartime emergency training program, 1940–41.

54 Wallis, comp., *Story of Pictou's Park Ships*, 12, from *Pictou Advocate*, 26 February 1942.

55 Salter, "Wartime Ship-Shaping in a Small Town," 17.

56 Lt Cdr A.D. Timson, RCN (rtd), discussion, Institution of Naval Architects, *Transactions* 88 (1946): 290.

57 *Dry Dock Bulletin* 1, no. 3 (December 1943): 19.

58 Marcil, *Tall Ships and Tankers*, 251–2; MacNeish, "Training Shipbuilders in Quebec," 19–20.

59 Ibid., 20–2.

60 Aubert, *Harlaka de mon enfance*, 63–4. I gratefully acknowledge Monsieur Aubert's kindness in receiving me at his home and talking about his first years at Davie Shipbuilding and Repairing.

61 *L'Écho de la marine* 3, no. 14 (29 September 1944): 1.

62 Sheila Anderson Papers, certificate of attendance.

63 Kimber, *Sailors, Slackers and Blind Pigs*, 178–83, 208.

64 *CS&MEN* 14, no. 10 (May 1943): 39.

65 *Dry Dock Bulletin* 1, no. 9 (August 1944): 13; *Dry Dock Bulletin* 1, no. 10 (October 1944): 9.

66 Wallis, comp., *Story of Pictou's Park Ships*, 12, from *The Fo'c'sle*, 6 January 1943.

67 LAC, RG 28, DMS History – Quebec Shipyards Ltd.

68 Mansbridge, *Launching History*, 75.

69 Steven, "United Effort in Cargo Ship Construction," 32; Robson, "Merchant Shipbuilding in Canada," 282.

70 DHH, Series 30: 8000, 75/270, interview by Lt Kerr with [Gordon F.] McDougall, general manager, Port Arthur Shipbuilding Co., 14 May 1945.

71 LAC, MG 30 B121, box 1, file 1–6, memorandum titled "Prospects for 1949," describing the firm's history.

72 Robson, "Merchant Shipbuilding in Canada," 283.

73 Wallis, comp., *Story of Pictou's Park Ships*, 103, from *The Foc's'le*, February 1945.

74 LAC, RG 27, box 434, file 5 [QUA reel 2478], acting deputy commissioner F.J. Mead, RCMP, to deputy minister of labour, 14 January 1944.

75 MacEachern, *George MacEachern*, 118–19.

76 Buxton, "British Warship Building and Repair," 86.

77 Douglas et al., *No Higher Purpose*, 304–5. Some of the incomplete work was due to failed deliveries of parts from Britain.

78 Robson, "Merchant Shipbuilding in Canada," 285.

79 D. Turner, discussion, Institution of Naval Architects, *Transactions* 88 (1946): 292.

80 Sir Amos L. Ayre, discussion, Institution of Naval Architects, *Transactions* 88 (1946): 288–9.

81 Lane, *Ships for Victory*, 412; *Dry Dock Bulletin* 1, no. 3 (December 1943): 32.

82 Canada, National War Labour Board, *Proceedings [of the] Inquiry into Labour Relations and Wage Conditions in Canada*, 1286.

83 DHH, Series 30: 8000, 75/270, interviews by Lt Kerr with Mr [Herbert S.] Hammill, president, VMD, 22 May 1945, and with Mr [Gordon F.] McDougall, general manager, Port Arthur Shipbuilding Co., 14 May 1945.

84 Robson, "Merchant Shipbuilding in Canada," 286.

85 Stevenson, *Canada's Greatest Wartime Muddle*, 66–89.

86 Ibid.

87 Lane, *Ships for Victory*, 412.

88 Compiled from weekly statistics published in *L'Écho maritime* (February–December 1943), in Eileen Reid Marcil Papers. *Canadian Transportation* 47 (April 1944): 219, reported an absenteeism rate of 11.8 per cent during the regular week, which rose to 16 per cent on Saturday.

89 Salter, "Wartime Ship-Shaping in a Small Town."

90 *Dry Dock Bulletin* 1, no. 10 (October 1944): 5.

91 Ibid.

92 *Dry Dock Bulletin* 1, no. 2 (October 1943).

93 Victoria Machinery Depot, *The Convoy* 2, no. 4 (August 1943): 1.

94 *Dry Dock Bulletin* 1, no. 3 (December 1943): 31.

95 CVA, Add. Mss. 304, box 530-C-3, file 21, Burrard Dry Dock, labour-management committee minutes, 14 June 1943.

96 LAC, MG 28 I103, box 54, file 3, report of board of conciliation in dispute between United Shipyards and Local 12, BISUC, 13 May 1944.

97 McInnis, *Harnessing Labour Confrontation*, 113–21.

98 LAC, RG 27, box 146, file 611.05: 20, Humphrey Mitchell to Howe, 18 February 1943, and Howe to Mitchell, 27 February 1943; ibid., copy of PC 167, dated 18 January 1944, authorizing establishment of labour-management committees in war-industries plants

99 LAC, MG 28 I103, box 54, file 2, David Côté reporting his conversation with Mr Brisco to A.R. Mosher, 1 September 1943.

100 Milward, *War, Economy, and Society, 1939–1945*, 107.

101 Bryce, *Canada and the Cost of World War II*, 327.

102 Canada, National War Labour Board, *Proceedings [of the] Inquiry*, 1027–28.

103 CVA, Add. Mss. 304, box 530-C-3, file 21, Burrard Dry Dock, labour-management committee minutes, 19 July 1943.

104 LAC, MG 30 B121, box 1, file 1-25, memorandum, H.T. Milne to D.A. Clarke, 28 November 1942.

105 Wallis, comp., *Story of Pictou's Park Ships*, 114, from *The Foc's'le*, 3 August 1943.

106 "Workmen's Compensation in Quebec, 1941," *Labour Gazette* 42 (1942): 1344.

107 Industrial accidents, nonfatal and fatal, in Canada as reported by provincial workmen's compensation boards were normally reprinted annually in the March issue of the *Labour Gazette* (see vols 40–6, 1940–46). See also BANQ-CAQ, E 62, 1986-01-002, box 1, "Rapports du commission des accidents du travail au Québec, 1939–1946," which reported 556,698 accidents between 1939 and 1945.

108 LAC, RG 28, box 104, file 2-1-6, telegram, Howe to R.B. Morley, 20 April 1942.

109 *L'Écho maritime* (February 1943): 6.

110 *L'Écho maritime* (June 1943): 1.

111 *CS&MEN* 16, no. 4 (November 1944): 142.

112 Compiled from the *Labour Gazette*.

113 Settle, "Halifax Shipyards, 1918–1978," 63–4.

114 Reported in *L'Écho maritime* (August 1943): 5–8.

115 BANQ-CAQ, E 24, 1960-01-040, box 211, file G36-42-43, Wilfrid Beaulac, director, Bureau de Québec du service d'inspection du travail, to Davie Shipbuilding and Repairing, 16 June 1943, my translation.

116 BANQ-CAQ, E 24, 1960-01-040, box 209, file A13-42-43, Beaulac to J. O'Connell-Maher, director, Service d'inspection des accidents du travail, 13 April 1942.

117 *CS&MEN* 15, no. 1 (August 1943): 80.

118 *L'Écho maritime* (April 1943): 10.

119 BANQ-CAQ, E 62, 1986-01-040, box 1, "Rapports annuelles du commission des accidents du travail, 1939–1946," reveals that compensation grew from approximately $10 million in 1939 to over $25 million by 1942.

120 McElroy and Svenson, "Basic Accident Factors in Shipyards," 13.

121 McElroy and Svenson, "Shipyard Injuries during 1943," 1004.

122 LAC, RG 27, box 268, file 1, "Statement of accidents."

123 *L'Écho de la marine* 3, no. 25 (24 November 1944).

124 McElroy and Svenson, "Basic Accident Factors in Shipyards," 13.

125 Canada, Government of, "Report of the Royal Commission on Shipbuilding in the Provinces of Quebec and Ontario," 25.

126 AO, RG 7-12, James F. Marsh, provincial deputy minister of labour, to Humphrey Mitchell, 18 July 1942; ibid., memo, Dr J.G. Cunningham, director, division of industrial hygiene, to J.R. Prain, chief inspector, Ontario Department of Labour, 1 September 1942; ibid., Prain to John S. Leitch, vice president and general manager, Collingwood Shipbuilding Co., 15 September 1942.

127 NVMA, Fonds 27, Burrard Dry Dock Clippings, vol. 6, *Vancouver Province*, 4 March 1942.

128 CVA, Add. Mss. 717, box 556-B-4, vol. 1, minute book, 27 May 1943.

129 *Dry Dock Bulletin* 1, no. 4 (January 1944): 23.

130 Ibid.; McElroy and Svenson, "Shipyard Injuries during 1943," 1004.

131 UBCSC, Trade Union Research Bureau Records, box 15, file 2, John C. Cosgrove, business agent, Local 2, BISUC, Victoria, to G.S. Culhane, secretary treasurer, Shipyard and General Workers Federation, 16 June 1944; ibid., box 14, file 5, Leonard Greenberg, MD, executive director of industrial hygiene, New York, Department of Labour, to Bert Marcuse, director, Pacific Coast Labour Bureau, 19 July 1944.

132 *Vancouver Sun*, 30 July 1942.

133 Driner, "Shipyard Health Hazards."

134 See, however, the case concerning Collingwood Shipbuilding Company, in AO, RG 7–12, memorandum, Cunningham to Prain, 1 September 1942.

135 Kossoris, "Work Injuries to Women in Shipyards, 1943–44."

136 Wallis, comp., *Story of Pictou's Park Ships*, 114, from *The Foc's'le*, 3 August and 1 September 1943.

137 Ibid., 116, from *The Foc's'le*, 28 November 1944.

138 *L'Écho maritime* (July 1943): 8; *L'Écho maritime* (November 1943): 8.

139 However, see UVA, Victoria Labour Council Fonds, series 4, box 4, Victoria and District Trades and Labour Council minute book, 5 August 1942, for a resolution that a letter be sent to the BC Workmen's Compensation Board drawing attention to accidents at Victoria Machinery Depot from tools and material dropping on men's heads and asking that the company supply men with "crash helmets."

140 NVMA, Fonds 97, box 3, file 16, *Ship-Construction Accident Prevention Regulations*; *Labour Gazette* 43 (1943): 689–90.

141 Robson, "Merchant Shipbuilding in Canada," 287.

142 *L'Écho maritime* (June 1945): 13.

143 See McInnis, *Harnessing Labour Confrontation*, 22.

144 Wade, "Wartime Housing Limited, 1941–1947," 42.

145 UBCSC, H.R. MacMillan Papers, box 99, file 16, private and confidential, C. Norman Senior, private secretary to the minister of pensions and national heath, to Major Len R. Andrews, office of the timber controller, 18 November 1940.

146 Prewar housing programs under the National Housing Act (1938) had been administered by the Department of Finance, which was permitted to continue administering the home-improvement plan under the National Housing Administration on a reduced level. See Bacher, *Keeping to the Marketplace*, 120–63.

147 NSARM, MG 20, box 3151, file 1, nos 584 and 590, Halifax District Trades and Labour Council, minute book, 10 April and 9 May 1941. See also Kimber, *Sailors, Slackers and Blind Pigs*, 53.

148 QUA, William Clifford Clark Papers, file N-2-5-4-2, memorandum, H.T. Mitchell to MacMillan, 6 January 1941; H.T. Mitchell Papers, Mitchell to wife, 17 January 1941.

149 LAC, RG 28, box 7, file 3 of 12, "DMS History of Wartime Housing Limited."

150 LAC, R1211-0-40-C, Wartime Housing Papers.

151 Wade, "Wartime Housing Limited," 44, 46. See also LAC, RG 28, box 7, file 3 of 12, "DMS History of Wartime Housing Limited," which claims 17,170 temporary houses were built by the end of 1944, when the corporation switched to construction of permanent homes for veterans.

152 Bacher, *Keeping to the Marketplace*, 123–4; Wade, *Houses for All*.

153 Mansbridge, *Launching History*, 96; Wade, "Wartime Housing Limited," 56n19.

154 Canada, DBS, *Census of Canada, 1941*, vol. 2, *Population*, table 7, gives Pictou's population as 3,069.

155 Sherwood, *Pictou Parade*, 36–7.

156 UBCSC, H.R. MacMillan Papers, box 100, file 17, MacMillan to J.P. Pettigrew, 2 April 1942.

157 *CS&MEN* 14, no. 1 (August 1942): 64; H.T. Mitchell Papers, Mitchell to wife, 15 June 1943.

158 Marcil, *Tall Ships and Tankers*, 253–4.

159 Bacher, *Keeping to the Marketplace*, 132.

160 Sherwood, *Pictou Parade*, 36; Wallis, comp., *Story of Pictou's Park Ships*, 22, from *The Foc's'le*, 2 February 1943.

161 *Dry Dock Bulletin* 1, no. 8 (June 1944): 23.

162 White, "Conscription City," 114; Kimber, *Sailors, Slackers and Blind Pigs*, 211.

163 Cuthbertson, "Pocketbooks and Patriotism."

164 Canada, DBS, *Canada Year Book, 1948–1949*, 1016.

165 For more, see Keshen, *Saints, Sinners and Soldiers*, 31–4.

166 Ibid., 113–14.

167 Victoria Machinery Depot, *The Convoy* 3, no. 6 (November 1944): 1.

168 *Dry Dock Bulletin* 1, no. 4 (January 1944): 23.

169 *Vancouver News Herald*, 23 March 1943.

170 See NVMA for a complete run of *The Wallace Shipbuilder*.

171 For more about *The Compass*, see Pritchard, "Fifty-Six Minesweepers and the Toronto Shipbuilding Company during the Second World War," 43.

172 Dufault, "L'Écho de la marine, 1944–1948," 21–6.

CHAPTER SEVEN

1 LAC, MG 28 I103, box 54, file 11, R. Woodbridge to N.S. Dowd, national secretary, ACCL, 30 November 1939.

2 Ibid., Dowd to Woodbridge, 9 December 1939.

3 Logan, *Trade Unions in Canada*, 133–4.

4 Heron, *Canadian Labour Movement*. This Marxist interpretation stresses the struggles within the labour movement more than the conflict between labour and government and between business and government.

5 McInnis, *Harnessing Labour Confrontation*, 43.

6 See Morton, *Working People*, 151–64, for a brief discussion of industrial-trade unionism in Canada before the war. See also Heron, *Canadian Labour Movement*, 175.

7 Abella, *Nationalism, Communism and Canadian Labour*, 51–3; Morton, *Working People*, 169.

8 McInnis, *Harnessing Labour Confrontation*, 43.

9 Rouillard, *Histoire du syndicalisme québécois des origines à nos jours*, table 4.5, 216.

10 Education committees of the Confédération des syndicates nationaux and the Centrale de l'ensignement de Québec, *History of the Labour Movement in Quebec*, 143.

11 Rouillard, "Mutations de la Confédération des travailleurs catholiques du Canada, 1940–1960," 245.

12 Ibid., 207–8.

13 LAC, RG 27, box 168, file 613.05: 3, letter to the editor from Norman Dowd, *Financial Post*, 18 September 1937. See LAC, MG 28 I103, CFL Fonds, box 110, for copies of *Labour Review*, the CFL's professionally produced journal from 1940 to 1942, which contained advertising from banks, companies, the Ontario government, and the Liberal Party of Canada! See also, LAC, box 54, file 1, Dowd to R. Woodbridge, 20 January 1939; Dowd doubted whether the CFL contained 5,000 members, although it claimed 50,000.

14 See Palmer, *Working-Class Experience*, 203–6, on the appearance of communism between the wars in Canada's labour movement. For accounts of communist organizing activities in Canada's trade unions, see White, *Hard Man to Beat*; and Smith, *Cold Warrior*.

15 See MacDowell, "*Remember Kirkland Lake*," 3–35, for a good survey of the Dominion government's approach to industrial relations.

16 Logan, *Trade Unions in Canada*, 521–3; Heron, *Canadian Labour Movement*, 70. See also, Lichtenstein, *Labor's War at Home*, 47–51; and Kersten, *Labor's Home Front*, 8, 28, 40, 46.

17 MacDowell, "*Remember Kirkland Lake*," 239.

18 See, for example, Heron, *Canadian Labour Movement*, 70.

19 MacDowell, *Renegade Lawyer*, 92–3.

20 Granatstein, *Canada's War*, 107, 252; Martin, *Very Public Life*, vol. 1, 215–16.

21 Pickersgill, ed., *Mackenzie King Record*, vol. 1, 310–11. For more on Mitchell, see Granatstein, *Canada's War*, 215, 221; Martin, *Very Public Life*, vol. 1, 286–7; MacDowell, *"Remember Kirkland Lake,"* 259n15; and McInnis, *Harnessing Labour Confrontation*, 31–2, 240n60.

22 Canada, National War Labour Board, *Proceedings [of the] Inquiry into Labour Relations and Wage Conditions in Canada*, 1286.

23 Stevenson, *Canada's Greatest Wartime Muddle*, 6, 12, 180n7.

24 Bothwell and Kilbourn, *C.D. Howe*, 162–5.

25 See MacFarlane, "Agents of Control or Chaos?"

26 Webber, "Malaise of Compulsory Conciliation."

27 McInnis, *Harnessing Labour Confrontation*, 184.

28 Betcherman, *Ernest Lapointe*, 296–300.

29 Jamieson, *Times of Trouble*, 276–95; Canada, DBS, *Canada Year Book, 1945*, 789.

30 Jamieson, *Times of Trouble*, 282.

31 LAC, MG 28 I103, box 55, file 9, A.G. Jacques, secretary-treasurer, Local 2, BISUC, to Dowd, 11 July 1940, reported that both Yarrows Limited and Victoria Machinery Depot were closed shops.

32 Webber, "Malaise of Compulsory Conciliation," 141; MacDowell, *"Remember Kirkand Lake,"* 239.

33 *Labour Gazette* 40 (June 1940): 656–7; Madsen, "Continuous Production in British Columbia Shipyards during the Second World War," 3–4.

34 NVMA, Fonds 27, box 561, union agreements and correspondence, 1939–46.

35 *Labour Gazette* 40 (December 1940): 1233.

36 *Labour Gazette* 40 (October 1940): 1007–9; *Labour Gazette* 40 (December 1940): 1234. See also Copp, "Rise of Industrial Unions in Montreal, 1935–1945," 858–9.

37 UMCP, IUMSWA, series 1, subseries 4, file 1, Ivan A. Emery to John Green, president, IUMSWA, 14 April 1937; *Shipyard Worker* 2, no. 5 (23 April 1937): 2.

38 LAC, RG 27, box 407, file 155 [QUA reel 2455].

39 *Labour Gazette* 41 (February 1941): 107.

40 Ibid., 109–10.

41 LAC, RG 27, box 407, file 156 [QUA reel 2457]; *Labour Gazette* 41 (February 1941): 107.

42 LAC, MG 28 I103, box 54, file 8, H. Forrest, local president, to Dowd, 20 November 1940; ibid., R.S. Woods, recording secretary, Local 4, to Dowd, 3 November 1941; ibid., monthly membership reports.

43 UVA, Victoria Labour Council Fonds, box 4, file 6, minute book, 1 June 1942.

44 *Labour Gazette* 41 (February 1941): 111.

45 *Labour Gazette* 40 (June 1940): 656–7.

46 *Labour Gazette* 41 (February 1941): 111–12.

47 See MacDowell, *"Remember Kirkland Lake,"* 240; and Stevenson, *Canada's Greatest Wartime Muddle*, 92.

48 LAC, RG 27, box 409, file 49 [QUA reel 2457], *Labour Gazette* 41 (July 1941); *Canadian Unionist* (August 1941).

49 LAC, RG 27, box 409, file 49; *Labour Gazette* 41 (October 1941); *Labour Gazette* 41 (May 1941).

50 QUA, Canada Steamship Lines Ltd, box 109, Kingston Shipbuilding Co. minute book, no. 2, 153.

51 BCARS, Add. Mss. 448, box 5, Department of Labour file, agreement dated 17 September 1941.

52 MacDowell, *"Remember Kirkland Lake,"* 82, 240.

53 See Nicholson, "Maritime Labour Irritation," 145.

54 *Labour Gazette* 41 (June 1941): 620.

55 *Canadian Transportation* 44 (December 1941): 698.

56 See PC 6931, 2 September 1941, for the order-in-council establishing the royal commission; and PC 7480, 25 September 1941, and PC 9272, 27 November 1941, for modifications of its terms. See also *Labour Gazette* 41 (September 1941): 1036.

57 See BANQ-CAQ, E 24, 1960-01-040, box 197, file G10-41-42, for the report of the conciliation board in the dispute between Morton Engineering and Dry Dock Company and its employees, who were members of Local 601 of the International Brotherhood of Boilermakers, dated 26 October 1941.

58 Some of this evidence may be found in LAC, RG 27, box 145, file 611.04: 22, exhibits 1 to 46 submitted to the royal commission to investigate wage rates and working conditions in shipyards in Quebec and Ontario.

59 Canada, Government of, "Royal Commission on Shipbuilding in the Provinces of Quebec and Ontario."

60 LAC, MG 28 I103, box 54, file 9, copy of PC 629, dated 26 January 1942.

61 *Labour Gazette* 42 (December 1942): 1374.

62 MacDowell, "1943 Steel Strike against Wartime Wage Controls."

63 LAC, RG 27, box 421, file 297 [QUA reel 2468], *Ottawa Morning Journal*, 24 September 1942.

64 LAC, MG 28 I103, box 65, file 3, application to CCL for local union charter, 13 November 1942; ibid., Thomas B. MacLachlan to Conroy, 16 November 1943; and ibid., copy of Ray Brunelle, Midland, to MacLachlan, 8 December 1942.

65 Ibid., MacLachlan to Conroy, 21 December 1942, and MacLachlan to Conroy, 9 January 1943; ibid., monthly report of local chartered union, October 1943.

66 Ibid., "certificate of counting of ballots," enclosed in MacLachlan to Conroy, 11 December 1943.

67 UMCP, IUMSWA, "National Office Charters, Local 34, Halifax"; *Shipyard Worker* 4, no. 11 (17 November 1939): 1; UMCP, IUMSWA, series 1, subseries 4, file 1, minutes of general executive board, 4–5 November 1939, Camden, New Jersey. Chiefly to disparage its efforts, James K. Bell mistakenly claimed the Halifax local was chartered in 1937; see Calhoun, *"Ole Boy,"* 25–6, 31.

68 UMCP, IUMSWA, box 5, file 82, Local 34, IUMSWA, official-reports sheets; thirteen of these monthly sheets exist for the period December 1939 to March 1941.

69 Ibid., J. O'Connell, president, Local 34, IUMSWA, to Philip H. Van Gelder, secretary, IUMSWA, Halifax, 6 July 1940.

70 Ibid., Van Gelder to Sibly Barrett, director, Steel Workers Organizational Committee, 12 August 1940.

71 LAC, MG 28 I103, box 64, file 11, C.H. Millard to Dowd, 9 September 1940; UMCP, IUMSWA, box 5, file 85, Van Gelder to Frank Meech, secretary, Local 34, IUMSWA, 10 September 1940; ibid., Meech to Van Gelder, 12 October 1940.

72 UMCP, IUMSWA, subseries 4, box 1, file 1, "Officers report to the seventh national convention," 23 September 1941, 10; UMCP, IUMSWA, subseries 5, file 82, Mosher to John Green, 18 January 1941, and Green to Murray Lowe, financial secretary, IUMSWA, 17 February 1941.

73 UMCP, IUMSWA, subseries 5, file 82, Frank Meech, recording secretary, Local 1, IUMSWA, to Van Gelder, May 1941.

74 LAC, MG 28 I103, box 65, file 9, telegram, Meech to Dowd, 16 April 1941.

75 Ibid., Mosher to James O'Connell, president, Local 1, IUMSWC, 29 April 1941.

76 LAC, MG 28 I103, box 65, file 12, agreement between T. Hogan Company and Local 1, IUMSWC, 8 July 1941. See LAC, MG 28 I103, box 64, file 11, for details of negotiating the agreement with Halifax Shipyards Limited.

77 LAC, MG 28 I103, box 65, file 14, "Memorandum of organization in the Halifax area," circa February 1942.

78 LAC, MG 28 I103, box 64, file 11, monthly "reports of local chartered union."

79 LAC, MG 28 I103, box 65, file 14, officials of Local 1, IUMSWC, to Conroy, 1 July 1942; *Ottawa Journal*, 29 August 1942.

80 For a sampling of the rich historiography of Nova Scotia's radical labour tradition, see Frank, "Cape Breton Coal Industry and the Rise and Fall of the British Empire Steel Corporation"; MacGillivray, "Military Aid to the Civil Power," 45–64; McKay, "Realm of Uncertainty," 3–57; Manley, "Preaching the Red Stuff," 65–114; Earle, "Down with Hitler and Silby Barrett"; and Stevenson, *Canada's Greatest Wartime Muddle*, chapter 5, "Coal Labour in Nova Scotia," 90–117.

81 This and following paragraphs are based largely on Chouinard, "Shipyard Struggles." See also Calhoun, *"Ole Boy,"* 24–5.

82 *Labour Gazette* 42 (December 1942): 1396–7.

83 LAC, RG 27, box 424, no. 416, H.P. Pettigrove to A. MacNamara, 7 December 1942.

84 LAC, MG 28 I103, box 65, file 5, application for charter for Local 7, BISUC, for workers at HMC Dockyard, 11 August 1943; ibid., monthly reports of membership in local chartered unions.

85 LAC, MG 28 I103, box 65, file 4, Shea to Conroy, 7 August 1943.

86 Ibid., Shea to Conroy, 17 August 1943.

87 Ibid.

88 Ibid., Shea to Conroy, 1 December 1943, enclosing wage rates currently paid to 283 workers at Clare Shipbuilding.

89 LAC, RG 27, box 430, file 342 [QUA reel 2474], memorandum of agreement between Local 6, IUMSWC, and Clare Shipbuilding Ltd, 16 September 1943.

90 LAC, MG 28 I103, box 65, file 4, monthly reports of local chartered unions, for Meteghan, Local 6, BISUC.

91 LAC, MG 28 I103, box 65, file 6, Donald MacDonald to Conroy, 14 October 1943; ibid., agreement between Cann's Marine Repair and Local 8, BISUC, 24 November 1943.

92 Calhoun, *"Ole Boy,"* 22.

93 MacEachern, *George MacEachern*, 109. According to a photograph in Calhoun, *"Ole Boy,"* 41, the first issue of the *Marine Worker* was published at St John on 7 May 1943 by Local 3 of the IUMSWC.

94 LAC, MG 28 I103, box 65, file 2, G.M. Dick to Dowd, 23 April 1942.

95 Ibid., Donald MacDonald to Conroy, 30 August 1942.

96 Ibid., Louis MacCormack, Local 2, BISUC, to Conroy, 20 August 1943; ibid., M.M. McLean to Conroy, 23 August 1943; *Halifax Herald*, 20 August 1943.

97 LAC, RG 28, box 256, file 196-13-3, "Report of the Controller of Ship Repairs and Salvage," period ending 31 August 1944.

98 LAC, MG 28 I103, box 65, file 5, Conroy to Wm.L. Lindsay, secretary, Local 7, BISUC, 20 March 1944.

99 LAC, MG 28 I103, box 65, file 8, Milfred Hubly to Conroy, 6 July 1944; ibid., application to CCL for a union-local charter, 20 September 1944; and ibid., Conroy to Hubly, 5 October 1944.

100 UVA, Victoria Labour Council Fonds, Jay Gilbert and Gary Carre, "Inventory," Victoria and District Labour Council, 1889–1983, 6–7.

101 The most detailed account of the controversy is Madsen, "Continuous Production," to which I am heavily indebted.

102 NVMA, Fonds 97, box 2, file 3, J.D.V. Kinvig binder for data on piecework; J.S. Marshall and Co. Ltd, *History of Burrard Dry Dock Company*, vol. 3, 222–3.

103 Mansbridge, *Launching History*, 73.

104 Walter Haydon, quoted in *Vancouver News Herald*, 26 January 1942.

105 J.S. Marshall and Co. Ltd, *History of Burrard Dry Dock*, vol. 3, 222–3.

106 UBCSC, H.R. MacMillan Papers, box 100, file 16, memorandum, MacMillan to Howe, 30 January 1942.

107 QUA, William Clifford Clark Papers, file N-2-4-5-2, copy of memorandum, H.T. Mitchell to MacMillan, 8 January 1941.

108 Wallis, comp., *Story of Pictou's Park Ships*, 82–3, from *The Fo'c'sle*, 13 September 1944.

109 See UBCSC, H.R. MacMillan Papers, MacMillan to Howe, 30 January 1942.

110 LAC, RG 27, box 268, file 1, list of exhibits, exhibit 23G, Royal Commission on Shipbuilding in Ontario and Quebec.

111 LAC, RG 28, box 77, file 1-1-162, Sheils to James Eckman, 12 March 1942.

112 AO, Floyd S. Chalmers Fonds, file 2-0-89, memorandum re: MacMillan, 5 February 1942.

113 Madsen, "Continuous Production," 6.

114 LAC, MG 28 I103, box 236, file 14, minutes of a conference of all shipyard-union delegates held in Victoria Hall, Vancouver, Wednesday, 25 March 1942; Madsen, "Continuous Production," 7.

115 LAC, RG 27 [reel T-10093], box 88, file 423.2: 10, pt 2, telegram, MacMillan to Humphrey Mitchell, 4 April 1942.

116 See note 112.

117 LAC, RG 27 [reel T-10093], box 88, file 423.2: 10, pt 2, Sheils to Bryce Stewart, deputy minister of labour, 11 April 1942.

118 See LAC, RG 27, box 418, no. 155, for a copy of PC 3636, 1 May 1942.

119 LAC, RG 27 [reel T-10093], box 88, file 432.2: 10, pt 2, M.M. Maclean to Mackenzie King, 13 May 1942, quoted in Madsen, "Continuous Production," 12.

120 CVA, Add. Mss. 362, box 551-D-7, file 7.

121 LAC, RG 27, box 418, file 155, *Vancouver Sun*, 23 June 1942; ibid., no. 157.

122 See ibid., file 157, for a copy of PC 5450, 25 June 1940.

123 Ibid., file 155, *Montreal Gazette*, 15 July 1942.

124 LAC, RG 27, boxes 268 to 270, contain the report of the royal commission and the proceedings of inquiry.

125 LAC, RG 27, box 418, file 156, "Shipyard Machinists Vote for 7-day Week," *Vancouver Sun*, 7 December 1942. See also *Victoria Times*, 15 December 1942.

126 LAC, RG 27, box 418, file 156, "Shipyard Work Plan Delay Protested," *Vancouver Sun*, 6 January 1943.

127 UBCSC, Trade Union Research Bureau Records, Boilermakers and Iron Shipbuilders Union, Local 1, marine workers and boilermakers scrapbook, box 10, file 18, *Vancouver Province*, 24 April 1943.

128 LAC, MG 28 I103, box 55, file 8, memorandum of agreement between VMD and Local 2, BISUC, 22 March 1943.

129 Ibid., A. McAuslane to Mosher, 30 April 1943.

130 Madsen, "Continuous Production," 24.

131 LAC, RG 27, box 418, file 156, *Vancouver Province*, 10 September 1942, reporting remarks made by Chris Pritchard.

132 Lane, *Ships for Victory*, figure 7, 64.

133 *CS&MEN* 13, no. 5 (December 1942): 62.

134 Abella, *Nationalism, Communism and Canadian Labour*, 80–3. For another view, see White, *Hard Man to Beat*, 177.

135 *Vancouver Province*, 2 January 1943; White, *Hard Man to Beat*, 40.

136 LAC, RG 27, box 417, file 129 [QUA reel 2463], "Shipyard Strikes at Vancouver."

137 LAC, RG 27, box 418, file 145, *Vancouver Province*, 19 June 1942.

138 See LAC, RG 27, box 417, file 129 [QUA reel 2463], "Shipyard Strikes at Vancouver," and "700 Shipyard Men Quit: Then Go Back to Jobs," *Vancouver Sun*, 10 July 1942. See also LAC, RG 27, box 418, files 145, 147, and 154 to 157 [QUA reel 2463], for details.

139 NVMA, Fonds 27, Burrard Dry Dock Clippings, vol. 5, file 571A, *Vancouver Province*, 6 January 1942.

140 White, *Hard Man To Beat*, 176.

141 CVA, Add. Mss. 717, box 556-B-4, minute book, vol. 1, 14 April and 20 May 1942.

142 NVMA, Fonds 27, Burrard Dry Dock Clippings from *Vancouver Province*, 2 and 4 January 1943.

143 "CCL Suspension of Boilermakers Invalidated," *Vancouver Province*, 20 March 1943.

144 See Abella, *Nationalism, Communism and Canadian Labour*, 80–5, for an account of these events from a social-democratic perspective. For a communist point of view, see White, *Hard Man to Beat*. The official union history by MacIntosh, *Boilermakers in British Columbia*, denies that communists ever led the union during the war.

145 UBCSC, Trade Union Research Bureau Records, box 61, file 12, "Formation Conference," 27 February 1944; Abella, *Nationalism, Communism and Canadian Labour*, 84–5.

146 White, *Hard Man to Beat*, 174.

147 See Morton, *Working People*, 179–84, for a strong expression of this view.

148 Heron, *Canadian Labour Movement*, 80. MacDowell, *"Remember Kirkland Lake,"* 237, attaches great importance to the CCL's apparent joining with the CCF as a threat to the federal Liberal Party. See also Robinson, *Measure of Democracy*, 135. For a contrary view that working-class actions rather than politics led government to legislate PC 1003, see Palmer, *Working-Class Experience*, 237; and McInnis, *Harnessing Labour Confrontation*, 40–1.

149 NSARM, MG 2, box 1503, file 391, Angus L. Macdonald diary, 1 September 1943.

150 Jamieson, *Times of Trouble*, 294; McInnis, *Harnessing Labour Confrontation*, 41–2.

151 Virtually every labour historian has written about PC 1003, but see McInnis, *Harnessing Labour Confrontation*, 41–2; and more important, Gonick, Phillips, and Vorst, eds, *Labour Pains, Labour Gains*.

152 This calculation is based on thirty-seven strikes in Quebec shipbuilding plants during the war as listed in Department of Labour files on strikes and lockouts. See LAC, RG 27, boxes 407 to 440.

153 For more on labour relations in Quebec's wartime shipyards, see Pritchard, "Long Angry Summer of '43."

154 See Copp, "Rise of Industrial Unions in Montreal," 857, 865–6.

155 Ibid., 847; MacDowell, "Formation of the Canadian Industrial Relations System during World War Two."

156 Canada, Department of Reconstruction and Supply, *Location and Effects of Wartime Industrial Expansion in Canada, 1939–1944.*

157 "Report of Board in Dispute between the Davie Shipbuilding and Repairing Company, Limited; Morton Engineering and Dry Dock Company, Limited; and George T. Davie & Sons,

Limited, Lauzon, Quebec, and Their Representative Employees," *Labour Gazette* 43 (June 1943): 771.

158 Ibid. For the full report, see LAC, MG 28 I103, box 53, file 8, Report of board of conciliation and investigation, 12 May 1943.

159 LAC, RG 27, box 429, file 211 [QUA reel 2472], assistant commissioner F.L. Mead, RCMP, to deputy minister of labour, 15 June 1943; and ibid., Quebec City, *L'Action catholique*, 15 June 1943; there are slight variations in the numbers reported in these two sources. See also LAC, MG 28 I103, box 73, file 4, M.M. Maclean to Mosher, 3 and 11 June 1943.

160 LAC, RG 2, registers, PC 5526, 15 June 1943, revoked PC 4893, 14 June 1943, and replaced it. See also LAC, RG 28, box 32, file 104, H.L. Clifford to Howe, 14 September 1943.

161 *Montreal Gazette*, 16 June 1943; Kennedy, *History of the Department of Munitions and Supply* (hereafter *History of DMS*), vol. 1, 404.

162 Canada, House of Commons, *Debates*, 3599, 14 June 1943.

163 "Strikes Hit 3 Quebec Shipyards," *Montreal Star*, 15 June 1943.

164 See MacDowell, "1943 Steel Strike against Wartime Wage Controls."

165 *Montréal La Presse*, 17 June 1943, my translation: "The strike must be settled simultaneously in the three shipyards; otherwise, there will be no possibility of agreement."

166 *Montreal La Presse*, 17 June 1943; *Sydney Post-Record*, 21 June 1943.

167 *Quebec Chronicle Telegraph*, 22 June 1943.

168 *Montreal Star*, 25 June 1943. The newspaper got the ships' names wrong; they were SS *High Park*, HMS *Prudent*, and HMS *Pert* rather than "Hyde Park," "Prejudice," and "Perth."

169 *Windsor Star*, 28 June 1943; *St. Thomas Times Journal*, 28 June 1943.

170 "Mitchell Is Wrong Say Labor Leaders," *Montreal Gazette*, 4 August 1943.

171 LAC, RG 27, box 430, file 249 [QUA reel 2473], director of industrial relations (DIR) report; *Labour Gazette* 43 (August 1943): 1122, 1123, 1126.

172 "Organizer Fined for Inciting Strike," *Ottawa Morning Citizen*, 19 August 1943.

173 LAC, RG 27, box 430, file 249 [QUA reel 2473], "Lettre Ouverte au Premier Ministre King."

174 "Labor Organizer David Coté Held for Urging Men to Continue Strike," *Montreal Gazette*, 24 July 1943.

175 LAC, RG 27, box 430, file 249 [QUA reel 2473], Department of Labour news release, 6 August 1943.

176 Ibid., DIR report, 2.

177 "Mitchell Is Wrong Say Labor Leaders," *Montreal Gazette*, 4 August 1943.

178 "Organizer Fined for Inciting Strike," *Ottawa Morning Citizen*, 19 August 1943; *Labour Gazette* 43 (September 1943): 1243.

179 LAC, RG 27, box 430, file 257 [QUA reel 2473], employment report, 22 July 1943.

180 Ibid., DIR report; ibid., F. Lafortune to Maclean, DIR, 27 July 1943.

181 *Labour Gazette* 43 (August 1943): 1123.

182 LAC, RG 27, box 430, file 257, telegram, H.A.R. Gagnon to commissioner, RCMP, 19 July 1943.

183 "Strikers Pelt RCMP Guards at Sorel Plant," *Montreal Gazette*, 20 July 1943.

184 "Le syndicat remporte une victoire à Sorel," *Montréal La Presse*, 20 July 1943; "La 'Marine Industries' annonce un règlement de la grève," *Montreal La Patrie*, 20 July 1943.

185 BANQ-CAQ, E 24 1960-01-040, box 240, file L29-42-43, J. Edouard Simard, vice president, Sorel Industries Ltd, to Edgar Rochette, ministre du travail, 17 February 1943. Of 4,339 employees, 3,518 cast ballots.

186 See BANQ-CAQ, E 24 1960-01-040, box 256, files G160 and G162-45-46, for some of this history.

187 LAC, RG 28, box 32, "DMS History–Quebec Shipyards"; ibid., Wilfrid Gagnon to J. de N. Kennedy, 26 October 1948.

188 Kennedy, *History of DMS*, vol. 1, 404; LAC, RG 28, box 32, "DMS History–Quebec Shipyards"; LAC, RG 28, box 32, Clifford to Howe, 14 September 1943.

189 LAC, RG 27, box 430, file 265 [QUA reel 2473], DIR report; ibid., file 271, DIR report; ibid., Mead, assistant commissioner, RCMP, to deputy minister of labour, 19 July 1943; *Labour Gazette* 43 (September 1943): 1242.

190 BANQ-CAQ, E 24, 1960-01-040, box 222, file A 40-42-43, W. Beaulac, directeur, to Gérard Tremblay, sous-ministre de travail, 14 December 1942 and 12 January 1943; ibid., Raymond A. Robic, chef du personnel, to Gérard Tremblay, 12 January 1944.

191 LAC, RG 27, box 434, file 433 [QUA reel 2477], strike report, 13 December 1943; ibid., undated RCMP report; ibid., commissioner S.T. Wood to deputy minister of labour, 26 November 1943; *Labour Gazette* 43 (December 1943): 1692.

192 LAC, MG 28 I103, box 65, file 7, Lionel P. Dion, secretary-treasurer, Local 9, IUMSWC, to Dowd, 8 August 1945.

193 *Montreal Gazette*, 29 July 1942.

194 McInnis, *Harnessing Labour Confrontation*, 39, 207n101.

195 Granatstein, *Canada's War*, 279–81.

196 See, for example, Palmer, *Working-Class Experience*, 236.

197 Morton, *Working People*, 170.

CHAPTER EIGHT

1 Canada, DBS, *Iron and Steel and Their Products in Canada, 1943–1945*, 52.

2 Kennedy, *History of the Department of Munitions and Supply* (hereafter *History of DMS*), vol. 1, 496–7.

3 No detailed history of the Canadian steel industry during the Second World War has been written, but valuable accounts may be found in Kilbourn, *Elements Combined*, ch. 10, 159–81; and McDowall, *Steel at the Sault*, ch. 8, 178–211. Kennedy's "Steel Control," in *History of DMS*, vol. 2, 209–34, is also helpful.

4 For more on the evolution of steel and its transformative effect on society, see the brilliant study by Misa, *Nation of Steel*.

5 Hughes, "Shipbuilding Materials." Tensile strength is the resistance of material to breaking under tension, the opposite of compressive strength.

6 Smith et al., "History of the British Admiralty Technical Mission in Canada" (hereafter "History of BATM"), 25.

7 Heron and Storey, "Work and Struggle in the Canadian Steel Industry, 1900–1950," 211.

8 Statistics for this period are located in Canada, DBS, *Iron and Steel and Their Products in Canada, 1943–1945*. Leacy, ed., *Historical Statistics of Canada*, R series, nos 693–704, does not include steel plate, sheet, and strip.

9 Canada, DBS, *Iron and Steel and Their Products in Canada, 1943–1945*, table 61, "Production and Factory Sales of Steel Plates, 1939–1945."

10 DHH, Series 30: 8000, 75/270, interview by Lt Kerr with Mr Isard, general superintendent, Yarrows Ltd, 22 May 1945; Isard claimed the cost of steel was only 8 per cent, even though plate was shipped from Hamilton, Ontario.

11 For quantities, see Canada, DBS, *Iron and Steel and Their Products in Canada, 1943–1945*, table 207, "Materials Used in Shipbuilding, 1943–1945." Babbit metal was a soft alloy of tin, antimony, copper, zinc, and usually lead, employed to line bearings.

12 MMGLK, German and Milne Papers, 1989.0044.0005.6, "List of Equipment and Materials – 15 vessels – quantities for one vessel, hull steel."

13 LAC, RG 28, box 171, "Canadian aggregate steel requirements for Canadian production programmes, 1 January–31 December 1944," 15 October 1943.

14 UBCSC, H.R. MacMillan Papers, box 100, file 16, MacMillan to Howe, 2 September 1942. According to Lane, *Ships for Victory*, 311, 77 per cent of a ship's hull is comprised of steel plate.

15 See note 12.

16 LAC, MG 27 III B20, box 57, file S-23-4, "UN Shipping Position as of 31 August 1942."

17 A complete list of these companies at the end of 1940 includes Burlington Steel Company Limited at Hamilton, Canadian Car and Foundry Company Limited at Longue Point, Quebec, Canadian Furnace Limited at Port Colborne, Canadian Tube and Steel Products Limited at Montreal, and Manitoba Rolling Mill Company Limited at Winnipeg.

18 Canada, DBS, "Monthly Report, Production of Iron and Steel in Canada," September 1939 and December 1941, table 9. Seven blast furnaces existed in 1939: one at Algoma, two at Canadian Furnace, two at Dosco, and two at Stelco. In September 1941 each of the four companies had three blast furnaces in operation, for a total of twelve.

19 Canada, DBS, *Iron and Steel and Their Products in Canada, 1943–1945*, table 61; LAC, RG 28, box 257, file 196-14(2), "Tentative Summary of Progress in the Canadian Primary Steel Industry from the Outbreak of the War, 1939 to 1941," E.A. Taylor, 18 October 1941.

20 Cox, *Canadian Strength*, 13–15. See also Bryce, *Canada and the Cost of World War II*, 27, 31, 338n38.

21 LAC, RG 28, box 261, file 196-14-13, "History of Steel Control," 1 November 1943 (hereafter "History of Steel Control"), 11; LAC, RG 28, box 195, file 196-2D-2, personal and confidential, F.H. Brown to J.G. Godsoe, 12 September 1944; Greene, ed., *Who's Who in Canada, 1943–44*, 1389.

22 This paragraph is indebted to McDowall, *Steel at the Sault*, 182–5, for a good account of Steel Control's activities.

23 LAC, "History of Steel Control," 5–6.

24 Lauderbaugh, *American Steel Makers and the Coming of the Second World War*, table 2.

25 LAC, RG 19, box 3988, file S-9-1, "Preliminary Report on the Canadian Steel Shortage," by Arthur G. McKee and Co. Engineers, Cleveland, Ohio, prepared in January 1941 for the DMS.

26 LAC, RG 28, box 171, "Report on Steel Requirement for 1941," revised, 6 March 1941. This report may be the source for the claim that prewar Canada imported one-third of its annual steel from the United States.

27 LAC, RG 28, box 257, file 196-14(2), "Tentative Summary of Progress in the Canadian Primary Steel Industry from the Outbreak of the War, 1939 to 1941," E.A. Taylor, 18 October 1941.

28 LAC, RG 28, box 22, "History of Steel Control, October 1st 1943 to October 31st 1945" (hereafter "History of Steel Control [addendum]"), 48, corrects the earlier "History of Steel Control," which states that the plate mill was being erected at the outbreak of war.

29 LAC, "History of Steel Control," 48; Kennedy, *History of DMS*, vol. 2, 223. Forbes, "Consolidating Disparity," 6, is the source of much error and confusion, as he claims the existence of a grand conspiracy by Howe and his officials to block the reopening of this plate mill. Any delay in deciding to rehabilitate the mill was brief and chiefly due to the uncertainty of the times.

30 Canada, House of Commons, *Debates*, 2104, speech by Howe, 2 April 1941.

31 Ibid., 1628, speech by Howe, 18 March 1941.

32 Forbes, "Consolidating Disparity," 7.

33 LAC, RG 28, box 195, file 196-2D-2, MacMillan to R.C. Berkinshaw, director general, priorities branch, DMS, 24 July 1941.

34 Ibid. box 257, file 196-14 (3), personal and confidential, Hoey, associate steel controller, to J.B. Carswell, director general, DMS office, Washington, 2 February 1943.

35 Ibid.

36 Kennedy, *History of DMS*, vol. 1, 242.

37 UBCSC, H.R. MacMillan Papers, box 100, file 16, memorandum, MacMillan to Howe, 10 October 1941; ibid., MacMillan's secretary to W.J. Bennett, Howe's executive assistant, 12 October 1941.

38 LAC, RG 28, box 256, file 196-13-3, report on ship repairs for period ending 31 October 1941.

39 Ibid., box 260, file 196-14-8, W.T.C. Hackett, secretary, Wartime Industries Control Board (WICB), to R.G. Berkinshaw, chairman, WICB, 17 October 1944; ibid., Hackett to Berkinshaw, 22 October 1942.

40 Canada, DBS, "Monthly Report on Steel Ingots," February 1946, table 1.

41 Canada, DBS, *Iron and Steel and Their Products in Canada, 1943–1945*, table 44, "Alloy Steel Ingots and Castings, 1939–1945."

42 Ibid., table 61.

43 "Canada's Steel Situation," *Canadian Machinery and Manufacturing News* 52 (December 1941): 135–7, 244.

44 Canadian Wartime Information Board, *Canada at War*, no. 45, "Recapitulation Issue" (July 1945): 74.

45 Kennedy, *History of DMS*, vol. 1, 239.

46 Ibid.

47 House of Commons, *Debates*, 132, speech by Howe, 22 May 1940.

48 NSARM, MG 2, box 1523, file 1157, "Imports of Steel Plate into Canada," sent by J.D. Dray to W.F. Drysdale, director general of munitions, 24 December 1940 (see table 3).

49 Lane, *Ships for Victory*, 314.

50 LAC, RG 19, box 3971, file B-2-8-9B, estimates of requirement, 10 February 1942.

51 UBCSC, H.R. MacMillan Papers, box 100, file 16, memorandum, MacMillan to Howe, 26 July 1941.

52 LAC, RG 28, box 260, file 196-14-8; see, for example, "Steel Budget for the Second Quarter of 1942 (April, May and June Combined) – March 2nd 1942."

53 Americans also encountered difficulties with this system. For an illuminating account of the problems securing efficient distribution of steel plate to the American shipbuilding industry, see Lane, *Ships for Victory*, 312–18.

54 McDowall, *Steel at the Sault*, 196.

55 Lauderbaugh, *American Steel Makers*, table 2.

56 Hennessy, "Rise and Fall of Canadian Maritime Policy, 1939–1965," 64, claims that shortages of specialized steel and other components presented a major bottleneck in Canadian ship production, and he accuses the steel controller of not using Canadian "milling capacity because small production runs for these components would disrupt larger programmes." He probably means rolling capacity and has misunderstood the controller's requirement that Canadian mills take the small orders so that American mills would receive only large ones.

57 LAC, RG 28, box 257, file 196-14(2), Hoey to Carswell, 2 February 1943.

58 Ibid., "Steel Orders Placed in the United States," 21 July 1942; H.T. Mitchell Papers, Mitchell to wife, 5 October 1942.

59 LAC, RG 28, box 257, file 196-14(2), F.B. Kilbourn to H.J. Carmichael, 22 October 1942. The allocation comprised 345,000 tons of carbon, 22,000 tons of alloy, and 500 tons of stainless steel.

60 LAC, "History of Steel Control," 64.

61 Stacey, *Arms, Men and Governments*, 176; Rosen, *Combined Boards of the Second World War*, 155. Rohmer, *Biography of Edward Plunket Taylor*, 131–2, indicates that Taylor found nothing to do on the board and used his appointment to return to Toronto and attend to his business affairs, which were badly in need of attention after a two-year absence.

62 See, for example, Hennessy, "Rise and Fall of Canadian Maritime Policy," 64n38.

63 Rosen, *Combined Boards*, 36–7; Hall, *North American Supply*, 366.

64 See LAC, RG 28, box 257, file 196-14(3), Carswell to Hoey, 25 January 1943, and Hoey's reply, 2 February 1943.

65 LAC, "History of Steel Control [addendum]," 35.

66 For this reason, ibid., table 61, shows higher annual production than is presented in table 8.4. Domestic production data for 1939 and 1940 are included as a reminder that this plate was not suitable for shipbuilding, as was the product of later years.

67 Kilbourn, *Elements Combined*, 170.

68 Canada, DBS, *Iron and Steel and Their Products in Canada, 1943–1945*, table 321, "Scrap Iron and Steel Used in Canada, 1930–1945." Steel furnaces used 1,826,911 net tons, iron foundries used 522,364 tons, iron blast furnaces used 64,624 tons, rolling mills used 49,773 tons, ferro-alloy furnaces used 38,959 tons, and artificial abrasives furnaces used 20,830 tons, for a total of 2,523,461 tons. According to table 322, "Consumption of Scrap Iron and Steel in Canada, 1941–1945," about 62 per cent (1,581,569 tons) was purchased and 38 per cent was made, or mill, scrap.

69 LAC, "History of Steel Control," 88.

70 LAC, RG 19, box 3988, file S-9-1, "Preliminary Report on the Canadian Steel Shortage," by Arthur G. McKee and Co. Engineers, Cleveland, Ohio, prepared in January 1941 for the DMS. According to Canada, DBS, *Iron and Steel and Their Products in Canada, 1943–1945*, table 322, "Consumption of Scrap Iron and Steel in Canada, 1941–1945," between 36 per cent and 45 per cent of all scrap consumed in Canada between 1941 and 1945 was made-scrap from the mills.

71 Canada, DBS, ibid., table 324, "Scrap Iron and Steel and Pig Iron Used in Steel Furnaces in Canada, 1930–1945."

72 See LAC, RG 28, box 258, for copies of all of Steel Control's formal orders.

73 Canada, DBS, *Iron and Steel and Their Products in Canada, 1943–1945*, tables 331 and 332.

74 LAC, "History of Steel Control," 111.

75 Ibid. A similar table separating cast iron and steel scrap may be found in Kennedy, *History of DMS*, vol. 2, 230, but I believe the data are less reliable.

76 LAC, "History of Steel Control," 93.

77 LAC, RG 28, box 256, file 196-13-1-0, Carswell to Berkinshaw, 3 June 1942.

78 Young, "Cheating the Nazis through Salvage," 31; LAC, RG 28, box 256, file 196-13(1), S.G. Godfrey, used-goods administrator, to Carswell, 25 July 1942; Carswell to Berkinshaw, 4 August 1942; and Berkinshaw to Carswell, 7 July 1942; see also L. Levin, scrap supervisor, Steel Control, to Carswell, 5 August 1942.

79 LAC, RG 28, box 256, file 196-13, Carswell to Howe, 28 May 1942.

80 LAC, RG 28, box 195, file 196-2D-2, E. Ashburner, engineer, DMS, to W.C. Blundel, 27 April 1942; ibid., steel subcommittee recommendation, 29 July 1942.

81 LAC, "History of Steel Control [addendum]," 72. Kilbourn, *Elements Combined*, 172–3, gives 250,000 tons drawn from the West between 1942 and the end of the war.

82 LAC, RG 2 7C, vol. 5 (reel C-4654), Cabinet War Committee minutes, 30 August 1941. See also LAC, RG 2 (register), for PC 8990, 18 November 1941.

83 LAC, RG 28, box 261, file 196-14(1), Kilbourn to Berkinshaw, assistant deputy minister, in charge of industrial controls, 28 May 1942.

84 LAC, "History of Steel Control," 104–6.

85 LAC, RG 28, box 260, file 196-14-1, Martin A. Hoey, "Steel Control in Canada," Ottawa, 30 March 1943.

86 *Harbour and Shipping* 24, no. 9 (September 1942): 323, gives 1,559,238 tons of steel ingots and castings manufactured during the first six months, compared with 1,551,054 tons for all of 1939.

87 LAC, RG 28, box 332, file 196-39-12, minister's desk book – Steel Control, circa June 1943.

88 Kilbourn, *Elements Combined*, 168.

89 *Canadian Machinery and Manufacturing News* 53 (February 1942): 125.

90 *Canadian Machinery and Manufacturing News* 53 (January 1942): 106; Canada, DMS, *Industrial Front*, vol. 5, 291.

91 LAC, RG 28, box 257, file 196-14(1), Kilbourn to Sheils, 7 April 1942; *CS&MEN* 13, no. 10 (May 1942): 50.

92 LAC, RG 28, box 257, file 196-14(1), J.H. Dougherty, assistant to the deputy minister, to Kilbourn, 22 June 1942; Canada, DBS, *Iron and Steel and Their Products in Canada, 1943–1945*, table 40, "Production of Steel Ingots and Steel Castings, 1935–1945."

93 LAC, RG 28, box 257, file 196-14, memorandum, Dougherty to Kilbourn, 10 February 1942.

94 Smith et al., "History of BATM," 46.

95 Glenn, "'Total War' in Steel."

96 LAC, RG 28, box 197, file 196-2W-3, MacMillan to Kilbourn, 2 March 1942.

97 Ibid., Kilbourn to MacMillan, 24 March 1942.

98 Ibid., Kilbourn to Howe, 26 March 1942.

99 LAC, box 257, file 196-14(1), R.D. Hamer, Aluminum Company of Canada Ltd, to Berkinshaw, 28 March 1942.

100 NSARM, MG 2, box 1500, file 278(12), Cabinet War Committee minutes, 23 September 1942.

101 UBCSC, H.R. MacMillan Papers, box 100, file 16, memorandum, MacMillan to Howe, 2 September 1942.

102 LAC, RG 28, box 195, file 196-2D-2, A. Cross, president of Dosco, to Henry Borden, coordinator of controls, 27 February 1943.

103 Hadley, *U-boats against Canada*, 152.

104 LAC, RG 28, box 257, file 196-14(2), Kilbourn to Sheils, 1 November 1942.

105 LAC, "History of Steel Control [addendum]," 37.

106 LAC, RG 28, box 256, file 193-13(1), Carswell to Borden, 23 October 1942.

107 LAC, RG 28, box 256, file 196-13(3), Carswell to Godsoe, 23 January 1945; LAC, RG 28, box 257, file 196-14(2), Kilbourn to Sheils, 1 November 1942, and Kilbourn to Sheils, 2 December 1942.

108 LAC, RG 28, box 195, file 196-2D-2, Borden to Kilbourn, 26 November 1942.

109 Kennedy, *History of DMS*, vol. 2, 215, reports a fivefold increase, whereas postwar statistics give a sevenfold increase; see Canada, DBS, *Iron and Steel and Their Products in Canada, 1943–1945*, table 61.

110 LAC, RG 28, box 257, file 196-14(2), Kilbourn to Sheils, 2 December 1942.

111 LAC, RG 28, box 332, file 196-39-12, minister's desk book – Steel Control, circa June 1943.

112 LAC, RG 28, box 171, "Steel budget for … 1942," dated 22 October 1941, 41.

113 LAC, "History of Steel Control," 23. On labour difficulties in the steel industry, see MacDowell, "1943 Steel Strike against Wartime Wage Controls."

114 LAC, RG 28, box 260, file 196-14-8, "Report on the Steel Supply Situation in Canada," by Sir John Duncanson and Earl A. Merson, August 1943.

115 Ibid., "Steel Control in Canada – A Report Presented to Sir John Duncanson, Steel Controller, British Ministry of Supply, on the Occasion of His Visit to Ottawa," by Martin A. Hoey, associate steel controller, Ottawa, 30 March 1943; LAC, RG 28, box 261, file 196-14-15, Hoey to Duncanson, 21 December 1943.

116 LAC, RG 28, box 261, file 196-14-15, copy of British high commissioner for United Kingdom to secretary of state for Dominion affairs, 27 November 1943.

117 LAC, "History of Steel Control [addendum]," 34.

118 LAC, RG 28, box 257, file 196-14(3), Hoey to Borden, 16 April 1943.

119 LAC, RG 28, box 257, file 196-14(2), G.L. Jennison, director, priorities branch, DMS, to G.J. Brown, WPB, 15 September 1943.

120 LAC, "History of Steel Control [addendum]," 13.

121 LAC, RG 28, box 332, file 196-39-12, minister's desk book – Steel Control, n.d.

122 LAC, RG 28, box 257, file 196-14(4), E.A. Taylor, field assistant, Steel Control, to G.L. Jennison, director, priorities branch, DMS, 13 October 1944.

123 LAC, RG 28, box 195, file 196-2D-2, "Distribution in Canada of Steel," attachment, Taylor to unknown, 31 August 1944; LAC, "History of Steel Control," 46.

124 In addition to the difference between actual and authorized imports, Canadian production and shipments never agree because mills carried stock on hand (i.e., not distributed) and because there were always rejects in the yards.

125 LAC, "History of Steel Control [addendum]," 84.

126 LAC, RG 28, box 171, "Steel Budget for … 1944," dated 15 March 1944.

127 LAC, RG 28, box 257, file 196-114(4), Hoey to Godsoe, 10 May 1944.

128 LAC, RG 28, box 171, "Canadian Aggregate Steel Requirements, October 1, 1944, to June 30, 1945," 21 July 1944.

129 LAC, RG 28, box 257, file 196-14(4), A.C. Anderson, deputy steel controller, to A.V. Blackadar, 4 July 1944.

130 *Canadian Transportation* 45 (April 1942): 237.

131 LAC, RG 28, box 256, file 196-14(2), "Steel Plate of Three Plate Mills Operating in Canada," circa April 1942.

132 LAC, RG 28, box 197, file 106-2W-3, Kilbourn to MacMillan, 24 March 1942.

133 On the hopeless situation at Dosco, see LAC, RG 28, box 195, file 196-2D-2, memorandum, F.H. Brown, minister's financial advisor, to Howe, 28 August 1944; T.F. Rahilly to Kilbourn, 5 September 1944; and Brown to Howe, 25 September 1944.

134 Ibid., Hoey to Godsoe, 4 July 1944.

135 Ibid.,, Brown to Godsoe, 2 September 1944, and Brown to C.E. [*sic*] Dewar, 2 September 1944.

136 Ibid., memorandum, Brown to Howe, 28 June 1944.

137 Ibid., confidential, Brown to Hoey, 29 June 1944, quoted in McDowall, *Steel at the Sault*, 200.

138 Ibid., memorandum, Rahilly to Kilbourne, 5 September 1944.

139 Ibid., Brown to Dewar, president, Wartime Shipbuilding Limited, 2 September 1944 and 22 September 1944.

140 Ibid., Hoey to Godsoe, 10 May 1944.
141 Ibid., Dewar to Carmichael, 28 February 1945.
142 Ibid., Dewar to Brown, 20 September 1944; LAC, "History of Steel Control [addendum]," 48.
143 Kennedy, *History of DMS*, vol. 2, 218.
144 McDowall, *Steel at the Sault*, 179.

CHAPTER NINE

1 Kennedy, *History of the Department of Munitions and Supply* (hereafter *History of DMS*), vol. 1, 239.
2 NVMA, Fonds 97, box 2, file 3, J.D.V. Kinvig binder, see under "standard-type ships"; *SR&SB* 26 (February 1943): 54; *L'Écho maritime* (July 1943): 6.
3 *CS&MEN* 14, no. 5 (December 1942): 61.
4 DUA, MS 4 106, box A, no. 67, Trenton Steel Works, "To date production costs for 9,300 ton[s of] cargo boat forgings," 31 December 1944.
5 Lane, *Ships for Victory*, 396.
6 Canada, DBS, *Canada Year Book, 1947*, 510; Milward, *War, Economy, and Society, 1939–1945*, 355.
7 Leacy, ed., *Historical Statistics of Canada*, R-12.
8 Howe, who often exaggerated, claimed 95 per cent of all materials in Canadian ships were locally manufactured, but this is not true of steel plate. For an example of one such claim, see *Canadian Transportation* 45 (November 1941): 637.
9 Tucker, *Naval Service of Canada*, vol. 2, 24; Kennedy, *History of DMS*, vol. 2, 236.
10 Ibid., vol. 1, 229.
11 Lane, *Ships for Victory*, 65.
12 For this and subsequent paragraphs, see LAC, RG 28, box 7, "A Brief History of Wartime Merchant Shipping Ltd., Montreal, December 31, 1943, with an Addendum on Wartime Shipbuilding Ltd., January 1944–February 1947" (hereafter "Brief History of WMSL"), typescript, 59–64.
13 Kennedy, *History of DMS*, vol. 1, 496.
14 *Canadian Transportation* 45 (November 1941): 638.
15 Wartime Merchant Shipping Limited acted under authority of a master supply contract dated 18 March 1942 between the minister, represented by War Supplies Limited, and the US Maritime Commission.
16 DHH, Series 30: 8000, 75/270, interview by Lt Kerr with George W. Allan, president, Canadian Sumner Iron Works, 18 May 1945.
17 *CS&MEN* 13, no. 10 (May 1942): 20.
18 LAC, RG 28, box 7, "Brief History of WMSL," typescript, 72.
19 *SR&SB* 26, no. 8 (August 1943): 58.
20 DHH, Series 30: 8000, 75/270, interview by Lt with G.W. Allan, 18 May 1945.
21 *Canadian Transportation* 45 (October 1942): 619.
22 LAC, RG 28, box 369, file 4-4-1224-1, contract, dated 30 January 1942. Stream anchors were carried as spares; they were often employed in large ships as a stern anchor. They had no permanent anchor cables, but if needed, one of the ship's wire hawsers was shackled on as cable, hence the special 4½-inch shackle in the order.
23 LAC, RG 58, series C-1, box 252, file 15, minutes of Privy Council re: WMSL, 5 November 1943.
24 *SR&SB* 28, no. 6 (June 1945): 49.
25 Robson, "Merchant Shipbuilding in Canada," 285.

26 Buxton, "British Warship Building and Repair," 86.

27 CTA, John Inglis Company Fonds, box 14, agreement by Marine Industries Ltd to purchase from John Inglis Co. one engine set, 14 March 1940.

28 Harland, "The 2750 IHP Corvette Engine," 188–91. The cylinder dimensions are: 18½-inch, 31-inch, and 38½-inch with a 30-inch stroke.

29 Lane, *Ships for Victory*, 396–8.

30 Harland, "The 2750 IHP Corvette Engine," 189.

31 Steven, "Building Marine Engines for 'Manufactured' Ships," 41–3.

32 DHH, Series 30: 8000, 75/270, interview by Lt Kerr with Mr Waltau, general superintendent, Port Arthur Shipbuilding Co., 14 May 1945.

33 Steven, "Great Lakes Yard Produces Naval Craft," 45.

34 CTA, John Inglis Company Fonds, box 351, copy of H.S. Van Patter, chief engineer, Dominion Engineering, to director of shipbuilding, DMS, 26 June 1940, re: corvette engines; ibid., box 17, telegram, R.G. McLiesh, John Inglis Co., to J.L. Brennan, Halifax Shipyards, 30 December 1943.

35 "Huge Marine Engines, Condensers Now Being Produced at Angus Shops," *Canadian Pacific Staff Bulletin*, 10 November 1943.

36 *Canadian Transportation* 47 (August 1944): 459.

37 Steven, "Building Marine Engines," 37–9.

38 LAC, RG 28, box 371, file 4-4-218, formal agreements between the DMS and Collingwood Ship-yards, Midland Shipyards, and George T. Davie and Sons, 8 July 1941; Sweeting and Gillham, *Ships of Midland*.

39 Dominion Bridge Company, *Of Tasks Accomplished*, 19.

40 LAC, RG 28, box 370, file 4-4-124-4, contract, dated 2 February 1942.

41 LAC, RG 28, box 369, file 4-4-124-1, contract, dated 10 February 1943.

42 J.S. Marshall and Co. Ltd, *History of Burrard Dry Dock*, vol. 3, 220–1, claims incorrectly that Burrard built engines for 10,000-tonners.

43 See Buxton, "British Warship Building and Repair," 90; Lane, *Ships for Victory*, 396–8.

44 Dominion Bridge Company, *Of Tasks Accomplished*, 31–2.

45 Ibid., 20.

46 Guthrie, *History of Marine Engineering*, 262; Rowland, *Steam at Sea*, 196.

47 Harland, "The 2750 IHP Corvette Engine," 191.

48 Barnes, comp., *Alfred Yarrow*, 101–2; and Guthrie, *History of Marine Engineering*, 263–6.

49 LAC, RG 28, box 364, file 4-4-123-1, contracts with John Inglis Co., dated 29 June 1943 and 20 January 1944, for thirteen sets of these boilers at $76,250 each.

50 LAC, RG 28, box 515, file 51-P-9, agreement with Page-Hersey Tubes Ltd, 29 January 1942. See also table 4.3.

51 LAC, RG 28, box 363, file 4-4-123-1, contracts with John Inglis Co., dated 28 June 1941 and 28 January 1942, for sixty-three Scotch marine boilers at $26,200 each.

52 LAC, RG 28, box 368, file 4-4-123-1, memorandum of agreement with Foster-Wheeler Ltd, 12 May 1942; LAC, RG 28, box 503, file 51-F-12, capital assistance to Foster-Wheeler Ltd, 28 March 1942; $81,000 was for extension of the boiler shop.

53 Babcock and Wilcox Ltd, *A History, 1844–1977*, 59, 68–9.

54 CTA, John Inglis Company Fonds, box 23, file 5, "Minutes of a Meeting of Boiler Manufactur-ers," 26 April 1943.

55 BANQ-CAQ, E 24, 1960-01-040, box 220, file L26-42-43, report to British minister of labour by British Shipbuilding Delegation [1943].

56 *Harbour and Shipping* 28, no. 9 (September 1945): 431.

57 NVMA, Fonds 97, box 2, file 3, J.D.V. Kinvig binder, see under "Victory ships."

58 Dominion Bridge Company, *Of Tasks Accomplished*, 20.

59 Salter, "Diesel Engines for Marine Power," 41–8.

60 Tucker, *Naval Service of Canada*, vol. 2, 45.

61 DHH, Series 30: 8000, 75/270, interview by Lt Kerr with Will Vivian, president and general manager, Vivian Engine Works Ltd, 18 May 1945.

62 BCARS, Add. Mss. 448, box 2, file on "General Lake."

63 LAC, RG 24, acc. no. 1983/84/167, box 3799, file NS-8200-449, memo from the secretary of the Naval Board, 25 April 1945.

64 LAC, RG 28, box 521, file 51-V-2, "Summary of Diesel Engine Production Schedule as at 31 October 1942."

65 "Launching of 50th Vivian Powered Steel Tug," *Harbour and Shipping* 27, no. 10 (October 1944): 449.

66 *Harbour and Shipping* 27, no. 3 (March 1944): 98; *Harbour and Shipping* 28, no. 4 (April 1945): 211.

67 *Harbour and Shipping* 23, no. 10 (October 1940): 311–13.

68 *SR&SB* 28, no. 6 (June 1945): 46–8.

69 According to Smith et al., "History of the British Admiralty Technical Mission in Canada" (hereafter "History of BATM"), 79–80, 84–5, the mission ordered sixteen of the 105-foot type between January and October 1941 and a further sixteen in January 1942; twelve of the 126-foot type were ordered on 18 December 1942 and twelve more on 19 February 1943. Three in the final order were later cancelled.

70 DHH, Series 30: 8000, box 80, file 9, *Preserver*; SHPS, P006, series 2, subseries 2, subsubseries 1, D25 Dwg No. W85-0-15, contracts 141 to 143, capacity plan.

71 Gillham, *Ships of Collingwood*; Heal, *Great Fleet of Ships*, 46.

72 Rance, *Fast Boats and Flying Boats*, 111; LAC, RG 28, box 390, file 18-18c-13, tender and agreement to purchase from Packard, dated 15 July 1941, six sets of spares for the model 4M-2500 marine engine.

73 Grayson, *Engines Afloat*, vol. 2, 152–3.

74 By April 1945 Packard had manufactured 12,115 of its 4M-2500 engines; ibid., 153–9.

75 Tucker, *Naval Service of Canada*, vol. 2, 509, 511, mistakenly identifies these engines as diesels.

76 Grayson, *Engines Afloat*, vol. 1, 86–8.

77 BCARS, Add. Mss. 448, box 3, Paul Driver, service engineer, to E. Mercer, managing director, Star Shipyard (Mercer's) Ltd, 25 February 1942, identifies Hall-Scott Motor Car Company as a division of American Car and Foundry Motors Company at Seattle, Washington.

78 LAC, RG 28, box 369, file 4-4-124-1, contract with Canadian Car and Foundry Co. Ltd, dated 22 October 1941, for eighteen stern frames for delivery between December 1941 and September 1942.

79 Hunt, "Story behind Sternframes," 479–81.

80 Dominion Bridge Company, *Of Tasks Accomplished*, 14.

81 DUA, MS 4 106, box A, no. 67, Trenton Steel Works, "To date production costs for 9,300 ton[s of] cargo boat forgings," 31 December 1944.

82 LAC, RG 28, box 257, file 196-14(2), items at Dominion Steel and Coal Co. Ltd, Trenton, to be forged by heavy presses, 27 July 1942.

83 LAC, RG 28, box 7, "Brief History of WMSL," typescript, 72–3.

84 Steven, "Kennedy Propellers Drive Canada's Ships," 33–4, 64.

85 LAC, RG 28, box 364, file 4-4-123-1, contract with John Inglis Company, Toronto, 30 March 1943, for fifty sets of ship pumps; LAC, RG 28, box 7, "Brief History of WMSL," typescript, 67.

86 LAC, RG 28, box 369, file 4-4-124-1, contract, dated 13 May 1942.

87 LAC, RG 28, box 364, file 4-4-123, contracts, dated 16 and 24 March 1942.

88 LAC, RG 28, box 369, file 4-4-124-1, contract, dated 19 March 1942.

89 Ibid., contract, dated 10 October 1941.

90 LAC, RG 28, box 7, "Brief History of WMSL," typescript, 74.

91 See CTA, John Inglis Company Fonds, box 22, file, Wartime Merchant Shipping – 1941, production manager, John Inglis Company, to Mr McKerlie, WMSL, 6 August 1941, re: purchase of more than 200 engines and valves from the Pulp and Paper Association.

92 Eileen Reid Marcil Papers, War Time Machine Shop Board of the Canadian Pulp and Paper Association, *News* 1, no. 12 (July 1944): 1.

93 LAC, RG 28, box 100, file 2-C-34, "Personnel of War Time Machine Shop Board," n.d.

94 Rowe, "Gold Mining and Shipbuilding," 628–9.

95 LAC, RG 28, box 370, file 4-4-124-1, contract, dated 23 February 1942.

96 Smith et al., "History of BATM," 47.

97 CTA, John Inglis Company Fonds, box 19, "Pumps for Victory Ships – 1942–43," file, F.Y. Walters to P.J. Baldwin, 18 February 1943, indicates John Inglis Company had subcontracted manufacturing of 64 and 192 pumps to Lake Shore Mines and Dome Mines, respectively.

98 Kennedy, *History of DMS*, vol. 1, 242.

99 CTA, John Inglis Company Fonds, box 16, P.J. Baldwin, operations manager, John Inglis Company, to Carswell, 23 June 1943.

100 Ibid., copy of Carswell to secretary of the Naval Board, 7 July 1943.

101 Lt Cdr A.D. Timson, RCN (rtd), discussion, Institute of Naval Architects, *Transactions* 88 (1946): 290; *SR&SB* 26, no. 8 (August 1943): 2.

102 *Canadian Machinery and Manufacturing News* 52 (December 1941): 197.

103 Steven, "Components Industry Helps Drive Canadian Ship Production Higher."

104 LAC, RG 28, box 7, "Brief History of WMSL," typescript, 73, shows $16,200 to Progressive Engineering and $34,400 to Letson and Burpee Limited.

105 *Canadian Machinery and Manufacturing News* 52 (December 1941): 198.

106 Greene, ed., *Who's Who in Canada, 1943–44*, 42.

107 "Engineering Works Expanded," *Harbour and Shipping* 24, no. 9 (September 1941): 293–4.

108 See LAC, RG 28, box 364, file 4-4-123-1, contracts with Letson and Burpee Limited and Link-Belt Limited, dated 28 June 1941 and 10 November 1942, respectively, for forty-two and twenty-eight standard, horizontal, direct, quick-warping, steam-driven windlasses for 4,700-ton freighters. The first contract called for delivery of three per month between August 1942 and September 1943, inclusive, for a price of $5,000 each.

109 LAC, RG 28, box 370, file 4-4-124-1, contract with E. Leonard and Sons, dated 7 April 1942.

110 Ibid., contracts with Stephens Adamson Manufacturing Company of Canada Limited, dated 28 June 1941 and 20 February 1942, for fifteen and eighteen steering gears and for eighteen anchor winches. See also *CS&MEN* 14, no. 10 (May 1943): 88, for United Steel Corporation's full-page advertisement showing 10½-by-12-inch cargo winches on a railway car ready for shipment and a 7-by-10-inch, double-drum, link, reversing hoisting winch.

111 Steven, "Fighting the U-boat Menace in Canada's Shipyards," 42.

112 *SR&SB* 26, no. 6 (June 1943): 34–7.

113 This section relies heavily on the complete report of the electrical department within the BATM, which is found in Smith et al., "History of BATM," 103–13.

114 Ibid., 108.

115 See the otherwise excellent article by Madsen, "Industrial Hamilton's Contribution to the Naval War," 37.

116 Rowe, "Gold Mining and Shipbuilding," 640.

117 For a list, see Smith et al., "History of BATM," 160.

118 Tucker, *Naval Service of Canada*, vol. 2, 255.

119 Madsen, "Industrial Hamilton's Contribution," 44–5.

120 For the complete story on radar, which is treated well elsewhere, see Middleton, *Radar Development in Canada*; and Zimmerman, *Great Naval Battle of Ottawa*, 32–3, 38–49.

121 Smith et al., "History of BATM," 142–3; Kennedy, *History of DMS*, vol. 1, 233–4.

122 See Rawling, "Challenge of Modernization." In December 1942 USS *Action*, a Collingwood-built corvette, was the first Canadian-built ship to receive hedgehog; see Smith et al., "History of BATM," 36, 81.

123 Rawling, "When the Simplest Thing Is Difficult," 3.

124 Smith et al., "History of BATM," 144.

125 McKay and Harland, *Flower-Class Corvette Agassiz*, 14.

126 See Crawford, "4[-inch] Naval Gun Mk XIX Arms Merchantmen."

127 Reid, *Arming of Canadian Merchant Ships in the Second World War*, 28, 38.

128 *Canadian Machinery and Manufacturing News* 53 (April 1942): 136; Crawford, "Railwaymen Build Naval Guns on Former Mud Flats."

129 Crawford, "Building Mounts for Twelve Pounder Naval Guns"; Crawford, "Western Railway Shop Builds Twelve Pounders."

130 LAC, RG 2 7c, vol. 10 (reel C-4874), Cabinet War Committee minutes, 30 September 1942.

131 Dominion Bridge Company, *Of Tasks Accomplished*, 58–65.

132 Smith et al., "History of BATM," 140. For more on the manufacture of Otis-Fensom and Bofors guns in Canada, see Madsen, "Industrial Hamilton's Contribution," 48–50.

133 Smith et al., "History of BATM," 27.

134 See *Canadian Machinery and Manufacturing News* 54 (September 1943): 99–106, 143–44, 190, for two articles on the manufacture of 4-inch Mk V gun mounts for Algerine minesweepers and the 2-inch naval pom-pom mount produced by Dominion Engineering Works. An additional item concerning the Mk XXIII naval gun mount appeared in *Canadian Machinery and Manufacturing News* 54 (December 1943): 159–62.

135 Madsen, "Industrial Hamilton's Contribution," 44.

136 Kennedy, *History of DMS*, vol. 1, 235.

137 LAC, RG 28, box 521, file 51-V-2, agreement between the DMS, Vivian Engine Works Ltd, Vivian Diesels and Munitions Ltd, and Will Vivian, 31 October 1942. See also, DHH, Series 30: 8000, 75/270, Vivian Diesels and Munitions Ltd, production of fire-control equipment for the RCN, contracts completed, Plant #2.

138 On the failure of Canadian-built radar sets, which were out of date when installed in Canadian ships and almost useless for spotting surface-cruising U-boats, see Milner, *North Atlantic Run*, 77–8, 122–4; Zimmerman, *Great Naval Battle*, 32–3, 38–49; and Douglas et al., *No Higher Purpose*, 305–7.

139 Milner, *North Atlantic Run*, 9, 37, gives a good account of the device's limitations.

140 Tucker, *Naval Service of Canada*, vol. 2, 24.

141 Kennedy, *History of DMS*, vol. 1, 232; Zimmerman, *Great Naval Battle*, 29–32, 85–6, 93.

142 Smith et al., "History of BATM," 101.

143 Ibid., 158.

144 See Rawling, "Forging Neptune's Trident," 220–2, for a serviceable account of the production of quartz crystals based on sources in LAC, RG 24, acc. no. 1983/84/167, box 2614, file 6120-85.
145 Smith et al., "History of BATM," 102.
146 Kennedy, *History of DMS*, vol. 1, 235.
147 Smith et al., "History of BATM," 101–2.
148 Ibid., 92–4, for this and subsequent paragraphs.
149 Ibid., 154–5.
150 See Milner, *North Atlantic Run*, 36, 265.
151 For more on this, see Zimmerman, *Top Secret Exchange*.
152 Carmichael, "War Production Nears Maximum," 175.

CHAPTER TEN

1 *Canadian Transportation* 43 (December 1940): 645.
2 Bélanger, *La construction navale à Saint Laurent, Ile d'Orléans*, 41–7.
3 Marcil, *Tall Ships and Tankers*, 238–9, 242.
4 Ibid., 200.
5 Ibid., 240, 515.
6 Freeman, *Canadian Warship Names*, 79–80.
7 Ibid., 137.
8 LAC, RG 28, box 29, file 5 of 6, Shipbuilding, ship and small-boat contracts.
9 DHH, Series 30: 8000, 75/270, interview by Lt Kerr with Mr Moran, superintendent and plant manager, Falconer Marine Industries Ltd, 22 May 1945.
10 SHPS, P006, series 2, subseries 2, subsubseries 1, file D2, 6, 7, and 8, contracts 77, 87, 88, and 89. The rebuilt tankers were named *Willowbranch*, *Cedarbranch*, *Pinebranch*, and *Oakbranch*.
11 "Shell Canada Limited," *Scanner* 7, no. 9 (1975): 1; Macht, *First 50 Years*, 22–3.
12 Tucker, *Naval Service of Canada*, vol. 2, 194, 529.
13 Ibid., 229; MacPherson and Burgess, *Ships of Canada's Naval Forces, 1910–1993*, 148, 153.
14 *L'Écho de la marine* 3, no. 16 (22 September 1944): 2.
15 The principal dimensions were a length (between perpendiculars) of 168 feet, moulded breadth of 32 feet, moulded depth of 14.5 feet, and approximate draft of 13 feet.
16 LAC, RG 28, box 460, file 30-1-54, contract with German and Milne, naval architects, dated 29 April 1942, to supply all detailed guidance, plans, and other services for construction of two new auxiliary oil tankers of 800 deadweight tons (dwt) for the naval service.
17 *Canadian Transportation* 46 (October 1943): 549.
18 Ibid.; Freeman, *Canadian Warship Names*, 210.
19 DHH, Series 30: 8000, box 32, file 6, *Dundurn*, "Brief history of CNAV *Dundurn*."
20 LAC, RG 28, box 256, file 196-13-3, report of ship-repairs and salvage controller for period ending 28 February 1943; Sawyer and Mitchell, *Oceans, the Forts and the Parks*, 35.
21 Heal, *Great Fleet of Ships*, 297; Halford, *Unknown Navy*, 31, 112–13, 228.
22 *SR&SB* 26, no. 8 (August 1943): 28.
23 DHH, Series 30: 8000, box 80, file 9, *Preserver*; Tucker, *Naval Service of Canada*, vol. 2, 195, 514.
24 See *Freshwater* 5, no. 2 (1990): 30, for an illustration of the "conduit bilge" system of construction.
25 *Canadian Transportation* 43 (July 1940): 385. For a photograph of MV *Lakeshell* in service, see *Canadian Transportation* 43 (September 1940): 489.

26 Heal, *Great Fleet of Ships*, 46–7.

27 LAC, RG 28, box 498, file 51-C-61, three contracts for capital assistance to Collingwood Ship-yards Limited, dated 16 March and 17 April 1943 and 4 January 1944.

28 Heal, *Great Fleet of Ships*, 237, 290, 294, and 300, correctly identifies the ships but confuses where they were built. See Gillham, *Ships of Collingwood*, 87–9.

29 Halford, *Unknown Navy*, 36–7.

30 Tucker, *Naval Service of Canada*, vol. 2, 61, 71.

31 Lambert and Ross, *Allied Coastal Forces of World War II*, vol. 1, 69.

32 Tucker, *Naval Service of Canada*, vol. 2, 71.

33 Ibid., 511.

34 Ibid., 509, mistakenly claims that Fairmile engines were diesels. See Hadley, *U-boats against Canada*, 36–7, 50, for the limitations of these vessels.

35 Tucker, *Naval Service of Canada*, vol. 2, 47–9.

36 Hadley, *U-boats against Canada*, 36, 50.

37 NSARM, MG 2, box 1524, file 1222, no. 6, "Nova Scotia Shipbuilding" [probable author and date: D.B. Carswell, March 1941].

38 NSARM, MG 2, box 1524, file 1221, no. 9, memorandum, "Construction of Wooden Mine-sweepers and Anti-Submarine Vessels in Eastern Canada," by Carswell to Shiels, undated, sent to A.L. Macdonald, 7 September 1940.

39 Gray, *Wood and Glory*, 28.

40 According to Duke and Gray, *Boatbuilders of Muskoka*, 135–6, the two firms parted company after building the first four Fairmiles, and Port Carling Boat Works continued to build seven more Fairmiles and two wooden minesweepers, while Minett-Shields built two 46-foot harbour craft.

41 See Muskoka Lakes Museum, Garth Tassie Papers, for a copy of the joint-venture agreement. Tassie was the accountant for Port Carling Boat Works Limited. The companies formed a joint venture rather than a partnership in order to continue business and trade as independent boat builders, but the venture was encountering serious difficulties by 1942.

42 Tucker, *Naval Service of Canada*, vol. 2, 514; "The Milner Boys Build Ships," *Shipping Register and North American Ports* 24, no. 9 (August 1942): 22–3.

43 LAC, RG 28, box 29, file 5 of 6, Shipbuilding, ship and small-boat contracts – Ontario.

44 Fossey, *Gidley-Grew & Bonnie Boat Company History*, 3, 5–8.

45 LAC, RG 28, box 459, file 31-4-44, DMS contract with Mac-Craft Co. Ltd to build three Fairmiles, 9 April 1942, and assignment, 25 July 1942.

46 Tucker, *Naval Service of Canada*, vol. 2, 510–11; *CS&MEN* 15, no. 4 (November 1943): 71.

47 Hunter, *Story of Hunter Boats*, 7, gives eleven, but thirteen are recorded in LAC, RG 28, box 29, file 5 of 6, Shipbuilding, ship and small-boat contracts.

48 Hunter, *Story of Hunter Boats*, 3–6.

49 Ibid., 12–13.

50 LAC, RG 28, box 29, file 5 of 6, Shipbuilding, ship and small-boat contracts – Ontario.

51 E-mail from Jim Taylor to author, 17 December 2007.

52 Canada, House of Commons, *Debates*, 214, 2 February 1942.

53 See Duke and Gray, *Boatbuilders of Muskoka*, 73–90, for a brief biography of Thomas Greavette, his boats, and his wartime relationship with Hans Sachau.

54 Information provided by Mr George Cuthbertson during a telephone conversation with the author, 14 August 2004.

55 LAC, RG 28, box 566, file 200-612, contract, 5 September 1944.

56 Don Hunter's later claim that the OFA was founded in 1941 (see *Story of Hunter Boats*, 11) is mistaken.

57 MSHS, Thomas Greavette Collection, minutes of meeting for the Ontario Fairmile Association, 18 July 1942.

58 Ibid., Minutes, 26 July 1942.

59 Ibid., Minutes, 20 May 1943.

60 Ibid., Minutes, 6 January 1944.

61 See *Canadian Transportation* 48 (November 1944): 627, for an account of the launching. The second minesweeper built at Honey Harbour, *Birch Lake*, was never commissioned but was completed as MV *Aspey III*.

62 MSHS, Thomas Greavette Collection, minutes, 19 December 1944.

63 Tucker, *Naval Service of Canada*, vol. 2, 164, 235.

64 LAC, RG 28, box 29, file 5 of 6, Purchases; MMGLK, Canadian Dredge and Dock Co. Fonds, 1979.0038, gate vessels, contract files; ibid., 1979.0037.0091, specifications; Ouderkirk and Gillham, *Ships of Kingston*, 81.

65 LAC, RG 28, box 29, file 5 of 6, Shipbuilding, ship and small-boat contracts – Ontario; LAC, RG 28, box 460, file 30-1-66, contract with Canadian Dredge and Dock Co., 28 December 1942, for the first two; MMGLK, Canadian Dredge and Dock Co. Fonds, 1979.0038, contract files.

66 BCARS, Add. Mss. 448, box 15c, contract for gate vessels with Star Shipyard (Mercer's) Ltd, 5 April 1943; Bélanger, *La construction navale*, 111–18.

67 See Freeman, *Canadian Warship Names*, for information on HMCS *Atwood, Brentwood, Eastwood, Greenwood, Inglewood, Kirkwood, Lakewood, Oakwood,* and *Wildwood*.

68 LAC, RG 28, box 29, file 5 of 6, Shipbuilding, ship and small-boat contracts.

69 Baird, *Under Tow*, 95–110, is both helpful and disappointing, for it is written without reference to sources and provides incomplete information about Canadian tug production during the war.

70 Ibid., 90.

71 LAC, RG 28, box 29, file 5 of 6, Shipbuilding, charters and purchases, 1939–45.

72 Eric M. Cordrey, "History of Russel Brothers Ltd., 1907–1982," www.russelbrothers.com.

73 Ibid.

74 LAC, RG 28, box 472, file 30-5-49, contracts with Russel Brothers, 20 April and 21 August 1942, for two and three tugs, respectively.

75 *Canadian Transportation* 46 (October 1943): 549.

76 *Canadian Transportation* 46 (September 1943): 499.

77 www.russelbrothers.com.

78 Baird, *Under Tow*, 95.

79 LAC, RG 28, box 461, file 30-1-112, contract with Canadian Dredge and Dock Co. Ltd, dated 20 September 1943, calling for two tugs to be delivered at Kingston before freeze-up in December 1944.

80 MMGLK, Canadian Dredge and Dock Co. Fonds, 1979.0038, contract files; personal communication from Edison Horton to author, 20 June 2007. The tugs were *Glenfield, Glenvalley, Glenella, Glenkeen,* and *Gleneagle*; all were powered by 6-cylinder Enterprise diesels.

81 *SR&SB* 28, no. 3 (March 1945): 53.

82 LAC, RG 24, acc. no. 1983/84/167, box 3799, file NS 8200-499(2), assistant director, general shipbuilding branch, to secretary of the Naval Board, 14 September 1945; www.russelboats.com.

83 LAC, RG 28, box 29, file 5 of 6, Shipbuilding, ship and small-boat contracts.

84 *Canadian Transportation* 43 (May 1940): 273; *SR&SB* 26 (May 1943): 68.

85 LAC, RG 28, box 472, file L30-5-48, contract with Montreal Dry Dock Ltd, 18 May 1943; LAC, RG 28, box 472, file L30-5-84, contract with German and Milne, 4 August 1943, to supervise construction of three tugs at Canadian Bridge Co. Ltd; Baird, *Under Tow*, 95, 98.

86 See MMGLK, German and Milne Fonds, for plans of the 1,000-hp tugs built for the RCN; reproduced in Baird, *Under Tow*, 100.

87 SHPS, P006, series 2, subseries 2, subsubseries 2, file D2, from survey of tugboat *Capitaine Simard*, acquired in 1946.

88 *Canadian Transportation* 46 (March 1943): 151–3.

89 Roberts and Tunnel, eds, *Canadian Who's Who, 1936–1937*, vol. 2, 1948; Shield and McMullen, *Ditchburn Boats*, 142.

90 *Financial Post*, 9 March 1940.

91 *Financial Post*, 2 and 9 March 1940. For an account of the bren-gun affair, see Stacey, *Arms, Men and Governments*, 101–2; and Mackenzie, "Bren Gun Scandal and the Maclean Publishing Company's Investigation of Canadian Contracts, 1938–1940."

92 Eben James II, W.A. Fraser's nephew, interview by author, Trenton, 12 April 2007.

93 LAC, RG 28, box 374, file 4-5-3, box 377, file 4-1-131, box 529, file 67-324, and box 592, file LT-FT2B-211, contracts with Central Bridge Co., dated 20 February, 13 June, 29 July, and 31 July 1941 and 12 January 1942.

94 LAC, RG 28, box 460, files L30-1-51 and 30-1-78, contracts with Central Bridge Co., dated 3 March and 3 June 1943.

95 Morton, "Canada Builds Tugs of War for the British Navy"; *CS&MEN* 15, no. 11 (June 1944): 4; Shield and McMullen, *Ditchburn Boats*, 145–9.

96 "Building of Invasion Tugs," *Canadian Transportation* 47 (September 1944): 517–18.

97 Eben James II, W.A. Fraser's nephew, interview by author, Trenton, 12 April 2007. At age eighteen, Mr James served as cook on board one of six tugs that made the journey to Baltimore during the summer of 1945. He remembers being in Baltimore when he learned of the dropping of the atomic bomb on Japan.

98 www.seawaves.com/newsletters/today_in_history_archive.htm.

99 *Canadian Transportation* 46 (March 1943): 151–2, 154; LAC, MG 27 III B20, box 42, file 5-9-25, D.W. Ambridge to Howe, 18 August 1943.

100 LAC, MG 27 III B20, box 42, file 5-9-25, Howe to Ambridge, 24 August 1943.

101 LAC, RG 28, box 569, file 200-1517 and file 200-1517/1, contracts with Central Bridge Ltd, 14 October, and with Russel Brothers, 24 October 1944, for forty and ten tugs, respectively; LAC, RG 28, box 571, file 200-1919, contract with Central Bridge, 3 May 1945, for twenty-five tugs.

102 MMA, MP 300.16.1, "List of vessels built by Smith and Rhuland."

103 Ibid., contracts with Smith and Rhuland, 2 May 1945, and with Industrial Shipping Co. Ltd, 3 May 1945, for five and ten 65-foot tugs, respectively.

104 MMGLK, Collingwood Shipbuilding Company Collection, 1982.0168.0030, Warrior tug contract, 2 April 1944, with Canadian Shipbuilding and Engineering Ltd.

105 LAC, RG 28, box 256, file 196-13-14, press release, DMS, 9 April 1945; Kennedy, *History of the Department of Munitions and Supply*, vol. 1, 495.

106 This and the following paragraphs are heavily indebted to Vernon, "RCAF Marine Craft." I gratefully acknowledge the assistance of graduate student Richard Goette, who gave me a copy of this article.

107 Douglas, *Creation of a National Air Force*, 2. For a map showing locations of bombing and gunnery schools, see ibid., 236–7.

108 LAC, RG 24, series E-1-b, box 5176, file 15-1-282, "Marine Craft Establishment Recommended for Western Air Command," appendix to Air Commodore A.E. Godfrey to Department of National Defence (DND) secretary for Air, 21 October 1940.

109 *Harbour and Shipping* 23, no. 10 (October 1940): 311–13; Vernon, "RCAF Marine Craft," 108.

110 LAC, RG 28, box 29, file 5 of 6, Shipbuilding, ship and small-boat contracts.

111 LAC, RG 24, series E-1-b, box 4984, file 643-16F-1, A.C. Beach, for chief of the air staff, to commanding officer, No. 13 Technical Detachment, Vancouver, 23 July 1942.

112 LAC, RG 28, box 390, file 18-16F-87, contract with LeBlanc Shipbuilding Co. Ltd, Weymouth, Nova Scotia, for one 114-foot supply and salvage vessel for the RCAF, 29 June 1943.

113 Vernon, "RCAF Marine Craft," 106–7.

114 LAC, RG 24, series E-1-b, box 3557, file 975-1-19. F/Lt J.C. Kelly for AOCinC/EAC to DND secretary for Air, 8 December 1943.

115 LAC, RG 28, box 29, file 5 of 6, Shipbuilding, ship and small-boat contracts – Ontario.

116 Graves, "'Hell Boats' of the R.C.N.," 36, citing LAC, RG 24, box 3830, file NNS 1017-1-15(2), Carswell to K.S. MacLachlan, 5 March 1940.

117 *Canadian Transportation* 43 (September 1940): 488.

118 Shield and McMullen, *Ditchburn Boats*, 142.

119 LAC, RG 28, box 436, file 22A, contract with Canadian Power Boat Company Ltd, 18 July 1940.

120 Vernon, "RCAF Marine Craft," 104. The others were M-231 *Malecite*, M-232 *Takuli*, M-233 *Abanaki*, M-234 *Montagnais*, and M-235 *Huron*.

121 MacPherson and Burgess, *Ships of Canada's Naval Forces*, 141. According to Vernon, "RCAF Marine Craft," these were M-407 *Abadick*, M-408 *Banoskik*, M-413 *Bras D'Or*, M-414 *Osoyoos*, and M-447 *Niktak*.

122 LAC, RG 24, series D-10, box 11048, file 27-1-7, Air Commodore A.L. Major for AOC to CinC/CNWA, Halifax, 7 September 1943.

123 Douglas, *Creation of a National Air Force*, 582; *CS&MEN* 15, no. 10 (May 1944): 36–7, 48.

124 Baker, "Notes on the Development of Landing Craft."

125 Baker III, *Allied Landing Craft of World War Two*, contains no mention of Canadian landing craft; nor do any of the British types mentioned have similar dimensions to the Canadian types.

126 Canada, House of Commons, *Debates*, 1698–9, 21 March 1944.

127 LAC, MG 27 III B20, box 42, file S-9-25, barge and cargo-lighter boatyards, 18 August 1943.

128 LAC, RG 27C, vol. 9 (reel C-4874), Cabinet War Committee minutes, 22 April 1942; Douglas et al., *Blue Water Navy*, 109.

129 LAC, RG 28, box 29, file 5 of 6, Shipbuilding, ship and small-boat contracts – British Columbia; Tucker, *Naval Service of Canada*, vol. 2, 86-7.

130 LAC, RG 28, box 29, file 5 of 6, Shipbuilding, ship and small-boat contracts – British Columbia.

131 LAC, RG 28, box 29, file 5 of 6, Shipbuilding, ship and small-boat contracts – British Columbia and Ontario; Leacock and Roberts, *Canada's War at Sea*, vol. 2, pt 3, 28, 93, 122.

132 *SR&SB* 28, no. 2 (February 1945): 23; Canadian Wartime Information Board, *Canada at War*, no. 45, "Recapitulation Issue" (July 1945): table 57.

133 LAC, MG 27 III B20, box 42, file 5-9-25, Ambridge to Howe, 25 August 1943.

134 Ron Marsh, "War-Born Barges Supplying Allies Designed by Local Naval Architect." An alternative account claims that Bill Roué, self-taught naval architect and designer of Canada's most famous ship, the *Bluenose*, created the lighter; see Joan E. Roué, *Spirit Deep Within*, 36–7. Bill Roué may well have been involved in the production of the barges in the Maritimes.

135 *CS&MEN* 15, no. 3 (October 1943): 82.

136 *SR&SB* 26, no. 11 (November 1943): 25–8.

137 Marsh, "War-Born Barges."

138 LAC, MG 30 III B20, box 42, file 5-9-25, barge and cargo-lighter boatyards, 18 August 1943.

139 Ibid., Ambridge to Howe, 25 August 1943.

140 Ibid., Humphrey Mitchell to Howe, 2 September 1943.

141 LAC, RG 28, box 29, file 5 of 6, Shipbuilding, ship and small-boat contracts – New Brunswick and Nova Scotia. The contractors were Eastern Woodworkers Limited at New Glasgow, Industrial Shipping Company Limited at Mahone Bay, J.A. Urquhart at Parrsboro, Irving Shipyards Limited at Buctouche, McMulkin and Son at Gagetown, and Ashley Colten at Gagetown.

142 Hunter, *Story of Hunter Boats*, 9–10, claims the Orillia plant built about 250 Mark IV pontoons.

143 LAC, RG 28, box 29, file 5 of 6, Shipbuilding, ship and small-boat contracts – Ontario.

144 Ibid. Unfortunately, I was unable to locate any photographs of these craft.

145 Edgar, "Canada, a Land of Little Ships."

CHAPTER ELEVEN

1 Kennedy, *History of the Department of Munitions and Supply* (hereafter *History of DMS*), vol. 1, 237.

2 Canada, Department of External Affairs, "Estimated Value of War Production," table 63. These data cover only war production and construction contracts placed by the Department of Munitions and Supply.

3 The order comprised twenty China coasters of 350 tons and fifteen of 1,250 tons.

4 Mansbridge, *Launching History*, 67; Halford, *Unknown Navy*, 263n2. I have included only six of nineteen vessels that Kennedy, *History of DMS*, vol. 1, 247, classifies as "All Others"; they represent the Great Lakes tankers built in 1944 with an approximate value of $6.6 million. The other thirteen vessels were most likely Warrior-class tugs, which are included in this chapter together with hundreds of others.

5 Heal, *Great Fleet of Ships*, 48, must be used with caution. He mistakenly attributes five cargo ships built by George T. Davie and Sons to Davie Shipbuilding and Repairing Company, locates Marine Industries Limited at Montreal, and claims (at page 159) that sixteen maintenance ships, rather than fifteen, were completed before the end of 1945.

6 LAC, RG 28, box 29, "Report on Canadian Shipbuilding," 6 July 1944.

7 Smith et al., "History of the British Admiralty Technical Mission in Canada" (hereafter "History of BATM"), 78. Dufferin Shipbuilding Company and North Van Ship Repairs Limited built these ships.

8 Ibid., 81–2; Tucker, *Naval Service of Canada*, vol. 2, 66–7.

9 LAC, RG 24, box 3842, file 1017-10-22(2), naval message from the British Admiralty delegation in Washington, DC, to CNS, 7 August 1942. Douglas et al., *Blue Water Navy*, 43, mistakenly reports that in 1942 the BATM ordered fifty-one corvettes from Great Lakes yards. In the autumn of 1941 the BATM ordered fifteen Revised corvettes and fifteen Algerine-class minesweepers from Great Lakes yards.

10 United States, Navy Department, Bureau of Ships, *Ships Data*, vol. 2, 108–9; these two patrol frigates, PF1 and PF2, were designated USS *Asheville* and USS *Natchez*.

11 Smith et al., "History of BATM," 83–6. Six minesweepers were later cancelled, leaving the fifty shown in table 11.3a.

12 LAC, RG 2 7C, vol. 12 (reel C-4875), Cabinet War Committee minutes, 28 April 1943, document no. 498.1; Tucker, *Naval Service of Canada*, vol. 2, 77–8, 509. For more on the Castle-class corvettes, see Elliott, *Allied Escort Ships of World War II*, 201–5, 371–2.

13 Smith et al., "History of BATM," 80.

14 Ibid., 84–5

15 Ibid., 87–90.

16 Ibid., 78, 80; Marystown Heritage-Museum Corporation, *History of Shipbuilding in Marystown, NL*, www.k12.nf.ca/discovery/Communities/acdrom/clarenville/shipbuilding.html.

17 See Sawyer and Mitchell, *Oceans, the Forts and the Parks*, 21–2, for a list of ships purchased from Canada by the United States and their delivery dates.

18 Hall, *North American Supply*, 223.

19 See tables 11.1, 11.2, and 11.6 and *Shipping Register and Shipbuilder* 27, no. 4 (April 1944): 19.

20 Tucker, *Naval Service of Canada*, vol. 2, 84.

21 Mansbridge, *Launching History*, 72. See LAC, RG 28, box 7, "A Brief History of Wartime Merchant Shipping Ltd., Montreal, December 31, 1943, with an Addendum on Wartime Shipbuilding Ltd., January 1944–February 1947" (hereafter "Brief History of WMSL"), typescript, 32–4, for a list of names and delivery dates.

22 Canada, House of Commons, *Debates*, 1308, Angus L. Macdonald, 9 March 1944.

23 Ibid., 1699, C.D. Howe, 21 March 1944.

24 Sawyer and Mitchell, *Oceans, the Forts, and the Parks*, 19.

25 Wilson, *History of Shipbuilding and Naval Architecture in Canada*, 52.

26 Ibid., citing "Canadian Shipbuilding and Ship Repairing Industry and Its Relation to Unemployment," *Canadian Railway and Marine World* (October 1930): 679. See also Weir, "Truly Allied Undertaking," 102–3.

27 Canada, House of Commons, *Debates*, 1388, Angus L. Macdonald, 9 March 1944.

28 Tucker, *Naval Service of Canada*, vol. 2, 38–9.

29 *Canadian Transportation* 44 (April 1940): 214.

30 "Approximate Cost of Ships in Canada," *SR&SB* 26, no. 4 (April 1943): 69.

31 See LAC, RG 28, box 7, "Brief History of WMSL," typescript, 11, for this and subsequent paragraphs. See also Kennedy, *History of DMS*, vol. 1, 492.

32 UBCSC, H.R. MacMillan Papers, box 100, file 17, MacMillan to Sheils, 5 May 1941.

33 LAC, RG 28, box 369, file 4-4-124, contract with St John Dry Dock and Shipbuilding Co., 10 May 1941, and supplemental contract, 8 May 1942.

34 LAC, RG 28, box 7, "Brief History of WMSL," typescript, 13–14.

35 See Lane, *Ships for Victory*, 458.

36 Canada, House of Commons, *Debates*, 697, Cleaver, chairman, War Expenditures Committee, 21 February 1944.

37 LAC, RG 28, box 7, "Brief History of WMSL," typescript, 76–87.

38 Ibid., 78. Bothwell and Kilbourn, *C.D. Howe*, 177–8, claim the worst case of attempted wartime profiteering was in shipbuilding. Their source is a postwar interview with Howe's financial advisor, but in view of the foregoing and the absence of any evidence, it is difficult to see how this occurred.

39 LAC, RG 28, box 7, "Brief History of WMSL," typescript, 85–6.

40 Ibid., 79–80, 85–6.

41 Lane, *Ships for Victory*, 473.

42 Mansbridge, *Launching History*, 85–6, cites the *Vancouver Province*, 23 February 1944, for a similar claim about West Coast yards being cheaper than East Coast ones, but the claim was mistakenly based on average estimated costs between two Montreal yards, one of which, United Shipyards, was the most expensive in the country.

43 LAC, RG 28, box 7, "Brief History of WMSL," typescript, 81.

44 Kennedy, *History of DMS*, vol. 1, 492.

45 Canada, House of Commons, *Debates*, 773, P.C. Black, 22 February 1944. Black, a member of the War Expenditures Committee, was quoting from the committee's report.

46 SHPS, P006, series 2, subseries 2, subsubseries 1, D24, "Cost of 3,600-ton ocean-going tankers up to November 30th 1945," André Kieffer, 26 December 1945.

47 I gratefully acknowledge the assistance of Professor Frank Lewis, Department of Economics, Queen's University, in creating table 11.13.

48 Canada, DBS, *Annual Industry Report: Iron, Steel and Their Products Group: The Shipbuilding Industry* (hereafter *Shipbuilding Industry*) (1939 and 1942), table 1 in each volume.

49 In December 1942, for example, *CS&MEN* 14, no. 5 (December 1942): 61, claimed a minesweeper required 350,000 man-hours of labour, whereas Hodgins et al., eds, *Women at War*, 102, claim a corvette required 375,000 man-hours.

50 This increase in man-hours per ton may also reflect the introduction of minesweeping trawlers, which although simple to build, broke the flow of corvettes from three inexperienced yards at Kingston, Midland, and Quebec City.

51 See note 11.

52 *Canadian Machinery and Manufacturing News* 52 (October 1941): 59.

53 Quoted in Weir, "Truly Allied Undertaking," 105. A joggle joint laps one steel plate over another to make a tight connection.

54 MMGLK, German and Milne Papers, 1989.0044.0005.5, Herbert J. Whitmill, superintendent, to Walter Lambert, German and Milne, 28 October 1941.

55 *Vancouver Daily Province*, 9 February 1942.

56 *Vancouver Sun*, 14 August 1942.

57 *L'Écho de la marine* 3, no. 17 (29 September 1944).

58 Mansbridge, *Launching History*, 75.

59 Lane, *Ships for Victory*, 826.

60 See Pritchard, "Fifty-Six Minesweepers and the Toronto Shipbuilding Company during the Second World War."

61 Marcil, *Tall Ships and Tankers*, 515–17, 523–4, 632–4.

62 Extrapolated from data on a graph printed in the shipyard newspaper *The Fo'c'sle*, 15 August 1944, in Wallis, comp., *Story of Pictou's Park Ships*, 78.

63 Robson, "Merchant Shipbuilding in Canada," 282–3.

64 Wallis, comp., *Story of Pictou's Park Ships*, 67.

65 Ibid., 1, from *The Fo'c'sle*, December 1944.

66 NVMA, Fonds 97, box 2, file 3, J.D.V. Kinvig binder, see under "riveting."

67 NSARM, MG 2, box 1524, file 1223, no. 3, Carswell to Norman Yarrow, 3 October 1940.

68 Robson, "Merchant Shipbuilding in Canada," 294; Lane, *Ships for Victory*, 235.

69 Elliott, *Allied Escort Ships of World War II*, 23.

70 Johnman and Murphy, *British Shipbuilding and the State since 1918*, 92.

71 Hall and Wrigley, *Studies of Overseas Supply*, 52.

72 Johnman and Murphy, *British Shipbuilding*, 91.

CHAPTER TWELVE

1 Johnman and Murphy, *British Shipbuilding and the State since 1918*, 85.

2 LAC, RG 2 7C, vol. 15 (reel C-4876), Cabinet War Committee, document no. 739, "Interim Report on Postwar Shipping Policy," 22 March 1944.

3 H.T. Mitchell Papers, Mitchell to wife, June 1943, recounts how Rannie was once cheered after talking to a group of welders at United Shipyards: "No boss was ever given a cheer at United before." On Leitch, see MMGLK, interview with Donald Page, *Jib Gems* 24, no. 2 (March 2009): 16.

4 According to the US Office of War Information, as of 1 October 1942, half of Canadian manufactured machine tools were being exported to the United States; see *Canadian Machinery and Manufacturing News* 53 (December 1942): 177.

5 This paragraph is indebted to Knox, "Engineer's Outline of RCN History: Part I," 113–15.

6 See Knox, "Engineer's Outline of RCN History: Part II," for an introduction to these postwar developments.

7 LAC, MG 27 III B20, box 57, file S-19-2(7), memorandum, W.J. Bennett to Sheils, 27 October 1943.

8 LAC, MG 27 III B20, box 42, file 5-9-25, Howe to Lord Leathers, 22 October 1943.

9 Ibid., Leathers to Howe, 15 November 1943.

10 See Ayre, "Merchant Shipbuilding during the War," 3, 13–14.

11 LAC, RG 2 7C, vol. 15 (reel C-4,876), Cabinet War Committee, document no. 739, "Interim Report on Postwar Shipping Policy," 22 March 1944; and document no. 740, "Report on Merchant Shipbuilding," 14 March 1944. See UBCSC, H.R. MacMillan Papers, box 100, file 15, MacMillan to R.A.C. Henry, 29 February 1944, for his view on the poor prospects for Canadian postwar shipping.

12 Lane, *Ships for Victory*, 574–6.

13 This paragraph is indebted to Conn, "Will Vivian, Pioneer Engine Builder," 22.

14 LAC, RG 2 7C, vol. 15 (reel C-4876), Cabinet War Committee minutes, 12 April 1944.

15 NVMA, Fonds 97, box 48, file 3, no. A-122-6, contract with Burrard Dry Dock Co., 30 April 1945; LAC, RG 28, box 256, file 196-13-4, press release, 12 May 1945.

16 LAC, RG 28, box 103, file 2-6-61, copy of C.L. Dewar, president, Wartime Shipbuilding Limited, to Horace H. German, 13 October 1944, closing the correspondence.

17 For more on these ships, see Mansbridge, *Launching History*, 99–100; and Marcil, *Tall Ships and Tankers*, 27-1.

18 LAC, RG 28, box 103, file 2-C-61, J. Edouard Simard to Prime Minister King, 24 April 1944; *SR&SB* 27, no. 4 (April 1944): 20.

19 See editorial in *CS&MEN* 15, no. 12 (July 1944): 25, attacking the Montreal Board of Trade's position.

20 UBCSC, H.R. MacMillan Papers, box 100, file 15, copy of Canadian Press report, 23 December 1944, of Michaud's remarks. See Halford, *Unknown Navy*, 236, for Michaud expressing the same view a year earlier.

21 Mansbridge, *Launching History*, 95–6. For a copy of the brief, see "Shipbuilders Representation to Government," *Canadian Transportation* 47 (October 1944): 565–71.

22 LAC, RG 28, box 103, file 2-C-61, Ambridge to Howe, 11 September 1944.

23 Mansbridge, *Launching History*, 104–6.

24 Hennessy, "Rise and Fall of Canadian Maritime Policy, 1939–1965" 81, citing LAC, RG 2 7C, vol. 16, Cabinet War Committee discussion, 5 October 1944.

25 See ibid., 96–8.

26 Milner, *Canada's Navy*, 166.

27 Quoted from Prime Minister Louis St Laurent's speech in the House of Commons in December 1949, in Clyne, *Jack of All Trades*, 139.

28 Bothwell and Kilbourn, *C.D. Howe*, 187–8.

29 Kennedy, *History of the Department of Munitions and Supply* (hereafter *History of DMS*), vol. 1, 386–7; Halford, *Unknown Navy*, 236, citing CS&MEN 16, no. 8 (March 1946): 31.

30 Kennedy, *History of DMS*, vol. 1, 502.

31 Ibid., 405.

32 Canada, Department of Reconstruction and Supply, *Disposal and Peacetime Use of Crown Plant Buildings*, 18–19, 28 (table 9).

33 Mansbridge, *Launching History*, 94–5. See Clyne, *Jack of All Trades*, for a full, if opinionated, discussion of the commission's work.

34 Norrie, Owram, and Emery, *History of the Canadian Economy*, 343.

Bibliography

PRIMARY SOURCES

Canada

BARRIE, ON
Private Archives
– Joe Fossey Collection (photographs)

COLLINGWOOD, ON
Collingwood Museum, 45 St Paul Street
– 911.1.22, Labour Agreement, Working Conditions, Plant Rules, etc., the Collingwood Ship-yards Ltd
– 991.24.4 to 991.24.22, Materials Estimates, 1940–1944

ESQUIMALT, BC
Esquimalt Municipal Archives (EMA), 1149A Esquimalt Road
– Yarrows Ltd Fonds
– Arthur J. Daniels Fonds

GRAVENHURST, ON
Muskoka Steamship and Historical Society (MSHS), Muskoka Boat and Heritage Centre
– Thomas Greavette Collection

HALIFAX, NS
Dalhousie University Archives (DUA), Isaac Walton Killam Library
– MS 4 106, Hawker-Siddley Canada Ltd/Trenton Steel Works Ltd Papers
– MS 4 171, Wagstaff and Hatfield Shipbuilding Company Papers
– MS 9 17, Marine Workers' Federation Records
Maritime Museum of the Atlantic (MMA), 6175 Lower Water Street
– MP 300.16.1, "List of vessels built by Smith and Rhuland"
– M 2002.9.1 a, b, and c, Boyd A. Gibson Collection (photographs)
Nova Scotia Archives and Records Management (NSARM), 6016 University Avenue
– MG 1, Halifax Harbour Commissioners
– MG 2, Angus L. Macdonald Fonds
– MG 3, Halifax-Dartmouth Industries Ltd Fonds

- MG 7, vol. 119, Shipping Registers, Notes of Protest
- MG 20, Halifax-Dartmouth and District Labour Council Fonds
- RG 73, Registry of Joint Stock Companies

KINGSTON, ON
Marine Museum of the Great Lakes at Kingston (MMGLK), 55 Ontario Street
- Canada Steamship Lines Fonds
- Canadian Dredge and Dock Co. Fonds
- Canadian Shipbuilding and Engineering Fonds
- Collingwood Shipbuilding Company Collection
- Francis MacLachlan Collection (photographs)
- German and Milne Papers
- *Jib Gems* (quarterly newsletter published by the museum)
- Port Arthur Shipbuilding Fonds
Queen's University Archives (QUA)
- A. ARCH 100, City of Kingston Archives
- A. ARCH 1004, Canada Steamship Lines Ltd
- A. ARCH 2007, William Clifford Clark Papers
- A. ARCH 2130, Norman Lambert Papers
- A. ARCH 2246, Canada Steamship Engineering Ltd (Kingston Shipyards)
- A. ARCH 2275, Grant MacLachlan Papers

LÉVIS, QC
Secteur des Arts et de la Culture, Archives privés historiques, Ville de Lévis, 4010 St-Georges
- Photographs from Davie Shipbuilding and Repairing Company

MIDLAND, ON
Huronia Museum, 549 Little Lake Park
- James Playfair Papers
- *Midland Free Press*, 1939–1945 (microfilm)

ORILLIA, ON
Museum of Art and History, 30 Peter Street
- Don Hunter photos and miscellaneous documents

OTTAWA, ON
Canadian War Museum Archives (CWMA)
- James Nicholson McLeod, shipwright foreman, United Shipyards
Directorate of History and Heritage (DHH), Department of National Defence
- Series 8: 1440–5
- Series 30: 8000/subseries 5, pt 3, dockyard file
- Series 30: 8200/construction of ships
- Series 33: 8280 Sydney files
- Series II: PRO/ADM 1 (copies)
- Series III: Navy narratives
- Card files: "Shipbuilding"

Library and Archives Canada (LAC), Government Documents
- Manuscript Groups: MG 27 III B20, C.D. Howe Papers; MG 28 I103, Trades and Labour Congress of Canada Papers; MG 28 I268, United Steelworkers of America Fonds; MG 30 A94, Jacob L. Cohen Papers; MG 30 B121, W. Harold Milne Fonds; MG 31 E12, Arthur J. Hill Papers
- Picture Division: Documentary Art Catalogue Cards
- R1211-0-40-C, Wartime Housing Papers
- Record Groups: RG 2, Privy Council Office; RG 2 a-1-a, Privy Council; RG 2 7C, Cabinet War Committee Papers and Minutes; RG 19, Department of Finance; RG 24, Department of National Defence, accession no. 1983/84/167, Naval Service Records; RG 27, Department of Labour; RG 28, Department of Munitions and Supply; RG 36/21, Canadian Mutual Aid Board; RG 46, Department of Transport; RG 58, Auditor General; RG 64, Wartime Prices and Trade Board; RG 117, Office of the Custodian of Enemy Property

OWEN SOUND, ON
Grey County Archives (GCA), 102599 Grey Road 18
- William Kennedy and Sons Collection
Owen Sound Marine and Rail Museum, 1165 1st Avenue West
- Russel Brothers Ltd Archives (available with additional archives on DVD)

PORT CARLING, ON
Muskoka Lakes Museum
- Garth Tassie Papers
Private Archives
- Garth Tassie papers and photographs in the possession of Paul Doddington

QUEBEC CITY, QC
Bibliothèque et Archives Nationales de Quebec – Central Archives Quebec (BANQ-CAQ), Université Laval, Ste Foy
- E 24, Fonds de Ministère du Travail, Commission des Accidents du Travail
- E 62, Commission de la Santé et Sécurité de Travail
Private Archives
- Eileen Reid Marcil Papers

RICHMOND, ON
Private Archives
- Ron Wallis Papers

SALT SPRING ISLAND, BC
Private Archives
- H.T. Mitchell Papers. Photocopies of extracts of Mitchell's wartime correspondence with his wife in the possession of Dr Kenneth Mackenzie

ST JOHN, NB
New Brunswick Provincial Archives
- Corporate records of St John Dry Dock and Shipbuilding Company

SOREL-TRACY, QC

Société Historique de Pierre-de-Saurel Inc. (SHPS)

- P001 Fonds Sorel Industries
- P006, Fonds de Marine Industries Ltd
- P189, Fonds Odette Vincent, Notes assembled during research for a doctoral thesis, "La construction navale au Quebec: Le cas de Marine Industries limitée, Sorel-Tracy, 1838–1985," begun 1995, abandoned following the candidate's death

TORONTO, ON

Archives of Ontario (AO), 77 Grenville Street

- C5, Gordon W. Powley Fonds (photographs)
- F-4153, Floyd S. Chalmers Fonds
- RG 6-15, Ontario Ministry of Finances, Interministerial and Intergovernmental Correspondence of the Ontario Treasury Department
- RG 7-12, Correspondence of the Deputy Minister of Labour
- RG 7-46, Correspondence of the Registrar of the Labour Court, 1943
- RG 7-60, Labour Court Case Files

City of Toronto Archives (CTA)

- No. 1297, John Inglis Company Fonds

Private Archives

- James Taylor Collection (photographs)

VANCOUVER, BC

City of Vancouver Archives (CVA), 1150 Chestnut Street

- Add. Mss. 251, Sheet Metal Workers International Association, Local 280 Fonds
- Add. Mss. 300, Vancouver Board of Trade Fonds
- Add. Mss. 304, International Brotherhood of Painters and Allied Trades Union, Local 138, Fonds
- Add. Mss. 362, Halford David Wilson Papers
- Add. Mss. 376, Gordon Brown Fonds
- Add. Mss. 507, Burrard Dry Dock Co. Ltd, 1941–1944
- Add. Mss. 558, Vancouver Metal Trades Council Fonds
- Add. Mss. 717, BC Marine Engineers and Shipbuilders Ltd Fonds
- Add. Mss. 902, Phyllis Turner Papers; box 38 contains Frank Ross Papers
- Boilermakers and Iron Shipbuilders Union Clippings
- City of Vancouver Photo Collection, 195-1 to 195-46

North Vancouver Museum and Archives (NVMA), 209 West 4th Street, North Vancouver

- Fonds 27, Versatile Pacific Shipyards (Burrard Dry Dock Co. Ltd)
- Fonds 97, J.D.V. "Doug" Kinvig
- Fonds 104, William J. Wardle
- Fonds 105, Matthew T. Davie
- Fonds 123, Lorne Davey
- Fonds 125, Tom Knox
- Fonds 143, Wartime Shipbuilding Ltd
- Fonds 157, Jock Mitchell
- North Vancouver Commissioner Fonds

University of British Columbia Library, Rare Books and Special Collections (UBCSC)
- Angus MacInnis Memorial Collection
- Angus MacInnis Papers
- H.R. MacMillan Papers
- MacMillan-Bloedel Ltd, Corporate Collection
- Marine Workers and Boilermakers Industrial Union, Local 1
- Trade Union Research Bureau Records
- Vancouver and District Labour Council Fonds

Vancouver Maritime Museum (VMM)
- Burrard Dry Dock Fonds
- Yarrows Ltd Fonds

VICTORIA, BC

British Columbia Archives and Records Service (BCARS), Corporate Registry Files
- Add. Mss. 9, Gerald Grattan McGeer Papers
- Add. Mss. 448, Star Shipyards (Mercer's) Ltd Fonds
- Add. Mss. 507, Victor S. Spencer, letter to
- Add. Mss. 1230, *History of Burrard Dry Dock Company*, J.S. Marshall and Co. Ltd, 7 vols
- Add. Mss. 1241, *History of Yarrows Limited*, J.S. Marshall and Co. Ltd, 4 vols
- Add. Mss. 1950, Victoria Motor Boat and Repair Ltd
- GR 1073, British Columbia, Department of Labour, Industrial Conciliation and Arbitration Disputes Files
- GR 1583, Certificate Registry Files
- GR 1976, Canada, Commission on the most effective methods to secure maximum production in the shipyards of British Columbia, 1942, microfiche (neg.)
- Tape 3976: 1–27, Marine Workers and Boilermakers Industrial Union, Local 1 (taped interviews with former shipyard workers, portions of which have appeared in Marine Retirees Association, *A History of Shipbuilding in British Columbia*)

City of Victoria Archives, 1 Centennial Square
- Photographic Archives

Maritime Museum of British Columbia (MMBC), 28 Bastion Square
- Miscellaneous re: Victoria Machinery Depot Ltd
- Copies of *The Convoy*, published monthly during the war by Victoria Machinery Depot

Private Archives
- Sheila Anderson Papers, in possession of her daughter Fiona Hyslop

University of Victoria Archives (UVA), McPherson Library
- Victoria Labour Council Fonds, 1904–1979
- Victoria Shipyard Workers Federal Union, Local 238, 1898–1956

United Kingdom

SOUTHAMPTON

Southampton Maritime Museum
- Canadian Power Boat Company Records (Hubert Scott-Paine Papers)

United States

COLLEGE PARK, MD
National Archives and Records Administration (NARA)
- RG 19, Records of the Bureau of Ships
- RG 38, Chief of Naval Operations – Naval Intelligence Reports
- RG 178, US Maritime Commission and War Shipping Administration
- RG 179, War Production Board
University of Maryland at College Park (UMCP), Hornbake Library
- Archives of the Industrial Union of Marine and Shipyard Workers of America (IUM3WA), Local 34, Halifax, Nova Scotia

Professional and Trade Journals

Canadian Machinery and Manufacturing News 50–6 (Toronto: Maclean, 1939–45). A complete wartime run is located at Queen's University, Stauffer Library.
Canadian Shipping and Marine Engineering News (CS&MEN) 10–16 (August 1939–July 1945). A not quite complete wartime run is located at Library and Archives Canada.
Canadian Transportation 42–8 (1939–45). A complete wartime run is located at Queen's University, Stauffer Library.
Harbour and Shipping 22–8 (Vancouver, 1939–45). A complete wartime run is located at the University of British Columbia, David Lam Library.
The Institution of Naval Architects. *Transactions* 81–9 (London, 1939–47). A complete wartime run is located in the Marine Museum of the Great Lakes at Kingston.
The North-East Coast Institute of Engineers and Shipbuilders. *Transactions* 55–61 (Newcastle-on-Tyne, 1939–46). Copies are located at the Marine Museum of the Great Lakes at Kingston.
Shipping Register and Shipbuilder (SR&SB) 26–8 (Montreal, 1943–45). An incomplete run is located at Library and Archives Canada.
The Society of Naval Architects and Marine Engineers. *Transactions* 47–54 (New York, 1939–46).

Shipbuilding Company and Trade Union Papers

Boilermakers and Iron Shipbuilders Union of Canada, Local 1, Vancouver. *The Main Deck.*
Burrard Dry Dock Company. *The Wallace Shipbuilder* (published from 1942 to 1945). Complete set at North Vancouver Museum and Archives.
Davie Shipbuilding and Repairing Company Ltd. *L'Écho maritime* (February 1943 to March 1945). Photocopies in the Eileen Reid Marcil Papers.
Ferguson Industries Ltd. *The Refitter* (14 of 22 issues from May 1944 to March 1946). Copies in Ron Wallis Papers.
Foundation Marine Ltd. *The Fo'c'sle* 1, 2 (6 January 1943). The first issue, dated 10 December 1942, appeared as *Shipping News*; published semimonthly until March 1945, for a total of forty issues. Copies in Ron Wallis Papers. Many pages are reproduced in Ron Wallis, comp., *The Story of Pictou's Park Ships* (Pictou, NS: Pictou Advocate, 2004).
Industrial Union of Marine and Shipyard Workers of Canada, Local 1, Halifax. *The Marine Worker* 2, no. 2 (January 1943). This mimeographed four-page paper was published from 1942 to 1944.

Marine Industries Ltd. *L'Écho de la marine* (published from 1944 to 1948). Complete set at Société Historique de Pierre-de-Saurel Inc., Sorel-Tracy, Quebec.

Prince Rupert Dry Dock Co. *Builders for Freedom* (first published October 1942). No copies located.

St John Dry Dock and Shipbuilding Co. *The Dry Dock Bulletin* 1, no. 1 (September 1943), to 1, no. 10 (October 1944). Copies at New Brunswick Museum, St John.

Toronto Shipbuilding Company. *Compass: To Keep Us on Our Course* 1, no. 1 (August 1942), to 2, no. 1 (August 1943). Copies in a single bound volume at Toronto Reference Library.

United Shipyards Ltd. *U.S.L. Journal.* No copies located.

Victoria Machinery Depot. *The Convoy.* Nearly complete collection at Maritime Museum of British Columbia, Victoria.

West Coast Shipbuilders Ltd. *Down Our Ways.* Complete run in City of Vancouver Archives, Add. Mss. 376, Gordon Brown Fonds.

Canadian Government Publications

Canada, Department of External Affairs. *Canadian War Data.* Ottawa: Department of External Affairs, 1946.

– "Estimated Value of War Production." Canadian Information Service Reference Paper No. 4. Ottawa: Department of External Affairs, 1946.

Canada, Department of Labour. *Labour Gazette* 39–47. Ottawa: King's Printer, 1939–47.

Canada, Department of Munitions and Supply (DMS). *The Industrial Front.* 4 vols. Ottawa: King's Printer, 1943–44.

– *Record of Contracts Awarded from July 14, 1939, to August 1941.* 20 vols. Ottawa: King's Printer, 1940–41.

– *Report on the Government-Financed Expansion of Industrial Capacity in Canada as of 31 December 1943.* Ottawa: DMS, 1944.

Canada, Department of Reconstruction and Supply. *Disposal and Peacetime Use of Crown Plant Buildings.* Ottawa: King's Printer, 1948.

– *Encouragement to Industrial Expansion in Canada: Operation of Special Depreciation Provisions, November 10, 1944–March 31, 1949.* Ottawa: King's Printer, 1948.

– *Location and Effects of Wartime Industrial Expansion in Canada, 1939–1944.* Ottawa: Directorate of Economic Research, Department of Reconstruction and Supply, 1 November 1945.

Canada, Dominion Bureau of Statistics (DBS). *Annual Industry Report: Iron, Steel and Their Products Group: The Shipbuilding Industry.* 1937–46. Not published in 1940 and 1941. Ottawa: King's Printer, 1937–46.

– *Canada Year Book, 1941–1948/49.* Ottawa: King's Printer, 1941–49.

– *Canadian Labour Force Estimates, 1931–1945.* Ottawa: King's Printer, 1951.

– *Census of Canada, 1941.* Vol. 2, *Population.* Ottawa: King's Printer, 1941.

– *Iron and Steel and Their Products in Canada, 1938 and 1939.* Ottawa: King's Printer, 1941.

– *Iron and Steel and Their Products in Canada, 1940–1942.* Ottawa: King's Printer, 1945.

– *Iron and Steel and Their Products in Canada, 1943–1945.* Ottawa: King's Printer, 1949.

– "Monthly Report on Steel Ingots." February 1946.

– "Monthly Report, Production of Iron and Steel in Canada." 1939–41.

Canada, Government of. "Royal Commission on Production in the Shipyards of British Columbia." 23 August 1942. Unpublished. Copies in LAC, MG 28 I103, box 236, file 13, and in NVMA, Fonds 27, box 554.

- "Royal Commission on Shipbuilding in the Provinces of Quebec and Ontario." *Labour Gazette* 42 (January 1942): 17–27.
Canada, House of Commons. *Debates*, 1939 to 1945.
- *Special Committee on War Expenditures.* Ottawa: King's Printer, 1944.
Canada, Mutual Aid Board. *Annual Report.* Ottawa: King's Printer, 1944–45.
- *Final Report.* Ottawa: King's Printer, 1946.
Canada, National War Labour Board (NWLB). *Proceedings [of the] Inquiry into Labour Relations and Wage Conditions in Canada.* Ottawa: NWLB, 1943.
Canadian Wartime Information Board. *Canada at War*, nos 1–45 (Ottawa, 1940–45). See especially issue no. 45, "Recapitulation Issue" (July 1945).
Goldenberg, H. Carl. *Government-Financed Expansion of Industrial Capacity in Canada.* Ottawa: King's Printer, 1945.
Library and Archives Canada, ArchiviaNet. *The Diaries of William Lyon Mackenzie King, 1893–1950.* http://King.collectionscanada.ca/EN/default.asp (accessed 19 June 2002).

SECONDARY SOURCES

Abella, Irving. *Nationalism, Communism and Canadian Labour.* Toronto: University of Toronto Press, 1973.
Anonymous. "Consolidation of Great Lakes Shipbuilding Companies." *Canadian Railway and Marine World* (January 1927): 26.
Anonymous. "Employment in the Shipbuilding Industry." *Monthly Labor Review* 58 (May 1944): 948–59.
Anonymous. "Shipbuilding in Canada during the Second World War." *Journal of Naval Engineering* 1 (1947): 6–10.
Archibald, Katherine. *Wartime Shipyard: A Study in Social Disunity.* Berkeley and Los Angeles: University of California Press, 1947.
Aster, Sidney, ed. *The Second World War as a National Experience.* Ottawa: Department of National Defence, 1981.
Aubert, Roland. *Harlaka de mon enfance: Autobiographie de Roland Aubert.* Lévis, QC: Éditions Apropos, 2003.
Ayre, Sir Amos L. "Merchant Shipbuilding during the War." Institute of Naval Architects, *Transactions* 87 (1945): 3–28.
Babcock and Wilcox Ltd. *A History, 1844–1977.* Cambridge, ON: Babcock and Wilcox Ltd, 1987.
Bacher, John C. *Keeping to the Marketplace: The Evolution of Canadian Housing Policy.* Montreal and Kingston: McGill-Queen's University Press, 1993.
Baird, Donald M. *Under Tow: A Canadian History of Tugs and Towing.* St Catharines, ON: Vanwell, 2003.
Baker, A.D., III. *Allied Landing Craft of World War Two.* Annapolis, MD: Naval Institute Press, 1985.
Baker, Elijah, III. *Introduction to Steel Shipbuilding.* 1st ed. New York and London: McGraw-Hill, 1943.
Baker, R. "Notes on the Development of Landing Craft." Institute of Naval Architects, *Transactions* 89 (1947): 218–58.
Barnaby, K.C. *100 Years of Specialized Shipbuilding and Engineering.* London: Hutchinson, 1964.

Barnes, Eleonor C. (Lady Yarrow), comp. *Alfred Yarrow: His Life and Work*. 1923. Reprint, London: Edward Arnold and Co., 1928.

Barnett, Corelli. *The Audit of War: The Illusion and Reality of Britain as a Great Nation*. London: Macmillan, 1986.

Beck, James Murray. *Pendulum of Power: Canada's Federal Elections*. Toronto: Prentice-Hall of Canada, 1968.

Behrens, C.B.A. *Merchant Shipping and the Demands of War*. London: HMSO/Longmans, Green and Co., 1955.

Bélanger, Diane. *La Construction navale à Saint Laurent, Ile d'Orléans*. St Laurent, QC: Bibliothèque David Gosselin, 1984.

Bellamy, Matthew J. *Profiting the Crown: Canada's Polymer Corporation, 1942–1990*. Montreal and Kingston: McGill-Queen's University Press, 2004.

Betcherman, Lita Rose. *Ernest Lapointe: Mackenzie King's Great Quebec Lieutenant*. Toronto: University of Toronto Press, 2002.

Bliss, Michael. *A Canadian Millionaire: The Life and Business Times of Sir Joseph Flavelle, Bart., 1851–1939*. Toronto: Macmillan of Canada, 1978.

– *Northern Enterprise: Five Centuries of Canadian Business*. Toronto: McClelland and Stewart, 1987.

Boas, William S. *Canada in World War II: Post-War Possibilities*. Montreal: W.S. Boas, [1945].

Borins, Sandford S. "World War II Crown Corporations: Their Functions and Their Fate." In *Crown Corporations in Canada: The Calculus of Investment Choice*, ed. J. Robert S. Prichard, 447–75. Toronto: Butterworth's, 1983.

Bothwell, Robert. "A Curious Lack of Proportion: Canadian Business and the War." In *The Second World War as a National Experience*, ed. Sidney Aster, 24–37. Ottawa: Department of National Defence, 1981.

– "'Who's Paying for Anything These Days?': War Production in Canada, 1938–45." In *Mobilization for Total War*, ed. N.F. Dreiziger, 59–69. Waterloo, ON: Wilfred Laurier Univeristy Press, 1981. Reprinted in Ronald G. Haycock and Barry D. Hunt, eds, *Canada's Defence: Perspectives on Policy in the Twentieth Century*, 119–28 (Toronto: Copp Clark Pitman, 1993).

– and W. Kilbourn. *C.D. Howe: A Biography*. Toronto: McClelland and Stewart, 1979.

Brown, David K. *A Century of Naval Construction: The History of the Royal Corps of Naval Constructors, 1883–1983*. London: Conway Maritime Press, 1983.

– *The Design and Construction of British Warships, 1939–1945: The Official Record*. Vol. 1, *Major Surface Vessels*. London: Conway Maritime Press, 1995.

Bruce, Jean. *Back the Attack: Canadian Women during the Second World War at Home and Abroad*. Toronto: Macmillan of Canada, 1985.

Bryce, Robert B. *Canada and the Cost of World War II*. Ed. Mathew J. Bellamy. Montreal and Kingston: McGill-Queen's University Press, 2005.

Bunker, John Gorley. *Liberty Ships: The Ugly Ducklings of World War II*. Annapolis, MD: Naval Institute Press, 1972.

Buxton, Ian L. "British Warship Building and Repair." In *The Battle of the Atlantic: 50th Anniversary International Naval Conference*, ed. Stephen Howarth and Derek Law, 80–100. London and Annapolis, MD: Greenhill Books and Naval Institute Press, 1994.

Cafferky, Shawn. "The Royal Canadian Navy's Drive for Diversification: Post-War Planning, 1943–1945." *American Neptune* 61, no. 4 (Fall 2002): 439–42.

Calhoun, Sue. *"Ole Boy": Memoirs of a Canadian Labour Leader J.K. Bell*. Halifax: Nimbus, 1992.

Canadian Shipbuilding and Ship Repair Association. *Annual Report.* 1947.

Canadian Vickers Limited. *Annual Report for Year Ending February 2, 1940.*

Carmichael, Harry J. "War Production Nears Maximum." *Canadian Machinery and Manufacturing News* 53 (December 1942): 175.

Carter, S. Maurice, ed. *Who's Who in British Columbia (Registered), 1944–45–46.* 6th ed. Vancouver: S. Maurice Carter, 1945.

Chappelle, Dean. "Building a Bigger Stick: The Construction of Tribal Class Destroyers in Canada, 1940–1948." *Northern Mariner* 5, no. 1 (January 1995): 1–17.

Chouinard, Craig. "Shipyard Struggles: The Origins of the Maritime Marine Workers Federation in Saint John, NB, 1937–1947." MA thesis, University of New Brunswick, 1975.

Clarke, J.Y. "Ship Construction and Repair." In *A History of Canadian Marine Technology,* 35–47. Ottawa: Eastern Canadian Section, Society of Naval Architects and Marine Engineers, 1995.

Clyne, J.V. *Jack of All Trades: Memories of a Busy Life.* Toronto: McClelland and Stewart, 1985.

Collard, Edgar Andrew. *Passage to the Sea: The Story of Canada Steamship Lines.* Toronto: Doubleday Canada, 1991.

Collins, David, et al., comp. *Esso Mariners: A History of Imperial Oil's Fleet Operations from 1899–1980.* Toronto: Imperial Oil, 1980.

Collins, Paul. "'First Line of Defence': The Establishment and Development of St. John's, Newfoundland, as the Royal Canadian Navy's Premier Escort Base in the Second World War." *Northern Mariner* 16, no. 3 (July 2006): 15–32.

Conn, David R. "Will Vivian, Pioneer Engine Builder." *Raincoast Chronicles,* no. 9 (Madeira Park, BC: Raincoast Historical Society, n.d.): 19–24.

Cook, Ramsay. "Canadian Freedom in Wartime, 1935–1945." In *His Own Man: Essays in Honour of Arthur Reginald Marsden Lower,* ed. W.H. Heick and Roger Graham, 37–53. Montreal and Kingston: McGill-Queen's University Press, 1974.

Cook, Tim. *Clio's Warriors: Canadian Historians and the Writing of the World Wars.* Vancouver: University of British Columbia Press, 2006.

Copp, Terry. "The Rise of Industrial Unions in Montreal, 1935–1945." *Industrial Relations/Relations Industrielles* 37, no. 4 (1982): 843–75.

Corkhill, Michael. *The Tonnage Measurement of Ships: Towards a Universal System.* London: Fairplay, 1977.

Cox, Corolyn. *Canadian Strength: Biographical Sketches.* Foreword by the Right Honourable C.D. Howe. Toronto: Ryerson Press, 1946.

Crawford, R.E. "Building Mounts for Twelve Pounder Naval Guns." *Canadian Machinery and Manufacturing News* 53 (March 1942): 61–5.

– "4[-inch] Naval Gun Mk XIX Arms Merchantmen." *Canadian Machinery and Manufacturing News* 53 (May 1942): 89–94, 152.

– "Railwaymen Build Naval Guns on Former Mud Flats." *Canadian Machinery and Manufacturing News* 53 (June 1942): 99–108.

– "Western Railway Shop Builds Twelve Pounders." *Canadian Machinery and Manufacturing News* 53 (September 1942): 67–71, 124.

Cuff, R.D., and J.L. Granatstein. *Ties that Bind: Canadian-American Relations in Wartime from the Great War to the Cold War.* 2nd ed. Toronto: Hakkert, 1977.

Cuthbertson, Wendy. "Pocketbooks and Patriotism: The 'Financial Miracle' of Canada's World War II Victory Bond Program." In *Canadian Military History since the 17th Century,* ed. Yves Tremblay, 177–85. Proceedings of the Canadian Military History Conference, Ottawa, 5–9 May 2000. Ottawa: Department of National Defence, 2001.

Daniels, C.J. "Off to Sea Again." *CS&MEN* 16, no.1 (August 1944): 37–41, 64.

– "Progress at Pictou." *CS&MEN* 16, no. 1 (August 1944): 46–7, 60.

Darlington, Robert A., and Fraser M. McKee. *The Canadian Naval Chronicle, 1939–1945: The Successes and Losses of the Canadian Navy in World War II*. Rev. ed. St Catharines, ON: Vanwell, 1998.

Dempsey, Lotta. "Women in War Plants." In *Women at War*, ed. J. Herbert Hodgins et al., 10–11. Montreal: Maclean, 1943.

– "Women Working on Ships and Aircraft." In *Women at War*, ed. J. Herbert Hodgins et al., 82–3. Montreal: Maclean, 1943.

Diamond, Sara. *Women's Labour History in British Columbia: A Bibliography, 1930–1948*. Vancouver: Press Gang, 1982.

Dionne, Bernard. "Les Canadiens français et les syndicates internationaux: La cas de la direction au Conseil des métiers du travail de Montréal (1938–1958)." *Revue d'histoire de l'Amérique française* 43, no. 1 (Summer 1989): 31–61.

Dominion Bridge Company. *Of Tasks Accomplished: The Story of the Accomplishments of the Dominion Bridge Company Limited and Its Wholly Owned Subsidiaries in World War II*. Montreal: Dominion Bridge Company, 1945.

Donald, W.J.A. *The Canadian Iron and Steel Industry: A Study in the Economic History of a Protected Industry*. Boston and New York: Houghton Mifflin, 1915.

Doughty, Martin. *Merchant Shipping and War: A Study in Defence Planning in Twentieth-Century Britain*. Royal Historical Society Studies in History No. 131. London: Swift Printers, 1982.

Douglas, W.A.B. "Conflict and Innovation in the Royal Canadian Navy, 1939–1945." In *Naval Warfare in the Twentieth Century: Essays in Honour of Arthur Marder*, ed. Gerald Jordan, 210–32. London: Croom Helm, 1977.

– and Brereton Greenhous. *Out of the Shadows: Canada in the Second World War*. Toronto: Oxford University Press, 1977.

– Roger Sarty, Michael Whitby, et al. *A Blue Water Navy: The Official Operational History of the Royal Canadian Navy in the Second World War, 1943–1945*. Vol. 2, pt 2. St Catharines, ON: Vanwell, 2007.

– Roger Sarty, Michael Whitby, et al. *No Higher Purpose: The Official Operational History of the Royal Canadian Navy in the Second World War, 1939–1943*. Vol. 2, pt 1. St Catharines, ON: Vanwell, 2003.

Dreesen, Waldemar C., et al. "Health of Arc Welders in Steel Ship Construction." Public Health Bulletin No. 298 (Washington: Government Printing Office, 1947).

Drent, Jan. "Labour and the Unions in a Wartime Essential Industry: Shipyard Workers in B.C., 1939–1945." *Northern Mariner* 6, no. 4 (October 1996): 47–64.

Driner, Philip. "Shipyard Health Hazards." *Journal of Industrial Hygiene and Toxicology* 26 (March 1944): 86–9.

Drushka, Ken. *H.R.: A Biography of H.R. MacMillan*. Madeira Park, BC: Harbour, 1996.

Dufault, Linda. "L'Écho de la marine, 1944–1948." *Le Carignan: Revue de la Société d'histoire de Pierre-de-Saurel* 1, no. 2 (September 1987): 21–6.

Duke, A.H., and W.M. Gray. *The Boatbuilders of Muskoka*. Erin, ON: Boston Mills Press, 1996.

Duskin, Gerald L., and Ralph Segman. *If the Gods Are Good: The Epic Sacrifice of the HMS Jervis Bay*. Annapolis, MD: Naval Institute Press, 2004.

Earle, Michael. "Down with Hitler and Silby Barrett": The Cape Breton Miners Slowdown Strike of 1941." In *Workers and the State in Twentieth Century Nova Scotia*, ed. Michael Earle, 109–43. Fredericton, NB: Acadiensis Press, 1989.

Eayers, James. *In Defence of Canada*. Vol. 2, *Appeasement and Rearmament*. Toronto: University of Toronto Press, 1965.

Edgar, Keith. "Canada, a Land of Little Ships." *CS&MEN* 15, no. 9 (April 1944): 36–8, 50.

Education committees of the Confédération des syndicates nationaux and the Centrale de l'ensignement de Québec. *History of the Labour Movement in Quebec*. Trans. Arnold Bennett. Montreal: Black Rose Books, 1987.

Elliott, Peter. *Allied Escort Ships of World War II: A Complete Survey*. London: Macdonald and Jane's, 1977.

Elphick, Peter. *Liberty: The Ships That Won the War*. Annapolis, MD: Naval Institute Press, 2001.

Evans, Gary. *John Grierson and the National Film Board: The Politics of Wartime Propaganda*. Toronto: University of Toronto Press, 1984.

Fisher, Robert C. "Canadian Merchant Ship Losses, 1939–1945." *Northern Mariner* 5, no. 3 (July, 1995): 57–73.

– "'We'll Get Our Own': Canada and the Oil Shipping Crisis of 1942." *Northern Mariner* 3, no. 2 (April 1993): 33–9.

Forbes, Ernest. "Consolidating Disparity: The Maritimes and the Industrialization of Canada during the Second World War." *Acadiensis* 15, no. 2 (Spring 1986): 4–27.

– and D.A. Muise, eds. *The Atlantic Provinces in Confederation*. Fredericton, NB: Acadiensis Press, 1993.

Forrestell, Diane. "The Necessity of Sacrifice for a National War: Women's Labour Force Participation, 1939–1946." *Histoire Sociale/Social History* 22, 4 (1989): 333–47.

Fossey, Joe. *Gidley-Grew & Bonnie Boat Company History: A Working Paper Trilogy & Overviews*. Barrie, ON: Joe Fossey, 2006.

Fox, Benjamin. "Alternating Current for Auxiliary Plants of Merchant Vessels." Society of Naval Architects and Marine Engineers, *Transactions* 54 (1946): 201–67.

Francis, Daniel, ed. *Encyclopedia of British Columbia*. Madeira Park, BC: Harbour, 2000.

Frank, David. "The Cape Breton Coal Industry and the Rise and Fall of the British Empire Steel Corporation." *Acadiensis* 7, no. 1 (Autumn 1977): 3–34. Reprinted in P.A. Buckner and David Frank, eds, *The Acadiensis Reader*, vol. 2, 2nd ed., 204–35 (Fredericton: Acadiensis Press, 1988).

Freeman, David J. *Canadian Warship Names*. St Catharines, ON: Vanwell, 2000.

Fudge, Judy, and Eric Tucker. *Labour before the Law: The Regulation of Workers' Collective Action in Canada, 1900–1948*. Toronto: Oxford University Press, 2001.

Fullerton, Douglas H. *Graham Towers and His Times: A Biography*. Toronto: McClelland and Stewart, 1986.

Gardiner, Robert, ed. *The Golden Age of Shipping: The Classical Merchant Ships, 1900–1960*. London: Conway Maritime Press, 1994.

Gaul, Weston. "Canada's Shipbuilding Industry." *Canadian Geographical Journal* 20 (Fall 1940): 56–73.

Gauvin, Luc. "Etude comparative des trois principals chantiers navals du Quebec." MA thesis, Université Laval, 1986.

German, Tony. *The Sea Is at Our Gates: The History of the Canadian Navy*. Toronto: McClelland and Stewart, 1990.

Gibson, Frederick, and Barbara Robertson, eds. *Ottawa at War: The Grant Dexter Memoranda, 1939–1945*. Winnipeg: Manitoba Records Society, 1994.

Gillham, Skip. *The Ships of Collingwood: Over One Hundred Years of Shipbuilding Excellence.* St Catharines, ON: Riverbank Traders, 1992.

Gilmore, James. "The St. Lawrence River Canals Vessel." Society of Naval Architects and Marine Engineers, *Transactions* 64 (1956): 111–61.

Glenn, Fergus. "'Total War' in Steel." *Canadian Forum* (July 1942): 114–16.

Glover, William. "The RCN: Royal Colonial or Royal Canadian Navy?" In *A Nation's Navy: In Quest of Canadian Naval Identity,* ed. Michael L. Hadley, Rob Huebert, and Fred W. Crikard, 71–90. Montreal and Kingston: McGill-Queen's University Press, 1996.

Gluck, Shawna Berger. *Rosie the Riveter Revisited: Women, the War and Social Change.* Boston: Twayne, 1987.

Gonick, Cy, Paul Phillips, and Jesse Vorst, eds. *Labour Pains, Labour Gains: 50 Years of PC 1003.* Winnipeg: Society for Socialist Studies, 1995.

Granatstein, J.L. *Canada's War: The Politics of the Mackenzie King Government, 1939–1949.* 1975. Reprint, Toronto: University of Toronto Press, 1990.

– *A Man of Influence: Norman A. Robertson and Canadian Statecraft, 1929–1968.* Ottawa: Deneau, 1981.

– *The Ottawa Men: The Civil Service Mandarins, 1935–1957.* Toronto: Oxford University Press, 1982.

– *Politics of Survival: The Conservative Party of Canada, 1939–1945.* Toronto: University of Toronto Press, 1967.

– and Desmond Morton. *A Nation Forged in Fire.* Toronto: Lester and Orpen Deny, 1989.

Gravel, Olivar. "Histoire de Marine Industrie Limitée." *Le Carignan: Revue de la Société d'histoire de Pierre-de-Saurel* 1, no. 2 (September 1987): 4–18.

Graves, Donald E. "'Hell Boats' of the R.C.N.: The Canadian Navy and the Motor Torpedo Boat, 1936–1941." *Northern Mariner* 2, no. 3 (July 1992): 31–45.

Gray, William M. *Wood and Glory: Muskoka's Classic Launches* Toronto: Boston Mills Press, 1997.

Grayson, Stan. *Engines Afloat: From Early Days to D-Day.* 2 vols. Marblehead, MA: Devereaux Books, 1999.

Great Britain, Ministry of Labour and National Service. *Women in Shipbuilding.* 1943. Copy in LAC, RG 28, box 256, file 196-13.

Green, Jim. *Against the Tide: The Story of the Canadian Seaman's Union.* Toronto: Progress Books, 1986.

Greene, B.M., ed. *Who's Who in Canada, 1927, 1943–44,* and *1945–46.* Toronto: International Publishing, 1927, 1944, and 1946.

Guthrie, John. *A History of Marine Engineering.* London: Hutchinson, 1971.

Hadley, Michael L. *U-boats against Canada: German Submarines in Canadian Waters.* Montreal and Kingston: McGill-Queen's University Press, 1985.

Halford, Robert G. *The Unknown Navy: Canada's World War II Merchant Navy.* St Catharines, ON: Vanwell, 1995.

Halifax Shipyards Ltd. *The Halship Saga: The War Effort of Halifax Shipyards Limited.* Halifax: Wallace Advertising, 1945.

Hall, H. Duncan. *North American Supply.* History of the Second World War Series. London: HMSO/Longmans, Green and Co., 1955.

– and C.C. Wrigley. *Studies of Overseas Supply.* London: HMSO/Longmans, Green and Co., 1956.

Hamilton, James H. "Shipbuilding in British Columbia." *Harbour and Shipping* 22, no. 10 (October 1939): 337–41.

Hamilton, Ross, ed. *Prominent Men of Canada, 1931–1932*. Montreal: National Publishing Co., 1933.

Hanington, Felicity. *The Lady Boats: The Life and Times of Canada's West Indies Merchant Fleet*. Halifax: Canadian Marine Transportation Centre, Dalhousie University, 1980.

Harland, John. "Corvette Boilers and the Whaler/Corvette Connection." *Argonauta: The Newsletter of the Canadian Nautical Research Society* 19, no. 2 (April 2002): 10–15.

– "The 2750 IHP Corvette Engine." *Warship* (1993): 188–91.

Harris, Carol. *Women at War, 1939-1945: The Home Front*. Stroud, UK: Sutton, 2000.

Harris, Daniel G. "Canadian Warship Construction, 1917–19: The Great Lakes and Upper St. Lawrence River Areas." *Mariner's Mirror* 75, no. 2 (May 1989): 149–58.

Hawkins, John. *The Life and Times of Angus L*. Hantsport, NS, and Windsor, ON: Lancelot Press, 1969.

Haycock, Ronald. "The Clash of Imperatives: Canadian Munitions Development in the Interwar Years, 1919–1939." In *Forging a Nation: Perspectives on the Canadian Military Experience*, ed. B. Horn, 235–69. St Catharines, ON: Vanwell, 2002.

Heal, S.C. *A Great Fleet of Ships: The Canadian Forts and Parks*. St Catharines, ON: Vanwell, 1999.

Heller, Ursula, and Barry Gray. *The Shipbuilders of Collingwood, a Photo-Documentation*. Collingwood, ON: Bennett Press, 1981.

Henderson, George F. *Federal Royal Commissions in Canada, 1867–1966: A Checklist*. Toronto: University of Toronto Press, 1967.

Henderson, T. Stephen. *Angus L. Macdonald: A Provincial Liberal*. Toronto: University of Toronto Press, 2007.

Hennessy, Michael A. "The Industrial Front: The Scale and Scope of Canadian Industrial Mobilization during the Second World War." In *Forging a Nation: Perspectives on the Canadian Military Experience*, ed. Bernd Horn, 135–54. St Catharines, ON: Vanwell, 2002.

– "Postwar Ocean Shipping and Shipbuilding in Canada: An Agenda for Research." *Northern Mariner* 1, no. 3 (July 1991): 25–33.

– "The Rise and Fall of Canadian Maritime Policy, 1939–1965: A Study of Industry, Navalism and the State." PhD diss., University of New Brunswick, 1995.

Heron, Craig. *The Canadian Labour Movement: A Brief History*. 2nd ed. Toronto: James Lorimer, 1996.

– *Working in Steel: The Early Years in Canada, 1883–1935*. Toronto: McClelland and Stewart, 1988.

– and Robert Storey. "Work and Struggle in the Canadian Steel Industry, 1900–1950." In *On the Job: Confronting the Labour Process in Canada*, ed. Craig Heron and Robert Storey, 210–44. Montreal and Kingston: McGill-Queen's University Press, 1986.

Hirshfield, Deborah. "Gender, Generation and Race in American Shipyards in the Second World War." *International History Review* 19 (1997): 131–45.

Hodgins, J. Herbert, et al., eds. *Women at War*. Montreal: Maclean, 1943.

Holt, W.J. "Coastal Force Design." Institute of Naval Architects, *Transactions* 89 (1947): 186–217.

Hughes, Charles H. "Shipbuilding Materials: Iron and Steel, Non-Ferrous Metals and Alloys." *Shipping Register and North American Ports* 2, no. 3 (March 1942): 26.

Hunt, Lionel A. "The Story behind Sternframes." *Harbour and Shipping* 27, no. 11 (November 1944): 479-81.

Hunter, Donald A. *The Story of Hunter Boats.* Barrie, ON: Mary Hunter, 2000.

Hurstfield, J. *The Control of Raw Materials.* History of the Second World War Series. London: HMSO/Longmans, Green and Co., 1953.

Hutchison, Bruce. "The Job Now Is to Make the War Effort Jell." *Vancouver Sun*, 25 November 1940.

Iacoveta, Franca, Roberto Perrin, and Angelo Principe, eds. *Enemies Within: Italian and Other Internees in Canada and Abroad.* Toronto: University of Toronto Press, 2000.

Industrial Reconstruction and Social Development Council. *Report of Conference on Post-war Reconstruction and Rehabilitation Called by B.C. Shipyard, March 11 and 12 1944.* Vancouver: East End Printers, 1944.

International Press. *Who's Who in Canada, 1917–1918.* Toronto: International Press, 1918.

Inwood, Kris. "The Iron and Steel Industry." In *Progress without Planning: The Economic History of Ontario from Confederation to the Second World War*, ed. Ian M. Drummond et al., 185–207. Toronto: University of Toronto Press, 1987.

Jamieson, Stuart Marshall. *Times of Trouble: Labour Unrest and Industrial Conflict in Canada, 1900–1966.* Ottawa: Queen's Printer, 1968.

Johnman, Lewis, and Hugh Murphy. "The British Merchant Shipping Mission in the United States and British Merchant Shipbuilding in the Second World War." *Northern Mariner* 12, no. 3 (July 2002): 1–15.

– and Hugh Murphy. *British Shipbuilding and the State since 1918: A Political Economy of Decline.* Exeter, UK: University of Exeter Press, 2002.

J.S. Marshall and Co. Ltd. *History of Burrard Dry Dock Company.* 7 vols. Typescript. Vancouver: n.p., n.d.

– *History of Yarrows Limited.* 4 vols. Typescript. Vancouver: n.p., 1964.

Jones, Richard. "Politics and Culture: The French Canadians and the Second World War." In *The Second World War as a National Experience*, ed. Sidney Aster, 82–91. Ottawa: Department of National Defence, 1981.

Kaplan, William. *Everything That Floats: Pat Sullivan, Hal Banks, and the Seamen's Unions of Canada.* Toronto: University of Toronto Press, 1987.

Kemp, Peter, ed. *The Oxford Companion to Ships and the Sea.* Oxford, UK: Oxford University Press, 1976.

Kennedy, Eleanor V. "Employment of Women in Shipyards, 1942." *Monthly Labor Review* 56 (February 1943): 277–82.

Kennedy, John de Navarre. *History of the Department of Munitions and Supply: Canada in the Second World War.* 2 vols. Ottawa: King's Printer, 1950.

Kersten, Andrew E. *Labor's Home Front: The American Federation of Labor during World War II.* New York and London: New York University Press, 2006.

Keshen, Jeff. *Saints, Sinners and Soldiers: Canada's Second World War.* Vancouver: University of British Columbia Press, 2004.

Kesselman, Amy. *Fleeting Opportunities: Women Shipyard Workers in Portland and Vancouver during World War II and Reconversion.* Albany: SUNY Press, 1990.

Kilbourn, William. *The Elements Combined: A History of the Steel Company of Canada.* Toronto: Clark, Irwin and Co., 1960.

Kimber, Stephen. *Sailors, Slackers and Blind Pigs: Halifax at War.* Toronto: Doubleday, 2002.

King, W.L. Mackenzie. "Canada's Defence Policy." *Canadian Defence Quarterly* 15, 2 (January 1938): 128–50.

Kinvig, John Douglas Gordon. *Family, Friends and Ships: Memoirs of J.D.G. Kinvig.* Vol. 1, *Birth to Retirement.* North Vancouver: Privately published, 1993.

Kluckner, Michael. *Toronto: The Way It Was.* Toronto: Whitecap Books, 1988.

Knox, J.H.W. "An Engineer's Outline of RCN History: Parts I and II." In *The RCN in Retrospect, 1910–1968,* ed. James A. Boutelier, 96–114 and 317–33. Vancouver and London: University of British Columbia Press, 1982.

Koisten, Paul A.C. "Mobilizing the World War II Economy: Labor and the Industrial Military Alliance." *Pacific Historical Review* 42 (1973): 443–78.

Konings, Chris. *"Queen Elizabeth" at War: His Majesty's Transport, 1939–1946.* Wellingborough, UK: Patrick Stephens, 1985.

Kossoris, Max D. "Work Injuries to Women in Shipyards, 1943–44." *Monthly Labor Review* 60 (March 1945): 551–60.

Lambert, John, and Al Ross. *Allied Coastal Forces of World War II.* Vol. 1, *Fairmile Designs and U.S. Subchasers.* London: Conway Maritime Press, 1990.

Lambert, Walter, and Horace German. *Floating Equipment Designed by Lambert and German.* Montreal: Lambert and German, 1932.

Lane, Frederick C. *Ships for Victory: A History of Shipbuilding under the U.S. Maritime Commission in World War II.* 1951. Reprint, Baltimore, MD: Johns Hopkins University Press, 2001.

Lane, Tony. *The Merchant Seaman's War.* Manchester, UK, and New York: Manchester University Press, 1990.

La Pedraja, René de. *A Historical Dictionary of the U.S. Merchant Marine and Shipbuilding Industry since the Introduction of Steam.* Westport, CT: Greenwood, 1994.

Latham, Barbara, and Roberta J. Pozdro. *Not Just Pin Money: Selected Essays on the History of Women's Work in British Columbia.* Victoria, BC: Camosun College, 1984.

Lauderbaugh, Richard A. *American Steel Makers and the Coming of the Second World War.* Ann Arbor, MI: UMI Research Press, 1980.

Leacock, Stephen, and Leslie Roberts. *Canada's War at Sea.* 2 vols in 1. Montreal: A.M. Beatty, 1944.

Leacy, F.H., ed. *Historical Statistics of Canada.* 2nd ed. Ottawa: Canadian Government Publishing Centre, 1983.

Lennon, M.J., and Syd Charenoff. *On the Homefront: A Scrapbook of Canadian World War Two Memorabilia.* Erin, ON: Boston Mills Press, 1981.

Lewis, Walter, and Rick Neilson. *River Palace.* Toronto: Dundurn, 2008.

Lichtenstein, Nelson. *Labor's War at Home: The CIO in World War II.* Cambridge, UK, and New York: Cambridge University Press, 1982.

Lindberg, Michael, and Daniel Todd. *Anglo-American Shipbuilding in World War II: A Geographical Perspective.* Westport, CT: Praeger, 2004.

Logan, Harold J. *Trade Unions in Canada: Their Development and Functioning.* Toronto: Macmillan of Canada, 1948.

Lynch, Thomas G. *Canada's Flowers: History of the Corvettes of Canada, 1939–1945.* Halifax: Nimbus, 1981.

MacDowell, Laurel Sefton. "The Career of a Canadian Trade Union Leader: C.H. Millard, 1937–1946." *Relations Industrielles/Industrial Relations* 43 (1988): 609–31.

- "The Formation of the Canadian Industrial Relations System during World War Two." *Labour/Le Travail* 3 (1978): 175–96. Reprinted in Laurel Sefton MacDowell and Jan Radforth, eds, *Canadian Working Class History: Selected Reading*, 2nd ed., 525–44 (Toronto: Scholars Press, 2000).
- "The 1943 Steel Strike against Wartime Wage Controls." In *Canadian Labour History: Selected Readings*, 2nd ed., ed. David J. Bercuson and David Bright, 295–315. Toronto: Copp Clark Longman, 1994.
- *"Remember Kirkland Lake": The Gold Miners' Strike of 1941–42.* Toronto: University of Toronto Press, 1983.
- *Renegade Lawyer: The Life of J.L. Cohen.* Toronto: University of Toronto Press, 2001.
MacEachern, George. *George MacEachern: An Autobiography.* Ed. David Frank and Donald MacGillivray. Sydney, NS: University College of Cape Breton Press, 1987.
MacFarlane, John. "Agents of Control or Chaos? A Strike at Arvida Helps Clarify Canadian Policy on Using Troops against Workers during the Second World War." *Canadian Historical Review* 84, no. 4 (December 2005): 619–40.
MacGillivray, Don. "Military Aid to the Civil Power: The Cape Breton Experience in the 1920s." *Acadiensis* 3, no. 2 (1974): 45–64.
Macht, Wally. *The First 50 Years: A History of Upper Lakes Shipping Ltd.* Toronto: Virgo Press, 1981.
MacIntosh, Robert. *Boilermakers in British Columbia.* Vancouver: International Brotherhood of Boilermakers, Iron Shipbuilders, Blacksmiths, Forgers and Helpers, 1976.
Mackay, Donald. *Empire of Wood: The MacMillan Bloèdel Story.* Vancouver and Seattle: Douglas and McIntyre and University of Seattle Press, 1982.
- *People's Railway: A History of Canadian National.* Vancouver: Douglas and McIntyre, c. 1992.
Mackenzie, David. "The Bren Gun Scandal and the Maclean Publishing Company's Investigation of Canadian Contracts, 1938–1940." *Journal of Canadian Studies* 26, no. 3 (Fall 1991): 140–62.
Mackenzie, H.M. "Sinews of War: Aspects of Canadian Decisions to Finance British Requirements in Canada during the Second World War." Paper presented to the Canadian Historical Association, June 1984.
Mackenzie, Kenneth S. "C.C. Ballantyne and the Canadian Government Merchant Marine, 1917–1921." *Northern Mariner* 2, no. 1 (January 1992): 1–14.
MacNeill, Jack. "Development of Pictou Foundry and Machine Company Limited." *The Refitter* 1, no. 3 (July 1944): 1.
MacNeish, Allan C. "Ship Construction at Quebec Yard." *CS&MEN* 13, no. 7 (February 1942): 11–14.
- "Shipyard Layout at Morton's." *CS&MEN* 13, no. 8 (March 1942): 11–13.
- "Training Shipbuilders in Quebec." *CS&MEN* 13, no. 7 (February 1942): 19–22.
MacPherson, Ken. *Frigates of the Royal Canadian Navy, 1943–1974.* St Catharines, ON: Vanwell, 1988.
- *Minesweepers of the Royal Canadian Navy, 1938–1945.* St Catharines, ON: Vanwell, 1990.
- "Naval Shipbuilding on the Great Lakes, 1940–45." *Freshwater* 3, no. 1 (Summer 1988): 10–14.
- and Marc Milner. *Corvettes of the Royal Canadian Navy, 1939–1945.* St Catharines, ON: Vanwell, 1993.
- and John Burgess. *The Ships of Canada's Naval Forces, 1910–1993: A Complete Pictorial History of Canada's Warships.* St Catharines, ON: Vanwell, 1994.

Madsen, Chris. "Continuous Production in British Columbia Shipyards during the Second World War." *Northern Mariner* 14, no. 3 (July 2004): 1–26.

– "Industrial Hamilton's Contribution to the Naval War." *Northern Mariner* 16, no. 1 (January 2006): 21–52.

Manley, John. "Preaching the Red Stuff: J.B. McLachlan, Communism and the Cape Breton Miners, 1922–1935." *Labour/Le Travail* 30 (Fall 1992): 65–114.

Mansbridge, Francis. *Launching History: The Saga of Burrard Dry Dock*. Madeira Park, BC: Harbour, 2002.

Marcil, Eileen Reid. *Tall Ships and Tankers: The History of the Davie Shipbuilders*. Toronto: McClelland and Stewart, 1997.

Marine Retirees Association. *A History of Shipbuilding in British Columbia*. Published on the occasion of the fifieth anniversary of the Marine Workers and Boilermakers Industrial Union, Local 1. Vancouver: College Printers, 1977.

Marsh, Ron. "War-Born Barges Supplying Allies Designed by Local Naval Architect." *Montreal Gazette*, 6 April 1945.

Martin, Paul. *A Very Public Life*. Vol. 1, *Far from Home*. Ottawa: Deneau, 1983.

Mason, Don. "Flat Tops for Britain." *CS&MEN* 15, no. 12 (July 1944): 34–5, 47.

Mayne, Richard O. *Betrayed: Scandal, Politics, and Canadian Naval Leadership*. Vancouver: University of British Columbia Press, 2006.

McAnn, Aida. "Maritime Women at Work in War and Peace." *Public Affairs* 7, no. 2 (Winter 1944): 117–22.

McDowall, Duncan. *Steel at the Sault: Francis H. Clergue, Sir James Dunn and the Algoma Steel Corporation, 1901–1956*. Toronto and Buffalo, NY: University of Toronto Press, 1984.

McElroy, Frank S., and George R. McCormack. "Shipyard Injuries and Their Causes, 1941." *Monthly Labor Review* 55 (October 1942): 680–96.

– and Arthur L. Svenson. "Basic Accident Factors in Shipyards." *Monthly Labor Review* 59 (July 1944): 13–23.

– and Arthur L. Svenson. "Shipyard Injuries during 1943." *Monthly Labour Review* 58 (May 1944): 1004–8.

McInnis, Peter S. *Harnessing Labour Confrontation: Shaping the Postwar Settlement in Canada, 1943–1950*. Toronto: University of Toronto Press, 2001.

McKay, Ian. "Realm of Uncertainty: The Experience of Work in the Cumberland Coal Mines, 1873–1927." *Acadiensis* 16, no. 1 (1986): 3–27.

McKay, J., and J. Harland. *The Flower-Class Corvette Agassiz*. St Catharines, ON: Vanwell, 1993.

McKee, Fraser. *The Armed Yachts of Canada*. Erin, ON: Boston Mills Press, 1983.

– "Princes Three: Canada's Use of Armed Merchant Cruisers during World War II." In *The RCN in Retrospect, 1910–1968*, ed. James A. Boutilier, 116–37. Vancouver and London: University of British Columbia Press, 1982.

– *Sink All the Shipping There: The Wartime Loss of Canada's Merchant Ships and Fishing Schooners*. St Catharines, ON: Vanwell, 2004.

McKenty, Neil. *Mitch Hepburn*. Toronto: McClelland and Stewart, 1967.

McLaren, T. Arthur. "Shipbuilding: Laughter and Tears." In *A History of Canadian Marine Technology*, ed. Society of Naval Architects and Marine Engineers, 57–77. Ottawa: Eastern Canadian Section, Society of Naval Architects and Marine Engineers, 1992.

– and Vickie Jensen. *Ships of Steel: A British Columbian Shipbuilder's Story*. Madeira Park, BC: Harbour, 2003.

McMann, Evelyn de R. *Canadian Who's Who Index, 1898–1984, Incorporating Canadian Men and Women of the Time.* Toronto: University of Toronto Press, 1986.

Mercogliano, Salvatore R. "The United States Merchant Shipping Offensive during the Second World War." *Northern Mariner* 11, no. 4 (October 2004): 27–47.

Metson, Graham. *An East Coast Port: Halifax at War, 1939–1945.* Toronto: McGraw-Hill Ryerson, 1981.

Middleton, W.E.K. *Radar Development in Canada: The Radio Branch of the National Research Council of Canada, 1939–1946.* Waterloo, ON: Wilfrid Laurier University Press, 1981.

Miller, Al. "Teeming with Enterprise: Augustus B. Wolvin's Life in the Great Lakes." *Inland Seas* 58, no. 1 (Spring 2002): 7–27.

Miller, Carman. "The 1940s: War and Rehabilitation." In *The Atlantic Provinces in Confederation*, ed. E.R. Forbes and D.A. Muise, 306–27. Fredericton, NB: Acadiensis Press, 1993.

Milner, Marc. *Canada's Navy: The First Century.* Toronto: University of Toronto Press, 1999.

– "The Historiography of the Canadian Navy, the State of the Art." In *UBI SUMUS? The State of Naval and Maritime History*, ed. John B. Hattendorf, 79–92. Newport, RI: Naval War College Press, 1994.

– "The Implications of Technological Backwardness: The Royal Canadian Navy, 1939–1945." *Canadian Defence Quarterly* 19, no. 3 (Winter 1989): 46–53.

– *North Atlantic Run: The Royal Canadian Navy and the Battle of the Convoys.* Toronto: University of Toronto Press, 1985.

– *The U-boat Hunters: The Royal Canadian Navy and the Offensive against Germany's Submarines.* Toronto: University of Toronto Press, 1994.

Milward, Alan. *War, Economy, and Society, 1939–1945.* London: Allen Lane, 1977.

Misa, Thomas J. *A Nation of Steel: The Making of Modern America, 1865–1925.* Baltimore, MD, and London: Johns Hopkins University Press, 1995.

Mitchell, R.B. "Sydney Harbour: The War Years, 1939–1945." In *More Essays in Cape Breton History*, ed. R.J. Morgan, 42–9. Windsor, ON: Lancelot Press, 1977.

Moir, Michael B. "Toronto's Shipbuilding Industry." In *Reflections of Toronto Harbour: 200 Years of Port Authority and Waterfront Development*, 89–97. Toronto: Toronto Port Authority, 2002.

Moore, Tom. "Organized Labour and the War Economy." In *Canadian War Economics*, ed. J.F. Parkinson, 170–9. Toronto: University of Toronto Press, 1941.

Morton, Desmond. *Working People: An Illustrated History of the Canadian Labour Movement.* 3rd ed. Toronto: Summerhill Press, 1990.

Morton, J. Alexander. "Canada Builds Tugs of War for the British Navy." *SR&SB* 27, 1 (January 1945): 32–4, 60.

Mowat, Farley. *The Grey Seas Under: The Perilous Rescue Missions of a North Atlantic Salvage Tug.* Toronto: McClelland and Stewart, 1958.

Musk, George. *Canadian Pacific Afloat, 1883–1968: A Short History and Fleet List.* Rev ed. London: Canadian Pacific, 1968.

Neary, Peter. "Canada and the Newfoundland Labour Market, 1939–45." *Canadian Historical Review* 62, no. 4 (December 1981): 470–95.

Newman, Peter C. *The Canadian Establishment.* Vol. 1. Toronto: McClelland and Stewart, 1975.

Newstead, Ralph. *Audels Shipfitter's Handy Book: A Practical Treatise on Steel Shipbuilding and Repairing for Loftsmen, Welders, Riveters, Anglesmiths, Flange Turners and All Ship Mechanics with Illustrations Showing Current Practice.* New York: Theo. Audel and Co., 1940.

Nicholson, J.W.A. "Maritime Labour Irritation." *Canadian Forum* 21 (August 1941): 143–4.

Norrie, Kenneth, Douglas Owram, and J.C. Herbert Emery. *History of the Canadian Economy*. 3rd ed. Scarborough, ON: Nelson Thomson Learning, 2002.

Oliver, Dean F., and Laura Brandon. *Canvas of War: Painting the Canadian Experience, 1914 to 1945*. Vancouver and Ottawa: Douglas and McIntyre and Canadian War Museum, 2000.

O'Neill, George. "The Workers Wrote the Title." *CS&MEN* 15, no. 8 (March 1944): 25–9, 44.

Osborne, Brian S., and Geraint B. Osborne. "Kingston's Women at War." *Whig-Standard Magazine* (10 November 1990): 8–11.

– and Donald Swainson. *Kingston: Building on the Past*. Westport, CT: Butternut Press, 1988.

Ouderkirk, Gerry, and Skip Gillham. *The Ships of Kingston*. Vineland, ON: Glenaden Press, 2007.

Overy, Richard J. *Why the Allies Won*. New York: W.W. Norton, 1996.

Owram, Doug. *The Government Generation: Canadian Intellectuals and the State, 1900–1945*. Toronto: University of Toronto Press, 1986.

Palmer, Bryan D. *Working-Class Experience: Rethinking the History of Canadian Labour, 1800–1991*. 2nd ed. Toronto: McClelland and Stewart, 1992.

Palmer, David. *Organizing the Shipyards: Union Strategy in Three Northeast Ports, 1933–1949*. Ithaca, NY: ILR Press of Cornell University Press, 1998.

Palmer, Joseph. *Jane's Dictionary of Naval Terms*. London: Macdonald and Janes, 1975.

Pennachio, Luigi G. "Exporting Fascism to Canada: Toronto's Little Italy." In *Enemies Within: Italian and Other Internees in Canada and Abroad*, ed. Franca Iacoveta, Roberto Perrin, and Angelo Principe, 52–75. Toronto: University of Toronto Press, 2000.

Pentland, H.C. "The Canadian Industrial Relations System: Some Formative Factors." *Labour/Le Travail* 4 (1979): 9–24.

Phillips, Paul A. *No Power Greater: A Century of Labour in British Columbia*. Vancouver: BC Federation of Labour and Boag Foundation, 1967.

Pickersgill, J.W. *The Mackenzie King Record*. Vol. 1, *1939–1944*. Toronto: University of Toronto Press, 1960.

Pierson, Ruth Roach. *"They're Still Women after All": The Second World War and Canada's Womanhood*. Toronto: McClelland and Stewart, 1986.

Plumptre, A.F.W. *Mobilizing Canada's Resources for War*. Toronto: Macmillan of Canada, 1941.

Poolman, Kenneth. *Escort Carriers, 1941–1945*. London: Ian Allan, 1972.

Principe, Angelo. "A Tangled Knot: Prelude to 10 July 1940." In *Enemies Within: Italian and Other Internees in Canada and Abroad*, ed. Franca Iacoveta, Roberto Perrin, and Angelo Principe, 27–51. Toronto: University of Toronto Press, 2000.

Pritchard, James. "The Beaver and the Bear: Canadian Mutual Aid, Ship Repairing and the Soviet Far Eastern Merchant Fleet, 1941–1945." *Northern Mariner* 20, no. 2 (April 2010): 129–47.

– "Fifty-Six Minesweepers and the Toronto Shipbuilding Company during the Second World War." *Northern Mariner* 16, no. 4 (October 2006): 29–48.

– "The Long Angry Summer of '43: Labour Relations in Quebec's Shipbuilding Industry." *Labour/Le Travail* 65 (Spring 2010): 47–73.

Quick, Paddy. "Rosie the Riveter: Myths and Realities." *Radical America* 9 (July–October 1975): 115–31.

Rance, Adrian. *Fast Boats and Flying Boats: A Biography of Hubert Scott-Paine, Solent Marine and Aviation Pioneer*. Southampton, UK: Ensign Publications and Southampton City Museums, 1990.

Rannie, John. "The 10,000 Tonner." *SR&SB* 27, no. 5 (May 1944): 25–7, 85; no. 6 (June 1944): 26–8, 68; no. 7 (July 1944): 35–6, 62.

Rapping, Leonard. "Learning and World War II Production Functions." *Review of Economics and Statistics* 47, no. 1 (February 1965): 81–6.

Rawling, William. "The Challenge of Modernization: The Royal Canadian Navy and Antisubmarine Weapons, 1944–45." *Journal of Military History* 63, no. 2 (April 1999): 355–78.

– "Forging Neptune's Trident." Author's typescript. N.d.

– "When the Simplest Thing Is Difficult: Manufacturing Depth Charges in Canada, 1933–1945." *Northern Mariner* 13, no. 2 (April 2003): 1–24.

Reeves, Wayne. "Regional Heritage Features on the Metropolitan Toronto Waterfront." Report to the Metropolitan Toronto Planning Department, Toronto, June 1992.

Reid, Max. *The Arming of Canadian Merchant Ships in the Second World War: Two Navies, the Same Ship*. Published for the Royal Canadian Naval Association, Defensively Equipped Merchant Ship Branch. Quyon, QC: Chesley House, 2003.

– "Canadian Wartime Merchant Shipping." In *A History of Canadian Marine Technology*, ed. Society of Naval Architects and Marine Engineers, 49–56. Ottawa: Eastern Canadian Section, Society of Naval Architects and Marine Engineers, 1992.

Rickover, H.G. "Alternating Current in the U.S. Navy." Society of Naval Architects and Marine Engineers, *Transactions* 49 (1941): 329–55.

Roberts, Charles G.D., and A.L. Tunnel, eds. *The Canadian Who's Who, 1936–37 and 1938–39*. Toronto: Trans Canada Press, 1937 and 1939.

Roberts, Leslie. *C.D.: The Life and Times of Clarence Decatur Howe*. Toronto: Clark, Irwin and Co., 1957.

Robinson, Daniel. *The Measure of Democracy: Polling, Market Research and Public Life, 1930–1945*. Toronto: University of Toronto Press, 1999.

Robson, John. "Merchant Shipbuilding in Canada." Institute of Naval Architects, *Transactions* 88 (1946): 280–94.

Rohmer, Richard, and E.P. Taylor. *The Biography of Edward Plunket Taylor*. Toronto: McClelland and Stewart, 1978.

Rosen, S. McKee. *The Combined Boards of the Second World War: An Experiment in International Administration*. New York: Columbia University Press, 1951.

Roué, Joan E. *A Spirit Deep Within: Naval Architect W.J. Roué and the Bluenose Story*. Hantsport, NS: Lancelot Press, 1995.

Rouillard, Jacques. *Histoire du syndicalisme québécois des origines à nos jours*. Montreal: Boréal, 1989.

– "Mutations de la Confédération des travailleurs catholiques du Canada, 1940–1960." In *Travail et Syndicalisme: Naissance et Évolution d'une Action Sociale*, 2nd ed., ed. James Thwaites. Quebec: Les Presses de l'Université Laval, 2002.

Rowe, R.C. "Gold Mining and Shipbuilding." *Canadian Mining Journal* 64, no. 10 (October 1943): 627–40.

Rowland, K.T. *Steam at Sea: A History of Steam Navigation*. New York: Praeger, 1970.

Roy, James A. *Kingston: The King's Town*. Toronto: McClelland and Stewart, 1952.

Runyan, T.J., and J.M. Copes, eds. *To Die Gallantly: The Battle of the Atlantic*. Boulder, CO: Westview Press, 1994.

Sager, Eric W., and Gerald E. Panting. *Maritime Capital: The Shipping Industry in Atlantic Canada, 1820–1914*. Montreal and Kingston: McGill-Queen's University Press, 1990.

Salmon, Stephen M. "British Competition: 'Canadian' Great Lakes Vessels Built in United Kingdom Shipyards, 1854–1965: An Archival Checklist." *Freshwater* 5, no. 2 (1990): 20–6.

- "Through the Shoals of Paper: An Introduction to the Sources for the Study of Twentieth Century Canadian Maritime History at the National Archives of Canada." *International Journal of Maritime History* 1, no. 2 (December 1989): 239–53.

Salter, A.E. "Diesel Engines for Marine Power." *CS&MEN* 15, no. 2 (September 1943): 41–8, 70.

Salter, Lynn. "Wartime Ship-Shaping in a Small Town." [Report to the?] Prince Rupert Northwest History Society, c. 1983. Vancouver Public Library, Special Collections, NW 338.9711 B93 Pam.

Sarty, Roger. "Admiral Percy W. Nelles: Diligent Guardian of the Vision." In *The Admirals: Canada's Senior Naval Leadership in the Twentieth Century*, ed. Michael Whitby, Richard Gimblett, and Peter Haydon, 69–95. Toronto: Dundurn Press, 2006.

- "The Ghosts of Fisher and Jellicoe: The Royal Canadian Navy and the Quebec Conferences." In *The Second Quebec Conference Revisited: Waging War, Formulating Peace: Canada, Great Britain and the United States in 1944–1945*, 143–70. New York: St Martin's Press, 1998.

- "The Origins of Canada's Second World War Maritime Forces, 1918–1940." In *Maritime Forces in Global Security*, ed. Ann L. Griffiths and Peter T. Hayden, 275–92. Halifax: Dalhousie University Centre for Foreign Policy Studies, 1995.

Sawyer, L.A., and W.H. Mitchell. *The Liberty Ships: The History of the "Emergency" Type Cargo Ships Constructed in the United States during World War II*. Cambridge, MD: Cornell Maritime Press, 1970.

- and W.H. Mitchell. *The Oceans, the Forts and the Parks: Merchant Shipbuilding for British Account in North America during World War II*. Liverpool, UK: Sea Breezes, 1966.

Saywell, John T. *"Just Call Me Mitch": The Life of Mitchell F. Hepburn*. Toronto: University of Toronto Press, 1991.

Schull, Joseph. *The Great Scot: A Biography of Donald Gordon*. Montreal and Kingston: McGill-Queen's University Press, 1979.

Scott, John Dick. *Vickers, a History*. London: Weidenfeld and Nicolson, 1963.

- and Richard Hughes. *The Administration of War Production*. London: HMSO/Longmans, Greene and Co., 1955.

Searle, Allan D. "Productivity Changes in Selected Wartime Shipbuilding Programs." *Monthly Labor Review* (December 1945): 1132–47.

Settle, Victor. "Halifax Shipyards, 1918–1978." MA thesis, Saint Mary's University, 1994.

Sherwood, Roland H. *Pictou Parade*. Sackville, NB: Tribune Press, 1945.

Shield, Harold, and Bev McMullen. *Ditchburn Boats: A Muskoka Legacy*. Erin, ON: Boston Mills Press, 2002.

Skold, Karen. "The Job He Left Behind: American Women in the Shipyards during World War II." In *Women, War and Revolution*, ed. Carol R. Berkin and Clara M. Lovett, 5–75. New York: Holmes and Meier, 1980.

Slater, David, with Robert B. Bryce. *War Finance and Reconstruction: The Role of Canada's Department of Finance, 1939–1946*. Ottawa: Privately published, 1995.

Smith, Doug. *Cold Warrior: C.S. Jackson and the United Electrical Workers*. St John's, NL: Canadian Committee on Labour History, 1997.

Smith, Edgar C. *A Short History of Naval and Marine Engineering*. Printed for Babcock and Wilcox Ltd. Cambridge, UK: Cambridge University Press, 1937.

Smith, F.M., et al. "History of the British Admiralty Technical Mission in Canada." Typescript. Ottawa: British Admiralty Technical Mission, 1946. Copy in LAC, RG 28, box 29.

Smith, Gaddis. *Britain's Clandestine Submarines, 1914–1915*. New Haven: Yale University Press, 1964.

Smith, Kevin E. *Conflict over Convoys: Anglo-American Logistics Diplomacy in the Second World War.* Cambridge, UK: Cambridge University Press, 1996.

Sobel, David, and Susan Meurer. *Working at Inglis: The Life and Death of a Canadian Factory.* Toronto: James Lorimer, 1994.

Society of Naval Architects and Marine Engineers, ed. *A History of Canadian Marine Technology.* Ottawa: Eastern Canadian Section, Society of Naval Architects and Marine Engineers, 1995.

Stacey, Charles P. *Arms, Men and Governments: The War Policies of Canada, 1939–1945.* Ottawa: Queen's Printer, 1970.

Stark, Robert C. "Bridge of Ships." In *Women at War,* ed. J. Herbert Hodgins et al., 98–103. Montreal: Maclean, 1943.

Stephens, Robert St George. "Reminiscences: The Naval Careers of Engineer Rear-Admiral G.L. Stephens, CBE, CB, CD, RCN, and Vice-Admiral R.S.G. Stephens, CD, RCN, 1910–1978." In *People, Policy and Programmes: Proceedings of the 7th Maritime Command (MARCOM) Historical Conference (2005),* ed. Richard H. Gimblett and Richard O. Mayne, 17–38. Winnipeg: Canadian Naval Heritage Press, 2008.

Steven, Thomas C. "Building Marine Engines for 'Manufactured' Ships." *CS&MEN* 15, no. 4 (November 1943): 37–43, 64.

– "Canada's Shipyards Are Helping to 'Finish the Job.'" *CS&MEN* 15, no. 1 (August 1943): 39–45, 72.

– "Components Industry Helps Drive Canadian Ship Production Higher." *CS&MEN* 14, no. 7 (February 1943): 27–9, 50.

– "Fighting the U-boat Menace in Canada's Shipyards." *CS&MEN* 14, no. 8 (March 1943): 41–5.

– "A Great Lakes Yard Produces Naval Craft." *CS&MEN* 15, no. 3 (October 1943): 43–50.

– "Kennedy Propellers Drive Canada's Ships." *CS&MEN* 14, no. 10 (May 1943): 33–8, 64.

– "Shipbuilders of the St. Lawrence." *CS&MEN* 15, no. 6 (January 1944): 24–31, 62.

– "United Effort in Cargo Ship Construction." *CS&MEN* 14, no. 4 (November 1942): 31–6.

– "Vickers Builds for Victory." *CS&MEN* 14, no. 9 (April 1943): 29–36.

Stevenson, Michael D. *Canada's Greatest Wartime Muddle: National Selective Service and the Mobilization of Human Resources during World War II.* Montreal and Kingston: McGill-Queen's University Press, 2001.

Sutton, George W., Jr. "Scott-Paine's Canadian MTBs." Reprinted from *Motor Boating,* September 1942.

Sweeting, Vern, and Skip Gillham. *The Ships of Midland.* Vineland, ON: Glenaden Press, 2004.

Taylor, Don, and Bradley Dow. *The Rise of Industrial Unionism in Canada: A History of the CIO.* Kingston: Queen's University Industrial Relations Centre, 1988.

Taylor, G.W. *Shipyards of British Columbia: The Principal Companies.* Victoria, BC: Morriss Publishing, 1986.

Taylor, Graham D. "A Merchant of Death in the Peaceable Kingdom: Canadian Vickers, 1911–1927." In *Canadian Papers in Business History,* vol. 1, ed. Peter Baskerville, 213–44. Victoria, BC: University of Victoria, 1989.

Tennyson, Brian, and Roger Sarty. *Guardian of the Gulf: Sydney, Cape Breton, and the Atlantic Wars.* Toronto: University of Toronto Press, 2000.

Terrell, Edward. *Admiralty Brief: The Story of Inventions That Contributed to Victory in the Battle of the Atlantic.* London: George G. Harrap and Co., 1958.

Thompson, Peter. "How Much Did the Liberty Shipbuilders Learn? New Evidence for an Old Case Study." *Journal of Political Economy* 109, no. 1 (February 2001): 103–37.

Thornton, Carole Paula. "Women of the Victoria Shipyards, 1942–1945: An Oral History." MA thesis, University of Victoria, 1998.

Todd, Daniel, and Michael Lindberg. *Navies and Shipbuilding Industries: The Strained Symbiosis*. Westport, CT: Praeger, 1996.

Toronto Harbour Commissioners. *Toronto Harbour: The Passing Years* Toronto: Toronto Harbour Commissioners, 1985.

Tracy, Nicolas. "Canadian Shipbuilding and Shipping Business: The State of the Scholarship." Research Report No. 11. Halifax: Canadian Maritime Transportation Centre, Dalhousie Ocean Studies Programme, 1985.

Tucker, Gilbert N. *The Naval Service of Canada: Its Official History*. 2 vols. Ottawa: King's Printer, 1952.

United States, Bureau of Labour Statistics. "Causes of Crane Accidents in Shipyards." *Monthly Labor Review* 58 (March 1944): 531–3.

– "Causes and Prevention of Injuries from Falls in Shipyards." *Monthly Labor Review* 57 (October 1943): 766–72.

– "Eye Injuries in Shipyards." *Monthly Labor Review* 57 (December 1943): 1151–4.

– *Wartime Employment Production and Conditions of Work in Shipyards*. Bulletin No. 824. Washington: Government Printing Office, 1943.

United States, Labour Department. *Shipyard Injuries and Their Causes, 1941*. Bulletin No. 722. Washington, DC: Government Printing Office, 1943.

United States, Maritime Commission. *The Postwar Outlook for American Shipping: A Report Submitted to the United States Maritime Commission by the Postwar Planning Committee, June 15 1946*. Washington, DC: Government Printing Office, 1946.

United States, Naval Historical Center. *Dictionary of American Naval Fighting Ships*. Washington, DC: Naval Historical Center, 1963.

United States, Navy Department, Bureau of Ships. *Ships Data: U.S. Naval Vessels*. Vol. 2, *Mine Vessels (Less CM & DM) Patrol Vessels Landing Ships and Craft, Navships 250-011*. Washington, DC: Government Printing Office, 1946.

United States, War Production Board. *Industrial Mobilization for War: History of the War Production Board and Predecessor Agencies, 1940–1945: Program and Administration*. Washington, DC: War Production Board, 1947.

Vancouver Sun. *Industrial British Columbia, 1945*. Vancouver: Vancouver Sun, 1945.

Vernon, J.E. "RCAF Marine Craft." In *Proceedings [of the] 4th Annual Air Force Historical Conference: 80 Years of Maritime Aviation in Canada*, ed. Office of Air Force Heritage and History, 101–12. N.p., 1998.

Von Der Porten, Edward. *The German Navy in World War Two*. 1969. Reprint, New York: Ballantine Books, 1974.

Wade, Jill. *Houses for All: The Struggle for Social Housing in Vancouver, 1919–1950*. Vancouver: University of British Columbia Press, 1994.

– "Wartime Housing Limited, 1941–1947: Canadian Housing Policy at the Crossroads." *Urban History Review* 15 (June 1986): 41–60.

Wallis, Ron, comp. *The Story of Pictou's Park Ships*. Pictou, NS: Pictou Advocate, 2004.

Ward, Wallace, and J. Alexander Morton. "Of Ships and Shipbuilding." In *Canada and the War at Sea*, pt 3. Montreal: A.M. Beatty, 1944.

Wartime Merchant Shipping Ltd. *Shipyard Terms*. N.p.: Wartime Merchant Shipping Ltd, 1942. Copy in Esquimalt Municipal Archives, Yarrows Ltd Fonds, 997.10.46.

Watson, A.W. "Corvettes and Frigates." In *Selected Papers on British Warship Design in World War II from Transactions of the Royal Institution of Naval Architects, 1947 and 1983*, ed. Rowland Baker. Annapolis, MD: Naval Institute Press, 1983.

Watt, Frederick B. *In All Respects Ready for Sea: The Merchant Navy and the Battle of the Atlantic, 1940–1945*. Toronto: Prentice-Hall Canada, 1985.

Webb, Roland H. "Burrard Drydock Co. Ltd: The Rise and Demise of Vancouver's Biggest Shipyard." *Northern Mariner* 6, no. 3 (July 1996): 1–10.

– "Wallace Burrard Versatile Hull List." In *Launching History: The Saga of Burrard Dry Dock*, by Francis Mansbridge, 197–208. Madeira Park, BC: Harbour, 2002.

– "Yarrows Ltd. and Burrard Dry Dock & Shipbuilding Ltd. Yard Hull Numbers." Typescript. 1993. Copy concerning only Yarrows in Esquimalt Municipal Archives, Yarrows Ltd Fonds.

Webber, Jeremy. "The Malaise of Compulsory Conciliation: Strike Prevention in Canada during World War II." *Labour/Le Travail* 15 (Spring 1985): 57–88. An abridged, edited version appears in Bryan D. Palmer, ed., *The Character of Class Struggle: Essays in Canadian Working-Class History*, 138–59 (Toronto: McClelland and Stewart, 1986).

Weir, Gary. "A Truly Allied Undertaking: The Progeny of Britain's Empire Liberty, 1931–43." In *The Battle of the Atlantic, 1939–1945: The 50th Anniversary International Naval Conference*, ed. Stephen Howarth and Derek G. Law, 101–17. London and Annapolis, MD: Greenhill Books and Naval Institute Press, 1994.

Whitby, Michael. "Instruments of Security: The Royal Canadian Navy's Procurement of the Tribal-Class Destroyers, 1938–1943." *Northern Mariner* 2, no. 3 (July 1992): 1–15.

White, Howard. *A Hard Man to Beat: The Story of Bill White, Labour Leader, Historian, Shipyard Worker, Raconteur: An Oral History*. Vancouver: Pulp Press Books, 1983.

White, Jay. "Conscripted City: Halifax and the Second World War." PhD diss., McMaster University, 1994.

– "The Homes Front: The Accommodation Crisis in Halifax, 1941–1945." *Urban History Review* 20, no. 3 (1992): 117–27.

– "'Pulling Teeth': Striking for the Check-Off in the Halifax Shipyards, 1944." *Acadiensis* 19 (1989): 115–41.

– "'Sleepless and Veiled Am I': An East Coast Canadian Port Revisited." *Nova Scotia Historical Review* 5, no. 1 (1985): 15–29.

Whitehurst, Clinton H., Jr. *The U.S. Shipbuilding Industry: Past, Present, and Future*. Annapolis, MD: Naval Institute Press, 1986.

Wickson, Ted. *Reflections of Toronto Harbour: 200 Years of Port Activity and Waterfront Development*. Toronto: Toronto Port Authority, 2002.

Williams, Robin. *A Vancouver Boyhood: Recollections of Growing up in Vancouver, 1925 to 1945*. Vancouver: Privately published, 1995.

Wilson, Garth. *History of Shipbuilding and Naval Architecture in Canada*. Ottawa: National Museum of Science and Technology, 1994.

Wright, Richard. *Freshwater Whales: A History of the American Ship Building Company and Its Predecessors*. [Kent, OH]: Kent State University Press, 1970.

Young, Ewart. "Cheating the Nazis through Salvage." *CS&MEN* 14, no. 11 (June 1944): 31–4.

Zimmerman, David. *The Great Naval Battle of Ottawa: How Admirals, Scientists and Politicians Impeded the Development of High Technology in Canada's Wartime Navy*. Toronto: University of Toronto Press, 1989.

– *Top Secret Exchange: The Tizard Mission and Scientific War*. Montreal and Kingston: McGill-Queen's University Press, 1996.

Index

Ships' names are listed under the kind of
vessel: ships, tugboats, or towing vessels

British Ministry of War Transport, 45, 50, 104, 108, 121, 122–3, 230, 242, 251, 266, 269, 270, 281–2, 283–4, 289–91, 307, 331
British Power Boat Company, 285, 287
British Purchasing Commission, 88
British Purchasing Mission, 20
British Supply Board of Canada, 20
Buffalo, New York, 243
Burbidge, Philip William, 81
Burdick, Arthur C., 69, 251, 330
burners, 168, 175
Burrard Dry Dock Company Limited (also called Burrard North Yard), xxi, 21, 23, 30, 36, 61–2, 66, 67, 69, 83, 95, 99, 115, 116, 134, 137, 141, 145, 148, 149, 154, 156, 160, 163, 171, 173, 186, 188, 192, 210, 220, 237–8, 257, 305, 312, 314, 316, 319, 320–1, 329, 330
Burrard (Vancouver) Dry Dock Company (also called South Burrard Dry Dock Company), 62, 83–5, 155, 185, 188, 190, 192, 305, 319–20
Byng, Governor General Lord, 47

Cabinet War Committee, 9, 19, 21, 27, 31, 32, 33, 42, 43, 102, 105, 110, 111, 121, 158, 169, 260, 288, 296, 304, 326–7, 329–30
Calgary, Alberta, 146, 217–18
Calgary Rolling Mills, 218
Campbell, Alec C., 51
Campbell, Lady, 28
Campbell, Pat, 162
Campbell, Wallace R., 20, 26, 32, 168
Campbellton, New Brunswick, 142
Canada, House of Commons, 19, 26, 28, 33, 129, 196, 282, 288, 308, 313
Canada Cement Company, 207
Canada Foundries and Forgings Limited, 68, 245
Canada Iron Foundries Limited, 220, 237
Canada Steamship Lines, 6, 24, 48, 51, 57, 58, 59, 60, 69, 70, 196, 268
Canada-United States Joint War Production Committee, 213
Canada West Coast Navigation Company, 58
Canada Wire and Cable Company, 255
Canadian Allis-Chambers Limited, 37, 234–6, 237, 247
Canadian and Catholic Confederation of Labour (CCCL). See Confédération des travailleurs catholique du Canada (CTCC)

Canadian army, 63, 256, 266, 273–4, 289, 290–1
Canadian Bridge Company, 269, 281, 282
Canadian Brotherhood of Railway Employees, 167
Canadian Car and Foundry Company, 52, 68, 239, 243
Canadian Comstock Company, 74
Canadian Congress of Labour (CCL), 136, 148, 167, 178, 180, 182–3, 187, 192–3, 194–5, 197–9
Canadian Dredge and Dock Company, 47, 48, 52, 93, 278, 280–1
Canadian Fairbanks Morse Company, 248. See also Fairbanks Morse Company
Canadian Federation of Labour (CFL), 167–8, 192
Canadian Forum, 220
Canadian Furnace Company, 219
Canadian Gauge Company, 250
Canadian General Electric Company, 254, 255, 257
Canadian Government Merchant Marine, 5, 62, 103, 330–1
Canadian Manufacturers Association, 18, 55, 168, 206, 278
Canadian Maritime Commission, 331
Canadian Mutual Aid Board, 115. See also mutual aid
Canadian National Railway (CNR), 52, 62–3, 69, 80, 99, 142, 260, 281, 330
Canadian National Steamship Company, 21, 99, 329
Canadian navy. See Royal Canadian Navy
Canadian Pacific Railway, 68, 284; Angus shops, 48, 236; Ogden shops, 48, 260
Canadian Power Boat Company, 24, 76–9, 138, 287
Canadian Pulp and Paper Association. See Pulp and Paper Association of Canada
Canadian Shipbuilding and Engineering Limited, 60, 330. See also Kingston Shipbuilding Company
Canadian Shipbuilding and Ship Repairing Association (CSSRA), 303, 328, 329–30, 331
Canadian shipbuilding industry value. See shipbuilding value
Canadian Shipping Board, 88, 326
Canadian Steamship Inspection Service, 88
Canadian Steel Workers Union, 179–80
Canadian Sumner Iron Works, 232–3

compulsory conciliation, 170, 173, 174, 194, 201

conciliation boards, 175, 195

condensers, 229, 231, 236, 238

Confédération des travailleurs catholique du Canada (CTCC), 167, 199–200

Congress of Industrial Organizations (CIO), 167

Conservative Party of Canada, 19, 193

Consolidated Engineering, 251

Consolidated Marine Companies Limited, 54

Consolidated Mining and Smelter Company, 236

constructive total loss, 106, 353n48

continuous production, 149, 184–90, 201, 321

contracts, 232. See also shipbuilding contracts

controller of ship repairs and salvage, 34, 41, 92–5, 106, 109, 123–4

conversions, 95, 96, 98–100, 113–18, 122–3, 268–70, 278. See also ship repairing

Co-operative Commonwealth Federation (CCF), 167, 193

copper and copper wiring, 229

coppersmiths, 143

corporatism, 167

corvettes, 22, 28, 29, 38, 42, 44, 57, 60, 61, 62, 65, 70, 80, 85, 118–19, 212, 220, 229, 234, 235, 238, 239, 250, 253, 260, 264, 271, 298, 309, 310, 317, 320, 327; Castle-class, 298; Flower-class, 7–8, 10, 18, 19, 70, 146, 234, 261, 293, 295, 296, 299, 300, 301, 304; Increased Endurance, 8, 10, 263, 293, 295, 298, 300, 301, 312; Revised, 8, 10, 41, 42, 204, 238, 260, 293, 295, 296, 297, 298, 299, 300, 301

cost-of-living bonus, 175, 197, 198, 199

cost plus fixed fee, 75, 87. See also shipbuilding contracts

Coté, David, 148, 198–9

counter sinkers, 175

Courrier de Sorel, 164

Courtney Bay, New Brunswick, 47, 48

Cousins, Ed, 113

Coverdale, William H., 51, 60

Cowie, Colonel Alfred Henry, 34, 40, 83, 91

Cox and Stevens, 329

Coyle, W.J., 177, 183

craft unions and unionism, 165, 170, 171, 194–200

Craig, David, 51

Crane Limited, 248

crash tenders, 285, 287–8. See also rescue launches

Crawford, Captain W.M., 251

Cribb, Ernest F., 289

Cross, Arthur, 209, 227

Crown corporations, 73, 75, 168

Cullwick, RCNVR, Electrical Commander A.G., 256

Cummins Engine Company, 280

Cunningham, William H., 282

Curry, RCN, Engineer Commander A.D.M., 18

Cuthbertson, Wendy, 161

cutters, 243, 266, 268, 273, 274, 275

Dalrymple, John, 84

Dartmouth, Nova Scotia, 101, 103, 120, 178–9, 183–4

Davie, Captain Allison, 50

Davie, Charles ("Charlie") Gordon, 56, 80, 88

Davie, George Duncan and Allison, 51, 55, 57

Davie and Sons, George T., 23, 55–7, 68, 76, 80, 88, 153, 175, 196, 221, 297, 310, 312, 314, 331

Davie Brothers, 57, 267

Davie Shipbuilding and Repairing Company, 6, 22, 23, 24, 30, 42, 50–1, 68, 76, 88, 143, 147, 151–3, 157, 158, 160, 162, 163–4, 171, 172–3, 175, 195, 196–7, 200, 212, 267, 310, 313, 314, 329

Davy, RCN, Engineer Captain A.C.M., 44

Dawson, Sir Trevor, 59

deck equipment, 250–3

Defence Industries Limited, 108, 258

Defence of Canada Regulations, 19

Defence Purchasing Board, 18, 20, 242

depot ships, 242. See also Fairmile depot ships

depreciation. See accelerated depreciation

depth charges, 236–7, 258–9. See also naval armament and equipment

derrick posts (also called Samson posts), 250

derricks, 253

derrick scows, 278, 279, 286

destroyer construction, 100–1

destroyers, 19, 42, 94, 103, 104, 118, 326; Tribal-class, 8, 18, 21, 42, 109–13, 125, 145, 239, 249–50, 326

Detroit, Michigan, 242, 243, 289

Detroit Shipbuilding Company, 21

Deveau, John F., 50

Dewar, C.L., 44, 227

Dick, G.M., 182

194–5, 197–9, 205, 218, 236, 243, 244, 245, 248, 250, 253, 255, 260, 264, 268, 294, 298, 320, 326

Pritchard, Chris, 188
productivity, 315–23. *See also* labour
    productivity
Progressive Engineering Works Limited, 250–2
propellers, 215, 229, 231, 245–7
propeller-shaft bearing, 244
propulsion machinery, 234–43
provision lighters, 22
PT-type boats, 288
Public Works, Department of, 268, 269
pulley blocks, 252–3
pulling boats, 266, 273, 274
Pulp and Paper Association of Canada, 248–9,
    252
pumps, 229, 247–50
punch operator, 175
Purdy Brothers, 94, 178
Pushie Machine Shop, 103

quartz crystal, 262
Quebec, Department of Labour, 152
Quebec, Workmen's Compensation
    Commission, 150
Quebec and Ontario Transportation Company,
    270
Quebec City, 80, 88, 100, 113, 123, 131–2, 142, 149,
    174, 185, 195–7, 199–200, 234, 236, 320, 321
Quebec labour strife, 194–200
Quebec Salvage and Wrecking Company, 107–8
Quebec Shipyards Limited, 75, 80–1, 145, 196–7,
    200, 331
Quebec-Sorel region, 177
quick write-offs. *See* write-off provisions
Quinte, Bay of, Ontario, 282–4, 287

radar, 257–8
Ralston, J. Layton, 21, 221
ramped cargo lighter, 288, 289. *See also* landing
    craft
range boats, 273, 277, 287
Rankin, Danny, 182
Rankin, John I., 52
Rannie, John, 92, 325
Ratcliffe, J.H., 71
Rawling, William, 258
Raymond, Avila, 52
reamers, 172, 175
Redfern, Charles, 40, 74
Redfern Construction Company, 74

Redfern Construction Company (Shipbuilding
    Division) Limited, 74, 331
Reed, William, 7, 9
refrigeration machinery, 307
refuelling launches and scows, 22, 266, 286
regional wartime labour boards, 168, 177, 184
Reid, John, 251
Reid, John A., 251
Reid, Max, 260
Reid, William J., 251
Reid, W.J., 251
repair barges, 106
rescue launches, 105, 106–9, 266, 285, 287–8
resident naval overseers (RNOs), 145
Richards, Mr Justice Stephen E., 155, 160, 188–
    90. *See also* royal commissions: continuous
    production in British Columbia
riggers, 172
riveters, 25, 104, 134, 142, 145, 154, 166, 172, 174,
    185; injuries, 134, 155
rivet heaters, 175
riveting, 319
Robbins and Meyers, 256
Robert Napier and Sons, 59
Robson, John, 147, 323
Roosevelt, President Franklin Delano, 33,
    200–1
"Rosie the riveter," 134
Ross, Frank Mackenzie, 29, 52, 64, 231;
    biography, 47–8
Royal Air Force, 24, 283–4, 287
Royal Canadian Air Force (RCAF), 20, 24,
    63, 76, 106, 108, 121, 242, 266, 273, 275, 277;
    marine craft, 285–8
Royal Canadian Army Medical Corps, 122
Royal Canadian Mounted Police (RCMP), 170,
    198, 199
Royal Canadian Navy (RCN), xxiii, 7, 18–19, 39,
    41, 42, 57, 63, 73, 76, 286, 78, 80, 94, 96–7, 102,
    109, 110, 111, 119–21, 124, 145, 155, 231, 241, 242,
    247, 253, 255, 256, 262, 267–8, 271, 273, 274,
    277, 278, 279, 283, 287, 296, 297, 298, 306, 326
Royal Canadian Navy Reserve, 146
Royal Canadian Navy Volunteer Reserve
    (RCNVR), 146, 255
royal commissions, 174, 177–8; continuous
    production in British Columbia, 154–5, 185,
    188–9; shipbuilding in Ontario and Quebec,
    130, 153, 175–7, 196, 201